Handbook of Hispanic Cultures in the United States: Sociology

Edited and introduced by Félix Padilla

General Editors: Nicolás Kanellos and Claudio Esteva-Fabregat

Publication of the *Handbook of Hispanic Cultures in the United States* was financed by the Instituto de Cooperación Iberoamericana, Madrid, Spain. Other support for this project was provided by the National Endowment for the Arts, a federal agency, the Mellon Foundation and the Lila Wallace-Reader's Digest Fund. The *Handbook of Hispanic Cultures in the United States* is a co-publication of the Instituto de Cooperación Iberoamericana and Arte Público Press.

Arte Público Press
University of Houston
Houston, Texas 77204-2090

Handbook of Hispanic cultures in the United States.
p. cm.
Includes bibliographical references and index.
Contents: Literature and art / edited by Francisco Lomelí – Sociology / edited by Felix Padilla.
ISBN 1-55885-101-1 : $60.00
1. Hispanic Americans. I. Lomelí, Francisco A. II. Padilla, Felix.
E184.S75H365 1994 973'.-0468 93-13348
CIP

The paper used in this publication meets the requirements of the American National Standard for Permanence of Paper for Printed Library Materials Z39.48-1984. 

Printed in the United States of America

Contents

Handbook of Hispanic Cultures in the United States: Sociology

General Introduction to the *Handbook of Hispanic Cultures in the United States*

Nicolás Kanellos and Claudio Esteva-Fabregat

The development of Hispanic communities within the United States has taken place during different periods of time. The first was initiated with the arrival of Spaniards and mestizos to the Florida territory (which extended as far west as today's Texas), at the beginning of the sixteenth century, and later to the present-day Southwest. The people coming from Spain and Mexico—Spaniards, *criollos*, *mestizos* and Indians—founded towns and villages along the present Southeast and the Great Southwest, and marked these areas culturally and contributed an historical Hispanic American way of life, an amalgamated society known by the name "hispano."

Since then, the generations of new colonists and the offspring of their unions interbred with the local Amerindians in the Southeast and Southwest. Later, especially during this century, more and more people from Mexico, Puerto Rico and Cuba came to the United States in search of better living conditions. Thus were born new Hispanic descendants in the United States; and today even newer Hispanic nationality groups are adding to this base: Spanish-speakers who are attracted as much by the tradition of freedom here as by the opportunity to find a better personal space in which to realize their dreams and potential.

In the past as in the present, the older Hispanic generations have joined the newer ones to form a population that is in principle united by at least one, if not two, common languages (Spanish and English) and by an historic culture which has allowed them to maintain their own ways of life as well as a unique interethnic cohesion, especially as regards customs, esthetics and ethos. In general, Hispanics today are a young and active population, renewing American vitality and contributing greatly to the national culture of the United States. And today, Hispanics live virtually in every part of the United States, existing as a veritable national subculture, thus contributing to the multiculturalism that enriches this country in all aspects of life.

The increasing political and economic strength of the Hispanic populations of the United States during the past decade has made Hispanic culture a force to reckon with both domestically and internationally. As consumers with billions of dollars of disposable income, as the majority of school children in the largest school systems, as the fastest growing segment of registered voters, the influence of Hispanics is pervasive in all sectors of American life. Domestically, the obvious signs of this influence are reflected in the growing political representation at city council, school board, mayoral, congressional and even cabinet-level positions. In the economy and popular culture, many segments of the business world and the media are increasingly becoming bilingual and bicultural. With the potential of hemispheric integrated economies, through such treaties as the North American Free Trade Agreement, the cultural and linguistic ties of U. S. Hispanics to Latin America will also become a premium in national life.

It is no wonder that Spain has been developing closer relations with its formerly long-lost cousins in the United States. There have been numerous cultural and economic initiatives to strengthen the ties of Spain with other Spanish American countries of origin, and with the U. S. Hispanic population. Much of the Quincentenary Celebration of the 1492 Encounter of Civilizations, in fact, highlighted historical and contemporary contributions of Hispanics to the development of the United States. The Spanish government and its departments of culture and education continue to sponsor cultural missions, exchanges and study programs for Hispanics of the United States. By no means is the information and culture flow a one-way proposition, only promoting the contributions of Spain to the

United States and to Hispanic Americans. Rather, the cultural development and even autonomy of U. S. Hispanics and Spanish Americans in the rest of the hemisphere are not only acknowledged but studied and celebrated through a myriad of programs on art, literature, politics and culture in Spain.

It is in this spirit that the *Handbook of Hispanic Cultures in the United States* originated as a project conceived of and funded by Spain's Instituto de Cooperación Iberoamericana, which traditionally devoted its attention specifically to cultural exchange with the countries of Spanish America and, in this particular case, with *hispanos* and their particular historical process and contemporary culture in the United States. As a result of various conferences held in Madrid between 1983 and 1990 with leading U. S. Hispanic community, political, cultural and educational figures, the idea was generated for the creation of an encyclopedia of Hispanic culture in the United States. In October, 1987, the Instituto sponsored a seminar on "Hispanic Communities in the United States" and concluded that there was a serious bibliographic gap regarding Hispanic culture in the United States. The Instituto thus resolved to produce an encyclopedic work on U. S. Hispanics, largely written by U. S. Hispanics, to coincide with the Quincentenary celebrations. After further discussions and debates—as well as belt-tightening due to budgetary constraints—the project was brought down to a more manageable size that would explore four major areas in a four-volume reference work: History, Anthropology, Sociology, Literature and Art. Two general editors were named, along with distinguished scholars to edit the individual volumes: Alfredo Jiménez of the University of Seville for History, Thomas Weaver of the University of Arizona for Anthropology, Félix Padilla of Northeastern University for Sociology, Francisco Lomelí of the University of California-Santa Barbara for Literature and Art. The individual editors were charged with bringing together teams of outstanding scholars to create this first and only comprehensive reference work on Hispanics from these four disciplinary perspectives.

In addition to the work of the editors and contributions to these volumes, this project would never have become a reality without the massive and concentrated efforts of Juan Olivas who, as Coordinator, exerted the diplomatic and cultural and bureaucratic brokering necessary to facilitate the work of scholars on both sides of the Atlantic Ocean. We want to mention as well Pilar Saro, Director of Cultural Relations of the Instituto, who was actively devoted to the project from the beginning, and Soledad Fuentes, her successor in this task. Moreover, the former Directors of the Instituto de Cooperación Iberoamericana, Inocencio Arias, Carmelo Angulo, Delfín Colomé, and the present Director, Javier Jiménez Ugarte, devoted to the project much effort and personal interest. Without them, this *Handbook* could not have become a reality.

The project since its inception has had a twofold mission: the preparation of a valuable reference work for use by students and the general public throughout the United States, and an eventual Spanish translation of the same by the Instituto de Cooperación Iberoamericana for publication and distribution in Spain and the rest of the Spanish-speaking world.

Thus, the present volumes are merely the initial phase of a far-reaching and ambitious project whose duration–and hopefully its impact–will be long lasting.

It is also the hope of the general editors, the project staff, the Instituto of Cooperación Iberoamericana and Arte Público Press that these volumes will help to dispel many of the myths and misinformation that have become real barriers to students in their quest to conceptualize their identity within the United States, as well as to contest the stereotypes of Hispanics that not only pervade our society but also reach Spain and Spanish America through the media. May the thought and documentation contained in these essays lead to greater understanding of Hispanic life and culture both within the school population and the society at large.

We intend this "handbook" to be a qualitative contribution to knowledge about the most significant aspects of Hispanic culture in the United States; in and of itself our "handbook" is highly representative of what may be called the Hispanic style of life within the prevalent social currents in the United States. It will allow the reader to understand the significance and personality of Hispanics from within the context of contemporary American society.

General Editors

Nicolás Kanellos	Claudio Esteva-Fabregat
Professor, Department	Professor Emeritus
of Hispanic and	Department of Cultural
Classical Languages	Anthropology
University of Houston	University of Barcelona

Introduction: the Sociology of Hispanic People

Félix M. Padilla

From the very first moments of incorporation into U. S. society, Hispanic people have fought persistently and heroically to assert and preserve our unique and important historical and cultural experiences. In both history and culture, we find visions and insights necessary to give meaning to our lives as descendants of the Spanish-speaking world, visions and insights that help us cope when we are stigmatized by the larger U. S. society, which characterizes and treats us as a "racial/ethnic minority," visions and insights that for the most part the larger U. S. society does not endorse and tries to force us into giving up. It is not difficult to realize that since incorporation into U. S. society, the Hispanic experience in the United States has been played out within the context of cultural and racial/ethnic conflict and friction.

There has never been any doubt that a good deal of our Hispanic experience is embedded in the general U. S. history and culture. It is also true that we will never know ourselves as Chicanos/as, Puerto Ricans, Cubans, Dominicans, Colombians, and others within the context of U. S. society until we become responsible for giving definition to that history. For a very long time our cultural experiences were not given much attention outside the various Hispanic communities. In cases when we were subjects of investigation and analysis as Puerto Ricans, Chicanos/as, Cubans, and others, we have been presented as passive and non-participants in our history or as belonging to a fatalistic culture. According to these treatments, we represent a type of people resigned to whatever destiny has to offer. In his criticism of social science depiction of Mexican Americans, sociologist Alfredo Mirandé sketches what has become the accepted characterization of all Hispanic people: "Suffice it to say that [mainstream social scientists] have created a mythical conception of Mexican Americans which sees them as (1) controlled and manipulated by traditional culture, (2) docile, passive, present-oriented, fatalistic, and lacking in achievement, (3) victimized by faulty socialization which takes place in an authoritarian family system, dominated by the cult of machismo, and (4) violent and prone to antisocial and criminal behavior" (1978, 295). Many examples can be found of this stereotypic account of Hispanics, but it is sufficient to illustrate one very popular account written nearly forty years ago by sociologist Saunders: "The Spanish-speaking person, by contrast [to whites] is likely to meet difficulties by adjusting to them rather than by attempting to overcome them. Fate is somewhat inexorable, and there is nothing much to be gained by struggling against it. If the lot of man is hard—and it frequently is—such is the will of God, incomprehensible but just, and it is the obligaton of man to accept it. . . . In the collective recollection of village life there is only the remembrance of men and women who were born, resigned themselves to suffering and hardship and occasional joys, and died when their time came (1954, 129).

In addition, as subjects of social science investigation, we were mostly stereotyped and stigmatized as undeserving "would-be Americans" who should "go back to their country" for being so indifferent and unwilling to abide by the American assimilationist dogma. If mainstream theoretical frameworks for thinking and writing about Hispanic people have persistently shared one major dimension, that commonality is: we have always been thought of as another "minority group" that will, in time, become part of the "melting pot" in much the same way European ethnics did years before. In other words, according to mainstream social science thinking and a great deal of popular view, Hispanic people will make it into the mainstream of the larger society when they agree to assimilation like other ethnic groups.

I began this introduction chapter with an overview of the ways Hispanic people have been characterized by mainstream social scientists, because the voices and writings of these individuals have served as accepted authorities on Cubans, Puerto Ricans, Chicanas/os, and others for quite some time. These were the voices and writings that became the "authoritative sources of information about Mexican Americans [and other Hispanics] for a wide variety of institutional agencies, from schools of medicine, departments of social welfare, to departments of employment and other governmental agencies. . . . [They were] used in the training of professionals as well as in race and ethnic relations courses in colleges and universities" (Romano 1968, 17-18).

Though remnants of this terrible chapter in the history of Hispanic stereotyping and stigmatization in U. S. society can still be found, (e.g., as professors we are looked at with much disdain when we speak in Spanish to our colleagues or students, particularly in places like the elevator of the buildings where we work), for the most part we have moved to a new and refreshing level of critical examination and analysis of Hispanic life and history. Political activism on the part of community residents and students in the last twenty-five years has been the major force of change, forcing colleges and universities throughout the country to consider Hispanic life and culture as central elements of the academic world. In the main, the admission door of the university was opened ever so slightly to enable some Hispanic students to enter. Once there, many worked earnestly to create structures and organizations for the recruitment and retention of students as well as for the academic study of Hispanic life. These efforts led to the creation of many of the Chicano/a, Puerto Rican, and Cuban research centers and academic departments and programs still functioning today. And of course, many of us are the products of these different organizations and programs.

The emerging, critical scholarship among Hispanic social scientists represents a direct challenge and attack to historic misconceptions and erroneous treatment by mainstream frameworks. Whether explicit or not, the critical writings of Hispanic social scientists begin and end by recognizing and taking very seriously the ways Hispanic people have responded to the melting pot approach to life in U. S. society, along with other similar assimilationist systems. These writers emphasize how these various integrationist ideas are out-of-line with the social, cultural, economic, and political interests and needs of Hispanic people. These writers pay attention to how Hispanic people have nurtured their own cultural ways of struggle and survival.

This central question will be apparent when reading the different chapters in this volume, which brings together Hispanic women and men who not only represent the outgrowth of efforts of community activism, but who continue to work to ensure that our cultural traditions and experiences are given the serious attention they deserve. These are some of the individuals who are truly committed to making sure that our stories as Puerto Ricans, Cubans, and Chicanas/os and others are told from our own perspectives, using the insights and intelligence of our grandparents, mothers and fathers, and neighbors to challenge standard social science perspectives that appear too distant from our everyday experiences to make a difference.

The sociology in this volume can be identified by the extent to which the theoretical perspectives and social issues presented and discussed are of major concern to the lives of Hispanic people. In addition the sociology of Hispanic people presented in this volume carries the ideological commitment of the various collaborators to improve the life chances of Hispanic people in a society in which they have suffered as victims of racial and ethnic discrimination. The work of the various collaborators represents far more than academic intellectual enterprising. It carries potential for progressive change and transformation. In brief, these chapters combine to form a sociology of Hispanic people built around the systematic study of social interaction and change among Hispanics and relations with the larger society, from the vantage points of Hispanic writers and people. And indeed, the volume's collected works represent alternatives for the many misrepresentations and misconceptions of Hispanic people in the United States, so popularized by mainstream writers.

After much consultation with various collaborators, we decided that the thrust of this volume should be geared to provide a structural or institutional as well as cultural examination of various leading dimensions of Hispanic life in U. S. society. I asked all the collaborators to frame their work in ways with which we could come to understand the Hispanic experience as it stems from the larger institutional arrangements of society and its own internal or cultural history. Specifically I asked them to consider the various ways Hispanic people have responded to conditions created by society's institutional arrangements; how they have utilized their culture to create opportunities for meeting the challenges presented by the larger social order; how they have interacted with other groups in society as well as with members from their groups and the kinds of realities they constructed from these various interactions. We all recognized that the most exciting part about using this sociological perspective is that it establishes the Hispanic experience in U. S. society within a dialectical context; that is, through this perspective we will be able to understand the Hispanic reality as not stemming only from the dictates of society's institutions, but more importantly existing as a live and participatory culture creating and responding to different challenges faced by people on a day-to-day basis. In this way, culture is not viewed as being static or fixed, but as undergoing a continuous process of change and growth.

An example of this dialectic approach is found in the opening chapter. José Hernández and Havidán Rodríguez introduce Hispanic demographics from a critical historical analysis, emphasizing racial and ethnic subjugation and subordination and sets of cultural responses on the part of different Hispanic groups. To understand how Hispanics have fared in U. S. society, according to Hernández and Rodríguez, they must be understood, first and foremost, as a "conquered people." The lands of those who would later become known as Hispanic people were conquered first by the Spaniards and later by the United States. Similarly, Hispanic people have represented a pool of cheap labor for U. S. industries. Hispanics have had to face the challenges of settlement and participation in U. S. society as second-class citizens.

Marisa Alicea echoes the views of Hernández and Rodríguez when she characterizes Hispanic immigration to U. S. society as "involuntary." She argues that Hispanic immigration, which constitutes a very large movement of people, has always been triggered by conditions larger that one person's individual choice. "Large scale migrations reflect the internal structure and political and economic dynamics of the sending nation. Such internal processes do not occur in isolation, but are themselves influenced by the position of the country within the world system. Both the internal origins of migrations and the countries to which they are directed are deeply conditioned by global relations. Recognizing this reality, this immigration discussion is also framed around the premise that the movement of [Hispanics] is occurring within one overarching economic and political system which is dominated by the United States. Historically, Latin America and its immigrants have provided cheap labor to the United States as well as a ready market. U. S. imperialist and economic interests in Latin America result in the economic and political impoverishment of these countries and the subsequent exodus of its people to the United States."

María de los Angeles Torres makes a similar case about Cuban settlement in U. S. society. "Cuban-Americans are popularly viewed as political exiles who are economically successful and conservative. Thus the myth of the golden exile. Yet serious studies have challenged the three tenets of this myth, which argue that Cubans leave Cuba because they are politically disaffected with the revolution; they are successfully self-employed; and they are politically conservative—especially in regard to U. S./Cuban relations. While the community undeniably bears the scars of thirty years of failed policies toward Cuba and of the island government's intolerance toward those who left, the Cuban-American reality is complex, often paradoxical and in transition. These changes are closely linked to a historical context which is defined in part by the internal situation on the island, the experience in the host country, international factors and the influx of new immigrants. It is also part of the larger matrix of U. S./Latin American relations."

In their chapter, Luis Falcón and Dan Gilbarg make it clear that labor participation among Hispanic workers in U. S. society has had a long history of exploitation and isolation, but also of success. They examine how Hispanic people have been active in the creation of opportunities for their own survival and well-being. Falcón and Gilbarg go on to establish Hispanic labor as "a significant force in the fabric of American society. In fact, their geographical concentration already makes them a sizable force in some of the largest metropolitan areas of the United States such as New York City, Los Angeles, and Chicago."

The various chapters on the political participation among Hispanics move beyond victim blaming. They do not ask, "why are Hispanics politically apathetic?" Instead, Maurilio E. Vigil establishes Hispanic political participation within "the basic structures and operation of the [U. S.] political system [which] historically [has] denied Hispanics [and other minorities] the full benefits of American society." In the chapter, "Puerto Ricans and the 'Door' of Participation in U. S. Politics," José Ramón Sánchez notes:

> If participation suggests an activity whereby citizens can approach government and influence, if not control, its actions, the truth is that the 'doors' that give access to government are not always open or open wide enough to permit all citizens entry. And like a house, the 'doors' of government exist to keep people out as well as to provide entry. Thus, while participation is an important aspect of democracy to study, one cannot fully comprehend how and why people participate without also having some knowledge of what doors exist and who they are designed to keep out. The 'doors' of government and who gains entrance and why are conceptualized here in the notion of political participation. . . . These assumptions about participation make Puerto Ricans in the United States a compelling and anomalous case study. The reason is that most studies of political participation of Puerto Ricans report that political participation, in all forms, is very low for this group.

> While some of these studies make an attempt to find causes for depressed participation rates in social and legal institutions, the notion that participation is something both desirable and necessary casts a long shadow of blame on Puerto Ricans themselves. . . . Ultimately, it is only by understanding how and whether Puerto Ricans were politically incorporated that an accurate image of their participation can emerge.

The chapters on Puerto Rican, Cuban, and Chicana women reflect the dynamics of gender relations within Hispanic people as well as racial oppression in the larger U. S. society. The writings focus on the struggles among Chicana, Puerto Rican, and Cuban women to be recognized for their contribution in the establishment and development of their communities as well as struggles to be heard within their own groups. "Work among Puertorriqueñas is not only what some of our women do in factories, stores, hospitals, schools, or offices—work activities for which they receive remuneration in the form of a 'pay' that often means just meager wages that hardly support them or their families," writes Altagracia Ortiz. "Work for Puertorriqueñas also has come to mean those kinds of constructive doings that have resulted in holding their families together, in building or reconstructing their communities here in America, in continuing their struggle to survive as a people with dignity—in spite of almost five hundred years of colonialism . . . and in spite of the alienating effects of a migration process that has uprooted thousands of Puerto Ricans from their native island and thrust them into American ghettos to live lives full of small, and sometimes not so small, indignities." Teresa Córdova proclaims: "Chicana feminists have struggled to find their voices—have struggled to be heard. Our struggles continue but our silence is forever broken. We are telling our stories and we are recording our triumphs and, by virtue of our presence, we are challenging our surroundings." Despite these early attempts to silence the voices of a developing feminist consciousness, *feministas* were very clear that their voices did not mean a disruption to the unity of La Raza, though it may have meant a disruption to a false unity based on the submission of women. Instead, "Men and women struggling together is a stronger foundation for a successful Chicano movement," Córdova asserts.

One final note is in order. Each collaborator accepted to present an examination of Hispanic life in U. S. society by focusing of one individual group or various groups in the aggregate. Of course the expertise of the writer was a major influence in the adaptation of a particular approach. Those who specialize on Cubans feel more comfortable writing about Cubans; those whose work is on Mexican Americans prefer focusing on Mexican Americans; those who make Puerto Ricans the central point of their work chose to write on the Puerto Rican experience.

Those who wrote on Hispanics in the aggregate are experts as well. Above everything else, their work recognizes the many differences that exist between Chicanos/as, Puerto Ricans, Cubans, and others as well as their shared experiences. In a way, those chapters that examine Hispanics in the aggregate present accounts comparing and contrasting various Hispanic groups as well as their individual (e.g., Cuban, Puerto Rican, Chicano/a) and collective (Hispanic) responses to their conditions in society.

It is also appropriate to indicate that, as I demonstrated in my chapter, there is an emerging, all-embracing identification among the various groups under what I call a Latino consciousness. Puerto Ricans, Mexican Americans, and Cubans and others are interacting with one another and creating new forms of identity as well as social, economic, and political agendas as one Latino group. This is part of the "blending" of identities discussed by Hernández and Rodríguez. It also shows Hispanics as people active in their histories, giving meaning and shape to their individual and groups conditions as they go about living their everyday lives.

Finally, this volume would never have been completed without the support of two friends and colleagues, Nicolás Kanellos and Juan Olivas. Their dedication to the project was felt by everyone of us—it triggered the kind of response required for such initiatives. I am also grateful for having worked with such an outstanding group of men and women—my collaborators were by far exceptional in their work. ¡Un millón de gracias a todos!

Bibliography

Mirandé, Alfredo

1978 "Chicano Sociology: A New Paradigm for Social Science." *Pacific Sociological Review,* vol 21, no 3, (July):293-312.

Romano, Octavio Ignacio

1968 "The Anthropology and Sociology of the Mexican Americans." *El Grito* (Fall):13-26.

Saunders, Lyle

1954 *Cultural Difference and Medical Care: The Case of the Spanish-Speaking People of the Southwest.* New York: Russell Sage Foundation.

Hispanics Blend Diversity

José Hernández

This history traces the development of the Hispanic community through five stages of social and economic change in the United States from 1776 to 1992. First a model is documented in a trend analysis of the first to the fourth stages. The proposed paradigm is completed with comments on the current demographic profile documented by Havidán Rodríguez in this book.

Global Origins and Colonial Inequality

The racial and cultural identity of Hispanics began hundreds of years ago, when people in the Americas, Europe, and Africa were not yet in contact. These origins remain visible, but Hispanics generally represent a blend of appearance and behavior called Latin American. The label's meaning refers to social patterns resulting from Spain's uniform style of managing its colonies, their geographic location, and a common experience of combining Spanish with other racial and cultural origins. The blend varies widely among Latin American nations, among regions within these nations, and among social classes in local areas. Because the same process took place in areas acquired by the United States long ago, the Hispanic identity has blended a diversity of racial and cultural origins and cultures, from its earliest beginnings.

The Native peoples (called Indians by European Americans) generally believe they originated in creation or reproduction by humans coming from the skyworld and have always lived in the Americas (e.g., North American Indian Travelling College 1984). Most scientific writers claim that the Natives migrated from Northern Asia to the Americas during the Ice Age (some 15,000 years ago) by way of a land bridge existing where the Bering Strait is located today (Hopkins 1982; Shutler 1983; Greenberg 1986). Considering the enormous diversity among the societies that followed, both versions could be true, and other origins may have been blended, as well. It is widely accepted that resulting cultures differed markedly from European ways of life at the time of contact, but that Native societies had comparable levels of human advancement and showed abundant evidence of the universal human quality of intelligence in response to diverse climates, terrain, and living conditions (Gordon 1971; Bryan 1978; Howe 1984; Fagan 1987).

Why, then, did the Europeans subjugate the Native nations? The first major reasons were a disparity in population size and a lack of immunity to contagious diseases—both placing the Natives at a disadvantage. An estimated 3 million Natives lived in 600 autonomous societies or nations, widely dispersed in what became the U. S. land area (Mooney 1928; Kroeber 1939). Such totals were typical of a region in a European nation and its towns at that time. Previously healthy Natives were vanquished by epidemics of measles, smallpox, and other imported illnesses that reduced their populations to totals readily outnumbered by the European invaders, regardless of whatever disparities may have existed in weapon technology (Quinn 1978; Wilson 1980).

Large numbers of Native deaths from epidemics also occurred in the conquest of Mexico and Central and South America. However, in these places the Native population was much larger; many more survived, and their subsequent expansion and blending with the colonizers from Spain became a major source of the Hispanic population (Rosenblat 1954, 1967; Calderón 1970).

The second major reasons were a belief in superiority firmly held by the Europeans and a belligerent attitude toward others. Seven hundred years of crusades against the Muslims, who invaded Spain from North Africa, resulted in a deeply rooted anger and greed in Spanish life. The final victory over the Muslims came just before Spain's discovery of America, setting the trend of European world control in motion. Racism was first directed to Spanish people of Arab identity and then to the Natives in America. When the Spanish considered the Natives to be insufficient for forced labor in the pursuit of their goals, they enslaved millions of Africans from south of the Sahara desert and brought them to their colonies in the Americas. The Africans who survived the boat trip from Africa became another significant source of the Hispanic population, which the Spanish structured as a caste system having four segregated levels (Wellman 1954; Picón 1962; Pérez 1976; Wilson 1990):

1. The pure Spanish from Spain
2. Spanish born locally of pure Spanish ancestry
3. Mulattos and mestizos
4. Enslaved Africans and pure Indians.

In time, myths developed to justify the inequality and conceal its origins in conquest. Belief in a natural inferiority of the Natives and Africans made denying education to people "of color" seem correct and convenient. Ignorance restricted their employment to manual labor, explaining why they remained poor. The strong pressure to assimilate Spanish culture eventually made racial categories secondary to the blend evolving from intermarriage with Natives and Africans. During more than three centuries of colonization most of the Latin American population gradually became racially mixed. Blended identities such as Dominican became inclusive in the independence process, making Native and African identities more marginal still.

For such reasons, historical data for Native and African origin populations in Latin America tend to underestimate their numbers, and Hispanics themselves are often confused by the racial divisions in American society, such as when they are identified in a demographic category separate from Whites, Blacks, Indians, and Asians, as an exclusive racial category.

Spain's colonization of what became the United States began about one hundred years before Great Britain and other European nations sent colonists to the North American east coast. Spain centered its management system in New Spain, or Mexico, and from there controlled the places from which Hispanics originate: Louisiana, Florida, Texas, California, Colorado, Utah, Nevada, New Mexico, Arizona, Guam, the Philippines, Cuba, Puerto Rico, Santo Domingo (the Dominican Republic) and Central America. This order follows the sequence of the Anglo American conquest, summarized here in stages of development as a conceptual model for analysis (Fanon 1963; Memmi 1991). The historical pattern of American policy shifted from (1) exclusive occupation of conquered lands, to (2) internal colonization as a conquered minority, to (3) restricted citizenship through statehood, to (4) external colonization by political dependence, to (5) subordination in a world economic system.

Stage 1: Exclusive Occupation, 1776-1834

At the beginning, Anglos found it desirable to become an exclusive population in conquered lands. When the United States established its independence, Spain and France claimed vast areas of North America but had only a small colonial population. The Native peoples had been reduced to less than a million (Steiner 1968), and about 100,000 Hispanics lived in the New Spain colonies that later became U. S. states (see Table 1). Their population and land use were tiny, compared with the U. S. potential for expansion by 4 million people. The prospect of conquest motivated Anglos to kill the inhabitants of conquered lands, march them to land beyond the frontier, or force them into servile labor, as they had done with the enslaved Africans. However, in step with this expansion, the population and land use of New Spain's colonies also expanded, and this made genocide less practical than subordination of Hispanics in the internal colony as conquered peoples (Moore 1970).

Louisiana was first colonized by the French, who explored the central and northern regions of North America and built forts along the St. Lawrence, Ohio, and Mississippi rivers and the Great Lakes. Spain acquired Louisiana by treaty in 1763, added it to New Spain, and claimed the coastal area from Texas to Florida. In that year the British colonists defeated the French in war and soon afterward rebelled to form the United States. The Americans always considered French claims to be theirs by victory, but in 1803 the United States paid France to formalize their ownership.

The Spanish population of about 30,000 could not stop the American takeover of Louisiana. Some His-

TABLE 1

Estimated Population of New Spain Colonies Later Conquered by the U. S., 1776-1800 Total Population of Spain 10 Million— of the U.S. 4 Million

New Spain Colonies Later U.S. States		New Spain Colonies Later U. S. Occupied	
Louisiana	30,000	Mexico	5,200,000
Florida	15,000	Guam	5,000
Texas	10,000	Philippines	3,500,000
California	15,000	Cuba	160,000
Colorado (+)	0	Puerto Rico	50,000
New Mexico	25,000	Santo Domingo	85,000
Arizona	5,000	Central America (*)	1,000,000
Total	100,000	**Total**	10,000,000

Sources: Nadal 1976; U.S. Bureau 1975; Centro 1981.
(+) Nevada and Utah had Spanish settlement after 1800.
(*) Included were Costa Rica, El Salvador, Guatemala, Honduras, and Nicaragua.

panics moved to other New Spain colonies, but most remained and blended their culture with people of French origin in a "Creole" identity that has endured two centuries of Anglo control. The state's name symbolized the blend—not "Luisiana" in Spanish, nor "Louisiane" in French—but a hybrid of both. Creoles also had various racial origins, but their peoplehood (or group identity) proved to be of greater importance than race in unifying the survivors (Dufour 1967).

From the start of Anglo contact with Hispanics, similarities became visible between New Spain and neighboring societies in the Southern United States. Both had agricultural economies organized in a latifundio, or plantation system, based on slave labor, and a new aristocracy oriented to lifestyles centered on family and leisure (Wertenbaker 1942; Keith 1977). The idea of gaining more wealth inspired Southern Anglos to steer American politics toward conquest of the Spanish colonies. Northern Anglos opposed this but planned the conquest of lands to the northwest. In the expansion that followed, Hispanics and Natives were targets for hostility both in conquest and as substitute objects in the rivalry between North and South. Until Hispanics moved in large numbers to the north central and northeastern cities during the 1950s, they were always considered part of Southern Anglo society, both within the United States and in nations occupied by Americans in subsequent times (Washburn 1973; Savage 1979).

The American takeover of Florida followed the U. S. purchase of land claims from Spain in 1819. This prompted the Southern Anglos to occupy the entire Southeast. When the state of Georgia enacted a law annexing Cherokee lands, this nation appealed to the U. S. Supreme Court. Justice John Marshall decided that the United States had the right to acquire such lands but that the Natives could keep part of them and eventually rule themselves, if and when the Anglos approved. This decision became U. S. policy for the Indian Reservations and the "Outlying Territories," or lands beyond the North American continent that were later taken for purposes other than integration by admission to statehood.

President Andrew Jackson then pressured Congress to pass the Removal Act, which approved using force to evacuate the eastern Natives to the Indian Territory later called Oklahoma. In the long walk, half the Natives died from exposure, hunger, and pursuit by American soldiers. When the Seminoles refused to leave Florida and march, the United States waged a war against them that was proportional, in time, cost, and death, to the American war in Vietnam 135 years later (McNickle 1973; Peters 1979).

What happened to the Hispanics in Florida during this period of violence is a topic for research. Migration from Spain from 1800 to 1819 increased their previous population of some 15,000. Some evidence shows that when the U. S. takeover occurred, most Hispanics returned to Spain or moved to Cuba (Douglas 1967). They may have been dislodged under pressure, as happened to the Natives. When the Removal was enacted in 1830, the Census counted 35,000 persons in Florida (U. S. Bureau 1975). How many of them were Hispanic is not yet known because until recent times, U. S. census data did not identify Hispanics. Perhaps Hispanic surnames could be identified in original records, but in such a repressive environment, Hispanics may have concealed their identity or avoided the census count. When Florida became a state in 1845 the population was described as made up entirely of the Anglos and enslaved Africans. However, the 1910 U. S. Census figures indicated 142,742 Hispanic residents (almost all native-born), suggesting a longtime presence in large numbers (see Table 3).

Stage 2: Internal Colonization, 1835-1859

The Chicanos or Mexican Americans gave the name Aztlán to southwest North America, north of Mexico. Like Chicano, the word Aztlán comes from the Aztec language and symbolizes the Native origins of a mestizo culture evolving during three hundred years of Spanish control. In California, Texas, and Colorado, most Native nations were integrated in the Hispanic mestizo society by the blending already described. In New Mexico and Arizona, Spain was unable to conquer some of the Native nations and allowed them to maintain a subordinate independence.

In Aztlán the Hispanic population was much smaller than in Mexico, before 1800. But it grew rapidly as soon as Mexico won independence from Spain in 1821 and encouraged its people to move northward. Mexico's independence also inspired the Aztlán peoples to develop their own peoplehood, a Chicano identity and autonomy, instead of loyalty to Mexico. Freedom from colonial rule and the caste system were as much the goals of the Chicano movement as a desire for independence and separate governments.

Independence was supported by the Anglo American immigrants who settled in Texas after 1821 and maintained ties with the U. S. South, with a view toward gaining control of Aztlán. Sam Houston urged the Anglo immigrant leaders to carry out President Jackson's plan for Texas to "trigger these United States into an explosion across the continent." After Texas was made a republic in 1836, it was readied for waging war against Mexico and for being annexed as a slave state. The Southern Anglos overcame opposition from Abraham Lincoln and other Northern leaders, and commanded the American forces. They treated both the Chicanos and Natives as substitutes for enslaved Africans in a Southern expansion that would use the conquered lands and wealth to dominate American politics. The Southern Anglo initiative blocked the Chicano wish for freedom from colonial and racial oppression. In the segregated society that followed the Anglo conquest, all Hispanics regressed to a lower caste level—regardless of color, previous social class position, or opinion on the American victory (Wellman 1962; Grebler 1970; Connor 1971; Acuña 1988).

As to power and position, Hispanics soon became a minority in number. In 1848 the Guadalupe Hidalgo Treaty ended formal war, and the United States pledged to respect Hispanic land titles and culture. Two years later, the U. S. Census showed a large increase in the population of Texas and California, resulting from the Gold Rush migration of Anglos who seized the farms, mines, and homes of the conquered peoples—the Natives, the Chicanos and Mexican Americans, and the Mexicans from Mexico. Hispanics were reduced to some 20 percent of the population (see Table 2).

Some Hispanics moved to supposedly vacant lands in southern Colorado. But as happened to the Natives who were there before them, the Hispanics also became a minority when Anglos discovered gold in 1858. Until 1854, when the U. S. bought Mexico's claim to a border area, Arizona was peopled mostly by Natives. The Spanish settlement in Tucson had been used as a transportation stopover from Mexico to California, and it continued attracting Mexicans. Only there and in New Mexico were Hispanics a numerical majority for a few decades after the U. S. conquest. By 1850 all Hispanics were less than 1 percent of the U. S. population and were simply ignored or considered by Anglo Americans as a residual fragment, compared with the vast amount of land acquired and its seemingly boundless resources (Fergusson 1964; Wagoner 1973; Abbott 1982; Caughey 1982).

TABLE 2

Estimated Hispanic Population of U. S. States and Territories Formerly Spanish or Mexican Colonies, 1850

Population of Mexico 8 million—of the U. S. 23.2 million of Hispanics and (% of Total Population*)

U. S. States	Population	%
Louisiana	50,000	(9.7)
Florida	?	
Texas	60,000	(28.2)
California	20,000	(21.5)
Occupied Territories:		
Nevada, Utah	?	
Colorado	5,000	(95+)
New Mexico	60,000	(96.8)
Arizona	5,000	(95+)
Total	200,000	(0.9)

Sources: Moore 1970; Acuña 1988; U.S. Bureau 1975; Centro 1981.
*U. S. Census population totals did not include native Americans.

Stage 3: Restricted Citizenship, 1860-1897

Soon after Anglos became a majority in a conquered land called a territory their control was secured by the area's admission to statehood. The state geographic domain provided Anglo rulers with freedom to organize politics to their advantage. Their influence extended to law enforcement through the use of state armed forces, such as the Texas Rangers, and a juridical system that was Anglo controlled. Taxation supported the government, which worked with Anglo business interests to establish the major forms of production and sale of goods. States competed with one another for political and economic power, which further strengthened "rings" of cooperation among the Anglos. This process of control eventually defined the social character of a state, which was also determined by the prevalent Anglo life-style. The local Anglo culture gave shape to the educational system, especially through the influence of state universities that were chartered as part of state politics and that trained the teachers who then worked in state-supported public schools. By 1900 statehood was firmly established in the thirty-five territories conquered after independence, except in Arizona, New Mexico, and Oklahoma (Wagoner 1970; Brown 1971; Ellis 1971; Fehrenbach 1980).

The Anglo Americans in California started the agribusiness pattern that combined factory methods of organizing work with the caste system traditional to the U. S. South and Latin America. Workers were recruited for routine tasks in coordinated teams as needed during seasonal stretches on farms and ranches and for the construction of buildings and railroads. Since wages and benefits were minimal, the workers became landless, impoverished migrants. Even when their jobs allowed permanent residence (as in the mines), they earned very little and depended on company stores and services. Upward mobility was for Anglos only, which meant that Hispanics were destined for a life of manual labor, as in the Spanish caste system.

When Hispanics proved insufficient in number for production, the Anglos recruited Asian peasants for the same kind of work as Hispanics. Asian immigrants were often employed separately by nationality groups, in order to stimulate competition and avoid coalitions. A divide-and-conquer policy was also applied to Hispanics. Peasants recruited from Mexico as temporary workers were seen as different from Chicanos and not as U. S. residents (Josephson 1934; LaFeber 1963; McWilliams 1964; Kitano 1974).

The stigma of defeat combined economic poverty with cultural alienation. A deeply rooted Anglo contempt for anything Hispanic ensued from the expansion, expressed in words such as old, quaint, lazy, dirty, backward. Rejected as having the negative personality features that Anglos despised in themselves, many Hispanics formed a negative self-image under Anglo pressure. Education in Spanish was denied, and Hispanics who learned English were still not allowed to advance, which served to fulfill the Anglo image of Hispanics as naturally inferior, people to be restricted to the bottom of society (Moore 1970; Vigil 1980).

Forced to keep to themselves, Hispanics blended their culture with Anglo values in a self-directed defiance to the conquest of mind and affirmed an American identity distinct from Anglo. Their alienation resembled that of the Asian immigrants, who were racially segregated and treated in the same way by Anglos in the California model of agribusiness development. Both the Hispanic and Asian experiences differed markedly from the assimilation of European immigrants—who faced an initial stigma as foreigners but eventually found acceptance as part of the Anglo population.

Victory in the Civil War shifted political leadership to the North during the period in which statehood was consolidated. The Northern version of the Manifest Destiny saw the United States as intended by God to bring enlightenment and progress to the rest of the world. It made the conquest seem morally right and the vast rewards a blessing. The Homestead movement attracted enough Anglos to ensure that states could be carved out of the north central region and added to the United States. In 1887 the Allotment Act applied the Homestead policy to Natives, aiming to provide a land base to live and practice farming in the Anglo manner, an idea that failed to take into account the great cultural differences. When Native people resisted the dismemberment of their communities into small individual lots, and refused to farm for profit instead of for provision, they lost their farms. This gave way to massive Anglo acquisition of the natives' allotment and reduced the natives to poverty on reservations (Brown 1971; Deloria 1969).

Slavery may have been abolished, and constitutional amendments may have proclaimed that former slaves were equal citizens, but the Civil War hardly put an end to racial oppression. The North attempted to unify statehood and bring about basic changes in the South through Reconstruction, but as Reconstruction failed in the 1870s, the African Americans returned to subordination, as Hispanics had, after the conquest of Aztlán. After that, Southern Anglos revised statehood to establish a caste system that endured one hundred years and functioned as the conservative standard for national policy in racial matters. Available manual work was paid at survival wages. Intimidation, negative images, and cultural alienation were promoted, with few chances of upward mobility for African Americans (Berry 1982).

The Southern policy extended to the Northern industrial cities, to which African Americans moved for end-of-the-line employment, while their outflow served to maintain an Anglo majority in the South. The reunited nation applied its policy of Manifest Destiny to overseas nations, benefiting from the experience of the South and the Southwest to exploit natural resources through forced racial discrimination. Northern complacency over the failure of Reconstruction and the allotment of Native lands supported Southern Anglo Americans in their drive to build an empire abroad in alliance with Great Britain, the major world power in the late nineteenth century. The external colonies would furnish the materials needed to develop the Northern industrial economy and be an outreach for Southern agribusiness. This association would establish the United States as a world power (Weinberg 1935).

The combined Northern and Southern methods of subordination were first applied to the Hawaiian Islands, an independent nation with a tropical climate, fertile soils, and Polynesian people. The Hawaiians suffered greatly from European "discovery" in 1778, and needed international trade. The Anglo Americans who immigrated to set up plantations acquired most of the productive lands by 1848. When the lower caste Hawaiian labor force proved insufficient for expansion, the United States arranged for Asian peasants to work in Hawaii as they had in California, when there were not sufficient numbers of Hispanics for menial work in agribusiness.

As happened in Texas, the Anglos who immigrated to Hawaii used political influence to weaken local authority, especially the monarchy. Anglo missionaries taught Hawaiians to reject their culture, speak English, and be loyal to the United States. In 1894 American marines and sailors were sent to Hawaii in order to overthrow the pacifist Queen Lilíuokalani. By then the Anglo and Asian immigrant populations were three times larger than that of native Hawaiians. No Hawaiians signed the annexation documents approved by the U. S. Congress during the initial period of the American war with Spain in 1898. The U. S. territorial government then sought to prepare Hawaii for statehood, under Anglo control

(Daws 1974; Pettigrew 1970; Blackman 1977; McGregor 1979; Dudley 1991).

Stage 4: External Colonization, 1898-1959

Americans were generally ready, eager, and proud to become a world power at the turn of the twentieth century. Their alliance with Great Britain defined both geographic domains and the methods of controlling distant nations. The United States would dominate the Caribbean and Central America, the Pacific Ocean islands, and the eastern coast of Asia. Experience in North American expansion would be combined with the British way of reorganizing culturally different populations for colonization in Egypt, India, Malaysia, and many other African and Asian nations (Foner 1972).

In order to support the U. S. external colonies and exchange manufactured items for raw materials in the world control system, the American populace would be reorganized, as well. People of color would function as an underclass, or substratum of cheap labor, locking them into economic failure. Greed and fear would strongly motivate Anglos to compete for upward mobility in social classes constructed by ethnicity and education, above internal colonies which included the Hispanic, Native, African, and Asian Americans.

From what remained of New Spain, the U. S. overseas expansion enveloped an additional total of some 9.7 million Hispanics: 7.1 million Filipinos, 1.6 million Cubans, 1 million Puerto Ricans, and 10,000 Chamorros in Guam (U. S. Bureau 1975). Starting with the 1900 Census, however, these Hispanics were not included in the U. S. population, reflecting the government's assumption that the outlying territories would not follow the former pattern of conquest, which led to integration by admission to statehood.

In the external colonies the Anglos were unlikely to form a majority by migration, and the large, "brown" populations had a pervasive land use. Their political status was consequently not in preparation for statehood but a product of expedience, as U. S. territorial administrations dealt with local concerns and a colony's functions in its geopolitical area. Citizenship for both residents and migrants to the United States was variously defined, but in no case equaled Anglo rights and privileges under Statehood. For example, the U. S. Census classified Filipinos by race, Cubans as immigrants, and Puerto Ricans by birthplace and parentage. Such policies divided Hispanics, lessened their visibility, and caused them confusion, uncertainty, and marginality (U. S. Bureau 1913).

Military activities became one of the primary functions of the external colonies. After a long, deadly war of occupation, the U. S. armed forces remained in the Philippines to further control the Pacific Islands and influence politics in Asia. As happened in Puerto Rico, U. S. military officers dictated basic decisions of local government in proclamations that the U. S. Congress later legitimized as territorial rule.

Building a canal connecting the Atlantic and Pacific Oceans simplified access to the colonies and places controlled. For this purpose the United States acquired part of Central America as an outlying territory called the Canal Zone and organized Panamá as a nation. Military bases such as Guantánamo in Cuba were built to safeguard the canal. Next, Hispanic men were inducted from the external colonies to serve in the U. S. military in World War I. By 1920 the external Hispanic communities had formed an authoritarian image of America from the actions of the Anglo servicemen. Ideals of Christianity, Western civilization, and democracy were said to justify military purposes for external colonies in the images projected by Anglo literature and social studies (Leech 1959; LaFeber 1978; Morales 1983; Pido 1986).

The American occupations reorganized farm production to focus on "cash crop" exports. As in California and Hawaii, Anglo companies gained ownership of the most productive land and controlled it by way of a local intermediary elite, usually persons having origins at the top of the Spanish caste system. Only survival wages were paid to the workers of color, who were given no chances for mobility or even subsistence farming. Their poverty provoked a migration to large cities such as Manila, Havana, and San Juan, which had a service economy with no room for additional unskilled labor. This brought about the rapid population growth of migrant settlements in city slums, with accompanying high levels of popular frustration and resentment.

U. S. territorial governments then encouraged limited migration to the United States as a solution. For example, soon after the war with Spain, the U. S. military and the "Big Five" sugar companies cooperated to recruit Puerto Ricans and Filipinos to work in Hawaii. Their migration originated a trend in which workers from external colonies have been regarded as a labor reserve for end-of-the-line employment in the United States, when and where the internally colonized labor force of color has been insufficient or unavailable (Centro 1979, 1986).

Americanization was imposed to acculturate the external colonies to their functions as outposts of the United States. General John Eaton, the first U. S. commissioner of public instruction in Puerto Rico, mandated English as the only language of communication and hired Anglo teachers from the rural South as supervisors, at twice the pay of the few Hispanics who qualified to continue as teachers (Negrón 1975;

Morales 1983). The same style of acculturation inculcated English as a national language and established an American educational system throughout the many cultural and linguistic areas of the Philippines (Pido 1986).

In time the conquest of mind succeeded, as ordinary persons came to see English and American "know-how" as a sure route to economic success, while they viewed things Hispanic as old-fashioned and inferior. Nevertheless, the harsh realities of colonization gave rise to the same alienation experienced by Chicanos after the conquest of Aztlán. Gradually a nativist awareness emerged, as people rediscovered traditional values and defined their identity as distinct from the Anglo culture they learned in school. Thus the social construction of the external colonies resembled the subordination of the conquered peoples within the United States, except that the outlying territories were defined as dependencies of secondary importance and never part of the U. S. population.

As these changes began to take shape, Hispanics within the United States increased to nearly 2 million. By 1910 more than a million descendants of Spanish colonists and Mexican immigrants lived in Texas, the largest Hispanic population by state. About 100,000 Hispanics lived in each of the other New Spain colonies conquered before 1850, except in Colorado. The Hispanic total was almost 2 percent of the U. S. population, and Hispanics continued as the nation's second largest minority after African Americans, who then numbered five times as many people (see Table 3).

TABLE 3

Hispanic Population in the U. S., 1910
U. S. Total Population, 91,972,266

			% Total Population			
Hispanic	**Total**	**%**	**Hisp.**	**Negro**	**"Indian"**	**Asian**
In the U. S.	1,743,217	100.0	1.9	10.7	0.3	0.2
Texas	1,059,127	60.8	27.2	17.1	0.0	0.3
Florida	142,742	8.2	19.0	4.0	0.1	0.0
New Mexico	123,820	7.1	37.8	0.5	6.3	0.2
California	112,219	6.4	4.7	0.9	0.7	3.3
Arizona	98,954	5.7	48.4	1.0	14.3	0.8
Louisiana	85,050	4.9	5.1	43.0	0.0	0.0
New York	26,341	1.5	0.3	1.5	0.1	2.0
Colorado	6,984	0.4	0.9	1.4	0.2	0.3
Other states	87,980	5.0	0.1	10.9	0.3	0.3

Hispanics	**Total**	**%**
Foreign born (+)	269,120	15.4%
Native of Foreign Parentage (+)	217,470	12.5%
Native of Native Parentage (*)	1,256,627	72.1%

Source: U. S. Bureau 1913.

(+) Percent by origin: 81.4% Mexico / 8.5% Caribbean Islands (in both groups) 7.0% Spain / 3.1% Central, South America

(*) Estimated by percent Hispanic in native of foreign parentage population in states above. The 1850 estimates, increased by 20 percent per decade, account for half. The rest are assumed to be descendants of immigrants from Mexico.

A cotton picker in 1933. (Photo by Dorothea Lange, Courtesy of the Library of Congress.)

Divide-and-conquer practices favored the movement of African Americans to northern states such as Illinois, Indiana, Michigan, Ohio, Pennsylvania, New Jersey and New York, and *not* to Texas, New Mexico, California, and Arizona–states with large Hispanic populations. For the same reason, few Hispanics lived in states that had *not* been Spanish colonies. Other racial minorities were also located in historical locations (e.g., Natives in Arizona and Asians in California). As a result, a single group made up the major non-Anglo population in each region and location, setting a pattern visible in the current population of the United States.

In time, however, small numbers of each racial and ethnic group moved to live in regions and locations in which another group was numerous. By 1910, for example, Cuban, Puerto Rican, and Dominican migrantsto New York City had formed the first Hispanic community in New York, a northern industrial city. Many of these people had been recruited to work in cigar factories and garment sweatshops. Such instances are typical of a general pattern in which limited opportunities gave rise to Hispanic communities

Mexican bracero during World War II. (Courtesy of Library of Congress.)

in almost every major city in the United States (e.g., Vega 1984).

By 1910 almost all Hispanics were native-born Americans, the majority having native-born parents who came from people added to the U. S. population by war. Most persons with a foreign identity had come from a Mexican immigration favored by surface travel and labor recruitment, as if from an external colony. From the Mexican Revolution until the Great Depression (1910-30) the immigration escalated, and more than a million moved from Mexico to California or the north central States. During the 1930s a U. S. repatriation program forced thousands to return, and the hard times discouraged more immigration. But most immigrants withstood the pressures to return, and their numbers greatly increased the Hispanic population, producing a new blend of peoplehood and culture (McWilliams 1939, 1964; Grebler 1966; Hernández 1966).

By 1940 one Hispanic in three had roots in the immigration from Mexico and a different sense of presence in America than citizens rooted in the nation's previous history. Most immigrants and their children lived in the barrios (segregated neighborhoods) of such metropolitan cities as Los Angeles and Chicago, in which Hispanics focused on Mexico as their nation of origin and on the urgency of finding jobs, housing, and survival. Their numbers grew rapidly during World War II, when workers were recruited from Mexico for factory work, and military service drew thousands of young Hispanics to the largest U. S. cities (Grebler 1970).

Labor shortages in rural areas also influenced grow ers to recruit *braceros* from Mexico, temporary farm workers with (or often without) contracts. Many braceros eventually settled in the Chicano villages that evolved from transient lodgings near farms, mines, and railroads and in the Mexican American barrios of towns and cities. Except in the Northeast and scattered communities, the immigration Mexicanized the life of most Hispanics and united Chicanos and Mexican Americans to form the largest segment of the national Hispanic population (Mirandé 1985; McWilliams 1990).

Once again Hispanics blended their diversity by integrating Mexican customs and the immigrants' outlook into a culture that evolved from Spanish colonial times. The Hispanic peoples were unified in a desire for social and economic progress within the system, as a segregated underclass accommodating itself to a low but essential position in the American industrial order. Manual workers nurtured values of hard work, honesty, and loyalty, and a middle class arose, made up of workers with sufficient education for important jobs in the Hispanic community, or as assistants to Anglos in the top jobs ascribed to Hispanics. This resembled the situation of Puerto Ricans in New York City (Sánchez 1983).

Community life and civic organizations made clear that U. S. citizenship was upheld as the symbol and means of belonging to the larger society. Anglo customs were blended with Hispanic values in the peoples' culture, especially during the 1950s, when thousands of small-town youth moved to find work in large city factories and services, and the social press to acculturate intensified. The blending of tradition with Anglo language and customs tended to unify Hispanics with different historical and immigrant origins and nationality life-styles, as members of communities having a sense of Latino peoplehood (Padilla 1985).

A blended culture and identity helped Hispanics deal with an often negative social environment. Communities frustrated from not sharing in the prosperity of the 1950s organized to break out of a segregated school and employment situation. Deep resentment followed the victimization of youth by soldiers in World War II and motivated efforts to stop the brutality sanctioned by Anglos, especially toward Hispanics who tried to organize farm workers or acted as political leaders. People insulted by the media tried to change the practice of using Hispanics as scapegoats for public problems in the news, as a failure model in editorials, and as a humorous image in advertisements (García 1989).

Hispanics forced to recurrently move–including farm workers and fringe groups in growth areas–sought to obtain permanent housing. "Operation Wetback" (another U. S. repatriation program starting in 1954) expelled nearly 4 million Mexicans from the United States, almost all without legal protection, and many of them U. S. citizens or legal residents. The social consequences of such intense discrimination and disruption resembled those of the historical conquests. Hispanics reoriented their efforts for the fight against injustice and began to analyze and understand the alienation transmitted through generations as an outcome of being conquered by the Spanish and the Anglo Americans (García 1980).

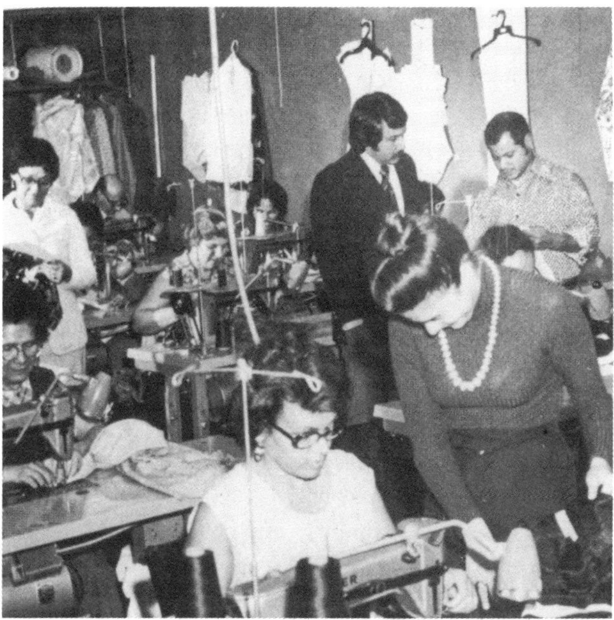

Puerto Rican garment workers in New York City.

Puerto Ricans experienced a similar conquest, when American political and economic influences displaced plantation workers in Puerto Rico and encouraged one third of the island's people to move to New York City and other northern cities during the 1950s. The Puerto Rican migrants felt that their American citizenship and loyalty in World War II would safeguard their belonging to U. S. society as equals. But since they were viewed by Anglos as racially mixed inferiors having negative traits (such as laziness and ignorance), Puerto Ricans were recruited for end-of-the-line work in factories or had to take this type of job, if they moved on their own. The migrants were uprooted from the external colony and replanted within the United States without public consideration as to the equity and consequences of the migration (Lewis 1974; Centro 1979).

Even the small Puerto Rican middle class was restricted by intense discrimination to live in crowded, deteriorating, and hazardous neighborhoods, in which segregated schools suppressed the desire to learn, excel, and become a successful citizen in American society. A resulting alienation became visible in such popular responses as yearning to return to Puerto Rico and the frequent use of hometown clubs. Again, by blending Anglo ways of acting with the enduring values of their peoplehood and culture, Puerto Ricans empowered themselves to survive, resist injustices, and contribute their accomplishments to their community life, as the second largest Hispanic nationality (López 1980; Rodríguez 1980).

Stage 5: Economic Subordination, 1960-1992

The Hispanic population grew rapidly during the second half of the twentieth century, partly as a result of family formation and reproduction among the people who had been added by war and occupation, and the Mexican immigrants. Another immigration was brought about by changes in American laws and social changes in Latin America, as people seeking to fulfill their wishes for freedom and prosperity left social restrictions and brought even greater diversity to the Hispanic population. The new immigrants differed from the Hispanics born in the United States in their experience of entry and social features such as nationality, politics, culture, language, education, occupation, and previous participation in the life of foreign nations (Maldonado 1985).

Background of Economic Subordination in Latin America

During the prosperity of the cold war with the Soviet Union, capitalist European nations joined Japan and the United States in a new colonialism based on the advantages of being "developed," in relation to nations previously colonized by a single power. For Africa, Asia, and Latin America the goals of "being like us" were packaged in humanitarian terms: education, health, and modernization. As formerly colonized nations became politically independent, these goals gave shape to Euro-American government and business standards that defined the quality of national life, mostly in terms of comparative income measures.

Development policies imposed Euro-American cultural norms on professional practices, textbooks, and city planning, housing, and transportation. Developed nations gained more control as they set up subsidiary businesses based on cheap labor in routine assembly work, the services required by innovations such as in tourism, and specialized work in bureaucracies. This new world dominance recognized the "Third World's" independence but stifled its liberation from colonial bonds. Dependency was transformed but remained forceful in subordinating the indigenous peoples and cultures of Africa, Latin America, and Asia. An ongoing inferior status was the main effect of the process of being labeled as underdeveloped—or, euphemistically, "developing."

A Cuban refugee at work in a restaurant in Tucson, AZ. (Courtesy of the *Texas Catholic Herald.*)

Although the Latin American independence movement of the nineteenth century attempted to break with colonialism, the new ruling elites were strongly European in cultural and racial identity and continued subordinating people of Native and African origins. As in the United States, slavery was abolished in the second half of the nineteenth century, but the land tenure in latifundios and similar institutions continued exploiting people of color. During the twentieth century social revolutions that aimed to unseat the traditional elite generally succeeded only in giving rise to a middle class with a limited mobility by exception to the enduring pattern of subordination. Moreover, the middle classes patterned their life after the elite and cooperated as intermediaries with the masses of people remaining in poverty at the bottom of the new world economic system (Furtado 1964, 1965, 1976).

Subordination Stimulates Immigration to the United States

Why did the new Hispanic immigrants come? Many were farm workers seeking an escape from a feudalism rejected in policy but continuing in practice. Limited attempts at land reform did not benefit those in the bracero caste of migrants. Latin American efforts to Hispanize peoples of Indian culture led many to seek a perceived cultural freedom in America. Immigrants from the urban working class were often attracted by family and barrio ties with Hispanics in the United States. Rapid population growth produced too many workers for the city jobs available, especially among persons disadvantaged by educational limitations and a lack of capital and technical support for local businesses. Immigrants with a bourgeois education felt alienated, because they saw Latin American economics as discouraging their new ideas and ambition. Where socialism inspired government ownership of utilities and initiatives in development, Latin Americans grew distrustful of bureaucracies and promises of plentiful jobs and better wages. Job scarcity became chronic, as capital-intensive projects took the place of labor-intensive factories that continually moved to places offering even lower wages. Those who stayed became part of an economy in which production was almost fully controlled by the consumerism of Euro-American development (Portes 1985).

The Cuban Revolution was the turning point in this stage of Hispanic history. Here, the United States lost a chance to show how basic economic and political reforms could lead Latin America out of feudalism and poverty. Instead Cuba served as a scapegoat for cold war tensions and as a failure model, contrary to the goals and aid programs of Euro-Americans in Latin America. In this case the Hispanics who came as refugees from the privileged classes in Cuba were strongly opposed to the social revolution. They gained power and success in U. S. Government, business, and the media, and public support as a success model for Hispanics. Later, public stigma degraded Cubans admitted by provisions for persons rejected by the revolution. This severely limited their chances to gain the success of earlier Cuban refugees and gave them an experience resembling that of undocumented Hispanics and the majority of the Hispanic immigrants seeking social mobility (Uriarte 1981, 1984; Pedraza 1985; Luzón 1987).

Opposition to the Cuban Revolution also strengthened support for oppressive dictatorships and escalated military interventions wherever social revolutions were likely. For example, the United States occupied the Dominican Republic in 1965 and pressured the government to approve the relocation of factories no longer seen as profitable in the northeastern and north central United States, because American workers demanded higher wages. Such moves often recurred in Latin American nations and displaced Hispanic factory workers, as the United States shifted to a new service economy requiring workers for menial tasks. For that purpose, Dominicans were encouraged to immigrate to the United States. The push to leave came from the job scarcity and inflation brought about by economic dependency and the Americanization made desirable by U. S. media and business (Hendricks 1974; Rosario 1990).

The caste system continuing from Spanish colonization also facilitated the use of cheap labor in the American plantations producing bananas and coffee in Central America. The revolution arose from long time injustices and the feudalism of the ruling families and despotic dictators. As in the Dominican experience, the United States favored conservatives relying on intimidation to suppress popular movements for change and imposed economic subordination. Massive violence was linked to the cold war, and the devastating results fostered the emigration of poor people as refugees (often undocumented) as well as middle-class people who left because of fear, resentment, and a desire for freedom and security. The new immigration laws and the image of prosperity projected by American television and retail vendors made the United States the destination preferred by most immigrants.

Causes and Effects of Subordination within the United States

While they still identified primarily with local nationality groups, Hispanics saw themselves as belonging to the underclass made up mostly of American citizens of color, with little power to move out of poverty, near-poverty, or a working-class status. When public policies and the media constructed a national Hispanic identity in the late 1970s and the 1980s, they assigned Hispanics a succession role at the bottom of the domestic economy, as the "second minority," less prepared for success and less worthy of correction for historical inequities than African Americans. "Hispanic" became a trendy label useful to the powerful and rich in order to divide and conquer, blame the victims of internal colonization, foster prejudice, and strengthen discrimination. This sealed the social destiny of Hispanics as the prototype of the "new immigrants," suitable for exploitation and subordination in a post-industrial economy, in the American "ethnic queue" of upward mobility. The principal causes and effects of the new domestic economy became facts of life in the fifth stage of conquest (Hernández 1990).

Geographic Concentration and Segregation

The Sunbelt economies grew in step with the world system, especially in Florida, Texas, and California. Prosperity was based on mobility and services, not on the production of goods. Massive infrastructure needs came about for transportation, housing, and communication. But Hispanics were relegated to marginal employment in the suburban society emerging from this economy. The role of manufacturing was not fully replaced by developing forms of production in northeastern and north central Rustbelt cities that were socially constructed by European immigrant subcultures and the influence of African American migration from the slavery of the Southeast. Here Hispanics were also placed in an end-of-the-line employment condition. Many had to seek out a precarious living in declining industries, the underground (unregulated or informal) economy, and welfare (Abbott 1981).

In both Sunbelt and Rustbelt, demographic data indicate that Hispanics remained in their historical places and in central city neighborhoods with limited economic potential, segregated from Anglo and African Americans, regardless of U. S. region. Social isolation meant more than a lack of participation in the nation's prosperity. It also supported the alienation rooted in the historical experience of conquest. This was true in Sunbelt states, which were former Spanish or Mexican colonies and had a lingering sense of defeat for Natives and Chicanos. Alienation was also a prevalent theme in the "Spanish" institutions that emerged in Rustbelt States, largely out of the public eye and serving as a substitute for the respect and genuine participation in society denied to Hispanics (Sections A-D Demographics: U. S. Bureau 1973-88; Rodríguez, Profile).

Structural Limitations in Occupation and Employment

The transfer of factory jobs to the Third World was only part of the structural factors in the new domestic economy. As the American public was reoriented to buy foreign-made goods, a deficit grew in the nation's international balance of payments, cheapening the dollar, and causing inflation led by imported luxuries and dependence on foreign oil. Due to the immense cost of the cold war and related "big-spender" attempts to reorganize the nation's domestic economy for world dominance, a runaway deficit developed in government budgets. At all levels, American politicians found themselves unable to provide for real solutions to employment and poverty problems through quality education for the disadvantaged, effective training and placement of workers.

Strong pressure developed to earn more money as life became more expensive. Upward mobility became more competitive and no longer influenced by ideals of social justice. The emphasis on such credentials as college degrees greatly increased. Massive increases took place in women's labor force participation, often under conditions of disadvantage, frustration, and conflict. The working class was reoriented to new roles in a consumer economy, by a shift to skilled manual or service jobs having a "glass ceiling" that prevented mobility to college-level professional work.

In such a vortex of negative causes, whatever progress took place among Hispanics came mostly from civil rights legislation, affirmative action, community organizations' efforts, and the new immigration law's educational preference, which selected the educated workers to be imported for the kinds of work Americans chose to avoid or for cheap-labor jobs below their educational level. The labor market for disadvantaged workers born in the United States contracted to a marginal condition, weakened even more by discouraged workers chronically unemployed, locked in poverty, and forced to survive on transfer payments, work in the underground economy, and dependence on others. As a result many Hispanics were submerged in poverty, while other segments of the nation prospered, typically Anglos in favored situations.

Income Deficiencies and Family Life Problems

As a result of the world economy, Americans were reoriented to rapid change, pressure to work, technology, and communication. This strengthened materialistic, selfish values and habituated them to seek easy comfort and feel good about their complacency. Nevertheless inflation, deficit spending, and deregulation led to a decline in real income, especially for the middle-class people who accepted a false vision of participating in a prosperity that favored only the rich. The same decline was felt by Hispanics at a time when they had accepted the vision of escaping poverty and moving into the middle class. Most found their chances severely damaged when the institutional means for upward mobility were reduced or eliminated in competition, or by the ineptness and incompetence of governments. Depending on their nationality, the Hispanic poverty rate was two to five times higher than for the Anglos. One-third stayed poor or near-poor, more than one-third belonged to the working class, less than one-third to the middle class. As living conditions reverted to the situation before the civil rights movement of the 1960s, their alienation intensified.

Alienation in turn had many negative family effects, particularly visible in the youth making up most of the Hispanic population. Hispanic fertility had declined to approach national averages, but early child-bearing remained customary. Most new immigrants were young adults. This meant that family dependency was greater than for Anglos, who typically postponed their family formation and did not receive a large number of youth from other nations. Hispanic households also had a higher rate of extended family members and women who were the only or principal provider. These solutions to the family stress brought about by the new economy were weakened by discrimination against youth and women. Children deprived of hope in schools and exposure to the larger society were motivated to leave school and get any job to help support the family and obtain things the family could not give them. More than half of Hispanic children were raised in this deprivation, and the trend was toward more.

Increasingly Restricted Potential for Mobility

Hispanics had less protection than other Americans against a decline in real earnings because they typically lacked wealth or accumulated money and social value that could serve as resources for coping with a changed economy. About half of Anglo households received income from savings and investments, the sale of a house, or secondary jobs, and a higher percentage received social security payments, considered "good"

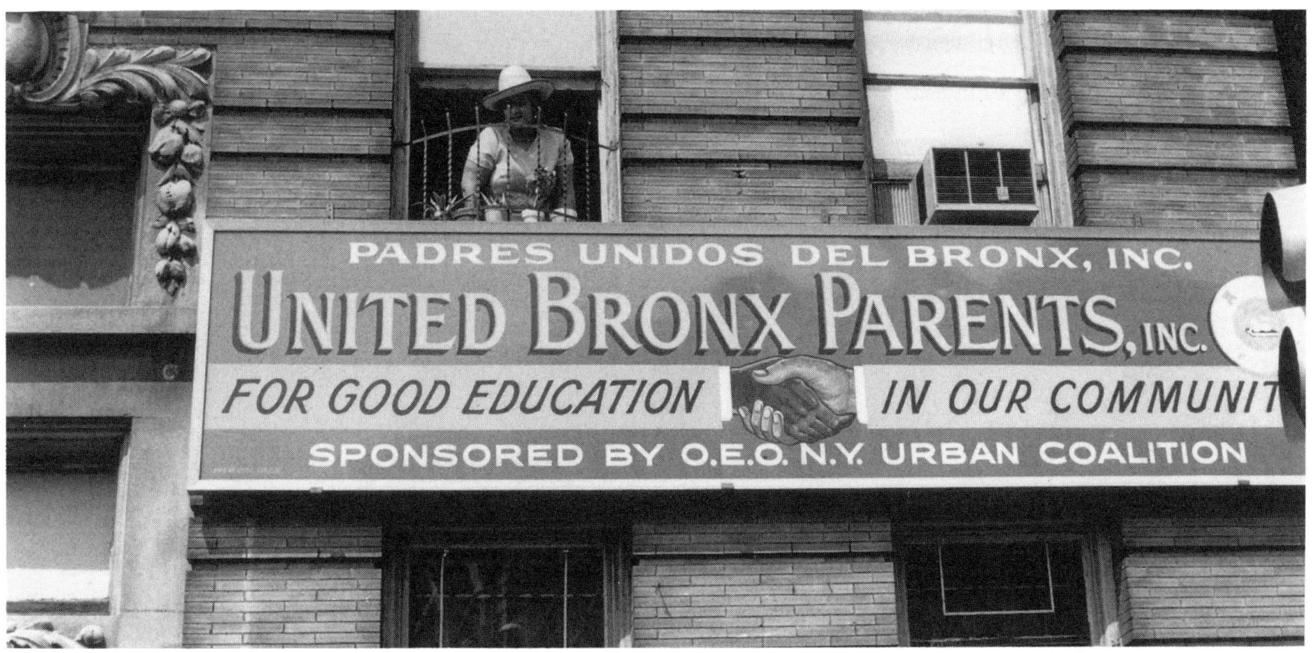

A community organization working for improvement of educational opportunity for Hispanics. (Courtesy of The Records of United Bronx Parents, Inc., Center for Puerto Rican Studies Library, Hunter College, CUNY.)

as a public money transfer. Hispanics depended more than Anglos on stigmatized sources of income, such as public assistance. Even so, information on eligibility showed that Hispanics received less public assistance than they could, based on economic needs. Regardless of nationality, the poverty percentage among Hispanic households was higher than the percentage of households receiving welfare. Wealth in terms of social value is not as easily reduced to a statistical indicator, but almost all the literature shows that the condition of being Hispanic was among the lowest in prestige and social acceptability. This also included intangibles such as the stereotypes in people's minds of the type of person who "should be given a break" or considered as a citizen worth helping when in trouble, if at all.

During the fifth stage of Hispanic history, formal education abounded as an activity in the "schooling society." Ironically, however, the quality of education declined in the United States, as a mediocre and incomplete education became the principal means of underclass placement. Most job requirements excluded Hispanics who were high school dropouts and many who were stay-ins having a partial college education. In addition, Hispanics generally had to be over-educated for the jobs assigned to them in the economy. For example, Hispanic college graduates typically held the kind of position held by an Anglo high school graduate.

Schools became the best example of discrimination, because the majority of teachers were Anglos, and Hispanics were hired only as an exception to the consistent pattern channeling them toward failure. Hispanic teachers typically had more preparation than needed for their job and worked in various additional tasks assigned to them by reason of being "a minority," and performed activities voluntarily, in order to compensate for school system inadequacies regarding Hispanic children.

Finally, a renewed vision of what it meant to be an Anglo arose from the world economy, including such beliefs as the supremacy of the English language and British-American culture. Because of the very meager knowledge and understanding given in American schools about Hispanic history and culture, most Anglos feared a "Spanish peril" when considering the size and growth of the Hispanic population. On a subconscious level they regarded Hispanics as the enemy, as if they could reverse history and take back the states once part of New Spain. Mass media and academic publications, manifested "hispanic" in what was said about Hispanics, usually with no real grounding in historical experience. Hispanics were pictured as the self-evident source of drug abuse, urban and school decay, and the underground economies. Such enormous devaluation of Hispanics intensified alienation and strengthened the Spanish language as a symbol of a people resisting continued conquest in the United States. Spanish was also supported by the social revolutionary background of the new immigrants, and their continued closeness to the nations of origin through television, continued family ties, and jet-travel visits.

Table 4 summarizes the Hispanic experience in the five stages of incorporation in the U. S. population. It

TABLE 4

Hispanic Responses to the Anglo Conquest

Stage	Dates	Kinds of Conquest	Hispanic Response
1	1776-1834	Exclusive Occupation	Continued Identity
2	1835-1859	Internal Colonization	Readjustment to Caste
3	1860-1897	Restriced Citizenship	Alienation
4	1898-1959	External Colonization	Community Organization
5	1960-1993	Economic Subordination	Empowerment

also lists the responses of ordinary people to the major kinds of conquest that have taken place as a result of Anglo dominance. Starting with the Hispanic reaction to the Southern occupation, a consistent pattern has been to affirm one's identity of origin in the Spanish colonies of the Americas. For most Hispanics this has meant having to cope with subordination to Anglos as a constant fact of life, in a condition similar to the previously oppressive situation under Spain. The underclass placement of Hispanics in politics, economy, and society came about as an effect of racial stigma. Among Hispanics this gave rise to long time feelings of rejection, isolation, and relegation to the bottom of a nation that prided itself on the victory of its Manifest Destiny.

Starting in the 1920s Hispanics formalized their efforts to gain civil rights and prevent discrimination by associating their members and pressuring the Anglos in authority to enact laws and policies facilitating desegregation and representation, equity in employment, and improvements in housing and education. Inspired by the civil rights movement in the 1960s, Hispanics participated in bringing about such changes, especially as their militancy urged Anglos to award grants and contracts to

A voter registration drive in East Harlem, 1960. (Courtesy of the Center for Puerto Rican Studies Library, Hunter College, CUNY.)

organizations seeking to diminish prejudice by reducing its effects in discrimination. For example, Hispanics pioneered a movement using bilingual methods of teaching to facilitate student success among non-Anglo groups in America. These efforts motivated a generation of Hispanics to specialize in human services and administration and expand their activities to form the national networks typical of organizations that arose or were strengthened in the 1970s. An intense drive of creative work followed in art, music, writing, Chicano and Puerto Rican Studies, symbols of cultural nationalism, and popular means of expressing peoplehood: flags, parades, and Spanglish idioms that told themselves and the world that "we're here to stay!" (e.g., Padilla 1987; Acosta 1988).

Hispanics have generally concluded that despite their many victories, organizational efforts to reduce the *effects* of the discrimination of conquest have not succeeded in uprooting the *causes* in prejudice, or the negative images retained by Anglos. Consequently Hispanics have redefined their national agenda toward gaining a genuine entitlement in public recognition of rights specific to themselves as citizens, a commitment to civic reform and action replacing the negative conditions that prejudice has effected with genuine institutional changes, and respect for cultural diversity in a more democratic society (Bruce 1986; Hernández 1990).

Perhaps the strongest force toward entitlement are the new Hispanic immigrants who entered after the civil rights movement and its organizational outcomes. In their experience, a decline in social and economic status often followed arrival in America, and the "catch-up" period seldom produced what they wanted from the beginning. They may have begun with an "invisible minority" identity, competing on the basis of personal competence in the business give-and-take and blending cultures by personal choice, instead of as a matter of group identity. However, many negative feelings resulted from their discovery of the same hostility and rejection that Hispanics had felt during the previous stages of conquest. Their responses typically replicated the sequence from continued identity through readjustment to caste and alienation but questioned the utility of community organization as the *only* means for solutions. In part their doubts may have arisen from feeling excluded from organizations founded by other nationality groups. But their responses seem influenced more by a perception of the Hispanic condition as a violation of the ideals of freedom and equality that inspired American independence and the values they sought to find in a nation that promised a change from the oppression and lack of opportunity they had left behind.

At present, Hispanics—those historically conquered and the new immigrants—are once again blending their diversity in a new realization that entitlement can be most effectively attained by empowerment. In this traditional approach to the improvement of life conditions, the element of power is defined as the ability to be self-determining and to influence others. Empowerment is a personal and group process to attain power by changing negative and destructive self-images to positive and constructive ones, taking effective actions to solve problems, helping others to change in their problem-solving mentality, and promoting group unity. With unity Hispanics empower themselves to: (1) influence the dominant Anglos in society, replacing negative images causing discrimination with favorable attitudes, (2) significantly improve their life conditions as a result of their own determination and initiative, and (3) reach a genuine equality that is based on the willingness of Americans to live out the principles on which the United States was founded as a decolonizing nation creating freedom and equality as fundamental values of a democratic society (Hernández 1974, 1992; cf. Josephy 1971; Akwesasne 1986; Champagne 1989).

Bibliography

Abbott, Carl
1987 *The New Urban America: Growth and Politics in Sunbelt Cities.* Rev ed Chapel Hill: U of North Carolina.

Abbott, Carl, and others
1982 *Colorado: A History of the Centennial State.* Rev ed Boulder: Colorado Associated UP.

Acosta-Belén, Edna, ed.
1988 *The Hispanic Experience in the United States.* New York: Praeger.

Acuña, Rodolfo
1988 *Occupied America: The History of Chicanos.* New York: Harper & Row.

Akwesasne Notes
1986 *Basic Call to Consciousness.* Rev ed Mohawk Nation.

Berry, Mary F., and John W. Blassingame
1982 *Long Memory: The Black Experience in America.* New York: Oxford UP.

Blackman, William F.
1977 *The Making of Hawaii: A Study in Social Evolution.* Repr of 1906 edition published by Macmillan. New York: AMS.

Brown, Dee
1971 *Bury My Heart at Wounded Knee: An Indian History of the American West.* New York: Holt, Rinehart & Winston.

Bruce-Novoa, Juan, and Renate von Bardeleben, eds
1986 *Missions in Conflict: Essays on U. S.-Mexican Relations and Chicano Culture.* Presented at the First International Symposium on Chicano Culture. Tubingen, Netherlands: Narr.

Bryan, Alan L., ed
1978 *Early Man in America from a Circum-Pacific Perspective.* Edmonton: U of Alberta.

Calderón Quijano, José A.
1970 *Población y raza en Hispanoamérica.* Sevilla: Real Academia Sevillana de Buenas Letras.

Caughey, John W., and Norris Hundley, Jr.
1982 *California: A History of a Remarkable State.* 4th ed Englewood Cliffs, NJ: Prentice-Hall.

Centro de Estudios Económicos y Demográficos.
1981 *Dinámica de la población de México.* 2d ed México: El Colegio de Mexico.

Centro de Estudios Puertorriqueños.
1979 *Labor Migration under Capitalism.* New York: Monthly Review.
1986 *Extended Roots: From Hawaii to New York; Migraciones Puertorriqueñas a los Estados Unidos.* New York: Centro de Estudios Puertorriqueños, City U of New York.

Champagne, Duane
1989 *American Indian Societies: Strategies and Conditions of Political and Cultural Survival.* Cambridge, MA: Cultural Survival, Inc.

Connor, Seymour V., and Odie B. Faulk
1971 *North America Divided: The Mexican War, 1846-1848.* New York: Oxford UP.

Daws, Gavan
1974 *Shoal of Time: A History of the Hawaiian Islands.* Repr of edition published by Macmillan, 1968. Honolulu: U of Hawaii P.

Deloria, Vine, Jr.
1969 *Custer Died for Your Sins: An Indian Manifesto.* New York: Macmillan.

Douglas, Marjory S.
1967 *Florida: The Long Frontier.* New York: Harper & Row.

Dudley, Michael Kioni, and Keoni Kealoha Agard
1991 *A Hawaiian Nation II: A Call for Hawaiian Sovereignty.* Waipahu, HI: Na Kané O Ka Malo P.

Dufour, Charles L.
1967 *Ten Flags in the Wind: The Story of Louisiana.* New York: Harper & Row.

Durán, Diego
1964 *The Aztecs: The History of the Indies of New Spain.* Originally published in 1588. Trans Doris Heyden and Fernando Horcasitas. New York: Union P.

Ellis, Richard N., ed.
1971 *New Mexico: Past and Present; A Historical Reader.* Albuquerque: U of New Mexico P.

Fagan, Brian M.
1987 *The Great Journey: The Peopling of Ancient America.* New York: Thames & Hudson.

Fanon, Fritz
1963 *The Wretched of the Earth.* New York: Grove.

Fehrenbach, T. R.
1980 *A History of Texas and the Texans.* New York: Macmillan.

Fergusson, Erna
1964 *New Mexico: A Pageant of Three Peoples.* 2nd ed New York: Knopf.

Foner, Philip
1972 *The Spanish-Cuban-American War and the Birth of American Imperialism.* New York: Monthly Review P.

Furtado, Celso
1964 *Development and Underdevelopment.* Trans Ricardo W. Aguiar and Eric C. Drysdale. Berkeley: U of California P.
1965 *Development and Stagnation in Latin America: A Structuralist Approach.* St. Louis: Social Science Institute, Washington U.
1976 *Economic Development of Latin America: A Survey from Colonial Times to 1973.* Trans Suzette Macedo. 2nd ed New York: Cambridge UP.

García, Juan R.
1980 *Operation Wetback: The Mass Deportation of Mexican Undocumented Workers in 1954.* Westport, CT: Greenwood P.

García, Mario T.
1989 *Mexican Americans: Leadership, Ideology, and Identity, 1930-1960.* New Haven: Yale UP.

Gordon, Cyrus H.
1971 *Before Columbus: Links between the Old World and Ancient America.* New York: Crown Publishers.

Grebler, Leo
1966 *Mexican Immigration to the United States: The Record and Its Implications.* Los Angeles: University of California Mexican-American Study Project, Division of Research, Graduate School of Business Administration, Advance Report 2.

Grebler, Leo, Joan W. Moore and Ralph C. Guzman
1970 *The Mexican American People: The Nation's Second Largest Minority.* New York: Free P.

Greenberg, Joseph H.
1987 *Language in the Americas.* Stanford, CA: Stanford UP.

Greenberg, Joseph H., and others
1986 "The Settlement of the Americas: A Comparison of the Linguistic, Dental, and Genetic Evidence." *Current Anthropology*, vol 27, no 5:477-97.

Hendricks, Glenn
1974 *The Dominican Diaspora: From the Dominican Republic to New York City; Villagers in Transition.* New York: Center for Education in Latin America, Teacher's College P, Columbia U.

Hernández, José
1966 "A Demographic Profile of the Mexican Immigration to the United States, 1910-1950." *Journal of Inter-American Studies,* vol 8, no 3 (July):471-96.
1974 *People, Power, and Policy: A New View on Population.* Palo Alto, CA: National Press Books.
1990 "Latino Alternatives to the Underclass Concept." *Latino Studies Journal,* vol 1 no 1, (January):95-105.
1992 *Conquered Peoples in America.* 4th ed Dubuque, IA: Kendall/Hunt Publishing.

Hopkins, David M., and others
1982 *Paleoecology of Beringia.* New York: Academic P.

Howe, K. R.
1984 *Where the Waves Fall: A New South Sea Islands History from First Settlement to Colonial Rule.* Honolulu: U of Hawaii.

Josephson, Matthew
1962 *The Robber Barons: The Great American Capitalists, 1861-1901.* Rpt from original 1934 ed New York: Harcourt, Brace.

Josephy, Alvin M., Jr.
1971 *Red Power: The American Indian's Fight for Freedom.* New York: American Heritage P.

Keith, Robert G., ed
1977 *Haciendas and Plantations in Latin American History.* New York: Holmes & Meier.

Kitano, H. H.
1974 *Race Relations.* Englewood Cliffs, NJ: Prentice-Hall.

Kroeber, Alfred L.
1939 *Cultural and Natural Areas of Native North America.* Berkeley: U of California P.

LaFeber, Walter
1963 *The New Empire: An Interpretation of American Expansion, 1860-1898.* Pub for the American Historical Association. Ithaca, NY: Cornell UP.
1978 *The Panama Canal: The Crisis in Historical Perspective.* New York: Oxford UP.

Leech, Margaret
1959 *In the Days of McKinley.* New York: Harper.

Lewis, Gordon K.
1974 *Puerto Rico: Freedom and Power in the Caribbean.* New York: Monthly Review P.

López, Adalberto
1980 *The Puerto Ricans: Their History, Culture, and Society.* Cambridge, MA: Schenkman.

Luzón, José
1987 *Economía, población, y territorio en Cuba (1899-1983).* Madrid: Instituto de Cooperación Iberoamericana.

Maldonado, Lionel, and Joan Moore, eds
1985 *Urban Ethnicity in the United States: New Immigrants and Old Minorities,* vol 29 of *Urban Affairs Annual Reviews.* Beverly Hills, CA: Sage Publications.

McGregor-Alegado, Davianna
1979 *Hawaiian Resistance, 1887-1889.* Master's thesis. U of Hawaii, Maui.

McNickle, D'Arcy
1973 *Native American Tribalism: Indian Survivals and Renewals.* Pub for the Institute of Race Relations. New York: Oxford UP.

McWilliams, Carey
1939 *Factories in the Field: The Story of Migratory Farm Labor in California.* Boston: Little, Brown.
1964 *Brothers under the Skin.* Rev ed Boston: Little, Brown.
1990 *North from Mexico: The Spanish-Speaking People of the United States.* Updated ed by Matt S. Meier. Orig ed pub by J. B. Lippincott, 1949. New York: Greenwood P.

Memmi, Albert
1991 *The Colonizer and the Colonized.* Trans. Howard Greenfeld. Expanded ed originally pub by Orion, 1965. Boston: Beacon P.

Mirandé, Alfredo
1985 *The Chicano Experience: An Alternative Perspective.* Notre Dame, IN: U of Notre Dame P.

Mooney, James
1928 "The Aboriginal Population of America North of Mexico." *Smithsonian Miscellaneous Collection,* vol 80, no 7.

Moore, Joan W., with Alfredo Cuellar
1970 *Mexican Americans.* Englewood Cliffs, NJ: Prentice Hall.

Morales Carrión, Arturo
1983 *Puerto Rico: A Political and Cultural History.* New York: W. W. Norton.

Nadal Oller, Jorge
1976 *La población española: Siglos XVI a XX.* 4th ed Barcelona: Ariel, Esplugues de Llobregat.

Negrón de Montilla, Aida
1975 *Americanization in Puerto Rico and the Public School System, 1900-1930.* Río Piedras: Editorial Universitaria, U of Puerto Rico.

North American Indian Travelling College
1984 *Traditional Teachings.* Cornwall Island, Ontario.

Padilla, Félix M.
1985 *Americans and Puerto Ricans in Chicago.* Notre Dame, IN: U of Notre Dame P.
1987 *Puerto Rican Chicago.* Notre Dame, IN: U of Notre Dame P.

Pedraza-Bailey, Silvia
1985 "Cuba's Exiles: Portrait of a Refugee Migration." *International Migration Review,* vol 19, no 1:4-33.

Pérez de Barrades, José
1976 *Los mestizos de América.* Madrid: Espasa-Calpe.

Peters, Virginia B.
1979 *The Florida Wars.* Hamden, CT: Archon Books.

Pettigrew, Richard F.
1970 *Imperial Washington: The Story of American Public Life from 1870 to 1920.* Repr of edition pub by Charles H. Kerr, 1922. New York: Arno P.

Picón Salas, Mariano
1982 *A Cultural History of Spanish America from Conquest to Independence.* Trans Irving A. Leonard. Repr of edition pub by U of California P, 1962. Westport, CT: Greenwood P.

Pido, Antonio J. A.
1986 *The Pilipinos in America: Macro/Micro Dimensions of Immigration and Integration.* New York: Center for Migration Studies.

Portes, Alejandro, and Robert L. Bach
1985 *Latin Journey: Cuban and Mexican Immigrants in the United States.* Los Angeles: U of California P.

Quinn, David B.
1977 *North America from Earliest Discovery to First Settlements: The Norse Voyages to 1612.* New York: Harper & Row.

Rodríguez, Clara E., and others
1980 *The Puerto Rican Struggle: Essays on Survival in the U. S.* Repr of edition pub by the Puerto Rican Migration Research Consortium, 1980. Maplewood, NJ: Waterfront P.

Rosario, Juan, Anneris Goris, and Francisco Angeles
1990 *Movimientos poblacionales en la República Dominicana.* New York: Centro de Investigación Dominicano.

Rosenblat, Angel
1954 *La población indígena y el mestizaje en América.* Buenos Aires: Editorial Nova.
1967 *La población de América en 1492.* Mexico: Np.
Sánchez Korrol, Virginia
1983 *From Colonia to Community: The History of Puerto Ricans in New York City, 1917-1948.* Westport, CT: Greenwood P.
Savage, Henry, Jr.
1979 *Discovering America, 1700-1875.* New York: Harper & Row.
Shutler, Richard, Jr., ed.
1983 *Early Man in the New World.* Beverly Hills, CA: Sage Publications.
Steiner, Stan
1968 *The New Indians.* New York: Dell.
U. S. Bureau of the Census
1913 *Thirteenth Census of the United States, 1910.* vol 1: *Population: General Report and Analysis.* Washington, DC: Government Printing Office.
1973 *Census of Population: 1970.* (a) "Persons of Spanish Origin," *Subject Report PC(2)-1C.* (b) "Family Composition," *Subject Report PC(2)-4A.* Washington, DC: Government Printing Office.
1974 "Persons of Spanish Origin in the United States," *Current Population Reports, Series P-20, no 264.* Washington, DC: Government Printing Office.
1975 *Historical Statistics of the United States, Colonial Times to 1970, Bicentennial Edition, Part 1.* Washington, DC: Government Printing Office.
1981 "Persons of Spanish Origin in the United States, March 1980 (Advanced Report)," *Current Population Reports, Series P-20, no 361.* Washington, DC: Government Printing Office.
1983 *Population Census: 1980.* (a) *General Population Characteristics, U. S. Summary, PC80-1-B1.* (b) *General Social and Economic Population Characteristics, U. S. Summary, PC80-1-C1.* Washington, DC: Government Printing Office.
1985 *Population Census: 1980.* "Marital Characteristics," *Subject Report PC80-2-4C.* Washington, DC: Government Printing Office.
1988 (a) "The Hispanic Population in the United States: March 1988 (Advanced Report)," *Current Population Reports, Series P-20, no 431.* (b) "Money Income and Poverty in the United States: 1987," *Current Population Reports, Series P-60, no 161.* Washington, DC: Government Printing Office.
Uriarte-Gastón, Mirén
1981 "The Economic and Political Context of the Cuban Emigration." Paper presented at the Latin American Studies Conference at Brandeis U, April.
Uriarte-Gastón, Mirén, and Jorge Cañas Martínez, eds
1984 *Cubans in the United States.* Monograph no 1. Jamaica Plain, MA: Centro de Estudios de la Comunidad Cubana.
Vega, Bernardo
1984 *Memoirs of Bernardo Vega: A Contribution to the History of the Puerto Rican Community in New York.* Ed César Andreu Iglesias. Trans Juan Flores. New York: Monthly Review P.
Vigil, James Diego
1980 *From Indians to Chicanos: A Sociocultural History.* St. Louis: Mosby.
Wagoner, Jay J.
1970 *Arizona Territory, 1863-1912: A Political History.* Tucson: U of Arizona P.
1973 *Early Arizona: Prehistoric to Civil War.* Tucson: U of Arizona P.
Washburn, Wilcomb E.
1973 *The American Indian and the United States: A Documentary History.* New York: Random House.
1975 *The Indian in America.* New York: Harper & Row.
Weinberg, Albert K.
1935 *Manifest Destiny: A Study of Nationalist Expansionism in American History.* Baltimore: Johns Hopkins P.
Wellman, Paul I.
1954 *Glory, God, and Gold: A Narrative History.* Garden City, NY: Doubleday.
1962 *Magnificent Destiny: A Novel about the Great Secret Adventure of Andrew Jackson and Sam Houston.* Garden City, NY: Doubleday.
Wertenbaker, Thomas J.
1942 *The Old South: The Founding of American Civilization.* New York: C. Scribner's Sons.
Wilson, James
1980 *The Original Americans: U. S. Indians.* Rev ed London: Minority Rights Group.
Wilson, Samuel M.
1990 *Hispaniola: Caribbean Chiefdoms in the Age of Columbus.* Tuscaloosa: U of Alabama P.

The Latino Immigration Experience: The Case of Mexicanos, Puertorriqueños, and Cubanos

Marisa Alicea

Introduction

This chapter provides an overview of the immigration of various Latino groups to the United States, specifically Puertorriqueños, Mexicanos and Cubanos, with information regarding key eras of immigration, patterns of settlement within the United States and the movement of these groups within the United States.

This discussion is framed around five premises: (1) that Latinos are relatively absent from choice in coming to the United States, (2) that the movement of immigrants is occurring within one economic and political system that is dominated by the United States, (3) that similar forces are at play in propelling the various Latino groups to come to the United States, (4) that the proximity of Latinos' homelands to the United States shapes their immigration patterns, and (5) that there is difficulty in labeling Latino immigrants as either "economic" or "political" immigrants.

Latinos are not voluntary immigrants to the United States. Mexican Americans in the Southwest, for example, entered American society as a conquered people following the U. S.-Mexico War of the 1840s. Puerto Ricans largely came into U. S. American society under conditions of less than perfect choice when Puerto Rico was taken over as an American colony after the Spanish American War of 1898. Although under circumstances different from that of Mexican Americans or Puerto Ricans, Cubans were not voluntary immigrants either. Many who came to the U. S. were reluctant exiles of the 1959 revolution.

Large-scale migrations reflect the political and economic dynamics of an immigrant's homeland but these internal processes do not occur in isolation. They are themselves influenced by the sending country's position within the world system (Portes and Bach 1985). That is, the direction and function of migration are influenced by global relations. Recognizing this reality, this immigration discussion is also framed around the premise that the movement of Latinos is occurring within one overarching economic and political system which is dominated by the United States. Historically Latin America and its immigrants have provided cheap labor to the United States as well as a ready market. U. S. imperialist and capitalist interests in Latin America result in the economic and political impoverishment of these countries and the subsequent exodus of its people to the United States.

For Mexicanos, U. S. imperialism resulted in the taking of its northernmost land and the abuse and exploitation of Mexican immigrants for U. S. economic gains. Mexicanos are victims of racial inequality and are a colonized labor force. As such, coercion and legal restriction limit Mexican immigrants' degree of economic freedom. In addition Mexican immigrants historically have been paid less than their nonminority counterparts for the same work and have been relegated into certain types of jobs considered to be for "minorities." The United States uses Mexicanos as a colonized reserve labor force (Barrera 1979).

As in the case of Mexicanos, the United States exploits and dominates the Puerto Rican homeland and its people. As a colony of the United States, Puerto Rico and its people are marginalized (Centro de Estudios Puertorriqueños 1979). Puerto Ricans are rendered an invisible people. In both their homeland and in the United States, Puerto Ricans lack jobs or real political inclusion.

Until the 1950s Cuba suffered a fate similar to that of Puerto Rico. Under U. S. rule, Cuba's economy stagnated which resulted in large-scale impoverishment and stifled the development of Cuba's political system. With the 1959 Cuban revolution came greater self-determination for Cuba and its people. However, since this time Cuban immigrants have been used by both the United States and the Castro government as political pawns. The U. S. desire to keep the Western Hemisphere free of communism has meant that Cuban immigrants or exiles have been used by the United States as examples of the "oppression of Cubans under the Castro regime" and to legitimize U. S. intervention in Cuba (Masud-Piloto 1988).

U. S. presence and influence in Mexico, Puerto Rico and Cuba have had a drastic impact on the immigration flow. U. S. exploitive and oppressive forces in these countries and homeland ruling elites' acceptance of these conditions shape immigration patterns. In this sense, the forces that propel Latinos to the United States are essentially the same.

The proximity of Latino immigrants to their native land shapes the migration patterns of Latinos. High levels of back-and-forth migration between the United States and Latin America characterize especially the Mexican and Puerto Rican immigration experience. Among these two communities a "dual home base phenomenon" has emerged. Puerto Ricans and Mexicanos maintain attachments to both the United States and their homeland.

Finally, it is difficult to label Latino immigration flows as political or economic. Movements that appear to be politically motivated have been found, with closer examination, to have economic roots. In addition, some immigration flows that at the start were clearly political evolve into economic migrations as people learn of the advantages of obtaining refugee status in the receiving country (Portes and Bach 1985).

Conversely, economic migrations may turn out to have direct political roots. National political decisions and policies of sending countries have consequences for the socioeconomic context in which individuals make decisions. Political decisions may induce migration, directly or indirectly, by constraining the economic opportunities available to the population (Portes and Bach 1985).

Mexican Immigration

Mexican immigration to the United States is characterized by inter-generational patterns, back-and-forth migration, and its constant flow since the mid-1800s. More importantly it is characterized by the colonization of Mexico and by a long history of exploitation and oppression of Mexican immigrants by the United States.

Pre-1900 Immigration

The story of Mexican immigration to the U. S. starts with the invasion of the United States into Mexico. Through a process of military conquest, which began in 1836 with the battle of San Jacinto and ended in 1853 with the Gadsden Purchase, Mexicans were incorporated into the United States.

A period of Anglo immigration into the northernmost part of Mexico preceded the process of U. S. military conquest. In 1810, Mexico began its struggle for independence from Spain. In an effort to increase the number of people loyal to its cause, the Mexican government in 1819 granted Anglo foreigners permission to settle in its northern region (Acuña 1972).

The Mexican government required Anglo immigrants to pledge their allegiance to the Mexican government and to adopt Catholicism. Anglo settlers initially accepted these conditions but soon defied them. Mexico's enforcement of these agreements was difficult because of the distance of the settlements from Mexico City and because of the internal "strife" common during the period (Baker 1965).

By 1830, Anglo-Texans outnumbered Mexicans. For every five Anglos, there was only one Mexican living in the region. Most entered the area illegally to cultivate cotton and import slaves.

Mexican officials, fearing that the United States would annex Texas, began to restrict Anglo settlement. Mexican soldiers were sent to the region to enforce Mexican laws including immigration laws. Customhouses also were set up along the borders. According to historian Eugene Barker (1965), by the 1830's Anglo-Texans began to see themselves in danger of coming under the rule of a people whom they believed were morally and intellectually inferior. This—together with a law passed in 1830 which prohibited the importation of slaves—aggravated the situation and led to increased Anglo-Texan defiance.

Conflicts between Anglo-Texans and the Mexican government culminated in the revolt of 1835-36, which created the Texas Republic that existed until 1845. The republic, while never recognized by the government of Mexico, was recognized by the U. S. government. It served as a pretext for further U. S. involvement in the region. In 1845, when the United States granted statehood to Texas, war was inevitable. A number of factors contributed to the Anglo settlers' push to gain their independence and the U. S. decision to go to war against Mexico: (1) attitudes of racial superiority, (2) Mexico's abolition of slavery, (3) and imperialist interests.

Businessmen motivated by their interest actively sought the war. The U. S. belief that Mexico was weak and torn by internal conflict also contributed to the U. S. decision to go to war (Estrada et al. 1985).

The war, which began in 1846, ended February 2, 1848, with the signing of the Treaty of Guadalupe Hidalgo. With a new border drawn, Mexico lost what today is Arizona, California, Colorado, New Mexico, Texas, Nevada, and Utah, as well as portions of Kansas, Oklahoma, and Wyoming. This area represented over half of Mexico's territory. The United States acquired an additional portion of land in the Gadsden Purchase of

1853, when Mr. Gadsden, a U. S. official, went to Mexico City to resolve a territorial dispute arising from the use of faulty maps in assigning borders at the end of the war. Gadsden purchased 45,000 square miles in what is now Arizona and New Mexico. The United States wanted this land to build a railroad to California.

Mexicans living in the acquired territory became foreigners in their own land. They were given one year to decide whether to relocate or remain in their native lands, accepting U. S. sovereignty. The U. S. government promised those that remained all the rights of U. S. citizenship. Very quickly, however, Mexicans who remained in the conquered territory were socially and economically displaced and rendered a colonized mobile labor force. The new power structure displaced Mexicans from their own land.

The process of military conquest, the presence of U. S. troops, racial violence, and government and judicial injustices served to establish Anglos in positions of economic and political power. In Texas wholesale transfer of land from Mexicans to Anglos took place. In addition, taxation, which under the Mexican government was based on the products of the land, was changed to taxation on the land itself. During bad seasons it was difficult to make enough money to pay taxes, so in this way Mexicans were dispossessed of their land (Barrera 1979).

Without land and political power, Mexicans were relegated to lower status jobs by the turn of the century. Anglos considered Mexicans a colonized labor force a national resource of the region that was to be controlled and exploited.

Mexican Immigration 1900-1930

There are no exact figures on the number of Mexicans that came to the United States prior to 1900. The open or unguarded border between the United States and Mexico meant migration to the newly acquired territories was essentially unrestricted. Estimates are that less than 10,000 came to the newly acquired territory. Between 1900 and 1930, however, over 700,000 Mexicans immigrated to the United States. Several factors contributed to the increase. By 1908, Mexican railroad connections could reach the entire United States, which made immigration easier. The outbreak of the Mexican Revolution in 1910 propelled many to the United States. More importantly, however, the need for cheap labor to work in the expanding industries of the Southwest is central to understanding the massive flow of Mexicans to the United States (Portes and Bach 1985).

From 1910 to 1920, during the period of the Mexican Revolution, the immigrants apparently included a significant number of middle-class and upper-class Mexican refugees, many of whom hoped to return to Mexico. Those who came included merchants, landowners, and intellectuals. The great majority, however, were the poor who came or were recruited to work in the United States, particularly in the Southwest where various industries were growing. According to Portes and Bach, "the sharp increase in the absolute number in the proportion of the inflow during the 1920s can be defined as a consequence of the consolidation of Mexico as the chief supplier of low wage labor for southwestern agriculture" (1985, 78-79).

The construction of dams and reservoirs in desert-like areas resulted in the expansion of agricultural lands and the need for cheap labor. The cotton crops of Texas and the fruit and vegetable farms of California required large numbers of farmworkers as well. Paid labor agents were sent by growers associations into the interior of Mexico to recruit laborers. Canners, meat packers, and food processors also required labor. Mexico was the chief supplier of low-wage labor not only for agricultural industries but also the herding, mining and railroad industries. Mining companies recruited Mexicans to mine the copper of Arizona and New Mexico, quartz in Arizona, Nevada, and Colorado, and petroleum in Texas. In addition, many of the early Mexican enclaves in cities such as Chicago, and Kansas City originated as labor camps for the railroads. By 1908, railroad companies were recruiting thousands of Mexicans to lay and maintain tracks (Barrera 1979).

The labor shortage created by World War I also resulted in a greater demand for Mexican labor, since curtailing immigration from Europe prevented any chance of new immigrant help coming to work in the fields. Another potential source of labor, the southern Negro, preferred migrating to large northern cities rather than to other agricultural areas.

Employers also brought in Mexicans as strike breakers, which obstructed unionizing efforts. In the United States of this period, Mexicans were hired for unskilled and semi-skilled jobs that offered little opportunity for upward mobility. Most of the jobs were seasonal in nature, and often Mexicans were paid less than their Anglo counterparts for the same work. In sum, the discrimination and inferior status they held in the conquered territories meant that Mexican immigrants received the same unjust treatment as the Mexicans already here.

During the first two decades of the 1900s, there were some important changes in the destinations of the new Mexican arrivals. Typically the immigrants of earlier years were bound for company towns or agricultural work camps somewhere in the border states. Texas, in particular, was a popular area of settlement and with time California became attractive as well. By the 1920s Mexicans began to settle outside this region in areas of the Midwest and the North. With immigration from Europe virtually at a standstill, metal-bending industries throughout the Midwest instead recruited Mexicans. Agriculture and meat packing plants also took them to different parts of the northern United States. Steel mills in Chicago, automobile assembly lines in Detroit and the steel industry in Ohio, Pennsylvania and Indiana all relied in part on Mexican labor (Estrada et al. 1985). For example, according to Escobar (1991), the first large-scale Mexican migration to northwest Indiana occurred when United States Steel in Gary and Inland Steel in East Chicago imported thousands of Mexicans to help break the great strike of 1919.

While Mexicans were considered by many as inferior, the economic needs of the Southwest and other regions of the country dictated their continued recruitment.

With the Great Depression came the closing of the border and the repatriation of thousands of Mexicans. With the decline of economic activity during this period, wage rates in agriculture and industry suffered. The general climate of insecurity and fear among the U. S. American people meant that Mexican immigrants were blamed for the ills of the country. These fears translated into the forced repatriation of thousands of Mexicans (Hoffman 1974). Estrada et al. (1985, 173) explained: "To reduce the public relief rolls and agitation to organize labor, the Mexicans became both the scapegoat and the safety valve in the Southwest. It is estimated that in the early years of the Depression (1924-30) more than 400,000 Mexicans were forced to leave the country under 'voluntary' repatriation."

Those repatriated included people from the Southwest and Midwest who had been recruited to the area by employers, had lived in the United States for many years, and in some cases had been born in the United States (Hoffman 1974). Unlike many post-World War II undocumented immigrants who knowingly entered in violation of immigration law, immigrants prior to the Great Depression entered the U. S. at a time when the government's views on immigration were in flux, moving from unrestricted entry to severe restrictions. Many found themselves confused by the tightening noose of regulations.

Contradictions: The Need for Labor and Exclusion

From 1900 to 1930, Mexicans were both admitted and deported, a pattern that resulted from the bewildering contradictions between racial and cultural prejudice, the exclusion mood in the country, and the need for cheap labor. Immigration policy toward Mexico and other countries of the Western Hemisphere exemplified this contradiction (Portes and Bach 1985).

Economic needs were always important and dictated the adoption of new immigration policies and/or the lack of enforcement of immigration policies. During World War I, when the need for labor increased, special exemptions from such immigration requirements as literacy and the head tax were issued every year between 1917 and 1920 to admit temporary Mexican miners, farm workers and railroad laborers. Many of these temporary workers one way or another remained in the United States.

In the National Origins Act of 1924, immigration from the Western Hemisphere was exempt from the National Origins quota system, but not without much debate. There were many who argued for restricting Mexicans and others from the Western Hemisphere from entering the United States. These included small farmers, labor unions and racists. Small farmers felt they could not compete with growers who hired cheap Mexican labor. While there were numerous legislative efforts to change the immigration law concerning Mexicans, those who opposed restriction prevailed.

According to Hoffman (1974, 29), the large-scale growers, railroad owners, chambers of commerce and business groups made a powerful case for their continuing need for Mexican labor, and therefore for unrestricted immigration. While racist sentiments prevailed as rationale for restricting Mexican immigration, they also served as reasons for bringing in members of this group. George P. Clements, manager of the Los Angeles Chamber of Commerce's department of agriculture, for example, advocated an open-door policy but did so using a racist argument. He stressed that it was safer to bring Mexicans into the Southwest because as aliens they could be easily deported. In contrast, if growers brought in "Negroes, Filipinos and Puerto Ricans" who were U. S. citizens, they would come to stay and become a menace (Hoffman 1974, 28).

As noted above, despite employers' recruitment efforts and desire for lax immigration laws, as soon as Mexican labor was no longer needed, as during the Great Depression, the border was closed and thousands of Mexicans were repatriated. These contradictions concerning Mexican immigration which began during the first half of the twentieth century continued into the second half.

Mexican Immigration: From World War II to the 1980s

With the onset of World War II, there was an increased need for both agricultural and industrial labor. In the Southwest, industrial owners once again reasserted their economic needs. Agribusiness in particular had a strong hand in shaping national legislation.

Probably the most significant event in Mexican immigration history was the adoption of the bracero program during and after World War II. The bracero program was a bilateral agreement between Mexico and the United States. The program, designed to supply labor for U. S. agriculturalists, underwrote Mexicans' travel costs, insured a minimum wage, and guaranteed jobs and equitable treatment (Galarza 1964).

Although the bracero program developed as a wartime agreement, it continued long after the war ended. The program continued in one form or another until 1964, the year the Immigration Act established quotas of 120,000 for all nations of the Western Hemisphere (Galarza 1964). The "successful" implementation and extension of this program demonstrates the immense power of agribusiness because the program, in effect, was a federal subsidy. More importantly, the program demonstrated continuation of the traditional U. S. manipulation and control of the flow of Mexican labor.

Together with those who came under the bracero program was a steady flow of undocumented workers. The greater enforcement of immigration law and increased control of the border meant more illegals were caught by the border patrol. In 1947 some 183,000 Mexicans were captured. By 1952 this number rose to 543,000. Yet despite increased boarder patrol, it was still possible to cross the boarder with the help of a "coyote," or with false papers. Some would get legal short-term papers and overstay.

Yet probably the one thing that contributed the most to the continuous arrival of undocumented Mexican immigrants was that they knew they could obtain jobs despite their immigration status. America's agribusiness continued to offer employment to all arrivals because it was not against the law to hire undocumented workers.

These workers were a mixed blessing for agricultural owners. While they did not have to pay the undocumented as much, undocumented workers were an unstable labor force because they were free to move around to seek higher wages, were not restricted to work in agriculture and could take jobs in urban districts (Estrada et al. 1985).

According to Galarza (1964), agricultural employers used the bracero program to regulate and expand their control over cheap labor and the undocumented. It was not uncommon for growers to transport the undocumented to the border and then immediately rehire them as braceros. In this way, growers transformed an unregulated labor supply into a legal and semi-controlled work force. Through the bracero program workers were more tightly bound to the agricultural sector.

In addition, once U. S. industries regulated the cheap labor force through the bracero program, it was easier to deport unwanted "illegal workers." When sentiments were high about the number of illegal workers, Operation Wetback, reminiscent of the repatriation program during the Great Depression, returned unstable workers to Mexico. Under this program some 3.8 million Mexicans were returned to Mexico from 1954 to 1959.

By 1960, with changes in the border states, Congress was more willing to listen to labor interests, religious groups, and others demanding the termination of the bracero program. Agricultural needs no longer dominated legislative thinking, most likely because of the rise of urban influence. Moreover, there was a steady and large-scale immigration of Mexican workers without papers—the so-called illegals.

The Immigration Act of 1965 set world quotas. Its intention was to change the basis for preferential admissions from national origin to family reunification and to occupational skills. A 20,000 annual limit was set. Despite the quotas, many more Mexicans came to the United States. There were enough loopholes in the law to allow people to come in if it was necessary. Immediate family members were exempt from the quota. In addition, immigration laws were administratively juggled to allow for the continuous admission of Mexican citizens as commuter workers (Estrada et al. 1985).

It is popularly believed that the undocumented who come to the United States are young (under thirty) men who have little education and are born predominantly in rural areas. However, studies show that these people do not necessary represent the most impoverished people in Mexico, nor are they necessarily going to work in the agricultural sector once they come to the United States (Portes 1979). An important segment of the undocumented workers are coming from non-rural origins, have relatively high levels of education, and have experience working in the industrial and service sector.

Mexican incorporation into the labor market not only includes temporary rural labor forces but also a lower tier urban proletariat. After the bracero program, for example, the uses of Mexican labor became more diversified. Increasingly, Mexicans moved toward urban employment, finding jobs in plant nurseries, construction firms, shipyards, cement companies, furniture factories, restaurants, hotels, motels, car washes, and butcher shops (Cornelius 1976).

A shift in the geographic distribution of Mexican immigrants accompanied this change. There has been greater distribution within the Southwest but also to areas outside the Southwest, particularly the Midwest. Tienda and Bean (1987, 138) report that a "substantial growth occurred in the population living in the North Central states, although by 1980 this population still represented only 9.3 percent of all persons of Mexican origin in the country."

Higher proportions of the Mexican-born population are found in the regions of the greatest concentration of this population. For example, 65 percent of the foreign-born Mexicans as opposed to only about 50 percent of the native-born live in the West, the region of greatest concentration among Mexican Americans. In addition, Mexicans who have been in the United States a short time are more concentrated in a few states, whereas those who have been in this country for a longer period of time have a state distribution more similar to that of native-born Mexican Americans (Tienda and Bean 1987).

Accompanying the shift in area of concentration from one region of the country to another after World War II was a greater concentration of Mexican Americans in metropolitan areas. The 1970s in particular was the decade of spatial consolidation for Mexicans within American cities (Tienda and Bean 1987).

Mexican Immigrants as a Reserve Labor Pool

The use and importance of Mexican labor in U. S. history is obvious, as is the discrimination and injustices that Mexicans received in the United States. One of the most comprehensive theories for understanding the reality of the Mexican-American experience is offered by Barrera in his book *Race and Class in the Southwest: A Theory of Racial Inequality*. According to Barrera (1979), during the second half of the nineteenth century, Chicanos emerged as a segmented labor force "that functioned within a colonial labor system"—a system that developed along racial and ethnic lines. Under this system Anglos systematically maintained Chicanos in a subordinate position.

Barrera identified five aspects of the colonial labor system. The first is "labor repression," whereby Anglos used coercion and legal restrictions to limit Chicano's economic freedom. For example, it was not uncommon for Chicano miners to have to buy goods from company stores where prices were high and wages low enough to create a permanent state of debt and dependency.

A second aspect discussed by Barrera has to do with the development of a "dual wage system" within various industries of the Southwest. Under this system, Mexican Americans received lower wages than Anglos for the same work (1979, 39-43).

"Occupational stratification" is a third aspect of the colonial labor system. According to Barrera, occupational stratification "refers to the practice of classifying certain kinds of jobs suited for minorities and others suited for non-minorities" (1979, 43). This system of stratification that developed in the Southwest maintained Chicanos at the lower end of the occupational ladder.

The fourth aspect of the colonial labor system is the use of minorities as a "reserve labor force." According to Barrera, a reserve labor force keeps employers from having to compete for labor and thus drives up wages. A group of unemployed workers can also be used by employers as leverage in bargaining with employees who threaten to or actually go on strike. Barrera further explained that minorities essentially act as buffers in poor economic times. Minorities are often among the last hired and first fired. This allows employers to lessen "the discontent of the potentially more dangerous non-minority workers" (1979, 48).

The overall effect of the colonial labor system was the subordination of Mexican Americans. Their subordination was no accident. It served many entrepreneurs and contributed to the economic development of the Southwest. But the experiences of Mexican Americans is incomplete without recognizing and understanding how U. S. involvement in Mexico contributes to the exodus of Mexicans to the United States. Portes and Bach (1985) provided some understanding of how the United States is responsible for the "push and pull factors" that bring Mexicans to the United States. Mexico's economy is increasingly controlled by foreigners, largely the United States. Nearly half of Mexico's 400 largest industries are predominantly U. S. owned. Portes (1979) pointed out that there are more subsidiaries of major U. S. corporations in Mexico than in any other Latin American country. Multinational companies generate over 25 percent of industrial production, especially in the most technological and dynamic branches. Mexico's foreign trade is dominated by the United States.

The industrialization of Mexico, largely through the presence of multinational corporations, has increased production of domestic goods but has failed to widen the consumer market through employment in the industrial sector. According to Portes (1979, 434), "In the eyes of the Mexican worker, the United States stands as the place where the benefits of an advanced economy, promised but not delivered by the present national development strategy, can be turned into reality."

Return Migration

As argued by Portes and Bach (1985, 80), cyclical migration patterns among Mexicans have been sustained by the fact "that neither employers nor migrants are generally interested in permanent resettlement." At the aggregate and individual level, Mexican immigration is characterized by cyclical migration patterns.

At the aggregate level, when there is a need for labor, Mexicans are recruited to the United States as in the bracero program. During periods of economic slowdowns, however, Mexican Americans are forcibly returned to their homeland, as in the repatriations of the Depression era and the deportations during Operation Wetback of 1954.

At the individual level, it is not uncommon for Mexican immigrants to have a period of work in the United States followed by periods of residence in Mexico. Temporal labor migration to the United States is deeply embedded in the social and economic fabric of Mexican communities. Mexican immigrants often send money home and make plans for their return.

Puerto Rican Immigration

For over a hundred years, Puerto Ricans have been immigrating to the United States. Much of the Puerto Rican community, if not the entire population, has experienced migration either directly or indirectly; i.e., most people know someone who has migrated. As of 1970, one out of every three Puerto Ricans had lived in the United States.

As among Mexicans, patterns of intergenerational migration are evident among Puerto Ricans. It is not uncommon to find families in which three generations have moved between the United States and Puerto Rico. The Puerto Rican migration experience is also characterized by a large, constant, and steady stream of Puerto Ricans returning back to their homeland and in some cases re-migrating to the United States.

The cyclical migration patterns of Puerto Ricans moving back and forth between the United States and Puerto Rico have been noted by government officials, school teachers, administrators, and social workers. Table 1 give some sense of the large-scale return migration to Puerto Rico.

The nature and resilience of the migration of Puerto Ricans to the United States must be understood within the context of the changing economic and political realities of Puerto Rico and the United States, particularly from the 1940s to the 1990s, a period of greater fusion of Puerto Rico's economy with that of the United States.

Furthermore, with the changing global economic system, both the United States and Puerto Rico are currently experiencing parallel or similar labor and economic conditions. In both countries the emergence of a service sector economy is leaving those with few skills either under- and unemployed or in jobs that offer low wages and little security. Puerto Ricans who lack skills find themselves confronted with similar economic problems in both countries.

Scholars of the Puerto Rican experience suggest that these conditions lead to the back-and-forth migration patterns of Puerto Ricans (Bonilla and Campo 1987). Unable to find jobs in Puerto Rico, they come to the United States. Once here they find themselves unable to "make it" and return to the Island. Thus, Puerto Rican migration flows should not be seen as occurring between two distinct, autonomous economic units but rather internal to a broader system to which both units belong (Bonilla and Campos 1987).

U. S. Occupation of Puerto Rico and Early Migration: 1898-1930s

In 1898 the U. S. took possession of Puerto Rico in the Spanish-American War. From the very beginning of the U. S. occupation of Puerto Rico, U. S. officials saw sugar as the most important investment. The United States needed sugar, and it was cheaper to grow in Puerto Rico than in Hawaii, the southern United States or other traditional sugar-cane-growing centers. The United States rapidly gained control of sugar production in Puerto Rico. Within the first seven years of U. S. occupation, three U. S. sugar companies, the Aguirre Central, The South Porto Rico Sugar Company, and the Fajardo Sugar Company, dominated Puerto Rican sugar production. Eastern Sugar Associated, which arrived in Puerto Rico in 1926, also came to dominate sugar production in Puerto Rico.

With the growth of commercial cultivation of sugar and the concentration of land, major structural changes occurred in Puerto Rico's class structure during the first decades of U. S. occupation. Small farmers had to sell their land and joined peasants who had long relied on access to land they did not legally own. In addition, unable to create sufficient jobs for Puerto Rico's population, agrarian capitalism on the Island institutionalized patterns of unemployment and underemployment (Centro de Estudios Puertorriqueños 1979).

Tobacco and needlework-manufacturing trades did grow slightly in the beginning of the nineteenth century, but neither employed a substantial part of the labor force. In addition, both of these industries quickly became outmoded. Cigars were replaced by the booming cigarette industry in the United States. The country's textile industry, which employed primarily women and children, had a short existence when new economic priorities were imposed in the 1940s.

Surplus labor populations created from agrarian capitalistic development were channeled by U. S. corporations to places such as the Dominican Republic, Cuba, Arizona, California and Hawaii. In 1903, for example, agents representing sugar cane growers of Hawaii came to Puerto Rico and contracted close to 1,000 men. In 1921 sugar cane growers once again recruited Puerto Ricans to work in the fields of Hawaii (Natal 1983).

Many Puerto Ricans who left from 1898 to the late 1920s had contractual arrangements to work in sugar cane and other fields. However, with the further development of the sugar economy and the imposition of U. S. citizenship in 1917, thousands more migrated to the mainland on their own, without organized contractual arrangements.

By the 1920s there were more than 4,500 Puerto Ricans living in New York City. Puerto Rican migration to New York City during the early 1900s included craftsmen and skilled workers who were politically conscious and literate. For example, the concentration of cigar companies in New York City attracted cigar makers who were active in Latin American politics of the time. The story of the cigar makers' immigration to the United States is best told in the book *Memorias de Bernando Vega*:

> The hours passed quickly. At around two in the afternoon I boarded the boat, the famous Coamo which made so many trips from San Juan to New York and back. I took a quick look at my cabin, and went right back up on deck. I did not want to lose a single breath of those final minutes in my country, perhaps the last ones I would ever have.
>
> Soon the boat pushed off from the dock, turned, and began to move slowly toward El Morro castle at the mouth of the harbor. A nun who worked at the women's home was waving adios from high up on the ramparts; I assumed she meant it for me. As soon as we were on the open sea and the boat started to pitch, the passengers went off to their cabins, most of them already half seasick. Not I. I stayed up on deck, lingering there until the island was lost from sight in the first shadows of nightfall.
>
> The days passed peacefully. Sunrise of the first day and the passengers were already acting as though they belonged to one family. It was not long before we came to know each other's life stories. The topic of conversation, of course, was what lay ahead: life in New York. First savings would come to return home with pots of money. Everyone's mind was on that farm they'd be buying or the business they'd set up in town . . . All of us were building our own little castles in the sky.
>
> When the fourth day dawned even those who had spent the whole trip cooped up in their cabins showed up on deck. We saw the lights of New York even before the morning mist rose. As the boat entered the harbor the sky was clear and clean. The excitement grew the closer we go to the docks. We recognized the Statue of Liberty in the distance. Countless smaller boats were sailing about in the harbor. In front of us rose the imposing sight of skyscrapers—the same skyline we had admired so often on postcards. Many of the passengers had only heard talk of New York, and stood with their mouths open, spellbound . . . Finally the Coamo docked at Hamilton Pier on State Island.
>
> First to disembark were the passengers traveling first class—businessmen, well-to-do families, students. In second class, where I was, there were them emigrants, most of us "Tabaqueros," or cigar workers. We all boarded the ferry that crossed from Staten Island to lower Manhattan. We sighed as we set foot on solid ground. There, gaping before us, were the jaws of the iron dragon: the immense New York metropolis.
>
> All of us new arrivals were well dressed. I mean, we had on our Sunday best. I myself was wearing a navy blue woolen suit (or "flus", as they would say back home), a borsalino hand made of Italian straw, black shoes with pointy toes, a white vest, and a red tie. I would have been sporting a shiny wristwatch too, if a traveling companion hadn't warned me that in New York it was considered effeminate to wear things like that. So as soon as the city was in sight, and the boat was entering the harbor, I tossed my watch into the sea . . . And to think that it wasn't long before those wristwatches came into fashion and ended up being the rage! And so I arrived in New York, without a watch. (1984, 5-6)

Puerto Rico's Industrialization and Migration Policies: 1942-1960

By the 1930s and 1940s in Puerto Rico, there was desperate need for restructuring the Island's economy. There was massive unemployment on the Island and widespread and desperate conditions of poverty. By this time, Puerto Rican and U. S. officials were proposing to move the Island's economy toward an industrial one as a way to improve Puerto Rico's economy and deal with severe poverty among the people. However, with implementation of massive economic transformations during the 1940s eventually came the increased fusion of the Puerto Rican and U. S. economy. In addition, economic changes in Puerto Rico promoted the migration of thousands of Puerto Ricans to the United States.

It was under the leadership of Luis Muñoz Marín, El Partido Popular Demócratico (The Popular Democratic Party), and Governor Ruxford B. Tugwell (then U. S.-appointed governor) that political, economic, and social changes occurred in Puerto Rico in an attempt to solve the economic ills of the Island. El Partido Popular proposed economic advancement through a combination of industrialization, migration, population control and the creation of new constitutional ties to the United States.

Leaders believed that industrialization would create a solid base for economic development and advancement and contribute to the gradual independence of the Island. Industrialization would also help reduce unemployment and increase workers' wages which were more immediate problems of the time.

The initial program for the industrialization of the Island was undertaken when the Economic Development Administration in Puerto Rico established the Fomento program in 1942. This program initially was a form of state capitalism, which organized insular companies. During its first four years, Fomento organized four major subsidiary corporations: the Puerto Rican Glass Corporation, the Puerto Rican Cement Corporation, the Puerto Rican Clay Products Corporation, and the Puerto Rican Shoe and Leather Corporation.

By the mid-1940s, however, it was clear that state capitalism and the industrialization programs established by Fomento were too limited to solve the Island's economic problems. The Fomento program did not create the number of jobs anticipated nor did it generate the necessary capital to raise the economic level of the Island (Centro de Estudios Puertorriqueños 1979).

In addition, the colonial bureaucracy was too limited for the administration and financing of industrialization. Consequently, on August 4 President Truman signed the Crawford-Butler Act, which permitted Puerto Rico to elect its own governor. In 1948, Luis Muñoz Marín, a leader of economic reform became the Island's first popularly elected governor. However, in the early 1950s, a peculiar and ill-defined political relationship between Puerto Rico and the United States was created and implemented under the name of commonwealth. As a commonwealth, Puerto Rico could elect its own governor but did not have voting members in Congress.

In addition to the political changes, the sale of state-owned industries and the passage of the 1947 Industrial Incentives Act marked a change in the tactics that would be used to industrialize the Island's economy. Instead of promoting state capitalism, Fomento became a program for promoting and encouraging private investment in the industrialization of the Island. To this end, El Partido Popular essentially opened the Island's market to American investors in light factory industries. It was anticipated and believed that private investment would broaden the industrial base of the colonial economy and create new jobs.

Under the new Fomento program efforts were made to induce U. S. companies and capital to Puerto Rico. This meant providing U. S. companies incentives for locating on the Island. The Industrial Incentives Act in 1947 allowed Puerto Rico to offer U. S. companies not only abundant and cheap labor but also generous tax exemptions. American industry owners learned about the advantages that Puerto Rico had to offer through a mainland advertising campaign known as Operation Bootstrap.

The construction of factory buildings and the pre-employment training of workers financed by the Puerto Rican government facilitated the establishment of U. S. companies in Puerto Rico. However, Puerto Rican leaders did not believe that political changes and industrialization alone would be enough to help create and stabilize Puerto Rico's economy. Leaders believed that the economic ills of Puerto Rico resulted from the Island's overpopulation; that is, overpopulation was used to explain the unemployment and underemployment problems of Puerto Rico not the inability of political and business officials to create jobs for Puerto Ricans (Centro de Estudios Puertorriqueños 1979).

Out of the overpopulation thesis or ideology emerged two solutions. One was to reduce fertility through family planning and the sterilization of women (Ramírez de Arrellano 1983). The second solution was to persuade thousands of Puerto Ricans to leave the Island. U. S. and Puerto Rican government officials attempted to alleviate the "surplus population" problem by encouraging Puerto Ricans to migrate. In sum, officials defined the unemployment and underemployment problems in Puerto Rico in such a way that they could deal with it. A North American consultant of Puerto Rico's Planning Board, Steven Zell, stated: "The improvement in the economic status of Puerto Ricans and the growth of the economy will be the result of influencing the migration process. Unemployment and migration are so interrelated that to concentrate the Planning Board's efforts on reducing unemployment without influencing migration will result in waste, inefficiency and failure."

After World War II, thousands of Puerto Ricans left the Island for the U. S. as contract workers. Steel corporations and other manufacturing industries as well as farmers contracted Puerto Ricans to the U. S. (Maldonado 1979). For example, in the 1950s the National Tube Company of Lorain, Ohio, and the Carnegie-Illinois Steel Corporation of Indiana contracted hundreds of Puerto Rican men to work in their factories and steel mills (*Gary Post Tribune* 1948). In the Midwest and East, Puerto Ricans were also brought in as contract farm workers. However, contract laborers represent only a small number of those who left Puerto Rico to come to the United States. It was the hundreds of thousands that followed without contract agreements that swelled the ranks of migrants. Puerto Ricans' U. S. citizenship status as well as low air transportation rates permitted by the Federal Aviation Administration, at the request of the Puerto Rican Government, facilitated the migration of Puerto Ricans to the United States.

Edward Rivera in his book *Family Installments* captured the reality of these times when he wrote:

> So now they had their "getaway money," as Papi was to mispronounce it a long time later, the funds for a one-way ticket, shopping bag, cardboard-suitcase, late-night flight to The North and just enough left over for roughly two weeks of room and board in a single room occupancy, which at first they mistook for a comedown hotel overrun with "disrespectful cockroaches," since at that point they had no way of knowing that the city they had fled to was also "a haven for vermin," an expression that might have been added to the famous one at the base of the Statue of Liberty. But they weren't complaining. Yet. In time they would join the unanimous legions, the brotherhood and sisterhood of displaced and misplaced ingrates who had escaped to El Bronx, or El Barrio, or Canarsie, or the run-down regions of Park Avenue, or wherever, and who had only themselves to blame for their situation. (Rivera 1982, 51)

According to Rivera, the sons, daughters, and wives of poor Puerto Rican men later joined them in New York:

> Chuito took an oxcart with us to San Juan, then a bus to the airport, where we sat and stood around a long time with hundreds of others who must have stuffed everything they owned into suitcases braced with rope and belts, and brown paper bags with cardboard handles. It was as if half the island were leaving on the same airplane, and the other, more melancholy half were there to see them off. (Rivera 1982, 68)

With the continued migration of Puerto Ricans to the United States, the Puerto Rican population in the U. S. more than quadrupled between 1940 and 1950. In 1940 69,967 Puerto Ricans lived in the United States. By 1950 this number had increased to 301,375, this included 226,110 persons of Puerto Rican birth and 75,265 born in the United States to Puerto Rican parents (see Table 2). Most Puerto Ricans moved to areas in the Northeast such as Boston, Philadelphia and New York, and to the Midwest, in particular Chicago (Wagenheim 1983).

The Persistence of Economic Problems and Migration: 1960-1970s

During the 1960s and 1970s, Puerto Rico's economic ills persisted despite efforts to industrialize the Island's economy and despite the massive migration and the sterilization of women on the Island. In addition, during the 1960s and 1970s, it became apparent that while thousands were leaving Puerto Rico, just as many were returning to the Island, exacerbating Puerto Rico's economic problems.

By the 1960s, industrialization resulted in a substantial rise in wage rates but the size of the labor force was stationary or declining. Between 1950 and 1960 average hourly earnings in manufacturing rose from 29 percent to 41 percent of the U. S. average and continued to rise; yet double digit unemployment rates of 13 and 16 percent persisted (Census 1980).

By the 1960s, it was also clear that U. S. companies that came to Puerto Rico did not establish firm roots. Once the term of their exemption status was exhausted, companies moved, leaving Puerto Rican workers unemployed. Furthermore, by this time, it was apparent that the Fomento program would not be enough to improve the Island's economy. The majority of the new manufacturing plants were branch plants of mainland manufacturing companies. Reynolds and Gregory showed that at the end of 1961, only about 10 percent of Fomento represented local investment (1965, 22). As a Centro study pointed out, "This meant that the price of labor and other commodities, as well as profit rations, were being determined by market relationship and economic policies in the United States rather than by relationships among local firms and their workers" (Centro de Estudios Puertorriqueños 1979, 128).

Consequently it was clear that the Fomento program and the Island's commonwealth status would not result in the development of a "Puerto Rican" economy. The program, in fact, had the opposite effect. As Bonilla and Campo (1987) suggested, by the 1960s it was unclear to what extent one could continue to talk about a "Puerto Rican economy." They further stated:

> Commonwealth status, it must be made clear, took the economy into a set of relations that could no longer be described or dealt with in terms of ideas about a foreign presence, penetration, control, or dependence. The result was closer to an effective fusion of economic systems . . .
>
> The point, of course, is not that command over decisions was placed abroad; that was the reality before Commonwealth. What Commonwealth did was to reaffirm and consolidate, within a framework of apparent increased autonomy, an obliteration of economic boundaries without effective, institutionalization provision for the minimal defense of local interests that federated states or independent nations are sometimes able to articulate. (Centro de Estudios Puertorriqueños 1979, 129-30)

The disintegration of Puerto Rico's economy was further exacerbated by leaders' efforts to encourage heavy industrial development in Puerto Rico. Heavy industry was supposed to create more jobs and raise the Island's economic level. But because industry had to be almost entirely financed from abroad, further internationalization of the Island's economy and erosion of Puerto Rico's already precarious economic base.

The demand for massive capital investment from abroad brought new actors into the picture. Throughout the 1960s and 1970s international conglomerates and multinational corporations with complex operations around the world began to replace smaller producers. These major corporations increasingly moved into positions of dominance in the Island's economy. However, even these efforts to attract heavy industry and to retain investments of U. S. companies and corporations were hampered by the U. S. recession of the 1970s and major realignments in the world economy. Other low labor cost locations were judged by major corporations to yield better profits. U. S. companies began to look less at Puerto Rico and more at foreign countries for setting up industries.

In sum, the Island's shift from agricultural capitalism to industrial modes of production did not reduce unemployment and underemployment rates in Puerto Rico. Puerto Rico's economic problems persisted. As in Mexico, foreign and largely U. S. industrialization failed to create sufficient jobs (Centro de Estudios Puertorriqueños 1979).

Furthermore, the return of thousands of Puerto Ricans to the Island added pressure to the job market and social services. In the early 1960s, net migration fell sharply (see Table 1). While thousands left Puerto Rico for the United States because of the lack of jobs, others returned (Hernández 1968; Cafferty 1975).

A plant closing in Michigan, which left hundreds of men unemployed in 1964, epitomized the fate that Puerto Ricans coming to the United States would have to face. In September of the same year, 230 Puerto Rican migrants were returned to Puerto Rico after the company they worked for closed down. *El Mundo* (The World) reported on the arrival of the Puerto Rican men to the Island, "Yesterday morning, at eight o'clock in the morning, the first 175 migrant workers of the 230 that remained stranded Saturday in Edmore, Michigan, returned when the company they worked for closed its doors" (Quiñones and Rodríguez 1964). Because the company did not pay the men, the Labor Department of Puerto Rico had to pick up the cost of returning the men to Puerto Rico.

Because of the problems return migrants created for Puerto Rico, a renewed emphasis was placed on family planning and the wholesale sterilization of women. In addition, some government officials advocated more active control of the migratory process by the insular government to ensure the best possible destinations for the migrating population and their permanent relocation outside of Puerto Rico.

Salvador Tío, a government official during the 1950s, advocated establishing Puerto Rican colonies in places such as Venezuela. Regardless of the feasibility of these ideas they do point to the concerns of rooting Puerto Ricans more firmly outside of the Island: "Puerto Rico can not continue emigrating farmworkers at will. It has to organize migrations that take into account our total character. It must transplant to adequate locations cross sections of our population. Under these conditions, any country interested in being populated would show an interest in receiving us" (Tío 1956, 127). Salvador Tío further stated: "What I said 9 years ago I say again, the absence of a clear migration policy has impeded the colonization of these extra ordinary human resources to locations more apt for their development and their involvement" (Tío 1956, 115). Tío pointed out that the similarities in language, vast unpopulated territories, and low population density ratios, as well as the availability of

TABLE 1

Migration between Puerto Rico and the United States

Fiscal Year	Travelers to U.S.	Travelers to Puerto Rico	Net Migration to U. S.
1920	19,142	15,003	4,139
1921	17,137	17,749	-612
1922	13,521	14,154	-633
1923	14,950	13,194	1,756
1924	17,777	14,057	3,720
1925	17,493	15,356	2,137
1926	22,010	16,389	5,621
1927	27,355	18,626	8,729
1928	27,916	21,772	6,144
1929	25,428	20,791	4,637
1930	26,010	20,434	5,621
1931	18,524	20,462	-1,938
1932	16,224	18,932	-2,708
1933	15,133	16,215	-1,082
1934	13,721	16,687	-2,966
1935	19,944	18,927	1,017
1936	24,145	20,697	3,448
1937	27,311	22,793	4,518
1938	25,884	23,522	2,362
1939	26,653	21,165	4,488
1940	24,932	23,924	1,008
1941	30,916	30,416	500
1942	29,480	28,552	928
1943	19,367	16,766	2,601

continued next page

TABLE 1, continued

Migration between Puerto Rico and the United States

Fiscal Year	Travelers to U. S.	Travelers to Puerto Rico	Net Migration to U. S.
1944	27,586	19,498	8,088
1945	33,740	22,737	11,003
1946	70,618	45,997	24,621
1947	102,136	67,011	35,125
1948	96,591	68,719	27,872
1949	113,440	79,379	34,061
1950	122,860	85,163	37,697
1951	136,101	92,956	43,145
1952	192,813	132,219	60,594
1953	237,953	161,701	76,252
1954	237,071	191,982	45,089
1955	242,608	211,369	31,239
1956	287,325	230,585	56,740
1957	334,392	287,632	46,760
1958	350,481	325,828	24,658
1959	412,674	377,382	35,292
1960	493,136	469,635	23,501
1961	518,162	501,344	16,818
1962	588,045	576,095	119,950
1963	615,287	605,788	9,499
1964	705,656	691,306	14,350
1965	840,960	825,020	15,940
1966	1,022,394	963,382	39,012
1967	1,217,543	1,080,323	47,220
1968	1,334,145	1,302,254	31,891
1969	1,505,892	1,494,31	11,582
1970	1,521,965	1,447,436	74,529
1971	1,495,587	1,479,447	16,140
1972	1,566,723	1,605,414	-38,691
1973	1,692,283	1,711,745	-19,462
1974	1,780,192	1,799,071	-18,879
1975	1,622,001	1,630,525	-8,524
1976	1,564,194	1,571,369	-7,175
1977	1,586,904	1,613,880	-26,976
1978	1,672,800	1,640,483	32,317
1979	1,871,350	1,845,946	25,404
1980	1,799,642	1,750,320	49,322
1981	1,751,403	1,723,811	27,592
1982	1,799,039	1,746,890	52,149

Source: Data from the Commonwealth of Puerto Rico Planning Board, published by Migration Division, Commonwealth of Puerto Rico Labor Department, based on statistics from the U. S. Immigration and Naturalization Service, Defense Department, Puerto Rico Port Authority, and Airlines and Steamship Companies operating in Puerto Rico. First printed in Wagenheim, 1983.

* A minus sign (-) denotes return migration from the U. S. to Puerto Rico

Note: Figures from 1920 through 1946 are for total passenger traffic between Puerto Rico and all other destinations (U. S., U. S. Virgin Islands and foreign nations) but the net migration figures accurately represent migratory trends between Puerto Rico and the U. S.

raw materials in Hispanic America, were conducive to the establishment of Puerto Rican colonies. (What he did not seem to recognize is that other forces may have been difficult to overturn. What dictated where Puerto Ricans went was deeper than any policy Puerto Rico could have developed.)

The United States and Puerto Rico's Economic Reality and Migration, 1970s-1980s

Today in Puerto Rico a service sector economy overshadows the industrial sector as the primary source of jobs. The United States also is experiencing the emergence of a service sector economy, leaving numerous Puerto Ricans, who have few skills, at the bottom of the socio economic ladder in both countries.

By 1982, with the decline in the number of jobs in production, 60 percent of Puerto Rico's work force was engaged in the service sectors compared to 30 percent in the 1970s. The primary employer within the service sector was the colonial government. In 1978, the colonial government had on its payrolls 40 percent of the employed work force in an attempt to slow the rise of unemployment. Unemployment figures soared from 11 percent in 1970 to 25 percent in 1983 (Census 1980).

The decline in the number of industrial jobs (from 20.6 percent in 1970 to 17.9 percent in 1980) has affected men and women differently. A higher proportion of women than men remain in industry. Women also obtain more of the new jobs created by the colonial government. In the 1980 fiscal period, 62 percent of new jobs went to women. However, they receive lower salaries than men at all levels (Bonilla and Campo 1987).

Women's salaries tend to trail those of men, except in manufacturing and technical jobs where the pay of women is about equal with that of men. Since women provide cheaper labor, there has been an increase in their employment, which places men in direct competition with women for the same jobs (Bonilla and Campo 1987).

Economic stagnation and the decline in the number of productive jobs has resulted in unemployment figures higher than 25 percent in 1983 not counting discouraged workers. Moreover, higher levels of education do not offer people a competitive advantage (see Table 3). On the contrary, at least through high school, unemployment is highest among those with the most schooling. In particular, higher levels of education among women do not offer them the same rewards as it does for men (Bonilla and Campo 1987).

Those who have low-ranking jobs within the service sectors receive few benefits. It also means that the middle class is further burdened with supporting the needs of the less privileged. Under these conditions, migration to the United States continues unabated. In 1980 over 2 million Puerto Ricans were living in the United States. This number represents an increase of 41 percent since 1970 (see Table 2 and also Table 4 for size of Puerto Rican population and areas of settlement).

Puerto Rico's transformation to a service economy is not unlike those shifts the United States is experiencing and may explain why thousands of Puerto Ricans return to Puerto Rico at the very same time that many leave the Island.

Even though Puerto Ricans left the island due to economic problems, in the United States, they faced economic and labor market conditions similar to those back home. Puerto Ricans were migrating to areas, primarily midwestern and northeastern cities, which were experiencing the same types of economic transformations as Puerto Rico. The decline in manufacturing jobs in the United States meant that Puerto Rican migrants would have trouble finding good jobs.

By the 1970s, cities such as New York, Chicago, Philadelphia, and Boston were experiencing large scales of disinvestment by large corporations first in preference of southern cities and later of international locations. These and other cities throughout the country lost their industries to places that offered cheaper labor and property. Blueston and Harrison (1980) calculated that although about one million new jobs were created in New York state (mainly service sector jobs) something over 1.5 million were destroyed by closings between 1969 and 1976 (Blueston and Harrison 1980).

Furthermore, Bonilla and Campo (1987) noted that in the 1980s New York state outdid Puerto Rico in the variety of fiscal incentives it offered to seduce investments. These findings depict the two sites as struggling against the same economic forces.

TABLE 2

Growth of Puerto Rican Population in the United States, 1910-1980

Year	Total	% Increase	Born in Puerto Rico	Born in U. S.
1910	1,513	-	-	-
1920	11,811	680.6	-	-
1930	52,774	346.8	-	-
1940	69,967	32.6	-	-
1950	301,375	330.7	226,110	75,265
1960	887,662	194.5	615,384	272,278
1970	1,429,396	61.0	783,358	646,038
1980	2,013,945	41.0	-	-

Source: Various Reports of the U. S. Census Bureau. First printed in Wagenheim, 1983. Note: Census reports between 1910 and 1940 did not offer a breakdown of Puerto Ricans born in Puerto Rico and born in the U.S. This data is not yet available, either, for 1980.

TABLE 3

Unemployment Rate by Education, 1981

Years of Schooling	Males	Females	Total
0	2.2	-	2.2
1-3	7.3	-	6.0
4-6	16.1	8.9	14.2
7-9	24.8	15.6	22.4
10-11	12.4	11.1	12.6
12	27.7	37.8	30.0
13 and more	8.8	22.2	12.0

Source: Puerto Rico 1981 - First printed in Bonilla and Campo, 1987. Note: Includes persons 16 years or older.

U. S. economic realignments and the rise of a service sector economy has left Puerto Ricans living in the United States on the bottom rung of the economic ladder. By the early 1970s, Puerto Rican scholars had begun to take notice of the economic and labor market conditions Puerto Ricans in New York City were up against. By the 1970s, it was clear that Puerto Ricans were not "making it". Rodríguez explains the mismatch between the arrival of Puerto Ricans to New York City and the economic and labor market conditions of the time:

> What are the root causes of Puerto Rican high unemployment, skewed occupational distribution, and low income? If we examine the economy and its relation to Puerto Ricans, we find a number of factors that contribute substantially to these phenomena.
>
> These include automation, suburbanization, sectoral decline, blue collar structural unemployment, racial and ethnic prejudice, restrictive union policies, inadequate education opportunities, and the near exclusion of Puerto Ricans from government employment.
>
> In a nutshell, here is how these factors operate and interact. Automation and the movement of surviving blue collar jobs to the suburbs and South, and to other countries have caused a sectoral decline in the number of manufacturing jobs available in New York City. Since these trends occurred more rapidly than out migration or the retraining of blue collar workers to fill white collar jobs, a severe problem of blue collar structural unemployment arose. (1980, 35)

The declining availability of low-skill job opportunities in the Northeast is a major factor in the deteriorating economic position of Puerto Ricans as a group.

In another study Bonilla and Campo (1987) depicted the economic and labor market conditions that Puerto

Ricans have faced in New York. Bonilla and Campo (1987) highlighted census figures of predominantly Puerto Rican neighborhoods in New York City that showed a decline in labor force participation rates of Puerto Rican men and women in the city. For example, according to 1980 census figures, the labor force participation rates for Spanish-origin women in Harlem and Mott Haven were 26.8 percent and 15.1 percent respectively. In 1970 the city-wide labor force participation rate for Puerto Rican women was 28.1 percent.

As a whole the economic conditions among Puerto Ricans in the United States actually worsened between 1970 and 1980. Puerto Rican families did better ten or twenty years ago as compared to today. In 1970 28.2 percent of U. S. Puerto Rican families lived in poverty. By 1980, this figure rose to 33.4 percent. Furthermore, according to the 1980 census, Puerto Rican families had a median annual income of $11,168. This was far below the figure for all non-Hispanic white families ($21,235) (Tienda and Bean 1987). Scholars such as Bonilla (1987) and Rodríguez (1980) have suggested that there is a mismatch between the opportunity structure in the United States and the skills of Puerto Ricans. Puerto Ricans are arriving in the United States at a time when the economic and labor market conditions in the United States are unfavorable for those who have little education and little or no skills. Thus Puerto Ricans find themselves unable to secure jobs that offer opportunities to improve their position.

TABLE 4

States with 10,000 or More Puerto Rican Origin in 1980

Rank	State	Percent Rate of increase 1970-1980	Number 1980	Number 1970
1	New York	7.6	986,389	916,608
2	New Jersey	75.3	243,540	138,896
3	Illinois	47.7	129,165	87,477
4	Florida	236.4	94,775	28,166
5	California	82.7	93,038	50,929
6	Pennsylvania	107.4	91,802	44,263
7	Connecticut	135.0	88,361	37,603
8	Massachusetts	227.7	76,450	23,332
9	Ohio	60.0	32,442	20,272
10	Texas	262.2	22,938	6,338
11	Hawaii	108.4	19,351	9,284
12	Indiana	36.8	12,683	9,269
13	Michigan	100.3	12,425	6,202
14	Wisconsin	44.6	10,483	7,248
15	Virginia	149.6	10,227	4,098
	Selected states	38.4	1,924,069	1,389,980
	United States	40.9	2,013,945	1,429,396

Source: Data from U. S. Census Bureau published in *El Diario,* September 17,1982, p.3 First printed in Bonilla and Campo, 1987.

TABLE 5

Persons of 5 Years of Age and Older Who Lived in the U. S. for 6 Months or More between 1970 and 1980, by Length of Stay

less 15 yrs.	6 mos-2 yrs.	3-5 yrs.	6 yrs.	Don't Report Length of Stay	Total
15 yrs.	23,954	18,780	22,111	16,653	81,498 (20.6%)
15-24	29,287	10,851	37,084	3,640	80,862 (20.4%)
25-34	37,592	17,832	36,277	1,320	93,021 (23.5%)
35-44	15,039	7,839	38,457	781	62,116 (15.7%)
45+	19,431	6,928	50,401	1,451	78,211 (19.8%)
Total	125,303 (31.7%)	62,230 (15.7%)	184,330 (46.6%)	23,845 (6%)	395,708

Source: Junta de Planificación de Puerto Rico, 1982.

Back-and-forth immigration patterns emerged under these economic conditions. Not all of those who return are of retirement age; some are young people in their productive years with and without children (see Table 5). The Puerto Rican Planning Board Survey in 1979 showed that the median age of the nonmigrant population was 21.6 percent, while among the Puerto Rican return migrant population the median age was 37.9. However, this figure for migrants might be inflated because the ages of their children were not included. Most of their children were born in the United States and are most likely categorized as migrants born in the United States of Puerto Rican parentage. Foreign-born immigrants have a median age of 39.6 years.

In sum, from the 1940s to 1980s, the U. S. domination of Puerto Ricans and the conditions of poverty that it created for this group resulted in the constant movement of Puerto Ricans to and from the United States (see Centro de Estudios Puertorriqueños 1979 and Maldonado-Denise 1984, which show how U. S. imperialism resulted in the massive migration of Puerto Ricans to the United States). This much movement between one country and another requires rethinking and reconceptualizing the Puerto Rican migration experience.

Among Puerto Rican migrants of the 1980s and 1990s is the development of the "dual home base" phenomenon (Alicea 1990), meaning that Puerto

Ricans have one home base in the United States and another in Puerto Rico. Each has its own set of resources in the form of relatives or friends on whom migrating individuals have some sort of claim for help. Puerto Ricans maintain a hold in each place to maximize resources and to respond to the needs of their extended family members. The concept of dual home base also means that Puerto Ricans maintain psychological attachments to both the United States and Puerto Rican society.

If "where people live" includes dual home bases as places where people fulfill their own and their families' needs, then the migration of Puerto Ricans to and from the United States is a continuation of extended patterns of home life and not a change in residence. Puerto Ricans must move to maintain family ties and responsibilities. Migration, quite literally, has become a way of life for them.

The development of dual home bases among Puerto Ricans of the 1980s resulted from two conditions. The first condition has to do with Puerto Ricans' status as a colonized people, while the second is related to an internal response among Puerto Ricans to structural factors emanating from Puerto Rico's political and economic domination by the United States.

The dual home-base phenomenon is a form of social organization that the United States imposed on Puerto Rico as economic opportunities failed to improve in both Puerto Rico and the United States. The U. S. imperialist and oppressive practices first resulted in the economic marginalization of Puerto Ricans, then the diaspora of the Puerto Rican people, and finally the development of complex family networks spread out between the United States and Puerto Rico. Various institutions of the United States and the colonial government in Puerto Rico, including military, educational, business and welfare institutions, propelled the dual home-base phenomenon.

However, dual home bases also represent a form of social organization that Puerto Ricans adopted to survive in the midst of social and economic problems and as resources, family members, and obligations spread out over space. That is, the dual home-base form of social organization represents an internal response on the part of Puerto Ricans to adverse conditions. Puerto Ricans create dual home bases as a way to maintain family ties and responsibilities to relatives.

The dual home-base conceptual framework emphasizes the constraining and enabling nature of social structures. The colonial relationship between Puerto Rico and the United States both propelled the Puerto Rican diaspora but also opened avenues for family ties to continue. Viewing the development of dual home bases as emerging from both structural forces and as an internal response of Puerto Ricans also emphasizes how human agents interact with, shape, and respond to forces representing aspects of the broader social and economic structure. The actions of Puerto Ricans as they move in response to their needs and the needs of extended family members redefines social space and shapes Puerto Rican reality (Alicea 1990).

Cuban Immigration

Cuban immigration, especially of the last thirty years, is often seen as separate and unique from that of the Mexican and Puerto Rican. Undoubtedly there are tremendous differences. The fact that most Cubans have entered as refugees has meant that the Cuban immigration experience has been very different from that of Puerto Ricans and Mexicans. Cubans' status as exiles, institutionalized by both the United States and the Cuban Government, is another key difference between Cuban immigration and that of Mexican and Puerto Ricans.

Yet seen within the context of the U. S. economic and political domination over Latin America, the immigration of Cubans, Mexicans, and Puerto Ricans has much in common. It has been the strong and oppressive presence of the United States in Cuba, Mexico, and Puerto Rico that has created reasons and avenues for leaving. Mexicanos, Puertorriqueños, and Cubanos move within an economic and political system dominated by the United States.

Early Cuban Immigration

One of the first migrations of Cubans to the U. S. dates back to the 1830s when Cuban cigar factory owners, attempting to avoid high U. S. tariffs, relocated their factories to Key West, Florida. With the relocation of these factories came many skilled workers and the development of the first Cuban communities in the United States.

It was not, however, until the waning years of the colonial Spanish rule of Cuba and the outbreak of the war of independence in October 1868 that more Cubans came to the United States. Roughly 100,000 Cubans sought refuge in the U. S. by 1869. The middle-class professionals and businessmen migrated to New York, Philadelphia, Boston, and Florida. In addition as the struggles for independence destroyed many tobacco plantations in Cuba, the migration of tobacco workers also increased from 1868 to 1878 (Poyo 1979, 1977).

One of the most interesting Cuban communities of the late 1800s emerged in Florida, when Vicent Martínez Ybor, a cigar factory owner, first relocated his factory from Havana to Key West and then to Tampa. Those who worked in the cigar factory were highly politicized. They were committed to Cuban's independence, active in local politics, and fought for the rights of immigrants. In fact, in the 1880s and 1890s, when José Martí (1853-1895), lived in exile in the U. S., he often visited Tampa to garner support from the cigar workers for the independence movement (Pérez 1978).

Many Cuban communities of the middle and late 1800s can be characterized by their active support of the Cuban independence movement. Tampa as well as other smaller Cuban communities in Ocala, St. Augustine, Jacksonville, Miami and New York, supported the Cuban independence movement, contributing thousands of dollars to the cause (Pérez 1978; Poyo 1979, 1977).

From the early 1900s until the Castro-led revolution of 1959, Cuban immigration to the United States fluctuated according to political and economic events in Cuba. From dictator Fernández Machados (1920s to 1930s) to the government of Fulgencio Batista, those who opposed the particular government in power sought refuge in the United States. Once a particular leader had been overthrown, then it was the loyalists of these leaders who would send them into exile in the United States.

However, the migration and diaspora of a community is made up of many groups. Oscar Hijuelos (1989) in his fictional book *Mambo Kings Play Songs of Love*, tells the story of the immigration of Cuban musicians in the 1940s. Early in the book he describes how two brothers learn of the advantages of immigrating to the United States:

> Tired of singing with the Havana Melody Boys, Cesar Castillo wanted to put together an orchestra of his own. Coming from a small town in Oriente, he had been inspired by the stories he'd heard about Cubans who'd left for the States. A woman from Hoguin had become an actress and gone to Hollywood, where she had gotten rich making films with George Raft and Cesar Romero . . . She made enough money to live in a radiant pink mansion in a place called Beverly Hills; and there was another fellow, a rumba dancer named Ernesto Precioso, whom Cesar had know from the dance halls of Santiago de Cuba and who had been discovered by Xavier Cugat, for whom he'd starred as a featured dancer in a Hollywood short with Cugat called *The Lady in Red* and with the pianist Noro Morales in *The Latin from Staten Island*. . . .
>
> But the most famous success story would be that of a fellow crooner whom the brothers knew from Santiago de Cuba, where they sometimes performed in dance halls and in the placitas, sitting out under the moonlight, strumming guitars. Desi Arnaz. He had turned up in the States in the thirties and established himself in the clubs and dance halls of New York as a nice, decent fellow and had played his conga drum, singing voice, and quaint Cuban accent into fame. . . .
>
> In any case, the scene might be better in New York. Musicians friends from Havana traveled north and found work in the orchestras of people like Cugat, Machito, Morales, and Arnaz. Cesar heard rumors and received letters about money, dance halls, recording contracts, good weekly salaries, women and friendly Cubans everywhere.
>
> The day the brother arrived in New York, fresh from Havana, in January of 1949, the city was covered in two feet of snow. Flying out of Havana on a Pan Am Clipper to Miami for $39.18, they then took the Florida Special north. In Baltimore they began to encounter snow, and while passing through a station in northern Maryland, they came across a water tower that had burst and blossomed into an orchid-shaped, many petaled cascade of ice. Pablo met them at Pennsylvania Station, and, hombre, the brothers in their thin-soled shoes and cheap Sears, Roebuck overcoats were chilled to the bone. . . . (31-33)

By 1959 well-defined Cuban communities developed in various parts of the United States, particularly New York and Florida. By the eve of Castro's victorious march into Havana, there were 40,000 Cuban-born Americans in the United States. Those who came prior to 1959 were a relatively heterogenous group. They included everyone from members of the ruling elite, out of favor at the time, to unemployed workers seeking jobs. The exiles who came after Castro were aware of these Cuban communities in the United States.

Cuban Immigration and the Revolution

The overthrow of dictator Fulgencio Batista and his supporters in 1959 was the event that set off the greatest migration of Cubans to the United States. Since Castro's victory, over 800,000 Cubans have come to the United States (See Table 6).

According to Boswell and Curtis (1983, 41) a key factor to understanding this exodus lies in "an appreciation for the pervasiveness and speed of the societal changes that took place as Castro consolidated his power between 1959 and 1962." Castro's efforts left no social sector untouched. Social, economic and political institutions were radically altered (Boswell and Curtis 1983; Fagen et al. 1968).

However, according to Masud-Piloto (1988), the Cuban immigration experience should also be understood by looking beyond the changes occurring within Cuba and to U. S. response to these changes. The fact that Cuba's revolution came at the height of the Cold War made the U. S. government determined to destroy it. Economic and political domination and control of Cuba was not something the United States wanted to give up easily.

According to Masud-Piloto (1988, 2-4), "Unable to change internal events in Cuba, the United States resolved to overthrow Fidel Castro by force and to embarrass his regime at any opportunity." Every administration from Eisenhower to Reagan has welcomed refugees from Cuba in order to further U. S. political objectives.

The decision to allow these refugees into the United States was not entirely motivated by humanitarian concerns but also by the desire to overthrow Castro with exile forces and to discredit the Cuban government. The United States has used Cuban immigrants as a way to speak out and attack communism. The belief that many of the exiles could easily be assimilated because they were professionals, educated and familiar with U. S. American culture also contributed to the decision to allow Cubans to come to the United States.

Castro, at the same time, encouraged or allowed periods of open migration as a way to help the revolution as well as hurt the United States for its stance against changes taking place in Cuba. The departure of those who opposed the revolution allowed Castro to consolidate his power. In sum, Masud-Piloto (1988) argued that these immigrants have been used as political pawns both by the United States and Cuba.

The Cuban immigration to the United States since the revolution can be divided into several eras. The first era, from 1959 to 1962, was touched off by Castro's triumphant victory. The Camarioca boatlift and the subsequent airlift from 1965 to April 1973 brought an additional 360,000 Cuban immigrants. The most recent and massive immigration occurred from May to September 1980.

TABLE 6

Cuban Migration to the United States, 1959-80

Year	Number
1959[a]	26,527
1960[b]	60,224
1961	49,961
1962	78,611
1963	42,929
1964	15,616
1965	16,447
1966	46,688
1967	52,147
1968	55,945
1969	52,625
1970	49,545
1971	50,001
1972	23,977
1973	12,579
1974	13,670
1975	8,488
1976	4,515
1977[c]	4,548
1978	4,108
1979	2,644
1980	122,061
Total, January 1, 1959 to September 30, 1980	793,856
Total, April 1, 1980 to December 31, 1980	125,118

Source: Sergio Díaz-Briquets and Lisandro Pérez, *Cuba: The Demography of Revolution* (Washington, D.C.: Population Refernce Bureau, vol. 36, no. 1, April 1981), p. 26.

[a] For 1959 the figures are for January 1 to June 30.

[b] For 1960 through 1976 the figures are for fiscal years beginning July 1, and ending June 30.

[c] For 1977 through 1980 the figures are for fiscal years beginning October 1 and ending September 30.

January 1959 to October 1962

First to leave Cuba after Batista's overthrow were the economic and political elite openly affiliated with the Batista government. Then, as agrarian reform laws were instituted in June 1959, the landholding aristocracy began to leave. By 1960, as the middle-class entrepreneurs began to feel the impact of urban reforms, they too left the island, followed by professionals and small merchants. During this period from June 1959 to October 1962, some 215,000 Cubans left their homeland (Díaz-Briquets and Pérez 1981).

Both Eisenhower's and Kennedy's policies toward Cuban immigrants were governed by the U. S. Cold War ideology. Essentially the intent of the U. S. open-door policy was "to destabilize Castro's government by draining it of vital human resources (such as physicians, teachers, and technicians) and to discredit the regime through encouraging the flight of thousands from a 'communist' to a 'free' country" (Masud-Piloto 1988, 1).

The U. S. strategy was initially successful. A massive exodus from a communist country to a capitalist one had a significant propoganda effect. In addition the departure of a large number of professionally trained and skilled individuals had a devastating effect on the Cuban economy. But the primary U. S. objective, to overthrow Castro, was not achieved (Masud-Piloto 1988).

The U. S. strategy to drain Cuba of its professionals, however, had a dual effect. While it temporarily drained Cuba of important human resources, it also allowed Castro to more easily consolidate the revolution and his power.

Probably no other action of the United States demonstrated more clearly its unrelenting attempt to discredit Castro and the Cuban revolution than the Cuban Children's Program established under the Eisenhower administration. Essentially the program emerged as a scheme to rescue Cuban children from communist indoctrination. In 1960 rumors spread throughout Cuba and the exiled community in Miami about Castro's revolutionary programs. "One of the most sensational and powerful of those rumors was the one about the 'patria potestá,' or the rights of parent over their children" (Masud-Piloto 1988, 39; Walsh 1971).

Although unfounded, the rumors were enough to set in motion the creation of the Cuban Children's Program. Under the program, Cuban parents were allowed to send their children unaccompanied to the United States to avoid communist indoctrination. Children were placed in foster homes or group homes. At first it was believed that the families would be separated for only a few weeks or months. However, the reunification of the children with their parents was prolonged as events in Cuba unfolded. The Bay of Pigs invasion and the Cuban Missile Crisis prolonged reunification. Many of the 14,048 children who came to the United States during the program waited up to twenty years to be reunited with their parents.

One of the key actions of the Kennedy administration regarding Cuban immigration was the adaptation of the Cuban Refugee Program under the Department of Health, Education and Welfare in December 1960. The program was to help refugees locate jobs, provide financial assistance to meet basic maintenance requirements, provide for essential health care, and provide funds for the resettlement of refugee areas outside of Miami. Under the program, various social service organizations, schools, and other institutions were eligible to receive funds to augment the unforeseen impact of the new refugees. The program also provided money to expand training and educational opportunities for Cuban refugees, including physicians, teachers, and those with other professional backgrounds.

The programs represented a wider commitment on the part of the United States to the Cuban immigrants. More importantly, as Félix Masud-Piloto (1988) argued, it played a key role in the political warfare the United States and Cuba waged against each other and the strategy to use the immigration experience to their respective political advantage. Kennedy sold the program as important to the fight against communism. Castro on the other hand saw the program as an attack against the Cuban government.

Amid the Cold War and political struggles between the United States and the Cuban government, Cuban refugees continued to arrive in Florida. Between 1959 and 1962 over 200,000 Cubans came to the United States. Those who came were not as heterogenous as previous groups had been, but they were not homogenous either. They were not all white-collar professionals (less than 40 percent were from white-collar classes). Nevertheless, when considered as a whole, the refugees who came between 1959 and 1962 were not representative of the entire Cuban population. As a group, immigrants who came during this period had a higher level of education than the Cuban population.

In 1962 the Cuban Missile Crisis brought an end to all direct flights between Cuba and the United States. The number of refugees dwindled rapidly between November 1962 and November 1965. The only way to leave the Island was through clandestine means or through third countries.

Despite the end of open emigration in 1962, about 56,000 still managed to make their way to the United States. About 6,000 of these immigrants were prisoners of war from the failed Bay of Pigs invasion who were released in exchange for shipments of badly needed medical supplies for Cuba. Another 6,700 of the 56,000 came through clandestinely. The remaining 43,300 left through third countries. This was a costly venture, because those who came through third countries were not automatically given legal status as compared with those who came directly from Cuba. They were subject to existing immigration restrictions and sometimes had to wait in the third country, usually Spain or Mexico, before being allowed to come to the United States (Boswell and Curtis 1983).

Camarioca, December 1965 to April 1973

A new chapter in Cuban immigration history began when the Cuban government announced in September 1965 that it would allow Cubans with relatives living in the United States to leave. The fishing port of Camarioca was selected as the point of departure. The boatlift that ensued brought about 5,000 new exiles to the United States.

The disorderly and sometimes dangerous and tragic ending of several voyages from Camarioca to Florida was a source of embarrassment to both the U. S. and Cuban governments. A Memorandum of Understanding established arrangements for an airlift, which was initiated December 1, 1965, and continued until April 6, 1973. During this period, two flights a day five days a week from Varadero Beach in Cuba brought over 340,000 to Miami, Florida.

Those who had close relatives already living in the United States were given priority. However, the Cuban government did not allow free exodus from Cuba. In an attempt to avoid past mistakes, it placed restrictions on those who could leave. Males of military age (17 to 26 years of age) or persons whose departure might create a disturbance to production or to social service could not leave. Highly trained individuals working in key occupations also were denied visas until they could be replaced (Boswell and Curtis 1983).

Several theories have been offered to explain Castro's decision to open the Camarioca port. The decision stemmed from the desire of the Cuban government to have open talks with the United States and to normalize diplomatic relations. Castro hoped that the boatlift would force the United States to make clear its immigration policy toward Cuba. The decision to open the Cuban port also resulted because the Cuban government wanted to ease internal problems by eliminating nonproductive Cubans. Finally, it was a way to provide a safety valve by letting dissidents go to the United States. Whatever the detailed reasons for Cuba's decision to allow the boatlift, it was apparent that it, like the United States, used the situation to further its own political objectives (Masud-Piloto 1988).

The United States continued to use the refugees to further its own political agenda. The boatlift and the subsequent airlift which came to be known as the Freedom Flights, were a great propaganda victory for the exiled Cuban community and the U. S. government. Once again media and government hype colored the situation as Cubans escaping communist oppression.

In the absence of clear U. S. immigration policy, both the boatlift and the airlift were treated as emergencies. Neither President Johnson nor President Nixon tried to normalize the immigration policy during the seven-year airlift.

At the same time it was becoming clear that refugees leaving Cuba for the United States could not be seen solely as political refugees but also as economic refugees. Those who were leaving Cuba seemed to be dissatisfied because of the economic situation and not the political repression (Portes and Bach 1985).

In 1973, the Cuban government unilaterally decided to end the airlift. Between 1973 and 1979 the only way to leave Cuba was once again through clandestine escapes or through third countries. The only exception to the end of sanctioned Cuban immigration came in October 1978 when Castro announced he would release 3,600 political prisoners. For seventeen months, until March 1980, former prisoners and their families flew to the United States. An estimated 10,000 to 14,000 persons took part in this exodus (Boswell and Curtis 1984).

Those who came from December 1965 to April 1973 were not as economically advantaged as in the previous exodus. Increasingly the lower middle class and urban working class were represented among the immigrant population. Despite this shift, the socioeconomic status and educational attainment continued to be above that of the Cuban population. Exiles were also disproportionately urban in origin. The proportion of blacks and mulattoes continued to be much lower than in the island's population (Boswell and Curtis 1984).

The Mariel Boatlift, May to September 1980

The occupation of the Peruvian Embassy in Havana in April 1980 triggered the largest ever Cuban immigration in a single year. On April 1, 1980, six Cubans crashed through the gates of the Peruvian Embassy with a bus and solicited and received political asylum. When Peruvian authorities refused the Cuban government's request to turn in the gate crashers, the Cuban government responded by withdrawing all guards and barricades from the embassy. It then announced that anyone who wanted to leave the country should go to the Peruvian Embassy. Within seventy-two hours, 10,000 people arrived at the embassy, a number unexpected by the Cuban or Peruvian governments.

Once this happened, Castro explained the government's position, declaring that as long as other countries provided for these individuals they could leave. Castro also used the opportunity to explain that the main motivation for the crowds at the Peruvian Embassy was economic and not political, an explanation soon accepted by the U. S. government (Boswell and Curtis 1984; Masud-Piloto 1988).

There were many reasons why people wanted to leave Cuba. The desire to reunite with family members already in the United States was one key factor. There were also those who were tired of having to sacrifice so much for the revolution or who were dissatisfied with the government. Masud-Piloto (1988, 80) and Boswell and Curtis (1984) explained that "consumerism" also played a role in people's desire to leave. Masud-Piloto writes, "Consumerism [was] long gone from Cuba's revolutionary austerity, but brought back for a short time during the 1979 dialogue, when Cuban exiles visited the island bringing expensive gifts and success stories about life in the United States."

Yet the United States continued to interpret the events in strictly political terms. Many saw the occupation of the Peruvian Embassy as the beginning of the end of the revolution. Once again the propaganda served to reaffirm anticommunist rhetoric. The occupation of the Peruvian Embassy was painted as a statement against communism. In the meantime the situation in the embassy worsened as thousands crowded into the facilities. To alleviate the situation, Castro asked people to leave the embassy and offered them passes to return home until their exit visas could be processed. About 3,000 moved back home temporarily until their paperwork was prepared. This action surprised U. S. government officials and forced them to grapple with the question: Were the motivations for leaving really political?

A group of Cuban exiles decided to travel to Cuba with more than 40 privately owned boats. They wanted to persuade the Cuban government to let them take the 10,000 in the Peruvian Embassy to Florida. To their surprise, the Cuban government decided to open the port of Mariel to anyone who wanted to leave the country. Exiles from Miami interpreted President Carter's open-arms policy as a signal to proceed with the boatlift. Within hours, in hundreds of boats, Miami Cubans arrived at Mariel Harbor hoping to pick up fellow Cubans. During the first week of the boatlift more than 6,000 Cubans arrived in Key West. By September 26, 1980, when the operation was suspended, 125,000 Cubans had come to the United States.

Carter, like Eisenhower and Johnson, reacted the same way to similar Cuban refugee crises. However, the situation during Carter's administration was different. Just five weeks before the Peruvian Embassy situation, U. S. immigration policy towards Cuba had become more clearly defined. The United States had passed a yearly quota of 19,500 refugees from Cuba under the Refugee Act of March 1980. In addition, it required individual case reviews before refugee status could be granted. Under the law, the U. S. defined refugees as people who were unable to return to their country for fear they would be politically, religiously or racially persecuted. As events surrounding the Peruvian Embassy transpired, it was clear that Cubans at the embassy were undocumented aliens seeking asylum, not refugees.

The question of what to do with the thousands of Cubans arriving in Miami was exacerbated by the reality that for months Haitians coming into the state had been denied refugee status. If the U. S. government granted refugee status to the Cubans, it would have to do the same for the 30,000 undocumented Haitians in the state. Refugee status also meant that all those eligible would qualify for federal aid. The prospect of massive Cuban and Haitian migration to Florida alarmed state and federal officials.

The Carter administration attempted to work with the Cuban government to make the exodus more orderly. First, the federal government declared it illegal for individuals in private vessels to bring Cubans from the Island to Florida. Many boats, however, continued to transport Cubans from Mariel Harbor to Key West.

The United States also requested that Castro close the Mariel Harbor and promised to start an airlift or boatlift. In an act of defiance, the Cuban government not only refused to close the port, but continued to announce that anyone who wanted to leave could do so as long as another country would receive them. Fidel Castro was determined to turn the Peruvian Embassy incident and the boatlift into a political victory for himself by embarrassing President Carter through defiance.

Faced with Castro's and the Cuban exiles' defiance, the federal government dealt with the Cuban exiles in a manner similar to earlier administrations—as a crisis. In May 1980, Carter declared a state of emergency in South Florida and set up a couple of tent cities in which to house homeless Cubans. The longer the exiles remained in the camps, sometimes for periods of several months, the more frustrated they became. Television news reports and daily newspaper accounts of violent confrontations between Cubans and the National Guard, the escape of known criminals and the destruction of federal property, triggered resentment toward the new immigrants.

As more and more Cubans poured into South Florida, the federal government continued to grapple with the question: Were Cubans motivated by economic or by political reasons? The Carter administration resisted granting refugee status to new arrivals believing that their motivations for leaving Cuba were largely economic and not political. Their fear of persecution came from having left Cuba, not because they had been persecuted by the government before leaving.

In June 1980, the status issue was settled with the creation of a new classification, "Cuban-Haitian entrant." Under this classification, new entrants were allowed to stay in the United Sates and after two years could adjust their status to "permanent resident alien." Furthermore, the new entrants would be eligible for medical services, supplemental income and emergency assistance benefits. State and local governments would be reimbursed for 75 percent of the program's costs.

As previously stated, close to 125,000 Cubans arrived in the United States from May to September 1980. Those who were processed by the federal government and released in Miami were not significantly different from previous immigrant cohorts. However, they were different from those who remained in the refugee camps. The group released from the camps had a high proportion of family groups and/or people with relatives in the U. S. In addition, a high proportion had been employed in Cuba before coming to the U. S. Those who went to the camps were younger and few had relatives in the United States. A large proportion were single men.

Sixteen percent reported having been incarcerated in Cuba. For both groups, however, the proportion of non-whites was significantly higher than in earlier waves of Cuban immigration (Portes and Bach 1985).

Those who came with the Mariel boatlift were not as well received as earlier Cuban immigrants. Castro and U. S. media hype created the impression that most of the those who came during this time were undesirables, prisoners, mentally ill, homosexuals, deafs and mutes, sick and old. The size of the immigration in such a short period of time also contributed to its negative image.

As in earlier periods, attempts were made to relocate those who came in the Mariel boatlift to other parts of the country. Recent statistics demonstrate, however, that they are moving back to the Florida area.

Driven by anticommunist ideology, the United States failed to develop clear immigration policies regarding Cuban refugees. It was more important to use Cubans as political pawns than to develop clear policies. Cubans were given refugee status not because it was truly believed that they were leaving Cuba for political reasons, but because they served a political end for the United States. While Cubans were allowed into the country, other groups, e.g., Haitians and Guatemalans, who came from politically torn countries backed by the United States, were not admitted (Masud-Piloto 1988).

Conclusion

As the United States and Latin American countries come to share more and more in common economically and culturally and become interdependent, it becomes increasingly difficult to describe Latino transnational migration as a process whereby people move from one system to another. For example, it becomes more and more difficult to argue that migrants move from a low-wage, peripheral society to a separate and distinct high-wage, core society (Portes and Bach 1985). Nor is it possible to assume that Latino migrants will eventually become fully integrated in the host society and abandon ties to the homeland.

Scholars explain that the cultural and economic similarities we see emerging among cities and rural areas throughout the world result from economic restructuring, globalization and the peripheralization of the core (Bonilla and Campo 1987). But as Goldring (1992, 2) explains, this process "can also be understood at an intermediate level of analysis. As people move back and forth across the border to the different places they inhabit, they participate in processes that change their physical and social environments."

Indeed, recent literature on Latino transnational migration and transnational migrant communities (e.g. Goldring 1992) highlight how groups maintain ties with their homelands and often create new kinds of communities that span international borders. Areas traditionally thought of as distinct become so closely tied together through the exchange of people, resources and information that they, in effect, become one community. As areas on each side of the border are transformed, boundaries traditionally drawn become blurred while new ones emerge. Coming full circle, this transformation then changes people's migration experiences. People move within extended notions of home and community. Structural forces in part shape the flow, direction and uses of Mexican, Puerto Rican and Cuban migrations, but it is also true that these groups shape the migration experience and in the process the spaces in which they travel.

Bibliography

Acuña, Rodolfo
1972 *Occupied America.* San Francisco, CA: Canfield P.

Alicea, Marisa
1990 "The Dual Home Base Phenomenon: A Reconceptualization of Puerto Rican Migration." *Latino Studies Journal* 1.3:78-98.

Andreu Iglesias, César, ed
1984 *Memoirs of Bernando Vega.* Translated by Juan Flores. New York: Monthly Review P.

Barker, Eugene
1965 *Mexicans and Texans, 1821-1835.* New York: Russell & Russell.

Barrera, Mario
1979 *Race and Class in the Southwest.* Notre Dame, IN: U of Notre Dame.

Bluestone, Barry, and Bennet Harrison
1980 *Capital and Communities: The Causes and Consequences of Private Disinvestment.* Washington, DC: Progressive Alliance.

Bonilla, Frank, and Ricardo Campos
1987 "Evolving Pattern of Puerto Rican Migration." Paper presented at Inter-University Seminar, Stanford, CA: Stanford U.

Boswell, Thomas D., and James R. Curtis
1983 *The Cuban-American Experience: Culture, Images, and Perspectives.* Totowa, NJ: Rowman & Allanheld.

Cafferty, Pastora San Juan
1975 "Puerto Rican Return Migration: Its Implications for Bilingual Education." *Ethnicity* 2:52-65.

Centro de Estudios Puertorriqueños, History Task Force
1979 *Labor Migration under Capitalism: The Puerto Rican Experience.* New York: Monthly Review P.

Cornelius, Wayne
1976 "Mexican Migration to the United States: The View from Rural Sending Communities." Working Paper.

Cambridge, MA: Center for International Studies, Massachusetts Institute of Technology.

Díaz-Briquetes, Sergio, and Lisandro Pérez
1981 "Cuba: The Demography of Revolution." *Population Bulletin* vol 36, (April):2-41.

Escobar, Edward J.
1991 "The Forging of a Community: The Latino Experience." *Latino Studies Journal* 2.1:38-57.

Estrada, Leobardo F., F. Chris García, Reynaldo Flores Macías, and Lionel Maldonado
1985 "Chicanos in the United States: A History of Exploitation and Resistance." In *Majority and Minority: The Dynamics of Race and Ethnicity in American Life.* Ed Norman R. Yetman. Boston, MA: Allyn & Bacon, pp 162-84.

Fagen, Richard R., Richard A. Brody, and Thomas O'Leary
1986 *Cubans in Exile: Disaffection and Revolution.* Stanford, CA: Stanford UP.

Galarza, Ernesto
1964 *Merchants of Labor: The Mexican Story.* Santa Barbara, CA: McNally-Loftin.

"Gary Works to Hire 500 Puerto Ricans."
1948 *Gary Post Tribune* (June 7):1.

Goldring, Luin
1992 "Blurring Borders: Community and Social Transformation in Mexico-U. S. Transnational Migration." Prepared for the conference on "New Perspectives on Mexico-U. S. Migration." U of Chicago, (October 23-24).

Hernández-Alvarez, José
1968 "Migration, Return, and Development." *Economic Development and Change* 16:574-87.

Hijuelos, Oscar
1989 *The Mambo Kings Play Songs of Love.* New York: Harper & Row.

Hoffman, Abraham
1974 *Unwanted Mexican Americans in the Great Depression: Repatriation Pressures, 1929-1939.* Tucson: U of Arizona P.

Junta de Planificación de Puerto Rico
1982 "Perfil demográfico y económico de la población inmigrante en Puerto Rico." San Juan, PR: Junta de Planificación.

Maldonado-Denis, Manuel
1972 *Puerto Rico: A Socio-Historic Interpretation.* New York: Vintage Books.
1984 *Puerto Rico y Estados Unidos: Emigración y colonialismo.* Santo Domingo, Republica Dominicana: Editora Corripio, C. por A.

Masud-Piloto, Félix R.
1988 *With Open Arms: Cuban Migration to the United States.* Totowa, NJ: Rowman & Littlefield.

Natal, Rosario Carmelo
1983 *Exodo puertorriqueno: Las emigraciones al Caribe y Hawaii, 1900-1915.* San Juan, PR.

Pérez, Louis A.
1978 "Cubans in Tampa: From Exiles to Immigrants, 1892-1901." *Florida Historical Quarterly* 2:129-40.

Portes, Alejandro
1979 "Illegal Immigration and the Internal System: Lessons from Recent Legal Immigrants from Mexico." *Social Problems* 26 (April):425-38.

Portes, Alejandro, and Robert L. Bach
1985. *Latin Journey: Cuban and Mexican Immigrants in the United States.* Berkeley, CA: U of California P.

Poyo, Gerald E.
1977 "Cuban Revolutionaries and Monroe County Reconstruction Politics, 1868-1876." *Florida Historical Quarterly 55*:407-22.
1979 "Key West and the Cuban Ten-Year War." *Florida Historical Quarterly 57*:289-307.

Quiñones Calderón, A., and Mandin Rodríguez
1964 "Llega el primer grupo de obreros migrantes." *El Mundo* (September 10):2.

Ramírez de Arrellano, A., and C. Seipp
1983 *Colonialism, Catholicism, and Contraception: A History of Birth Control in Puerto Rico.* Chapel Hill: U of North Carolina P.

Reynolds, Lloyd G., and Peter Gregory
1965 *Wages, Productivity and Industrialization in Puerto Rico.* Homewood, IL: Richard D. Irwin.

Rivera, Edward
1982 *Family Installments: Memories of Growing Up Hispanic.* New York: Penguin Books.

Rodríguez, Clara E.
1980 "Economic Survival in New York City." *The Puerto Rican Struggle.* Eds Clara E. Rodríguez, Virginia Sánchez Korrol, and José Oscar Alers. New York: Puerto Rican Migration Research Consortium, pp 31-46.

Tienda, Marta, and Frank Bean
1987 *The Hispanic Population of the United States.* New York: Russel Sage Foundation.

Tío, Salvador
1956 "La emigración: Cambios sugeridos en la política publica." *La Torre* 4:113-36.

U. S. Bureau of the Census
1980 "General Social and Economic Characteristics-Puerto Rico." Selected Tables. Washington, DC: Government Printing Office.

Wagenheim, Kal and Leslie Dunbar
1983 "Puerto Ricans in the U. S." Minority Rights Group-Report no 58. New York.

Mexicans, Puerto Ricans, and Cubans in the Labor Market: An Historical Overview

Luis M. Falcón and Dan Gilbarg

Introduction

The labor market experience of Latinos in the United States is a diverse one. This diversity is reflected in differential economic trajectories and overall social position for the different groups. The timing of historical events such as migration and the changing characteristics of economic sectors have combined with the characteristics of these immigrant groups to create histories of disadvantage and isolation—but also of success. A reflection of this diversity is the debate surrounding the use of terms such as Hispanics, Latinos, and Latin Americans to refer to the totality of groups living in the United States who trace their ancestry or birth to some country in Latin America. As emphasized in this chapter, the experiences of the different Hispanic groups in the U. S. labor market are distinct and require to be understood as such.

As a whole, Hispanics are still a small percentage of the total U. S. labor force. In 1991 Hispanics accounted for under 7.7 percent of the total civilian labor force in the United States (U. S. Bureau of the Census 1991). Close to 10 million workers in the 1991 labor force were of Hispanic origin. On the other hand, the rapid rate of growth of the Hispanic population and labor force during the last two decades presage increasing importance for this group. For example, Hispanics filled about 20 percent of all new jobs created in the United States during the 1980-87 period, with Hispanic employment increasing by over 2 million workers during the same period (Cattan 1988). The U. S. Bureau of Labor Statistics predicts that the Hispanic labor force will grow by 74 percent by the year 2000 and constitute about 10 percent of the U. S. labor force.

Given these trends, the Hispanic population will become a significant force in American society. In fact, their geographical concentration already makes them a sizable force in some of the largest metropolitan areas of the United States, such as New York City, Los Angeles, and Chicago. This chapter overviews the experience in the U. S. labor market of the three largest Hispanic groups in the United States—Mexican Americans, Puerto Ricans, and Cuban Americans. We focus on the interplay between structural conditions and the characteristics of these Hispanic groups.

Historical Experiences and the Labor Market

Many factors have contributed to distinguish the situation of the different Hispanic groups. Their pattern of settlement is one of the most distinctive aspects of the Hispanic presence in the United States. Mexican Americans, Puerto Ricans, and Cubans have been part of migratory flows that have peaked at different points in time, have evolved because of different political and economic factors, and have flowed to different geographical areas. This section focuses on the settlement process of the three groups and their insertion into the U. S. economy.

Mexican Americans

Mexican Americans constitute the oldest Hispanic-origin population in the United States. The presence of a Mexican-origin population dates back to the colonial era of the United States. The territories where today a majority of the Mexican-American population is concentrated were once part of Mexico. Mexicans became a minority group within the United States as a result of the annexation of those territories. The Mexican-American war of 1846-48 was the military event that led the United States to seize the northern part of Mexico. Of the estimated 86,000 to 116,000 Mexicans who resided in the northern part of Mexico and were involuntarily incorporated into the United States, a full range of social classes was represented, including a considerable group of large and small landowners.

However, by 1900, these property-owning classes had largely disappeared. Over two-thirds of the landholdings were transferred to Anglos through a combination of coercion, intimidation, force, and fraud. This process was sanctioned by U. S. land courts and commissions that were set up to hear land claims. Traditional claims were rejected, and original owners were required to prove their ownership in court. The procedures of these courts were biased against the original owners: the burden of proof fell on them, the courts were conducted in English and in locations less accessible to Mexican landowners, and standards of legal proof were based on U. S. law rather than Mexican law under which the land had originally been acquired.

This dispossession from the land, together with the displacement of much of the traditional middle classes of artisans and merchants into manual occupations, laid the foundation for the establishment of Mexicans as a labor force limited to low-skilled and low-paid jobs. The main sources of employment for Mexicans during this period were in agriculture, the railroads, and mining. In agriculture, Mexican workers were a key segment of the labor force in the developing cotton and fruit and vegetable industries, as well as the traditional cattle and sheep ranching. In mining, Mexicans were employed in the large-scale, mechanized copper, silver, gold, and lead mines. Mexicans were also employed in the construction and maintenance of the vastly expanding network of railroads that began to crisscross the Southwest by the end of the nineteenth century. In a number of these industries, Mexicans displaced Chinese workers as the preferred source of cheap labor when the Chinese immigrants were excluded from the United States after 1882.

At this time, Mexican workers were limited to unskilled jobs. For example, in ranching, Mexicans were the cowhands, but only Anglos were the overseers. When mechanization occurred in the mines and on the farms, Mexicans remained in the unskilled jobs while only Anglos became the machine operators. In the railroads, Mexicans worked in construction and the maintenance of tracks, while only Anglos worked as engineers, motormen, and conductors. On the farms, Mexicans picked the crops but only Anglos served as counters and packers in the sheds. Anglos were also employed as unskilled labor, but were paid more than Mexicans for the same work. In the laundries, Mexican women were excluded from jobs as markers, sorters, checkers, or supervisors. Other minorities such as native Americans, African Americans, and Chinese were treated the same as Mexicans in this dual wage and segmented occupational system. While most Mexican workers were men at this time, women began to enter the labor force around 1880. They also worked in agriculture in cases where entire families picked crops, engaged in laundry and domestic work, and served as operatives in the packing and canning industries that developed in conjunction with agriculture.

Mexican mine workers in Arizona during the early 1900s. (Courtesy of the Mexcian Heritage Project, Arizona Historical Society Library.)

A migrant work camp.

By 1900 the Mexican population in the Southwest had expanded to roughly half a million people. This was mostly a result of natural increase rather than migration from Mexico. However, beginning in 1900, immigration began and picked up steadily until 1930. In the 1920s, an average of 50,000 Mexican immigrants a year came to the United States, mainly to Texas and California. On the one hand, conditions in Mexico favored emigration. The rural population in Mexico was being rapidly expropriated from the land by commercial agricultural interests, while industrialization did not proceed apace. Population increased rapidly. Inflation was heavy and real wages were falling. On the other hand, southwestern U. S. employers engaged in heavy recruitment campaigns for Mexican workers to meet their rapidly increasing demands for cheap labor. During this period Mexican immigrant labor became the main source of cheap labor in the Southwest.

Much of the demand for Mexican labor continued to come from agriculture. With the Reclamation Act of 1902 and the opening up of new land due to irrigation, the continuation of a shift from extensive to intensive uses of land, the further development of the cotton and fruit and vegetable industries, and the introduction of new crops such as beet sugar, agricultural labor demands soared. In addition new railroads continued to be built, the lumber industry was further developed, mining continued to be developed, and the new oil industry grew rapidly in Texas and California. Industries also developed around the extractive industries–canning, oil refining, the building of mine equipment, ore smelting, machine shops stimulated by the needs of the oil industry, textile mills, and meat packing. Nevertheless, industry in the Southwest was still fairly weak by industrial standards.

General efforts to restrict immigration during this period did not apply to Mexican immigrants. Immigration restrictions were passed in 1917, which required paying an eight-dollar head tax and taking a literacy test, but Mexican immigrants were explicitly exempted from these requirements. In 1924, when a national origin quota system was established, Western Hemisphere countries such as Mexico were not included. Generally speaking, the need southwestern employers had for cheap labor took precedence over any efforts by nativist or labor groups to restrict Mexican immigration.

During this period, the dual wage and segmented occupational system that was established in the nineteenth century continued. This system characterized labor relations not only in rural areas but, for the most part, in cities as well, as rapid urbanization occurred. Here, Mexican males worked mainly on unskilled laboring jobs in construction and road work and in manufacturing. Even skilled workers were usually restricted to such positions as helpers. Women continued to work mainly as unskilled or semi-skilled operatives in laundries, garment factories, and food processing plants and as service workers (domestics, waitresses). Some women also worked in clerical and sales positions. The dual wage system was implemented in many, but not all, cases.

With the Depression of the 1930s, the policy of encouraging Mexican immigration shifted dramatically. Now there was a labor surplus rather than labor short-

Southern Pacific Railroad workers, World War II. (Courtesy of the Arizona Historical Society Library.)

age. Anglo labor was available to work as cheap labor—especially migrants from the Dust Bowl. As a result, half a million Mexicans were returned to Mexico, either as a result of compulsion or encouragement. Initially, in 1931, some 80,000 were either deported or left voluntarily on threat of deportation. The remainder left on the basis of repatriation campaigns, in which Mexicans were persuaded to leave. Los Angeles County was particularly hard hit, as reflected in the sharp decline of Mexicans from 80 percent to 20 percent of California's farm labor force.

With World War II, matters turned around again. Once again Mexican labor was needed, and once again immigration was encouraged. This time, a special program was instituted—the bracero program—to stimulate and regulate immigration. This program was periodically extended until its demise in 1964. The numbers involved were large—each year from 1951 to 1964, at least 181,000 braceros were allowed, with a maximum of over 444,000. Braceros were employed in the railroads and agriculture until 1946, and then only in agriculture. In 1960 an estimated 26 percent of the seasonally hired labor force were braceros, as were 10 percent of the entire farm labor force in the Southwest.

For employers there were several advantages of the bracero program. Workers were required by contract to remain on the farm—they could not migrate to the cities. In addition braceros could not unionize. Employers were only permitted to use braceros if there was a labor shortage; but there was always a shortage of Anglo workers at the low wages paid by the growers. During the period of the bracero program, farm labor wages and housing conditions deteriorated.

The bracero program finally came to an end in 1964. The Kennedy administration was more attuned to the interests of organized labor than prior administrations, which helped to account for this. But in addition farm labor demand had declined somewhat due to increased mechanization. Growers now had sufficient alternatives to meet their needs for cheap labor—specifically, undocumented workers.

The bracero program was a catalyst for undocumented migration. First, it encouraged Mexicans to migrate to northern Mexico, with expectations for an opportunity to enter the United States. When many of these Mexicans were turned away from the bracero program, they entered the United States anyway as undocumented workers. Second, the Immigration and Naturalization Service (INS) followed a policy of "drying out" undocumented workers—they would apprehend them, only to allow them to reenter the country legally as braceros. Thus, undocumented migration was officially sanctioned. Third, the bracero program along with other migration resulted in the establishment of social networks in the United States which encouraged still more Mexicans to immigrate, so that the migration became self-sustaining.

Until about the 1950s Mexican undocumented migrants presented high rates of cyclical migration where residence in the United States and in Mexico varied according to seasonal periods. During the last few decades, this pattern has changed as the Mexican immigrant labor force has acquired a more urban character.

The type of housing available for the bracero program. (Courtesy of Library of Congress.)

While there is still a large cyclical component, patterns of settlement are such that Mexican communities have sprouted in areas away from the initial settlement in the Southwest–particularly in the midwestern states.

Puerto Ricans

Puerto Ricans represent a peculiar situation in the context of the Hispanic experience in the United States. While Puerto Ricans have been citizens of the United States since 1917–and accordingly are not subject to the vagaries of United States immigration laws–they share many characteristics more commonly associated with immigrant groups. Despite almost a hundred years of U. S. presence on the island of Puerto Rico, in cultural, linguistic, and racial terms Puerto Rico is indeed a Latin American society. Therefore, despite their condition as citizens, Puerto Ricans who migrate to the mainland United States bring with them cultural and social differences that separate them for the native population where they settle.

As with many other immigrant groups, the migration of Puerto Ricans has been a migration of laborers. The first migrations of Puerto Ricans began prior to the Spanish-American War and were composed of small landholders and peasants departing for other areas in Latin America such as the Dominican Republic, Cuba, and Venezuela. These early migration flows were mostly a response to the uncertain working conditions in the Puerto Rican agricultural economy by the closing of the nineteenth century. However, it is not until after Puerto Rico becomes a possession of the United States that there is a more organized flow of laborers out of the Island. During the first decade of the twentieth century there were organized efforts by labor recruiters to bring Puerto Rican workers to agricultural areas in Hawaii, Mexico, and Cuba. The expeditions to Hawaii were by far the largest ones, with thousands of Puerto Rican workers committing themselves to a long trip by land and sea enticed by promises of guaranteed income and benefits. Puerto Rico's economy was undergoing a rapid realignment throughout this period as a shift was made from a pre-capitalist coffee "hacienda" system to labor-intensive sugar production. Because of the seasonal nature of sugar production it was difficult for workers to survive on part-year employment. In addition, the employment-generating capacity of this industry fell short from the needs of a growing labor force. The population of the island of Puerto Rico grew by about 18 percent during every decade of the 1900-30 period. Emigration was seen as a potential solution to the problems of unemployment and population growth by the colonial administration and was encouraged in official statements (Falcón 1991). By the 1930s there were already several established communities of Puerto Ricans on the U. S. mainland (Sánchez-Korrol 1983).

The bulk of the Puerto Rican migration, however, does not take place until the 1940s and 1950s. This time, rather than places in Latin America and the Pacific, the main point of destination is the United States. The 1917 Jones Act, which granted citizenship to all residents of Puerto Rico, was instrumental in facilitating the access of Puerto Ricans to the mainland. Earlier, in 1904, the United States Supreme Court had already determined that citizens of Puerto Rico were not "aliens to the United States and entitled to enter the country without obstruction" (History Task Force 1979).

Between 1940 and 1960, Puerto Rico's economy underwent a process of transformation from a sugar-producing economy–with tobacco growing and needlework as the other two major areas–to an industrialized export-oriented economy (see Falcón 1991; History Task Force 1979). The agrarian economy of Puerto Rico was plagued with problems. The seasonal character of sugar, tobacco, and coffee production left workers idle for large parts of the year. In addition competition from other area economies had contributed to stagnation in the levels of production. Puerto Rico's population had grown rapidly since about 1930. The increase in the working age population was surpassing the job-generating capacity of the economy. Consequently unemployment and underemployment were widespread. By the time of industrialization, forces were already in place to facilitate uprooting of rural populations to urban areas.

In the decade of the 1940s, over 150,000 Puerto Ricans migrated to the United States. The following decade, during the 1950s, 430,000 Puerto Ricans migrated to the United States. This massive outflow of Puerto Ricans took place during the point in time when the Puerto Rican economy was undergoing its most radical changes. The History Task Force (1979) has noted that it was rather peculiar to see the "unusual spectacle of a booming economy with a shrinking labor force and . . . shrinking employment." This outmigration facilitated the transition of the Puerto Rican economy to industrialization since it served as a pressure valve to reduce the tension between the number of jobs and the number of available workers.

Most of these migrants were headed to the east coast of the United States, primarily to New York City. A migration of unskilled and semi-skilled laborers, Puerto Ricans were attracted by the possibilities of employment in the manufacturing sector and other sectors that were enjoying the post-World War II economic boom. Many Puerto Ricans migrated to find employment in jobs requiring few skills, such as are commonly found in the service sector. A substantial number of Puerto Ricans began migrating regularly as part of a Puerto Rican version of the "bracero" program. The outmigration of Puerto Rican workers was an integral part of the model of economic development opted for by the Puerto Rican government during the 1940s (see Falcón 1990; History Task Force 1982). By the closing of the 1940s the Puerto Rican Department of Labor had established a migration office in New York City. The Labor Department took an active role in monitoring the contracts signed by Puerto Rican agricultural workers and in facilitating the migration process. Thousands of Puerto Rican agricultural workers migrated every year to work in the farms throughout the New England region.

While the flow of Puerto Ricans to work in agricultural jobs was substantial it was in manufacturing that Puerto Ricans were to concentrate. For example, by 1964, 52 percent of all Puerto Rican workers in the United States were employed in the manufacturing sector. At the time of arrival of the bulk of the Puerto Rican migration to New York City, the manufacturing sector was already a sector in the midst of employment decline. In New York City the number of jobs in the manufacturing sector declined by 92 percent between 1950 and 1960 (U. S. Department of Labor 1975). This process of employment decline continued during the 1960s, when manufacturing employment declined by 20 percent. Between 1972 and 1982 manufacturing employment declined by 21 percent. What is interesting about this process of employment decline in manufacturing in New York City is the way that it would impact the livelihood of the Puerto Ricans in the New York economy. The rapid entrance of Puerto Ricans into manufacturing employment links their economic situation to the stability of that particular sector of the economy. From then on, as manufacturing employment fluctuated, so did the employment trends for the Puerto Rican population on the mainland.

Cuban Americans

The Cuban presence in the United States did not begin with the triumph of the Cuban revolution in 1959. Cuban communities were already in existence in cities in New Jersey and Florida. The Cuban presence goes back to the nineteenth century when Cuban and Puerto Rican revolutionaries in New York City strategized on ways to achieve the liberation of their respective countries from their colonial condition. Miami, the city which is today the heart of the Cuban community in the United States, has had a significant Cuban presence going back to the 1930s, when many commercial and financial transactions with Cuba were conducted via Miami. Nonetheless, the majority of Cubans currently in the United States did not arrive until after the 1960s.

In contrast to the Mexican-American and Puerto Rican experience, the migration of Cubans has been essentially a one-way flow and not rooted in systems of labor recruitment but on a radical political change (Portes and Bach

A birthday party in East Harlem. (Courtesy of the Justo A. Marté Collection, Center for Puerto Rican Studies Library, Hunter College, CUNY.)

1985). The 1959 Cuban revolution was a precipitating factor in the consolidation of the Cuban presence in the United States. The factors which eventually led to the fleeing of hundreds of thousands of Cubans have been discussed extensively elsewhere (Llanes 1982; Boswell and Curtis 1984; Pedraza-Bailey 1985; Gann and Duignan 1986) and will not be covered here. The initial post-revolution exodus included mostly the upper classes of Cuban society and its most highly skilled labor force. This initial migration received extensive support from the U. S. government, which saw a diplomatic edge in assuring the adequate settlement of Cuban refugees. Programs where put in place to assist this process. These programs included the re-training of workers to prepare them to perform in the U. S. labor market, medical benefits, welfare, and tuition assistance for those wishing to continue their education.

Since the Cuban migration was a response to radical systemic changes within Cuban society, the flow of refugees was by no means a cross-section of the population of Cuba at the time. Cuban refugees in general were more likely to be older, more highly educated, more likely to have been engaged in professional or trade occupations, and more likely to be of the white race than the actual racial distribution in the Cuban population. Notwithstanding the settlement assistance on the part of the U. S. government, these characteristics were to substantially impact the settlement process for the Cuban refugees.

The Cuban exodus has varied substantially over time with some important consequences for the adjustment of

Puerto Rican Day parade in Newark, New Jersey, 1964. (Courtesy of the Center for Puerto Rican Studies Library, Hunter College, CUNY.)

Cuban refugees. The initial flow left Cuba legally right after the revolution between 1959 and 1962. Over 200,000 Cubans migrated to the United States during this period. The preponderance of members of the professional class—particularly from economic and political sectors—earned this initial flow the name of "the Golden Exile." The Bay of Pigs incident in 1961 and the Missile Crisis in 1962 increased the tensions between the United States and Cuba and put a halt to the legal outflow of Cubans. There was a break in the migration of Cubans that lasted until 1965 when the "freedom flights" began. Between 1965 and 1973 daily flights from Cuba to Miami brought close to 300,000 Cubans to the United States. Priority was given to those with family members already in the United States. In contrast to the earlier flow, this was a less selective group of refugees. For example, the percent of professionals among the refugees declined from 31 percent in 1962 to 18 percent in 1967 (Boswell and Curtis 1983). Nonetheless, refugees as a whole had higher levels of education and occupational attainment than the Cuban population, were more likely to come from urban areas, and African Cubans continued to be underrepresented among them (Portes and Bach 1985).

After 1973 the Cuban government once again put a stop to the outflow of refugees. Between 1973 and 1979 few Cubans left the country, and those who did so went to third countries such as Mexico and Spain. In 1980, however, a third wave of refugees landed in the United States as a result of the opening of the Mariel port to those Cubans willing to leave their country. Close to 125,000 Cubans arrived in the United States between May and September 1980. The characteristics of the Mariel arrivals were much closer to those Cubans who had arrived during the 1970s than to the earlier 1960s flow. Many were from urban areas and had been formerly employed in urban manufacturing, construction, and service sectors (Portes and Bach 1985). In other respects they were different. There was a large number of single young adult males—a small proportion of those had criminal records. There was also a higher proportion of African Cubans—some estimate as high as 30 percent of the total flow.

Large-scale Cuban migration has stopped since 1980. Even though there are significant Cuban exile communities in Mexico, Spain, Venezuela, and Puerto Rico, the flow of Cuban refugees was primarily directed to the mainland United States. The cities of Miami (Florida), Union City (New Jersey), and New York (New York) account for the majority of the Cuban population on the mainland. Miami is nationally recognized as the center of the Cuban settlement. Over half a million Cubans live in the Miami area.

Some of the key factors that distinguish the Cuban population on the mainland from the Mexican and Puerto Rican groups have already been identified. Rather than a continuous flow of migrants with some return migration, Cuban migration has been unidirectional and composed of a series of waves of refugees. The initial settlement of an entrepreneurial-professional community together with the high spatial concentration provided the basis for the emergence of an ethnic enclave economy (Portes and Manning 1986). The original enclave economy was largely composed of ethnic shops and restaurants that catered to the Cuban community. By the 1970s, however, the Cuban enclave economy expanded dramatically, largely spurred by the increased access to capital and the presence of a large pool of low-wage laborers provided by more recent waves of arrivals. Between 1967 and 1982 the number of Cuban-owned firms in Dade County (where Miami is located) increased from 919 to about 12,000.

The economic expansion of the enclave was primarily in the areas of light manufacturing (apparel, cigars, footwear), construction, and finance and insurance (Portes and Manning 1986). Part of this growth has been based on the ascension of Miami into an international role in financial transactions. Miami has increasingly become a center for international trade with Latin America and the Caribbean (Wilson and Martin 1982), and Cubans have been central to this process. International trade contributed to the creation of thousands of jobs in the financial and information processing sectors. A key factor to this "success story" has been the use of the ethnic enclave for labor, credit, and as a market. Wilson and Martin (1982) present evidence as to the high level of integration between Cuban-owned firms. Cuban businesses were more likely to conduct transactions of goods or financial resources with other Cuban firms than with non-Cuban firms.

While Cubans present a picture of socioeconomic success relative to the situation of Puerto Ricans and Mexicans, there is considerable stratification within the Cuban community. We have mentioned that one key factor to the growth of the Cuban enclave is the presence of a large pool of ethnically similar low-wage labor. The outcome of this is the presence of a substantial proportion of the Cuban labor force that is working class. Stepick and Grenier (1993) conclude that Cubans are over-represented in the manual occupations like laborers and craftsmen and in service jobs. The availability of the Cuban labor force, they suggest, has been the basis of the continued expansion of the construction and manufacturing industries in Miami while elsewhere in the United States those same sectors have experienced stagnation. Many businesses, particularly in the manufacturing sector, relocated to Miami due to the availability of a low-wage labor force and the accessibility of international markets.

Hispanics in the Labor Force

The context of immigration described in the earlier section suggests that a distinctive set of conditions surrounds the presence of Hispanic subgroups in the labor force. These contextual differences translate into different patterns of labor force attachment for the three main groups. This section presents a brief overview of the labor market attachment of Hispanics workers by examining changes in labor force participation rates (LFPR) and unemployment rates over time.

Table 1 presents rates of labor force participation and unemployment for Hispanic males and females for the period 1969 to 1991. There has been a general trend toward declining LFPR among all groups except for Mexican males. Mexican men consistently present a higher rate of participation than the non-Hispanic population and other Hispanic groups. At the other end, Puerto Rican males present the lowest level of participation of all four groups in 1991. Notice, however, that as recently as 1969 Puerto Rican males had a LFPR as high or higher than that of the other groups. This pattern is consistent with the argument that Puerto Rican workers have experienced a narrowing of economic opportunity for employment during the last two decades.

In terms of unemployment, Hispanics—with the exception of Cubans—experience much higher unemployment than the non-Spanish population. Puerto Rican males again seem to fare the worst, with unemployment rates at times twice the non-Spanish rate. Cubans, on the other hand, seem to be less sensitive to unemployment fluctuations than Mexicans or Puerto Ricans. This argument is consistent with the hypothesis that the ethnic enclave economy protects Cubans from external market forces.

The situation of Hispanic females is similar to that of Hispanic males. Females, in general, have lower rates of LFPR than males. Mexican and Cuban females present a higher rate of participation than Puerto Rican females. Also notice that the labor force participation of Cuban

Table 1

Labor Force Participation and Unemployment Rates for Hispanic Males and Females

Males: Percentage in Labor Force

Year	Non-Spanish Total	Hispanic Origin: Mexican	Puerto Rican	Cuban
1969	79.4	80.0	82.7	78.6
1976	75.3	79.3	66.4	77.2
1982	74.8	83.5	71.9	72.8
1989	74.4	82.2	69.6	76.3
1991	73.9	79.6	66.4	73.3
% Unemployed				
1969	2.7	5.5	6.4	2.0
1976	7.7	10.5	14.3	12.0
1982	10.1	12.9	20.5	8.8
1989	5.5	8.3	12.1	6.4
1991	7.8	11.7	11.9	5.2

Females: Percentage in Labor Force

Year	Non-Spanish Total	Hispanic Origin: Mexican	Puerto Rican	Cuban
1969	52.3	38.4	38.8	48.7
1976	47.0	43.9	30.5	47.9
1982	52.3	49.1	34.9	47.5
1989	57.0	52.7	41.7	49.1
1991	57.4	50.6	42.2	55.1
% Unemployed				
1969	4.7	7.4	6.1	0.9
1976	8.3	14.0	14.0	10.9
1982	8.7	14.0	12.1	13.7
1989	4.9	8.8	5.0	5.7
1991	5.9	9.2	8.3	8.0

females has been consistently higher over time than that of other Hispanic groups. Unemployment rates for Hispanic women tend to be uniform, although higher than for non-Spanish women.

Median earnings for Hispanic workers and Hispanic families during the 1969 to 1990 period are presented in Table 2. Mexicans, Puerto Ricans, and Cubans present disparate trends in median earnings over time. Mexican males and females exhibit the lowest individual earnings of all Hispanic groups. Puerto Rican males have the highest median earnings among men, and Cuban women among females. In general, Mexicans present the most disadvantaged picture in terms of earnings, and it seems to be worsening over time. The situation for Puerto Rican and Cuban males and females, on the other hand, seems to have improved over time. The discussion in the next section will address the reasons for some of these trends.

Median family earnings present a rather different situation. Despite a rather positive situation at the individual level, Puerto Ricans families present the most disadvantaged situation in terms of family median earnings. The median earnings of a Puerto Rican family in 1990 was only 50 percent of the median earnings of a non-Hispanic family. That is in contrast to 64 percent for Mexican families and 87 percent for Cuban families. Furthermore, the Puerto Rican situation seems to be getting worse over time.

This overview suggests that the situation of the two largest groups–Mexicans and Puerto Ricans–may have worsened during the last two decades. However, the picture is somewhat confused by the apparent improvement in individual median earnings while there is a decline in family median earnings for these two groups. When coupled with declining rates of participation for Puerto Ricans and stable ones for Mexicans, the situation becomes more complex. A series of factors considered essential to understand these divergent trends in the labor market for Hispanics is addressed in the following section.

TABLE 2

Median Income/Earnings by Sex, Nationality, and Year.

	In Dollars				**Ratio of Hispanic/ Non-Spanish**			
Nationality	**1969**	**1976**	**1982**	**1990**	**1969**	**1976**	**1982**	**1990**
				Males				
Non-Hispanic	-	8,981	13,759	22,207	-	-	-	-
Mexican	-	6,450	10,397	12,894	-	0.72	0.76	0.58
Puerto Rican	-	6,687	9,206	18,193	-	0.74	0.67	0.82
Cuban	-	7,074	8,561	17,455	-	0.79	0.62	0.79
				Females				
Non-Hispanic	-	3,394	5,482	12,438	-	-	-	-
Mexican	-	2,750	4,933	9,286	-	0.81	0.90	0.75
Puerto Rican	-	3,837	4,698	11,702	-	1.13	0.86	0.94
Cuban	-	3,407	4,682	12,904	-	1.00	0.85	1.04
				Family				
Non-Hispanic	8,011	-	22,800	36,330	-	-	-	-
Mexican	5,488	9,546	16,900	23,240	0.69	-	0.74	0.64
Puerto Rican	4,969	7,290	11,300	18,008	0.62	-	0.5	0.5
Cuban	6,383	11,772	18,000	31,439	0.8	-	0.79	0.08

Key Issues Surrounding the Hispanic Presence in the Labor Force

The discussion that follows intends to answer three questions. First, why has the economic progress that Hispanic workers made relative to whites since World War II given way to increased inequality in recent years? Second, why have the two largest Hispanic groups–Puerto Ricans and Mexicans–fared so poorly in recent years? Why did the labor market situation of Puerto Ricans so sharply deteriorate from 1970 through the mid-1980s? Why did the economic position of Mexicans sharply decline in the 1980s after improving in the 1970s? And third, how do we account for the varied labor market outcomes of the major Hispanic groups–Mexicans, Puerto Ricans, and Cubans?

As Bean and Tienda (1988) point out, there are several types of factors that may account for some of these trends and differences in group labor market outcomes. First, there are the individual characteristics that workers bring with them to the labor market, such as education, English language proficiency, and labor market experience. Second, there are the characteristics of the labor markets within which workers must function. For example, labor markets vary according to the availability of different types of jobs and composition of the work force. Workers living in different regions may find themselves competing in labor markets that offer different degrees of opportunity. Economic developments such as deindustrialization, suburbanization, and the spatial decentralization of industry from central city to suburb have occurred in different ways and to different degrees in various labor markets. And third, there are differences in how workers with the same individual characteristics are treated in identical labor markets because of discrimination based on skin color, nationality, or bias against immigrants.

To these factors, we would add other important considerations. As discussed earlier, migration patterns vary from group to group and can have a substantial impact on labor market outcomes. Family structure also varies across groups and greatly influences economic conditions. Each group has its characteristic historical mode of insertion into the U. S. economy, and this may impact the status and progress of future generations. Finally, forms of discrimination in other areas than the labor market, such as schooling and housing, have an important influence.

The Impact of Educational Differences

Clearly, among the major factors influencing labor market outcomes are the qualifications that workers bring with them to the job. Primary among these is the level of a worker's education. Educational attainment differences are dramatic when comparing Hispanic groups and the majority population in the United States. In 1991, while 78.4 percent of the U. S. population age twenty-five and above had at least a high school education, only 61.0 percent of Cubans, 58.0 percent of Puerto Ricans, and 43.6 percent of Mexicans had such education. While 21.4 percent of the U. S. population age twenty-five and above had college degrees, only 18.5 percent of Cubans, 10.1 percent of Puerto Ricans, and 6.2 percent of Mexicans had such degrees (U. S. Bureau of the Census 1991).

Many studies have attempted to measure the effects of educational differences on labor market outcomes. For example, DeFreitas (1985) found that education played the primary role in accounting for differences in the type of employment between Mexicans and non-Hispanic whites. Roos and Hennessey (1983) found that differences in level of education were responsible for half of the gap between the earnings of Anglo and Mexican males in California. Neidert and Tienda (1981) found that for each additional year of education, the annual earnings of Puerto Ricans increase by 2.8 percent, Mexicans by 4.3 percent and Cubans by 5.9 percent.

While education generally contributes to positive labor market outcomes, it benefits some groups more than others. For example, Tienda (1983a) found that when compared to Hispanic immigrants, U. S.-born Hispanics received twice as much in earnings from each additional year of education. DeFreitas (1985) found that while education played the primary role in accounting for differences in type of employment for Mexicans, it only played a secondary role for Puerto Ricans. Reimers (1985) found that the returns from education for Hispanic women are particularly low. Education had the greatest influence on labor market outcomes for Hispanic males born in the United States, especially Mexicans and Cubans.

The benefits of each additional year of education also vary depending on the level of education involved. Neidert and Tienda (1981) estimated that the increment in earnings expected from an additional year of elementary education is 1.9 percent per year or lower for the

A bilingual education class in California, 1980.

three major Hispanic groups, compared to 4.5 percent to 4.7 percent for a year of high school education and 7.8 percent to 11.0 percent for a year of college education. In addition, for some groups the benefits of education accrue mainly as a result of obtaining a degree. Neidert and Tienda also found that Mexicans with some college earned little more than simple high school graduates, and Mexicans with some high school made little more than eighth-grade dropouts.

While education clearly makes a difference for Hispanic workers, other factors may override the impact of education. Consider the relative positions of Puerto Ricans and Mexicans. Puerto Ricans present considerably greater educational attainment than Mexicans. Nonetheless, Mexicans have higher median family incomes ($23,240 versus $18,008) and lower family poverty rates (25.0 percent versus 37.5 percent) than Puerto Ricans (U. S. Bureau of the Census 1991). In addition, Puerto Rican educational attainment is rising more quickly than among Mexicans. This can be seen from examining the figures for twenty-five to thirty-four-year olds (U. S. Bureau of the Census 1991). In 1991 71.8 percent of Puerto Ricans in this age group had high school diplomas compared to only 50.5 percent of Mexicans. Close to 12 percent of Puerto Ricans had college degrees, compared to only 7.4 percent of Mexicans. Yet comparisons between Puerto Rican and Mexican labor market outcomes showed that Puerto Ricans are falling further behind Mexicans rather than catching up, at least until the last half of the 1980s.

We should consider not only the impact of education on educational achievement but also the possible influences of labor market outcomes on education. Ogbu (1974) argued, for example, that a major factor accounting for low levels of educational achievement among Mexicans is the lack of economic incentives for such achievement. The economic value of education is not as clear to Mexican children as to Anglo children, because the returns to education are lower. This leads to problems with motivation for the child and may also compromise the extent of parent encouragement. Thus, the problem of improving educational attainment cannot be separated from that of reducing discrimination in the labor market.

The Effects of English Language Proficiency

The recency of the Hispanic migration and the still continuing inflow of new arrivals contribute to the immigrant character of Hispanic communities. One indicator of this immigrant character is the extensive use of the Spanish language. A survey of Hispanics done by the Census Bureau in 1976 indicates that only 68 percent of Mexicans and 65 percent of Puerto Ricans report good English language proficiency, while 17.6 percent of Mexicans and 9.0 percent of Puerto Ricans report no knowledge of English (Tienda and Neidert 1981b). Cubans also have relatively low levels of English language proficiency (Portes and Bach 1985). These self-reports probably overestimate the extent of facility in English. The largest proportion of Mexicans are native born, which favors knowledge of English. Puerto Ricans have the advantage of learning some English as part of their public schooling on the Island.

How does English language proficiency effect the labor market outcomes of Hispanic workers? Tienda and Neidert (1981) found that Hispanic workers with good to excellent English competency attain average occupational status of approximately nine to twelve points higher than those with limited English ability. However, it is difficult to determine how much of this effect is actually due to knowledge of English and how much to the higher educational levels of those who speak more English. When employers decide to hire a high school educated Hispanic worker who speaks English, it may be due to the education, language skills, or a combination of both. Independent of education, English language proficiency only increased the average occupational status of Hispanics by four points in Tienda and Neidert's study—a modest amount, but the combined effect of the two may be somewhat greater.

English proficiency should be expected to affect employment chances in some types of jobs much more than others. For example, lack of knowledge of English may not usually prevent a worker from being hired to work in the fields or factories. However, lack of English proficiency may exclude workers from service jobs where contact with English-speaking clients or customers is involved. Waldinger (1989) provides an example in the case of hospital work in New York City: while Hispanic workers have made little progress in entering employment in hospitals, Jamaican immigrants who are native English speakers have entered this sector in large numbers. Similarly, poor English language skills may be an obstacle to working in some jobs in the retail sector, with the exception on eighborhood stores primarily serving Hispanic customers.

Economic Restructuring and Hispanic Workers

The U. S. economy has been undergoing a massive process of decline and restructuring in recent years. The decline is reflected in deterioration of the U. S. position in international competition, massive deindustrialization in certain manufacturing industries where the United States has historically been preeminent, declining real wages, relatively high rates of unemployment, and an increase in the ratio of part-time to full-time jobs. This decline has occurred unevenly throughout the economy, however, reflecting a process of restructuring. While the manufacturing sector has declined, the service sector has grown. In addition, while manufacturing in the Rustbelt (northeastern and north central states) has declined, manufacturing in the Sunbelt (southern and southwestern states) has continued to grow. Employment not only in manufacturing but also in wholesale and retail trade has shifted from the central cities to the suburban fringe of metropolitan areas, especially in the Rustbelt. While Rustbelt cities have seen an overall decline in entry-level jobs that do not require a high school diploma, these same cities have experienced an increase in knowledge-intensive jobs requiring at least some college education (Kasarda 1983, 1985, 1989).

These changes may account for some of the trends and comparisons cited above. To begin with, the general decline experienced by the U. S. economy has extended to all groups to one extent or another, whites as well as Hispanics and other minorities. For example, if we compare poverty rates from 1979 to 1987, while Hispanic rates increased from 20.3 percent to 25.7 percent, as mentioned above, African American rates increased from 27.8 percent to 29.4 percent, and white rates increased from 6.9 percent to 8.1 percent (Statistical Abstract of United States 1990).

However, these trends have affected different groups in varying ways, depending on their location geographically and in the socioeconomic structure. To begin with, a much higher proportion of Hispanics live in the central cities rather than the suburbs in our large metropolitan areas. This is particularly the case for Puerto Rican residents of metropolitan areas, 80 percent of whom live in the central city. It is also the case for Mexicans (55 percent) and Cubans (41 percent) (Bean and Tienda 1988). In contrast to African Americans, this is true more for economic reasons than due to outright discrimination (Cuciti and James 1990), but discrimination in housing is still a factor, particularly for Puerto Ricans (Massey and Bitterman 1985).

Yet the trend in the economy, especially in Rustbelt areas, has been movement of employment—both manufacturing and retail and wholesale jobs—from the cities to the suburbs. (Kassarda 1983, 1985, 1989). At the same time, the population of the largest northern and north central cities (New York, Chicago, Philadelphia, Detroit) has increased by 1 million, with the fastest rate of increase being for Hispanics. Yet much of this minority population is poorly educated, which, according to Kasarda, creates a spatial mismatch between skill requirements and educational credentials.

Farley's 1987 study of the contribution of these factors to racial differences in unemployment between non-Hispanic whites and African Americans and Hispanics lends support to this "spatial mismatch" theory. In metropolitan areas with 3 percent Hispanics or greater, he found that the extent to which jobs have become suburbanized had a particularly important impact on the gap in Anglo-Hispanic unemployment. Those areas that had experienced the highest rates of job suburbanization also showed Hispanics being worse-off than Anglos in the level of unemployment. The extent of concentration of Hispanics in the central city and the degree of racial inequality in education also had statistically significant effects on the differences in unemployment. Overall, these three factors—all stressed in Kassarda's analysis of the spatial mismatch between skill requirements and educational credentials—explained about a third of the total difference in unemployment between Hispanics and Anglos in these metropolitan areas.

In addition, regional differences are very important. While manufacturing has declined in Rustbelt cities, it has remained stable or even risen in Sunbelt cities (Cuciti and James 1990). For example, if we examine the period 1958-82, New York City's employment in production jobs in manufacturing declined from 677,000 to 311,000. Most of this decline was experienced from 1967 to 1982, when production jobs declined by half. Similar stories can be told for other RustBelt cities such as Philadelphia, Chicago, or Baltimore. On the other hand, during the same 1967-82 period, production jobs in Los Angeles rose by 3 percent, in Dallas by 21 percent, and in Houston by 109 percent. Combining manufacturing, retail, wholesale, and selected services to estimate the impact on entry-level jobs, New York experienced a loss of 393,000 and Philadelphia a loss of 171,000 jobs in the 1963-82 period, compared to gains for Los Angeles (212,000), Dallas (122,000), and Houston (371,000) (Wacquant and Wilson 1991). Cuciti and James' study of the twenty-six largest southwestern cities confirm this analysis. They found that from 1972 to 1982 production jobs in manufacturing and jobs in wholesale trade increased in twenty-one of these cities, while jobs in retail and overall employment increased in all twenty-six. This pattern of uneven economic change across regions of the country had a differential impact on Hispanics. On the one hand, Puerto Ricans were concentrated in the Rustbelt, where economic decline has been most pronounced. On the other hand, Mexicans are concentrated in the Sunbelt, where economic fortunes have been better.

This, in part, helps to explain the particular difficulties that Puerto Ricans have experienced in the labor market. Puerto Ricans who migrated to New York City in large numbers in the 1940s and 1950s overwhelmingly obtained jobs in the manufacturing sector, especially in the apparel industry. This was a largely unionized sector with wages that at the time were more in line with those in more monopolized industries. But precisely at that time, this sector began its precipitous decline. As a consequence of suburbanization, automation, and international competition, employment in the apparel and related products sector declined by 21.5 percent in the years from 1950 to 1960 (Falcón 1990). In the 1960s and 1970s, as mentioned above, the process continued at a rapid pace. In 1960, 26.8 percent of all employment in New York City was in manufacturing. By 1984 this figure had fallen to only 12.5 percent (Falcón and Gurak 1992). As a consequence of the resulting displacement from manufacturing, joblessness increased and labor force participation rates rapidly declined for both Puerto Rican men and women.

On the other hand, while the quantity of jobs available to Mexicans in the Southwest may be greater than those available to Puerto Ricans in the Northeast, the quality of jobs may be quite low. As indicated earlier, Mexican workers make considerably lower wages than Puerto Ricans. One reason may be the prevailing wages in the labor markets of the Southwest. Tienda (1983a) estimates that Mexicans with identical characteristics living in relatively high-wage areas (mainly outside of the Southwest) make 12 percent more than those living in relatively low-wage areas. Thus, while the labor markets of the Northeast may contribute to the lower employment rates of Puerto Ricans, the labor markets of the Southwest may contribute to the lower wages of Mexicans.

The situation of Cubans is distinct from that of Mexicans and Puerto Ricans.The presence of an ethnic economic enclave has tended to insulate Cuban workers from the instability experienced by Hispanic workers in the open market. A substantial number of the jobs that have appeared in the Miami area during the last two decades have been a result of relocation from the Rustbelt area. Many companies have moved to Miami in search of a nonunionized work force. This has been the case in the textile and construction industries (Stepick and Grenier 1992). Working-class Cubans have benefited from the presence of a thriving manufacturing industry in the Miami area. The economic expansion experienced by the Miami economy has provided opportunity for Cuban entrepreneurs to start businesses in the service sector that cater to the growing financial and construction sectors.

Family Structure

One of the major factors influencing family income is the structure of the family. Two-parent families have many economic advantages over female-headed families. This is true for the population as a whole and for Hispanic families in particular. For the overall population, while the general poverty rate for families is 10.7 percent, the poverty rate for female-headed families is 33.4 percent. For Hispanic families, the general poverty rate is 25.0 percent, while 48.3 percent of female-headed Hispanic families are poor (U. S. Bureau of the Census 1991).

Hispanic groups differ greatly in the tendency to establish female-headed families. The proportion of such families among Cubans (19.4 percent) and Mexicans (19.1 percent) was similar to the population as a whole (17.0 percent) in 1991 (U. S. Bureau of the Census 1991). However, a far larger number of Puerto Rican families (43.3 percent) were headed by women. The high proportion of female-headed households is a major contributor to the higher poverty rate experienced by Puerto Rican families. The high frequency of single-parent families among Puerto Ricans is a relatively new development. The proportion of female-headed Puerto Rican households almost doubled between 1970 and 1986 (Falcón 1989). This presents a serious problem, given the lower levels of labor force participation among Puerto Rican women and the narrow set of opportunities faced by women in the labor market.

While the poverty rates for Mexican and Puerto Rican families headed by couples are almost identical (17.1 percent versus 17.4 percent), the much larger proportion of female-headed families among Puerto Ricans results in substantially higher rates of poverty (Bean and Tienda 1988). The Puerto Rican poor population is largely composed of women and children. As of 1991 female-headed households accounted for 75.5 percent of the all poor Puerto Rican families (U. S. Bureau of the Census 1991). This helps to explain why poverty rates have risen among Puerto Ricans in the 1970s and 1980s despite sharp increases in educational attainment.

A strong argument can be made that the declining labor market opportunities for Puerto Ricans undercut the economic basis for marriage and was the chief contributor to this increase in female-headed households. The general argument connecting employment and family structure was made by Wilson (1987), who argued that the rise in female-headed families among African Americans is a consequence of the declining pool of "marriageable males"—that is, African American men with jobs. Since Wilson developed this thesis, a considerable amount of evidence has been accumulated to support it. For example, Testa (1989) found that employed fathers in Chicago are twice as likely to marry the mother of their first child than those who are not employed. Among Hispanics, the one group that has experienced sharply deteriorating employment opportunities in the 1960s, 1970s and 1980s—Puerto Ricans—is precisely the group that has also experienced sharply increasing rates of female-headed households. Falcón et al. (1990) found that Puerto Rican and Dominican female heads of household in New York City were more likely than those who remained with their partners to have had last partners who were unemployed at the time of their union. Cuciti and James (1990) found in their comparative study of twenty-six southwestern cities that the correlation between the size of the marriageable pool of males and the frequencies of female-headed families was even higher for Hispanics than for African Americans.

The differences in family structure are reflected in comparative figures concerning the number of wage earners in each family. Bean and Tienda's (1988) study of the 1980 Census found that 50 percent of Mexican families had two wage earners, compared to only 35 percent of Puerto Rican families. Bean and Tienda also found that while 15 percent of Mexicans had three wage earners or more in the family, this was true for only 7 percent of Puerto Ricans.

One issue that arises concerning family structure is also the substantial difference in family size between Mexican families on the one hand and Puerto Rican and Cuban families on the other. The average size of the Mexican family is 4.06 persons, compared to 3.37 for Puerto Ricans and 2.81 for Cubans (U. S. Bureau of the Census 1991). This larger family size means that median per capita family income is actually not much higher for Mexicans ($5,724) than for Puerto Ricans ($5,344). Does this mean that large family sizes cause higher rates of poverty for Mexicans? Bean and Tienda (1988) indicate that for the majority of Mexican families, this is not the case. They found that poverty rates are similar for Mexicans of different sized families with five members or less. One possible reason for this may be that with larger families there are typically more wage earners or hours worked as well. However, they did find that poverty rates were higher in those families that have six or more members than in smaller families. In such cases, there may simply not be additional resources available that can be utilized for the purpose of increasing family income.

Modes of Incorporation and the Enclave Economy

While the factors already discussed account for some of the economic differences between Hispanic groups, they are by no means the whole story. Consider in particular the advantageous position of Cubans in comparison to Mexicans. Simple differences in group characteristics do not account for the far greater economic achievements of Cubans. For example, consider language proficiency. Here, a comparative study of Mexican and Cuban immigrants who all arrived in the United States in 1973 (Portes and Bach 1985) shows similarly low levels of knowledge of English, yet the Cuban immigrants had achieved considerably more economically six years after immigration than the Mexican immigrants. Or consider differences in socioeconomic background. While Cuban immigrants in the 1960s were primarily from the middle and upper classes, those of the 1970s were primarily from the working classes, more similar to the backgrounds of immigrants from Mexico (Portes and Bach 1985). Yet these working-class immigrants from Cuba advanced much more rapidly than their Mexican counterparts. Neither are the differences accounted for by family structure. The proportion of female-headed families is similarly low for both Mexicans and Cubans, yet Cuban rates of economic achievement are far higher (U. S. Bureau of the Census 1991). Nor can the differences between Cubans and Mexicans be explained by the differences in the labor markets in which they find themselves, since the Southwest and Florida are both regions where the economy and entry-level jobs are expanding.

What then could account for the differences between the experiences of the Cuban and Mexican immigrants? Portes and Truelove (1987) argued that the key is differences in the manner in which each group has been incorporated into the U. S. economy. On the one hand, Mexicans were brought into the U. S. economy to engage in menial labor for low wages for Anglo employers (Barrera 1979). By contrast, the Cuban working-class immigrants of the 1970s were incorporated to a large degree into a Cuban enclave economy already established by the earlier waves of Cuban immigrants, who were more likely to come from a more privileged background. This ethnic enclave economy made it possible for a much higher proportion of Cubans than Mexicans to become self-employed or to work for ethnic employers who could provide them greater opportunities for training and mobility (Portes and Bach 1985).

The Cuban immigrants of the 1960s brought with them entrepreneurial skills and capital that enabled them to quickly establish a substantial Cuban-owned business sector in South Florida. In addition, the U. S. government facilitated setting up this business sector with loans and other forms of support, so that Cuban prosperity in the United States could be used as a showcase in the propaganda battle against communism in Cuba. By contrast, Mexican immigrants came mainly from peasant and urban working-class backgrounds (and received no such support from the U. S. government), making establishment of such a business sector much more difficult. The resulting differences are reflected in statistics cited in Portes and Truelove, which show that in 1984, five out of the ten largest Hispanic industrial firms and four out of the ten largest Hispanic banks were owned by Cubans, despite the small proportion (5 percent) that Cubans constitute of the total Hispanic population. Census figures showed that in 1977 Cubans owned proportionately 250 percent more businesses than Mexicans.

These economic realities were reflected in Portes and Bach's comparative study of a sample of Cuban and Mexican immigrants. In 1979, six years after immigrating to the United States 21.2 percent of the Cubans were self-employed, compared to only 5.4 percent of the Mexicans. Over 36 percent of the Cubans were employed by other Cubans, compared to only 14.6 percent of the Mexicans employed by other Mexicans. Thus, nearly three-fifths of the Cubans were self-employed or worked in Cuban-owned firms, compared to one-fifth of the Mexicans working in Mexican-owned firms. While incomes for Mexican and Cuban workers employed by Anglo-owned firms were comparable, incomes in the Cuban-owned enclave were considerably higher, especially for owners but also for workers. Furthermore, many of these workers were being taught skills and gaining connections that would enable them to branch out and open their own businesses in the future. Clearly, the existence of an ethnic enclave economy provides opportunities to an ethnic group for socioeconomic success.

The Impact of Immigration

Hispanic communities in the United States are constantly in flux as new immigrants arrive and older ones

A mass citizenship swearing-in ceremony in Houston, Texas, 1987. (Courtesy of the *Texas Catholic Herald*.)

may relocate to other areas. In addition, these communities change because of the arrival of new Hispanic groups to the area or the presence in the labor market of non-Hispanic immigrants. The situation of established Hispanic groups is not independent of the presence of other groups in the area. What impact does this have on labor market conditions for Hispanics?

First, we need to compare the economic status of immigrants and natives. Although labor market participation rates are higher for immigrants than for native workers, earnings are lower and poverty rates are higher. For example, Mexican immigrants had a poverty rate 4.8 percent higher than Mexican natives according to the 1980 census (Bean and Tienda 1988). Close to 33 percent of Hispanic immigrants were poor in 1979 (Jensen 1989). These lower earnings result primarily from the lower levels of educational attainment of immigrants and their lower levels of English language skills. For example, Mexican immigrants from 1970 to 1980 averaged 6.9 years of schooling, while Puerto Ricans averaged 9.6 years and Cubans 9.7 years (Tienda, Bach, and Jensen 1989). These figures are about 2 to 3 years lower, on the average, than for their U. S.-born counterparts. In addition, Hispanic immigrants typically earn less than U. S.-born Hispanics in their initial years in the new country, even when they have the same characteristics. According to Tienda (1983a), it takes 10 to 15 years for Mexican immigrants to be treated the same as natives in the labor market. Borjas (1981) estimates that this occurs much faster for Cuban immigrants but takes 25 years for Puerto Ricans.

The effect, then, of continual streams of immigration is to bring down the overall level of English language proficiency, education, and earnings for each group. This is one reason that Wilson (1987) predicted that Hispanics will fare worse than African Americans in the coming years. While net African American migration to the cities from rural areas of the South stopped by 1970, so that now more African Americans are returning to the South than leaving, the migration of Mexicans and Puerto Ricans to the U. S. mainland proceeds on a large scale. Wilson argued that not only does this lower the overall economic profile of the group but that the large and increasing numbers entering particular localities also can foster a hostile reaction that can intensify discrimination. In addition, large and continuing migrations make it difficult for a large portion of the group to take advantage of special economic niches, such as the case of Jamaicans in hospital work cited earlier, because the numbers of workers to be integrated into the work force far exceed the jobs that can be found in such niches (Lieberson 1981).

As indicated in the earlier discussion contrasting Cuban and Mexican immigrants, groups are able to advance economically at different rates. This is not a function of differing rates of cultural assimilation (e.g., English language acquisition) but rather a matter to a large degree of the different ways in which each immigrant or migrant group is incorporated into the economy. For Cubans, we have seen that a majority of immigrants are able to advance quickly because of their absorption into the ethnic enclave. While those outside of the enclave may have experiences that are more similar to Mexican immigrants (employment in low-wage, dead-end jobs), the existence of the enclave increases employment rates, wage rates, and opportunities for mobility for the immigrants as a whole.

On the other hand, Mexicans do not have the advantage of being able to assimilate into a substantial Mexican subeconomy. For this reason they must depend to a greater extent on the Anglo-controlled economy. This makes them more vulnerable to economic fluctuations, which may contribute to the higher unemployment rates experienced by Mexican immigrants, reduces their opportunities for mobility, and lowers their relative wage levels.

Portes and Truelove (1987) suggested that different modes of incorporation also account for different labor market experiences for Puerto Ricans and Mexicans. They point out that while Mexicans continue to be the preferred source of cheap labor in the American Southwest, Puerto Ricans have been displaced in this role by other immigrant groups—notably Colombians and Dominicans—in the New York/New Jersey area.

Puerto Rican migrants initially entered labor markets in New York City, which, in contrast to those in the Southwest, were largely unionized and which paid wages that at the time were competitive with those earned in other more monopolized manufacturing industries. By contrast, Mexican immigrants were initially incorporated into the lowest paying, nonunionized menial jobs. Furthermore, Puerto Ricans are U. S. citizens and thus are less vulnerable than Mexican immigrants, many of whom not only lack citizenship but are also undocumented. Because many of the Mexican immigrants are undocumented and use the low-wage conditions of their initial incorporation into the U. S. labor force as their base of comparison, they are a relatively reliable and exploitable group that continues to be viewed as desirable to Anglo employers in secondary sector jobs. By contrast, Puerto Ricans are seen by employers as less pliable and have been displaced by newer Hispanic immigrants, such as Dominicans and Colombians, as the preferred cheap labor force.

This process occurred in conjunction with the transformation of the apparel industry in New York City into which Puerto Rican workers initially were incorporated. Increasingly the industry became more automated and jobs more routinized in response to increased international competition. A unionized and relatively high-paid industry increasingly gave way to nonunion shops dependent for their survival on hiring at (or below) minimum wage under sweatshop conditions (Waldinger 1989). Puerto Rican as well as African American and white workers who had previously worked in the industry were displaced, and new immigrants grateful for a chance for any employment and comparing their conditions of work to even worse conditions in their home countries took their places.

This preference for Dominican and Colombian over Puerto Rican labor may apply not only to long-term Puerto Rican residents of New York, who remember the relatively high-paid unionized manufacturing jobs into which they were initially incorporated. It may also apply to more recent migrants from Puerto Rico. These workers are accustomed to far higher pay scales on the Island than are Dominicans, Colombians, or Mexicans in their home countries (Falcón and Gurak 1992). In addition they continue to have the advantage of being U. S. citizens because of the unique historical relationship between the United States and Puerto Rico, in contrast to the frequent vulnerable status of other Latin American immigrants.

Aponte (1991) and Wilson (1991) described similar dynamics in Chicago. Here, Mexican immigrant workers were preferred for low-status jobs to African Americans in the 1980s. The Mexicans, unlike African American workers, are vulnerable as many are undocumented. At the same time, the base of comparison for the Mexican immigrants are wages of less than a dollar an hour in Mexico, while African American workers are accustomed to working in what was once a thriving center for heavy industry, which provided many opportunities for minorities in unionized, relatively high-paid, semiskilled production jobs. This accounts for the high rate of employment for Mexican workers in Chicago, even in the face of rapid deindustrialization and the shift of entry-level jobs from city to suburb.

This may help to explain differences in employment rates and in wage levels. On the one hand, we would expect employment rates to be higher among Mexicans than Puerto Ricans or African Americans. On the other hand, we would expect earnings to be higher among Puerto Ricans and African Americans who work—this is in fact the case.

To understand the comparative impact of migration on labor market outcomes of different groups, we need to consider two additional factors. First, the proportion of immigrants/migrants varies depending on the group. We can only speculate on the effect of these different proportions on labor market outcomes. For example, the proportion of foreign born in the Puerto Rican population is much higher than for Mexicans. This may have the effect of depressing the economic profile of Puerto Ricans as a whole more than for Mexicans. The large working-class Cuban immigration of the 1970s and 1980s also has the effect of bringing down overall economic status, but because of the exceptionally high status of earlier

Cuban immigrants (primarily those from professional, managerial, and property-owning classes in pre-revolutionary Cuba) and the possibilities for mobility within the enclave economy, the overall economic picture for Cubans is still relatively strong (Portes and Bach 1985; Grenier and Stepick 1992).

We should also consider one other way that migration patterns may affect group labor market outcomes. For Puerto Ricans and Mexicans, there is considerable two-way migration between the U. S. mainland and the home country. This is particularly the case for Puerto Ricans, who do not have to contend with obstacles to crossing borders. This can have effects on the economic profile of the U. S. community if there is selectivity involved in these migrations. There is some evidence that this may in fact be the case for the two-way migration between Puerto Rico and the United States (Falcón and Gurak 1990). On the one hand, those who leave the United States for Puerto Rico are more likely to have better education, more employment experience, more stable marital unions, and lower fertility than those who remain on the mainland. On the other hand, those same characteristics (higher education, employment experience, etc.) are less associated with those who migrate from the island to the mainland. Falcón and Gurak offer this pattern of selectivity in migration as one possible explanation for the somewhat more favorable condition of Dominicans compared to Puerto Ricans in New York City (1992).

Labor Market Discrimination

Discrimination in the labor market is a recurring theme in the history of minority populations in American society. Hispanics have been no exception to this dynamic. As Bean and Tienda (1988) pointed out, such discrimination may occur on the basis of accented or imperfect English, mestizo racial characteristics or dark skin color, Spanish surnames, or other visible ethnic traits. While most would recognize historical discrimination against Hispanics, some would argue that today, with the advent of antidiscrimination laws and affirmative action, that such discrimination is insignificant. Instead, the case could be made that the disadvantaged position of Hispanics can be explained on the basis of differences in group characteristics such as education or language proficiency, or in the labor market conditions faced by different groups. William Julius Wilson (1987), for example, made this point when he argued that market forces and class position may be more important than race in explaining the situation of the African American poor. A similar argument can be made for the disadvantaged situation of some Hispanic groups.

Typically, researchers attempt to determine if discrimination exists by accounting (controlling) for all other labor market and individual level characteristics deemed important in explaining, for example, differences in average earnings. If any of the gap in earnings between the groups remains unaccounted for this is usually attributed to discrimination. For example, consider Hispanics and whites who are born in the United States, who live in the same region, who have the same levels of education, and who all speak English fluently. Are their earnings the same or are they different? If they are the same, then we can conclude that the differences between Hispanic and white earnings are attributable to differences in group characteristics. However, if despite similar characteristics whites continue to have higher incomes than Hispanics, then these studies assume that this difference is attributable to something other than group characteristics—namely, discrimination.

Studies that tried to determine the existence of discrimination have usually looked at three different outcomes—earnings, unemployment rates, and occupational status. For example, Tienda (1983) examined the role of discrimination in accounting for differences in the earnings of Hispanic and non-Hispanic white men. She studied the impact of a variety of factors on earnings differentials, including levels of education, English language proficiency, hours worked, job experience, marital status, region and average wage rates, and unemployment rates of the local labor market. She found that differences in education, weeks worked, language proficiency, and residence in areas with high concentrations of Hispanics had the most significant impact of all the variables considered. However, even when all of these factors were taken into account, a considerable income gap remained. For example, for native-born men, these variables accounted for almost 80 percent of the income gap for Mexicans and Anglos, leaving 20.5 percent to be accounted for by discrimination. As for foreign-born men, some 27.6 percent of the gap between Mexicans and whites was accounted for by discrimination.

In another study, Reimers (1985) found that wage discrimination accounted for 18 percent of the differences in earnings of Puerto Rican and Anglo men. On the other hand, she found that only 6 percent of the Mexican-Anglo male earnings gap was a result of discrimination, while there was no gap at all for Cubans and Anglos with identical individual characteristics. For women, she found that the returns from education for Hispanic women were much lower than for white women. On the other hand, Puerto Rican and Cuban women who lived in the Northeast were able to make more money than white women with identical characteristics due to higher earnings they were able to obtain in manufacturing employment.

Stolzenberg (1990) presented evidence for discrimination, showing that equal increments of education and

English language proficiency contribute less to the earnings of Hispanics than for whites. For example, the penalty for poor English language skills on earnings is 24 percent for Hispanics but only 9 percent for whites. Stolzenberg also found a higher degree of discrimination at lower educational levels than higher. He estimated that if Hispanic men speak English well and have completed at least twelve years of education then the pay gap with whites with the same characteristics and living in the same region is 7 percent, but if the men speak English poorly and have only eight years of schooling, then the earnings gap is twice as high, 14 percent. Neidert and Tienda (1981) found similar results—for example, while returns for a year of elementary education for white men are usually found to be about 5 percent, the returns for Hispanic men were 1.9 percent (for Mexicans) or lower.

We should keep in mind that these and other similar analyses of earnings underestimate the impact of discrimination on economic outcomes, because they exclude from their samples those workers who do not have earnings to compare. Unemployed workers or those who have dropped out of the labor force are not included because they do not have earnings. The exclusion of these workers biases the results of these studies, since the proportion of such workers is higher among Hispanics than among Anglos.

There is some evidence that the gap in unemployment rates is also, in part, a product of discrimination. DeFreitas (1985) compared unemployment rates for Anglo and Hispanic males. As indicated earlier, he found that education played a major role in accounting for differences in unemployment between Mexicans and Anglos. Yet even here, 69.1 percent of the unemployment gap was not accounted for by education and other individual characteristics. In the case of Cubans, 43.9 percent of the difference was unexplained while for Puerto Ricans, individual characteristics had little bearing on the differences in unemployment rates.

These are only a few of several studies that support the conclusion that discrimination, at least for Mexicans and Puerto Ricans, continues to be a significant contributing factor to the racial inequality in labor market outcomes. However, the assumption made in such studies that the unexplained difference in labor market outcomes is attributable to discrimination is open to interpretation. It is difficult to be certain whether the remaining differences have to do with discrimination or something else. There is always the possibility that some unmeasured factors account for all or some of the unexplained differences. For example, in the DeFreitas research cited above, it is likely that differences in the job opportunities available in local labor markets—which go unmeasured in the study—account for much of the differences. In the case of Puerto Ricans, higher unemployment rates may be dependent on their concentration in the New York City labor market, as indicated earlier. Second, it can be argued that there is little reason to believe that the level of discrimination against

Demonstrators supporting the national boycott against grapes in 1973 to improve working conditions for farm workers. (Courtesy of the *Texas Catholic Herald.*)

one Hispanic group is so much different than the level of discrimination against another. Even if one believed that discrimination is stronger against one group or another due to any one of a number of factors (e.g., the higher prevalence of dark-skinned Puerto Ricans), it could be argued that the differences in actual discrimination could not be sufficiently large to account for the large variation in the degree of discrimination found in these studies.

However, these objections can be answered by those who would argue that these studies do measure discrimination, albeit imperfectly. First, some of the research, such as the study by Tienda cited above, do a better job of including a range of possible factors in their analysis, including differences in local labor markets, thus reducing the chances that significant unmeasured factors have been left out. Second, some of the largest between-group differences in measured discrimination are found between Cubans, who according to some studies (Reimers 1985) are not discriminated against, and Mexicans and Puerto Ricans who are. But this result is fully consistent with the existence of the Cuban enclave economy, which allows a majority of Cubans to insulate themselves from the discriminatory treatment of Anglo employers, and which in fact may actually allow Cubans to be treated more favorably than Anglos within the Cuban subeconomy (Portes and Truelove 1987). Those Cubans who must work outside the subeconomy may experience as much discrimination as Mexicans, but since this is only a minority of Cuban workers, and since this experience is compensated for by more favorable treatment in the enclave, the overall analysis will not reveal the existence of this discrimination. In view of these arguments and the overall consistency of the results indicating discrimination against Puerto Ricans and Mexicans, we would argue that the general results indicated by the statistical studies of discrimination have strong support.

It is also important to remember that the full effect of discrimination against Hispanics cannot be measured by simply examining labor market discrimination (Bean and Tienda 1988). Also important are various forms of prelabor market discrimination, particularly in education but also in housing. There is a large literature emphasizing the role of discrimination in teacher expectations, tracking assignments, and the use of standardized testing in influencing educational outcomes for racial minorities. Some focus on Hispanics (Ogbu 1974). In housing, discrimination in Rustbelt cities restricts Hispanics to the inner cities, thereby making it more difficult to obtain entry-level jobs that are increasingly located in the suburbs. This is particularly a problem for Puerto Ricans (Massey and Bitterman 1985). In addition, such discrimination confines Hispanic children to inferior inner-city schools. Thus, the full impact of discrimination on labor market outcomes occurs not only on the job but in housing and schools.

Summary

A variety of factors that help to account for the labor market outcomes of Hispanic groups have been examined. These factors provide a context to answer the questions posed initially regarding the decline of Hispanic economic conditions, the intensification of racial inequality with whites, and the disparate outcomes between Mexicans, Cubans, and Puerto Ricans.

Economic Decline of Hispanics in the 1980s

First, how can the economic decline experienced by Hispanics in the 1980s be accounted for? First, as mentioned earlier, this is partly a function of the decline experienced by all groups in the 1980s, including whites, as a result of a declining economy. Wages declined in general, as well as for Hispanics. Employment declined in general, including for Hispanics. Part-time work increased in general and for Hispanics as well.

Second is the differential impact of economic restructuring. The decline of the urban Rustbelt economies has had a particular impact on any groups that happen to be concentrated in these communities. This has had particularly negative consequences for Puerto Ricans, who are concentrated within the central cities of Rustbelt communities, especially New York City.

The economic restructuring has had other effects that fall particularly hard on Hispanics. For example, the job market has increasingly been polarized into higher and lower paying jobs, with the shrinking of the number of middle-income jobs. Groups with relatively low levels of education have been hurt by this development, since education is typically required for the higher paying jobs. The value of the high school diploma and even some college is great, negatively affecting Puerto Ricans and (even more so) Mexicans with their low rates of college graduation (Falcón and Hirschman 1992; Ojeda et al. 1991).

Third is the increasing instability of Hispanic households as manifested in a rising proportion of single-parent families, again especially for Puerto Ricans, but also for Mexicans as well (Cuciti and James 1990). This in turn, as indicated earlier, is influenced by the declining economic opportunities available to young Hispanic men and women.

Inequality Between Hispanics and Whites

How can the widening of the earnings gap between Hispanics and whites during the 1980s be explained? First, a major gap in educational attainment continues to explain a large part of the difference. This gap has gotten larger due to the stagnation of Mexicans, the largest Hispanic group. This is particularly serious in an economy where educational credentials are increasingly at a premium. A simple continuation of existing educational differentials will produce increased economic inequality under such circumstances. As indicated above, this inequality in education is partly a consequence of discrimination and is also in part a response to unequal opportunities in the job market, constituting a vicious circle. Second, the continuing influx of immigrants continues to exert a downward pull on Hispanics that does not occur for whites. Immigrants are also faring more poorly in the job market, with historically unprecedented rates of poverty. While the poverty rate for Hispanic immigrants in 1969 was 24.8 percent, this figure had risen to 32.5 percent by 1979 (Jensen 1989). Third, there are the continuing realities of job discrimination, whereby people of different groups are treated differently in the labor market even when they have the same characteristics. The continuation of hiring based on racial preference continues to favor whites. While this has less effect on Cubans because of the insulating character of the Cuban enclave, it has a substantial effect on Mexicans and Puerto Ricans, who continue to show fewer returns for their educational achievements than whites. Ojeda et al. (1991) argued that rates of wage discrimination between Hispanics and Anglos in the same industries and with the same individual characteristics increased in the 1980s, especially for those certain educational levels (high school graduates only) and younger workers.

Furthermore, the proportion of single-parent families has risen at a much faster rate for Hispanics than for whites or African Americans. Between 1980 and 1985 the proportion of female-headed families among Hispanics rose by 16 percent, compared to only 4 percent for African Americans (Cuciti and James 1990). The end result is more rapid growth in poverty levels because of the higher probability of poverty associated with female-headed households.

Differences Among Hispanic Groups

The most distinctive pattern found within the Hispanic experience in the labor market is the differential rate of socioeconomic success experienced by Cubans relative to Mexicans and Puerto Ricans. Some potential explanations to this divergence have already been discussed. First, Cubans have the highest level of educational attainment of the three groups. Second, even for those Cubans without much education, the existence of the Cuban enclave economy provides some protection from regular economic forces. This enclave economy provides some additional incentives to becoming self-employed or obtaining managerial positions even for those from modest backgrounds and with little formal education. Third, Cuban families are typically headed by married couples, which in turn reflects the strength of the economic opportunities available to Cuban males and females.

The differences between Mexicans and Puerto Ricans are a bit more complex to explain. On the one hand, Mexicans have more employment opportunities for both males and females. This is reflected less in official unemployment figures than in differential labor market participation rates for both men and women. As a consequence of the poor labor market participation rates for men, female-headed families are far more common among Puerto Ricans than among Mexicans. Both for this reason and due to the limited employment opportunities available for Puerto Rican women, these women have high rates of welfare dependency.

The difference in Mexican and Puerto Rican labor market opportunities is primarily a function of geographical concentration. Puerto Ricans are concentrated in the central cities of the Rustbelt, where entry-level jobs are declining. Mexicans are concentrated in the Sunbelt, where the economy is stronger all-around. However, in addition to this, the favorable employment experience of Mexican immigrants in Chicago as well as the lack of representation of Puerto Ricans in certain low-wage sectors in New York City where other Hispanic immigrants (such as Dominicans) predominate indicate that employer preferences may also play a role.

This is not the entire story, however. While the employment opportunities for Mexican men and women in menial jobs are stronger than for Puerto Ricans, Puerto Ricans have more opportunities to get higher status positions. This is a function of the higher educational attainment of Puerto Rican workers. In addition, those Puerto Ricans who do work at menial jobs are typically working in sectors of the labor market where the wages are higher than is the case for Mexicans.

The resulting effects are higher earnings for those Puerto Ricans who do work and greater representation in higher status positions. For example, in 1990 median earnings for Puerto Rican males were $18,193, compared to $12,894 for Mexican males. Median earnings for Puerto Rican women were $11,702, compared to $9,286 for Mexican women. Only 20.1 percent of Mexican men and 9.8 percent of Mexican women earned $25,000 or more, compared to 37.1 percent of Puerto Rican men and 16.7 percent of Puerto Rican women. About 12 percent of Puerto Rican men and 22 percent of women are in managerial and professional specialty positions, compared to 8.9 percent of Mexican men and 14.1 percent of Mexican women (U. S. Bureau of the Census 1991). Falcón and

Hirschman (1992) compared Puerto Ricans to Mexicans and Cubans and found that Puerto Rican males and females not only have the largest proportion of earners in the $25,000 or more category but have also experienced the largest increase in that category during the last decade. That is despite having the highest poverty rate of all three groups.

Thus, Puerto Rican families have a far greater range of income than do Mexican families. This is largely a function of the characteristics of Puerto Rican workers interacting with the occupational and income polarization taking place in the labor market on the East Coast, a pattern very different from the one taking place where Mexicans concentrate. These patterns of income distribution reflect the different pattern of incorporation of Mexicans and Puerto Ricans into the labor markets in the geographical regions in which they reside.

How to Improve the Labor Market Situation of Hispanics

The review presented here suggests some potential avenues to address the problems faced by Hispanics in the labor market and to alleviate their poverty altogether. First, measures could be taken to improve the employment conditions of low-wage workers. These include substantially raising the minimum wage, which has fallen further and further behind the cost of living in recent years. In addition, the size of the Earned Income Tax Credit by which workers with low incomes can earn credits from the federal government needs to be raised further. These actions would particularly benefit Mexicans but would also help the smaller numbers of low-wage Puerto Ricans and Cubans.

Second, measures could be taken to improve the economic situation of female-headed families, which is a pressing issue for Puerto Ricans but also to a lesser extent for Mexicans. These include (1) a vast expansion of low-cost, subsidized day care so that single mothers can work; (2) the development of a national health care system so that single mothers do not require welfare in order to obtain health insurance for their families; (3) a major commitment to public and subsidized housing so that rents are affordable–the major factor accounting for the rapid increase of homelessness among single mothers and their families in the 1980s was skyrocketing rents combined with cutbacks in federal housing programs; (4) better job opportunities for women so that work is a viable alternative for single mothers with responsibilities for children.

Third, measures could be taken to provide better employment opportunities for young men. This would reduce poverty among two-parent families and would provide the conditions for establishing stable unions between men and women. These increased jobs could be provided through strategies to stimulate economic expansion and through jobs programs whereby men and women are hired to do socially necessary tasks, such as educating and caring for our children, providing health care, rebuilding our cities, cleaning up our environment.

Fourth, steps need to be taken to improve the opportunities for schooling available to Hispanics. The model of successful schools such as the Hernández School in Boston (Ribadeneira 1990) that stress high teacher expectations, effective bilingual education, hiring of Hispanic teachers, cooperative learning methods, encouragement of parent involvement, and the use of mixed-ability grouping needs to be expanded on a broader scale.

As suggested above, the improved job picture would provide the conditions not only to strengthen families but to increase the incentives for education. In addition, the underlying causes of crime in poor communities–lack of opportunity and hopelessness–would be attacked. Finally, steps need to be taken to reduce discrimination against Hispanics in the labor market. Key to this is the strengthening of antidiscrimination enforcement machinery and a renewed commitment to affirmative action in hiring and promotions.

Bibliography

Aponte, Robert
1991 "Ethnicity and Male Employment: A Test of Two Theories."

Barrera, Mario
1979 *Race and Class in the Southwest.* South Bend, IN: U of Notre Dame P.

Bean, Frank, and Marta Tienda
1988 *The Hispanic Population in the United States.* New York: Russell Sage Monograph Series.

Borjas, George J.
1981 "Hispanic Immigrants in the U. S. Labor Market: An Empirical Analysis." *Hispanic Origin Workers in the U. S. Labor Market.* Ed Marta Tienda.

Boswell, Thomas D., and J. R. Curtis
1984 *The Cuban American Experience.* Totowa, NJ: Rowman & Allanheld.

Cattan, Peter
1988 "The Growing Presence of Hispanics in the U. S. Work Force." *Monthly Labor Review,* vol 111 (August), pp 9-14.

Cuciti, Peggy, and Franklin James
1990 "A Comparison of Black and Hispanic Poverty in Large Cities of the Southwest." *Hispanic Journal of Behavioral Sciences,* 12:50-75.

Falcón, Luis M.
1991 "Migration and Development: The Case of Puerto Rico." *Determinants of Emigration from Mexico, Central America, and the Caribbean.* Eds Sergio Diaz-Briquets and Sidney Weintraub. Boulder, CO: Westview P, pp 145-87.

Falcón, Luis M., Douglas T. Gurak, and Yanmin Gu
1990 "A Comparative Analysis of Female-Headship Among Puerto Ricans and Dominicans in the New York Area." Paper presented at Annual Meetings of the American Sociological Association, Washington, DC, (August).

Falcón, Luis M., and Douglas T. Gurak
1992 "Features of the Hispanic Underclass: Puerto Ricans and Dominicans in New York City." Unpublished ms.

Farley, John E.
1987 "Disproportionate Black and Hispanic Employment in U. S. Metropolitan Areas." *American Journal of Economics and Sociology*, 46:129-50.

Gann, Lewis H., and Peter J. Duignan
1986 *The Hispanics in the United States.* Boulder, CO: Westview P.

Guhleman, Patricia, Marta Tienda, and Marion Bowman
1981 "An Employment and Earnings Profile of Hispanic Origin Workers in the United States, 1976." *Hispanic Origin Workers in the U. S. Labor Market.* Ed Marta Tienda.

Jensen, Leif
1988 "Poverty and Immigration in the United States, 1960-1980." *Divided Opportunities: Minorities, Poverty, and Social Policy.* Eds Gary D. Sandefur and Marta Tienda. New York: Plenum P.

Kassarda, John D.
1983 "Caught in the Web of Change." *Society*, 21:41-47.
1985 "Urban Change and Minority Opportunities." *The New Urban Reality.* Ed Paul Peterson. Washington, DC: Brookings Institute.
1989 "Urban Industrial Transformation and the Underclass." *Annals*, 501:26-47.

Llanes, José
1982 *Cuban-Americans: Masters of Survival.* Cambridge, MA: ABT.

Maldonado, Lionel A.
"Altered States: Chicanos in the Labor Force." *Ethnicity and the Work Force.*

Massey, Douglas S., and B. Bitterman
1985 "Explaining the Paradox of Puerto Rican Segregation." *Social Forces*, 64:306-31.

Neidert, Lisa J., and Marta Tienda
1981 "Converting Education into Earnings: The Patterns among Hispanic Origin Men." *Hispanic Origin Workers in the U. S. Labor Market.* Ed Marta Tienda.

Ogbu, John
1974 *The Next Generation.*

Ojeda, Raúl Hinojosa, Martin Carnoy, and Hugh Daley
1991 "An Even Greater 'U-Turn': Latinos and the New Inequality." *Hispanics in the Labor Force: Issues and Policies.* Eds Edwin Meléndez, Clara Rodríguez, and Janis B. Figueroa. New York: Plenum P.

Ortiz, Vilma
1986 "Changes in the Characteristics of Puerto Rican Migrants." *International Migration Review*, 20.3:612-28.

Pedraza-Bailey, Silvia
1985 *Political and Economic Migrants in America: Cubans and Mexicans.* Austin: U of Texas P.

Portes, Alejandro, and Cynthia Truelove
1987 "Making Sense out of Diversity: Recent Research on Hispanic Minorities." *Annual Review of Sociology*, 13:359-85.

Portes, Alejandro, and Robert D. Manning
1986 "The Immigrant Enclave: Theory and Empirical Examples." *Competitive Ethnic Relations.* Eds Susan Olzak and Joanne Nagel. Orlando, FL: Academic P.

Portes, Alejandro, and Robert L. Bach
1985 *Latin Journey: Cuban and Mexican Immigrants in the United States.* Berkeley: U of California P.

Reimers, Cordelia W.
1985 "A Comparative Analysis of the Wages of Hispanics, Blacks, and Non-Hispanic Whites." *Hispanics in the U. S. Economy.* Eds George Borjas and Marta Tienda. Orlando, FL: Academic P.

Roos, Patricia A., and Joyce F. Hennessy
"Assimilation or Exclusion: Japanese and Mexican Americans in California." *Sociological Forum*, 2:278-305.

Roth, Dennis M.
1983 "Hispanics in the Labor Force: A Brief Examination." *The Hispanic Population of the United States: An Overview.* Congressional Research Service. Washington, DC: U. S. House of Representatives.

Stepick, Alex, III, and Guillermo Grenier
1993 "Cubans in Miami." *Poor Latino Communities in the United States: Beyond the Underclass Debate.* Eds Raquel Pinderhughes and Joan Moore. New York: Russell Sage.

Stolzenberg, Ross M.
1990 "Ethnicity, Geography, and Occupational Achievement of Hispanic Men in the United States." *American Sociological Review*, 55:143-54.

Testa, Mark, Nan M. Astone, Marilyn Krogh, and Kathryn M. Neckerman
1989 "Employment and Marriage Among Inner-City Fathers." *Annals*, 501:79-81.

Tienda, Marta
1981 *Socioeconomic Attainment and Ethnicity.* Washington, DC: U. S. Department of Labor.
1983a "Market Characteristics and Hispanic Earnings: A Comparison of Natives and Immigrants." *Social Problems*, 31:59-72.
1983b "Nationality and Income Attainment among Native and Immigrant Hispanic Men in the United States." *Sociological Quarterly*, 24:253-72.

Tienda, Marta, and Lisa J. Neidert
1981a "Market Structure and Earnings Determination of Native and Immigrant Hispanics in the U. S." *Hispanic Origin Workers in the U. S. Labor Market.* Ed Marta Tienda.
1981b "Language, Education, and the Socioeconomic Achievement of Hispanic Men." *Hispanic Origin*

Workers in the U. S. Labor Market. Ed Marta Tienda.

Tienda, Marta, and Leif Jensen
1988 "Poverty and Minorities: A Quarter Century Profile of Color and Socioeconomic Disadvantage." *Divided Opportunities: Minorities, Poverty, and Social Policy.* Eds Gary D. Sandefur and Marta Tienda. New York: Plenum P.

U. S. Bureau of the Census.
1991 "The Hispanic Population in the United States," *Current Population Reports*, Series P-20, no 449. March 1990. Washington, DC: Government Printing Office.

Wacquant, Loic J. D., and William J. Wilson
1989 "Poverty, Joblessness, and the Social Transformation of the Inner City." *Welfare Policy for the 1990s.* Eds Phoebe H. Cottingham and David T. Ellwood. Cambridge, MA: Harvard UP.

Waldinger, Roger
1987 "Changing Ladders and Musical Chairs: Ethnicity and Opportunity in Post-Industrial New York." *Politics and Society*, 15:378-402.

Wilson, Kenneth L., and W. Allen Martin
1982 "Ethnic Enclaves: A Comparison of the Cuban and Black Economies in Miami." *American Journal of Sociology,* 88.1.

Wilson, William J.
1987 *The Truly Disadvantaged: The Inner City, the Underclass, and Public Policy.* Chicago: U of Chicago P.
1991 "Poverty, Joblessness, and Family Structure in the Inner City: A Comparative Perspective."

Latinos in American Politics

Maurilio E. Vigil

Latinos or Americans of Hispanic descent are at the "cross-roads" of political power as the end of the twentieth century approaches. The much heralded "decade of Hispanics," the 1980s, came and went with only marginal progress in the political arena. Even the perennial optimist former New Mexico governor Toney Anaya admitted that Hispanics may face the prospect of "growing in numbers without growing in power." While conceding that Hispanic population growth has been phenomenal, Anaya pointed out that "long, slow and tedious registration drives . . . [have produced] very small numbers of new Hispanic voters" (Anaya 1989).

While Latinos have been regarded as an important political ethnic group since the onset of the Chicano movement of the 1960s, this has been largely based on the expectation that the group would realize its political potential. That potential has been based on demographic data (birthrate and immigration patterns) that have consistently identified Hispanics as the fastest growing ethnic minority group in the United States. While Hispanics have made notable gains in almost every sector of American political life, they are still far from achieving even median levels of participation in politics and far from enjoying the benefits of American citizenship.

This chapter is about how Latinos have fared in the American political system. In particular it investigates the involvement of Hispanics in traditional electoral politics, describes the types of national and community-level activist organizations that Hispanics have created, and the response of American society to the political initiatives and interests of the Hispanic people.

The book *Hispanics in American Politics* (Vigil 1987) was the first comprehensive treatment of all Hispanics (Mexican Americans, Cuban Americans, Puerto Rican Americans, and other Hispanic Americans) as a single political interest group. The present effort explores the current status and progress of the group in American politics.

In many ways the story of Hispanics in politics provides a penetrating vantage point from which to gauge the nature and operation of the American political system. That vantage point reveals, for example, that the basic structures and operation of the political system have historically denied Hispanics (and other minorities) the full benefits of American society. It is true that the American political system has favored White-Anglo-Saxon-Protestants (WASP), particularly the rich and powerful, that "majority rule" has often meant "minority oppression," and that racism persists in the hearts of many Americans. It is also true, however, that the political system has been susceptible to change and to remedy historical wrongs. The federal civil rights legislation of the 1960s along with landmark federal court decisions in affirmative action, voting rights, and civil liberties since then have brought significant political change.

This report begins by providing a demographic political profile of Hispanics. Brief historical sketches of each Hispanic group highlights their origin, the circumstances of their arrival or presence in the United States, and the level of political integration into American society. The study then examines the most important themes in Hispanic politics. It updates the *Hispanics in American Politics* book by describing the most important recent political developments among the three major Hispanic groups. It examines Hispanic voting patterns in the 1988 and 1990 elections; considers the nature and extent of Hispanic office holding in national and state governments; reviews developments involving Hispanic organizations; and reports within all of these sections on the most important developments in public policy making affecting the Hispanic community.

A Demographic Political Profile of Hispanic Americans

The number of Hispanics in the U. S. population increased by 38.9 percent in the period 1980 to 1989. The increase was four times greater than that of the national population, which grew by 9.5 percent in the same period. Thus while the overall American population remained fairly stable, that of Hispanic Americans nearly doubled in size. Hispanics now number 22 million and make up 9 percent of the total U. S. population of 250 million (U. S. Census 1990). Hispanics are now the second largest ethnic minority group (African Americans are higher), and their greater growth rate will make them the largest ethnic group shortly after the year 2000. These statistics alone are significant in a political system in which population and votes contribute to political power. However, in order to effectively assess the present and future influence of Hispanics in American politics we need to know more about their geographic distribution, their socioeconomic status, and the attitudes of Hispanics toward the political system.

Urban Concentration of Hispanics

Hispanics are overwhelmingly concentrated in urban areas. More than 90 percent live in urban areas as compared to 73 percent for non-Hispanics. Furthermore, most of the urban Hispanics are concentrated in some of our largest metropolitan centers across the nation. As shown in Table 1, Hispanics (mostly Mexican Americans) in Los Angeles make up 29.3 percent of the population; in New York (mostly Puerto Ricans), they make up 13.8 percent of the population; in Miami (mostly Cubans), they make up 28 percent of the population; in Chicago (mostly Mexican Americans), they make up 9.9 percent of the population; in San Antonio (mostly Mexican Americans), they make up 51 percent of the population; and in El Paso Hispanics (mostly Mexican Americans) have the highest percentage of the total population, with 62.5 percent. These figures explain why presidential candidates who ordinarily concentrate their campaigns in large urban centers have targeted Hispanics as a potential pivotal vote in the large cities. The figures also suggest an increasing importance of Hispanics in big-city politics in the years to come.

TABLE 1

Largest Metropolitan Areas for Hispanic Population

Rank	SMSA	1988 Hispanic Population	Percent Hispanic	Predominant Hispanic Group
1.	Los Angeles/Anaheim, CA	4,072,700	29.3	MA[a]
2.	New York, NY	2,499,200	13.8	PR[b]
3.	San Francisco/Oakland, CA	893,500	14.7	MA
4.	Miami, FL	858,500	28.0	Cuban
5.	Chicago, IL	811,100	9.9	MA
6.	Houston, TX	667,500	18.5	MA
7.	San Antonio, TX	667,000	51.4	MA
8.	San Diego, CA	425,700	17.9	MA
9.	Dallas/Fort Worth, TX	400,200	10.7	MA
10.	El Paso, TX	319,375	62.5	MA
11.	Phoenix, AZ	305,300	14.8	MA
12.	Denver, CO	200,400	18.8	MA
13.	Albuquerque, NM	127,764	33.8	MA

Source: U. S. Bureau of the Census. *Statistical Abstract of the United States, 1990.* No. 38. Washington, DC. 1990, p. 33.

[a]MA: Mexican Americans.

[b]PR: Puerto Ricans.

Political Implications of Hispanic Distribution by States

The Hispanic population, moreover, is heavily concentrated in just nine states, some of which are the most populous states (such as California, New York, Florida, Illinois, and Texas) in the Union. The authors of the 1989 *National Roster of Hispanic Elected Officials* (NALEO) have speculated on the political significance of Hispanic population growth and its concentration in the nine states. These nine states comprise a total of 193 of the 270 electoral vote majority needed for election to the presidency (see Table 2). According to NALEO calculations, a gain or loss of 3.6 percent of the Hispanic vote in Texas, for example, translates into a 1 percentage point gain or loss for any presidential candidate in that state. Similarly a 6.3 percent change in the Hispanic vote in California, 8.7 percent in New York, 7.1 percent in Florida, 12.2 percent in New Jersey, and 16.5 percent in Illinois could alter the outcome by 1 percent in each of these electoral vote rich states (NALEO 1989). Thus, in a close election the Hispanic vote could prove pivotal in the outcome of the race in any one of these states and in the election of the president of the United States.

While these demographic data provide encouraging prospects for Hispanics, there are several disturbing features in the Hispanic population data reported by NALEO. One is the comparative youth of the Hispanic population. The median age of Hispanics is 25.5 years. This means that 35 percent of Hispanics are below the prime voting age. Put another way, 20 percent of all Hispanics of voting age are in the population group (18 to 24) that participates least in the electoral process as compared to 14 percent for the population as a whole.

A second disturbing demographic characteristic is that a large segment of the Hispanic population in the United States is ineligible to vote because they are not citizens. Table 3, which compares Anglo, black, and Hispanic nonvoters in the November 1988 election, shows that over half (52 percent) of all Hispanics legally in the United States did not vote because they were ineligible. Consequently, absence of U. S. citizenship among Hispanics continues to be the single greatest obstacle to Hispanic political participation in the United States (NALEO 1989).

TABLE 2

Percent of the 1988 Hispanic Vote Needed to Make a 1 Percent Shift in the Statewide Vote

State	Hispanic Vote 1988	Percentage Needed To Make 1% Shift[a]	Electoral Votes,1988
Arizona	119,288	5.6%	7
California	826,621	6.3	47
Colorado	136,608	5.6	8
Florida	361,449	7.1	21
Illinois	153,936	16.5	24
New Jersey	140,955	12.2	16
New Mexico	161,043	1.8	5
New York	411,250	8.7	36
Texas	853,522	3.6	29
TOTAL			**193**
Electoral Votes need to Win Presidency		270	

Source: U. S. Census Bureau. Compiled by NALEO Educational Fund.
[a]These percentages assume that the vote shifts represent movement from one party to the other. In other words, elections are viewed as a zero sum game in which a shift of one vote represents a net gain of one vote for one party and a net loss to the other party. To calculate the number of new voters needed to alter results, double these percentages.

Even among Hispanics eligible to vote, the turnout of 46 percent in the November 1988 elections was lower than the 61 percent recorded for non-Hispanics. The subordinate socioeconomic condition of Hispanics presents a third demographic characteristic that is disturbing to advocates of Hispanic political participation. Most scholarly studies have shown a positive correlation between such socioeconomic indicators as level of education and income and levels of political participation. The poverty rate of Hispanics in 1989 was 23.7 percent as compared to 9.4 percent for other Americans. The proportion of

TABLE 3

A Comparison of Anglo, Black and Hispanic Nonvoters in the November 1988 Elections

	NONVOTERS (%)	NONCITIZEN	NONCITIZEN AS % OF NONVOTERS
Anglo	62,492,000 (41%)	6,849	11%
Black	9,548,000 (48%)	730,000	8%
Hispanic	9,183,000 (71%)	4,815,000	52%

Source: U. S. Census Bureau, Series P-20, No. 435, 1989.

Hispanic families maintained by single parents was 30 percent as compared to 20 percent for non-Hispanic families. The educational attainment of Hispanics has improved over the past decade, but it is still far below that of non-Hispanics. Among Hispanics aged 25 to 34, 60 percent have finished high school compared to 89 percent of non-Hispanics. The proportion of Hispanics 25 years or older who had completed four or more years of college in 1988 was 10 percent as compared to 21 percent for non-Hispanics (U. S. Census *The Hispanic Population* 1990). Thus, the continued subordinate socioeconomic condition of Hispanics will probably translate into lower levels of political interest, activity, and participation in political affairs.

Hispanic Population by Subgroup and Geographic Distribution

Mexican Americans are the largest and fastest growing of the Hispanic subgroups. They totaled 12.6 million in 1989, a rise of 45 percent from 1980. There were also 2.3 million Puerto Ricans, a rise of 17.5 percent from 1980, and 1.1 million Cubans, up 33.8 percent from 1980. "Other" Hispanics in the American population, numbering 4.1 million, had increased by 36 percent since 1980.

California has by far the most Hispanics, 6.8 million or 34 percent of the total population in the United States. Texas follows with 4.3 million. Most of the Hispanics in these two states are Mexican Americans. Other states with large Hispanic populations are New York, 1.9 million (primarily Puerto Rican); Florida, 1.6 million (mostly Cuban); New Jersey, 638,000 (mostly Puerto Rican); Arizona, 725,000; New Mexico, 549,000; and Colorado, 421,000, with Mexican Americans predominating in the latter four states (U. S. Census *The Hispanic Population* 1990).

Several factors account for the current geographic distribution of the Hispanic population in the United States. Mexican Americans are most heavily concentrated in the southwestern states of California, Texas, New Mexico, Arizona, and Colorado. All these states are located in what was once Mexican territory, and this partly accounts for the large Mexican-American population. Moreover, continued immigration from Mexico after the Mexican War accounts for the majority of the Mexican-American population in the United States today. This "immigrant" Mexican-American population settled in the southwestern states due to the proximity to Mexico (McWilliams 1949). Mexican-American settlement in states outside of the Southwest is primarily the result of migratory patterns followed by agricultural migrant workers from Mexico in the United States.

Heavy Cuban concentrations in Florida are, of course, due to the proximity of that state to the island country of Cuba. Cuban emigration to the United States began in the 1930s as political refugees escaped the dictatorship of Gerardo Machado and continued in the 1950s with similar escapees from the oppressive dictatorship of Fulgencio Batista. The greatest migration occurred following the Cuban Revolution and the establishment of Fidel Castro's Cuban communist state in 1959. This time, however, the émigrés were primarily middle- and upper-class Cubans who sought temporary sanctuary while they awaited the demise of the Castro dictatorship. These hopes faded after the failure of the Bay of Pigs invasion, thus many Cubans resigned themselves to permanent settlement in the United States (Torres 1988).

Migrations of Puerto Ricans to New York began in the early 1900s and was encouraged by a unique economic arrangement that allowed Puerto Ricans free movement between the United States and the commonwealth. Puerto Rican workers were even encouraged to migrate to the United States by recruiting efforts of such organizations as the War Manpower Commission during World War II and the Commonwealth Office in the 1950s (Jennings 1977).

Political Status of Hispanics

More Hispanics are involved in conventional forms of political participation than ever before. There are more Hispanics voting; involved in political party activity; campaigning for national, state and local offices; and holding both appointive and elective offices than ever before in U. S. history. By 1990 more than 3,700 Hispanics held local elective office. However, the overall political participation rates of Hispanics, as a whole, remain woefully inadequate and far below the U. S. population. As our data for Hispanic voting and office holding will later show, much progress remains to be made.

Political status, it should be understood, goes beyond voting and office holding. A very important measure of political power is representation in administrative and appointive public office. Hispanics achieved their first federal cabinet-level appointment in 1986 when President Ronald Reagan appointed Lauro Cavazos as secretary of the Department of Education. When President George Bush assumed office in 1989, he retained Cavazos in the cabinet and also appointed former New Mexico congressman Manuel Luján as secretary of the Department of the Interior. In 1990 Cavazos resigned from the cabinet.

However visible the electoral achievements and top-level appointments (such as Cavazos and Luján) may be, they conceal the absence of Hispanics from the administrative bureaucracy where much of the allocation of values occurs in American politics. It also helps explain why, despite outward signs of progress in the political status of Hispanics, the everyday lives of Hispanics remains unchanged.

These dismal conclusions, however, should not deter Hispanics, for it has been shown before in the American political system (as in the labor movement) that sustained progress in the electoral arena is the first step to progress in the policy arena. It is on this premise that much of the foregoing discussion and analysis of the progress of Hispanics in the American political arena is based. Before such an analysis is undertaken, however, it is appropriate to consider the diversity of this group.

Pío Pico, last Mexican governor of California.

Hispanic Diversity

Hispanics constitute the most diverse ethnic group in American politics. No other American minority group is characterized by equal differences in race, economics, migration history, national origins, and regional separation as Hispanics.

David S. Broder once convened a meeting of Hispanic leaders to discuss Hispanic identity and behavior. He found uncertainty and described Hispanics as "diffused . . . divided . . . disunited . . . hard to define . . . their numbers uncertain . . . " (Broder 1981). The explanation for this condition is derived from origins in quite different national cultures. Unlike other American immigrant groups such as the Irish or Italians, Hispanics did not originate in any one nation; instead, the "histories, immigrant experiences, and economic standings of the groups vary tremendously" (Broder 1981). While Puerto Ricans and some Mexican Americans are American citizens by birthright, Cubans arrived in the United States as "privileged" political refugees who nourished hopes of returning to Cuba after Castro was deported. Many Mexicans find themselves in an uncertain status in the United States. Some are legal residents whose long residence has qualified them for amnesty but not citizenship, others are temporary residents working in the United States to support a family back in Mexico. Others are simply "illegal," more courteously referred to as "undocumented aliens."

Even some of the subgroups that comprise the Hispanic community are characterized by diversity. Mexican Americans in New Mexico, for example, differ widely from their cousins in California, Arizona, and Texas in their Spanish dialect, in their historical experience, in their economic and occupational status, and even in self-identification. Most refer to themselves as "Spanish-American" rather than Mexican American (Gonzales 1967).

The Hispanic groups also differ in their socioeconomic condition. Although some have been quite successful economically (especially Cubans and Mexican Americans), the majority of them continue to experience poverty and discrimination. The basis of unity for Hispanics therefore lies in their common experience (with variations) of Spanish language, surnames, and culture. Any effort to analyze the potential for a Hispanic political coalition must begin by acknowledging this diversity in origin, nationality, and culture. Moreover, it is necessary to discuss the historical experience of each group (see Chapter 2).

The Hispanic Vote

It is said that "voting" is the "most universal political act." If this is true, then Hispanics have some distance to travel before they reach the universal level of participation.

It is appropriate then, to begin a narrative of Hispanic politics with the topic of the Hispanic vote. Unlike the black vote, which has exhibited remarkable cohesion by supporting the Democratic party in the last three presidential elections, the Hispanic vote has yet to show such cohesion and support for one party. George Bush and Ronald Reagan won their presidential elections even though they lost (with the exception of Cubans) the overall Hispanic vote; but even if the Democrats had won, Hispanic claims upon the Democrats would have been

A voter registration campaign in New York City. (Courtesy of the Center for Puerto Rican Studies Library. Hunter College, CUNY.)

diminished by the less than overwhelming support given that party by Hispanics.

Conditions and Importance of the Hispanic Vote

The significance of Hispanic voting in presidential elections will determine whether Hispanics can become, like blacks, a pivotal vote in a close election; it will also determine the claims Hispanics can make on the winning party as a reward for the group's support. Because Hispanic support has benefited the Democratic party, it is assumed that they will receive more favored treatment from the Democrats and will generally agonize during periods of Republican hegemony. The Republican party, nevertheless, mounted a sustained drive for Hispanic support in the 1980s.

Hispanic voting in presidential elections is tied to such external forces as national and international events, economic conditions, the influence of mass media, and political organization. It is also influenced by internal factors such as political values, voter awareness, political leadership, and political awareness and participation. All of these factors constitute the political environment under which Hispanics will vote. Under normal conditions Hispanics tend to favor the Democrats, but alterations in the norms could yield a reversal in the historical pattern or could affect the margin of Hispanic support the Democrats receive.

This section examines Hispanic voting in national and state elections. One section that focuses on the 1988 presidential election enables us to see the impact that the Hispanic vote is having in national elections. Another section that focuses on the 1990 "off-year" election provides a closer look at Hispanic voting patterns at the state level. This part on Hispanic voting attempts to uncover trends in Hispanic voter preference and offers explanations for those trends. It explores the possibilities for and obstacles to a more cohesive and viable Hispanic vote. The Hispanic vote in a presidential election assumes importance not only as a barometer of Hispanic political participation and as a symbolic expression of Hispanic values and preferences, but from a national perspective serves as a measure of the power the group wields in determining the outcome of an election and in making claims upon government. The Hispanic vote at the state and local level expresses the degree of Hispanic organization and cohesion that was marshalled to secure victory for specific Hispanic candidates.

A meeting between César Chávez and Robert Kennedy. (Photo by George Ballis.)

Hispanic Vote in the 1988 Presidential Election

Although completely reliable public opinion polls measuring Hispanic voter preferences in national elections are not yet available, a preliminary picture of Hispanic voter preferences has begun to appear in the national polls conducted by the major television networks following presidential elections. In 1988 all three television networks conducted exit polls as part of their general election coverage, and all attempted to identify distinct voter preferences among ethnic groups on a national level. Some of the polls, however, failed to include Hispanic samples in key representative states; thus their utility for the present analysis is limited.

Also in 1988 the Southwest Voter Research Institute conducted its first extensive exit polling of Mexican-American voters in California, Texas, and New Mexico. By combining, comparing, and cross checking these various polling results one is able to discern some distinct patterns in Hispanic voting, offer some preliminary observations on the impact of the vote, and suggest its implications for Hispanics, the parties, and the candidates.

Although Republican George Bush won the 1988 Presidential election with fairly overwhelming electoral and popular vote margins, Democratic candidate Michael Dukakis, won the Hispanic vote with substantial majorities. All three national exit polls conducted by the major television networks showed Dukakis winning the Hispanic vote (see Table 4). The CBS and ABC news polls showed Dukakis with an identical score of 69 percent to Bush's 30 percent, while the NBC poll showed Dukakis with 66 percent to Bush's 34 percent. The CBS and ABC poll results show much greater support for Dukakis in 1988 than the support received by Democratic candidate Walter Mondale in 1984, while the NBC News poll showed nearly identical Hispanic support of 68 percent and 66 percent for the Democratic candidate in 1984 and 1988 respectively. All poll results affirm the continued overall support of the Democratic party by Hispanics even though individual state patterns may differ.

How do Hispanic voter preferences compare with whites and blacks? Table 5 offers a comparison of the 1980 and 1984 voter preferences of white, Hispanic, and black voters. Although Hispanics gave their support to Democratic party candidates Carter in 1980, Mondale in 1984, and Dukakis in 1988, the margin was less than overwhelming when compared to the black vote. The 82 percent Carter received in 1980, the 89 percent Mondale received in 1984, and the 88 percent Dukakis got in 1988, clearly indicate that although the black community is itself a coalition of diverse localized and specialized subgroups, it shows remarkable collective expression as "the black vote" in national elections. Such is not the case with Hispanics.

TABLE 4

Hispanic Vote for President, 1984-88 National Polls

	NBC News	CBS New York Times	ABC Washington Post
1984			
Mondale (D)	68	61	56
Reagan (R)	32	37	43
Sample *N*	390	219	286
% of Voters	3	2	3
1988			
Dukakis (D)	66	69	69
Bush (R)	34	30	30
Sample *N*	437	442	684
% of Voters	4	3	3

Source: Southwest Voter Research Institute, *Southwest Voter Research Notes*, Vol. 2, No. 6, Sept.-Dec. 1988. Also *NBC News Decision 88* General Election Exit Poll Results, and CBS News/New York Times Survey, National Exit Poll, Table 1, November, 1988.

Hispanics gave the incumbent Jimmy Carter only a slight majority of 55 percent in the 1980 presidential election; Mondale, 56 percent in 1984; and Dukakis, a larger 69 percent in 1988. Although Bush waged a more concerted drive for Hispanic votes, he received less support overall from Hispanics than did Ronald Reagan in 1980 and 1984.

The distribution of the Hispanic vote over different regions of the country or by states is difficult to determine, because no single national exit poll conducted by any of the networks or other organizations sought or obtained data for every state with a large Hispanic population. Consequently, it is necessary to piece together this data from the available exit poll results that were conducted by the three television networks and also by the Southwest Voter Research Institute (SVRI), which conducted exit polls in Texas, California, and New Mexico.

TABLE 5

Comparison of 1980, 1984 and 1988 Exit Poll Results White, Hispanic and Black Voters

Candidate/ Year	Whites %		Hispanics %		Blacks %	
1980						
Reagan (R)	55		37		13	
Carter (D)	34		55		82	
Anderson (I)	9		7		4	
1984						
Reagan (R)	63		44		11	
Mondale (D)	37		56		89	
1988	(CBS)	(NBC)	(CBS)	(NBC)	(CBS)	(NBC)
Bush (R)	59	60	30	34	11	12
Dukakis (D)	40	40	69	66	85	88

Source: ABC News Polling Unit, "ABC News Poll—Year End Wrapup," 1985; *NBC News Decision 88* General Election Exit Poll Results and CBS/News New York Times Survey, National Exit Polls, Table 1, November 1988. ABC News conducted the most extensive polls in 1980 and 1984 by ethnicity, but did not include such a comprehensive poll in 1988, thus NBC News and CBS polls are used for comparison in 1988.

Table 6 presents a summary of the exit poll results pertaining to Hispanic voters. The national poll results, as indicated before, show that Hispanics remained loyal to the Democratic party by giving Dukakis a majority of between 66 percent to 69 percent of its vote. The valid-

TABLE 6

1988 National and Statewide Hispanic Exit Poll Results (All Numbers are in Percents)

	CBS[a]		NBC[b]		SVRI[c]		ABC[d]	
	Bush	Dukakis	Bush	Dukakis	Bush	Dukakis	Bush	Dukakis
National	30	69	34	66	–	–	30	69
California	29	70	34	66	25	74	–	–
Texas	27	72	24	76	17	83	23	76
New Mexico	32	66	–	–	31	69	28	71
Florida	–	–	72	28	–	–	–	–
New York	–	–	24	76	–	–	–	–

Source: CBS News/New York Times Survey, National Exit Poll November, 1988; NBC News, *Decision 88* General Election Poll Results; and Southwest Voter Research Institute, *Southwest Voter Research Notes*, Vol. 2, No. 6 Sept-Dec, 1988.

[a]CBS News exit poll included national results and the states of Texas, California and New Mexico.
[b]NBC News exit poll included national results and the states of California, Texas, Florida and New York.
[c]SVRI exit poll was restricted to California, Texas and New Mexico.
[d]ABC News exit poll provided only national total, no state results.

ity of the different polls is reflected by the fact that the results are within 4 percentage points for both candidates. The heavy concentration of Mexican-American voters in California, Texas, and New Mexico and the support they gave Dukakis indicate that southwestern Hispanics remain loyal to the Democrats.

Interestingly, Dukakis's greatest margins ranged from 72 percent in the CBS poll to 76 percent in the NBC poll. New York's predominantly Puerto Rican voters also gave the Democrat Dukakis a substantial majority of 76 percent to the 24 percent they gave Bush in the NBC exit poll. The Cuban community of Florida remained the only Hispanic group that supported the Republican party as reflected in the 72 percent received by George Bush, compared to 28 percent for Dukakis in the NBC poll.

The Hispanic Vote in the 1990 "Off-Year" Election

If the 1988 presidential election underscored Hispanic loyalty to the Democratic party, then the 1990 off-year elections not only reinforced that trend but clearly exhibited an erosion of Republican support in the Cuban community. In 1988 Hispanic support had been partially responsible for Republican victories in the governorships of Florida, Texas and California. Accordingly Republicans developed an "outreach" strategy to capture greater Hispanic support for the 1990 elections. After assuming the chairmanship of the Republican National Committee in 1989, Lee Atwater outlined his Sunbelt strategy, which included capturing at least 30 percent of the Hispanic vote in Texas and California and consolidating its support among Cubans in Florida (Parker 1990). The Hispanic vote would help Republicans retain the governorship in those key states and assure favorable congressional redistricting in the early 1990s which would help the Republicans gain seats in Congress. All three states had seen substantial population increases, which would result in additional congressional seats. Indeed the Bush administration's appointment of Hispanics to top-level government positions was part of the strategy to gain Hispanic support. However, on November 6, 1990, the Republican strategy was shattered. Hispanic voters contributed to major Democratic party gubernatorial victories in Texas and Florida. In Texas they gave overwhelming support to Democrat Ann Richards, while in Florida the conservative Republican Cuban voters deserted fellow Hispanic Bob Martínez to help his Democratic opponent to victory. Only in California did Republican senator Pete Wilson register modest gains among Hispanics, which contributed to his narrow victory over Democrat Diane Feinstein (Parker 1990).

In Texas, Hispanics (primarily Mexican Americans) gave former secretary of state Ann Richards an overwhelming 77 percent of the vote against only 22 percent for her Republican opponent, Clayton Williams. The Hispanic vote assuredly helped Richards become the first woman governor in Texas in recent history. Williams had courted the Hispanic vote, airing radio commercials addressing the audience in Spanish. However, when Hispanics voted they gave Williams less support than they had given Bush (23 percent) in 1988. Hispanics' rejection of Williams was apparently due to several gaffes that eroded the 40 percent Hispanic support he reportedly had in early preelection polls. One stinging criticism of Williams, revealed late in the "nasty" campaign, was the fact that Williams had not paid income taxes in 1989. According to Robert Brishcetto, executive director of the Southwest Voter Research Institute, Williams "really didn't cut through the surface . . . He certainly spoke Spanish, but that's not sufficient . . . and I think Hispanics were unable to identify with a millionaire who didn't pay his taxes last year" (Parker 1990).

Williams's most serious gaffe was when he joked that he had often traveled across the Mexican border to visit Mexican prostitutes. Richards correctly seized on that admission, which she interpreted as a lack of respect for Hispanics. Indeed, many Hispanics were offended by the prostitute remark and vented their anger in a vote against Williams.

The final factor that damaged Republican chances in Texas was their failure to field any Hispanics on their state-level ticket while the Democrats were running popular attorney and state representative Dan Morales for attorney general. Morales was elected along with Richards, thus becoming the highest Hispanic elected official in recent Texas history (Parker 1990).

In Florida, Robert Martínez, who was swept into office in 1988 under a tide of Cuban support, was swept out of office in 1990 by the same Cuban current. Martínez had antagonized many voters, including Cuban professionals and entrepreneurs, by his advocacy and enactment of new taxes, including a comprehensive new sales tax on services such as dry-cleaning and newspaper advertising. Pro-choice groups also targeted Martínez for his support of some of the toughest anti-abortion legislation in the country. Estimates of Hispanic voting against Martínez varied. Robert De Posada, a coordinator with the Republican party's Hispanic outreach program, estimated that as many as 65 percent of Cuban voters may have voted for Lawton Chiles, while only 35 percent voted for Martínez. Others estimated that Martínez may have polled a majority of Cuban votes (as high as 59 percent), but his support was not as overwhelming as he needed in order to retain the governorship.

Martínez was soundly defeated by Chiles in several precincts in Dade County (Miami), the heart of Cuban country, and also in Orlando, Florida's heavily Hispanic precincts (Parker 1990). In either case, Martínez's defeat was atributed to the Cuban vote or lack of it in 1990. Martínez received some consolation later when President George Bush appointed him as the new "drug Czar" to coordinate the government's anti-drug efforts. Martínez had established a reputation for his tough anti-drug policies, which stressed tough penalties, law enforcement, and prison construction over treatment and prevention (*Albuquerque Journal* December 1, 1990).

California was the only state where Republican prospects for Hispanic votes were realized. It is estimated that Republican senator Pete Wilson received 32 percent of the Hispanic vote, which was better than George Bush's 27 percent in 1988. The added Hispanic votes were sufficient to help Wilson win in the closely contested election (Parker 1990).

In New Mexico, Hispanic voters maintained their record as the staunchest Democratic supporters and as a core vote of the Democratic party. The Republican candidate, Frank Bond, campaigned extensively in the northern Hispanic counties and emphasized his Hispanic linkages (as a native of Santa Fe with a graduate degree in Spanish literature). He narrated Spanish political advertisements that were broadcast in Spanish radio stations and pointed out that his Spanish-speaking ability would enable him to "communicate" better with Hispanics. Bond's efforts fell short as liberal Democrat Bruce King carried every Hispanic county with wide margins. King, for example, carried Santa Fe county with 11,000 votes, Río Arriba with 4,700 votes, and San Miguel with 4,000 votes. Of no small importance for King was that his running mate (in New Mexico the governor and lieutenant governor run as a team) was Casey Luna, a popular and well-known Hispanic car sales agent. Hispanics also captured four other state-level elective offices in New Mexico, those of secretary of state (Stephanie Gonzales), state auditor (Robert Vigil), land commissioner (Jim Baca), and corporation commissioner (Eric Serna) (*Albuquerque Journal* November 7, 1990).

The impact that Hispanic voters had in the outcomes of the above elections indicate that, even with less than overwhelming participation and cohesion, Hispanics are able to swing an election one way or another in a key state and that the major parties can no longer ignore their political importance.

A Profile and Issue Orientations of Hispanic Voters

In addition to providing some insight into the candidate and partisan preferences of Hispanic voters, some of the recent public opinion polls have provided us with a better picture of the demographic character of Hispanic voters and their issue orientations. Table 7 contains a summary of exit polling conducted by the Southwest Voter Research Institute among Mexican-American voters in California, Texas, and New Mexico following the 1988 presidential election. Although the table does not provide data for Cubans and Puerto Ricans, it does provide a very comprehensive view of the Mexican-American voters. Statistics that are of special interest are that Hispanic women outnumber men as voters in all three states and that from one-fourth to one-third of Hispanic voters are union members. Almost half of Hispanic voters are under 35 years of age, suggesting to parties and candidates that age and gender are two additional factors to consider in appealing to the Hispanic vote. Just over half of the Hispanic voters have completed no more than a high school education, and no more than one-fifth are college graduates. About one-fifth of Hispanic voters (over one-half in Texas) earn incomes of less than $10,000, which would be considered poverty level, and over two-thirds of Hispanic voters earn less than $30,000. Although low levels of education and income have both been associated with non-participation among Americans, their socioeconomic conditions have apparently not deterred Hispanics from voting participation. Although more Hispanics identify as liberals than conservatives, most apparently do not consider themselves as ideologues, as half identify as "in betweens" in identifying ideological preferences. As evidenced by their voting, three-fourths of Hispanics identify as Democrats and less than one-fifth as Republicans.

The issue orientations of Hispanic voters present some contrast to those of Americans in general and even to those of blacks, particularly in regard to those concerns that have been related to their ethnicity. Table 8 summarizes the responses by Hispanic, Anglo, and black voters to questions asked during an exit poll conducted by Southwest Voter Research Institute following the 1988 presidential election.

On several social issues Hispanics closely approximated black sentiments reflecting the similarities in their socioeconomic background. For example, three-fourths of Hispanics favored a national health insurance program, compared to four-fifths for blacks and only three-fifths of Anglo voters. Hispanics also showed great support for federal day-care funding (72 percent), with 68 percent of blacks and only 58 percent of Anglos favoring such a program. Hispanics, like blacks, were similarly opposed to cutting social programs in order to reduce the budget deficit.

On issues of direct concern to Hispanics, they were more polarized from blacks and Anglo voters. For example, on the issue of granting temporary amnesty to Central American refugees, over half of Hispanics expressed support, as compared to only 45 percent of Anglos and

TABLE 7

Profile of Mexican-American Voters California, Texas and New Mexico

Category of M-A Voters	California %	Texas %	New Mexico %
Gender			
Males	48	47	48
Females	52	53	52
Union Membership			
Union Members	38	26	35
Non-union Members	62	74	65
Age Groups			
18-25	19	20	16
26-35	29	29	25
36-45	20	21	27
46-55	14	14	13
56-65	11	10	11
66+	7	6	7
Education			
Not H.S. Graduate	24	27	15
H.S. Graduate	25	30	38
Some College	31	25	28
College Graduate	14	12	12
Post Graduate	6	5	7
Household Income			
Less than $10k	16	28	21
$10-$20k	22	23	26
$20-$30k	18	20	20
$30-$40k	18	13	14
$40-$50k	12	8	10
$50k or more	14	8	10
Ideology			
Liberal	27	28	27
Conservative	23	24	22
In between	50	47	51
Party Affiliation			
Democrat	72	76	73
Republican	18	9	17
Independent-Dem.	7	10	7
Independent-Rep.	2	4	3

Source: Southwest Voter Research Institute, Exit polls conducted on November 8, 1987, in California, Texas and New Mexico.

blacks. Seventy percent of Hispanics expressed support for increased spending on bilingual education, as compared to 28 percent for Anglos and 45 percent for blacks. On the issue of declaring English as the only official U. S. language, both Anglos (65 percent) and blacks (51 percent) supported such a proposal, while 70 percent of Hispanics opposed such a declaration. These two issues indicate that Hispanic voters are most united on issues pertaining to the preservation of their language, which also finds them most polarized from other groups. Hispanics also showed greater support for making abortion illegal than other groups, although a greater number of respondents (43 percent to 41 percent) seemed to favor legalized abortion.

The 1988 Southwest Voter Research Institute exit poll also revealed some interesting findings relative to media use by Hispanic voters in the Southwest. English language media (television, radio, and newspapers) were the most frequently utilized by Hispanics as a source of information. About 86 percent of Hispanic families rely on English language television, 78 percent rely on English radio, and 84 percent rely on English language newspapers for information on news and politics. Meanwhile, about 28 percent rely on Spanish television and radio as an often-used informational source. Fewer Hispanics (about 19 percent) rely on Spanish language newspapers for information on news and politics. These figures sug-

TABLE 8

Views on all Selected Issues, in 1988 by Ethnicity in the Southwest

Issue	% Hispancis	% Anglos	% Blacks
Temporary Amnesty for CA[a] Refugees			
Favor	52	45	45
Oppose	26	30	29
Not sure	22	25	26
Cut Social Programs to Reduce Deficit			
Favor	20	29	18
Oppose	62	54	67
Not sure	18	16	15
Increase Spending on Bilingual Education			
Favor	70	28	45
Oppose	18	56	36
Not sure	12	16	19
English as Only Official Language of U. S.			
Favor	21	65	51
Oppose	70	25	37
Not sure	9	10	13
National Health Insurance			
Favor	75	59	79
Oppose	13	28	12
Not sure	12	13	13
More Federal Funding for Day Care			
Favor	72	58	68
Oppose	17	29	22
Not sure	11	12	9
Abortion Illegal Except for Rape/Incest			
Favor	41	33	35
Oppose	43	57	52
Not sure	16	10	13

Source: Southwest Voter Research Institute, 1988 Exit Poll results.

[a]CA: Central American.

gest that the best way to reach Hispanic voters is through traditional English language media, particularly television and radio. It also suggests that about 30 percent of Hispanics (perhaps the older population) will rely on Spanish language TV and radio for information (*Southwest Voter Research Notes* Sept.-Dec. 1988).

While the Hispanic vote has been incohesive as a swing vote in national politics, the data shown in this section have clearly demonstrated how the Hispanic vote may play such a role in the future. The concentration of Hispanics in the large electoral vote states like New York, Florida, Texas, and California make them a pivotal vote in a close election. Their impact on a national election could also be underscored by the key role Hispanics played in the gubernatorial election outcomes in Texas, California, and Florida in 1990.

In addition to impacting on national and state elections Hispanic voting continues to manifest itself in state and local elections with the re-election of the Hispanic congresspersons and state-level executives in New Mexico and Texas. There are many other instances throughout the country where Hispanic voter participation, as described above, has contributed to the election of Hispanics to congressional, state, and local offices. These will be described in succeeding sections on Hispanic elected officials.

A voter registration poster showing that education is a leading concern among Hispanics.

While it is still true that overall Hispanic voter participation remains below that of Americans as a whole, this data underscores the progress that Hispanics have made and are making in voter participation.

Hispanics in National Office

Undoubtedly the most dramatic political progress Hispanics made in the decade of the 1980s was in national office. At the dawn of the decade in 1980, Hispanics could count just five Hispanic congressional representatives and not a single cabinet member, although there were a few Hispanics in subcabinet positions in the administration of President Jimmy Carter. At the twilight of the decade in 1989, two Hispanics sat in President George Bush's cabinet, Secretary of Education Lauro Cavazos and Secretary of the Interior Manuel Luján. Moreover, the number of Hispanic members of Congress had increased to ten. At least four of the new seats were the product of congressional redistricting, which created new "Hispanic" congressional districts in California, Texas, and New Mexico.

Although it is difficult to equate political presence with political power, the more prominent role of Hispanics is an acknowledgement by national political leaders such as President Bush of the potential pivotal role that Hispanics can play in national elections. It is also encouraging that the number of Latino voices in Congress may assure a greater acknowledgement and sensitivity to the group in public policy making. In view of the precedent-setting standard, it is appropriate to begin by considering the appointment of the two Hispanic cabinet members.

Ronald Reagan appointed Lauro Cavazos, a Mexican American born in Texas and president of Texas Tech University, as secretary of education in September 1988, an appointment accompanied by expected fanfare. President Reagan called Cavazos a "sterling example of the magnificent contributions Hispanic Americans have made to our national life" (Reagan 1988). Some Hispanic leaders, however, questioned the timing of Reagan's nomination of Cavazos in the waning days of his administration as a token gesture to bolster the candidacy of George Bush in Texas. Representative Albert Bustamante, chairman of the Congressional Hispanic Caucus, commented that "people will see it [the appointment] for what it is," and pointed out that the appointment was an effort to draw attention away from a dismal Reagan record of cutbacks in federal education funding.

To offset charges that the Cavazos appointment had been a temporary expedient to gain political leverage

Former Congressman and Secretary of the Interior Manuel Luján.

and to fulfill a campaign pledge he had made in July 1988, Bush retained Cavazos in the cabinet after assuming office in 1989. However, Bush surprised more than a few people when he selected a second Hispanic, Manuel Luján, the recently retired Republican congressman from New Mexico, as his secretary of interior.

The appointment of Luján, however, was not solely prompted by his ethnicity. One of the more qualified persons for the position, Luján had served many years in the House Interior Committee and was the ranking Republican on the committee when he retired. Cavazos's and Luján's tenures in the cabinet were distinguished more for their precedent-setting nature than for particularly inspired leadership. Neither made dramatic progress in his department, and a mid-1990 media assessment of the performance of cabinet members yielded both a median to low rating. Nor did Cavazos or Luján offer initiatives from their departments aimed at addressing special needs of Hispanics. Cavazos instead angered many Hispanic leaders when he suggested in a 1990 speech that Hispanic parents did not take enough interest in their children's education. He was also criticized for his advocacy of policies to allow parents to select the school their children attended. Having antagonized the very constituency that his appointment was designed to satisfy, Cavazos found himself as an object of criticism by education leaders such as Albert Shanker of the American Federation of Teachers (AFT), who labeled Cavazos as ineffective. Such criticisms culminated in Cavazos resigning in December 1990 (Cavazos 1990).

Hispanics in Congress

As indicated before, the decade of the 1980s was marked by the increased representation of Hispanics in the U. S. House of Representatives. A brief review of the history of Hispanics in Congress and a review of recent developments sets in perspective the current status of Hispanics and the Congressional Hispanic Caucus (CHC) in Congress.

Hispanics have been represented in Congress since the early part of the nineteenth century and almost continuously since the middle of the nineteenth century. Joseph Marion Hernández was the first Hispanic ever to serve in Congress. He was the first delegate selected to represent Florida after the creation of the Florida Territory in 1822.

The next Hispanic to serve in Congress was José Manuel Gallegos, a priest who was elected as New Mexico's first territorial delegate to Congress, serving from 1853 to 1855. In the next sixty years of territorial status, eight other Hispanics would represent New Mexico in Congress. During their tenure these Hispanics made numerous and persistent efforts to secure statehood for New Mexico, and that status was finally achieved in 1912.

Two years later New Mexico elected Benigno "B.C." Hernández to its single seat in Congress. Congressman Hernández thus became the first of several Hispanics to represent New Mexico in Congress, making it the only state to have almost uninterrupted representation by a Hispanic in Congress. The distinction of being the first Hispanic to serve as a regular member of Congress goes to Romualdo Pacheco of California, who served from 1879 to 1883 (Vigil 1990).

In 1929 Octaviano A. Larrazolo became the first Hispanic to serve in the Senate, when he was elected to fill the unexpired term of Senator A. A. Jones who had died in office. Larrazolo had previously served as governor of New Mexico in 1919-20.

Dionisio "Dennis" Chávez, who represented New Mexico in the House from 1931 to 1934 and was appointed to the Senate in 1935, was the first Hispanic to serve in both houses of Congress. Chávez served in the U. S. Senate longer than any other person in New Mexico's history, from 1935 until 1962, when he died in office. During his tenure Senator Chávez sponsored legislation and pursued programs that were quite important for the Hispanic people. Between 1944 and 1948 he sponsored a bill calling for the creation of a federal Fair Employment Practices Commission, and he labored only to see the bill defeated by a staunchly conservative Senate. He was a strong supporter of the 1957 Civil Rights Act—the first civil rights legislation since Reconstruction, which created the Civil Rights Commission. He also supported the 1960 Civil Rights Act, which authorized the federal courts to appoint referees to help blacks register to vote.

Chávez was no longer in the Senate when Congress enacted the milestone Civil Rights Act of 1964 and the Voting Rights Act of 1965, but his earlier participation surely helped lay the basis for them. Chávez was also a strong advocate of organized labor and social legislation on behalf of the indigent, elderly, and poor (Luján 1990).

In 1964 New Mexico congressman Joseph M. Montoya succeeded to the Senate seat vacated by the death of Senator Chávez. Montoya, who had just been reelected to his fourth term in Congress when Chávez died in 1962, defeated Republican Edwin L. Mechem, who had been appointed to Chávez's seat. Montoya thus became the third Hispanic U. S. senator.

Montoya sponsored the Bilingual Education Act of 1968 and the amendments of 1974. He also sponsored the bill creating the Cabinet Committee on Opportunities for the Spanish Speaking, a bill for the training of bilingual persons in the health professions, and a bill creating a commission on alien labor. Furthermore Montoya was a strong supporter of the Voting Rights Act of 1965 and the amendments of 1970 and 1975 and other civil rights legislation of the period. He was also a consistent supporter of social legislation benefiting minorities, the elderly, labor, and consumers. Montoya was defeated in 1976 by political novice and former astronaut Harrison Schmitt. Montoya died shortly after leaving office, and since then, no Hispanic has served in the Senate (Vigil 1990).

Henry B. González (D-Texas).

The decade of the 1960s was an important turning point for Hispanics in Congress. Prior to this time only one or two Hispanics (mainly from New Mexico) had been elected to Congress. This changed in the 1960s as several Hispanics from other states were elected to the House. These individuals organized the Congressional Hispanic Caucus (CHC) in 1976, and several remain in Congress as powerful committee chairs.

Henry B. González, elected in 1961 from the 20th District (San Antonio) in Texas is chairman of the House Banking, Finance, and Urban Affairs Committee. The colorful, eccentric González triggered the congressional probe that uncovered the savings and loan scandal.

Ernesto "Kika" de la Garza, elected to Congress in 1964 from the 15th district in south Texas (McAllen, Edinburg) occupies the chair of the House Agriculture Committee and has been involved in most agricultural policy adopted since the 1980s.

Edward Roybal, elected from California's 88th congressional district (Los Angeles), has been the most outspoken advocate of Hispanics in Congress and, as chair of the Select Committee on Aging, has been a major instigator of policies for the elderly.

Puerto Ricans were represented in Congress in the 1960s by Herman Badillo and in the 1980s by Robert García, both of whom represented a district from the Bronx.

The 1980s witnessed dramatic developments that doubled the size of Hispanic congressional representation and the membership of the CHC. The 1980 census revealed population growth and shifts that increased representation of several Sunbelt states. The redistricting process, done in the shadow of the 1975 Voting Rights Act, had the effect of creating several new congressional districts with Hispanic concentrations, which resulted in the election of two additional Hispanic representatives. From the Los Angeles, California, area, Matthew "Monty" Martínez and Esteban Torres were elected in 1982. In Texas Solomon Ortiz was elected from a Brownsville/Corpus Christi district in 1982, and Albert Bustamante from San Antonio joined him in 1984. New Mexico qualified for a new 3rd district in 1980, to which Bill Richardson was elected after Manuel Luján shifted over to a new 1st district, encompassing populous Bernalillo (Albuquerque) County. When Luján retired in 1988, Hispanic efforts to retain the seat failed.

Three Hispanics entered Congress recently. One is José Serrano, a New York state assemblyman who was elected to replace García as congressman from New York's South Bronx district. Serrano thus became the third Puerto Rican to serve in Congress and to represent

"Kika" de la Garza.

the 18th district, which is made up equally of Puerto Rican and black voters (*Congressional Quarterly* 1990).

Another recent addition to the Hispanics in Congress is Ileana Ros-Lehtinen, a Cuban American elected in a 1989 special election to the seat vacated by the late Representative Claude Pepper. Ros-Lehtinen, a former Florida state senator, thus became the first Cuban-American woman ever in Congress and the only Republican and woman in the Congressional Hispanic Caucus (*Albuquerque Journal* 1989).

Ileana Ros-Lehtinen.

In 1991 Ed Pastor was appointed to the seat vacated by Morris Udall, thus becoming Arizona's first Hispanic congressman.

The Congressional Hispanic Caucus

The Congressional Hispanic Caucus (CHC) was organized in December 1976 by the five Hispanics then serving in the U. S. House of Representatives. The objectives of the Caucus were to advance the interests of Hispanics through public policies and to enhance public awareness of Hispanic issues and problems.

The primary mover for the organization of the caucus was Herman Badillo, the Puerto Rican congressman from New York, who saw it as a means to encourage greater unity among Hispanic groups in the nation, as well as in Congress. The stated purpose of the caucus was "to monitor legislation and other government activity that affects Hispanics" and "to develop programs and other activities that would increase opportunities for Hispanics to participate in and contribute to the American political system." Most importantly the CHC was founded "to reverse the national pattern of neglect, exclusion and indifference suffered for decades by Spanish-speaking citizens of the U. S." and to fulfill the need for the development of a "a national policy on the Spanish-speaking" (CHC "History" 1981).

Through the 1970s, the size of the CHC remained at the five regular members of Congress, who were joined by three Hispanic delegates from American Trust Territories, including Jaime Fuster of Puerto Rico, Ben Blas of Guam, and Ron de Fugo of the Virgin Islands. By 1985 the size of the caucus had increased to its peak membership of ten regular members and the three delegates. The only other recent change was the retirement of Congressman Luján in 1989, but Republican representation in the CHC was restored with the election of Ros-Lehtinen in 1989.

The CHC and Hispanic Public Policy

Even with its new members, however, the CHC has had difficulty agreeing about priorities, programs, and policies that affect Hispanics. It has been unable to arrive at a coherent national Hispanic policy or to develop the necessary legislative agenda, and it lacks the unity to carry it out. Because of the different personalities, backgrounds, and philosophies of the members, the caucus has had difficulty presenting a united front. Washington correspondent Paul Weick described the CHC as "more of an informal arrangement than an organized group," a handful of independent-minded members who had been in Congress a long time and who worked in tandem only when it was convenient (Weick 1983).

Of the many public policies affecting Hispanics in the United States, two are particularly prominent: immigration reform and the English as official language policy. The impact the CHC has on both policies may ultimately determine the importance of this organization as an advocate for Hispanics. Immigration reform was a high-priority policy concern in Congress in the 1980s, and the role of the CHC in the evolving policy has been rather marginal.

In 1983 several members of the CHC lobbied against the Simpson-Mazzoli Immigration Bill and were able to suspend action in the House and thus prevent its passage that year. Two CHC members appeared in a press conference following the suspension, claiming it as "a major victory" and "the first cohesive win" for their diverse group. The caucus, however, was subsequently criticized for being an obstacle to immigration reform and for vetoing the only solution offered to address the national problem of illegal immigration. Even in this victory the Caucus indicated differences of opinion among members. Congressman Manuel Luján said, "Everyone [in the Caucus] is opposed to the Simpson-Mazzoli Bill, but each of us has different reasons." The CHC only postponed action on immigration reform, for Congress continued debating the matter through the 1980s.

When the 99th Congress finally passed the Immigration Reform and Control Act of 1986 (IRCA), the CHC was unable to present a united position and its members split five to four on the issue. Although the bill provided amnesty to illegal aliens in the country before 1982 as favored by some members, it also provided for penalties to employers who knowingly hire illegal aliens, a provision opposed by most members. CHC members were able to push for some antidiscrimination safeguards, but overall, IRCA's passage underscored the CHC's inability to achieve consensus and leadership in a policy matter of great concern to Hispanics.

In 1990 pressure for further revision of immigration reform caused Congress to once again debate the issue. While the major reforms increased the number of visas available to about 700,000 per year (an increase of some 40 percent) and gave preference to certain professionals (scientists, engineers, and top-level managers), CHC members focused on two issues of concern to Hispanics.

Although IRCA had generally accomplished its purpose of curbing the number of illegal aliens entering the country, CHC members were disturbed that a serious side-effect of the law was causing widespread discrimination against Hispanics. A study conducted by the General Accounting Office (GAO) revealed that as many as 1.3 million of the 4.6 million employers surveyed admitted that they somehow discriminated against job applicants who appeared "foreign born" out of fear of incurring huge INS fines, which are levied against employers who violate IRCA (*Albuquerque Journal* 1990).

Edward Roybal.

Congressman Edward Roybal introduced a bill to repeal the employer sanctions provision of IRCA, but the bill became stalled in the Judiciary Committee. CHC members were unable to generate further support to repeal employer sanctions.

CHC members, again led by Congressman Roybal, were more successful in defeating the provision in the Immigration Reform Bill of 1990 that called for a three-state pilot program to test the use of a "tamper proof driver's license system" to be used as a test for employment. The provision included in the Senate-passed version of the immigration bill was criticized by Hispanic congressmen, who called it the first step in the creation of a national identification card. Summoning images of Nazi death camp tattoos and South African passbooks, Hispanics won a procedural vote to keep the bill from coming to the House floor. Only after the sponsors agreed to eliminate the provision for the pilot program was the bill allowed to proceed to the House floor, where it eventually passed (*Albuquerque Journal* 1990).

A second policy issue of concern to Hispanics and one that may yet test the influence of the CHC in national politics is the "English First Movement." An increasing number of states and communities have adopted "English as official language" resolutions. Such resolutions, which appeal to the nativistic preferences of WASP Americans, are guised in patriotic rhetoric supportive of core American values such as liberty, freedom and equality. Although the resolutions nominally call for recognizing English as the sole language to be used for public documents and conduct of official public business, the implications for Hispanics are far greater. For example, they would preclude the printing of any documents in Spanish even if Hispanic population numbers would warrant it. It could also mean prohibitions against the use of Spanish by government officials in dialogue with Hispanic clients in need of social services or Spanish translations for Hispanic defendants in a court trial. By inference it could also threaten bilingual education programs throughout the country as a way of fostering an English-only society.

By 1990 seventeen states including California, Florida, Illinois, Arizona, and Colorado had passed such resolutions. California overwhelmingly adopted its English language constitutional amendment in the November 4, 1986, election. Since 1986 there have even been several congressional resolutions introduced on the issue, so the CHC will again find itself tested as an effective bulwark on behalf of Hispanics.

In the 101st Congress, English-as-official language bills were introduced in both Houses. Senator Richard Shelby (D-AL) the sponsor, denied any intent to discriminate against any group, but simply claimed he wanted to "maintain the benefits of a single official language of the government of the United States." Representatives Bill Emerson and Ike Skelton of Missouri also introduced a similar bill. Representative Norman Shumway (R-CA) introduced a resolution, co-sponsored by sixty-nine other representatives, to propose a constitutional amendment to make English the official language of the U. S. government (Beck 1990).

While both bills and the resolutions did not pass in 1990, the issue will invariably re-emerge in Congress and may well prove to be the biggest challenge faced by the CHC.

Internal Differences within the CHC

Some CHC members have had difficulty embracing caucus positions. Congressman González, for example, perceives that his role is to represent his district constituency, not serve as regional or state spokesman for Hispanics. This may account for González's decision to withdraw from active caucus membership in 1987. As one of only two Republican caucus members, Congressman Luján saw it as too oriented toward liberal programs and the Democratic party and on occasion considered resigning for this reason. Republican congresswoman Ros-Lehtinen may encounter similar differences.

Even beyond partisan differences, "the diversity is so great [among members], that it would be very difficult to arrive at a consensus," according to Margarita Roque, a legislative assistant to the caucus (Roque 1987). Because of these differences, the group ruled that unless all members agree, no caucus position is adopted. Such a rule, of course, enables one representative to veto any proposal even if supported by all the remaining members.

The Hispanic Caucus cannot and does not operate like the Congressional Black Caucus, which is not as diverse in its background and policy orientations. Nevertheless, according to Roque, caucus members do make a conscious effort to work together whenever possible (Roque 1987). This oversensitivity to minority member concerns is a drawback that has prevented the caucus from taking a more aggressive position on some issues of concern to Hispanics.

Though the Congressional Hispanic Caucus can certainly serve as a means to power, its history suggests that, measured by its own goals, it has not wielded much political influence. An analysis of the CHC, however, should consider the wider circumstances under which it wields political power, the limits of that power, and the objectives it seeks.

On this basis it is possible to evaluate the CHC on three levels: first, as a unified political group operating within the Congress; second, as a loose group of individual congressional representatives who wield individual power that is beneficial to Hispanics; and third, as a collective group of representatives who wield collective influence as representatives of the Hispanic community in national politics.

On the first level it is clear that, aside from a fairly concerted effort in opposition to the Simpson-Mazzoli Bill, the CHC has not functioned as a unified group within the Congress. The inability of the caucus to present an alternative to the immigration reform bill, even if they were united in their opposition to it, was an embarrassing admission of their lack of unity. This was further manifested by their failure to press for repeal of the "employer sanctions" provision of IRCA, even after evidence surfaced of widespread discrimination against Hispanics.

The CHC has probably functioned closer to the second level of analysis, that is, as a loose coalition of Congressional representatives who wield individual power. Several veteran members, particularly González and de la Garza, never saw it as more than a loose coalition; they remained basically parochial in their loyalty to their home districts. Because they have achieved substantial seniority, placing them in committee chairmanships, Congressmen de la Garza and González have been able to get things done for their constituents without tapping the resources or advantages offered by the caucus.

It is difficult to quantify the exact benefits received by Hispanics as a result of the efforts of these House members because their work often benefits the public at large. Their advocacy of programs or policies is based on a desire to help both their immediate district constituents (which include Hispanics) and the wider Hispanic community.

On the third level, the CHC has not yet achieved the desired visibility as a collective advocate for Hispanic Americans. This is probably due to its lack of success in determining policy in any given area and to its inability to speak cohesively on any issue, due to its characteristic disunity.

Still, some progress has been made. A permanent CHC staff is in place and has begun to perform a variety of services for member representatives and Hispanics. This staff will likely push for greater cooperation among Hispanic House members and their staffs.

A method of financing CHC activities has been established with the annual banquet held during Hispanic Heritage week in September. A CHC Institute to coordinate the caucus educational programs and other activities has been created, and the CHC has gained visibility among Hispanic organizations and is recognized for its policy-making orientations in Washington. Moreover, the CHC Washington staff and the CHC Institute have begun to serve as a clearinghouse for collecting and disseminating information on Hispanics, including a *National Directory of Hispanic Elected and Appointed Officials* and its *Guide to Hispanic Organizations*. It also provides information on educational scholarships and fellowship programs for Hispanics.

The long-run effectiveness of the CHC will be determined by its ability not only to defeat proposals that are adverse to Hispanic interests, but also by its ability to develop and present cohesive alternative proposals. It is apparent that the CHC presently lacks such a decision-making mechanism.

Moreover, because of its small size and because of the importance of consensus building in the day-to-day operation of Congress, it is vital that the CHC present a united front on any issue it addresses. Even the slightest hint of internal dissension will greatly diminish its effectiveness in persuading other House members that the caucus position truly represents the Hispanic position.

Its inability to present a united front on a variety of issues deprives it of a very important strategic tool. Because of its small membership size, CHC's strength is insignificant, except in very close roll-call votes. Rather, unity is important because of its potential influence on the other 425 House members, some of whom have sizable Hispanic constituencies or who may be sensitive to Hispanic concerns. The caucus has already targeted many of these representatives by inviting them to become honorary members of the CHC, but it can probably improve the means used to communicate with them by a more formal process.

It is likely that a roll-call analysis would reveal a very high rate of congruence in the voting records of caucus members, with the exception of Ros-Lehtinen. We have the paradox of describing the CHC as a group that exhibits a high degree of congruence in voting and positions because of similar partisan and/or constituency interests, not because of their membership in the caucus.

In summary, the Congressional Hispanic Caucus has not yet achieved the level of influence hoped for by its organizers and desired by the Hispanic community. It is, however, still in its developmental stage, and the entry of additional Hispanic House members may be the needed catalyst for change. Indeed, projections of population changes reported by the 1990 census indicate that Hispanics may gain one or more seats in Congress. Four Sunbelt states with large Hispanic populations, California, Texas, Florida and Arizona, will pick up a total of fifteen seats in Congress after the 1990 census. If 1980 reapportionment patterns are repeated, Hispanics will gain some of those seats (Parker 89).

One thing is certain: the potential for the development of the Hispanic community as a powerful political group hinges upon the successful transformation of the CHC into a leading Hispanic organization.

Hispanics in Public Office: State and Local Levels

Like their progress in national office holding, Hispanic progress in state and local office has been systematic and recent. Until the 1970s Hispanic office holding was restricted to some legislative, county, municipal and school board positions in New Mexico and Texas and more limited and isolated cases in California, Colorado and Arizona. Since the 1970s an increasing level of registered voters, greater political awareness, and the combined effects of the 1965 and 1970 Voting Rights Acts, which have eliminated barriers to voting, have been improving the fortunes of Hispanics. This section reviews the nature and extent of elective office holding by Hispanics historically through the 1990s and highlights some important recent Hispanic victories in state and local politics and their implications for the future.

Historical Sketches of Hispanic Office Holding at State and Local Levels

New Mexico has always been the exception to the low levels of voter participation and office holding that has generally been the case among Hispanics. New Mexico was the first state to elect both a Hispanic U. S. senator and congressman. It is also the only state that has had sustained representation by Hispanics in Congress, in state office, in the state legislature, and in county and local offices since it became a state (Vigil 1984). New Mexico can serve as a model for Hispanic populations in other states.

A Hispanic, Ezequiel C. de Baca, was New Mexico's first lieutenant governor (serving from 1912 through 1915) and its second governor, elected in 1916. Octaviano A. Larrazolo became New Mexico's fourth governor in 1919 and was later elected to the U. S. Senate. In addition to the many aforementioned Hispanics who served in both houses of Congress throughout New Mexico's history (see Hispanics in national office), several other Hispanics served in various state offices. Since 1912 they have averaged about 30 percent of the membership of both houses of the legislature. Hispanics, moreover, have been well represented in county and municipal governments and school boards in New Mexico.

In all circumstances the presence of Hispanics in New Mexico state and local office was made possible by high levels of participation and support from Hispanic voters (Vigil 1978). Yet, during the 1970s, New Mexico also experienced a new surge of political participation even beyond already high levels. In 1974 Jerry Apodaca became the first Hispanic since Larrazolo to win the governorship. What was equally impressive about these four years (1975-78) was the fact that Hispanics also held five additional elective positions in New Mexico state government (attorney general, secretary of state, land commissioner, corporation commissioner, and state auditor) and two positions in the state supreme court and state court of appeals, respectively (Vigil 1978). In 1982 Toney Anaya became the fourth Hispanic and the second in recent history to be elected governor of New Mexico.

Both Apodaca and Anaya used their positions as the highest ranking elected state officials to articulate Hispanic problems and concerns, enhance the visibility of Hispanic politics, and to urge greater unity among the diverse Hispanic communities. Both also suffered adverse public response from their non-Hispanic constituency in New Mexico for their activism (Vigil 1987).

Next to New Mexico, Texas is the other state that has experienced a moderate level of Hispanic participation in political office holding, particularly at the local level. However, Hispanic participation in Texas has not been spread out over the entire state but has been most concentrated in particular areas with large Hispanic populations and a tradition of political involvement, such as San Antonio, Corpus Christi, and Laredo among other south Texas regions. Hispanic political activism in these Texas communities began in the 1920s, with the creation of groups such as the League of United Latin American Citizens (LULAC), despite the harsh political environment.

After World War II political activity accelerated, with LULAC becoming more activist politically and with new groups forming, such as the American GI Forum, a leading civic action group. Notable success was achieved in Hispanic voter registration and office holding in the 1960s through the Political Association of Spanish Speaking Organization (PASO), which worked within the structure of the Democratic Party.

In the 1970's, following the Chicano movement, La Raza Unida Party (LRUP) emerged and spread from its base in Crystal City and Zavala County into a state-level minor party, which held a state party nominating convention in 1972 and fielded a slate of candidates for state office headed by gubernatorial candidate Ramsey Muñiz,

LULAC Council Number 1 in 1940.

a lawyer from Waco, Texas. LRUP again fielded candidates in the 1974 statewide elections and succeeded in winning most county offices in Zavala County (Vigil 1978). In recent years Hispanic political activity has been channeled through traditional parties (especially the Democratic party), but the experience with PASO and LRUP were important in the political development of Hispanics in Texas.

In California, Hispanic political activity before the 1980s was sparse and limited to local governmental positions. Early community development and political organizational activity was begun by the Community Service Organization (CSO) in the 1940s and continued by the Mexican American Political Association (MAPA) in the 1960s. One of the few early attempts by Hispanics for state office in California occurred in 1954, when CSO sponsored the candidacies of Edward Roybal for lieutenant governor and Henry López for secretary of state. Both candidates lost, a fact attributed to lukewarm Democratic party support for the Hispanic candidates. This defeat contributed to the creation of MAPA, which was more politically neutral than CSO, which had affiliated with the Democrats.

One of the organizers of CSO and MAPA was Roybal, who served as a Los Angeles city councilor from 1949 to 1962, when he was elected to Congress. MAPA activities in the 1960s also contributed to the elections of two state assemblymen, three superior court judges, and three municipal court judges and other local officials. Its most important victory was the election of Roybal to Congress (Vigil 1978).

In Arizona, the election of Raúl Castro as governor in 1974 would appear to represent a significant measure of Hispanic influence in that state. That election, however, was a unique occurrence and, rather than reflecting widespread Hispanic influence and support, was largely a personal achievement of Castro himself. Castro, a son of Mexican immigrants, settled in Tucson, Arizona, in 1916. A graduate of the University of Tucson Law School, he embarked on a brilliant career as district attorney for Pima (Tucson) County (1954-58); judge of the superior court (1958-64); and then served as U. S. ambassador to El Salvador and Boliva. After returning to Arizona and entering private law practice, Castro was elected governor in 1974 as a Democrat in one of the more conservative states in the Union. Although Castro received overwhelming support from Hispanics, he won as a moderate Democrat who received support from conservative as well as moderate Democrats and Republicans (Vigil 1978).

As in Texas, California, and Arizona, Hispanic political activity in Colorado was limited to local-level office holding in particular regions of the state, in this case rural southern Colorado communities such as Pueblo and Trinidad. The political cultures of a few southern Colorado counties such as Las Animas (Trinidad) resembled that of northern New Mexico. Notable Hispano patrones were men such as Casimiro Barela, José Urbano Vigil, Teodoro Abeyta, José Aguilar, and J. M. Madrid. Barela of Las Animas, the archetype patron, served on different occasions as justice of the peace, sheriff, assessor, treasurer, and probate judge. In 1876 he was elected to the Colorado state senate, where he served until his death in 1920 (Taylor and West 1973).

Although lacking sufficient numbers to impact Colorado state government, Hispanics have retained county and municipal level offices and represented other counties in the state legislature through the twentieth century. Federico Peña was elected mayor of Denver in 1983, thus becoming the highest ranking Hispanic elected official in Colorado in modern history.

The political fortunes of Puerto Ricans in New York have not been as great as those of the Mexican Americans in the Southwest. Although there are, as indicated earlier, over a million Puerto Ricans in New York (about 10 percent of the population), only about 30 percent are registered to vote. This has meant that relatively few Puerto Ricans have been represented in New York City government in a few city council positions. Instead, the political success of Puerto Ricans has been more closely entwined with single individuals.

The earliest of these was Herman Badillo, who represented the 21st District (the South Bronx) in Congress. Badillo, the first Puerto Rican politician to achieve national stature, was born in Caguas, Puerto Rico, in 1929 and migrated to New York as a youngster. Educated at City College of New York and Brooklyn College, where he received his law degree in 1954, Badillo entered law practice in 1955. In 1962 he served as deputy commissioner of the New York City Board of Real Estate and later as commissioner of the New York City Department of Relocation (1962-65). He then served as president of the Borough of the Bronx from 1966 to 1969. Badillo was elected to the 92nd Congress in 1970 and served four terms through 1977. After Badillo's retirement from Congress, he served as New York's deputy mayor for management (1978) and deputy mayor for policy (1979) and in 1983 was appointed as chairman of the Governor's Commission on Hispanic Affairs for the state of New York (Vigil 1987).

Badillo was succeeded as the sole Puerto Rican in the House of Representatives by Robert García in 1979. García, who had served one year in the New York state assembly and twelve years in the state senate, represented a congressional district from the South Bronx. García remained in Congress until 1990, when he resigned after being convicted of extortion in connection with the Wedtech Scandal. García's conviction was later

Herman Badillo.

overturned by the U. S. Court of Appeals (*Wall Street Journal* 1990).

Because of their comparatively recent presence in sizable numbers in the Unites States, Cuban Americans have had less time to develop a history of political participation. Already, however, because of their higher education and economic status, Cuban Americans have begun to make their mark in Florida politics. They were a significant force in the mayoral elections of Maurice Ferré and Xavier Suárez in Miami, Robert Martínez in Tampa, and Raúl Martínez in Hialeah. That their influence will continue to be felt in state, county, and municipal level offices in Florida is evident by Robert Martínez's victory for governor in 1986.

Hispanic Elected Officials in the 1980s

As of 1989 there were 3,783 Hispanic elected officials (HEO) in the United States. This is an increase of 581, or 18.1 percent, from the 1985 total of 3,202. Although the number of HEOs is less than 1 percent of the total number of elected officials in the United States (504, 404), the number for Hispanics is larger than in the past, and they are concentrated in a few states. In the seven states with the greatest number of Hispanic elected officials (Arizona, California, Colorado, Florida, New Mexico, New York, and Texas) as shown in Table 9, the number of HEOs has increased by 2,249, or 175 percent, in the sixteen-year period between 1973 and 1989. Just in the past four years (1985-89), the number of HEOs has increased by 504, or 17 percent.

TABLE 9

Hispanic Office Holders by Selected States 1973 -1989

State	1973	1989	Number of Increase	% of Change
Arizona	95	268	173	+182
California	231	580	349	+151
Colorado	125	208	83	+66
Florida	13	62	49	+377
New Mexico	366	647	281	+77
New York	10	71	61	+610
Texas	565	1,693	1,128	+200
Total	1,405	3,529	2,124	+151

Source: NALEO Education Fund, *1989 National Roster of Hispanic Elected Officials.*

The greatest increase in actual numbers of HEOs in the sixteen-year period was in Texas, where 1,128 more Hispanics were in office in 1985 than in 1972. Part of the reason for the sharp increase in office holders in Texas is due to the fact that with 254 counties with 1,200 elected officials and over 12,000 municipal governments, Texas affords much more office holding than other states like California, which has only 58 counties and 500 municipalities. Also, intensive voter registration drives following the elimination of many restrictive barriers in the last ten years have greatly increased the number of Hispanics seeking elective office. What is encouraging is that all states except New Mexico have seen increases of over 100 percent. New York increased its number of elected Hispanics by 710 percent, even though the number of HEOs (71) is far below what it should be as a proportion of the population. Florida also increased by 376 percent, even though its number of HEOs (62) is also below its population ratio. New Mexico only increased by 77 percent, but that is because of its already high number of elected officials. However, even there, the 281 additional officials is a large increase. California has also made notable progress, increasing its number of HEOs by 349 or 151 percent (NALEO Roster 1989).

Table 10 shows that the number of HEOs is distributed throughout the country, although many states have only one or a few Hispanic elected officials. The greatest concentration of HEOs is in the southwestern states of Texas (1,693), New Mexico (647), California (580), Arizona (268), and Colorado (208). Three states, Texas, New Mexico, and California, in fact, account for over 75 percent of the HEOs in the whole country. This is because Texas (20 percent) and California (30 percent) have the largest Hispanic populations, and New Mexico has the highest proportion of Hispanics (37 percent) in its population. Midwestern states such as Illinois with 41 and Michigan with 10 are also beginning to see a rise in

TABLE 10

Hispanic Elected Officials by State, 1989

State	Hispanic Elected Officials
Alaska	2
Arizona	268
Arkansas	1
California	580
Colorado	208
Connecticut	17
Delaware	2
Florida	62
Hawaii	1
Idaho	2
Illinois	41
Indiana	9
Iowa	1
Kansas	7
Louisiana	7
Maryland	1
Massachusetts	7
Michigan	10
Minnesota	5
Missouri	4
Montana	4
Nebraska	4
Nevada	5
New Jersey	53
New Mexico	647
New York	71
Ohio	8
Oklahoma	5
Oregon	10
Pennsylvania	9
Rhode Island	1
South Carolina	1
Texas	1,693
Utah	4
Washington	18
Wisconsin	5
Wyoming	10
Total	**3,783**

Source: NALEO Education Fund, *1989 National Roster of Hispanic Elected Officials.*

Hispanic elected officials. The nature of elected offices currently held by Hispanics suggests a pattern that deserves analysis. Table 11 shows that the great majority (97 percent) of HEOs held office at the local level. This indicates that Hispanics have as yet been unable (outside of New Mexico) to make significant inroads in state and national office. On the other hand, it also indicates that there is a large pool of talented HEOs who are beginning to receive local-level training and experience in elective positions and who may make further inroads into the state and national scene in the years to come. Table 11 also shows that by far the greatest number of HEOs are in school boards (35.4 percent), municipal government (31.1 percent), law enforcement/judicial positions (15.2 percent), and county government (8.9 percent).

One interesting statistic not reflected in Table 11 relates to the gender of HEOs. Stereotypes about Hispanic culture would suggest that few women participate in political affairs. The truth is that more Hispanic women vote than men; and while the number of Hispanic women in public office is underrepresented, the proportion of Hispanic women to Hispanic men is the same as in the American population as a whole. Also, Hispanic women hold a similar percentage (20 percent) of elective offices as women in the national population (NALEO Roster 1989).

In 1989 Florida was the only state with a Hispanic governor (Bob Martínez) and New Mexico the only state with other state Hispanic elective officials. These include Rebecca Vigil-Girón, secretary of state; and Eric Serna and Jerome Block, corporation commissioners. Martínez, as indicated earlier, lost his governorship in 1990, while New Mexico retained five state elected officials, and Texas gained one.

Of the various elective positions, service in the state legislature is particularly important because of its direct role in policy making and as an entrée to state and national office. Thus a review of HEOs in state legislatures is most appropriate.

In 1990 Hispanics held a total of 127 state legislative positions, spread out over nineteen states. New Mexico had the greatest number of Hispanics in its legislature, with 15 of 42 members in the state senate (36 percent)

TABLE 11

Hispanic Elected Officials by Level of Government and Office Held, 1989

Office Held	Number	Percentage
Federal Level		
U. S. Senators	0	0.00
U. S. Representatives	10	0.26
State Level		
Governors	1	0.03
State Executives	4	0.11
State Legislators	128	3.38
Local Level		
County Officials	338	8.93
Municipal Officials	1,178	31.14
Law Enforcement/Judicial	575	15.20
School Boards	1,340	35.42
Special Districts	209	5.52
Total	**3,783**	

Source: NALEO Education Fund, *1989 National Roster of Elected Officials.*

and 25 of 70 members in the house (36 percent). Furthermore, Hispanics controlled powerful legislative positions: Representative Ray Sánchez was speaker of the house and Senator Manny Aragón was president pro tempore of the state senate. Arizona had the second highest proportion of Hispanics in its legislature, 5 of 30 senators (17 percent) and 5 of 60 state representatives (8 percent). Texas had 6 Hispanics in the 31-member senate and 19 Hispanics in the 150-member house. California had 3 Hispanics in the 40-member senate and 4 in the 80-member state assembly. Colorado had 4 Hispanics in the 30-member senate and 7 in the 65-member house of representatives.

In New York the predominantly Puerto Rican community had 1 member in the state senate and 5 members in the state house of representatives. In Florida Cubans had elected 2 state senators and 8 state representatives. Illinois had 1 Hispanic in the state senate and 2 members in the state house of representatives. Kansas and Washington each had 1 Hispanic in the state senate and 1 member in the state house of representatives. Nevada had 1 Hispanic in the state senate and Connecticut had 3 Hispanic members in the state house of representatives. Finally, Alaska, Indiana, Massachusetts, Montana, New Jersey, Pennsylvania, and Rhode Island each had 1 Hispanic in the state house of representatives (NALEO Roster 1989).

Regionally the greatest concentration of Hispanic state legislators is among Mexican Americans in the Southwest. Although Hispanics are underrepresented in all states, these numbers reflect an awareness of the importance of state legislative office both for policy making and as stepping stones to higher elective office. In Puerto Rico virtually all the elected officers from the governor to the senate and house of representatives are Puerto Ricans, as expected.

Surely the most publicized gains achieved by HEOs in American politics in the 1980s were in mayoral elections particularly those of Henry Cisneros in San Antonio and Federico Peña in Denver. Although Cisneros did not seek reelection in 1989, Hispanics picked up the mayoral position in Albuquerque and retained it in Miami.

As of 1990 there were three Hispanic mayors in major metropolitan centers in the United States, Peña of Denver Xavier Suárez of Miami, and Henry Saavedra of Albuquerque, New Mexico. Peña, first elected in 1983, was reelected in 1987 but did not seek reelection in 1991. Suárez defeated another Hispanic, Maurice Ferré in 1985, and was reelected in 1989. Louis Saaverda was elected in 1989 in a runoff election over fellow Hispanic Pat Baca.

As indicated in Table 12, the total number of Hispanic mayors in 1989 was 245. The size of the municipalities with Hispanic mayors varied between medium-sized cities to towns and villages. The large number of mayors in specific states such as Texas (81), California (44), New Mexico (45), Arizona (16), and Colorado (16) is significant; moreover, quite a number of Hispanics head moderate-sized cities with populations of 25,000 or more. The respectable number of Hispanics in this most important of municipal offices indicates that Hispanics have been quite willing to tackle and citizens have been willing to entrust them with those important executive positions. Table 12 also indicates that Hispanics are well represented in county executive and judicial/law enforcement positions.

In retrospect, the most recent statistics on HEOs shows that the trend reflecting a slow but steady increase has continued through the 1980s. In the 1980s Hispanic legislative representation has increased so that they are at least minimally represented in nineteen states. Also encouraging are the increased representation of Hispanics in mayoral positions in large and medium-sized cities.

TABLE 12

Hispanic Elected Officials at the Local Level, 1989

Local Level	AZ	CA	CO	FL	NM	NY	TX	Other
County Officials								
Supervisor	9	8	0	0	0	0	0	0
Treasurer	1	1	5	0	16	0	21	1
Commissioner	0	0	10	1	43	0	100	6
Assessor	1	1	4	0	18	0	17	1
Clerk/Recorder	2	3	6	0	18	0	38	2
Auditor	0	1	0	0	0	0	0	0
Coroner	0	1	1	0	0	0	0	0
Legislator	0	0	0	0	0	2	0	0
Total	**13**	**15**	**26**	**1**	**95**	**2**	**176**	**10**
Municipal Offices								
Mayor	16	44	16	7	45	0	81	16
Vice Mayor	13	6	0	2	0	0	0	0
Council Member	76	121	67	23	172	4	359	95
City Clerk/Secretary	0	4	0	0	0	0	2	4
Treasurer	0	5	0	0	0	0	0	0
Total	**105**	**180**	**83**	**32**	**217**	**4**	**442**	**115**
Judicial/Law Offices								
Judge/Magistrate	23	50	1	10	67	5	193	20
Sheriff/Marshall	4	3	3	1	13	0	19	4
Constable	9	0	0	0	0	0	115	2
Clerk	2	0	0	0	0	0	0	0
Attorney	3	0	1	0	2	0	25	0
Total	**41**	**53**	**5**	**11**	**82**	**5**	**352**	**26**
School Board	92	293	51	3	165	51	611	74
Special District	7	29	32	3	42	2	83	11
Total	**258**	**570**	**197**	**51**	**601**	**64**	**1664**	**236**

Source: NALEO Education Fund, *1989 National Roster of Hispanic Elected Officials.*

While Hispanic political influence at the national level of government may still be in question, the data presented in this section illustrates that their participation in state and local government is encouraging. Nevertheless, the mere presence of Hispanics in positions as legislators, mayors, and city council members does not in itself guarantee favorable programs and policies for Hispanics. The need is for Hispanics to become participants in biethnic or multiethnic coalitions that control government. Hispanics have reached the first rung on the ladder of political success, and only increased mobilization and coalition-building will assure greater success in the future.

Hispanic Organizations

Hispanic organizations have been the vanguard of the Hispanic struggle for social, political, and economic opportunity in the United States. They have been active in every environment–social, legal, political, religious, business, and professional–and every level of government in addressing the problems and concerns of Hispanics.

There are two general functions performed by ethnic organizations. One is the advancement of group consciousness that leads to greater cohesion and political power; the other function is the provision of goods and services which address the needs and concerns of the minority. There are several ways in which the organization enhances group consciousness. The ethnic organization emphasizes core values such as history, culture, and language. It employs symbols such as folk heroes, songs, and emblems to encourage group identification. The organization also generates dialogue and provides other forums of communication enabling different segments of the group to identify with each other's problems. These forums also help groups find a common ground, generating resources and laying the ground rules for strategies of action. Ethnic organizations are frequently formed in specific business, occupational, or legal environments. In these cases the organization strives to improve the availability or delivery of specific types of services to the ethnic group.

Hispanic organizations, contrary to common assumptions have been plentiful but have faced inherent obstacles in advancing the interests of Hispanics. Among the difficulties have been the dearth of knowledgeable and skilled leadership, limited fiscal resources, and a constituency not always attuned to participatory democracy. In recent years all of these deficiencies have been somewhat ameliorated, and some Hispanic organizations have begun to make significant progress. One continuing problem is that up to now most Hispanic organizations have been formed around the particular Hispanic subgroups–Cubans, Mexican Americans, or Puerto Ricans rather than representing the entire Hispanic community.

In studying contemporary Hispanic organizations, the student is first impressed by their great number and diversity, contradicting the popularly held perception of Hispanics as a group that engages in limited organizational activity. Because of the many organizations involved, it is impossible to consider all of them in this brief summary. This section, therefore, provides a brief profile of some of the more prominent Hispanic organizations. A somewhat more cursory case study of MALDEF reveals the inner structure and workings of perhaps the most important Hispanic organization.

National Civic Action Groups

The League of United Latin American Citizens (LULAC) is the oldest and largest Hispanic organization. Founded in 1927, LULAC is headquartered in Corpus Christi, Texas, and has chapters in thirty-four states. LULAC's broad goal is to unite efforts of civic action groups to assist Hispanic Americans. It has been involved in litigation on behalf of Hispanics to end discrimination in employment, education, and public accommodations. Throughout its history, LULAC has been characterized by uneven and sporadic leadership and activity. In some circumstances it has been in the forefront of civic action, while in others it has resembled little more than a docile community service group. It has also been characterized by internal strife, as in the 1990 convention when it

Raúl Yzaguirre, Executive Director of the National Council of La Raza.

became bitterly divided over the election of its national director (*Albuquerque Journal* 1990).

The American GI Forum, founded in 1948, has served as a leading advocate for Hispanic issues, veterans' programs, and civil rights. Among its programs for Hispanics are the veterans' outreach program, the education foundation, the National Economic Development program, and Project Ser–Jobs for Progress, co-sponsored with LULAC. At its peak, the GI Forum had chapters in 23 states with over 20,000 members. Unlike its counterpart (LULAC), the GI Forum has been more visible on the local rather than national scene (Vigil 1974).

The National Council of La Raza (NCLR) is a broad-based service organization comprised of 100 affiliated groups which have coalesced into NCLR to advance the social and economic well-being of Hispanics. It works for public policy community assistance programs, special projects, and media attention favorable to Hispanics. NCLR publishes a bimonthly journal, *Agenda*, and holds an annual convention. NCLR's member organizations serve over 1 million people. It has a staff of forty operating offices in Chicago, Phoenix and Albuquerque (CHC *Guide to Hispanic Organizations* 1981).

The National Association of Latino Elected and Appointed Officials (NALEO) was established in 1975 to bring together Hispanic public officials in an effort to inform Hispanics of issues affecting them and to register Hispanic voters. NALEO sponsors research, conferences, programs, and information dissemination designed to increase awareness about Hispanics in American society and to increase civic and political participation within the group. Indeed one of the important contributions of NALEO is the publication of its *National Roster of Hispanic Elected Officials* (CHC *Guide to Hispanic Organizations* 1981).

Business Organizations

Recognizing that many of the socioeconomic problems of Hispanics stem from economic disadvantage attributable to insufficient capital resources, some Hispanic organizations have targeted economic development as a way to address the group's problems. Probably the largest Hispanic business organization is the U. S. Hispanic Chamber of Commerce (USHCC), organized in 1979 to coordinate all state and local Hispanic chambers of commerce into a national organization. The USHCC like its well-known forerunner, the U. S. Chamber of Commerce serves to advocate the interests of business, except that its primary concern is directed toward Hispanic businesses.

Probably the most successful Hispanic business organization is the National Economic Development Association (NEDA). Formed in 1970, NEDA grew to a total of twenty-five offices in fourteen states by 1981, with an annual budget of over $3 million. Funded by grants from the federal Minority Business Development Administration (MBDA) and the Small Business Administration, NEDA provides technical assistance to Hispanics developing new business as well as assisting the expansion of minority business (Vigil 1974).

Professional Associations

Other Hispanic organizations have developed in specialized occupational fields, the most prominent being Incorporated Mexican-American Government Employees (IMAGE). IMAGE seeks equal status and achievements for Hispanics in government work.

In the religious field the *Padres Asociados para Derechos Religiosos, Educativos, y Sociales* (Associated Priests for Religious, Educational, and Social Rights) or PADRES, the Spanish word for priests, is made up of Hispanics in the priesthood. This group has endeavored to alter Catholic Church policy to make it more responsive to its Hispanic clientele, who comprise one-quarter of the 52 million Catholics in the United States. It has also sought to increase the number of Hispanics in high-echelon church positions, such as bishops. In 1970 there were no Hispanic bishops in the United States. Since its formation, PADRES has effectively lobbied for the selection of seventeen new Hispanic bishops across the country (Vigil 1974).

One of the Hispanic organizations in the present category of professional organizations has distinguished itself both for its breadth of reform activity and for its success on behalf of Hispanics. For this reason it is appropriate to offer a more in depth look at the Mexican-American Legal Defense and Education Fund (MALDEF).

MALDEF: A Case Study

The Mexican-American Legal Defense and Education Fund

(MALDEF) is probably the best known of the Hispanic professional organizations. Organized in 1968, MALDEF is the Hispanic counterpart of the NAACP, engaging in litigation on behalf of Hispanics. Operating from a national office headquarters in downtown Los Angeles and four regional offices in San Francisco, Chicago, San Antonio and Washington, DC, MALDEF is administered by a president and general counsel under the supervision of a thirty-member Board of Directors. Although MALDEF maintains a staff of attorneys in each regional office, they are supplemented by lawyer members of the organization and a national network of referral lawyers from private law firms, corporations, and businesses who provide pro bono services.

A recent MALDEF publication states its broad objective in simple terms as being "to promote and protect the civil rights of Hispanics living in the United States" (MALDEF *Annual Report* 1987-88). MALDEF has employed several strategies in its effort to accomplish its goals, but the most important is the "litigation program" designed to implement legal action to eliminate discriminatory practices. The procedural strategy has been to initiate "class action" suits involving one or more Hispanics representing a larger group. In addition to sponsoring (initiating) litigation, MALDEF has also participated in cases as "intervenor," that is, as an outside interested party, and through amicus curiae (friend of the court) briefs.

The MALDEF objective is to select cases directed at traditional barriers to Hispanics such as abridgment of civil rights, inequalities in educational opportunities, discrimination in employment and education, police brutality, political exclusion in voting and electoral laws, and inequities in public service. MALDEF litigation and advocacy programs are divided into three main areas, including education employment and political access (Vigil 1990).

MALDEF's Education Program

Recognizing that education is the key to political, economic and social opportunity for Hispanics and alarmed at the extremely high dropout ratios among this group, MALDEF has concentrated on addressing traditional educational problems such as inequities in school finance and segregation that have adversely affected Hispanics. One of its more important victories occurred in the case of *Plyler v. Doe* (1982). In this case the school board of Tyler, Texas, acting in conjunction with a 1975 Texas state law that stipulated that local school districts could not receive state funds to finance the education of children of illegal aliens, tried to charge the children of illegal Mexican aliens for education received in Tyler public schools. The law allowed school districts to bar attendance altogether or to charge the parents for the education. Accordingly the school board decided to charge the parents of some forty Mexican children the sum of $1,000 per year per child. Unable to pay the $1,000, all of the children dropped out of school. MALDEF filed suit on behalf of sixteen of those children, claiming the law violated the equal protection clause of the Fourteenth Amendment of the Constitution. The state opposed the suit arguing that any person who is in the state illegally is technically not within the state's jurisdiction, thus the Fourteenth Amendment did not apply. The Supreme Court in 1982 ruled in favor of MALDEF and the Mexican children, stating that the children of illegal aliens have an inherent right to free public education, which is considered a fundamental national policy (*MALDEF Newsletter* April 1986).

Reflecting MALDEF's antisegregation efforts was a 1986 lawsuit against the San Jose, California, schools (*Vásquez v. San Jose United School District*). MALDEF charged that the school district discriminated against Hispanic students by means of segregation. Initially U. S. District Judge Robert Peckham ruled against the Hispanics, saying that while the district was ethnically imbalanced, the school board had acted "without segregative intent." An appeal to the U. S. 9th Circuit Court of Appeals overturned Peckham's ruling, saying that the school district "had intentionally kept Hispanic students segregated since 1962." The court ordered the school to end segregation over a five-year period, cease school closures in Hispanic neighborhoods, and directed it to initiate bilingual education and dropout prevention programs. The court also appointed an official monitor to assure compliance with the order (MALDEF *Annual Report* 1986).

In 1984 MALDEF initiated a federal lawsuit against the state of Texas (*Edgewood v. Kirby*) challenging the constitutionality of a public school-funding formula that discriminated against low-income and minority students who live in areas with low-property valuations. The suit charged violation of the equal protection clause of the Fourteenth Amendment, the right to an education, and uniform taxation under the Texas state constitution. In 1985 the Texas state legislature, at least in partial response to the lawsuit, appropriated an additional $1 billion per year for education. After evaluating the effects of the increased funding and noting some improvements, MALDEF attorneys based in San Antonio decided to pursue the case because of inherent inequities in the school-funding formula. The amended case finally went to trial in Travis County, Texas, in early 1987. On April 27, 1987, Judge Harley Clark ruled in favor of MALDEF, declaring that the school-funding system was unconstitutional under the Texas constitution. The state of Texas and fifty-five school districts filed an appeal to Judge Clark's decision in early 1987, and oral arguments were heard in the Texas Court of Appeals in April 1987. The case was ultimately settled in favor of MALDEF (Hernández 1988).

MALDEF Employment Programs

Hispanics have suffered every conceivable form of discrimination, exploitation, harassment, and abuse in the work place. They have been denied employment opportunity and job security. They have often been denied job training and other opportunities to develop job skills that would ensure their advancement and promotion to higher paying and managerial positions. Even if they achieved equal training and experience, Hispanics have been denied "equal pay for equal work." As employment circumstances dictate many other facets of life, such as home, school, and social life, one can appreciate the importance of employment. Unemployment or underemployment dictates the harsh social environment in which many Hispanics live.

MALDEF has addressed employment problems through litigation, negotiation, and advocacy. In the 1980s MALDEF sponsored or assisted in presenting the case of Hispanics involved in litigation that challenged discriminatory patterns in hiring and promotions by three large supermarket chains the H. E. Butt Company of San Antonio and Ralph's Supermarkets and Lucky Stores in California. All three cases resulted in victories for Hispanics.

In the case *Davis v. City of San Francisco*, MALDEF attorneys intervened on behalf of Chicano firefighter applicants in a class-action employment discrimination suit against the San Francisco Fire Department. In February, 1987, the U. S. District Court ruled that entry-level and promotional exams indeed discriminated against Hispanics, and the court directed that new selection procedures be devised, that no further appointments be made from an existing list based on prior exams, and that the city engage in expanded recruitment efforts for minorities (MALDEF *Annual Report* 1986 and 1987).

In a multistate case, MALDEF won a settlement on a discrimination suit filed against the western region of the National Park Service (NPS). The agreement called for the NPS to develop an affirmative action policy aimed at hiring and promoting Hispanics at all levels of employment throughout the western region of the NPS (California, Arizona, Nevada Hawaii and Guam).

In another type of employment issue, MALDEF filed an amicus curiae brief in the case of *Gutiérrez v. Debubovay*. In this case the Huntington Park, California, municipal court had a "speak English only" rule for its employees, which prohibited all employees from conversing in any language other than English except when engaged in translation duties. The bilingual court clerk who filed the suit challenged the rule because of the need to speak Spanish when serving the public. The court held that the rule was not justified by business necessity and had a disparate impact on Hispanics, violating Title VII of the 1964 Civil Rights Act (MALDEF *Annual Report* 1987-88).

MALDEF's Political Access Program

As indicated before, Hispanics (outside of New Mexico) have historically avoided political involvement and generally have had low registration and voter turnout. This has been reflected in the comparatively small number of Hispanic elected officials. Chicano leaders and organizations have long recognized, however, that active participation in the political process, beginning with registration and voting and extending into office holding and other forms of electioneering is essential for the future progress of the group. Politics is seen as the means by which Hispanics can begin to influence or participate in the decision-making process that leads to public policies in education employment, housing, and civil rights, which they need for future progress. For too many years discriminatory electoral arrangements and apathy have kept Hispanics out of the voting booth and without effective representation in capitals, courthouses and city halls. Accordingly, MALDEF has made the elimination of barriers to the political process a top priority in its litigation and advocacy programs. MALDEF has engaged in various lawsuits involving voting rights violations, including arbitrary and restrictive registration requirements and explicit voting procedures in conflict with the Voting Rights Acts of 1965, 1970 and 1975. The lion's share of MALDEF litigation and intervention has been directed, however, at apportionment, districting and gerrymandering problems. At-large election systems have especially been targeted because of their discriminatory effect on Hispanic representation on city councils, school boards and county commissions.

Shortly after the 1982 redistricting of the Los Angeles City Council, the U. S. Department of Justice filed suit, and MALDEF intervened in the case of *United States and Carrillo v. Los Angeles*, arguing that the districting plan gerrymandered the Hispanic vote. MALDEF presented evidence showing that in over 100 years only two Hispanics had been elected to the city council, despite the fact that the group had been increasing in population and in 1980 made up one-third of the population. The suit resulted in the creation of a second predominantly Hispanic district in northeastern Los Angeles and the consolidation of Hispanic strength in the San Fernando Valley when the city council adopted a new districting plan in July, 1986.

In a follow-up lawsuit to the city council action, MALDEF filed a similar lawsuit in August, 1988, against the Los Angeles County Board of Supervisors, charging the county with discrimination against Hispanics in its 1981 reapportionment plan. The suit charged that the districting plan, which did not contain a single "Hispanic district," effectively disenfranchised the 2 million Hispanics in Los Angeles County who make up 35 percent of its population (MALDEF *Annual Report* 1987-88).

In June, 1990, federal district judge David V. Kenyon ruled that the five Anglos in the Los Angles County Board of Supervisors had drawn district lines to keep Hispanics from being elected to the board in violation of the Voting Rights Act (*Albuquerque Journal* June 8, 1991). As a result of the subsequent redistricting, the first Hispanic, Gloria Molina was elected to the Los Angeles Board of Supervisors (*Hispanic* 1991).

In 1985, after participating in several lawsuits challenging at-large voting systems in New Mexico, MALDEF helped draft precedent-setting legislation that required that city councils, county commissions and school boards beyond specific populations to elect their members by single-member district. The law, which affected 70 percent of the local governing bodies, had the immediate effect of canceling a number of pending lawsuits. As a result of the newly established single-member districts, several Hispanics were elected to governing bodies that had never before been represented by a Hispanic.

One of the most publicized victories was in the case of *Gómez v. City of Watsonville.* In that case MALDEF challenged the at-large voting scheme that had denied Hispanics representation on the city council despite the fact that they comprise 49 percent of the population. In July, 1988, the Ninth Circuit Court of Appeals found that the at-large mayoral and city elections impermissibly diluted the voting strength of Hispanics in Watsonville in violation of Section 2 of the 1975 Voting Rights Act (*MALDEF Newsletter* 1989).

Education, employment and political participation are the triad of factors that have been the main thrust of MALDEF's efforts on behalf of Hispanics, and those combined factors will determine the future of the group in American society. The American historical legacy of Hispanics has largely been one of political exclusion and subordination, inequities in educational opportunity, and discrimination in employment. Because of its central role in pursuing change in these crucial areas of concern to Hispanics, MALDEF has placed itself squarely in the vanguard of the Hispanic struggle.

Poster for a women's conference sponsored by MALDEF.

Educational Organizations

A number of Hispanic educational groups have emerged both to advance interests of Hispanics in the educational field and to promote better educational opportunity and special programs (e.g., bilingual education) for Hispanics. *Aspira* of America, a Puerto Rican organization primarily concentrated in the New York, New Jersey and Pennsylvania area, seeks to improve educational opportunity for Hispanics. The National Association for Chicano Studies (NACS) has, since 1972, sought to build Chicano political, cultural, and educational awareness. Much of its effort is to improve and encourage Hispanic research and to encourage dissemination of new findings in Hispanic history and culture.

Women's Groups

Hispanic women's groups have emerged to advance the particular interests of Hispanic women, who suffer a dual minority status. Examples are Mexican-American Women's National Association (MANA), organized in 1976 to advance the status of Mexican-American women, and the Chicana forum, which is oriented toward advancing Chicanas in business and economic development. Another organization is the National Chicana Foundation, whose main thrust is in education and career advancement of Hispanic women. The National Association of Cuban-American Women (1972) and the National Conference of Puerto Rican Women (1972) have fought for equal rights for women of their specific groups and for Hispanic women in general. Both support the Equal Rights Amendment and seek to improve the status of Hispanic women in the nation's economic social and political life (CHC *Guide to Hispanic Organizations* 1981).

Partisan Political Clubs

There are a number of Hispanic political organizations that have emerged to encourage Hispanic political participation. These groups have launched voter registration drives, have developed programs to advance Hispanic issues and have encouraged Hispanics to seek political office. Some of the groups have maintained independence from political parties while others have actively served the interests of and have been supported by one of the major parties.

The Mexican-American Political Association (MAPA) is the oldest (1960) of the nonpartisan Hispanic organizations. It has launched voter registration drives and supported Mexican-American candidates and issues. The Republican party has made its appeals to Hispanics through groups like the Republican National Hispanic Assembly, the Mexican-American Republicans of Texas, and the Hispanic Republicans of Michigan, whose avowed aims are to recruit Hispanics to the Republican party to educate Hispanics about the American political process, to register Hispanic voters in the Republican party, and to support Republicans for office. Similarly, the Democratic party has worked through such groups as the multistate Hispanic-American Democrats (HAD), Mexican-American Democrats of Texas (MAD), and the Michigan Spanish-Speaking Democrats all of which have sought to increase Hispanic voter registration and support for the Democratic party (Vigil 1990).

This section has shown that the number and activities of Hispanic organizations is significant enough to consider them an important and instrumental part of Hispanic political, social and economic fortunes in the years to come.

Conclusion

The quincentennial observance of Columbus's discovery and exploration of the New World is an appropriate time for reflection on the status of Hispanics in American society. Surely one of the most important legacies of Columbus's discovery is a recognition of the important place Hispanic peoples occupy in American life. That legacy, however, is tempered by the continued subordinate status of Hispanics in American society as of 1992. Nevertheless, while the practices of American society have not lived up to the lofty ideals and principles of the Bill of Rights, Hispanics can savor their improved political status.

Hispanics continue to face formidable obstacles to the realization of their true political potential in the United States. Among these are external institutional policies and procedures discussed in this essay that continue to impair Hispanics. Also included are internal problems among Hispanics themselves. Hispanics are not a monolithic group of people with a single leader or set of leaders and a single agenda. They are an amorphous, fractionalized group with a diverse historical background and socioeconomic circumstances, variable leadership, and a plethora of concerns and problems. Indeed, although we have preferred the term Hispanic, it is not entirely true that Hispanics are truly a "political community."

Hispanics have not yet achieved "national" political prominence, although some influence has been acquired individually and somewhat vicariously by particular Hispanic leaders with varying levels of commitment to Hispanic problems and concerns. Even in the states, progress has been uneven; few states approach the prominence of Hispanics in New Mexico.

Although Hispanics have benefited from government policies in such areas as bilingual education, they are besieged by others such as immigration reform and the English as Official Language movement.

Nonetheless, the "seeds" for a political community exist in the common Hispanic cultural heritage—the language, the surnames, the religion, among other cultural manifestations which have been acknowledged by the people themselves and exploited by politicians and political parties.

Among the various topics and themes discussed in this article, several developments are encouraging for the future of Hispanics in American politics. Probably the most encouraging is the organized effort to register Hispanic voters. A recent estimate placed the number of Hispanic registered voters at 3.4 million, which was less than 60 percent of those eligible to vote. While this is less than the 67 percent registration for Americans as a whole, it is an improvement over previous levels.

It has also been demonstrated that advances in Hispanic voter registration have resulted in significant increases in the number of Hispanic elected officials. It can be assumed that these officials will, at least perfunctorily, address problems and issues of concern to Hispanics.

The emergence of a new style of Hispanic politician—the young, urbane, middle-class, college-educated professional—is another important development. This new leader builds on his Hispanic base of support by appealing to a broad cross section of voters—whites, ethnics, women, business, labor and single-issue groups—for further support.

Also important in the new Hispanic politics are the new organizations that have emerged to advance the interests of Hispanics through traditional lobbying strategies, protest politics, or, as in the case of MALDEF, litigation in the courts. These organizations will serve as the vanguard for the political mobilization of Hispanics and for the cross-group coalitions that will serve as the basis for the development of the Hispanic political community.

It is ironic that on the quincentennial anniversary of Columbus's discovery the United States is undergoing a distinct "Latinization" and that Hispanics are on the verge of becoming the largest ethnic minority in a nation of minorities. Since 1850 Hispanics have waged a determined effort to carve their place in American society and life. In the past two decades it has become clear that Hispanics will become a large and important ethnic group in American society. It has also become apparent that Hispanics are determined to share in the social and economic prosperity of American society as well as the political freedoms, liberty, justice and equality that are part of the American heritage.

Bibliography

Beck, Joan
1990 "Declare English Official Language of U. S." *Albuquerque Journal*, (October 16).

Broder, David S.
1981 *Changing the Guard: Power and Leadership in America*. New York: Penguin Books.

"Bush Names Hard-Liner Drug Czar."
1990 *Albuquerque Journal*, (December 1).

"Cavazos Forced to Quit."
1990 *Albuquerque Journal*, (December 13).

"Cavazos Resigns from Cabinet."
1990 *Las Vegas Daily Optic*, (December 12).

CBS News/New York Times Survey
1988 "National Exit Poll," (November 8).

Congressional Hispanic Caucus
1981 Guide to Hispanic Organizations. New York: Philip Morris Public Affairs Department.

"Cuban-American Win Boosts GOP."
1989 *Albuquerque Journal*, (August 31).

García, F. Chris, ed
1988 *Latinos and the Political System*. Notre Dame, IN: U of Notre Dame P.

Hernández, Antonia
1988 "La Opinión de MALDEF." *Réplica: The Spanish Language Magazine*, vol 19, no 870, (December):16-17.

Hernández, Beatriz
1981 "The History of the Congressional Hispanic Caucus." Washington, DC: Congressional Hispanic Caucus.
1991 "Shaking the House Down." *Hispanic*, (July):12-15.

"House Facing the New Year with Three Seats to Fill"
1990 *Congessional Quarterly*, (January 6):49-50.

"Immigration Reform Bill Boosts Visas, Workers"
1990 *Albuquerque Journal*, (October 28).

"Internal Strife Spells Trouble for Hispanic Groups"
1990 *Albuquerque Journal*, (May 3).

Jennings, James
1977 "The Puerto Rican Community: Its Political Background." *Puerto Rican Politics in New York*. Washington, DC: UP of America.

Kenworthy, Tom
1989 "González's Pugnacious Populism: House Chairman Draws Blood with S & L Hearings." *Washington Post*, (December 6).

"King Wins Third Term: Democrats Capture Executive Offices"
1990 *Albuquerque Journal*, (November 7).

Luján, Roy
1990 "The Groundwork for Civil Rights Legislation: The Fair Employment Practices Bill." Paper presented at the 1990 National Social Science Association Conference. Washington, DC, (November 7-10).

McWilliams, Carey
1949 *North from Mexico*. Philadelphia, PA: Lippincott.

Mexican American Legal Defense and Education Fund (MALDEF)
1986 *MALDEF Newsletter*. (April).
1986-87 *MALDEF Annual Report*.
1987-88 *MALDEF Annual Report*.
1989 *MALDEF Newsletter*. (January).

Moore, Joan
1970 *Mexican Americans*. Englewood Cliffs, NJ: Prentice-Hall.

NBC News
1988 "Decision '88: General Election Poll Results." (November 8).

"New Education Secretary First Hispanic in Cabinet"
1988 *Albuquerque Journal*, (September 21).

"New Member Profiles: Jose E. Serrano"
1990 *Congressional Quarterly*, (March 24):937.

1989 National Roster of Hispanic Elected Officials
1989 Washington, DC: National Association of Latino Elected Officials (NALEO) Educational Fund.

O'Connor, Karen, and Lee Epstein
1984 "A Legal Voice for the Chicano Community: The Activities of the Mexican American Legal Defense and Education Fund, 1968-82." *Social Science* Quarterly, (June).

Parker, Richard
1990 "Census Expected to Help Minorities Win Election Races." *Albuquerque Journal*, (August 25).
1990 "Employer Sanctions a Lingering Sore Spot." *Albuquerque Journal*, (October 8).
1990 "Hispanics Give Republicans Cold Shoulder." *Albuquerque Journal*, (November 18).

"Rep. Garica, Convicted in Scandal, Quits Congress"
1990 *Wall Street Journal* (January 3).

Robertson, John
1989 "Saavedra's Anglo-Backed Win Fuels Ethnic Factor Debate." *Albuquerque Journal*, (November 5).

Roque, Margarita
1987 Legislative Assistant to the Congressional Hispanic Caucus. Telephone interview, (October 5).

Southwest Voter Research Notes
1988 San Antonio: Southwest Voter Research Institute, vol 2, no 6, (September-December).

Special Edition: California Exit Poll Results
1988 San Antonio: Southwest Vote Research Institute, vol 2, no 7, (September-December).

Special Edition: New Mexico Exit Poll Results
1988 San Antonio: Southwest Voter Research Institute, vol 2, no 8, (September-December).

Special Edition: Texas Exit Poll Results
1988 San Antonio: Southwest Voter Research Institute, vol 2, no 9, (September-December).

Taylor, William B., and Elliott West
1973 "Patron Leadership at the Crossroads: Southern Colorado in the Late Nineteenth Century." *Pacific Historical Review* vol 42, no 3, (August):335-57.

Torres, María de Los Angeles
1988 "From Exiles to Minorities: The Politics of Cuban Americans." *Latinos and the Political System*. Notre Dame, IN: U of Notre Dame P.

U. S. Bureau of the Census

1989 "The Hispanic Population in the United States: March 1988." Washington, DC: Government Printing Office.

1990 "The Hispanic Population in the United States: March 1988." Washington, DC: Government Printing Office.

Vigil, Maurilio E.

1974 "Ethnic Organizations among the Mexican Americans of New Mexico: A Political Perspective." Ph.D. Diss, U of New Mexico.

1978 *Chicano Politics*. Washington, DC: UP of America.

1980 *Los Patrones: Profiles of Hispanic Political Leaders in New Mexico History*. Washington, DC: UP of America.

1984 *The Hispanics of New Mexico: Essays on History and Culture*. Bristol, IN: Wyndham Hall P.

1984 "Hispanics Gain Seats in the 98th Congress, after Reapportionment." *International Social Science Review*, vol 59, no 1, (Winter):20-30.

1987 *Hispanics in American Politics*. Lanham, MD: UP of America.

1990 "The Congressional Hispanic Caucus: Illusions and Realities of Power." *Journal of Hispanic Policy*, vol 4:19-30.

1990 "The Ethnic Organization as an Instrument of Political and Social Change: MALDEF, a Case Study." *Journal of Ethnic Studies*, vol 18, no 1, (spring):15-32.

Weick, Paul

1983 "Different Issues, Personalities, Hurt Unity of Hispanic Caucus." *Albuquerque Journal*, (December 18).

Weyr, Thomas

1988 *Hispanic USA: Breaking the Melting Pot*. New York: Harper & Row.

Puerto Ricans and the Door of Participation in U. S. Politics

José Ramón Sánchez

In 1990 the U. S. Congress considered a bill to simplify voter registration procedures and expand the pool of voters. This bill, however, never made it out of the Senate, although a House version (HR 2190) was passed that February. Why did the legislature of this staunchly democratic nation reject a proposal to expand citizen participation? The Bush administration and its supporters in the Congress argued that the problems with the bill were that it would increase the potential for voter fraud and create a severe fiscal burden for the states. One overlooked reason is that both Democrats as well as Republicans possess the Madisonian fear of an "excess of democracy." The registration bill could have been set aside precisely because it would produce more voters. The role played by this traditional American fear of mass participation not only explains what happened to this bill but why Puerto Ricans as a group don't seem to participate in U. S. politics at rates comparable to other groups.

No democratic capitalist society expects or has practiced the complete enfranchisement of its citizens. Switzerland, for example, that showcase of Western democracy, did not grant women the right to vote until 1971 (Therborn 1983, 264). Participation may be the key moral and philosophical principle behind democracy, but it has not always been the behavioral norm. If participation suggests an activity whereby citizens can approach government and influence, if not control, its actions, the truth is that the doors that give access to government are not always open or open wide enough to permit all citizens entry. And like a house, the doors of government exist to keep people out as well as to provide entry. Thus, while participation is an important aspect of democracy to study, one cannot fully comprehend how and why people participate without also having some knowledge of what doors exist and who they are designed to keep out. The doors of government and who gains entrance and why are conceptualized here in the notion of political incorporation. This chapter reviews the history of political participation by Puerto Ricans in the United States, but it does so in relationship to how Puerto Ricans have been incorporated into the U. S. political process, considering not only what Puerto Ricans have done to influence government but what they have been permitted to do in politics by the laws and political institutions of this nation.

Participation and Puerto Ricans

People participate in politics because they want to take part in and influence what goes on there. Jack Nagel defines participation as "actions through which ordinary members of a political system influence or attempt to influence outcomes" (Nagel 1987, 1). Defined in this broad way, participation seems both desirable and necessary for all citizens of a democracy. These assumptions about participation make Puerto Ricans in the United States a compelling and anomalous case study. The reason is that most studies of political participation among Puerto Ricans report that political participation, in all forms, is very low for this group (see NPRC 1983). While some of these studies make an attempt to find causes for depressed participation rates in social and legal institutions, the notion that participation is something both desirable and necessary casts a long shadow of blame on Puerto Ricans themselves. Most people ask: "Why don't Puerto Ricans want to participate?" and "Why are Puerto Ricans different?" But what if Puerto Rican efforts at participation are thwarted by the closing of political "doors"? Ultimately, it is only by understanding how and whether Puerto Ricans were politically incorporated that an accurate image of their participation can emerge. This chapter begins with a review of the history of Puerto Rican participation and then turns in the latter part to a discussion of the political incorporation Puerto Ricans experienced through the Liberal party and public housing. What we find is that this close look at the history of Puerto Rican political experiences themselves suggests Puerto Ricans do not simply have a dislike of participation. Puerto

Ricans have historically made deep personal and collective investments to participate in the political process. But they have not always been welcomed or heard.

Participation

Puerto Ricans have lived in New York City since the nineteenth century, although not in large numbers until after the First World War. Like any community, the rate of political participation and how participation takes place has varied over the years. Three distinct periods can be identified: The pre-World War I period, when Puerto Rican political attention was basically directed at Puerto Rico and the Caribbean. The period between the two World Wars, when Puerto Rican political organization and participation appeared to mushroom. Then, ironically, as the number of Puerto Ricans in New York City and the United States mushroomed, especially after the Second World War, participation rates plummeted. But the history of participation for Puerto Ricans over this period provides some clues to why participation declined.

This chapter concentrates on the political history of Puerto Ricans in New York City since the vast majority of Puerto Ricans in the United States have lived in that city. It was only in 1980, for the first time, that only 49 percent of continental Puerto Ricans resided in New York.

Pre-1898 Period

The few records and reports that exist on the Puerto Rican community living in New York City prior to 1898 suggest that it was small in size and not very involved in electoral city politics. Many Puerto Ricans came to New York City during the 1860s as a result of the mercantile trade in sugar and molasses between Puerto Rico and the United States. Most of these migrants settled in the Chelsea section of Manhattan with other Latin Americans. While they ignored New York City politics, like any exile community of a colonized nation, Puerto Ricans directed their political energies to gaining Puerto Rico its independence from Spain.

In 1868 a rebellion broke out in the Puerto Rican town of Lares, as Puerto Rican leaders launched what they hoped would be a revolutionary war of independence against Spain. That rebellion, called El Grito de Lares, was planned the year before in New York City by exiled Puerto Rican leaders, including Emeterio Betances and Ruiz Belvis. These Puerto Rican leaders in New York were, moreover, concerned not only with the status of Puerto Rico but with that of Cuba as well. Puerto Ricans in New York City worked with the Republican Society of Cuba to plan an 1868 revolt in Cuba as well as in Lares, Puerto Rico, against Spanish rule (Falcón 1984, 19). Puerto Ricans were, thus, not very involved in New York City politics, but they were very much involved and active in the politics of the Caribbean.

The interest of Puerto Ricans in New York City in the political affairs of Puerto Rico and the Caribbean continued throughout the rest of the nineteenth century. Puerto Rican educator Eugenio María de Hostos and Puerto Rican physician Julio J. Henna arrived in New York in 1869 and gave new life to the Puerto Rican and Cuban independence forces. In 1873 independence forces again invaded Cuba. That effort, however, failed to liberate the island from Spain.

Cuban independence became the main priority for Puerto Ricans as well as for Cubans living in New York during the 1890s. The arrival in New York of Cuban revolutionary José Martí in 1885 inspired the exiles into more concerted action. Independence for Puerto Rico was not forgotten but became a secondary issue to that of Cuba. This was illustrated by the creation in 1895 of a Puerto Rican Section *within* the Cuban Revolutionary Committee. By 1898 the U. S. occupation of Puerto Rico and the unsuccessful efforts of section president Julio Henna to negotiate more autonomy for Puerto Rico from the United States led to the dissolution of the Puerto Rican Section.

As early as 1893, working-class members of the Puerto Rican community in New York City began to organize themselves. This reflected the growing presence of working-class Puerto Ricans in the city and the need to address political issues concerning New York. Falcón reported that "in 1893, one of the first organizations of Spanish and Latino cigar makers, the Populist Committee, was formed in New York by Antonio Molina, Pachín Marín, and others to begin their involvement in U. S. electoral politics" (1984, 20). These efforts by Puerto Ricans to become more involved in New York City politics continued through the turn of the century.

World War I to World War II

After the U. S. occupation of Puerto Rico, the migration of Puerto Ricans to the United States expanded. Between 1900 and 1909, 2,000 Puerto Ricans were estimated to have journeyed to the U. S. mainland to stay (Calzada 1979, 144). By 1919 the Puerto Rican population in the United States was estimated to be at about 11,000, almost all of them in New York City. Another account, however, put the estimate of Puerto Ricans in New York City in 1918 at 35,000 (Iglesias 1977, 144).

The New York City that confronted Puerto Ricans at the time was dominated by the Tammany political machine of Richard Croker. Reform mayor John Purroy Mitchell, however, took office in 1914, but political reforms made little difference in how the city treated Puerto Ricans. "Under both machine and reform poli-

Political activist Bernardo Vega, c. 1940. (Courtesy of the Jesús Colón Papers, Center for Puerto Rican Studies Library, Hunter College, CUNY.)

tics," Falcón wrote, "Puerto Ricans remained at the periphery of party politics in New York during this period" (1984, 22).

One of the first reports of Puerto Rican voter registration patterns came from Puerto Rican labor and political activist Bernardo Vega. Although it is unclear what his sources were, Vega estimated the number of Puerto Ricans registered to vote in 1918 as about 7,000. The vast majority of Puerto Ricans were Democrats, though Vega found that "no serious effort was made [by the Democratic party] to organize the community and utilize its citizenship rights" (Iglesias 1977, 155). If Vega's registration number is correct, the two population estimates mentioned above yield a low of 20 percent and a high of 66 percent of all resident Puerto Ricans (adults and children) registered to vote in 1918.

Bernardo Vega also reported that an estimated 30,000 Puerto Ricans were registered to vote in 1940 (Iglesias 1977, 251). Since there were 61,463 Puerto Ricans in New York City in 1940, about half of all Puerto Ricans were registered to vote in New York City (Handlin 1962, 142). Whatever the exact number, the increase in registered voters paid some dividends. In 1937 Puerto Ricans in East Harlem elected Oscar García Rivera, a Republican and the first Puerto Rican elected official in the United States, to the New York State Assembly. The Republicans had selected García Rivera as their candidate as part of a strategy designed to upset the entrenched Democratic party (Baver 1984, 67). Republican support, however, was later withdrawn when García Rivera's voting record in the assembly proved to be too progressive for them. García Rivera's election signaled, in any case, the political maturation of the Puerto Rican community in New York City.

Puerto Ricans developed a variety of political and social organizations in the 1920s and 1930s. Aside from self-help and cultural organizations, Puerto Ricans also created two distinct types of political organizations (see Table 1). Puerto Ricans organized both radical, militant political groups and groups oriented towards the established, sometimes machine-based, political process.

By anyone's stocktaking, the proliferation of social and political groups in New York City was a very impressive achievement for a community that averaged around 35,000 before 1940. There were, for example, 10 organizations devoted to political affairs (or 1 per 3,500 Puerto Ricans). Also, while not every one of these groups lasted the entire period, the total number of civic organizations (whether political, social, or cultural) was 34, or about 1 for every 1,000 Puerto Ricans. In comparison, there were about 1,177 political clubs for all of New York City between 1927 and 1933. These clubs not only organized voting in the general population but served as social service agencies (Peel 1935, 320). This means that there were about 1½ clubs for every 10,000 New Yorkers, far less than the rate of political club organizing by Puerto Ricans at the time.

Most of the political clubs organized by Puerto Rican leaders such as Carlos Tapia were generally patronage mechanisms. Some of them were alledgedly involved in selling to the local "bookies" the protection of Brooklyn's Democratic machine in exchange for generous political contributions (Baver 1984, 6). The average Puerto Rican, however benefited from the work of the Tapia clubs and the Democratic political machine. For example, despite an estimated population of only 61,000 Puerto Ricans in New York City during 1940, half of all Puerto Ricans (of all ages) were registered to vote. In exchange for their votes, Puerto Ricans appeared to get government services and jobs. Over 400 Puerto Ricans, for example, were working in federal and local agencies in the late 1920s (Vega 1984, 147). The high voter registration rate also helped get Puerto Ricans elected to public office.

The first Puerto Rican elected official in New York City, Oscar García Rivera, won the assembly seat in 1937 in the 17th district in East Harlem. García Rivera was elected on the Republican ticket; however, after García Rivera's voting record in the assembly proved too progressive for the Republicans, they withdrew their support,

TABLE 1

Puerto Rican and Latino Organizations in New York City, WWI-WWII

Organization	Founded	Purpose
La Prensa	1918	Daily newspaper
Asociación Puertorriqueña	1922	Social
Alianza Obrera Puertorriqueña	1922	Economic, political
Alianza Puertorriqueña	1922	Social
Club Betances	1922	Social
Club Caborrojeno	1922	Social
Club Democrata Hispanoamericano	1922	Political, social
Club Latino-americano	1922	Social
Club Videro	1922	Social, political
El Club Hijos de Borinquen	1923	Social, political
Federation of Porto Rican Democratic Clubs of New York	1923	Political
The Puerto Rican Brotherhood of America	1923	Social, political
Porto Rican Chelsea Democratic Clubs	1923	Political
Porto Rican Political Club	1923	Political
Comite de Defensa de Puerto Rico	1924	Political
Nueva York Sporting Club	1924	Social, sports
Caribe Democratic Club	1925	Political
Casa de Puerto Rico	1925	Culture, economics
Ateneo Obrero	1926	Culture, economics
Hermandad Puertorriqueño	1926	Social, charity
Club Esperanza	1926	Social
El Grafico	1927	Spanish newspaper
El Machete Criolla	1927	Spanish newspaper
Metropolis	1927	Spanish newspaper
Camara de Comercio Hispaña	1928	Economic
Liga Puertorriquena Hispaña Eugenio Maria de Hostos	1928	Political, culture
Circulo Cultural Cervantes	1930	Theater
Pan American Women's Association	1930	Social, culture
Club Caridad Humanitaria	1930	Women, charity
Comision Pro Centenario de Hostos	1930	Culture
Mision Episcopal Hispana-Women's Auxiliary Group	1930	Charity
Sociedad de Mujeres Puertorriqueños	1930	Civic, culture
Emergency Unemployment Relief Committee, So. Bronx Headquarters	1932	Welfare, civic
Asociación de Empleados Civiles de Correo	1935	Social, economic
Spanish Association for the Blind	1935	Charity
Club Artes and Letras	1940	Culture

and García Rivera was reelected in 1938 as a candidate of the radical American Labor party, which had been founded and supported in large part by garment unions. García Rivera's election symbolized the political growth of the Puerto Rican community between the wars. Puerto Rican political organizing had become more oriented to labor and grass roots interests as well as to independence from the Tammany political machine. The Porto Rican Brotherhood, for example, established in 1923 in response to the growing needs and interests of the Puerto Rican barrios, was an attempt by Puerto Ricans "to define their own problems and needs and devise their own solutions" (Rodríguez-Fraticelli et al. 1990, 36).

Puerto Ricans began to discard political clubs during the 1930s. Instead, they began to join the movement for political reform in New York City, which at the time consisted of independent Democrats, fusionists, laborites, Marxists, and Republicans (Shefter 1985). When García Rivera lost his reelection bid in 1940, however, Puerto Ricans lost an important voice and leader.

Some argue that the void in political leadership was filled by Congressman Vito Marcantonio, an Italian. A leader of the American Labor party, Marcantonio represented East Harlem's 7th Congressional District during the 1935-37 and 1939-50 terms of office. Marcantonio was more than a congressman, however. He was a vehement and outspoken defender of Puerto Rican community interests in New York as well as an advocate of political independence for Puerto Rico. More important was the fact that Marcantonio's radical politics were lodged within a machine political style adapted from Marcantonio's participation, during the early 1920s, in the old La Guardia Club (Wakefield 1959, 262; Shefter 1986). As a result of Marcantonio, the Puerto Rican community became more politically active in elections as well as more militant.

Marcantonio "combined a personal, pragmatic style of 'machine politics' with a progressive legislative program based on radical principles" (Jackson 1983, 50). But rather than distribute patronage jobs or contracts to minor political leaders and a select few loyal followers, Marcantonio's "machine" was geared to fighting on behalf of Puerto Rican and other East Harlem residents when they had problems with their landlords or local government offices. Residents understood that unlike the corrupt Tammany machine, Marcantonio's political machine operated with a very simple principle: "people had problems: an intransigent landlord, a real or imagined conflict with civil service regulations, discrimination, unfair treatment by the city, state, or federal bureaucracy: and the congressman offered his services" (Schaffer 1966, 191). By offering his services to anyone who came by the office with no requirements that they contribute or join the ALP, Marcantonio and his multilingual staff indirectly built a large, loyal following that repaid his help with campaign workers and votes on election day. The loyalty of Puerto Rican votes came in handy during Marcantonio's reelection bid.

The Democratic and Republican parties engaged in an extremely unusual collaborative effort in 1947 to get rid of Marcantonio. In 1947 the New York State legislature passed the Wilson-Pakula Act that prohibited anyone from gaining the nomination of both the Democratic party and the American Labor party, something Marcantonio had done often before (Carter 1965, 314). Limited to just the ALP line, Marcantonio was forced to run against both a Republican and a Democrat in a predominantly Democratic district. Despite this legislatively sanctioned repression, in 1948 Marcantonio won reelection to the U. S. Congress by a margin of close to 5,000 votes (Carter 1965, 370). Though "opposed by all the organized power of anti-communism," Marcantonio didn't lose the 1948 election largely because of the formidable support he received from Puerto Rican and other East Harlem voters (Schaffer 1966, 196). Ironically, a Columbia University study reported that same year that Puerto Ricans could not and did not want to be organized politically (Mills 1948). This disjunction between fact and professed knowledge suggests how slippery the concept of participation is to observation and understanding.

In the late 1940s C. W. Mills and his colleagues at Columbia University declared that "the Puerto Ricans have no such organizational tradition, and no 'organized' Puerto Rican community seems to exist in New York City" (1948, 105). How could a community possessing so many political, social, and cultural organizations in the 1920s and 1930s be reduced to such apparent helplessness? Part of the answer lies in the nature of the Columbia study itself. It was a survey of Puerto Rican migrants, not of Puerto Rican organizations. Thus they reported that "only 108 out of the 1113 migrants belong to general organizations; only 6 percent of all the migrants belong to organizations which could be called Puerto Rican" (1948, 105). Even if the number of organizations in 1947 stayed the same as in the 1920s, the influx of Puerto Rican migrants coming to New York City during the 1940s would have increased the number of newly arrived Puerto Ricans unable or uninterested in participating. Existing Puerto Rican organizations "disappeared" against the background of the huge tidal wave of migration that occurred after the war. It may also be true that the poorer Puerto Ricans who migrated during the 1940s did not create as many organizations as the earlier migrants. The conditions of this last migration and the status of the newer migrants in the New York City political economy may help us to understand whether this was the case.

The Mills study did show that Puerto Rican migrants who had been in New York City the longest participated in political organizations at slightly higher rates than those who were more recent arrivals. About 16 percent of early Puerto Rican male migrants, for example, compared to 12 percent of more recent Puerto Rican male migrants belonged to political organizations (Mills 1950, 106). One obvious interpretation of this difference in participation is that newer migrants must go through an adjustment process. New migrants do not have sufficient experience to know how and where to participate. The problem with this explanation is that Puerto Rican migrants between the wars apparently created organizations without having much experience in New York. Also, new Puerto Rican organizations were created during the 1950s, though it is not clear that the newer migrants created them or that these organizations helped to increase participation among Puerto Ricans.

During the 1950s, the Migration Division of the Department of Labor of the Commonwealth of Puerto Rico (Migration Office) and the government of Puerto Rico played a very prominent role in developing Puerto Rican organizations in New York City. The Migration Office, for example, helped to create the Hispanic Young Adult Association (HYAA) (Rodríquez-Fraticelli 1990, 38). HYAA was composed primarily of young Puerto Ricans trained in social work who wanted to organize Puerto Ricans around local New York issues and to develop a new Puerto Rican leadership. Their hope was to use education and "effective social intervention" to solve the problems of the Puerto Rican community. HYAA eventually began to more closely identify with Puerto Ricans and in 1956 became the Puerto Rican Association for Community Affairs (PRACA). The Migration Office also helped to found the Council of Puerto Rican and Spanish American Organizations of Greater New York in 1952. This latter organization incorporated dozens of civic, social, cultural, religious, and fraternal organizations. The council served as an umbrella organization for all these smaller groups and every year sponsored stations near polling places to advise Puerto Ricans about their civic duties and literacy qualifications (Senior 1961, 101).

The council's efforts demonstrated that Puerto Ricans in the 1950s would register and come out to vote. Senior reports that "the Puerto Rican vote in New York City rose from about 35,000 in the 1954 election to about 85,000 in 1956" (1965, 102). During this time Puerto Rican and Hispanic registration in the city increased to about 175,000. Puerto Rican organizations, like the Spanish American Organization Council, estimated that there were 260,000 potential Puerto Rican voters in New York at that time (*New York Times* May 6, 1956, 48: 1). These numbers must be considered suggestive since there is no alternative confirmation of the estimate.

The 1950s also saw a proliferation of community organizations based on the specific hometown in Puerto Rico that was the origin or birthplace of Puerto Rican migrants in New York City. Thus Puerto Rican towns like Mayaquez and Caguas were honored in spirit by Puerto Rican *ausentes* in New York. About seventy-seven such hometown organizations in New York City were organized under an umbrella organization called El Congreso del Pueblo (Council of Hometown Clubs). The Congreso, like the clubs, was a voluntary, self-supporting organization. These organizations and their leaders not only provided important services to Puerto Ricans but began to provide Puerto Ricans in New York with an important footing for becoming politically involved in city politics.

Rosa Estades called the Puerto Rican hometown clubs "the greatest single innovation in the pattern of organization of the community [that] appeared during the fifties" (1978, 39). Indeed the clubs became a wonderful mechanism for maintaining cultural ties to the Puerto Rican heritage. It was also a vehicle for community organization that respected and mobilized on the basis of the natural, small town allegiance possessed by recent migrants from a newly industrializing Puerto Rico. Finally the hometown clubs were also an effective mechanism for the delivery of services (in housing, employment, finances) to the new migrant as well as for the delivery of cash and goodwill back to Puerto Rico. Thus, Gerena Valentín, a prime organizer of these clubs and the Congreso, explained that the organizing principle was kinship: "cuando organizaba por pueblas, pues venían los primos, hermanos, toda la familia" (Valentín 1989, 33).

The hometown clubs were also political organizations. The Congreso, for example, "was at the forefront of the struggle for better housing, [and] led mass protests and demonstrations against police brutality, racism and discrimination" (Rodríguez-Fraticelli et al. 1990, 41). Gilberto Gerena Valentín, who led the Congreso during this period, explained the political activism of the Congreso as a product of its working class membership. Thus, Valentín declared: "El Congreso era fundamentalmente una organización de clase trabajadora. . . . La clase media y burguesa no tenían ningún rol en este tipo de cosa porque le temían" (Valentín 1989, 33). One of the most important contributions of the Congreso and other organizations was the development of *El Desfile Puertorriqueño* (The Puerto Rican Day Parade).

The political importance of parading seems apparent. Communist regimes parade battalions of soldiers and weapons to demonstrate their might to foreign nations and internal dissidents. Capitalist nations like the United States have ticker-tape parades for heroes in order to remind its ordinarily market-driven, individualistic citizens of their common commitment and identity as one nation. While the hero may be on parade, it is the community and nation that are being celebrated. Puerto Ricans too have political as well as cultural reasons for parading.

The Puerto Rican Day Parade was started in 1959 (Rodríquez-Fraticelli 1990) as an offshoot of a Desfile Hispano, which began in 1955 and represented all Latino groups in New York. By the late 1950s Puerto Ricans not only began to conceive of their needs and interests in singular Puerto Rican terms but sought to express the unique aspects of Puerto Rican life and political desires. The Puerto Rican Parade was, thus, a coming-out party. It asserted the particular existence and goals of the growing Puerto Rican community in New York City. There are obvious political benefits to this. Public officials were made aware of the particular problems and demands of the Puerto Rican community. The process of organizing the parade and recruiting participants is also political. Communication between various Puerto Rican groups improves even if only on a marginal basis, since Puerto Ricans must see and hear each other as they march. The parade also creates a sense of group solidarity as everyone waves *la bandera* and exchanges smiles of pride and goodwill about their Puerto Rican heritage. Gerena Valentín, an organizer of the Parade Day, described how important it was to get as many Puerto Ricans of all backgrounds to participate, "Cuando organizamos el Desfile, tuvimos una lucha inmensa para que esta gente se envolvieran" (1989, 33).

Parades also create political advantages with respect to the non-Puerto Rican community. The participation of city mayors and other elected officials in the parade allows Puerto Ricans to make contact with public officials and draw their attention to Puerto Rican community needs. Rosa Estades explained that Puerto Rican leaders found that "in the organization of the 'Desfile' they [Puerto Ricans] made valuable political contacts both in New York and in Puerto Rico" (1978, 39).

Parades not only convey information and demands by a community, they also provide an opportunity for political participation. Parades allow a community to proclaim its distinctive, separate existence. But it is also true that a parade makes this proclamation through a benevolent, even entertaining medium. Ultimately parades assert not separation but integration into the wider society. This view of parades is consonant with the view that ethnicity is not primordial but an identity that emerges historically as people grope to make sense of their place in society. A parade in that sense is a "coming-out party." K. N. Conzen argued that the parade played just such a role in the nineteenth-century creation of a German ethnic identity in the United States. A variety of different classes and groups came together at that time to form a "German" identity. These people started a German Day Parade in order to defend, celebrate, and bind themselves together and, thus, enter "as a group into American public life" (Conzen 1989, 41).

The Puerto Rican Day Parade was a "coming-out party" for the emergence of Puerto Ricans as an ethnic group. Rosa Estades describes the parade as an inclusive organization, "a predominantly grassroots movement; it is a day for 'el pueblo' even though most Puerto Ricans belonging to all social classes participate and follow its progress" (1978, 40). Parade Day started at a time when Puerto Rican life in New York City had begun to come unhinged. The migrants had come to New York City for what they thought would be a temporary stay to amass wealth and return to *la Isla*. But the possibility of return on some permanent basis began to fade even as opportunities for employment in New York City began to disappear (see Padilla 1958, 301). The parade was not only a nostalgic reflection and celebration of Puerto Rican cultural traditions but an attempt to implant and keep these traditions firmly rooted here in New York City.

Parade Day tried to make being Puerto Rican something valuable not only to Puerto Ricans but to non-Puerto Ricans as well. New York City became *La Gran Manzana* even if only for one day. What was being asserted, or implanted, in the consciousness of other New Yorkers wasn't only Puerto Rican culture but the political and social contribution of Puerto Ricans to life in this city. Puerto Ricans were asserting that they were part of this city even as they celebrated their differences. Parades, in this sense, have become the preferred method for the city's unmelted pot of ethnic-racial groups to establish ties to each other. The parading of group uniqueness has become a shared New York City tradition.

The participants in the Puerto Rican parade marched with clothing, colors, music, and joy associated with Puerto Rican culture. But they also marched with banners representing public schools in the Bronx, community organizations in East Harlem, social clubs from Williamsburg, Boy Scouts, garment workers in the ILGWU, Aspira of New York, etc. In these symbolic and concrete ways Puerto Ricans established their ties and contribution to life in New York City. Many commentators point to the presence in the parade of mayors from towns in Puerto Rico as proof of how deeply political it is (see Estades). They fail to realize, however, that the politics were also about New York. The participation of all those grass roots organizations conveyed an important message about what it meant to be *Puerto Rican in New York City*. As Estades once said, "the history of the organization of the 'Desfile' follows the ups and downs of the development of the community, reflecting the difficulties of the organizational life of the districts as they struggle for a place in the life of the city" (1980, 87).

The institution of the parade prepared Puerto Ricans and non-Puerto Ricans alike for the next stage of participation. This stage was the federal government-sponsored attempt in the 1960s to get the poor involved in trying to overcome their own poverty, called the War on Poverty Program (WPP). President Lyndon B. Johnson hired Sargent Shriver to start the WPP and get the poor and other groups involved in alleviating poverty. For this purpose, Shriver identified the groups that would be included as "governmental groups, philanthropic, religious, business, and labor groups, and the poor" (Lowi 1969, 84). The plan called for the "maximum feasible participation" of the poor in the decision-making process of programs like the Community Action Program and the Job Corps. Puerto Ricans were naturally drawn to these programs by their twin promise of participation and ending poverty.

The Puerto Rican Forum was the first Puerto Rican organization to take advantage of the new programs. In 1964 the Forum designed a proposal to create the Puerto Rican Community Development Project (PRCDP). The PRCDP was a "clearinghouse for a variety of self-help programs" (Rodríquez et al. 1990, 41). The plan was to fund about sixty community-based groups that would help to increase family income, reduce poverty, improve education, and strengthen family life, cultural and community organization. After a series of challenges from city government officials and some Puerto Ricans in PRCDP who disagreed over strategy, the PRCDP came into existence in 1965 with an approach based on community action. Rodríquez-Fraticelli and Tirado argued that "during the early years, the PRCDP was a militant organization. It helped organize and worked closely with grass roots organizations, such as the United Bronx Parents. It also organized and actively participated in mass demonstrations to protest violations of Puerto Rican civil rights in New York City" (1990, 42). This militancy declined, however, as the PRCDP became controlled by a conservative faction in the early 1970s.

Many different Puerto Rican organizations were created or benefited from the War on Poverty Program. The Office of Economic Opportunity, which was the main agency in the War on Poverty, funded the creation of Community Corporations to allow the poor "to assert their influence in the community decision-making process from which they had been excluded" (Kramer 1969, 13). Seven areas in New York City with high concentrations of Puerto Ricans were served by community corporations: the South Bronx, Hunts Point, Lower East Side, Midwest Side, East Side, Sunset Park, and Williamsburg. These corporations established anti-poverty programs or funded existing groups in their area. They decided how to allocate city, state, and federal funds to programs. Out of the 26 community corporations in New York City, Puerto Ricans gained control of 10 (Estades 1978, 56). Control here means that Puerto Ricans either had a majority of the members in the corporation's locally elected board of directors, a Puerto Rican served as the corporation's executive director, or both. As a result of this influence, over 200 Puerto Rican organizations were funded through these corporations (Estades 1978, 56). A number of already-existing Puerto Rican organizations benefited from this funding. The Puerto Rican Forum, Aspira, and the Puerto Rican Family Institute are three such examples.

Along with helping to maintain and create Puerto Rican community organizations, the War on Poverty Program also helped to establish new political leaders, including Ramón Vélez in the South Bronx. Vélez has been described as a "poverty-crat" and "machine politician" because of how he used poverty organizations to amass political power. The War on Poverty provided a great opportunity for patronage politics. The community corporations controlled funds and jobs in economically poor communities. The corporations were also governed by a board of directors elected by local residents. During the early 1960s Vélez was quick to see the possibility of trading funding and jobs for votes. As a result, by the late 1960s Vélez controlled most of the antipoverty programs in the South Bronx. The core of Vélez's power was the Hunts Point Multi-Service Center and the Hunts Point Community Corporation. From this base, Vélez himself or a subordinate controlled "twenty different anti-poverty community and ethnic groups" (Bavers 1984, 72). Vélez was not, however, the only one to devise a patronage system. On a smaller, sometimes less organized, scale such patronage was prevalent throughout the War on Poverty period (Kramer 1969). Puerto Ricans and other poor people were encouraged to participate in antipoverty politics. But they were usually limited to electing corporation directors with the promise of receiving special services or jobs in local antipoverty agencies.

The War on Poverty programs, like the PRCDP, did little to change the poor conditions in which Puerto Ricans lived. Rodríquez and Tirado argued that the problem was that the war fostered the bureaucratization of Puerto Rican organizations. Bureaucratization created paid labor in place of voluntary labor. As a result, "dependent on government funds, many groups grew more conservative as their fortunes became increasingly tied to the political power structure" (Rodríguez et al. 1990, 42). Alfred López offers a more caustic explanation for the failure: "The War on Poverty was a war on us: the leadership, the outspoken, the educational, the strongest and the most confident" (1973, 307). The War on Poverty, in this sense, did not fail. It accomplished its mission of decimating Puerto Rican and other poor communities. But whatever the failures and the reasons for it, the War on Poverty Program did have some impact, however transitory, on political participation.

There are no reliable figures on community participation levels during the War on Poverty period, but existing information suggests that there was some increase in participation. Some analysts argue, for instance, that Model Cities, like many programs in the War on Poverty, allowed for limited participation. Model Cities allowed "citizens to advise or plan ad-infinitum but retain for powerholders the right to judge the legitimacy or feasibility of the advice" (Arnstein 1972, 116). Fifteen cities in the United States were, in fact, able to achieve this limited degree of citizen participation. Many public officials and political scientists, on the other hand, saw this level of participation in the War on Poverty as an unfortunate diffusion of governmental authority. For this reason, political scientist Theodore Lowi characterized the war as a "delegation of power" to citizens (1969, 234). Lowi, however, exaggerated the degree of delegation. In reality, the average citizen had little power.

While there was participation by the poor in the War on Poverty Program during the late 1960s, it isn't clear that this participation included people who did not otherwise already participate in the mainstream political process. The number of community residents who took part in community corporation elections was generally unimpressive. Not many turned out to vote. Berndt's study of community corporations in various cities shows this. In St. Louis, for instance, "15 percent typically cast votes" (Berndt 1977, 66). Others have reported voter turnouts in many communities that peaked at less than six percent of the resident population (Greenstone et al. 1973, 192). And those who voted in community corporation elections were not drawn from the masses of apathetic and poor residents. They were generally activists and those with a practical interest in local politics. Berndt says they were mostly "business-oriented residents." Efforts were made in New York City to ensure that at least one-third of the community corporation's board be low-income residents. Despite this, the great "majority of the representatives to the NPCs (Neighborhood Poverty Council) were middle- or upper middle-income residents" (Greenstone et al. 1973, 175). The War on Poverty, thus, did not seem to significantly increase the rate of participation among the poor. But it did provide an important environment for Puerto Ricans and others to learn about how to influence the political process. Rivera says that Puerto Ricans became "more familiar with New York City politics and various service agencies affecting life standards in places like East Harlem" (Rivera 1984, 62). Much of that learning, however, was limited to middle-class elements in the Puerto Rican community. That, of course, disappointed democratic ideals and War on Poverty objectives. The War on Poverty, nonetheless, changed the nature of politics in the United States.

The impact of the War on Poverty was basically subtle. These programs drew community attention to government and the idea that solutions to problems like poverty could be found there. While these discoveries were important for increasing participation, they weren't longlasting. But the War on Poverty also had some practical impact. López mentions that they served as a mechanism for identifying talent (raw or developed) in the community. The War on Poverty, thus, "gobbled up almost all the black and Puerto Rican talent that was existent during this talentless period" (1973, 302). The community participants also got a lot of practice in the art of politics and organizing. Estades, for example, stated that "larger numbers of Puerto Ricans also learned to speak up in neighborhood and city-wide meetings, and to organize for representation of community needs" (Estades 1978, 56). Many of these Puerto Ricans became involved in local electoral politics. Between 1972 and 1976, for instance, Puerto Rican activists in East Harlem were "able to elect 3 district leaders and one state assemblyman and to seize control of several institutional bodies (the local school board, community planning board, and health advisory board)" (Monte 1984, 67). Even the patronage systems of a Vélez had some positive impact. The local control of jobs was an incentive for increased participation (Estades 1978, 57). Jobs were a tangible objective for people who may have felt alienated from the wider political community. It was also not enough. Many Puerto Ricans who became involved in War on Poverty programs or who became interested observers began to note that, in complex ways, poverty continued unabated.

This period of government-sponsored political participation at the local level lasted until the early 1970s. Much of the research on the changes in poverty produced by the War on Poverty suggests that the achievements were mixed. There were, for instance, some absolute declines in the poverty population. The number of persons in poverty (according to government definitions) declined from 38 million to 23 million in the period from 1962 to 1973 (see Plotnick et al. 1975, 81). Despite this decline, analysis of the ability of families with different income levels to meet basic needs suggests that poverty, on a relative basis, stayed fairly constant over that same period. Between 1965 and 1972, for instance, the incidence of poverty among persons in the United States was 15.6 percent with only a slight dip to 14.6 percent in 1966 (Plotnick et al. 1975, 85). The relative incidence of poverty is a more accurate statement of the negligible social impact of War on Poverty efforts. For many residents of the Puerto Rican barrios, this failure to end poverty was blamed on the bureaucratic structure of the programs, corrupt politicians, or both. From this recognition came a turn to more militant politics.

The War on Poverty Period to the Present

There had been radical political groups in the Puerto Rican community before the Young Lords emerged in Chicago and New York City in 1969. New York City had, for instance, the *Movimiento Pro Independencia* (MPI) and later the Puerto Rican Socialist party (PSP). The Young Lords, however, were important because of their ideological and practical stance towards electoral participation. The Lords claimed a commitment to what they called "barrio politics." Pablo Guzmán, a leader in the Lords, argued that "barrio politics" was about "winning supporters to the 'extra-legal' approach—taking over failed institutional symbols, fighting police in the streets, establishing survival programs, demonstrating in the 'barrio'" (Guzmán 1980, 126). How effective the Lords were in getting Puerto Ricans involved in such "extra-legal" politics is hard to say. The Lords had a substantial and active membership. Lords chapters were created in the Puerto Rican communities of Boston, Philadelphia, Chicago, Hartford, Bridgeport, Newark, Hoboken, Rochester, Buffalo, Cleveland, and Detroit. This active membership was also responsible for creating Lords programs in health and free breakfast. Many of these communities were, of course, affected by the Lords' militant actions. But the degree of impact is hard to gauge. Guzmán, the Lords leader, suggested that the impact was ephemeral. By the late 1970s, he wrote that "a new generation [of Puerto Ricans], barely five years younger than we, came into adolescence practically untouched by our words and almost ignorant of our deeds, for no new deeds were forthcoming" (Guzmán 1980, 127). Guzmán also argued that a decline in Puerto Rican voting rates during the 1970s was a product of the Lords' "barrio politics." Puerto Ricans, according to Guzmán, didn't vote because they consciously rejected that form of participation. Though Guzmán exaggerates the impact of the Lords, changes in electoral participation among Puerto Ricans did occur in the 1970s.

The 1960s period of political mobilization and activism came to a close and appeared to leave Puerto Ricans less rather than more interested and integrated into the political system. That is at least the conclusion made by many in a series of new social science studies to come out at that time to explain Puerto Rican politics. The early 1970s are, thus, the object of an unusual number of studies. But the understanding of why Puerto Ricans do or do not participate was not necessarily improved by these studies.

Much of the research on Puerto Rican participation in the early 1970s demonstrated that Puerto Rican rates were low in comparison to other groups. Dale Nelson, for example, showed in one study that the percentage of New York Puerto Ricans who voted in local elections during 1973 was 70 percent (Nelson 1980, 105). This voting rate was low not only in comparison to Jews, at 88 percent, and the Irish, at 90 percent, but low in comparison to similarly situated groups. Blacks, for instance, voted at a rate of 78 percent and Cubans at 79 percent. The situation for Puerto Ricans, however, was not so dire in other forms of participation. Nelson ignored, for instance, that Puerto Ricans contacted public officials to get help or lodge complaints at rates that were twice those of Dominicans and Cubans, though at less than half the rate for Jews, the Irish, and blacks (Nelson 1980, 105). Puerto Ricans in the Nelson study were, furthermore, more likely than almost any other group to join organizations, sign petitions, and attend protests. Twenty-two percent of Puerto Ricans, for example, attended protests compared to 17 percent for Jews, 16 percent for the Irish, 22 percent for blacks, 11 percent for Dominicans, and 9 percent for Cubans (Nelson 1980, 105). This research suggests, as Guzmán has argued, that Puerto Ricans were turned off to participating in the formal political process (i.e., voting) but that they were still interested in raising their political voices through less formal ways. Some of these conclusions are supported by other studies.

Cohen and Kapsis studied Puerto Rican participation in voluntary organizations during the early 1970s period. This study attempted to prove that "similarly deprived ethnic groups," such as Puerto Ricans and blacks, would tend to have comparable levels of political participation. The findings were, however, that Puerto Rican participation was lower than that of blacks. Cohen and Kapsis found that only 22 percent of Puerto Rican males belonged to voluntary associations like churches, PTAs, block associations, etc. This compares with 39 percent of black males and 42 percent of white males (1978, 1066). The authors conclude from this that Puerto Ricans, unlike blacks, lack "activist norms" that encourage participation in voluntary associations (1978, 1066). A closer look at the data reveals again, however, how subjective data analysis and interpretation can be.

It isn't clear that Puerto Ricans lack any such "activist norms" or even that they necessarily participate less given the nature of the participation opportunities they have available. The Cohen and Kapsis data, for example, summarizes participation for Puerto Ricans, blacks, and whites across a wide range of voluntary associations—from churches to political groups. Many of these types of associations are closed to Puerto Ricans for a variety of reasons. Except for the Pentecostal church, there are few churches that can be called "Puerto Rican churches." Puerto Ricans don't control their religious institutions to the same extent that blacks and whites do theirs (see Stevens-Arroyo 1980). Few Puerto Ricans also complete high school and go on to college, minimizing their chances of joining a fraternal organization.

Few Puerto Ricans also own their homes. As late as 1987 only 11.5 percent of all Puerto Ricans in New York City owned their homes, compared to 25 percent of blacks and 37 percent of whites (Stegman 1987). It is not surprising, thus, that the percentage of Puerto Ricans participating in homeowners groups is generally small. In all, of the eleven types of voluntary associations studied by Cohen and Kapsis, there are four categories with little Puerto Rican participation because they are not normally found in the area of social life these groups represent or advocate. The participation rate was, however, better for Puerto Ricans in those associations representing areas of social life that involve Puerto Ricans.

The participation of Puerto Ricans in parents organizations, ethnic organizations, tenant associations, and political groups was comparable if not higher than that of whites and blacks in the Cohen and Kapsis study. For example, the participation of Puerto Rican males in parents groups is 5 percent. This is similar to the rate for white males (6 percent) and similar to black males (8 percent) (Cohen and Kapsis 1978, 1063). Puerto Rican women are also active in parents groups at rates comparable to other women. Over 13 percent of Puerto Rican women in the Cohen and Kapsis study joined parents groups like the PTA, compared to 13 percent of white women and 25 percent of black women. Except for parents groups, however, Puerto Rican women's participation in public life is almost nonexistent, according to this study. Contrary to anecdotal information, this study claims that Puerto Rican women do not participate in political groups. Puerto Rican men, on the other hand, do participate in political groups at a rate of 5 percent, which is the same as that of black and white men.

Studies like the one by Cohen and Kapsis suggest that it is hard both to assess the level of Puerto Rican political participation compared to other groups as well as to establish reasons to explain them. Puerto Ricans may participate as much or more compared to other groups, depending on what one counts as participatory activity. For example, since the Puerto Rican community is primarily made up of parents and renters, it is natural to expect Puerto Ricans to be more active in parents associations and tenants groups than in other types of groups. A better comparison can also be made if one distinguishes between Puerto Ricans who are registered and those unregistered to vote. Puerto Ricans registered to vote are generally more active in parents and tenants groups than those who are not registered. A 1987 study of Puerto Ricans in New York City found that 16 percent of registered Puerto Ricans were members of educational organizations, compared to only 9 percent of unregistered Puerto Ricans (Government of Puerto Rico 1988). Similarly, 11 percent of registered Puerto Ricans were members of tenants groups compared to only 5 percent of unregistered (Government of Puerto Rico 1988). These differences are not only significant but suggest the unlikelihood that a lack of "activist norms" is responsible for low participation among Puerto Ricans.

Puerto Ricans do participate significantly in those areas of social life where they are already included. Research on Puerto Ricans that ignores this is wrongheaded. Eugene Cornacchia ignored it in his study of participation among different ethnic groups in New York City during the early 1970s. Cornacchia stated that "Puerto Ricans frequently have been found to be particularly inactive in communal participation" [i.e. nonvoting politics] (1985, 111). Among the communal activities Cornacchia studied, Puerto Ricans had very low activity rates in organizational membership, contacting officials, and signing petitions. But again the evidence does not show that Puerto Rican participation was consistently low across all fronts. While Puerto Rican activity was low in the areas just mentioned, Cornacchia also reported that almost 16 percent of Puerto Ricans in his study attended political protests. This rate of participation compares very favorably with the rates for WASPs (15 percent), Jews (24 percent), American blacks (16 percent), West Indian blacks (10 percent), and other Hispanics (7.5 percent). Thus, while Puerto Ricans may be unwilling, unable, or prevented from organizing themselves, signing petitions, or contacting public officials, there is little reluctance on their part to exercise their right to protest. This relatively high rate of protest among Puerto Ricans should not be underestimated, since protesting requires a greater investment of personal energy and commitment than petition signing. Cornacchia, however, seemed to ignore the significance of what his own study reported. His comments on these facts are basically dismissive, for he stated, "While American Blacks and Puerto Ricans are not the most inactive groups in terms of protest activity, they are much lower than anticipated" (1985, 116). It is unclear, however, why Cornacchia assumed protest activity would be higher for Puerto Ricans.

Participation does not always produce political power. Cohen and Kapsis appeard to understand this paradox. They stated, "While Puerto Rican and Hispanic organizational activity has been on the rise with respect to organizations associated with the 'War on Poverty,' it has not, at least at the time of our survey, been translated into community problem-solving organizational activity generally" (1985, 115). But the impact of the War on Poverty on power for Puerto Ricans was actually more complicated. The War on Poverty period did have a longterm impact on Puerto Rican participation rates. What's not clear, however, is whether the impact was positive or negative.

In terms of formal participation, a dramatic increase was recorded in the number of Puerto Rican registered voters in this War on Poverty period. About 200,000 new Puerto Rican voters were added to New York's voting rolls during 1972. This achievement can be largely attributed to the work of an organization called the *Cruzada Cívica del Voto,* a collection of Puerto Rican organizations including the daily newspaper *El Diario de Nueva York* and the Puerto Rican Development Project (Estades 1978, 59). This registration drive was helped by the 1972 passage of a law lowering the voting age to eighteen as well as by the strengthening of organizations and the emergence of new Puerto Rican leaders as a result of the War on Poverty. In fact, Herman Badillo, the first Puerto Rican U. S. congressman, benefited most from these processes. Badillo ran for mayor in 1973 and came in a strong second in the primaries, largely because of the larger bloc of Puerto Ricans who were registered and turned out to vote. Writing around that time, Rosa Estades believed that "this increase in registration makes the Puerto Rican bloc a potentially significant one in New York City politics" (1978, 86). That potential was never realized, however. Puerto Rican participation in many different forms declined, often involuntarily, into the 1980s.

By the late 1970s, the Puerto Rican community could boast the election of more Puerto Ricans to public office but a declining rate of participation in the electoral process. Five Puerto Ricans won election to the New York State Assembly in 1978 alone. The voter turnout by Puerto Ricans in those five assembly districts, however, was consistently low compared to other districts. Angelo Falcón, for example, recounted: "The five Puerto Rican winners of the State Assembly seats averaged 6,513 votes each, with the highest polling 9,653. Among white Assembly victors, the lowest vote getter received 10,294 votes, more than the highest Puerto Rican candidate for Assemblyman" (Falcón 1980, 33). The decline in participation was not only in Puerto Rican voter turnout but in registration rates. In 1982 only 35 percent of the Puerto Rican/Latino voting age population were registered to vote in New York City (Falcón 1985, 16). This compares with 39 percent of blacks and 49 percent of whites who registered. As happens in presidential election years, the registration rates of Puerto Ricans, blacks, and whites all increased during 1984. The rate for Puerto Ricans and Latinos increased to 52 percent, blacks to 56 percent, and whites to 60 percent (Falcón 1985, 16). Over the long run, however, Puerto Rican participation declined and not only in New York City.

Puerto Ricans residing outside of New York City participated at equally low levels. Census data on voter turnout rates during the 1980 election show consistently lower rates for the Spanish-origin population in the Northeast and Middle Atlantic portions of the United States, where Puerto Ricans represent the vast majority of voter-eligible Latinos (U. S. Department of Commerce 1982). Puerto Ricans and Spanish-origin came out to vote in those areas at rates that were about 20 percent lower than for whites and about 10 percent lower than blacks (ibid.). This reduced voter turnout was true of Puerto Ricans and other Spanish-origin compared to other groups at all age categories.

Curiosity about why so many Puerto Ricans were not voting and generally seemed to participate less grew during the 1980s. Interestingly, Puerto Ricans themselves, even those not registered to vote, believed that voting was an important political act. In one 1987 survey, 97 percent of all registered and 87 percent of all unregistered eligible Puerto Ricans believed that voting was important (Government of Puerto Rico 1988, 3). But if voting was so important to Puerto Ricans, why weren't more of them registered? As in the early 1970s, Puerto Ricans showed a greater propensity in the late 1980s to participate in the political process in ways other than voting. As many Puerto Ricans as Mexican Americans signed petitions to support particular causes (LNPS 1990, 14). This was almost three times the rate for Cuban Americans. Puerto Ricans were also more likely than any other Latino group to attend public meetings or demonstrations supporting group interests. About 14 percent of Puerto Ricans attended meetings and demonstrations for their group, compared to 9 percent of Mexican Americans and 6 percent of Cuban Americans (LNPS 1990, 14). At the same time that Puerto Ricans attended meetings and demonstrations to support their group interests, Puerto Ricans were also less likely to do so on behalf of particular political candidates. Only 5 percent of Puerto Ricans did so in this study (LNPS 1990, 14). This rate is extremely low when compared to other Latino groups as well. Fully 22 percent of Mexican Americans and 17 percent of Cuban Americans attended meetings and rallies in support of particular candidates (LNPS 1990, 14). These differences suggest that the decline in Puerto Rican participation was not totally their choice.

Compared to other Latinos, Puerto Ricans don't attend meetings, rallies, volunteer, or contribute money to further the career of a politician or the objectives of a group or community that they believe excludes them as members. Puerto Ricans, however, are willing to do all of those things to support political candidates, causes, and organizations that represent Puerto Rican interests and concerns. Does this make Puerto Ricans more shallow or self-interested than other groups? I don't think so. These differences in the way Puerto Ricans participate can be best explained by exploring an aspect of the participatory process that is largely ignored in the literature—the issue of "doors." Puerto Ricans may simply participate less when they encounter too many closed political "doors."

Another History of Participation: The Incorporation of Puerto Ricans

In one interesting study of political participation among Puerto Ricans and other Latinos in New Jersey during the early 1980s, Kenneth Greene offered different explanations for political behavior involving voting and "contacting officials" in this population. This study found higher rates of voting and contacting in this Puerto Rican community than other studies have found for other Latinos and minorities. High rates of voting were explained by Greene as a function of residence in Hispanic areas and higher socioeconomic status. Puerto Ricans in this study had "greater resources and a greater sense of political involvement that translates into higher levels of voting" (1990, 304). Contacting behavior was explained differently. The author found that the highest rates of contacting were among those Puerto Ricans and Latinos who were older, more educated, and resided in predominantly white neighborhoods (1990, 305). Specifically, Greene suggested a possible causal process: "Group membership and residence in predominantly white neighborhoods place Hispanics within networks of individuals who possess greater political skills and information. . . . Location in networks which enhance political awareness is an important buttress to their personal resources and contributes substantially to their contacting behavior" (Greene 1990, 305).

While it certainly seems plausible that residence in an area with many politically skilled and connected individuals could enhance contacting skills and behavior, the explanation is ultimately unsatisfactory. Greene assumed but did not demonstrate that there are more politically skilled people in white suburbs than in the inner city. That may or may not be the case in general or for any particular city or suburb. Even if it were true that there were more politically skilled people in the New Jersey suburb Greene studied, it is wrong to assume that simple residence in that community would give Puerto Ricans a political education in contacting. Greene needed to show that Puerto Ricans and Latinos interacted in cultural, social, and political ways with politically skilled whites to make an effective case for this transference of political skill. The ultimate implication of this line of reasoning is that Puerto Ricans and Latinos were integrated or accepted by whites in the suburbs. While this is certainly possible, it raises issues about race, racism, and social class which point in a direction Greene did not and could not go.

As a rule most studies of participation seem unable, as Nagel put it, "to get outside the heads of survey respondents" (1987, 42). The general inclination is to study the beliefs, characteristics, and attitudes of individual citizens and to ignore the role that organizations and social structures play in motivating, assisting, and informing participation. This is no less true of studies on Puerto Rican political participation. Puerto Ricans are blamed for lacking "activist norms" (Cohen and Kapsis), or rejecting formal participation (Cornacchia), or for lacking political skills because they unfortunately reside in non-white areas

(Greene). Aside from the work of researchers like Falcón and García-Passalacqua, structural and organizational factors are virtually ignored in the study of Puerto Rican political participation. But a focus on such factors opens an entirely different view of the history of the nature and course of political participation for Puerto Ricans.

Structures of Participation

Every community has features "whether natural or artificial, that are normally beyond the control of groups or individuals and that change rarely, slowly, or not at all" (Nagel 1987, 42). We call these features "social structures." Electoral laws and the political party system are obvious examples of relatively permanent structural features in society. There are a few studies that explore the impact of such structures on Puerto Rican participation. Less obvious are the structural roles played by class and race in determining participation. But though the impact is less obvious, these too have worked to limit Puerto Rican participation.

Electoral participation has declined for all Americans, and not only for Puerto Ricans, over the last fifty years. Voter registration and turnout are so low in the United States that Ronald Reagan's landslide presidential victory was based on only 30 percent of the votes of the potential electorate. Registration and turnout numbers have been historically higher in presidential election years than at other times. Voter turnout was historically highest in the United States during the nineteenth century. The highest voter turnout was 83 percent in the 1876 presidential election (Hellinger and Judd 1991, 85). The highest in the modern era was 65 percent in the 1960 presidential election (Hellinger and Judd 1991, 86). Turnout has dropped consistently, however. In the 1988 presidential election, for example, only 50 percent of eligible voters turned out to vote (Hellinger and Judd 1991, 86). The low voter turnout of Puerto Ricans in the United States can thus be largely attributed to more general processes affecting all voters in the United States. Despite this broader context of voter turnout decline, the consistently lower turnout of Puerto Ricans compared to other groups in the United States fuels efforts to find plausible explanations specific to this group.

Structural features become most noticeable when one steps back from the familiar and compares one political system to another. That is precisely what Angelo Falcón did in the seminal work "Puerto Rican Political Participation: New York City and Puerto Rico" (1980). Comparing the electoral and political party systems in Puerto Rico and New York City, Falcón found that Puerto Ricans participate in electoral politics at much higher rates in Puerto Rico than in New York City. The most prominent explanation for this difference was structural:

Angelo Falcón, president of the Institute for Puerto Rican Policy.

"The combination of widespread patronage practices and party control over an important part of the voting structures greatly increases material incentives to participate" (1980, 40). The political parties in Puerto Rico, in contrast to their counterparts in New York City, mobilize citizens on election day to come out to vote. The registration process also encourages participation, since the Puerto Rican government itself conducts frequent registration drives. In addition, a strong patronage system links participation to government jobs and benefits. As a result, voting patterns in Puerto Rico, according to Falcón, refute the most common explanations for low Puerto Rican participation in the United States. Participation rates are 20 points to 30 points higher in Puerto Rico regardless of socioeconomic or educational level, urban-rural residence, gender, and race.

A study by Juan M. García-Passalacqua elaborates and validates the Falcón argument that political structures account for the difference in voting between Puerto Rico and New York City. For Passalacqua, social structures don't simply facilitate or encourage participation. They compel it. Passalacqua argued:

> The political elite in Puerto Rico has used to the utmost its power in the Legislative Assembly to assure heavy electoral turnouts. For many years until 1977, the vote was compulsory under law, and one lost the right to vote if it was not exercised. Election day is, by law, an *official holiday* in which all employees are excused from work,

> stores, and shops of all kinds, must remain closed, public events are prohibited, and there is a prohibition, strongly enforced, on the expenditure of liquor. Thus, there is very little to do in Puerto Rico on the first Tuesday after the first Monday in November every four years *but to vote* and then await the results. (1983, 43)

The external compulsion of the electorate, according to Passalacqua, goes way beyond these elements.

The political parties in Puerto Rico have developed extensive control over certain factors that compel and promote heavy turnouts. The total electorate of about 2 million people in the early 1980s, for instance, was divided into groups of no more than 260 potential voters. Each of these units is assigned a volunteer by each political party to organize them. These volunteers keep a census, register, and mobilize voters. The parties also utilize *público* drivers (of taxis and buses) to take voters to demonstrations, to register, and to vote. Once in power, a political party controls and dispenses government jobs (25 percent of the economy), health services, personal loans, bail financing, and other services. Most of the compulsion come from the pressure that "family ties, parental authority, male marital authority, employer's authority and job supervisor's authority" have on getting Puerto Ricans to "register, attend party functions and vote" (Passalacqua 1983, 45). The end result is, according to Passalacqua, that Puerto Ricans in Puerto Rico vote more often than Puerto Ricans in New York City. But they vote more often because they are forced. Indeed, Passalacqua says that this compulsion makes Puerto Ricans more interested in voting than in choosing (1983, 47). Do Puerto Ricans in New York City vote less often, then, because they lack such external compulsion?

Ever since Rousseau proposed the idea of forcing citizens to be free, compulsion has been a despised but hidden, often accepted, feature of democratic society. Chinese peasants may be prodded to vote by gun-toting militia-men and soldiers. But then force of a more subtle kind has been employed in the West too. Until 1970, for example, citizens in the Netherlands were fined for not voting. That was enough to keep turnout rates there in the upper 90 percent range. The difference in coercion between a soldier and a tax is considerable but besides the point. Both are attempts to "force them to be free." The problem with this, as Nagel has pointed out, is that "coercion and constraint restrict personal liberty" (1987, 64). But I wonder if other issues besides the ethical and moral one of freedom are also involved here?

In the United States, like in Puerto Rico, there have been many examples of citizens forced to participate in politics. Most major American cities, for example, have experienced periods, if not entire histories, when citizen participation was compelled by the patronage dispensed by "political machines." What is often overlooked, however, is that there is also a long history in the United States of citizens forced *not to* participate. Women and African-Americans are two obvious examples. But the maintenance and creation of barriers that keep people from participating in elections is much broader. The decline in participation recorded for all Americans over the years may mean that voters are being "disappeared." Those in power may act or not act to keep the average citizens passive. The reason for this may be as Walter D. Burnham has argued that "the preservation of the existing stratification of power, status, and income in the U. S. could only be promoted by a politics so organized that there are vast pools of nonparticipant lower-class people at one end of the participation continuum and . . . *hyper-active Republican* participants at the other" (Burnham 1982, 154). What is hard to figure out here is what accounts for the amount of nonparticipation seen in Puerto Ricans? Did Puerto Ricans pose a special threat to the existing stratification of power, or were they simply victimized more than other lower-class people by the efforts of power wielders to keep and make them all nonparticipants? The question is, thus, the reverse of that studied by Passalacqua. He explained how the political parties and the government of Puerto Rico mobilize Puerto Rican citizens to vote. We want to know what powers in the United States promote nonparticipation among Puerto Ricans. It may not be possible to get real answers to this question but asking it certainly changes the entire interpretation of Puerto Rican political participation in the United States.

The decline in participation among Puerto Ricans is a complex issue, as discussed earlier. And it is likely that this decline, however much only apparent or real it is, results from the closing of political "doors." The problem is, however, that efforts to limit participation are not always as obvious as efforts to increase it. No radio broadcasts are made to announce new limits on participation. Usually one can only point to processes that have only an indirect or inadvertent impact on political participation. There have been many instances of this type in Puerto Rican history, though most of these have been overlooked and gone unstudied. Two examples that come to mind are Puerto Rican experiences in New York with the Liberal party as well as with public housing. In both cases Puerto Ricans lost or were denied real opportunities and resources that could have increased political participation.

Puerto Ricans have traditionally been excluded from positions of influence within the International Ladies' Garment Workers' Union (ILGWU). They have also found leadership positions within the Liberal party, the political arm of the ILGWU, closed off to them. By 1960, it had become clear that the Liberal party leadership had no intention of maintaining an active, mass following. Membership in the Liberal Party, for instance, plunged earlier from a high of 118,000 in 1949 to about 66,000 in 1954 (Flournoy 1956, 104). The Liberal party did count on a loyal group of voters, mostly old ex-garment workers and reformers, but the predominantly Puerto Rican and black garment workers who were nominally members of the ILGWU did not become active or willing followers of the party. As Shefter stated, "The Liberal Party had close ties with the ILGWU and the millinery union but these unions supplied the party with money more than manpower" (1986, 68).

Support for the Liberal party from Puerto Rican and black garment workers was involuntary. A number of reports indicate that Puerto Rican and black workers were usually "forced" by the union to make contributions to the Liberal party (Galíndez 1969). Much as the ILGWU contributed union funds to Israel and Jewish causes without rank and file approval, the union also contributed the votes of garment workers as well as part of their wages to the Liberal party (Laurentz 1980, 218).

At its peak as a membership party in the mid-1950s, and with the organizing help of Encarnación Padilla de Armes, who coordinated the Spanish Division, the Liberal party could boast that Puerto Ricans represented 15 percent of its members (Baver 1984, 10). Whereas old Jewish ILGWU locals like the Cloak Pressers could boast a 65 percent enrollment in the Liberal party, locals with predominantly Puerto Rican and black workers usually had no more than a 20 percent enrollment (Flournoy 1956, 72). The Liberal party, like the ILGWU, remained firmly controlled by an elite white (basically Jewish) leadership who saw Puerto Ricans and blacks as mere pawns in the effort to maintain economic and political power (Laurentz 1980). The Liberal party did not want Puerto Ricans to become members, since they were no longer interested in being a mass-based party. Though its leaders believed otherwise, ultimately, this strategy did not prove to be enough to save the party. The Liberal party's efforts in local reform politics helped to destroy the old political machine and to institute professional government in the city. These changes benefited the emerging corporate finance sector of the economy more than manufacturing, especially not apparel manufacturing. Ultimately these changes undercut the foundations of power from under the union and the party.

Political parties, like government, have a tremendous history of fragmentation and proliferation in New York City (see Wood 1961). Wallace Sayre and Herbert Kaufman counted fifty-two different "independent bodies" or parties alone that appeared on New York City voting machines in the forty years preceding 1960 (1960, 193). Many of these were small splinter groups, sometimes merely individuals, that were organized simply to capture a single office. These third "parties" generally disappeared quickly, leaving basically unaffected the local terrain of political power dominated and held by Democrats and to a lesser extent by Republicans. Unlike other third parties, the Liberal party and its parent organization, the American Labor party, did play a significant role in New York State politics during the 1950s. But its power was something Puerto Ricans themselves never got to exercise. Most of the major elections for city, state, or national offices in the post-WW II period were decided in New York State by the Liberal party (Sayre and Kaufman 1960, 187). Votes from the American Labor party or the Liberal party have been credited with providing the margin of victory in New York State in each presidential election between 1936 and 1956, in the New York State governor's elections of 1938 and 1954, in the three U. S. Senate races between 1936 and 1954, in the mayoral elections of Fiorello LaGuardia in 1937 and 1941, in Robert Wagner's mayoral victories of 1953 and 1957, as well as in John Lindsay's 1965 victory for mayor (Sayre and Kaufman 1960, 191; Shefter 1985: 79). The importance of the American Labor and Liberal party goes farther than this string of electoral victories, however. As the political arm of the ILGWU, the Liberal party controlled and manipulated Puerto Rican and other garment workers' votes while promoting anti-worker policies, such as a restraint on the minimum wage. More importantly, the Liberal party actually helped demobilize labor and de-politicize working-class interests even as the union was itself becoming more politically active (see Shefter 1986).

This policy of labor demobilization was made particularly evident by the events that led to the creation of the Liberal party. The Liberal party appeared for the first time in New York during 1944 when ILGWU and Amalgamated Clothing Workers Union (ACWU) leaders broke with the American Labor party because of its increasingly radical politics under the leadership of Vito Marcantonio. The Liberal party went on to become as politically successful as the American Labor party.

The establishment of the ALP in 1936 had challenged reformist union policies and leaders. One of those challenged was John L. Lewis who advocated political lobbying and participation by unions, but only within the two major political parties (Degler 1959). The emergence of the American Labor party, then, not only challenged the norms of political participation acceptable to established union leadership but created the possibility of developing a political voice for labor independent of the two major parties. It was this threat of independent politics for labor that led later to the collusive efforts of the Democratic and Republican parties to destroy the ALP (Shefter 1985, 59).

The ILGWU and the Liberal party pioneered the use of "political unionism" in the post-WW II period. This new political style marked a separation not only from the radical activism of the ALP but also from the conservative, interest-group style of the AFL-CIO. Gompers and the AFL eventually accepted the idea of labor union participation and support for parties and politicians in an attempt to create legislation protecting syndicalist rights and economic benefits for workers. The ILGWU, however, entered the political arena feet first with the ALP and then with the Liberal Party. In the Liberal party the ILGWU created a vehicle for carrying forth a centralist version of political unionism.

Years later, Gus Tyler, an assistant president of the ILGWU and resident researcher, introduced philosophical principles that he hoped could tie together the divergent strains of political activism present within the ILGWU. Tyler said that the union must be defined *sui generis* as "a political entity" and even as "enforcing agencies . . . performing government functions in a specialized way and in specialized zones improper or inconvenient for government itself to undertake" (Tyler 1968, 92). Tyler's reasoning was consonant with the post-war period of new labor and workplace legislation. The wage and hour laws, for instance, provide an example of the public, state-like functions unions are often required to perform. Without the monitoring and policing actions conducted by labor unions, most employers would likely try to chisel at wage and hour regulations. Tyler saw this delegation of state responsibility to the unions not as a burden or liability but as a symbol of the institutional partnership between state and union. The increased interventionist role of the state from the New Deal period onward was interpreted by Tyler as an unmistakably progressive change for unions and their workers. He envisioned the unions joining with the "benevolent state" to control and manage the evils of capitalism and meet working-class needs. This managerialist view of a labor-state partnership was founded on the rush of post-war labor legislation. But it was a foundation that political and economic forces had begun to erode even as it was being constructed.

Though the ILGWU believed in a state-union partnership, the fragmentation of capital into many independent, competitive units as well as the fragmentation of the state into disparate institutions and different levels of government created contrasting conditions of existence for labor which, given the passage of time and spatial change, made a fiction of the idea of state management and benevolence. Even if it wanted to, the state could not guarantee labor a geographically balanced relationship with capital. The capitalist state has very little actual control over the mobility and investment decisions of capital (see Harvey 1985). This deficiency in state power severely destabilized the ILGWU's progressive program of managerial government reform. And it made possible the spectacle of a union like the ILGWU that simultaneously became one of the first to oppose the war in Vietnam yet condoned the operation of sweatshops in the United States (Laurentz 1980).

What is ironic about the growth of bureaucratic government and municipal employee power since Wagner is that the ILGWU and the Liberal party participated and encouraged processes that ultimately undermined the basis of their political and economic power. The Liberal party in particular became a mere shell of a party. By the late 1960s it could still deliver the votes of old retired garment workers, radicals, and East Side liberals, often in exchange for patronage, but it did not represent any formidable social force within the city. It had few organized clubs. Observers noted that "Liberal Party control seems to rest in very few hands, and the absence of local political clubs ensures that no faction will arise to seriously challenge that control" (Adler et al. 1975, 10). The Liberal party had become a political farce. This is what David Dubinsky must have sensed when he decided to pull ILGWU sponsorship from the Liberal party in 1966 (Costikgan 1966). Today it is the unions, especially the municipal employee unions, that control city politics. The parties, like the manufacturing and construction unions, play minor roles. The municipal unions do most of the basic legwork in political campaigns, running telephone banks and supplying campaign workers and experts. The municipal unions have become, according to labor analyst Norman Adler, "the only institutional memory left in New York City politics" (*Newsday* July 6, 1988).

During its heyday, however, the Liberal party could have done for Puerto Ricans what it did for Jews and what the black church did for blacks. It could have provided an independent voice and instrument for the political interests of the Puerto Rican community. The Liberal party instead became an instrument of domination over the Puerto Rican community during the 1950s and 1960s. The only times it showed more than token interest were when it directed Padilla de Armas to develop Puerto Rican political clubs and when the party supported the candidacy of José Lumen Román for city council. The Liberal party's reasons for endorsing Román, in fact, demonstrate how the party was more interested in manipulating than in organizing and mobilizing the Puerto Rican community.

After Marcantonio's death Puerto Ricans had few elected leaders who instilled confidence and provided authentic leadership. When they were not being ignored, Puerto Ricans either had their leaders chosen for them or had their own candidates defeated by opponents backed by the powerful Democratic political machine. For example, the election of a Puerto Rican named Felipe Torres to the state assembly representing the Morrisania and Mott Haven sections of the Bronx in 1953 came about because he had been selected for the seat by Ed Flynn, who was the boss of the Bronx Democratic Club (Wakefield 1959, 266). A year later, in 1954, Antonio Méndez became the first Puerto Rican district leader for the Democratic party in East Harlem only because there had been a shake-up in the local party office. Tammany Hall boss Carmine DeSapio had removed Sammy Kantor as district leader after he had refused to support Robert Wagner for mayor in the previous year. DeSapio replaced Kantor with Méndez, according to Wakefield, both because DeSapio was scrupulously aware of the growing Puerto Rican population of East Harlem and because he believed that Tony Méndez had "no recognizable ambitions of a political future beyond the one assigned him by DeSapio" (Wakefield 1959, 268)

The Liberal party was once, however, the vehicle for a failed effort by Puerto Ricans themselves to elect one of their own. In 1957 the Liberal party announced the party's endorsement of José Lumen Román, a Puerto Rican, for the city council seat from East Harlem. The party's intentions, however, did not aim simply at making Román the only elected Puerto Rican official in the city. The Liberal party's actions in this case actually resembled an earlier byzantine episode in which the Republicans had made Oscar García Rivera their candidate for assembly in 1937 simply to upset the Democrats.

Román, a reporter, had written numerous articles and testified before the McClelland Committee against the exploitation of Puerto Ricans by racket unions in New York City. Since many of these unions were members of the ILGWU and connected to the Liberal party, Román would seem to be the least likely choice as Liberal party candidate for office. But the party endorsed him anyway in an attempt to score a blow against Tammany Hall. Like the Republican affair with Oscar García Rivera, the Liberal's endorsement was an empty gesture, an act full of "despair and hope by the out-of-office political groups to score an upset over the older, entrenched minorities represented by the ruling Democrats" (Wakefield 1959, 267). Román needed time, money, and campaign workers in order to register and get Puerto Ricans out to vote. Though Román was lacking in all three of these resources, the Liberal Party did not help him. The result was that Román lost the election. Román lost by almost 27,000 votes to the incumbent, Democrat John Merli. His loss thus obscured what was creditably, in the eyes of some observers, a solid and real challenge by Puerto Ricans to the Democratic party machine (Wakefield 1959). The Román candidacy, in fact, produced numerous defections from the Democratic party by loyal Puerto Rican activists, who could no longer tolerate the politics of obedience summed up in the motto of the Tony Méndez Club that said "I am a Democrat first and a Puerto Rican second" (Wakefield 1959, 270). More important, perhaps, was the fact that the Román election campaign was manned not only by defected Puerto Rican activists but also by Puerto Rican and other members of the New York Hotel Trades Council and Local 485 of the International Union of Electrical Workers. These workers distributed leaflets, petitioned voters, and arranged rallies for Román. The Puerto Rican members of Local 485 demonstrated their independence from "bosses" not only in this campaign but also in the spontaneous work action conducted both against their employer, the Metzer Company in the Bronx, and their union. Though this raw political energy didn't prove to be enough to get Román elected, it did give the Democrats good reason to become concerned.

Roman's followers were stubborn. After Román's defeat, many frustrated Puerto Ricans talked about starting a "Spanish Party," having become convinced by their campaign experiences that "they could trust only themselves" (Wakefield 1959, 278). In response the established machine tried to demonstrate to the Puerto Rican community of East Harlem that they were still in control by giving the 1958 Democratic party nomination to José Ramón López and eventually electing him to the state assembly district of East Harlem. By 1963 the Democrats had added two more Puerto Ricans to the assembly, Carlos Ríos and Frank N. Torres, who succeeded his father. Elected office in city government itself somehow remained off limits to Puerto Ricans until the 1965 election of Herman Badillo to the Bronx Borough president's office.

Today Puerto Ricans have more elected officials but less participation. Puerto Ricans have, as Shefter says, been selectively incorporated into the New York political system. The Liberal party played a role in this. Other parties and institutions may have played a similar role in other places. The outcome is that the "doors" these institutions protect have permitted Puerto Ricans to be *represented* but not fully *incorporated* into the political system. Public housing has played a similar role.

Political participation has been associated with homeownership and length of residence. Pomper and Semekos thus stated, "We expect higher turnout among persons who own, rather than rent, their homes; who have lived longer in their current town or city; and who have lived longer in their current specific homes" (1991, 13). Staying put increases voter turnout. The reason is that "when people move, many tasks are more important than registering to vote" (Wolfinger 1991, 25). This means that the housing condition and residential mobility of Puerto Ricans are important factors affecting their participation. The facts are that Puerto Ricans are generally renters rather than owners and have a high rate of residential mobility.

According to the 1987 New York City Housing and Vacancy Survey, Puerto Ricans were less likely than other groups to own their home. Less than 12 percent of all Puerto Ricans in New York City in 1987 own their home. This compares with 18 percent for other Latinos, 25 percent for blacks, and 37 percent for whites (IPR 1989, 16). The vast majority of Puerto Ricans are, thus, renters, and more likely to move from their homes and neighborhoods. (A comparable condition exists at the national level. Only 24 percent of all Puerto Rican households in the United States own their home. This compares with 47 percent of Mexican Americans and 66 percent for all non-Latinos [U. S. Census 1989].) The housing turnover rate for Puerto Ricans was, in fact, higher than for any other group. Between 1984 and 1989, 51 percent of all Puerto Ricans in New York City moved from one apartment to another (U. S. census 1989). Only 33 percent of blacks and 29 percent of whites moved in that same period. This high degree of "internal migration" destroys opportunities for all kinds of participation. Registration to vote in New York State must take place sixty days before the primary election and thirty days before the general election. A poor family, forced to move involuntarily because of crime or dilapidated housing, is not likely to see voter registration as an immediate necessity. In addition, frequent internal migration wreaks havoc on community organizations. Groups are likely to find much of their membership relocating and becoming unavailable to the organization. This not only weakens organizational continuity and resources but creates a persistent recurring need to recruit new members. Much of the decline in voting and participation in other political activities among Puerto Ricans can, thus, be attributed to high internal migration. But the reasons for this are not simply that Puerto Ricans are too poor to afford home ownership and, thus, are unfortunately more likely to reside in rental housing that is often subject to deterioration, abandonment, and destruction. Puerto Rican housing conditions are also the result of policies and social processes that target them specifically as a group.

Home ownership leads to residential stability. But so does residence in public housing. Rents in public housing are set according to family income. That keeps the cost down. Public housing is also kept in much better condition than the private housing stock, especially of comparable rents. For this reason, the tenant turnover rate in public housing is historically very low, generally about 3 percent of all units per year. Puerto Ricans, however, do not enjoy the social and economic benefits provided by public housing at a rate equal to their level of poverty and housing need.

Currently about 27 percent of all public housing tenants in New York City are Puerto Rican. Though the number of Puerto Ricans in public housing seems substantial, many more Puerto Ricans deserve to be and are not in public housing. They have been kept out by an admissions philosophy that the Housing Authority has been reluctant and slow to discard. Unlike other social service agencies, the Housing Authority insists on playing the role of public landlord. It is more concerned with maintaining buildings than with providing shelter for the neediest portion of the population. This has cost Puerto Ricans the sound housing they so desperately need.

Since the very first days of the public housing system in New York City in 1936, the Housing Authority has preferred applicants who could be called "deserving poor" because they had jobs and "intact" families. This admissions policy has hurt Puerto Ricans because, since the 1950s, the authority has apparently labeled them a "non-deserving" though poor group. This policy has been demonstrated repeatedly in the courts.

A number of recent court actions has exposed the biased nature of the admissions process used by the Housing Authority. In 1976, for example, Latinos in Williamsburg, Brooklyn, won a class-action suit against the Housing Authority (see *Williamsburg Fair Housing Committee, et al. v. New York City Housing Authority, et al.* S.D.N.Y. 76 Civ. 2125 (CHT)). The court, in this case, found the Housing Authority guilty of discriminatory admissions practices. Relief was granted by way of a consent decree, which required that the Housing Authority eliminate the use of a quota system that kept Puerto Ricans and Latinos out of public housing in South Williamsburg. Despite the consent decree, the Housing Authority continued to admit applicants to public housing on the basis of racial quotas. This policy maintained a concentration of 75 percent to 90 percent white in South Williamsburg public housing. As a result, in 1989 the Southside Fair Housing Committee (representing Latinos and African Americans) started new legal proceedings against the Housing Authority. That motion produced another agreement with the Housing Authority to eliminate racial quotas. All signs suggest, however, that the Housing Authority continues to drag its feet.

The authority's use of racial quotas to admit tenants is not limited to the public housing projects of Williamsburg. The Housing Authority has used quotas since the 1950s and for all of its projects. That is the basis of the latest legal charges leveled against the authority. In December 1990 the Legal Aid Society asked the U. S. District Court to intervene to stop "the systemic discrimination practiced by the Authority" (S.D.N.Y. 90 Civ. 628 [PNL]). Among the plaintiffs in this case was a Jeanette Vargas. This Puerto Rican woman with two children was homeless and living in emergency housing when she was denied admission to a Sheapshead Bay project that is 69 percent white and has many vacant apartments. The Housing Authority instead steered her to a predominantly minority project in the East New York section of Brooklyn.

The problem for most Puerto Ricans, however, is not that they get steered by the Housing Authority away from white projects and to projects that are mostly African American and Latino. The problem is also that many Puerto Ricans who deserve to be admitted into public housing are being excluded.

Joseph Christian, the chair of the Housing Authority in 1983, claimed that the proportion of Puerto Ricans among the tenants of public housing had stayed fairly even (at about 25 percent) since 1968 and that this record indicated" a fairly constant figure and a constant commitment" by the authority to the Puerto Rican community. But that constant proportion over time says just the opposite. Since 1968, both Puerto Rican housing needs and poverty levels have increased dramatically. What the Housing Authority has done, thus, is to stand pat while conditions have worsened for Puerto Ricans.

Puerto Ricans, for instance, had the lowest median household income among all renter groups in the city during 1986 at $9,000 a year. Comparisons to other groups reveal, moreover, that poverty is growing among Puerto Ricans. Thus, while the median income of Puerto Rican renters was 50 percent that of white city renters in 1977, the 1986 median for Puerto Ricans had dropped to only 40 percent that of white renters. In contrast, the median income of African-American renters was 68 percent that of whites in 1986 and hasn't changed much since 1977, when it was 67 percent of the white median. A "constant commitment" by the Housing Authority, thus, seems totally inappropriate, given the deepening crisis of poverty in the Puerto Rican community. The authority's record when measured against Puerto Rican housing needs is also very poor.

Puerto Rican housing conditions are worse today than they were twenty-nine years ago. Over 24 percent of all Puerto Rican households in 1987 were living in "seriously under-maintained" housing. This was twice the proportion observed for Puerto Ricans in 1960. In contrast, only 20 percent of African American and less than 8 percent of white households lived in such uninhabitable quarters in 1987.

Rent also takes a big bite out of Puerto Rican incomes to pay for what are very bad apartments. The median gross rent-to-income ratio for Puerto Ricans was 35 percent in 1987, compared to 29 percent for African Americans and 26 percent for whites. The rent burden for Puerto Ricans was thus 20 percent higher than that of African Americans and 30 percent more than whites. The rent burden on Puerto Ricans has also increased absolutely and relatively compared to the past. While the rent burden for Puerto Ricans has stayed fairly constant since the late 1970s, it is much higher than it was in 1960. Then, the Puerto Rican median rent-to-income ratio was only 20 percent, while that of all city households was 18 percent.

The Puerto Rican community thus has experienced extreme and accelerating rates of poverty and lives in poor and expensive housing. But this critical level of need has not produced increased admission to public housing.

If the proportion of Puerto Ricans to all public housing tenants increased by just 10 percent more than the 27.6 percent in 1983, much of the gap between Puerto Rican and African-American housing quality and price would be reduced. That 10 percent increase in public housing tenure would translate into a 5 percent increase in the proportion of all Puerto Ricans in the city who live in public housing and thus pay more reasonable rent and live in better quarters. A 5 percent decrease means that about 50,000 Puerto Ricans would no longer pay more than 30 percent of their income for rent. It also would mean that 5 percent fewer Puerto Ricans would have to live in under-maintained housing. This would lower the percentage of Puerto Ricans living in such poor quality housing to 29 percent, the rate at which African Americans are at now. While African-American housing conditions are generally also poor, reaching the African-American level would actually mark an improvement for Puerto Ricans.

So the question remains, if Puerto Rican housing needs are so great and the potential impact of expanded public housing tenure so substantial, why hasn't the Housing Authority and the Dinkins administration been more responsive? The Housing Authority makes it hard to get answers to this question. The authority structure makes the public housing system a secret enclave, immune from the close scrutiny of the general public. The best guess as to why Puerto Ricans don't get admitted in greater numbers to public housing has to do with the authority's management policy and the political weakness of the Puerto Rican community.

The Housing Authority continues to prefer applicants who could be called "deserving poor" because they have jobs and "intact" families. The Housing Authority has doggedly kept alive this philosophy of serving poor "submerged middle-class" applicants rather than the neediest, even though it has come under attack by different liberal groups and by demographic and economic changes affecting the city. Thus, Joseph Christian, the chair in 1983, reaffirmed the essence of this management philosophy when he described public housing "as a stepping stone, a way station for families to gather strength en route to the middle class." One impact of this philosophy is that it excludes Puerto Ricans from sound, affordable housing and residential stability. The high internal migration that Puerto Ricans experience because they are limited to poor quality and relatively expensive inner-city housing weakens their chances of participation in community organizations and electoral politics. The indirect impact of Housing Authority admissions practices is to reduce Puerto Rican political participation.

Participation and Choice

The closing of political doors experienced by Puerto Ricans in the Liberal party, with public housing, and with other institutions discourages rather than automatically limits participation. The element of choice still exists. But the choice everyone basically has is the option to either try to solve the problems or to simply quit the system. Albert O. Hirschman described this as "voice" or "exit" (1970). We can either participate to change things (voice) or drop out and/or leave our community, city, or society (exit). Our decision whether to voice or exit is not made in a vacuum, however. Social institutions and structures will promote or discourage people to voice or exit. We have seen how Puerto Rican participation has been discouraged by social structures and specifically by the Liberal party and public housing. Many people have argued, however, that the decision to participate is affected more by the ease of exit that Puerto Ricans in the United States enjoy (by returning to Puerto Rico) compared to other groups in the United States. Puerto Ricans participate less because *exit*, in this case, overwhelms *voice*.

It has become popular to explain the deep poverty and powerlessness among Puerto Ricans as a unique condition, attributable to the unlimited opportunity to return to Puerto Rico. Thurow, for instance, explains the Puerto Rican lack of economic success to the "ability to go home again, to go back to Puerto Rico whenever one chooses without any fear that one will not be allowed to re-enter the U. S., undercuts the feeling that many immigrants have that they must succeed in the U. S. because there is no home to which they can return" (1986). Tienda and Díaz make a similar claim about Puerto Rican social participation. They argue that what distinguishes Puerto Ricans "from other inner-city minority groups is their circular migration between the island and the United States, which severely disrupts families and schooling, leading inevitably to a loss of income" (1987). But it isn't necessarily true that ease of exit discourages participation in the economy or in politics. It can stimulate participation. People will participate more when ease of exit diminishes the possibility of "retaliation from authorities or others who dislike the participant's policies or tactics" (Nagel 1987, 45). Thus, the possibility of escape to Puerto Rico can increase participation by weakening the threat of possible retaliation. The empirical evidence, however, is inconclusive about whether Puerto Rico, in fact, serves as an escape-valve or as a sanctuary from politics.

The 1987 survey of Puerto Ricans in New York City by the government of Puerto Rico revealed that although a large percentage of Puerto Ricans in New York were interested in political developments in Puerto Rico, not many Puerto Ricans actually did much traveling to Puerto Rico, and there was very little difference in response between registered and unregistered Puerto Ricans. Among registered voters, for example, a majority (57 percent) stated that they were "interested to very interested" in political developments in Puerto Rico (Government of P.R. 1988, 10). This compares with 46 percent of the not registered who had such interest. While Puerto Ricans may be interested in political developments in Puerto Rico, they don't seem to have any more time or energy to follow political events there than they do in New York City. The report states that "the majority of both the registered (63%) and non-registered (54%) indicated they did not closely follow or did not follow at all events in Puerto Rico" (Government of P.R. 1988: 10). This suggests that while Puerto Rico may occupy a position of intellectual and emotional importance to Puerto Ricans in the United States, it may not have everyday, practical impact on their lives. This study, for instance, reported that very few of the registered (13 percent) or the non-registered (12 percent) Puerto Ricans in New York City actually traveled to the Island more than once a year (Government of P.R. 1988, 10). In addition, "18 percent of the registered and 21 percent of the non-registered stated they never visited Puerto Rico" (Government of P.R. 1988, 10). Thus, there does not seem to be as much "circular migration" as some analysts have predicted. It is probably more accurate to describe it as "ambiguous migration," since a large proportion of Puerto Ricans have plans to eventually move to Puerto Rico: 44 percent of the registered and 51 percent of the unregistered (Government of P.R. 1988, 10). Most Puerto Ricans, nonetheless, saw New York City rather than Puerto Rico as home. Over 51 percent of the registered and 47 percent of the unregistered stated that New York was their home, while only 38 percent of the unregistered and 28 percent of the registered stated that Puerto Rico was home.

Despite the ambiguity, however, New York City is not a comfortable home for Puerto Ricans. Few Puerto Ricans, for example, felt that the Puerto Rican community had been accepted by most other Americans (only 39 percent of the unregistered and 45 percent of the registered). And 62 percent of Puerto Ricans registered to vote felt that Puerto Ricans were discriminated against compared to 59 percent of the unregistered Puerto Ricans (Commonwealth 1988, 9). The differences between the attitudes of Puerto Ricans registered and not registered to vote are clearly minor. Those who have chosen to express their needs and interests (voice) don't appear to see themselves and American society very differently from those who decline to participate (exit). We do not know from the report whether the same people in this study who are not registered are also the ones who travel to Puerto Rico often, plan to move there, or think of Puerto Rico as their home. But there is some intuitive logic to the idea that if Puerto Ricans don't feel at home in New York City, they are less likely to become involved in its political affairs. Pomper and Semekos suggest such a connection as an explanation for why Americans in general don't participate.

Pomper and Semekos argue that voting participation hinges not on individual characteristics such as education or attitude but on community solidarity. Voting is in this sense very similar to bake sales. In both cases "the expected benefits may be very small and the costs are irrelevent. Both acts are expressions of community solidarity, a sharing and a ritual" (Pomper and Semekos 1991, 10). People don't vote when they lack real integration into their local community. That is what Puerto Ricans experience but not so much because Puerto Rico offers an easy exit. Puerto Ricans lack integration into community life in New York City because of some of the factors described above. Political parties, like the Liberal party, exclude, manipulate, and demobilize them. Housing conditions are such that Puerto Ricans are especially vulnerable and made restless by the deterioration of the private housing market. Puerto Ricans also lack control of religious institutions that could help create a sense of community solidarity. The lack of community solidarity would help explain why it is that, though Puerto Ricans consider New York City home, many still have plans to eventually move to the Island. Puerto Rico provides a sense of identity and community life, even if sometimes only as a dream, because New York City, and the United States in general, is so inhospitable. Puerto Ricans don't vote, then, for a simple but daunting reason: they have come to think they don't belong in the United States.

Bibliography

Adler, Norman, B. Blank, and R. Peel

1975 *Political Clubs in New York.* New York: Praeger.

Arnstein, Sherry

1972 "A Ladder of Citizen Participation." In *The City in the Seventies.* Ed Robert K. Yin. Itasca, IL: F. E. Peacock.

Bavers, Sherrie

1984 "Puerto Rican Politics in New York City: The Post-World War II Period." *Puerto Rican Politics in Urban America.* Eds James Jennings and M. Rivera. Westport, CT: Greenwood P.

Berndt, Harry

1977 *New Rulers in the Ghetto: The Community Development Corporation and Urban Society.* Westport, CT: Greenwood P.

Burnham, Walter D.

1982 *The Current Crisis in American Politics.* New York: Oxford UP.

Calzada, José L.

1979 "Democratic Aspects of Migration." *Labor Migration under Capitalism: The Puerto Rican Experience.* History Task Force. New York: Monthly Review.

Carter, Robert F.

1965 "Pressure from the Left: The American Labor Party, 1936-1954." PhD Diss Syracuse U.

Christian, J.

1983 Chair of NYCHA. "Address on the New York City Housing Authority." LaGuardia Archives, Queens, NY.

Cohen, Steven M., and Robert E. Kapsis

1978 "Participation of Blacks, Puerto Ricans, and Whites in Voluntary Associations: A Test of Current Theories." *Social Forces,* vol 56 (June):4.

Conzun, Katheleen N.

1989 "Ethnicity as Festive Culture: 19th-Century German America on Parade." *The Invention of Ethnicity.* Ed Werner Sollers. New York: Oxford UP.

Cornacchia, Eugene

1985 "Ethnicity and Modes of Participation: White Ethnics, Blacks, and Hispanics in New York City." PhD Diss Fordham U, Bronx, NY.

Costikgan, Roy

1966 *Behind Closed Doors: Politics in the Public Interest.* New York: Harcourt, Brace & World.

Degler, Carl

1959 *Out of Our Past: The Forces That Shaped Modern America.* New York: Harper & Row.

Estades, Rosa

1978 *Patterns of Political Participation of Puerto Ricans in New York City.* Rio Piedras, PR: U of Puerto Rico.

1980 "Symbolic Unity: The Puerto Rican Day Parade." In *The Puerto Rican Struggle: Essays on Survival in the U. S.* Eds C. Rodriguez et al. New York: PR Migration Research Consortium.

Falcón, Angelo

1980 "Puerto Rican Political Participation: New York City and Puerto Rico." Repr Institute for Puerto Rican Policy.

1984 "Early Puerto Rican Politics in New York City, 1860-1945: Prolegomenon to a History." In *Puerto Rican Politics in Urban America.* Eds James Jennings and M. Rivera. Westport, CT: Greenwood P.

1985 "Black and Latino Politics in New York City: Race and Ethnicity in a Changing Urban Context." Discussion Paper. New York: Institute for Puerto Rican Policy, October.

Flournoy, Houston I.

1956 "The Liberal Party in New York State." PhD Diss Princeton U.

García-Passalacqua, Manuel

1983 "Mythology and Practice of Puerto Rican Electoral Participation." In *Strategies for Increasing Voter Participation in Puerto Rican Communities in the Continental U. S.* Washington, DC: National Puerto Rican Coalition.

Government of Puerto Rico, Migration Division
1988 "Puerto Rican Voter Registration in New York City: A Comparison of Attitudes between Registered and Non-Registered Puerto Ricans." New York: Commonwealth of Puerto Rico.
Greene, Kenneth
1990 "Political Participation among Hispanics: Voting and Contacting in a Northern County." *Journal of Urban Affairs,* 12:3.
Greenstone, J. David, and Paul E. Peterson
1973 *Race and Authority in Urban Politics: Community Participation and the War on Poverty.* New York: Russell Sage Foundation.
Guzmán, Pablo
1980 "Puerto Rican Barrio Politics in the United States." In *The Puerto Rican Struggle: Essays on Survival in the U. S.* Eds C. Rodríguez et al. New York: PR Migration Research Consortium.
Handlin, Oscar
1962 *The Newcomers: Negroes and Puerto Ricans in a Changing Metropolis.* New York: Anchor Books.
Harvey, David
1985 *The Urbanization of Capital: Studies in the History and Theory of Capitalist Development.* Baltimore, MD: Johns Hopkins UP.
Hellinger, Daniel, and Dennis R. Judd
1991 *The Democratic Facade.* Pacific Grove, CA: Brooks/Cole.
Hirschman, Albert O.
1970 *Exit, Voice, and Loyalty: Responses to Decline in Firms, Organizations, and States.* Cambridge, MA: Harvard UP.
Iglesias, César Andréu, ed
1977 *Memorias de Bernardo Vega.* Rio Piedras, PR: Ediciones Huracán.
Institute for Puerto Rican Policy (IRP). *Towards a Puerto Rican/Latino Agenda for New York City, 1989.* New York: IPR.
Jackson, Peter
1983 "Vito Marcantonio and Ethnic Politics in New York." *Ethnic and Racial Studies,* vol 6 (January):1.
Jennings, James, and M. Rivera, eds.
1984 *Puerto Rican Politics in Urban America.* Westport, CT: Greenwood P.
Kramer, Ralph
1969 *Participation of the Poor: Comparative Case Studies in the War on Poverty.* Englewood Cliffs, NJ: Prentice-Hall.
Latino National Political Survey (LNPS).
1990 *Preliminary Explorations from the Pilot Survey.*
Laurentz, Robert
1980 "Racial Ethnic Conflict in the New York City Garment Industry, 1933-1980." PhD Diss. State U of NY at Binghamton.
López, Alberto
1973 *The Puerto Rican Papers: Notes on the Reemergence of a Nation.* New York: Bobbs-Merrill.
Lowi, Theodore
1969 *The End of Liberalism: Ideology, Policy, and the Crisis with Public Authority.* New York: W. W. Norton.
Mills, C. W., C. Senior, and R. K. Goldsen
1950 *The Puerto Rican Journey: New York's Newest Migrants.* New York: Harper & Row.
Nagel, Jack
1987 *Participation.* Englewood Cliffs, NJ: Prentice-Hall.
National Puerto Rican Coalition (NPRC).
Strategies for Increasing Voter Participation in Puerto Rican Communities in the Continental U. S. Washington, DC: NPRC.
Nelson, Dale C.
1980 "The Political Behavior of New York Puerto Ricans: Assimilation or Survival?" In *The Puerto Rican Struggle: Essays on Survival in the U. S.* Eds C.E. Rodríguez et al. New York: PR Migration Research Consortium.
Padilla, Elena
1958 *Up from Puerto Rico.* New York: Columbia UP.
Peel, Roy V.
1935 *The Political Clubs of New York City.* New York: Putnam.
Plotnick, Robert D., and Felicity Skidmore
1975 *Progress against Poverty: A Review of the 1964-1974 Decade.* New York: Academic P.
Pomper, Gerald, and Loretta A. Semekos
1991 "Bake Sales and Voting." *Society,* vol 28 (July/August):5.
Rivera, Monte
1984 "Organizational Politics of the East Harlem Barrio in the 1970s." In *Puerto Rican Politics in Urban America.* Eds. James Jennings and M. Rivera. Westport, CT: Greenwood P.
Rodríquez, Clara, V. Sánchez-Korral, and J. O. Alers, eds
1980 *The Puerto Rican Struggle: Essays on Survival in the U. S.* New York: PR Migration Research Consortium.
Rodríquez-Fraticelli, Carlos, and Amilcar Tirado
1990 "Community Organizations in New York." *Boletín,* 2:6.
Sayre, Wallace, and H. Kaufman
1960 *Governing New York City.* New York: Russell Sage Foundation.
Schaffer, Alan
1966 *Vito Marcantonio: Radical in Congress.* Syracuse, NY: Syracuse UP.
Schefter, Martin
1985 *Political Crisis/Fiscal Crisis: The Collapse and Revival of New York City.* New York: Basic Books.
1986 "Political Incorporation and the Extrusion of the Left: Party Politics and Social Forces in New York City." In *Studies in American Political Development,* vol 1. New Haven, CT: Yale UP.
Senior, Clarence
1965 *The Puerto Ricans: Strangers—Then Neighbors.* Chicago: Quadrangle Books.
Stevens-Arroyo, Antonio M.
1980 "Puerto Rican Struggles in the Catholic Church." *The Puerto Rican Struggle: Essays on Survival in the U. S.* Eds C. Rodríquez et al. New York: PR Migration Research Consortium.
Therborn, Goran
1983 "The Rule of Capital and the Rise of Democracy." In

States and Societies. Eds David Held et al. New York: New York UP.

Thurow, Lester
1986 "Latinos Enter Mainstream Quickly." *Los Angeles Times, (March* 16), Part IV.

Tienda, Marta, and William A. Díaz
1987 "Puerto Ricans' Special Problems." *New York Times,* (August 28), Section I, 31:3.

Tyler, Gus
1968 *The Political Imperative: The Corporate Character of Unions.* New York: MacMillan.

U. S. Bureau of the Census
1982 *Voting and Registration in the Election of November 1980.* Washington, DC: Government Printing Office.
1989 *Current Population Survey*. Washington, DC: Government Printing Office.

Valentín, Gilberto Gerena
1989 "Mi Gente: Gilberto Gerena Valentín." Interview in Center for Puerto Rican Studies Boletin. vol 2:5.

Vega, Bernardo
1984 *Memoirs of Bernardo Vega: A Contribution to the History of the Puerto Rican Community in New York.* Ed César A. Iglesias. New York: Monthly Review P.

Wakefield, Dan
1984 *Island in the City: The World of Spanish Harlem.* New York: Arno P.

Wolfinger, Raymond E.
1991 "Voter Turnout." *Society,* vol 28, (July/August):5.

Wood, Robert C.
1961 *1400 Governments: The Political Economy of the New York City Metropolitan Area.* Cambridge, MA: Harvard.

The Politics of Cuban Emigrés in the United States

María de los Angeles Torres

Immigrant communities have a very complicated and often ambivalent relationship to their country of origin. Maintaining and rebuilding a relationship with a homeland left behind is not an easy matter. Politics further complicates this difficulty, particularly for exiles living in a host country antagonistic to their homeland. While banishment as a form of punishment has been used by many societies, the modern-day phenomenon of political exiles has been closely related to the Cold War.

The contemporary search for a more productive economic system and a more democratic and just society presents an opportunity to review this phenomenon. Ensuing discussions within nations as well as among nations can include the participation of political exiles. Given that the conflict between exiles and their homeland is often reflective of deeper problems, exiles can and sometimes should play a role in the resolution of problems. What role and to what effect depends on many factors. But given the dangerous potential of a rise of authoritarianism, it is particularly important to understand the dynamics and the trajectory of exile political organizations. This understanding is also important in order to promote a positive contribution from exile communities.

The resettlement of people from one land to another has been part of human history. Natural disasters, wars, and economic, social, and political conditions have many times created situations that forced people to relocate. With the rise of an international economic system,these movements developed a unique set of dynamics closely related to the international division of labor. Thus, the movement of people and the communities they developed in new lands were closely related to the movement of labor and capital globally. Population exchanges were politicized by the procedures developed by nation-states. With the nation-state also came a new set of conditions that defined the rights of individuals, particularly in relationship to the state. Citizenship became a right to be granted or denied by the state, nationalism a way of laying claim to political legitimacy. The notion of national citizenship was intricately woven into the nation-state, which also included the concept of homeland in many instances.

In the case of Cuba, a small island in the Caribbean, the movement of people in and out was historically linked to the island's relationship to international powers. In this context, Cubans also struggled to establish an independent nation. The search for nation has defined the politics of the island as well as the politics of Cubans abroad.

Throughout the 1800s Cubans in the United States organized political organizations aimed at influencing the question of the political status of the island. In the mid-1800s Cubans in the United States organized pro-annexationist organizations that found support among Southern slave-owners. In the late 1800s, emerging groups called for the independence of the island. Therefore, the politics of exile were part of the fabric of the emerging Cuban communities in the United States. Even before the "Spanish-American" War of 1898, while Cuba was still a colony of Spain, its economy was more closely linked to the United States than to its colonial masters. Investors from the United States had already expanded into the sugar industry, and their larger sugar mills had driven many Cuban owners into bankruptcy. From 1887 to 1907 most of Cuba's sugar and tobacco was sold to the United States (Pino-Santos 1973).

Therefore, Cubans did not flock in great numbers to Madrid but rather to New York, New Orleans, Philadelphia, Key West, and Tampa. Although the 1910 U. S. Census identified only 15,133 Cubans, a special report to the U. S. Senate on people entering the United States from 1899 to 1910 compiled data on 44,211 Cubans (U. S. Congress 1910). Most Cuban immigrants in the late 1800s were tobacco workers, although some were also manufacturers. Class division characterized the Cuban community from its inception.

The contemporary nexus between Cuban Americans and the United States must first be understood within the larger framework of U. S./Latin American relations, for it is this superseding dynamic that in the first instance defines the linkage between the United States and Cuba and subsequently defines Cuban immigrants and the United States. This linkage has been one in which the United States has tried to impose hegemony by force and ideology on the people of Cuba. It has been characterized by racism and economic and political manipulation.

Today almost a tenth of Cuba's population lives in the United States. Over 0.5 million Cuban Americans live in South Florida. Another 0.5 million are spread out across the United States with important concentrations in New York, New Jersey, Illinois, and California. The majority of Cubans who live in the United States today migrated after the 1959 Cuban revolution. Cuban Americans are popularly viewed as political exiles who are economically successful and conservative. Thus the myth of the golden exile. Yet serious studies have challenged the three tenets of this myth, which argue that Cubans leave Cuba because they are politically disaffected with the revolution; they are successfully self-employed; and they are politically conservative— especially in regard to U. S./Cuba relations. While the community undeniably bears the scars of thirty years of failed policies toward Cuba and of the island government's intolerance toward those who left, the Cuban-American reality is complex, often paradoxical, and in transition. These changes are closely linked to a historical context that is defined in part by the internal situation on the island, the experience in the host country, international factors, and the influx of new immigrants. It is also part of the larger matrix of U. S./Latin American relations.

The Origins of the Post-Revolutionary Emigré Community

The Cuban revolution produced a restructuring of class and power relations that redefined Cuban society. Policies were instituted that greatly redistributed wealth and benefits of society. While the revolution of 1959 was deeply rooted in the struggle to define a nation and institute a just social program, it had major ramifications for U. S. hegemony in the Caribbean. This in turn had an impact on the post-World War II standoff between the Soviet Union and the United States. Therefore, the dynamics set in place by an internal revolution were played out on the world arena. This affected the movement of people out of the island and consequently the politics of emigré communities. Although the duality of immigrant/exile was forged on the politics of Cuban Americans since the 1800s, this historical dynamic became trapped in the sharply divided world politics of the 1950s.

Therefore, the relationship of Cuban Americans to their homeland after the revolution must be understood within a framework which analyzes U. S. and Cuban national security interests, how these influenced the formation of the politics of the community, and how internal community dynamics in turn evolved. The broader framework of homeland politics—its organizational and ideological articulation—must be understood in this context. National security interests on both sides of the Florida Straits have drawn the boundaries in which unfold the dilemmas of race and class, immigrant and exile, and individual and community. The origin and continued development of the Cuban emigré community in the United States is intricately woven in past U. S./Cuba relations and in internal Cuban policies toward dissent. Therefore a resolution of conflict between both nations and the continued political opening on the island necessarily will include a resolution of the conflict between community and homeland.

U. S. National Security Interests

The revolution in Cuba did challenge U. S. hegemony in the Caribbean. It called for a reordering of political power to protect Cuban national interests, not U. S. interests. The United States reacted by trying to remove the revolutionary leadership from power. U. S. intervention relied on military, ideological, political and economic tactics.

U. S. involvement in Cuban affairs was nothing new. But unlike interventions prior to World War II, U. S. reactions to the Cuban revolution were intermeshed with the crusade to stop communism from spreading in the Western Hemisphere. State structures in which foreign policies emerged and were implemented had dramatically changed after World War II, giving rise to the national security state (Barnet 1973; and Landau 1988). The mood of the U. S. public had been infected by fanatical anticommunism.

When the Cuban revolution triumphed in 1959, an estimated 124,000 Cubans were living in the United States. Of these, 100,000 had registered at the Cuban consulate. As the revolutionary government moved leftward and came into increasingly sharp confrontation with the United States, between 1959 and 1962, approximately 215,000 more people left the island (Díaz-Brisquet et al. 1981).

For the first time in U. S./Cuba relations, Cuban emigrés became a critical component in foreign policies aimed at overthrowing and discrediting the Cuban revolution (Arguelles 1982). Cuban emigrés came to fulfill many functions for the United States (Forment 1984). Given the concentration of these activities in national security agencies, these relationships were forged within the evolving national security state.

Exiles: A Cover for U. S. Intervention

As early as spring 1959 Richard Nixon proposed arming and otherwise supporting an exile force for direct military intervention against Fidel Castro. He also succeeded in getting CIA and FBI approval of his recommendation (Williams 1962). By March 1960 the CIA had issued a top-secret report entitled "A Program of Covert Action Against the Castro Regime," which included the following policy options:

- Creation of . . . a responsible and unified Cuban government in exile
- A powerful propaganda offensive
- A covert intelligence and action organization in Cuba to be responsible to the exile opposition
- A paramilitary force outside of Cuba for future guerrilla action. (Wyden 1979)

On March 17, 1960, Eisenhower approved CIA policy which directed that measures be taken to help organize, train and equip Cuban refugees so they could act at the proper time (Szulc 1961). Still there were several concerns. One was the reaction of other Latin American countries. U. S. officials had clearly been stung by anti-Americanism, as evidenced by Allen Dulles's testimony to a Senate Committee on Foreign Relations in 1958 regarding the protests that met Nixon on his tour of Latin America that year (U. S. Congress 1958). Thomas Mann, assistant secretary for InterAmerican Affairs, wanted to thoroughly conceal American sponsorship (Wyden 1979, 100). There was also concern from the CIA about reaction from the press and other agencies, such as the state and justice departments, since its charter prohibited the agency from operating inside the country (Wyden 1979, 76). The new president, John F. Kennedy, wanted to make sure that if it failed, it would not be perceived as his fault, but rather that of the Cuban exiles. According to Williams, "he was also concerned for his power, his externalization of evil, and his urge to control the future while still in the present" (Williams 1962, 152). Therefore, plausible deniability—the ability to conceal involvement—was important. These sets of international, bureaucratic, and political concerns contributed to institutionalizing practices that created Cuban exiles—and made Miami a foreign city on U. S. soil.

Emigrés: An Army

Cuban emigrés provided the human resources to implement a military strategy against Cuba. Estimates of the number of Cubans trained in military action range from 2,000 to 15,000 (Arguelles 1982, 31). The most dramatic action taken was the Bay of Pigs invasion. Training took place both in the United States and in Central America. Operatives received a monthly pension for their families.

Cuban President Fidel Castro.

After months of training in Guatemala and the United States, the Bay of Pigs invasion launched in April 1961 failed in its attempt to overthrow Castro's government (see Johnson et al. 1964). It also failed in concealing U. S. involvement. But it did create an experienced and trained military force that throughout the 1960s provided the CIA with small teams with which to carry out a covert war against Castro (U. S. Congress 1975).

These military actions institutionalized a series of practices that cemented the military functions Cuban emigrés could fulfill for the U. S. state. It contributed to creating institutions which on the one hand made Cuban emigrés part of U. S. foreign policies and on the other made sure they remained foreigners.

Massive Immigration: Ideological Functions

After the Cuban revolution, the United States became the country of first asylum for the first time in history. Although Cubans leaving Cuba were not expelled from their country per the classic exile definition, and there was no imminent threat to their person (as the international definition of asylum requires), they nonetheless were defined as refugees by U. S. immigration officials (Tabori 1972). The reasons for this can be found in the foreign policy objectives traced by the Eisenhower and Kennedy administrations.

While immigration is usually viewed as a domestic phenomenon closely linked to labor demand, it is also a product of foreign policies (Bach 1985). In fact in the case of Cuba, some have argued that immigration flows from the island to the United States can be categorized according to particular foreign policies (Scalan and Loescher 1983). Evidence indicates that there is a close connection between foreign policy objectives and Cuban immigration–particularly the need to show the failure of the revolution.

The ideological campaign against the Cuban revolution started very early. The political discourse of the time was cast in the anticommunist language of the l950s and is best represented in a State Department document released days before the Bay of Pigs invasion. The themes that run throughout this report include the betrayal of the middle class by the revolution, the establishment of a communist beachhead in the Western Hemisphere, the delivery of the revolution to the Sino-Soviet bloc, and the assault on the hemisphere (U. S. Department of State 1961).

A key strategy in showing the revolution's failure to live up to democratic ideals was the emigration of thousands of Cubans, particularly middle-class Cubans. The facilitation and encouragement of Cuban migration to the United States was part of a context that included humanitarian concerns, desire to overthrow the revolution with Cuban exiles, and the need to embarrass the Cuban Government. The now-famous line "voting with your feet" was institutionalized into a strategy by the Eisenhower and later the Kennedy administrations. As U. S. Representative Walter Rudd claimed: "Every refugee who comes out (of Cuba) is a vote for our society and a vote against their society" (Piloto 1988). Massive migration of professionals in particular proved to the world that the revolution was failing and specifically betraying the middle class. In the policy debate about whether or not to facilitate Cuban immigration to the United States, until the l980s those arguing that Cuban immigration showed the world the failure of communism had won out (Domínguez 1988). Therefore, from the early days of the revolution, the U. S. Government facilitated and politicized immigration.

This was implemented by creating special immigration policies and programs to facilitate and encourage migration. Special visa waivers and resettlement programs for the post-revolutionary immigration were part of the strategy to use Cuban immigrants to discredit the Cuban revolution (Hernández 1980; and Pedraza-Bailey 1985). In 1961 the United States brought more than 15,000 Cuban children to this country through the State Department-sponsored "Peter Pan Operation." The Catholic Church and the U. S. Chamber of Commerce in Havana convinced Cuban parents that if they did not send their children to the United States, the revolutionary government would send them to the Soviet Union. Once in the United States, children could claim their parents under the family preference stipulations of the immigration laws (Walsh 1971).

In its efforts to encourage Cuban immigration to the United States, the government set up special programs that included food, clothing, medical care, and cash benefits. As Richard Brown, the director of the Office of Refugee and Migration Affairs, stated: "Our assistance demonstrates in concrete form to the enslaved millions in Communist-dominated lands the inherent humanity of a free society." In a January 14, 1962, State Department bulletin, he made reference to Kennedy's statement that "the successful reestablishment of refugees is importantly related to free world political objectives" (Pedraza-Bailey 1985, 155). Over two billion dollars were estimated to have been spent on the refugee program (Arguelles 1982, 30). The U. S. government also expected that the stay of Cubans on U. S. soil would be a temporary situation.

Later, other programs to ease integration into U. S. society were established such as the Department of Health, Education, and Welfare's scholarship fund to help Cubans pay for college education. Unlike that of other Latin American immigrants, the entry and settlement of Cubans into North American society was greatly facilitated by the U. S. government. For Cubans, it paid to be a political refugee (Pedraza-Bailey 1985, 75).

Political refugees fleeing communist-controlled countries showed the world the horrors of communism and the desire for democracy. Symbolism is an integral part of ideology. Emigrés provided images for the rationale for continued U. S. foreign policies aimed at containing communism and expanding the forces needed for battle. While the principal functions of Cuban emigrés were military and ideological, the massive emigration out of Cuba drained the economy of much-needed professionals. Therefore, the emigré movement also had an economic function.

Cuba and Outgoing Emigration

While U. S. foreign policies were major factors in shaping the politics of Cuban exiles, Cuban security policies have to be added to the matrix as well. Most countries include defense of their national territory as a fundamental part of their national security. Developing countries also include economic development as part of their national security interests. Scholars analyzing Cuba's national security dispute with the United States have shown how the United States violated both: it invaded Cuba directly, and it imposed an economic blockade that affected Cuba's ability to develop economically (Treto 1988). Within this definition, Cuban emigration represented a threat to Cuba's national security in that many who left initially took physical and human resources. They also joined an invasion of the island.

Given this definition, Cuban scholars often analyze Cuban emigration solely in the context of U. S./Cuba relations (Miyar Bolio 1991; and Arce Rodríguez 1991). This context is critical for understanding the fomentation of immigration and the utilization of emigrés to fulfill functions for the U. S. state, but it does not allow for an understanding of the internal dynamics at work within Cuba which also contributed to creating an exile.

After 1959 internal dynamics within Cuba provoked a restructuring of power and class relations that led to a redistribution of land and resources. Economic changes, such as agrarian and urban reforms, spurred a momentum that contributed to people leaving the country. While Cuba's reaction to those leaving the country was in part a response to U. S. actions aimed at destabilizing the revolution, it had its own internal logic as well (Valdez 1990). Revolutionary justice was quickly dispensed, and many civil rights were suspended. The death penalty was used often, and incarceration of political opponents became a common practice. By 1965 more than 20,000 political prisoners were jailed (Domínguez 1978). Internal policies therefore contributed to making dissent from the revolutionary government difficult and mostly impossible. For opponents, leaving the country was one of the remaining options. This option is still used today as sentenced prisoners such as María Elena Cruz Varela, a poet and leader of Criterio Alternativo, an internal dissident group, are given the option of remaining in jail or leaving the country ("Cuba da opción a Cruz Varela" 1991, 1).

Just as Cuban emigrés have fulfilled a set of functions for the U. S. state, so have they for the Cuban state. The post-revolutionary government has always publicly maintained that the construction of socialism was "Una tarea de hombres libres" (A task for free men), yet simultaneously it set up legal mechanisms to punish those who left without authorization. So the emigration's purpose was twofold: first to reinforce control of the population through political and legal mechanisms, and second, to externalize dissent and attempt to render it impotent (Shain 1989).

Loyalty Test: Political Functions of Emigration

The issue of leaving or staying in Cuba provided the new government with a political rallying point with which to mobilize support for the revolution (Pérez 1984). In the early days of the revolution Fidel Castro stated: "Those who escape their duty, taking the road to the north, have lost the right to be worthy sons of the fatherland" (*New York Times* 1960). From the beginning the Cuban revolution manifested a very hard line toward those who left the country. Leaving was akin to treason. Those leaving were called *Gusanos*, a double entendre referring to both the duffel bags carried by people as they left and to being a low-life. For a country accustomed to taking a ferry from Cuba to Florida, honeymooning in Miami, and maintaining a very close relationship to the United States, this was a drastic turn.

Leaving or staying—as well as a person's position on those who left—became a litmus test for loyalty to the revolution. For instance, when a great number of professionals started leaving the country and the loss started to have a visible impact on Cuba's economy, a political campaign was launched to identify remaining on the island with patriotism. At a rally at the University of Havana, President Dortico asked those present to stand up and take an oath that they would stay and give their services to the nation (Alarcón 1991). Revolutionary cadres were also discouraged from maintaining contact with their relatives who left. Party militants were explicitly prohibited from writing to relatives.

The reaction of Cuba's leaders toward those who migrated were institutionalized into policies. As early as 1961 a law was passed that authorized the Ministry of the Interior to give exit and reentry permits to those leaving the country. If a person was not back by the time allotted by the reentry permit, their leave was considered a "definitive abandonment" of the country, and thus the state had the right to confiscate all their property (Gaceta Oficial de la República de Cuba 1962). Persons who migrated were not allowed to return to visit; thus, the punishment for leaving the country was permanent banishment.

Exile was a penalty used by the Spaniards during the colonial period. Those who challenged Spanish authority were banished from the country. While the Cuban practice has roots in its colonial past, it contradicts contemporary immigration laws, which were put into effect by a U. S. military governor in 1901. This law, an exact copy of U. S. immigration law, does not recognize dual citizenship; therefore once a Cuban citizen, always a Cuban citizen. Cubans—persons or the children of persons born in Cuba—living abroad are considered Cuban, and when traveling to Cuba must do so on a Cuban passport. However, because of the law of "definitive abandonment," these persons have no property or social rights.

In a strange sort of way the community abroad helped dramatize the "exceptional" character of the Cuban revolution. It also helped create an image of the permanence of the revolution. But time gave way to some of these measures, and in the 1970s, when Cuban emigrés lobbied the Cuban government to allow return visits, the Cuban emigré acquired a new function—bearer of economic hard currency.

Externalizing Dissent: National Security Served

The exodus of exiles helped consolidate the revolution politically by externalizing dissent and rendering it impotent (Pedraza-Bailey 1985, 148). By accepting large numbers of Cubans, the U. S. government inadvertently helped facilitate the formation of a more politically pliable population (Domínguez 1978, 137).

Adversity that has been denationalized loses its legitimacy, particularly in a situation in which nationalism is an important element of mobilization. Often home country governments cast these adversaries as "traitors" for leaving, thereby delegitimizing their exodus. This is particularly true if the host country is at war or is antagonistic to the home country. The Cuban revolution is a classic example: it delegitimized those leaving. It legally defined their exit as "definitive." And the host country was a historical as well as contemporary "enemy" of the nation. In 1960 Raúl Castro analyzed outgoing migration as "the normal exodus that takes place when the people take the power in their own hands and liquidate exploitation and the privileged classes. Their departure does not damage the revolution, but fortifies it as it is a spontaneous purification" (*New York Times* 1961). In addition, the ever-present threat of the counterrevolution from "el exilio" helped rationalize the need for national security agencies within Cuba in charge of protecting the revolution.

The conflict between the United States and Cuba required an expansion of Cuban governmental capabilities to meet an external threat (Domínguez 1978, 37). This has been true in the expansion of national security agencies within Cuba and in particular in dealing with those who leave. This includes the Ministry of the Interior, which encompasses immigration services and internal and external intelligence apparatus. It also includes offices within other ministries, such as the Ministry of Foreign Affairs and ICAP, El Instituto de Amistad con los Pueblos and the Cuban Communist Party. While externalizing dissent has its benefits, it also has its cost. Besides the obvious loss of human resources, the actions of revolution fueled an "exile," which in the long run may have externalized opposition at the same time that it institutionalized it.

Internal Community Factors and Exile Politics: The Political Economy of the Cuban-American Community

The Cuban community in the United States is also a product of the fragmented national elite that was overthrown. Most of this sector of Cuban society left after the revolution, bringing with them experience, knowledge, habits, and, in many cases, relationships that over time have been replicated within North American society. As this sector has matured, it has realigned in some instances and developed its own economic and political interests.

The development of the Cuban-American exile has also been influenced by the internal dynamics of the community as well as the larger society's reaction to the community. For as intimate as the relationship between the exile power formation and U. S. foreign policy has been, sectors within the community began to incur their own interests in this political arrangement (Portes and Bach 1985).

While for the first wave of immigrants, there has been a net downshift in their economic and social position in the United States compared to where they were in Cuban society, Cubans have built an impressive economic base in Miami and other cities (see Jorge and Moncarz 1981). The ethnic economic enclaves in part have been built on the ability to extract cheap labor from Cuban workers. Therefore, the institutionalized political power that first emerged from a relationship with state foreign policies helped ethnic capital as well. Many of the exiles' political activities began to acquire a function of internal control of the community, which greatly benefited the emergence of the enclave economy that relied on cheap labor (Arguelles and McGoin 1980).

Post-revolutionary migration has been heterogeneous, yet the first waves included an over-representation of professionals and skilled workers. Once in the United States, some professionals were not able to transfer their skills, yet many did. The class background, as well as the rearrangement of class within the United States, created a community in contact with sectors of U. S. society that historically had been exclusively white.

Throughout the United States, and in particular South Florida, Cubans were not welcomed with open arms. Unlike federal policy that encouraged migration, local and state governments and communities often rejected Cuban exiles, particularly when it was clear that they were in the United States to stay. Given the class background of the initial wave of immigrants, this dynamic tended to reinforce nationalism (Gómez-Quiñones 1977). The experience of being a privileged exile and an unwanted immigrant at the same time created an ambivalent position for Cubans in the United States in which issues of homeland and ethnicity continued to intermingle with politics.

Cubans have long been politically active in the United States. Exile politics have either supported or opposed U. S. policies toward Cuba, depending on the moment. In general, Cubans are highly politicized (Azicri 1982). Most have lived through a revolutionary period in their homeland where crucial political decisions were common.

Cuban-American politics, while traditionally diverse, unfolded within a political culture that had little tolerance for dissent. Opponents of the revolution were not only ultra-right landowners and business people, but social and Christian Democrats as well. It was the militarization of this opposition by the United States and the promotion of hard-line policies on both sides of the Florida Straits that encouraged antidemocratic tendencies within the community (Forment 1984). Having gained control of the media, many businesses, and the electoral arena, these forces sought to impose a single, rigid anti-Castro viewpoint, using intimidation and violence to silence opponents.

There is a close connection between the politics of the Cuban-American community and U. S. policies toward Cuba. In the early l960s there was a shared strategic political goal of overthrowing the revolution. This coincided with U. S. policy at the time. But this "strategic uniformity" obscured the ideological pluralism that characterized the opposition (Casal 1979; and Azicri 1982).

National security apparatus and policies had a dominant influence on the creation of exile politics of the post-revolutionary Cuban community. Foreign policies aimed at overthrowing and discrediting the Cuban revolution were in part implemented through Cuban emigrés (Arguelles 1982). Once in the United States, many Cuban emigrés participated in U. S.-backed military actions such as the Bay of Pigs. The U. S. intelligence network gave life to the first political organizations and actors in the Cuban community. In fact, it was CIA agents who handpicked the leaders of the "government in exile" that was supposed to take over the government in Cuba after the Bay of Pigs invasion (Wyden 1979).

"The Frente," formed in a hotel room at the Statler Hilton in New York City, originally included Manuel Artime, the CIA's golden boy; Justo Carrillo; Manuel Antonio de Varona, former prime minister of Cuba and president of the senate; José Ignacio Rasco, a university professor and leader of the new Christian Democratic Party; and Aureliano Sánchez Arango, former minister of education and foreign relations. The last two were still in Cuba. Frank Bender, the CIA man in charge of the Cuba group, hosted the meeting (Johnson et al. 1964, 29).

But conflicts erupted. Men in the training camps in Guatemala felt that The Frente did not represent them and went on strike. The dissolution of The Frente led to a new civic political structure called "El Consejo Revolucionario Cubano." This time more liberal sectors of the opposition were included like Manuel Ray, Castro's former minister of public works; and José Miró Cardona, who had been the prime minister (Johnson et al. 1964, 62). The role of the political organization was essentially propagandistic. On the day of Bay of Pigs, April 17, 1961, the members of El Consejo were locked in barracks at a military camp. They were not even told that the invasion was underway.

After the 1959 revolution, immigrants from Cuba were those most adversely affected by the programs of the revolution. Not all Cubans left Cuba because they were dissatisfied with the revolution, but it was a deciding factor for the initial wave of immigrants in the early 1960s. As such, Cuba thus remained the central concern of emigré politics for many years. They did not intend to make the United States their permanent home. The first Cubans to leave the island clung to the belief that the revolutionary government would be toppled and they would return to Cuba (Fagen et al. 1968). In 1961, after the failure of the U. S.-sponsored Bay of Pigs invasion, those hopes began to fade.

Until 1965, the year the Cuban government defeated the internal counterrevolution, several groups led raids on the Cuban coast, smuggled arms and newspapers into Cuba, and maintained an active fund-raising drive among Cubans in the United States. Many times, fund-raising was done through extortion and threats of being fired if a worker did not contribute to the weekly drives (Arguelles 1980). Terrorism, as a form of activism, became ingrained in the political life of the community.

From 1962 to 1965, politics were fragmented as U. S. policy changed toward Cuba, and Cuba defeated the internal armed opposition. In the following years there was a general depoliticization toward Cuba in the Cuban-American community. The conflict between terrorism and depoliticization set in place a dynamic of political tension in the community, which created opportunities for different political tendencies to emerge.

Summary of Theoretical Framework

In this context, the relationship of Cuban Americans to Cuba acquired a political significance not normally ascribed to an immigrant community's relationship to its homeland or to the politics that emerge from this relationship. On the one hand, the relationship emerged from a revolution that challenged U. S. hegemony. This has meant that the relationship of this community to the state—host and home—is located in national security interests. However, it is also a community of non-white immigrants from a country that historically had been dominated by the United States and whose inhabitants therefore had been seen as inferior (*Our Islands and Their People* 1900s). In the process of domination, a people are deemed inferior by nature of their race, ethnicity, religion, or nationality. While Cubans may be white or black, race in the United States is constructed as "other," and all Cubans fall into that category—even those who support U. S. policies.

The Cuban exile is a distinct political formation fundamentally anchored in foreign policy objectives of the U. S. government and internal policies of the Cuban state. Exiles provided the United States military resources and ideological cannon fodder. As long as Cuban emigrés were exiles and not a part of the United States, the administration could deny involvement in the military actions being taken against the revolution. As exiles they provided "plausible deniability" to the CIA and other governmental agencies involved in the planning and execution of the covert war against the Castro regime.

After the 1959 Cuban revolution, U. S. policies politicized the process of immigration and militarized opposition to the revolution. They thus were institutionalizing repressive methods of political participation—particularly those focused on Cuba—within an evolving U. S. immigrant community. Further, the exiles also fulfilled the ideological functions of providing evidence that communism was a repressive system and that they preferred to flee to a free country. Legal definitions within the United States as well as aid packages for the community contributed to creating a distinct exile formation.

Cuban state policies contributed to this phenomenon as well. By politically defining leaving the country as treason, exiles provided the emerging revolutionary government with a rallying point. Externalizing opposition allowed the Cuban government to get rid of its dissidents in a fashion that essentially rendered them impotent to launch a legitimate challenge to the government, which increasingly relied on nationalism to consolidate its power. A force tied to one of the nation's historical enemies had no chance in mounting a popular claim against the government. The interaction between U. S. foreign policy objectives and domestic security policies in Cuba fueled the creation of a community abroad in exile. The close interaction between national security agencies within Cuba and the United States and the emigrés left a mark on the kinds of political organizations and ideologies that consolidated in the community. The class background of the emigrés and the conflict faced within the United States contributed to increasing nationalism in the community. While continuing a historical tradition of a duality of immigrant/exile, the post-revolutionary emigré community developed distinct characteristics owing to its original ties to national security interests in a Cold War era.

This is not to say that emigrés are passive actors in events concerning their homeland, but that generally speaking, they are not the dominant force in carving out the strategic policies for states. Further, this perspective does not deny that emigré groups acquired their own interests that at times ran contrary to state interests, but that ultimately the state has the upper hand—for power defines politics—and emigré groups do not enjoy a monopoly on power. Fulfilling symbolic and ideological functions for the state can create power, but the utilization of that power ultimately has to concede to larger state interests.

The study of the development of Cuban-American emigré politics is more a study of the development of state structures and ideologies. It is also a study of how emigré homeland politics evolves in the context of international confrontation between host and homeland.

Cubans in the 1970s: Pluralization and Dialogue

Even though l965 was the year of the dramatic exodus of thousands of Cubans through the port of Camarioca, by then it was fairly clear that the Cuban revolution was around to stay. That year the Cuban government announced the capture of the last remnants of the counterrevolution. The Johnson administration seemed less committed to toppling the revolution than President Kennedy had been. The grandiose plans for military action were abandoned along with the military role for Cuban Americans, even though terrorist actions continued to be encouraged.

For most Cuban exiles, life in the United States had not turned out to be as glittering as they expected. Though they received overt and covert aid unprecedented in U. S. immigration programs, even politically palatable immigrants faced discrimination and racism. As hopes of returning to Cuba faded, Cubans turned their concerns to life in the United States. Exile struggles took the backburner as more immediate struggles emerged. Class divisions sharpened, and advocacy groups seeking better social services emerged. As life in the United States created new needs and interests in such political activities, entrance into the political system was predictable.

Unexpectedly Cuban political activities were highly diversified, not monolithic as the popular image suggests. During the first years of exile political activity focused on returning to Cuba and defeating the revolution. As time passed the revolution consolidated, and political activities increasingly became related to emerging social services for needy sectors, such as the elderly and youth (Casal and Prohias 1973). Those working with the elderly joined forces with Miami-based senior citizens to advocate for quality medical care for its members. A University of Miami group of psychologists was one of the first to participate in national Latino social service advocacy organizations (Szapocznick et al. 1979).

Those groups that did not focus on the Cuban revolution were met with hostility from those who did. These Cubans felt threatened by organized activities that could be interpreted as abandonment of the exile cause. Yet the community as a whole was less concerned with returning to Cuba than with making it in the United States. This reformist tendency continued to grow. While in the social service sectors, normalization of relations was not a concern; the lack of concern with overthrowing the revolution placed these groups on the more liberal side of the political spectrum. Their demands for more government-supported services for the needy were evidence that Cubans were facing problems in the United States.

In questioning the inefficiencies of the United States, some individuals involved in social service organization did begin to question whether or not the revolution in their homeland had resulted in gains for the poor. The social service movement was not generally concerned with foreign policy, yet its activities tended to ally it with those that were. Both sectors were challenging the monolithic control held by Cuban conservatives, who were primarily interested in overthrowing the Cuban revolution and either ignored or denied the social and economic problems facing the community in the United States.

The process of pluralization of the exile community (Díaz 1970), as the diversification of politics has been called, was especially evident among young people. Confronted with the civil rights and antiwar movements, a significant number of Cuban students on North American campuses experienced a radicalization process that was to have surprising political implications in the long run.

The first signs of this movement were in publications such as *Nueva Generación* and the more politically defined *Areito* and *Joven Cuba. Joven Cuba* called on Cubans to become part of the civil rights struggles of the black and Latino communities. *Areito*, first published in Miami, was more concerned with building bridges between Cubans in the United States and Cuba. An organization called *Jóvenes Cubanos Socialistas* emerged in Puerto Rico (Grupo Areito 1979; Díaz 1979). Their radical stance of calling for a normalization of relations with Cuba was echoed by other sectors of the community as well. In the early 1970s debate ensued as to whether or not Cubans should hold a dialogue with the government they had left.

Young Cubans interested in returning to Cuba clustered around these various groups and publications. After intense lobbying efforts, the Cuban government started granting a small number of visas. In 1977 the Cuban government shifted its policy and granted the Areito group fifty-five visas. From this initial group, the Antonio Maceo Brigade was organized (*Areito* 1978).

The visit of these young Cubans to Cuba had a tremendous impact on the government and people of Cuba, who had not been willing previously to open communications with Cubans who had left the revolution (Díaz 1978). The Antonio Maceo Brigade trip paved the way for future dealings between the Cuban government and Cuban communities abroad. Both in Cuba and the United States, the myth of a monolithic Cuban community had been shattered.

Cubans Abroad in Dialogue with the Cuban Government

The Cuban community, which in the 1970s had appeared unchanging to most observers, was in fact increasingly polarized in regard to its vision of relations with the revolution. They nevertheless had various concerns that necessitated at least some conversations with the Cuban government. These concerns included traveling to Cuba to visit relatives, reunifying families, and releasing political prisoners.

In September, 1978, President Fidel Castro announced that he would hold conversations with representatives of the Cuban communities abroad (*Areito* "Interview" 1979). The "Dialogue," as these conversations were named, occurred for several reasons: There was a climate of rapprochement between the United States and Cuba. The United States had lifted the travel ban it had imposed on its residents. The Cuban government and the United States had traded "Interests Sections," a sort of embassy through third countries, as a step toward reestablishing full diplomatic relations. Also, the Cuban government had consolidated its power and thus was in a better position to deal with people who had left the country. Finally, there were Cubans abroad ready to hold a dialogue with the Cuban government (Casal *Areito* 1979).

The impact that the easing of tension between the United States and Cuba had on this process cannot be understated. As part of a new human rights strategy toward Latin America, the Carter administration's willingness to explore the development of relations with Cuba created the political space for those Cuban Americans who had been lobbying both governments to establish relations. Although the tendency for rapprochement with the revolution had already developed in the Cuban community, it did not consolidate until relations between Cuba and the United States became a political probability. The larger context of U. S./Cuba relations defined the political possibilities.

The Dialogue was held in two sessions, in November and December 1978. The agenda included the release of political prisoners, permission to leave the island for these prisoners and former political prisoners and their families, the reunification of divided families, and the right of Cubans living abroad to visit their relatives on the island. Representing the religious, labor, youth, professional, and business sectors of the Cuban community, 140 participants attended the meetings.

The Antonio Maceo Brigade presented the Cuban government with a more radical agenda, which included the right of repatriation, the right to study in Cuba, the creation of an institute within the Cuban government to represent the interests of Cuban communities abroad, the opportunity to participate in social and professional organizations within Cuba, and the establishment of exchanges between Cubans on the island and abroad (*Baragua* 1979).

In January 1979 the Cuban government started releasing 400 political prisoners each month. This lasted approximately one year. The United States accepted jailed prisoners and their families but refused to grant visas to former political prisoners and their families. They were told that they had to apply through the regular Latin America quota. For most people, this represented a wait of anywhere from three to eight years. In 1965 under similar circumstances, the Cuban government opened up the port of Camarioca to those wishing to pick up their relatives. This time another "Camarioca" solution was discussed as a possibility if the United States did not grant visas. Another agreement between the Cuban government and Cubans abroad resulted in the visit to Cuba of over 120,000 Cubans. It was clear that while Cubans abroad had broken with the revolution, they were interested in being able to visit their families and their homeland. Committees to defend and implement the accords of the Dialogue sprang up throughout the United States and in Puerto Rico, Venezuela, Mexico, and Spain (Azicri 1979).

Much to the chagrin of organizers of the Dialogue and the groups that emerged during this period, visitors often came back more embittered than they had been before going to the island. Many felt that the Cuban government was exploiting their desire to see their relatives by charging outrageous prices which, at one time reached $1,500 for a one-week visit from Miami, even if a traveler stayed with relatives. The Cuban government viewed visits by relatives as a source of foreign exchange. Special stores were opened where visitors could pay top dollar for consumer goods in short supply to give as presents. The corruption they encountered throughout the island required them to hand out still more money and further antagonized them. Contrary to the explicit hopes of those organizing the exchange, the trips did not encourage good will.

Nevertheless, the willingness of the U. S. and Cuban governments to negotiate changed the political climate between the countries. Cuban-American organizations calling for normalizing relations found that their demands were now politically acceptable and therefore carried a level of legitimacy. In these new conditions, Cuban-American organizations working toward reestablishing relations with their homeland flourished (Gómez 1979). The increased contact with Cuba also spurred professional and cultural interest among Cubans inside and outside of Cuba. For a time the tendency for rapprochement became important outside the initial youth sector which had prompted it, although its articulation into a mass movement was tempered by both the political climate in Cuba and by terrorism within the Cuban community in the United States.

An interesting political development was the formulation of the Cuban-American Committee. This group, composed of a broad cross section of professionals, was the first official Cuban-American lobbying group in Washington. They circulated petitions, met with political representatives, and held press conferences. Unlike past political organizations of the Cuban community, the Cuban-American Committee was involved in "políticas a la americana."

In 1979 the Committee presented the State Department with a petition signed by over 10,000 Cubans asking for a speedy normalization of relations between the United States and Cuba. As a significant number of Cubans welcomed the relaxation of relations with Cuba, groups who were still trying to overthrow the revolution felt more and more isolated. Their promises of invasion and return to the island were no longer relevant. The Cuban community had come to understand that the revolution was an irreversible process.

The counterrevolutionary groups reacted violently to these developments. Their first point of attack was on the participants of the Dialogue. In 1979, "Omega 7," one of the most active terrorist organizations, claimed credit for over twenty bombings aimed at Dialogue participants' homes and businesses. They sent communiqués to the Miami offices of the Associated Press and United Press International, vowing to kill any Cuban who traveled to Cuba. In April, 1979, Omega 7 claimed credit for the assassination of Carlos Muñiz Varela, a twenty-six-year-old member of the Antonio Maceo Brigade who coordinated the offices of Viajes Varaderos in Puerto Rico, an agency involved in arranging travel to Cuba. In November of the same year, in Union City, New Jersey, the organization killed another participant of the Dialogue, Eulalio Negrín (Stein 1979, 1980). Although these groups were successful in intimidating many Cuban Americans, their reliance on terrorism clearly demonstrated that they were isolated.

In response to these threats, more liberal-minded Cuban Americans launched an unprecedented national campaign against terrorism, which demonstrated that they had learned how to use the political system. Cuban Americans successfully lobbied several congressmen to set up special congressional hearings on Cuban-American right-wing terrorism. They had Mel King introduce a resolution in the Massachusetts House of Commons condemning terrorism. They were also instrumental in assuring that Rutgers University's Constitutional Legal Clinic document cases of intimidation and assassinations (Schneider 1979). Because of this campaign, the White House eventually set up a special FBI task force and named Omega 7 the most dangerous group in the United States (Herman 1980).

The political legitimacy received by those calling for a rapprochement with the revolution contributed to shifting the political spectrum in the Cuban community. Supporters of the Dialogue had successfully organized a base of support in the Cuban community that expanded the political spectrum. The demand for normalizing relations with Cuba at least recognized that there was a government with which Cuban Americans could negotiate. It also recognized that Cuban Americans were in the United States to stay. Since political space in the community had expanded, organizations that advocated for the needs of Cuban Americans were no longer susceptible to the charges that they were abandoning the cause of toppling the Cuban government. They were no longer targets for the right.

With this expanded political space, new issues emerged. For one, the Cuban community became a vocal supporter of bilingual programs in Dade County, a clear departure from mainstream North American opinions. There was even support from the Miami community for bilingual voting materials. Further, an unprecedented number of Cubans became naturalized citizens of the United States, a necessary requirement for voting. Within the Democratic party, a new organization, Hispanic American Democrats, formed in 1979 (García 1980). It attempted to unify Latinos under the same banner. Traditional Cuban-American Democrats as well as representatives from the Dialogue movement played a key role. No longer did conservative Cubans monopolize the contacts with the political structures.

The political developments in the Cuban community were accompanied by parallel ideological currents. Especially significant was the change in self-definition from an exile people to a community. In some sectors the definition went further and included a conception of Cubans as a minority group within the United States. Few Cubans continued to refer to themselves as exiles. This reflected the changing international relations as well as the changing political focus for Cuban Americans.

Cuba was still very much at the center of political debate and life in the Cuban community. New forms of political participation emerged, however, which related to the status of Cuban Americans as U. S. citizens. New political concerns such as the defense of First Amendment rights grew. Perhaps most significantly, the use of electoral and pressure group methods of political participation by Cuban-American progressives in the 1970s changed the rules of politics in the community. These activities proved to be effective and set a new standard on how to conduct the political business of the Cuban community.

Cuban Americans in the 1980s: Entering Mainstream Politics

Cuban Americans entered the 1980s in the limelight of the Mariel immigration. The community trips to Cuba had crystallized a generalized discontent about the economic situation in Cuba. With visitors bringing consumer goods and dollars, the black market surged. Those who did not have relatives abroad resented those who did. The release of political prisoners exacerbated tensions in Cuba; the United States dragged its feet processing visa applications, and Cuban policy did not facilitate the integration of former political prisoners into the work force.

The immigration of 120,000 Cubans and the rise of a conservative president combined to reverse the liberalizing trend that had developed during the Carter administration. For the first time in years many Cuban Americans perceived that the Cuban revolutionary government could fall. This fueled the traditional right-wing groups, who quickly organized paramilitary camps (Taylor 1982). This counterrevolutionary tendency combined with the consolidation of the New Right in the White House; the result was to halt the new diplomacy that had developed in the Cuban community during Jimmy Carter's term. The groups that emerged in the Reagan era can be called anti-Dialogue.

The Reagan administration developed more sophisticated plans for Cuban Americans and Nicaraguans to fight a covert war in Nicaragua; it also actively promoted Cuban Americans to key positions throughout government and the Republican Party (Bailon 1983; Sweeney 1983). The general trend of the 1970s toward electoral political participation coincided with the Republican strategy for making Cuban Americans key actors in the administration. In the 1980s, Cuban-American political participation in lobbying and in partisan and electoral activities proliferated. For the right this was carried out under the legitimacy of the Republicans; for the progressives it had been done in coalition with other minority groups.

As early as fall 1980 key Republicans had their eyes on Cuban Americans. This was especially evident in operatives of the New Right whose ideology had coincided with that of conservative Cuban Americans in past political relations. Roger Fontaine, former Latin American adviser to the National Security Council, stated that what was needed in Washington was a strong conservative Cuban-American lobby group (Arguelles and Torres 1983). A few months after the 1980 presidential election, a group of Cuban-American businessmen and ideologues formed the Cuban-American National Foundation.

The board of directors of the foundation consisted of male leaders of Miami's financial and import-export sector. Directors and trustees of the board each made sizable contributions to fund the foundation's budget (financial reports of the Cuban-American National Foundation are on file at the Federal Election Commission, Washington, DC). Many of the companies represented on the board benefited from trade and investments in Latin America. They also benefited from Reagan's policies toward Latin America that explicitly aim to protect investments abroad.

Jorge Mas Canosa, president of Church and Tower Construction Company, was the first president of the board. The board named Frank Calzón as its first executive director. He had been the former director of On Human Rights, a Washington-based group that had been dedicated to publishing materials and lobbying Congress on human rights violations in Cuba. Roger Fontaine had also been on its board of directors.

During its first year of operation the Cuban-American National Foundation spawned two other organizations: the National Coalition for a Free Cuba, a political action committee first headed by Frank Hernández, president of Argo-Tech International (a company involved in agribusiness with Latin America); and the Cuban-American Public Affairs Council, a lobbying group.

Although the Cuban-American National Foundation claims to be nonpartisan, the projects it has lobbied for closely resemble many of Reagan's. Perhaps most indicative of the foundation's links to the administration and the New Right were its activities related to the passage of Radio José Martí, the administration's radio station beamed at Cuba. While the idea of the project first appeared in a report on Latin America by the Santa Fe Group (Tambs 1980) (a conservative ad hoc think tank, which surfaced during the 1980 presidential election to elaborate policy recommendations for Ronald Reagan and subsequently for the National Security Council), the White House initiated the radio project, and Paula Hawkins, then Republican senator from Florida, introduced it in the Senate. As a means of developing support for the project, the president formed the Commission of Broadcasting to Cuba. He named two Cuban Americans to the commission: Tirso de Junco and Jorge Mas Canosa.

Even though the bill initially faced opposition, especially from North American broadcasters, a final version authorized the Voice of America to establish the Radio Martí program. The Cuban-American National Foundation played a key role for the administration in gathering nationwide support for the bill. After its passage, the president named Ernesto Betancourt, a member of the foundation's speakers bureau, as its first director.

The Cuban-American Committee lobbied against the bill. This time they were not met with terrorists but with an organized lobbying effort. However, for the Cuban-American groups that had lobbied for an easing of tensions between the two governments, Reagan's project had the effect of worsening relations. The Cuban government responded by suspending agreements it had previously reached with the Reagan administration on the return of Mariel prisoners and on exit visas for political prisoners.

The Cuban government also suspended the accords of the Dialogue and for a year did not allow Cuban Americans to visit the island. Although in part this was meant to be a message to the Cuban community, it showed that the Cuban government had not fully developed a coherent policy toward the Cuban communities outside of Cuba. Their action surprised supporters of the Dialogue, for it in effect aligned the Cuban government with the most reactionary forces in the Cuban community who had consistently fought against the travel of Cuban Americans to Cuba (Pérez-Stable 1985). The Cuban government's suspension of the accords of the Dialogue forced the Cuban Americans who supported it to refocus their political activities. Those who stayed in the realm of trying to better relations with Cuba were relegated to negotiating the number of visas and the price of trips.

The Cuban-American National Foundation also helped the Reagan administration lobby for a variety of other foreign policy projects. These included aid to the contras, support for the Grenada invasion, and funds for the antigovernment rebels in Angola. They were also instrumental in helping Reagan pass his Caribbean Basin Tax Plan, which directly benefited the businessmen on the board. Clearly the foundation was a product of a maturing economic base in Miami and its merger to Cuban-American conservative ideologues (Zaldívar 1986).

The Republicans not only accepted Cuban Americans as lobbying supporters, they also actively promoted many of them to key policy positions within the government and the party hierarchy. The highest-level appointments included José Sorzano, the second president of the board of directors of the foundation, who became ambassador to the Economic and Social Council of the United Nations, and Otto Reich, who was named to various diplomatic posts. Not all appointments have been concentrated in the realm of foreign policy, however—some have been in institutions with domestic policy functions (Directory 1983).

Cubans have also been placed in key positions within the Republican party. The powerful Republican Finance Committee invited Carlos Benítez, also on the board of the Cuban-American National Foundation, to join its other nine members. In many states Cubans direct the Republicans' Hispanic Assemblies. In fact, in 1983, the Party replaced the president of the National Hispanic Assembly, Fernando C. de Baca, a Mexican from New Mexico, with Tirso de Junco, a Cuban from California. Cubans in Florida have provided the Republican party with a base with which to attempt to establish itself in Democratic party-controlled states. The electoral strategies have generally relied on fielding numerous Cuban-American candidates against Democrats. In 1982 this included running Manuel Yglesias against Congressman Claude Pepper.

With these Cuban appointments and candidates, the Republicans attempted to build the image that they have Latino support. Cuban Americans have thus been very valuable to a party that since the 1960s has had a serious problem with minorities. Their relationship with the Republicans has signaled the changing function of Cuban Americans from merely foreign policy actors to domestic policy actors as well.

Despite all the political successes of the Reagan-aligned Cuban Americans, this group was not able to elect a mayor in Miami. In 1985 Xavier Suárez became the first Cuban-born mayor of Miami. In the first round of the elections, Maurice Ferré, a national Democrat and Puerto Rican incumbent, came in third. The run-off was between Raúl Masvidal, a vocal supporter of Reagan and member of the board of directors of the Cuban-American National Foundation, and Xavier Suárez. Miami voters opted for Suárez. Yet by 1989 the lobbying clout of the foundation found an electoral expression. Along with the Republican National Committee it succeeded in electing Ileana Ros-Lehtinin to fill the Congressional seat opened by the death of Claude Pepper.

While the Republicans did garner more than 90 percent of the Miami Cuban-American vote in the 1980 presidential election, they did not fare as well with Cuban Americans in northern and midwestern cities. Percentages for the Republicans ranged from 65 percent in New York to 68 percent in Chicago (Gómez 1985; Southwest Voter Registration 1984). In part these regional differences are due to the role that Cubans who support domestic programs, which better distribute the goods of society as well as foreign policies that are less interventionist, have played vis-a-vis other minorities in the electoral arena. This has been possible in cities outside Miami, where the right wing is less dominant and where there are fewer acts of political repression against progressive activists.

Cubans in these cities are a minority of other Latinos. Thus, Cuban Americans have had a shared experience with other Latino communities that has impacted on their political world view. Cuban Americans in urban areas have also suffered the severe cutbacks of federal services and are less likely to be supportive of the Reagan administration. This has resulted in a diversity of political opinions and organizations.

In the 1980 presidential election, progressive Cubans formed an unprecedented Cuban-American Democrats Committee. They lobbied the party with a document produced by the Cuban-American Committee outlining a series of policy issues affecting Cuban Americans as well as other Latinos (Gómez 1984). These included high school dropout rates, better services for the elderly, day care needs, and bilingual educational opportunities for the young. It outlined concerns over immigration policy. In a section on foreign policy, they also supported peaceful solutions to the crisis in Central America and the Caribbean.

The lack of opportunity to develop a more humane and less interventionist foreign policy based on the rights of Latin American countries to choose their destiny, as well as the Cuban government's reversal of a Dialogue policy, forced Cuban Americans interested in relations with Cuba to concentrate on local issues, which in turn have provided the basis for them to build coalitions with other minorities. Many progressive Cubans were radicalized in minority community movements—these past political relations have eased the process of building bridges with these other communities.

In cities outside of Miami, progressive Cubans have participated in building minority electoral coalitions. In Chicago, a small but significant group of Cuban-American Democrats participated in the 1983 mayoral elections. Over 50 percent of Cubans voted for Harold Washington, despite a well-organized campaign by the Cuban right in support of the Republican candidate, Bernard Epton (Midwest Voter Registration 1983; Santillán 1989). In Boston, Cubans also played an important role in Mel King's campaign for mayor. In Philadelphia and Atlanta, progressive Cubans are a part of the largely minority urban coalitions that control those municipal governments. To date the most impressive documentation of this trend is the result of the 1987 Chicago mayoral election. Both in the primary and general elections, the Cuban-American community was the Latino community that gave Harold Washington the highest proportion of their vote. In the 1980s, progressive Cubans joined coalitions with other Latinos and African Americans. The 1970s polarization of the Cuban community is being played out in a broader political arena in the 1980s.

The Coming Decades

In the spring of 1990, the Bush Justice Department announced that they might grant Orlando Bosch, well-known anti-Castro terrorist, entrance into the United States. That same week a powerful bomb exploded outside Miami's *Museo de Arte Cubano Contemporáneo*, whose director, Ramón Cernuda (also U. S. spokesperson for the Cuban Commission on Human Rights and National Reconciliation, an island-based human rights group), advocates a revision of U. S./Cuba relations. In the last years Cernuda has been a frequent target of anti-Castro terrorists. He has also suffered the wrath of political terrorism from the federal government and the Cuban-American National Foundation, the well-connected right-wing lobbying group.

What is ironic about the targeting of Cernuda is that he, like other anti-Castro activists, advocates an end to totalitarianism in Cuba and the one-man rule of Fidel Castro. But unlike others, Cernuda believes that the best way to bring about political change in Cuba is not through confrontation, but rather by ending U. S. economic and diplomatic hostility against Cuba, since this would encourage the opening of the island's political space (Cernuda 1990). This puts Cernuda at odds with Jorge Mas Canosa (president of the Cuban-American National Foundation) and the Bush administration, and it allies him with Cuban Americans who advocate better relations between Cuba and the United States.

The Cernuda bombing shows that while Cuban Americans may in fact be concerned about a domestic agenda, and may in fact be negotiating even a foreign policy agenda within the confines of traditional policy arenas, Cuba will continue to be a concern of the community. Further, the political culture of the community, especially as it is manifested in regard to resolving issues pertaining to Cuba, has been heavily influenced by practices legitimized by the U. S. state.

For Cuban Americans, whether emigrés from the 1950s or 1990s, or for that matter for those born in the United States, Cuba continues to be an unresolved problem. While the dominant tendency in the host country government has been to follow a policy of confrontation with the Cuban government, in the community there has been more support for a humanitarian solution to the conflict between the United States and Cuba on those issues affecting the community and relatives on the island. And while the discourse around the issue of homeland has often been defined by the administration in power in Washington and Cuba's policies toward that community, there are independent community interests in resolving the conflict. Yet the dominant (not necessarily majority) opinion has usually been against negotiations.

Broadly speaking, there are two currents of thought in the Cuban community on how to relate to Cuba: one supports a dialogue, or an engagement with the government, and the other is against a dialogue. In this section I will briefly describe each of these positions, which are by no means monolithic, and point out the consequences each holds for U. S./Cuban relations and community development.

Dialogue

In part because of the void created by hard-line political positions in the Cuban community, groups emerged in the mid-1970s that began calling for a normalization of relations with the Cuban government. These voices were a combination of young Cuban Americans, whose experience as a minority in the United States had led them to question their identity and reevaluate their relationship with their homeland and consequently with the government, and organizations and individuals interested in developing a relationship with Cuba to facilitate family contact.

The groups and individuals advocating a respectful yet meaningful relationship with their homeland have throughout the years built very important relationships with key individuals on the island. While there are some officials who are leery of the independent thinkers and artists, there is a growing counterpart to this tendency in Cuba. As the Cuban revolution is forced to redefine itself, a debate about nationhood and what constitutes the Cuban nation has emerged. A key component of this debate is the relationship to those who have left. Therefore, for the first time since 1959, there is a broad-based debate about the relationship with those who left. Those involved inside the island are looking for linkages with honest, nationalist elements outside.

A U. S. initiative to negotiate these issues for the Cuban-American community may provide a major breakthrough in the impasse. In fact, the resolution to these issues will have profound implications not only for U. S. policies but also for the internal reordering of ideology, politics, and economics in Cuban society. For Cuba to develop a humanistic and comprehensive policy toward its "communities abroad" will mean that, for starters, they will have to give up the notion that all those who leave are traitors. For this to happen, there will have to be meaningful forms of dissent within Cuba beyond leaving the country or risking jail. And this will be a major step toward a more democratic political system. A less politically charged atmosphere on the island will contribute to normalizing community politics as well.

The Bush administration never fundamentally altered its policies toward the Cuban government; and while the Clinton administration has not pursued the embargo as aggressively as past administrations, it has not made major changes in U. S. Cuban policies (Brenner and Landau 1990). However, profound transformations, both external and internal to the island government as well as in the Cuban-American community, are creating interesting opportunities for a change. There is no doubt that Cuba's revolution is at a crossroads. A critical part of their economic and political frame of reference is in flux. State-controlled planned economies all over the world are decentralizing and privatizing. One-party political structures are giving way to multiparty representation. Cuba's trade relations with Eastern Europe and the former Soviet Union have undergone drastic alterations.

What is certain is that Cuba will not continue to exist as we have known it for thirty years. The ideological and practical aspects of these changes are already beginning to have a profound impact on Cuban society. The economy has been reorganized from a wartime plan called *El plan especial en tiempo de paz,* which has meant fewer goods (parallel markets are gone), cutbacks in services (critical medicine is missing from the pharmacy shelves and transportation services have been severely curtailed), and layoffs in all but the agricultural sector. The crumbling of the ideological framework that has held the island together for thirty years has created a full-fledged crisis of legitimacy for the present government. The scramble for a new one has opened up the political debate. Government officials are not unaware of the need for change, and indeed they have initiated a series of reforms. But profound changes through official channels are unlikely, given the inherent conservatism of party functionaries as well as the centralization of power. And past political repression and the lack of a political culture of grass-roots activism severely constrain the possibilities of change through other channels. Yet young intellectuals and workers, who feel, they have nothing to lose and much to preserve are challenging those who they feel have lost touch with revolutionary principles. With the backdrop of the collapse of an entire economic system, in the midst of a tremendous battle for the succession of power, a most fascinating ideological struggle to redefine "revolution and nation" is taking place.

A key component of this redefinition is the relationship to those who have left. While officials have renewed the rhetoric against those who live abroad and in fact have christened new critics with the term" new gusanos," those at the vanguard of new thinking in Cuba are saying that those who have left are part of the nation and should be brought into discussions about the future of the island's economics, politics, and culture. At the cutting edge of this debate are artists and intellectuals who are personally affected by the economic and political crisis facing the island. The scarcity of papers and materials has forced intellectuals and think tanks to find publishing outlets abroad. Several years ago a book published abroad and not on the island was looked at with suspicion. Today, those being forced to publish outside are advocating for changes in political practices that have defined Cuban culture as only that which is created on the island.

Other artists and professionals have been forced to leave the country in search of employment. They do not feel that they are breaking with the revolution, and as such they are interested in redefining the official relationship with those abroad. Further, the call for reconciliation with those who have left is echoed by every major internal opposition group. These sectors call for an easing of U. S. pressure on the island, for they understand that a more open political space is more conducive to real discussions and change.

It is interesting to note that the debate about the relationship to the island is also occurring in the communities abroad. Over the last several years, several groups have emerged in Miami specifically calling for the resolution of some of these issues. But there are constraints.

Anti-Dialogue

The possibility of change in Cuba has recharged those advocating the traditional exile agenda. These anti-Dialogue forces are composed of two main tendencies: those who advocate the overthrow of the Cuban government through military actions and those who advocate its destruction through economic and political isolation.

In response to a realignment in the political center of the community, organizations opposed to a Dialogue with the Cuban government staged a march in Miami in spring 1991. Their purpose was to unify the exile community under the banner of an end to Fidel and no Dialogue with the Cuban government. When Cuba executed a member of a three-man infiltration team in January 1992, right-wing political organizations in Miami launched a petition drive advocating no prosecution of exiles involved in military expeditions. Days before the 1992 presidential election, they succeeded in having the Cuban Democracy Act, which called for tightening the embargo, signed into law.

Both in Cuba and in the Cuban-American community, debate about the future of Cuba or U. S./Cuba relations is extremely difficult. In Cuba, while broad discussions took place in 1991 within a process initiated by the party, publicly people are rallied to expouse an increasingly hardening official position, which makes debate or dissent difficult. Human rights activists are accused of being agents of the U. S. Government and are jailed under laws prohibiting the right of assembly (*Juventud Rebelde* 1992).

In 1990 the FBI named Miami the capital of U. S. terrorism as eighteen bombs went off in the homes and businesses of Cuban Americans working to better relations with Cuba. Hard-line organizations such as the Cuban-American National Foundation accuse supporters of better relations with Cuba of being agents of the Castro government.

Advocates of better relations with Cuba are also limited by their narrow political agenda. While criticizing U. S. policies that create obstacles to a normal relationship between the community and Cuba, they are generally silent about Cuba's policies, which have divided the community. Further this silence has reduced the possibilities of forming a left-to-center coalition in the Cuban-American community, which could challenge the right.

The center of the community, on the other hand, includes groups that advocate for a democratization of Cuba and the community. Unlike the extreme right, which has no contacts in Cuba, advocates of human rights in Cuba have built relationships with opposition groups on the island. This relationship has had a significant impact on the politics of these groups, which tend to be much more in tune with what is actually happening in Cuba (Cernuda 1991). In addition, these human rights groups do not see themselves as the leaders of a future government in Cuba, but rather they recognize that solutions to Cuba's future ought to be generated from inside the island. Nevertheless, the politicization of human rights issues by the United States puts to question the authenticity of these groups.

Nevertheless, despite these constraints, there may be a reason to look at these issues in the Cuban-American community in a new light. There are generational changes occurring in the community, as well as changes introduced by new immigrants from the 1980s, who are bringing at least a more contemporary vision of Cuba and their relationship with homeland. Profound transformations are under way on the island as well.

The lack of political expression about these issues and the almost total lack of support from those in power in Havana, Miami, and Washington to resolve the needs of the Cuban-American community have left an agenda of unresolved issues, which deeply affect the 1 million Cuban Americans living in the United States. Undeniably, better U. S./Cuba relations would help create an atmosphere in which these unresolved issues could be negotiated. The resolution of these issues can help the community rid itself of the old obsession that blinds it and prevents it from seeing its real interests and allies. Resolving these issues will not only help normalize relations between the community and Cuba, it will also help normalize the politics of the Cuban-American community. For, regardless of the future of Cuba, a Cuban-American community in the United States will be a permanent feature, and issues of homeland and new emigrés will be part of the political agenda for everyone involved.

Bibliography

Acta Final del Dialogo entre representativos de la comunidad cubana en el exterior y el gobierno cubanos.

Alarcón, Ricardo

1991 July interview with Ricardo Alarcón, Cuban ambassador to the United Nations and former student leader at the University of Havana during this time.

Alzaugaray Treto, Carlos

1988 "La seguridad nacional de Cuba y el diferendo con los Estados Unidos." Instituto Superior de Relaciones Internacionales. Raúl Roa García.

Arce Rodríguez, Mercedes

1991 "La política de Cuba hacia la comunidad cubana-americana: Una evaluacion de los años 80." Paper presented at the 16th Congress of the Latin American Studies Association, Washington, DC, (April).

Areito

1978 Issue is dedicated to Antonio Maceo Brigade. *Areito*, vol 4, nos 3-4 (spring).

1979 "Un análisis pragmático del diálogo entre la Cuba del interior y del exterior." Max Azicri. *Areito,* 5.19-20:4.

1979 "Interview with President Fidel Castro." *Areito,* vol 6, (September).

Arguelles, Lourdes

1982 "Cuban Miami: The Roots, Development, and Everyday Life of an Emigré Enclave in the National Security State." *Contemporary Marxism,* vol 5, (summer): 27-44.

Arguelles, Lourdes, and Gary McGoin

1980 "El Miami cubano." *Areito,* 7.28:4-15.

Arguelles, Lourdes, and María de los Angeles Torres

1983 "La comunidad cubana en la política de los Estados Unidos." *Material de Trabajo.* Havana, Cuba: Centro de Estudios Sobre América, no 4.

Azicri, Max

1981 "The Politics of Exile: Trends and Dynamics of Political Change among Cuban-Americans." *Cuban Studies/Estudios Cubanos*), pp 53-73.

Bach, Robert
1985 "Western Hemispheric Immigration to the United States: A Review of Selected Research Trends." Hemispheric Migration Project, Occasional Paper Series, Center for Immigration Policy and Refugee Assistance, Georgetown University and the Intergovernmental Committee for Migration, (March), p i.

Bailon, Bob
1983 Personal interview with Bob Bailon, Republican National Committee, (May).

Baragua
1979 Vol 1, no 1, (spring):2.

Barnet, Richard
1973 *The Roots of War: The Men and Institutions behind U. S. Foreign Policies.* Baltimore, MD: Pelican P.

Brenner, Philip, and Saul Landau
1990 "Passive Aggressive." *NACLA,* vol 24, no 3, (November).

Casal, Lourdes
1979 "Cubans in the United States." *Revolutionary Cuba in the World Arena.* Ed Martin Weinstein. Philadelphia, PA: Institute for the Study of Human Issues, p 121.
1979 "Invitación al diálogo." *Areito,* vol 6, (September).

Casal, Lourdes, and Rafael Prohias
1973 *The Cuban Minority in the United States: A Preliminary Report on Need Identification and Program Evaluation.* Boca Raton: Florida Atlantic U.

Cernuda, Ramón
1990 Personal interview with Ramón Cernuda, June 30.
1991 A series of interviews with Ramon Cernuda, spokesperson for Elizardo Sanchez's organization.
1991 "Cuba da opción a Cruz Varela: prisión o exilio." *El Miami Herald,* (December 10):1.

Díaz, Guarione
1970 "El proceso de pluralización del exilio cubano." *Nueva generación,* (November).

Díaz, Jesús
1979 *Del exilio a la patria.* Havana, Cuba: UNEAC.
1978 Director. *55 Hermanos* (documentary film). ICAIC.

Díaz-Brisquet, Sergio, and Lisandro Pérez
1981 "Cuba: The Demography of the Revolution." *Population Bulletin,* no 36, (April):2-41.

A Directory of Hispanic Appointees in the Reagan Administration
1983 Washington, DC.

Domínguez, Jorge
1978 *Cuba: Order and Revolution.* Cambridge, MA: Harvard UP.
1988 "Cooperating with the Enemy? U. S. Immigration Policy toward Cuba." Paper presented at the annual meeting of the Latin American Studies Association, New Orleans, LA.

Fagen, Richard, R. Brody, and T. O'Leary
1968 *Cubans in Exile: Disaffection and Revolution.* Palo Alto, CA: Stanford UP.

Forment, Carlos
1984 "Caribbean Geopolitics and Foreign State Sponsored Social Movements: The Case of Cuban Exiles' Militancy, 1959-1979." In *Cubans in the United States.* Eds Miren Uriarte-Gastón and Jorge Canas. Boston: Center for the Study of Cuban Communities in the United States, pp 65-102.

Gaceta Oficial de la República de Cuba
1962 Ley no 989. Miércoles, (December1):23705.

García, Franklin
1980 Personal interview with Franklin García, a founding member of HAD, Austin, TX, (June).

Gómez, Manolo
1984 *Cuban-Americans, Hispanics, and the 1984 Presidential Election.* Washington, DC: Cuban-American Committee.
1979 "El exilio pide relaciones con Cuba." *Areito,* 5.19-20:7-9.
1985 "The Hispanic Vote in the Election." *U. S.-Cuba Bulletin,* vol 3, no 1, (February):1-6.

Gómez-Quiñónez, Juan
1977 "On Culture." *Revista Chicano-Riqueña.*

Grupo Areito
1979 *Contra Viento y Marea.* Havana, Cuba: UNEAC.

Herman, P.
1980 "Highest Priority Given by U. S. to Capture Anti-Castro Group." *New York Times,* (March 3):1-3.

Hernández, Rafael
1980 "La política imigratoria de Estados Unidos y la revolución cubana." *Havana, Cuba: Centro de Estudios Sobre América,* no 3.

Johnson, Haynes, Manual Artime, José Pérez San Román, Ernesto Oliva, and Enrique Ruiz Williams
1964 *The Bay of Pigs: The Leaders' Story of Brigade 2506.* New York: W. W. Norton.

Jorge, Antonio, and Raúl Moncarz
1981 "A Case of Subutilization and Dislocation of Human Capital Resources: The Cubans in the United States." Working paper, Human Resources and Development Program, College of Business, U of Texas, San Antonio.

Juventud Rebelde
1992 (January 5):12.

Landau, Saul
1988 *The Dangerous Doctrine: National Security and U. S. Foreign Policy.* Boulder, CO: Westview P.

Masud-Piloto, Félix
1988 *With Open Arms: Cuban Migration to the United States.* Totowa, NJ: Rowman & Littlefield.

Midwest Voter Registration and Education Project

Miyar Bolio, and María Teresa
1993 *Exit Poll, 1983 Chicago Mayoral Elections.*
1991 "La política de Cuba hacia la comunidad cubana en el contexto de las relaciones Cuba-Estados Unidos, 1959-1980." Paper presented at Latin American Studies Association Working Group Meeting, Havana, Cuba, (January).

New York Times
1960 November 12. Cited in *Political and Economic Migrants in America: Cubans and Mexicans.* Sylvia Pedraza-Bailey. Austin: U of Texas P, 1985, p 149.
1961 July 23. Cited in *Political and Economic Migrants in America: Cubans and Mexicans.* Sylvia Pedraza-Bailey. Austin: U of Texas P, 1985, p 150.

Our Islands and Their People (a book of photographs of the early 1900s demonstrates how the United States viewed the people of Cuba).
Pedraza-Bailey, Sylvia
1985 *Political and Economic Migrants in America: Cubans and Mexicans.* Austin: U of Texas P.
Pérez, Lisandro
1984 "Migration from Socialist Cuba: A Critical Analysis of the Literature." *Cubans in the United States.* Eds Miren Uriarte-Gastón and Jorge Canas. Boston: Center for the Study of Cuban Communities in the United States, pp 12-22.
Pérez-Stable, Marifeli
1985 "Diversidad y política de cubanos." *El Miami Herald, (*October 7):1.
Pino-Santos, Oscar
1973 *El asalto a Cuba por la oligarquía financiera yanqui.* Havana, Cuba: Casa de las Américas.
Portes, Alejandro, and Robert Bach
1985 *Latin Journey: Cuban and Mexican Immigrants in the United States.* Berkeley: U of California P.
Santillán, Ricard
1989 "Latino Politics in the Midwestern United States, 1915-1986." *Latinos in the Political System.* Ed Chris García. Notre Dame, IN: U of Notre Dame P, pp 99-120.
Scalan, John, and Gilbert Loescher
1983 "U. S. Foreign Policy, 1959-1980: Impact on Refugee Flow from Cuba." *Annals, AAPSS,* vol 467, (May):116-37.
Schneider, Elizabeth
1979 "The Basis of and Need for a Coordinated Federal and State Investigation and Prosecution of Cuban Exile Terroism." Rutgers Law School, Constitutional Litigation Clinic, (May).
Shain, Yossi
1989 *The Frontier Loyalty.* Hanover, CT: Wesleyan UP.
Southwest Voter Registration and Education Project
1984 *Analysis of the 1984 Presidential Vote.*
Stein, Jeffrey
1979 "Army in Exile." *New Yorker,* September 10:42-49.
1980 "Inside Omega 7." *Village Voice,* (March 10):1-5.
Sweeney, Bernie
1983 Personal interview with Bernie Sweeney, Coordinator, Ethnic Liaison Office for the Republican Party, (May).
Szapocznick, José, Javier Lasaga, and Priscilla Perry
1979 "Outreach in the Delivery of Mental Health Services to the Elderly." *Hispanic Journal of Behavioral Sciences,* 1.1:21-40.
Szulc, Tad
1961 *New York Times,* June 13.
Tabori, Paul
1972 *The Anatomy of Exile: A Semantic and Historical Study.* London: Harrap.
Tambs, R., ed.
1980 *A New InterAmerican Policy for the Eighties.* Washington, DC: Council on InterAmerican Security.
Taylor, S.
1982 "Latins Training in U. S. Raise Questions of Criminal and International Law." *New York Times,* (January 18).
U. S. Congress
1975 "Alleged Assassination Plots Involving Foreign Leaders: An Interim Report of the Select Committee to Study Governmental Operations." Report No. 94-465. 94th Cong, 1st Sess November 20.
U. S. Congress, Senate
1910 "Report to the Senate by the Commission on Immigration."
U. S. Congress, Senate Committee on Foreign Relations
1958 *Executive Sessions of the Senate Foreign Relations Committee (Historical Series).* vol 10. 85th Cong, 2d Sess.
U. S. Department of State
1961 "Cuba." *Department of State Publication 7171, Interamerican Series 66.* Washington, DC: Government Printing Office, (April).
Valdez, Nelson
1990 "Cuban Culture: Between Betrayal and Death." Unpublished paper, (November).
Walsh, Monsignor Bryan
1971 "Cuban Refugee Children." *Journal of InterAmerican Studies and World Affairs,* vol 13, nos 3-4 (July-October).
Williams, William Appleman
1962 *The United States, Cuba and Castro.* New York: Monthly Review P, p 122.
Wyden, Peter
1979 *Bay of Pigs: The Untold Story.* New York: Simon & Schuster, p 25.
Zaldivar, Ricardo A.
1986 "A Cuban Lobby Courts Allies, Reaps Clout." *Miami Herald, (*August 11):1.

Educational Experiences of Hispanics in the United States: Historical Notes

William Vélez

The United States of America is an advanced industrial society where, in spite of technological and economic achievements, one can still find extreme levels of socioeconomic inequality. In making the ideological assumption that the country is moving towards a meritocracy in which ability and individual effort count for more than privilege and inherited status, schools have been seen as playing a central role as an important avenue of mobility for disadvantaged groups and individuals (Bell 1973). The studies of Featherman and Hauser indicate a substantial reduction in the correlation between parents' social status and years of schooling completed, suggesting an educational system increasingly governed by meritocratic selection in which ascriptive factors are declining in importance (Feathernam and Hauser 1978; Hauser and Featherman 1977). However, the historical record shows that access to educational institutions has not been free of the fetters of ascriptive factors like race and national origin.

Of all the major racial, ethnic groups in American schools, Hispanics experience the highest dropout rates. In 1989, 41.2 percent of Hispanics twenty to twenty-one years old had not completed high school, as compared to only 15.6 percent of non-Hispanic whites and 16.8 percent of blacks (National Center for Education Statistics 1991). Some of the most frequent reasons given for the high attrition rates among Hispanic students include their relative poverty, their concentration in large urban public school systems, lack of English proficiency, and a disproportionate number of Latino families headed by women (Fernández and Vélez 1985; Vélez 1989). To understand the educational experiences of Hispanics in the United States one has to look at the historical context of ethnic relations within the different regions of the United States. The availability and quality of schools has always depended on the political and socioeconomic position of Latinos vis-à-vis the Anglo majority.

This chapter illustrates the educational histories of Hispanics in the United States by focusing on the experiences of Mexican Americans in Texas and Puerto Ricans in New York. These are the two largest national origin groups among Latinos, accounting for about three-fourths of all Hispanics (García and Montgomery 1991). The most recent population census shows Texas and New York to have some of the largest concentrations of Latinos in the nation.

From Dominating to Dominated: Texas Mexicans Struggle for Educational Equality

What is now the state of Texas was once part of Mexico. Mexican authorities, as a strategy to repel continuing Indian raids, opened their northern province to Anglo colonization. By the mid-1830s the Anglo population had become a numerical majority, and in 1836 Texas Mexicans lost political control when Texas became an independent nation. A new socioeconomic and political order where Anglos dominated and Tejanos occupied a subordinate position was created.

As Anglos consolidated their political and economic power throughout the state, they extended their dominance in the cultural domain by restricting the use of Spanish. In 1870 the state legislature passed a new school law mandating English as the language of instruction for all public schools. Coupled with extreme poverty and poor public school facilities, the new law made schooling unavailable for most Mexican children.

Formal education before the final quarter of the 1800s, when public schools were first established, was mostly limited to wealthy Tejanos (Texas Mexicans) enrolled in religious institutions and private Mexican schools (San Miguel 1987). The Incarnate Word of

Brownsville, established in 1853, was probably the earliest Catholic school attended by Tejanos. Founded by four Catholic nuns, this religious convent accepted females between the ages of five and eighteen years of age. San Miguel offers this description about the Incarnate Word school: "Tuition was fifteen dollars a month in 'Mexican coin' for boarders, and from fifty cents to three dollars a month for day scholars. Music, painting, plain sewing, fine needlework, and embroidery were some of the subjects taught" (9).

A parochial school for boys, St. Joseph's College, was established in Brownsville in 1872. The school experienced recurring financial problems, and in 1887 the sisters of the Incarnate Word assumed operation of St. Joseph's. Other religious schools existed in San Antonio.

Private Mexican (founded by Mexican nationals) schools were found mostly in the border counties. According to San Miguel (1987), they had three major purposes: (a) maintain a Mexican "spirit" in the youth of the border by imparting Mexican ideas and ideals, (b) uphold these ideals by imparting knowledge of Mexican national traditions and history, and (c) arouse racial pride in the youth.

In the latter part of the nineteenth century private Texas Mexican schools began to appear in the educational horizon. For example, in Hebbronville the Mexican population of Jim Hogg County maintained the Colegio Altamira, founded in 1897 with an enrollment of over 100 children.

For poor Tejano parents, however, public schools were the only alternative. School officials showed indifference and antipathy towards Texas Mexican children, and it was mostly in some urban areas where community pressures forced them to provide these children with school facilities. In a pattern that would be repeated for many decades, these schools were usually segregated, overcrowded, and lacked adequately trained staff and school equipment. In the rural areas the few public schools available were called "rancho schools," and their poor conditions are aptly described by San Miguel (1987) in the following manner:

> In some South Texas counties the rancho school buildings were jacales, thatched-roofed huts with dirt floors. There were neither blackboards nor desks of any kind; the children wrote on slates and sat on crude backless benches or boxes. Teaching was generally conducted in Spanish, since the children did not know any English. Teachers were rarely trained and teaching positions were usually based on political rather than educational considerations. (12)

The language barrier discouraged many Mexican children from attending. To deal with this problem, a group of parents in El Paso encouraged Olivas V. Aoy, an elderly Spaniard, to establish a private school in 1887 where children could learn English and be prepared to attend public schools. The Mexican Preparatory School, as it was known, was so popular with Tejano parents that it was soon incorporated into the public school system on a segregated basis. In Brownsville school officials responded to the large number of non-English-speaking children by enacting a local policy that postponed the English-only policy until the fourth grade.

The first three decades of the twentieth century saw a number of developments in the Texas economy that would have profound implications for the educational fortunes of the Tejano population. The rapid expansion of the lumber and oil industries and the development of commercial agriculture in West Texas and in the south near the Rio Grande led to rapid economic development. The paternalistic, almost feudal ranch society based on cattle raising would slowly give in to commercial farmers transplanted from the North and the Midwest, with its emphasis on contractual agreements and wage labor.

Developments in Mexico would also play a role, as millions of rural peasants were dispossessed of their communal lands, leading to the Mexican Revolution of 1910. As a result, Mexican immigration to the United States increased greatly between the years 1900 and 1930. Many of the newcomers settled in Texas, and their children were deliberately excluded from schooling. Seasonal production encouraged an agricultural economy based on migrant family labor. Under a system of exploitative wages, the migrant family was encouraged or forced to supply the labor of their children to sustain itself. Thus, as a matter of basic survival Mexican parents often kept their children at work (González 1990). Many boards of education simply denied admission to migrant children, placing them outside of the protection of educational rights mandated by the state. When admitted, Mexican children were frequently forced to attend the first grade for two years due to language and irregular attendance. As with many Texas Mexican children, Mexican migrant children were placed in segregated classrooms for the first several grades. The great majority of Mexican migrant children never went beyond the primary grades, as a study of Hidalgo County (Warburton, Wood, and Crane 1943) illustrates: "The ages of the enrolled children reflected the brevity of the school experience of most children of field workers in the valley. Seldom were children enrolled before they were 7 or 8 and usually by the time they were 14 they had withdrawn" (35).

The growing numbers of Mexican and Tejano children made it more difficult for school officials to hide their lack of access to adequate public education. For example, in 1928 a study revealed that about 40 percent of the Tejano school-age children in Texas had not been provided with any educational facilities during the 1927-28 school year (Manuel 1930). Where facilities were provided, Texas Mexican children showed large attrition rates and low achievement levels.

Curricular reforms began in the 1920s aimed at providing Texas Mexican children with vocational education (San Miguel 1987). Agriculture classes, industrial training, and home economics instruction were widely offered to Texas Mexican children by 1929. Thus, schools were used to train Mexican Americans to be domestics, farm hands, and occupy the lower rungs of the manufacturing sector. For example, the Lanier Junior School in San Antonio offfered courses such as "sewing, cooking and art work for girls; machine shop practice, auto repair, auto painting, top making, sheet metal work, plain bench and cabinet work in wood and a department in which type-setting and job printing are taught for boys" (San Antonio Public Schools Bulletin 1924, 70).

Another aim was to assimilate or Americanize the Mexican student population, as reflected in the extension of the existing English-only policy into the private schools and into the classroom. The main vehicle for Americanization was language instruction. As an example of this, one finds the words of Laura Frances Murphy (1939), a teacher from Grandfalls, Texas, who wrote that in that system's Americanization program, "first place has been given to the susbstitution of English for Spanish in school life" (23). The ultimate goal was the obliteration of Spanish language usage in the community. Elaborate sytems of rewards and punishments were instituted in many schools to discourage the use of Spanish. In the Mexican schools of Harlingen, the principal organized an English club, restricting membership to children who had not spoken Spanish in the previous six weeks. This club would hold picnics and other activities on a regular basis and would expel members caught speaking Spanish (Taylor 1930). The message received by the Mexican child was that his family, community, and culture were hindrances to educational attainment, and "school policies treated the culture of the Mexican child as unworthy of equality with the dominant culture" (González 1990, 45).

The ascension to political power by the Anglo farmers during the 1920s meant the imposition of numerous controls to keep the Mexican work force tied to the land (Montejano 1987). Increased educational levels were seen as a threat to this goal, as the growers felt more educated Mexicans would unionize and ask for higher wages or migrate to the cities. In their study of Hidalgo County, Warburton, Wood, and Crane (1943) reported a widespread "attitude that school attendance should not be allowed to interfere with the supply of cheap farm labor" (31). An example of this concern is the lax enforcement of the compulsory law school. School officials put no effort in enforcing the school attendance law on Mexicans. The words of a school official reported by Paul Taylor (1930) illustrate this kind of attitude: "We don't enforce the attendance law. The whites come all right except one whose parents don't appreciate education. We don't enforce the attendance on the whites because we would have to on the Mexicans."

There was also an ethnic self-interest behind this policy, as enforcement of the attendance law would have forced many school boards to build new schools to accommodate the large number of Mexican children out of school. Since the apportionment of state funds was based on the number of local children between the ages of six and seventeen, many districts would include Mexicans in their school census and then did little to provide educational facilities for them. In effect, they would use most of the funds apportioned to Mexican children to support the schools attended by white children (San Miguel 1987). Thus, exclusion was a windfall for the Anglo community, a fact illustrated by these words from Pauline Kibbe (1946):

> One central West Texas school district last year (1945) reported 2,000 children of school age in the district and collected the State apportionment on that basis, whereas the total seating capacity of school buildings in the district was 1,350. The State of Texas is not morally justified in contributing to that district on the scholastic enumeration basis, when it is obvious that 650 children could not attend school if they so desired. It so happened that the Latin American children in the district numbered 650. (94-95)

In the majority of school districts where school officials accepted Mexicans in the system, two strategies were used to accommodate the children. The first one was to establish separate facilities, or "Mexican" schools. The second strategy involved establishing separate classes within the Anglo schools. Local officials usually gave two sets of reasons for separating Mexicans from Anglos. The first one emphasized the perception among Anglo parents that Mexicans had lower standards of cleanliness and were socially and economically inferior. The second set of reasons argued that separation was to the advantage of Mexicans, since due to their language deficiencies Mexican children could not effectively learn in the presence of English-speaking peers. Separate facilities were needed to enable the Mexican children to learn English better.

Still another discriminatory policy prevalent in some rural districts was to provide transportation only for Anglo children (Taylor 1930). Finally, segregation usually meant that the few Mexican children who advanced through the elementary grades had to stop their education, since they were not allowed to transfer to the Anglo schools for advanced work. This practice is illustrated by the comments made to Taylor (1930) by an Anglo informant:

> There are two Mexicans in the eighth grade. I suppose they will just have to teach them the ninth grade next year [in the Mexican school]. . . . They would not let them go over to the American school. The Americans here have always held that the Mexicans are here just to work. They say that if the Mexicans came to the American school they would make it so hot for them they would not stay. (376)

San Miguel (1987) argues that these exclusionary practices were at "cross-purposes" with the assimilationist curricular practices of the day. The exclusionary practices were designed to maintain differences existing between Anglos and Mexicans at the social level, while instruction was supposed to Americanize the culturally distinct Mexican student. Another interpretation is to see schools as promising a nonexisting avenue of socioeconomic mobility in exchange for the tacit acquiescence of Mexican students in the extirpation of their language and culture.

The civil rights of Mexicans were also violated in other sectors of society. In the political arena Mexican Americans were prohibited or discouraged from participating. Early in the twentieth century the Democratic party approved the practice of the "White Man's Primary Association" by suggesting that county committees require primary voters to affirm that "I am white person and a Democrat" (Montejano 1987). Poll taxes, literacy tests, elimination of interpreters at the voting polls, and outright intimidation were some of the practices disfranchising Texas Mexicans.

It was in response to these discriminatory conditions that the League of United Latin American Citizens was founded in 1929. Organized by middle-class Mexican Americans, LULAC would play an important role in securing political and educational rights for Texas Mexicans. The organization's constitution declared that one of its aims was "to assume complete responsibility for the education of our children as to their rights and duties and the language and customs of this country; the latter insofar as they may be good customs" (cited in Montejano 1987, 71). The original founders had an assimilationist perspective and adopted English as the official language of the organization while at the same time advocating racial pride.

LULAC made its first legal challenge to segregation in 1930, in a case known as *Independent School District v. Salvatierra.* The Del Rio Independent School District had practiced segregation on the basis of ancestry for a long time and had recently obtained funding to build a new senior high school. It did not have any plans to admit Mexican children into the new building and instead was planning to add five rooms and an auditorium to the two-room "Mexican" school. The court sided with the district, since it found that the segregation was based not on national origin grounds but on allowable educational grounds.

Disheartened by this decision, LULAC members changed their strategies, emphasizing the politics of "persuasion." What this meant was an emphasis on dealing directly with school officials and lobbying state legislators in support of bills having an impact on the education of Mexican Americans (San Miguel 1987). Organizing parents into advocacy groups was another strategy followed by LULAC. It would take a world war and a new leadership to return to the litigation strategy.

World War II created a group of politically conscious Mexican-American veterans who would launch vigorous protests against segregation. Being the most decorated ethnic group of World War II, Mexican Americans decided to fight the discrimination they found when they returned home. To accomplish this, Hector P. García, a medical doctor, and a group of veterans launched the American GI Forum on March 26, 1948. The GI Forum would join forces with LULAC in the years to come to obtain equality in education for Mexican Americans.

The first legal assault on segregation would be won not in Texas but in California. With assistance from LULAC, several Mexican Americans challenged the practice of school segregation in the Ninth Federal District Court in Los Angeles on March 2, 1945. The suit, known as *Méndez v. Westminster School District,* charged that a number of school districts in Orange County were denying Mexican and Latino children their constitutional rights by being forced to attend separate "Mexican" schools. On February 18, 1946, the court ruled against the district, and under appeal the decision was upheld fourteen months later, on April 14, 1947. This was a very important victory from a legal standpoint, since the court reinterpreted the Plessy "separate but equal" doctrine. The presiding judge, Paul J. McCormick, made a distinction between physical equality (facilities) and social equality. The existence of separate facilities was unconstitutional because it fostered social inequality. Moreover, McCormick found no evidence that showed segregation aided in the development of English proficiency. Thus, he ruled that the segregation of Mexican children lacked legal and educational justifications (González 1990).

The Méndez case had repercussions in other states, as illustrated by what happened in Texas. On April 8, 1947, the attorney general of Texas, Price Daniel, issued a legal opinion prohibiting the separate assignment of Mexican-descent children in the state's public schools "where segregation is based solely on race" (San Miguel 1987). However, the opinion contained language that allowed separation based on language deficiencies and other individual needs as ascertained by "properly conducted tests," especially during the first three grades.

Segregation not only meant inferior facilities for Mexican-American children but reached areas such as extracurricular activities and teacher quality, as teachers in the Mexican schools were poorly trained, poorly paid, and less experienced compared to those in the schools for Anglos.

An important victory against segregation was won by a group of parents in Central Texas with the help of LULAC and the American GI Forum. In *Delgado v. Bastrop Independent School District,* the court unmistakably ruled that placing students of Mexican ancestry in different buildings was arbitrary, discriminatory, and illegal. The Delgado decision was important because it placed responsibility on local and state officials for condoning or aiding segregation. On the day of the court's ruling, the state superintendent of public instruction issued a series of regulations and instructions that stipulated that segregation as mandated by the state constitution applied only to blacks. In addition the superintendent made the following points: "(1) Segregation practices based on national origin were unconstitutional, arbitrary, and discriminatory; (2) separate classes were to be formed in the first grade for any students who had language difficulties 'whether the students be of Anglo American, Latin American or any other origin'; and (3) all educational agencies, including the State Department of Education, were to take 'all necessary steps to eliminate any and all segregations that may exist' in these districts" (San Miguel 1987, 126).

Despite the court decision and strong language issued from the state's highest education official, most local school districts failed to correct segregation for a long time to come. A long series of legal battles were won in state and federal courts, but local districts found numerous evasive administrative schemes to circumvent court decisions. For example, "one district established separate classes for Mexican Americans within the Anglo school while another established segregation based on the 'language handicap' of the non-English-speaking children" (San Miguel 1987, 126-27).

Towards the late 1950s LULAC redirected its efforts away from litigation and into curricular change aimed at promoting English language instruction for Mexican-American preschool children. Towards that goal they established and promoted the Little Schools of the 400 whose primary objective was to teach Mexican-American preschool children 400 essential English words that would enhance their probabilities of completing the first grade. Begun in the summer of 1957 with only sixty pupils, its phenomenal success led to its expansion during the summer of 1958, when an average of 402 children per month were taught. The program received state sponsorship in May 1958 and continued its successful operation for some years, but it gradually declined in importance and was eventually superseded as a result of such federal programs as Title I and Project Head Start.

The creation of the Mexican American Legal Defense and Education Fund (MALDEF) in 1968 brought back the strategy of using the legal system to advance the educational opportunities of Mexican Americans. MALDEF'S first legal victory in Texas came as a result of its challenge of the expulsion of sixty-two students by the Edcouch-Elsa High School in Hidalgo County. In December 1968 the court agreed with MALDEF that the expulsion violated the students' constitutional right to protest and ordered school officials to reinstate the students.

Perhaps one of the most important cases in which MALDEF played a role was *Rodríguez v. San Antonio Independent School District,* in which Mexican-American parents challenged the Texas system of financing public education. A three-judge panel wrote an opinion in December 1971 declaring the Texas school finance system unconstitutional under the equal protection clause of the Fourteenth Amendment. However, on March 12, 1973, the United States Supreme Court reversed the decision, ruling that school finance is a matter of the states and best left to the political process.

One of the primary concerns of MALDEF was eliminating segregated schools for Mexican Americans. Surprisingly it had to go to court to undo the actions of the Department of Health, Education, and Welfare, which had designated the Office for Civil Rights (OCR) to enforce the antidiscrimination provisions of the Civil Rights Act of 1964. Taking an uninformed and shortsighted biracial approach to desegregation plans and treating Mexican Americans as white, OCR was negligent and unwilling to seek the elimination of "Mexican" schools in communities with few if any

African-American students. This situation allowed some school districts to appear to have "integrated" schools by pairing blacks with Mexican Americans while leaving the all-Anglo schools intact. In order to change this, MALDEF sought court decisions declaring Mexican Americans as an identifiable ethnic minority group that had been subjected to a system of pervasive official discrimination. The crucial decision was rendered by the U. S. Supreme Court in 1973 in *Keyes v. School District Number One, Denver, Colorado,* declaring Mexican Americans as an identifiable minority for desegregation purposes.

Integration by itself could not guarantee equal educational opportunity for all Mexican-American children, since many of them were Spanish speaking and could not be integrated into the regular classroom. It was necessary to address the special needs of these children by implementing a new curriculum, one that was designed to deal with linguistic handicaps. The crucial legal decision that paved the way for demanding bilingual programs was the 1974 Supreme Court ruling in the *Lau v. Nichols* case. The Court ruled that bilingual education was to be provided to facilitate equal access to the instructional program of students with language deficiencies. In many cases, however, desegregation plans conflicted with the implementation or continuity of bilingual programs. The closing of some minority schools often meant the dismantling of bilingual programs coupled with the busing of Mexican-American children to white neighborhoods. In addition, attending desegregated settings had very little academic payoff for Mexican-American children. These realities led Mexican-American parents to shift their support away from desegregation and in the direction of bilingual education programs.

During the 1970s a number of legislative measures to mandate bilingual programs were introduced in the Texas legislature. Through the leadership of state representative Carlos Truan, the state legislature approved bills requiring bilingual programs in the first three grades in 1973. Active opposition from state political leaders and the lack of support and cooperation from local and state education officials prevented the expansion of bilingual programs to subsequent grades.

A federal judge would provide the right motivation for state legislators to pass a truly comprehensive bilingual program. On January 9, 1981, six years after a lawsuit filed by MALDEF, Judge Wayne Justice found that the state bilingual education plan for Mexican-American students was "wholly inadequate" (*U. S. v. State of Texas* 1981, 41). Judge Justice ordered the state to outline a plan of "relief" that required bilingual instruction for all Mexican-American children of limited English proficiency in the public schools. But the state of Texas appealed the decision and the state legislature rejected proposals by Senators Truan and García to enact new bilingual education legislation. Finally, on June 1, 1981, the Texas legislature approved S.B. 477, the bilingual education expansion bill. With the governor's signature on June 15, it became law. San Miguel (1987) described the main features of the bill in the following way:

> This bill mandated bilingual education from kindergarten through the elementary school grades for school districts with twenty limited English proficient students at the same grade level. The bill also directed school districts having twenty or more LEP children to offer other transitional language programs through the eighth grade and English language immersion programs at the high school level. (208)

The struggle is not over, however. In October 1989 more than 1,000 Mexican-American students walked out in protest from Austin High School in the Magnolia Park neighborhood in Houston (Suro 1992). Their grievance centered on the belief that their school was not as good as the ones in Houston's white neighborhoods. School officials acceded to many of the protesters' demands, including removal of the principal. A Hispanic principal was appointed, as well as Spanish speaking staff and counselors. Under the sponsorship of a Houston-based natural gas and pipeline company, a dropout prevention program was initiated. This illustrates how difficult it is for Latinos to obtain equal educational opportunity in the United States.

The Puerto Rican Struggle for Equal Educational Opportunity

As a result of the war between Spain and the United States in 1898, Puerto Rico was declared an American territory. Puerto Ricans have been U. S. citizens since 1917, when Congress passed the Jones-Shafroth Act. The political status of Puerto Rico is that of a commonwealth, and while retaining some local autonomy, Puerto Rican affairs have been closely controlled by American business interests and federal agencies. The growth of huge sugar plantations during the first three decades of this century considerably reduced the number of small farmers. With the demise of Puerto Rico's subsistence economy the ranks of the unemployed grew considerably, and the stage was set for migration to jobs on the U. S. mainland.

Although Puerto Ricans have been present in New York since the nineteenth century, their heaviest migration occurred in the 1946-64 period. Initially Puerto

Ricans formed communities in East Harlem, the Brooklyn Navy Yard areas, the South Bronx, and the Lower East Side. They are now geographically dispersed throughout the United States but remained heavily concentrated in the New York area until the 1970s. As in the case with previous immigrant groups of an earlier era, the city of New York's public schools failed to adjust to the needs of culturally different children with limited English proficiency. The schools hired few Puerto Rican teachers, and then only as non-teaching auxiliary staff, and forced an immersion approach on Puerto Rican students. Giving in to pressure from the Puerto Rican community in 1954 the New York City Board of Education obtained the funds to study the "Puerto Rican" problem.

This study, known as the "Puerto Rican Study," lasted three years and in its final report recommended proper screening, placement, and periodic assessment of non-English-speaking children (Santiago-Santiago 1987). These recommendations were ignored as they were never implemented at the system level, leaving it up to the discretion of the local schools to follow them.

The abysmal failure of the city's schools to educate and graduate its Puerto Rican students is reflected in their large dropout rates, estimated at between 80 percent and 85 percent throughout the 1960s. By 1969 Puerto Ricans constituted 22 percent of the student population but filled less than 1 percent of all teachers and guidance positions. A study conducted by the Puerto Rican Forum in 1964 concluded that Puerto Ricans had the lowest educational attainment of any minority group in New York (Puerto Rican Forum 1964).

In spite of rampant exclusion and discrimination by New York's political institutions, by the 1950s Puerto Ricans were beginning to win elected offices, and with the formation of the Puerto Rican Forum in 1957, the Puerto Rican community developed agencies and organizations that concerned themselves with the difficulties their children were having in school. One of these, Aspira of New York, would play a major role in the legal battles to come in the 1970s. When it became clear that the Board of Education had taken inadequate measures to meet the needs of Puerto Rican children, as yet another study (Jenkins 1971) had conclusively demonstrated, Aspira of New York decided to litigate. In 1972 the Puerto Rican Legal Defense Fund filed a suit on behalf of Aspira of New York (*Aspira v. Board of Education of the City of New York*). The suit persuasively argued that Puerto Rican children had been denied their right to equal educational opportunity by the board as a function of their ethnicity and language. It also petitioned to implement a bilingual educational program. This suit resulted in the Aspira Consent Decree, signed by both parties on August 29, 1974. It required that the NYC Board of Education comply with the following conditions (Santiago-Santiago 1978):

1. Implement the stipulated bilingual education program
2. Identify and classify those children whose English language deficiency prevented them from fully participating in the learning process and who could participate more effectively in Spanish
3. Promulgate a policy of minimum educational standards to all districts and high schools in the school system, and
4. Apply its maximum feasible efforts to obtain the necessary numbers of teachers and the funds required to implement the program by September 4, 1975, to all children entitled to the program as defined by the decree

Thus, after stiff resistance from the New York City Board of Education, the community finally obtained some changes in the way the schools treated its limited-English-proficiency students. As Fitzpatrick (1987) observed, "The effectiveness of the Puerto Ricans as a a community will depend greatly on their ability to organize cohesively and interact politically" (166).

However, bilingual programs and the decentralization of the city's schools has not proved to be an effective remedy for the high dropout rates affecting Puerto Rican students in New York City (Fitzpatrick 1987). Furthermore, the city schools continue to deny bilingual education to many language minority children. After ten years under the consent decree, the Educational Priorities Panel (1985) severely criticized the New York City school system after making the following discovery: "New York schools are still not providing any legally required language instruction to more than 44,000 limited-English proficient students, almost 40 percent of all those entitled to services. Furthermore, only 30 percent of entitled students receive the full bilingual education that is prescribed by law" (1).

Conclusion

Hispanics in the United States have fought long and hard to attain educational equality. Mexican Americans in the Southwest had to initially overcome the exclusionary and discriminatory practices of public school systems. Their use of the political and legal systems resulted in the elimination of the discriminatory practice of assigning Chicano children to inferior school buildings and classes separate from Anglo children. However, school districts have continued many administrative practices that deny Latino students equal access to resources. One of the ways in which districts spend less money on Hispanic students is through their staffing policies. In 1986 black and Hispanic groups initiated a lawsuit in Los Angeles, California, contending that the district's staffing policies have resulted in the concentration of experienced, higher-paid teachers in mostly white neighborhoods, depriving minority children of equal access to educational resources. Thus, predominantly black and Hispanic schools end up with disproportionate numbers of inexperienced and undercredentialed teachers. The lawsuit *Rodríguez v. Los Angeles Unified School District* also alleges that minority students are more likely to be placed in overcrowded schools. Recently the district's board of education gave its approval to a proposed consent decree that would equalize resources in schools districtwide by the beginning of the 1997-98 school year (Schmidt 1991).

Some of the factors associated with a growing militancy among Latinos include political and organizational bases of power. The presence of Mexican-American and Puerto Rican elected officials has had an impact on educational policies and practices. Organizations such as LULAC, MALDEF, and Aspira provided the sustained attention and efforts that resulted in numerous and successful legal challenges to the discriminatory practices of educational systems.

More recently, both Chicanos and Puerto Ricans have advocated bilingual education as the most appropriate instrument for attaining equal educational opportunity. Bilingual programs make instruction understandable for language minority children. Support for bilingual education and its implementation is also seen as a way to maintain and promote ethnic pride and awareness, as the cultural heritage of Chicanos, Puerto Ricans, and other Latinos are introduced into the curriculum. In clear conflict with the assimilationist goal of creating an "American" identity historically held by U. S. public schools, Latinos appear desirous of retaining their language and culture.

Impressive as the gains in educational equality have been, Latinos are still far from enjoying complete equality in educational opportunity. The reasons for this situation are many and complex. School officials have been extremely creative in designing administrative techniques for circumventing antidiscrimination mandates. And even when apparently implementing potentially beneficial programs such as bilingual education, school districts have been able to maintain the assimilationist character of the curriculum. They have accomplished this by stripping bilingual education of its cultural components and refusing to hire native speakers. In addition, by limiting access to students with limited skills in English, school systems have provided access to only a small minority of Latino students. In doing so, the equally urgent needs of the rest of the language minority students who do not qualify for special programs have generally been ignored. Thus, for many administrators, to serve Latino students means only to provide bilingual education. The system, as Rodríguez (1989) commented, has a great capacity to resist change: "The system incorporated the change thrust upon it, as a result of Hispanic struggles, by altering the nature of the change. It created and proposed its own programs for groups it determined to be deserving. It altered the symbolic meaning of the original concept of bilingual education: the strengths of bilingualism and biculturalism came to be viewed as disabilities" (141).

Because schooling in the United States serves a sorting function, differentiating students early in the game according to their perceived occupational destinations, school administrators have always used another mechanism that negatively affects Latino students: curriculum tracking. Only those students who enroll in an academic track in high school are very likely to take the college-oriented courses that greatly increase the odds of college admission. While half of all white high school seniors are in a college preparatory curriculum, only one of every four Chicano students is enrolled in the same track (Vélez 1989). While track assignments appear to be based on fair meritocratic criteria, the strong negative association between poverty and academic aptitude translates in diminished educational opportunities for Latino students.

Perhaps the biggest educational issue in the last decade of the twentieth century is school financing. The United States has always had a very decentralized approach to educational governance and finance. In practice this has resulted in the federal government deferring most of its regulatory powers to the states. It is not coincidental that the federal department of education attained cabinet level only recently. In the past, most states have allowed local municipalities and counties to run their school systems, as they see fit, with little, if any, supervision on the part of the state commissioner (or superintendent) of education. School boards have relied very heavily on the local property base (to collect taxes) to finance public education. This situation has created enormous disparities in the availability of monies for schools between wealthy and relatively poor districts. In Texas, for example, the 150,000 students living in the state's poorest districts receive educations costing half that of their 150,000 wealthiest counterparts (Kozol 1991). Although many states have tried to address these inequities in the form of increases in state dollars for public education, it has not been enough to correct intrastate disparities. The formulas used to provide state aid for the poorer districts usually assume a minimum level of resources, or the point at which less affluent systems can provide a "basic" education, but not an education on the level found in the rich districts. In states where the legislature ignored the situation, such as Texas, legal challenges had to be mounted in federal courts against the state system of school financing.

Increases in state dollars for school financing have been accompanied by an erosion of local control of schools. In the last two decades many states have aggressively tried to improve and control local schools through expanded regulation. In turn, this has made it easier to mount legal assaults against the states for maintaining funding inequities within their borders. Given the reluctance of the federal branch of government to support or regulate public schools, the best hope for obtaining equal educational opportunity for Latino children lies with school finance reform at the state level. Coupled with meaningful curriculum reform aimed at providing a true multicultural learning environment, most Latinos see school finance reform as an important step in this nation's commitment to provide equality of opportunity for all its children.

The historical record strongly suggests that educational systems have denied equal educational opportunity to Latinos in the United States. A major reason for this unequal treatment has been the structural (or economic sector) demand of keeping Latino workers constrained to a limited set of occupations or, in the case of the Southwest, employed as agricultural workers. Thus, past educational policies of exclusion and discrimination were based on oppression and economic exploitation. The development and militancy of the Latino communities has undermined the most egregious forms of discrimination. Although the number and proportion of college-educated Latinos has increased in the last decades, unacceptably high numbers of Latino youth still fail to graduate from high school. The success of this ongoing struggle for equality of educational opportunity depends on a constant vigilance on the part of Latino communities throughout the United States to fight and eradicate discriminatory practices. One also hopes that a feeling of declinining state of readiness to compete in global markets and a general consensus that schools are in a deep crisis will compel the political and economic elites to devote more attention and resources to the education of all American children.

Bibliography

Bell, Daniel
1973 *The Coming of Post-Industrial Society*. New York: Basic Books.

Educational Priorities Panel
1985 "Ten Years of Neglect: The Education of Children of Limited English Proficiency in New York Public Schools." New York: Interface.

Featherman, David L., and Robert M. Hauser
1978 *Opportunity and Change*. New York: Academic P.

Fernández, Ricardo, and William Vélez
1985 "Race, Color, and Language in the Changing Public Schools." In *Urban Ethnicity in the United States: New Immigrants and Old Minorities*. vol 29, of *Urban Affairs Annual Review*. Eds. Joan W. Moore and Lionel A. Maldonado. Beverly Hills, CA: Sage Publications, pp 179-186.

Fitzpatrick, Joseph P.
1987 *Puerto Rican Americans: The Meaning of Migration to the Mainland.* Englewoods Cliffs, NJ: Prentice-Hall.

García, Jesús M., and Patricia A. Montgomery
1991 "The Hispanic Population in the United States, March 1991." *Current Population Reports*, Series *P-20, No. 455*. Washington, DC: Bureau of the Census, (October).

González, Gilbert G.
1990 *Chicano Education in the Era of Segregation.* Philadelphia: Balch Institute P.

Hauser, Robert M., and David L. Featherman
1977 *The Process of Stratification.* New York: Academic P.

Jenkins, Mary
1971 "Bilingual Education in New York City." New York: New York City Board of Education, Office of Recruitment and Training of Spanish-Speaking Teachers.

Kibbe, Pauline R.
1946 *Latin Americans in Texas.* Albuquerque: U of New Mexico P.

Kozol, Jonathan
1991 *Savage Inequalities: Children in America's Schools.* New York: Crown.

Manuel, H. T.
1930 *The Education of Spanish-Speaking Children in Texas.* Austin: U of Texas P.

Montejano, David
1987 *Anglos and Mexicans in the Making of Texas, 1836-1986.* Austin: U of Texas P.

Murphy, Laura Frances
1939 "An Experiment in Americanization." *Texas Outlook*, 23.11:23-24.

National Center for Education Statistics
1991 *The Condition of Education, 1991.* Washington, DC: U. S. Department of Education.

Puerto Rican Forum
1964 "The Puerto Rican Community Development Project: A Proposal for a Self-Help Project to Develop the Community by Strengthening the Family; Opening Opportunities for Youth and Making

Full Use of Education." New York: Puerto Rican Forum.

Rodríguez, Clara
1989 *Puerto Ricans: Born in the U. S. A.* Boston: Unwin-Hyman.

San Antonio Public Schools Bulletin
1924 "The Public Schools of San Antonio." Vol 2, no 1:70.

San Miguel, Guadalupe, Jr.
1987 "Let All of Them Take Heed," *Mexican Americans and the Campaign for Educational Equality in Texas, 1910-1981.* Austin: U of Texas P.

Santiago-Santiago, Isaura
1978 *A Community's Struggle for Equal Educational Opportunity: Aspira v. Board of Education* (Monograph no 2, Office of Minority Education). Princeton, NJ: Educational Testing Service.
1987 "Aspira v. Board of Education Revisited." *American Journal of Education,* vol 95.

Schmidt, Peter
1991 "L. A. Decree Would Equalize Resources among All Schools." *Education Week,* (December 11):1, 11.

Suro, Roberto
1992 "Generational Chasm Leads to Cultural Turmoil for Young Mexicans in U. S." *New York Times,* January 20, p A11.

Taylor, Paul S.
1930 "Mexican Labor in the United States: Dimmit County, Winter Garden District, South Texas." *University of California Publications in Economics,* vol 6, no 5. Los Angeles: U of California P.

United States v. State of Texas
1987 Docketed, No. 5281 (E. D. Tex. June 3, 1975) (motion to enforce decree and for supplemental relief); docketed, No. 5281 (E. D. Tex. January 9, 1981) (memorandum opinion).

Vélez, William
1989 "High School Attrition among Hispanic and Non-Hispanic White Youth." *Sociology of Education,* vol 62:119-33.

Warburton, Amber A., Helen Wood, and Marian M. Crane
1943 "The Work and Welfare of Children of Agricultural Workers in Hidalgo County, Texas." *U. S. Department of Labor, Children's Bureau Publication No. 298.* Washington, DC: Government Printing Office.

Mexican-Heritage Families in the United States

Maxine Baca Zinn

Massive changes in population trends are reshaping the United States by creating a multiracial, multicultural society. The 1980s became the decade of diversity, when the minority population rose to an all-time high of 25 percent of the population. The 1990 census confirmed that the non-Hispanic, white population no longer unerringly reflects the nation's character. Today, one in four people in the United States is black, Hispanic, Asian, or native American. The Hispanic population figures prominently in this demographic transformation.

The phenomenal growth of the Latino population in the United States has become a frequent media topic. In magazines and newspaper stories, Latinos are typically touted as the fastest growing racial ethnic category—destined to surpass African Americans shortly after the turn of the century. Despite such recent attention, the family patterns of this fastest growing minority group are misunderstood. In popular images, Latino families are "known to be" especially close-knit even in adversity, weathering poverty better than families of other racial ethnic backgrounds (Estrada 1989, 15). These myths only obscure the reality of family life among Mexican-origin people.

This chapter examines Mexican-heritage families from several different vantage points. First, I present some defining characteristics of the Mexican-origin population and provide historical overview of Mexican family life in the Southwest. Then I discuss social science perspectives on Mexican-heritage families and examine how they have changed over time. This is followed by a brief discussion of contemporary family patterns and trends. The chapter then turns to a critical examination of family dynamics and concludes by asking how Mexican-heritage families are affected by social and economic changes in the broader society. Two fundamental themes guide this inquiry of Mexican-heritage families: First, their development has been strongly influenced by social, political, and economic forces in the larger society. Second, family life shows ongoing patterns of adaptation to suit the needs and lifestyles of the Mexican-origin population. These themes point to change and continuity in Mexican-origin family patterns. They challenge much conventional thinking about Mexican families in this society, especially the view that minority family patterns are the force most responsible for racial subordination in American society. This chapter, on the other hand, underscores the qualities within minority family arrangements that have served as sources of adaptation and survival.

Social science and the media tend to lump various Hispanic groups together under the hybrid label "Hispanic." This can obscure important differences between the groups. In reality, U. S. Hispanics show both similarities and variability. While most Hispanics share a common language and cultural ancestry, the diversity among Hispanics makes it difficult to speak in generalities. Since it first gathered information on Hispanics in the 1960 Census, the Census Bureau has modified its method of identifying the Hispanic population with each decennial census. Consequently, intercensual comparisons are somewhat uncertain. For most data collection activities, including the census, self-identification is used to identify Hispanics. If an individual indicates that he or she is of "Spanish Origin" on the census form, that is sufficient to include the person in the Hispanic population (O'Hare 1989, 7-8). It was not until the mid-1980s that we began to receive detailed, individualized data on the major Hispanic groups (Aponte 1991, 1). Where family issues are concerned, trends and indicators ought to be fully disaggregated to reveal the varied circumstances that create different patterns.

In 1991 Hispanics or Latinos numbered 22.4 million, 9 percent of the U. S. population. Several characteristics distinguish Mexicans from other minorities in the United States. First, they make up the largest segment of the diverse groups that comprise the Latino population. In 1991, 64 percent of all Hispanic Americans were Mexican Americans, 4.9 percent were Cubans, 13.7 percent were Puerto Ricans, 13.7 percent were

Central Americans, and 6.9 percent were "other Hispanic" (U. S. Bureau of the Census, 1991, 1). These groups differ in patterns of marriage and divorce, poverty rates, female headship, and fertility patterns. The Mexican-origin population continues to receive migrants in waves that have made America a "permanently unfinished" society (Portes and Rumbaut 1990). Mexicans have been at the forefront of newcomers making their way into the United States. While immigration from Mexico is not a new phenomenon, it has changed in important ways. Originally it was a rural flow. Today it has become mostly urban with 88 percent of the new arrivals going to metropolitan areas. In addition, the flow of Mexican immigration is formed overwhelmingly by urban workers, farm laborers, and their families (70 percent). Only 6 percent of the new arrivals are professionals (Portes and Rumbaut 1990, 41). In some areas, large-scale immigration is changing the proportion of Mexicans born in the United States and those who are immigrants. For example, in 1960, immigrants were a rarity among the Mexican population in California, since 82 percent of all Mexican were born in the U. S. Today, because of massive immigration to California, the ratios are nearly reversed (Hayes-Bautista 1991, 10).

In 1990 the concentration of immigrants was so high as to form virtually a new population with family characteristics that differ from the native-born Mexicans or "Chicano" brethren. Although immigration has become a major social trend, little attention has been given to the difference between native-born and foreign-born families (Romo 1986). Along with continued immigration, the Mexican population will continue to grow disproportionately, due to high birth rates and a young age structure. Women of Mexican origin have the highest fertility levels of any Hispanic group and higher fertility levels than non-Hispanic whites (Bean and Tienda 1987). Taken together, these distinguishing characteristics of Mexican-origin families present compelling challenges to students of the family.

In this chapter, the terms "Mexican-heritage," "Mexican-origin," and, for simplicity, "Mexican," include those who have been in the United States for several generations as well as the immigrant population. Native-borns (Chicanos) and immigrants are both labeled "Mexicans" by the wider society. Whether they are the descendants of families that lived in what is now the Southwest since the time of independence or arrived this year is not important. Rather it is the social construction of the category "Mexican" as a racial group that is important. Social relations with Mexicans are institutionalized. People identified and labeled as Mexicans are treated differently, that is, as a distinct racial minority group.

As a social category, Mexicans experience distinctive treatment in virtually all areas of social life. Conditions associated with labor force participation have profound consequences for well-being. People of Mexican heritage fall well behind non-Hispanic whites on most indicators of status and well-being. They face obstacles to entering the economic mainstream of society. They have lower levels of educational completion, lower incomes, lower standards of living, and lower life expectancy. These inequalities reflect ongoing patterns of institutional discrimination that create serious problems for families. Like blacks, Asians, and Native Americans, Mexicans are defined in racial terms. They are viewed as different from and inferior to whites. Being set apart for unequal treatment by virtue of their common ancestry fosters the development of unique Mexican cultural and ethnic characteristics. Both race and ethnicity are important for the social placement and the lived experiences of Mexican-heritage people.

The Historical Context

Mexicans involuntarily became part of the United States through military conquest at the termination of the Mexican-American War. The war of conquest converted Mexicans into foreigners in their own land. The treaty of Guadalupe Hidalgo signed in 1848 granted American citizenship to Mexicans living in what is now the Southwest. Although Mexicans were an integral part of the Southwest before they became immigrants, the American take over resulted in their gradual displacement from their land and their incorporation into a foreign labor force. North American expansion did not stop at military conquest. The colonization of the indigenous Mexican population was accompanied by the beginnings of industrial development, the growth of agriculture, ranching, railroads, and mining in the region. Rapid economic growth in what had been northern Mexico soon needed labor from the portion of the country left south of the Rio Grande. Southwest growers and railroad companies began to send recruiters into the reduced Mexican republic, offering free rail travel and wage advances as incentives for workers to come north (Portes and Rumbaut 1990, 225-26).

With the coming of the railroads and the damming of rivers for irrigation, the Southwest became an area of economic growth, but the advantages accrued mainly to Anglos. Mexicans no longer owned the land; now they were the source of cheap labor, an exploited group at the bottom of the social and economic ladder. As Mario Barrera has summarized: "Dispossession from the land . . . depleted the economic base of Chicanos and put them in an even less favorable position to exercise influence over the political process. In addition, it

The Lugo family, residents of Bell Gardens, California, ca. 1988. (Courtesy of the Los Angeles County Museum of Natural History.)

had other far-ranging consequences, including facilitating the emergence of a colonial labor system in the Southwest, based in large part on Chicano labor" (Barrera 1979, 33). What emerged in the nineteenth-century Southwest was a segmented labor force that Barrera refers to as a colonial labor system. "A colonial labor system exists where the labor force is segmented along ethnic and/or racial lines, and one or more of the segments is systematically maintained in a subordinate position" (Barrera 1979, 39).

Contract laborers moved back and forth across the Rio Grande with little official resistance. Such movements across the new border were a well-established routine in the Southwest before they became redefined as "immigration," and then as "illegal" immigration. Contrary to the conventional portrait of Mexican immigration as a movement initiated by the desires of the migrants themselves, the process had its historical origins in North American geopolitical and economic expansion that first restructured the neighboring nation and then proceeded to organize subordinate labor flows out of it (Portes and Rumbaut 1990, 226). Yet external conquest and induced labor streams do not explain everything we need to know about this migration. Family arrangements and kinship organization shaped Mexican migration in important ways. For example, studies have documented that a major predictor of the probability of labor migration was prior migrant experience by the individual and his or her kin. Families pass on their knowledge of the different aspects of migration and its expected rewards to younger generations (Portes and Rumbaut 1990, 231).

Whether natives of northern Mexico or immigrants from southern Mexico, Mexican-heritage people were largely a peasant population whose lives had been defined by a feudal economy and daily struggle on the land for economic survival. Patriarchal families and elaborate systems of kinship and co-parenting (*compadrazgo*) were the rule. The family consisted of a network of relatives including grandparents, aunts, uncles, married sisters and brothers and their children, and also *compadres* (co-parents) and *padrinos* (godparents), with whom Chicanos actively maintained bonds.

Family roles in the nineteenth century were strongly gendered. Women did domestic work and cared for children within the home, while men did productive work outside the household. Exceptions to this pattern could be found in rural areas, where women tended gardens or looked after domestic animals (Barrera 1979). This division began to break down as more and more women entered the paid labor force. The entrance of women into the labor market was stimulated by the dire economic situations that affected so many Chicano families after 1870. Albert Camarillo has described how traditional patterns of employment and family responsibilities were altered in Santa Barbara, California:

> The most dramatic change was the entrance of the Chicana and her children as important wage earners who contributed to the family's eco-

> nomic survival. As male heads of household faced persistent unemployment, their migrations to secure seasonal work in the other areas of the country or region became more frequent. In these instances the Chicana assumed the triple responsibilities of head of household, mother, and wage earner. No longer able to subsist solely on the income of the husband, the Chicana and her children were forced to enter the unskilled labor market of Anglo Santa Barbara. The work they performed involved domestic services and agriculture-related employment. (Camarillo 1979, 91)

During the 1800s, Chicanas were incorporated into the agricultural labor market as entire families entered the pattern of seasonal and migratory fieldwork. Initially Chicanas and their children were employed as almond pickers and shellers and as harvesters of olives. During the almond and olive harvests, men were usually engaged in seasonal migratory work. There were seasons, however, especially in the early summer, when the entire family migrated from the city to pick fruit. Chicano family labor had become essential for the profits of growers. Families would often leave their homes in Santa Barbara for several weeks, camping out in the fields where they worked (Camarillo 1979, 93).

Large-scale immigration from Mexico greatly expanded the Mexican/Chicano presence in the Southwest. Migrating in a chain-like pattern, Mexican family units were reconstructed in the United States. This provided an increase in the Chicano labor force. This abundant supply of cheap labor was "placed" in the labor force according to gender. Men were incorporated into the segmented labor market in agriculture, and ranching, mining, railroads, and as common laborers in urban industrial occupations. Women were incorporated into the segmented labor market as domestics, in canneries and packinghouses, in the textile industry, and in the agriculture industry (Camarillo 1979, 221). The gender system of work prevailed throughout the Southwest. Historian Mario García found that in El Paso, Texas, for example, from 1890 through 1920, women worked mainly as servants and laundresses, in garment factories, and as cooks and dishwashers.

Race and gender inequalities placed Mexican-heritage women in subordinate work outside the home. In addition, a distinctive system of Mexican patriarchy controlled their activities in the private sphere. As both daughters and wives, Mexican women were instructed to be obedient and submissive to their parents and husbands. Domesticity and motherhood were primary virtues. Whether or not they labored outside the home, they were subject to a sexual division of labor in which their primary task was to care for their husbands and children and to accept subordination as a natural condition. The "private" patriarchy meshed neatly with the patriarchy of the Southwest economy. Wage-earning mothers and daughters were responsible for domestic duties. The work women did outside of the home was considered less important than that of men. Their wages only supplemented those of men. Despite these conditions, the wage

The Manuel Amado family in late nineteenth-century Tucson. (Courtesy of the Arizona Historical Society Library.)

labor of Mexican-heritage women contributed greatly to family adjustment in a colonized setting (García 1980).

Besides their roles as workers, wives, and mothers, women in particular guarded Mexican cultural traditions within the family—not consciously, but as a matter of practice (García 1980, 128). Certain customs practiced during the 1920s by Mexican immigrant families throughout the Southwest promoted Mexican tradition. These included folklore, songs, and ballads, birthday celebrations, saints' days, baptisms, weddings, and funerals in the traditional Mexican style. Through the family, Mexican culture was nurtured.

Immigration to the United States during the nineteenth and early twentieth centuries served to replenish both the Mexican population and their cultural traditions in the areas of settlement. The large presence of poor immigrant families in southwestern cities gave rise to studies portraying Mexican family life as a social problem for American society.

This thinking was rooted in the emergence of family study as a new field. Family study emerged out of a deep fundamental belief in the need to study and ameliorate social problems (Thomas and Wilcox 1987, 27). During the 1920s and 1930s the "social problems" approach to family life led to studies of Mexican immigrants that highlighted (a) their foreign patterns and habits, (b) the moral quality of family relationships, and (c) the prospects for their Americanization. A prominent sociologist of the time, Emory Bogardus, observed that fathers had primitive attitudes concerning large numbers of children, and mothers had fatalistic attitudes, viewing children as gifts from God. These primitive family relationships were seen as natural representations of the lower class culture (Bogardus 1934, 25).

Mr. and Mrs. Castro, Mexican immigrants to Houston soon after the turn of the century. (Courtesy Houston Metropolitan Archives, Houston Public Library.)

Social reforms of the times favored the enforced modernization of the Mexican immigrant family:

> Teachers of Americanization, directors, settlements workers, and visiting nurses, should make the most of the opportunity they have in bringing to the Mexican the right attitude toward his family. . . . The Americanization of the women is as important as that of the men. They are harder to reach, but are more easily educated. They can realize in a moment that they are getting the best end of the bargain by the change in the relationships between men and women which takes place under the new American order. "Go after the women" should become a slogan among Americanization workers, for after all, the greatest good is to be obtained by starting the home off right. . . . The man's moral qualities may be doubtful, but at least the womenfolk and the children are undefiled. (White 1923, 33-35)

Social reformers, social workers, and sociologists of the early twentieth century assumed that Mexicans and other minorities should and would eventually become acculturated and take the family characteristics of middle-class white Americans. This was to become a guiding theme in the study of Mexican-origin families.

Changing Frameworks for Thinking about Mexican Families

In examining the sociology of Mexican-heritage families, we can distinguish between a cultural approach that focuses on traditional family patterns inherited from the Mexican past and a structural approach that focuses on family patterns emerging in the United States. The difference between these two approaches lies in whether Mexican culture or systems of social organization are the primary units of analysis. The cultural approach emphasizes family patterns passed down from generation to generation, such as close-knit family forms, male dominance, and other traditionally "Mexican" ways of relating within families. In the past such patterns were viewed as cultural exceptions to the rule of standard family development. The reasoning was that traditional "cultural baggage" created serious problems for Mexican families.

In the past twenty years scholars have critically examined this culturally deficient model of Mexican-heritage families. New approaches have found that alternative family patterns do not reflect deviance, deficiency, or disorganization. Instead of representing outmoded cultural forms handed down from generation to generation, Mexican family lifestyles often reflect adaptive responses to social and economic conditions. What were once labeled culturally deficient family patterns may now be viewed as family strategies that serve as solutions to constraints imposed by economic and social structures in the wider society (Baca Zinn and Eitzen 1990). Of course the long-standing interest in cultural patterning of family life continues alongside a "social adaptation" approach. Greater attention is now given to the social situations and contexts that affect Mexican families (Vega 1990, 1015).

Structural approaches explore the close connections between the internal dynamics of family life and external conditions such as changing labor markets and political systems. A growing population emanating from massive immigration and high fertility, combined with transformations in the economy, have required new perspectives. In the 1980s the frameworks shifted "from a stereotypic model of family life, characterized by rigidity, authoritarianism, and a patriarchal structure, to a social adaptation perspective based on themes of family metamorphoses, resilience, flexibility, and cohesion in the face of changing social environments and economic circumstances" (Berardo 1990, 6).

Contemporary Patterns and Trends

Evidence accumulated over the past two decades reveals that Mexican-origin families are undergoing many of the transitions facing U. S. families in general. Yet there are important differences. The continuing influx of immigrants from Mexico combines with systems of class and racial inequality to produce hardships not faced by mainstream families.

Several characteristics of the Mexican-origin population create severe disadvantages for family living. Mexicans in this country lag behind the white population on most measures of socioeconomic status. This is not surprising since many are immigrants, and immigrants typically have low status. Making generalizations about Mexican-origin families is particularly complex, because it involves assessing two distinct groups: native-borns and foreign-borns. On most indicators of well-being, native-born Mexicans are better off than their foreign-born counterparts (O'Hare 1989). Although native-born Mexicans are better off in general, some studies reveal counter-intuitive trends about the family patterns of immigrant families. David Hayes-Bautista (1990) discovered that over time and generation, "positive" family characteristics become weakened. Studying census data on Mexican immigrant families, this sociologist discovered high rates of family formation, low welfare dependency, and high labor force participation. In successive generations, these characteristics appear to become weakened.

Low-status occupations and high unemployment have especially serious consequences for family life, because they translate into low incomes and high poverty rates. Median family income for Mexican-origin families in 1989 was $22,245, compared with the non-Hispanic median income of $35,183, (U. S. Bureau of the Census *Current Population Reports* 1991). While

Mrs. Dolores Venegas, Los Angeles. Mexican Mother of the Year in 1969, with her husband, Miguel. They emigrated to the United States in 1927. (Courtesy of the *Texas Catholic Herald*.)

the median family income for Mexicans is below that of non-Hispanics, per-person income is actually lower, because Mexican-origin people tend to have large families. In 1989, 25.7 percent of Mexican-origin families had incomes below the poverty threshold, compared to only 9.2 percent of non-Hispanic families (U. S. Bureau of the Census 1991). A large proportion of poor Mexican families have members in the work force. "In 1987, around 72 percent of all Mexican-origin families in poverty had at least one member in the work force. Yet it was not enough to bring them over the poverty line (Aponte 1991, 12).

Marriage and Divorce

Marriage is very much the norm for Mexicans. Compared with other Hispanics and non-Hispanics, Mexicans (both women and men) are likely to be married. Their age at first marriage is also somewhat lower than both other Hispanics and non-Hispanics (22.8 for males, 20.9 for females). Marriage patterns have often led to conjectures that Hispanics in general and Mexicans in particular have more stable families than others. The evidence does not support this assumption. William Vega reports that:

> Bean and Tienda's review of 1980 census data found negligible variations in rates of marital disruption between non-Hispanic Whites, Mexican Americans and Cuban Americans, but Puerto Rican rates that are much higher than those of the other groups. Although other investigators. . . . had reported lower divorce rates for Mexican Americans, Bean and Tienda point out that when separation is included in marital disruption, such differences disappear. (Vega 1990, 1016)

Fertility and Family Size

As noted earlier, an important characteristic of Mexican-origin families is their large size. Average household size for Mexicans in 1989 was 4.1, compared with 3.8 for all Hispanics and 3.1 for non-Hispanics (U. S. Bureau of the Census 1991). Among Hispanic subgroups, Mexican families had the highest proportions of families with 5 or more members. About one of every six Mexican families had 6 or more members.

Although steadily declining, high rates of childbearing among Mexican-origin women are evident in all age categories and levels of education. The persistently high birth rate among Mexican women has been variously interpreted in terms of religion, class, and culture. With reference to religion, the question is whether Mexicans as a group overwhelmingly self-identify as "Catholic," confirming the national pattern of Catholics being less supportive of contraceptives and more positive about large families. The second explanation has emphasized the generally low socioeconomic status of Mexicans in the United States, explaining that their low income and lack of education make fertility control difficult for them. The third interpretation focuses on a cultural explanation to account for high fertility; that is, values are assumed to be different from others in terms of the way large numbers of children are perceived. Contrasting evidence can be found for each explanation (Andrade 1980). New evidence shows that increasing proportions of Mexican women approve of and/or use birth control when they are available (Moore and Pachón 1985, 105).

Type of Family

The large increase in the number of families headed by women is one of the most important social developments of the past decade. A small but growing proportion of Mexican-origin families are headed by women. Still, female-headed households are less prevalent among Mexicans (19.6 percent in 1989, compared to 23.1 percent among Hispanics in general) and slightly more prevalent than among non-Hispanics (16.0 percent in 1989). There is a clear relationship between household composition and economic well-being. Female-headed households are especially vulnerable. In 1989, 49 percent of Mexican-origin families in poverty were maintained by women (U. S. Bureau of the Census 1991).

Family Structure and Gender Relations

Traits commonly associated with Mexican-origin families in the United States are (a) familism, an assortment of beliefs and behaviors associated with family solidarity and the extended family, and (b) a gender-specific division of labor.

Familism

For decades, familism has been considered to be a defining feature of the Mexican-origin population. Presumably family is one of the strongest areas of life, more important for Mexicans than for Anglos. This pertains not only to the nuclear family, but also to a wider circle of relatives, the extended family that includes aunts, uncles, grandparents, cousins, in-laws, and even compadres (Alvirez and Bean 1976, 277).

Familism contains four key components. The first component, demographic familism, refers to macro-characteristics of Chicano families, such as family size, whereas the second component, structural familism, measures the incidence of multigenerational households, or extended households. The third component, normative familism, taps the value Mexican-heritage people place on family unity and solidarity. Fourth, behavioral familism refers to the level of interaction between family and kin networks (Ramírez and Arce 1981).

Compadrazgo is another feature of familism among Chicanos and Mexicans. It refers to two sets of relationships with "fictive kin": (1) *padrinos y ahijados*, or godparents and children; and (2) parents and godparents who become *compadres* or co-parents. The compadrazgo system of godparents enlarges family ties by creating connections between families. According to Richard Griswold del Castillo, "Godparents were required for the celebration of major religious occasions in a person's life: baptism, first communion and marriage."

At these times, godparents "entered into special religious, social and economic relationships with the godchild as well as the parents of the child." They acted as co-parents "providing discipline and emotional and financial support when needed." As compadres, they were expected to become the closest friend of the parents and members of the extended family (Griswold del Castillo 1984, 40-44).

Familism was thought to be a Mexican cultural pattern handed down through the generations. However, recent research has found that the Mexican-origin extended family has important roots in racial and economic conditions of U. S. society, where it is often a response to historical conditions of economic deprivation (Alvírez and Bean 1976; Hoppe and Heller 1973). Many studies offer evidence that extended families are vital in facilitating the adaptation of Mexicans within this society.

Research has consistently discovered, for example, that kinship networks are considerably involved in the migration of Mexicans to the United States (Samora and Lamanna 1975; Macklin 1976; Wells 1976). These studies document the process of chain migration, of using kin to locate housing, employment, and to link migrants to the new society. Important parallels can be found in Mexicans' past and present reliance on a network of kinship obligations. Alejandro Portes and Robert Bach (1985) found that 50 percent of Mexican Americans use families in the first three years of post-immigration residence. Other studies have concluded that "binational, intercommunity linkages are sustained through resilient family network ties" (Alvarez 1987; Massey et al. 1987 reported in Vega 1990, 1017).

Strong evidence exists for the relationship between structural familism and socioeconomic conditions (see Baca Zinn 1983 and Vega 1990 for reviews related to the socioeconomic functions of extended families). In their study of extended households among whites, blacks, and Hispanics, Ronald Angel and Marta Tienda found that Chicanos and low-income Chicano women who head families were more likely than Anglo Americans to form such households (Tienda and Angel 1982). Moore (1971) has shown that Mexican Americans in Los Angeles rely on kin for financial assistance and that the use of kin for financial need did not decrease with time in the city. Other studies have shown how the networks are used among Chicanos, Anglos, and blacks. Ronald Wagner and Diana Shaffer discovered large kinship networks of Chicana heads of households permitting a unique pattern of "resource specialization":

A Mexican family at mass in Houston, Texas. (Courtesy of the *Texas Catholic Herald.*)

> Parents are turned to in circumstances of dire necessity such as illness, when the woman might move in with the parents, or more commonly the mother might live with her temporarily, take care of the children, and fix the meals. Parents are also most often relied on for borrowing money. . . . Siblings tend to be utilized for those problems that are best met through people of one's own generation. Those women with cars, for example, turn to brothers as often as to a commercial garage for repairs. . . . Significant siblings were turned to for advice (usually a sister) more often than parents. People of one's own generation usually have a more empathetic understanding of problems one may be facing, since they may be confronting similar problems themselves. (Wagner and Shaffer 1980)

An important question has been whether Mexican familism operates primarily as an exchange system for socioeconomic marginality or as a system of emotional support. Evidence exists for both. Charles Mindel has found emotional support to be of great importance for Chicanos. These findings lead him to posit that the kinship system provides different functions for blacks and Chicanos:

> The differences between blacks and Mexican Americans . . . provide some interesting insights concerning the nature of kinship relations for these two groups. Mexican Americans appear to have large families and therefore engage in more extensive kinship interaction. Blacks, on the other hand, appear to have smaller families and interact with them less, but they use their kin in a more instrumental fashion as a mutual aid and support system. . . . The black kinship system appears to function primarily as an instrumentally oriented system open to a wide range of geographically near and distant kin. The Mexican-American system appears to be more socioemotional than instrumental with its emphasis on interaction with large numbers of kin. (Mindel 1980, 28-29)

Mindel concludes that non-Hispanics migrate away from kin and Hispanics migrate toward them. Socioeconomic differences may create variations in familism among Mexican-origin people. As with blacks, those with higher socioeconomic status may retain strong patterns of kin interaction by choice. They use their families not only for instrumental assistance but for the socioeconomic support that relatives provide.

Gender, Power and Family Activity

No assumption is more deeply ingrained in scholarly and popular thinking about Mexican-origin families than that of male dominance. *Machismo,* the Mexican masculinity cult, has long been thought to be responsible for many of the family and socialization patterns that create problems for Mexicans. The term *machismo* has gained popular usage in American society, referring to exaggerated masculinity, physical prowess, and male chauvinism. In the social science literature about Mexicans and Chicanos, *machismo* is the primary concept used to explain family structure and inadequate personality development. It is based on the assumption that exaggerated masculinity represents a compensation for cultural inferiority (Baca Zinn 1982, 2). Early research on Mexican families in the United States focused on the "macho-dominated" authoritarian Mexican-American family in which the male demands complete deference, respect, and obedience from his wife and children.

From the vantage point of the 1990s, the findings of these early studies "sound like ludicrous stereotypes—projections of the scholars' individual racism rather than valid indicators of the culture and its people" (Segura and Pierce 1991). While such stereotypical writings about overcompensating men and submissive women have given way to more balanced empirical works on gender, questions about male domination continue to be important. Although themes of patriarchy remain, the nature of male dominance is different from that described in earlier studies.

A wave of revisionist work on marital power conducted in the 1970s and 1980s found that wives and husbands share in family activities and decision making (Grebler Moore and Guzmán 1970; Hawkes and Taylor 1975; Cromwell and Cromwell 1978; Baca Zinn 1980; Ybarra 1982). These studies refute the stereotype of macho-dominated Mexican-origin families, but they do not dispute that gender is still a major determinant of family activities. Marital role relationships in Mexican-origin families are neither male dominated nor egalitarian, but like families in general, they reveal a range of patterns between these opposing models. Certain social conditions appear to be associated with greater equality for wives. The most striking is that of wives' employment. Again, there are parallels between historical and current patterns. Griswold del Castillo (1979), in his historical work on the Los Angeles barrio from 1850 through 1890, found that increased female involvement outside the family altered the role of women in the household as well as relations between women and men.

Maxine Baca Zinn (1980) found that wives' education and employment gave them certain "rights" within the family. And Leonarda Ybarra (1982) found many different patterns of decision making—from a patriarchal role-segregated structure to an egalitarian or joint structure, with many combinations between these two polar opposites evident. But Chicano couples in which both partners were in the labor force were more egalitarian than couples in which only the husband was employed. Linda Whitford (1980) found that employed women took on a variety of innovative behaviors by being part of a new social network that offered jobs, income, and information. These behaviors altered their own lives as well as those of their families. These findings support the importance of wives' employment in the contest for marital power.

Yet employment by itself does not eradicate male dominance nor transform women's subordinate roles. This is one of the main lessons of Patricia Zavella's landmark study, *Women's Work and Chicano Families* (1987). She found ongoing power struggles in the families of Chicano cannery workers in the Santa Clara Valley of California. Cannery jobs did give women some leverage in the home. Yet, as seasonal part-time work, their jobs were defined as an extension of their household responsibilities and did not fundamentally transform family roles. This study shows how the impact of women's work on the family is bound up with broader systems of class and racial inequality. Chicano working mothers faced occupational segregation by race and gender on the job and the double day at home. Although financial incentives kept wives employed, they were workers in a declining industry, still economically dependent upon husbands. These structural conditions supported and reinforced male dominance within the family.

Different kinds of work and different work settings also influence the balance between work and family. A comparison of Cuban women in Miami and immigrant women in Los Angeles reveals important differences. Patricia Fernández Kelly and Anna García found different outcomes for these women, despite similar gender role expectations about female employment in both groups. Immigrant Mexican women in Los Angeles found themselves in a process of proletarianization, "where their labor was required for family survival, whereas many Cuban women left the labor force when short-term goals of improving living standards were attained" (Kelly and García 1989 reported in Vega 1990, 1920).

In the past decade, important feminist insights about patriarchy within families has been incorporated into studies of Mexican-origin families (Baca Zinn 1990). Gender roles will continue to be a primary area of study. In fact, gender is emerging as pivotal for understanding how Mexican-origin people (both women and men) experience a variety of social settings beyond those of family and paid labor. For example, migration to the United States is strongly shaped by gender. In a comprehensive review of gender and migration, Silvia Pedraza (1991) has sketched the role gender plays in the decision to migrate, the composition of the migration flows, and the incorporation of women and men within the new society. Among Mexicans, gender relations shape women's and men's migration in surprisingly different ways. Whereas the conventional thinking assumed that women passively follow their husbands to the United States, new research shows otherwise. In a study questioning the power relations between Mexican women and men, Pierrette Hondagneu-Sotelo (1993) has discovered a complex process in which gender faciliates and restrains migration and is itself rearranged by movement to the United States. She has also discovered that patriarchy is not an all-pervasive, monolithic factor that renders Mexican women powerless as they move to this society. Although patriarchal systems and ideals influence the migration process, patriarchal relations are fluid. Structural changes alter the conditions of daily life and enable women to persuade, subvert, and diminish patriarchal relations in the new settings.

The Impact of U. S. Social Trends on Mexican Families

In the last quarter century, families throughout society have been affected by some fundamental changes including family composition, the participation of women in the workforce, patterns of marriage and divorce, and the proportion of households headed by women. These trends will continue to transform families, and Mexicans will be no exception. Like families throughout society, Mexican-origin families will be bombarded by economic and demographic upheavals. The following social forces will have serious consequences for Mexican-origin families: (1) the structural transformation of the American economy from one based on manufacturing to one based on information and services, and (2) immigration patterns, policies, and relations between the U. S. and Mexican governments.

Family stability is severely threatened by trends in the United States that are transforming its economy, redesigning and redistributing jobs, exacerbating inequality, and reorganizing cities and regions. New technologies and industrial restructuring are affecting the lives of people in virtually all social categories. However, the magnitude of structural transformation is different throughout society. Minorities are especially hard hit by technology and the changing distribution of jobs. The effects of these changes are most visible in three areas: (1) the changing distribution and organization of jobs, and the tendency for the newly created jobs to be low-paying, (2) the trend toward women's rising rates of labor force participation, and (3) the trend toward poverty and unemployment. Each of these trends is related to industrial restructuring and has created changes in the family patterns of Mexicans.

The dramatic reversal in economic progress and income distribution since the mid-1970s has been called "The Great U Turn" (Harrison and Bluestone 1988). All minority groups and especially Latinos have experienced an even greater U-Turn, even though Latinos have expanded their share in the workforce (Ojeda 1990). As a firmly established blue collar work force, Mexicans have tended to work in economic sectors most vulnerable to cyclical unemployment and in some manufacturing industries that are threatened with decline. They have been affected by plant closings created by the flight from the West and Southwest for cheaper locales in other parts of the world. Although most of the Mexican-origin population lives in areas with booming economies, they do not always profit from regional growth. Many of the growth industries that employ Mexicans pay poorly and have weak unions. Thus, while growth does create jobs, many are in service and low-wage manufacturing. Few in the population have enough training for high-wage jobs in the new industries (Moore 1989).

The impact of economic restructuring on Mexicans has been and will remain uneven. Where plant closings and factory layoffs have been studied among Mexican-origin workers, predictable family stresses and disruptions have been documented (Castro 1990). In other cases industrial restructuring has been found to generate employment. Many Mexican-origin women have found their work opportunities expanded in electronics and apparel factories. Such work often creates new forms of race and gender exploitation and offers only marginal income. But it also allows many Mexican women to keep their families afloat when their husbands have lost their jobs due to economic reorganization (Zavella 1984). Changes in industrial employment affect women and men differently, and these patterns have staggering effects on family life.

As industrial restructuring reorganizes work, women in all social categories are drawn into the labor force. Mexican women are no exception. Of the 54.7 million women in the civilian labor force in 1988, 3.6 million, or 6.5 percent, were of Hispanic origin. Of this 3.6 million, 58.5 percent were of Mexican origin (U. S. Department of Labor 1989, 1). This represents an important departure from the earlier patterns. Mexican-origin women have historically had among the lowest rates of labor force participation. This increase in women's employment has created far-reaching changes in family life, but it has not stabilized Mexican families nor diminished the impact of poverty. Like women in the larger society, Mexican women have experienced both rising levels of employment and higher poverty rates that are associated with the growth of female-headed households. Although Mexican-heritage people have the highest proportion of married couple families, they are not immune to the feminization of poverty. Almost half of the 18.5 percent of female-headed households in 1988 were below the federal poverty level. Poor female-headed households with or without the support of extended kin create severe problems for mothers and their children.

During the 1980s all Hispanic groups experienced a decrease in real median family income. To a large extent, this was due to changes in the larger economy that polarized the occupational structure into "good" jobs and "bad" jobs. Few in the Mexican-origin population have enough training for high-wage jobs. They are dropping further behind in education and training just when jobs are requiring more technical knowledge and higher levels of education. This is one of the most crucial barriers to family well-being. Mexicans (along with other Latino ethnic groups) have the highest rates of school drop-outs in the country. Undereducated people suffer in the employment world, and their families pay a high price.

Low levels of educational completion are partly the result of immigrant status. The Mexican-origin population will continue to receive migrants. This is a matter of great significance insofar as it contributes to sustained differences in the social and economic characteristics of the Mexican-origin population in the United States. The level of well-being among Mexicans depends on the impact of immigration policies in regulating the flow of workers from Mexico to the United States and on the success of the migrants in securing employment (Sandefur and Tienda 1987).

These are truly extraordinary times for family study. Accelerated social changes that are affecting families in all racial categories are creating widespread variation in "the American family." The growing diversity of family life offers the potential to sharpen, as never before, our understanding of how families are related to the larger social world. In this renewed concern for how families respond to and absorb external changes, the Mexican-origin family can be a stimulus to our understanding of "the family." Although racial inequalities produce strong differences in many aspects of family life, the study of minority families can generate important insights for all families. Families may respond in a like manner when impacted by larger social forces. To the extent that minorities and others experience similar pressures, they may respond in similar ways, including the adaptation of their family structures and other behaviors.

Contemporary family studies have taken insufficient account of the Mexican experience. In the mainstream of family scholarship, minority families are too often marginalized as special "cultural" cases. Mainstream scholarship has not questioned how the study of minority families can generate insights for family dynamics in general. Instead of judging all racial ethnic families against a mainstream family model, we must now recognize that diversity is the predominant pattern. Mexican-origin families can teach us much about the interplay between families and society, about how people with severely constrained options and choices, nevertheless forge family lives that are suited to their own needs and lifestyles.

Bibliography

Alvarez, Robert
1987 *Families: Migration and Adaptation in Baja and Alta California from 1800 to 1975.* Berkeley: U of California P.

Alvírez, David, and Frank D. Bean
1976 "The Mexican-American Family." In *Ethnic Families in America.* Eds Charles H. Mindel and Robert W. Habenstein. New York: Elsevier Scientific, pp 271-92.

Andrade, Sally
1980 "Family Planning Practices of Mexican Americans." *Twice a Minority: Mexican American Women in the United States.* Ed Margarita Melville. St. Louis, MO: Mosbey.

Angel, Ronald, and Marta Tienda
1982 "Determinants of Extended Household Structure: Cultural Pattern or Economic Need?" *American Journal of Sociology,* 87:1260-1383.

Aponte, Robert
1991 "Urban Hispanic Poverty: Dissagragations and Explanations." *Social Problems,* 38.4:516-28.

Arce, Carlos
1978 "Dimensions of Familism and Family Identification.'' Unpublished paper presented at the National Conference on the Hispanic Family, Houston.

Baca Zinn, Maxine
1980 "Employment and Education of Mexican-American Women: The Interplay of Modernity and Ethnicity in Eight Families." *Harvard Educational Review,* vol 50, no 1, (February):47-62.
1982 "Chicano Men and Masculinity." *Journal of Ethnic Studies,* vol 10:29-44.
1982 "Familism Among Chicanos: A Theoretical Review." *Humboldt Journal of Social Relations,* 10:224-38.

Baca Zinn, Maxine, and D. Stanley Eitzen
1990 *Diversity in Families.* Second Edition. New York: Harper & Row.
1990 "Family, Feminism, and Race in America." *Gender & Society,* vol 4, no 1, (March):68-82.

Barrera, Mario
1979 *Race and Class in the Southwest.* Notre Dame, IN: U of Notre Dame P.

Bartz, K., and E. Levine
1978 "Childrearing by Black Parents: A Description and Comparison to Anglo and Chicano Parents." *Journal of Marriage and the Family,* vol 40, (November):709-19.

Bean, Frank D., and Marta Tienda
1987 *The Hispanic Population of the United States.* New York: Russell Sage Foundation.

Berardo, Félix M.
1991 "Family Research in the 1980s: Recent Trends and Future Directions." In *Contemporary Families: Looking Forward, Looking Back.* Ed Alan Booth, Minneapolis, MN: National Council on Family Relations.

Bogardus, Emory
1934 *The Mexican in the United States.* Los Angeles: U of Southern California P.

Camarillo, Albert
1979 *Chicanos in a Changing Society: From Mexican Pueblos to American Barrios in Santa Barbara and Southern California, 1884-1930.* Cambridge, MA: Harvard UP.

Cromwell, Vicky L., and Donald E. Cromwell
1978 "Perceived Dominance in Decision Making and Conflict Resolution Among Anglo, Black, and Chicano Couples." *Journal of Marriage and the Family,* vol 40, (November):749-59.

Eitzen, D. Stanley, and Maxine Baca Zinn
1989 *The Reshaping of America.* Englewood Cliffs, NJ: Prentice-Hall.

Estrada, Richard
1989 "Myths of Hispanic Families' Wellness." *Kansas City Star,* (September 10):15.

García, Mario T.
1981 *Desert Immigrants: The Mexicans of El Paso, 1890-1920.* New Haven: Yale UP.
1980 "La Familia: The Mexican Immigrant Family, 1900-1930." In *Work, Family, Sex Roles, Language.* Eds Mario Barrera, Albert Camarillo and Frances Hernández. Berkeley: Quinto Sol International, pp 117-40.

Grebler, L. et al.
1970 *The Mexican American People: The Nation's Second Minority.* New York: Free P.

Griswold del Castillo, Richard
1981 "Chicano Family History and the Life Course Analysis: San Antonio, Texas, in 1960." Paper presented at the Pacific Sociological Association, Portland, OR.
1984 *La Familia,* Notre Dame, IN: U of Notre Dame P.

Hawkes, Glenn R., and Minna Taylor
1975 "Power Structure in Mexican and Mexican-American Families." *Journal of Marriage and the Family,* 37:807-11.

Hayes-Bautista, David
1989 "Latino Adolescents, Families, Work, and the Economy: Building upon Strength or Creating a Weakness?" Paper prepared for the Carnegie Commission on Adolescent Development, Washington, DC.

Hondagneau-Sotelo, Pierrette
1993 "Overcoming Patriarchal Constraints: Reconstituting Gender Relations among Mexican Immigrant Women and Men." *Gender & Society.*

Hoppe, Sue Kier, and Peter Heller
1975 "Alienation, Familism, and the Utilization of Health Services by Mexican-Americans." *Journal of Health and Social Behavior,* 16:304-14.

Kelly, Patricia F., and Anna García
1989 "Power Surrendered and Power Restored: The Politics of Home and Work among Hispanic Women in Southern California and Southern

Florida." In *Women and Politics in America*. Eds. Louise Tilly and Patricia Gurin. New York: Russell Sage Foundation.

Luzod, Jimmy A., and Carlos H. Arce
1979 "An Exploration of the Father Role in the Chicano Family." Paper presented at the National Symposium on the Mexican American Child, Santa Barbara, CA.

Macklin, Barbara June
1976 *Structural Stability and Culture Change in a Mexican American Community*. New York: Arno P.

Massey, Douglas, Rafael Alarcón, Jorge Durand, and Umberto Gonzales
1987 *Return to Aztlán*. Berkeley: U of California P.

Mindel, Charles H.
1980 "Extended Familism among Urban Mexican Americans, Anglos, and Blacks." *Hispanic Journal of Behavioral Sciences*, 2:21-34.

Moore, Joan
1989 "Is There a Hispanic Underclass?" *Social Science Quarterly*, 70:265-84.
1971 "Mexican-Americans and Cities: A Study in Migration and the Use of Formal Resources." *International Migration Review*, 5:292-308.

Moore, Joan W., and Hary Pachón
1985 *Hispanics in the United States*. Englewood Cliffs, NJ: Prentice-Hall.

Ojeda, Raúl Hinojosa
1990 "An Even Greater 'U Turn': Latinos and the New Inequality." Paper presented at the Inter University Program's Conference on Latino Research Perspective in the 1990s, Pomona, CA.

O'Hare, William P.
1989 "Assimilation and Socioeconomic Advancement of Hispanics in the U. S." Population Reference Bureau Staff Working Papers.

Pedraza, Silvia
1991 "Women and Migration: The Social Consequences of Gender." *Annual Review of Sociology*, 17:303-25.

Portes, Alejandro, and Robert L. Back
1985 *Latin Journey*. Berkeley: U of California P.

Portes, Alejandro, and Rubén G. Rumbaut
1990 *Immigrant America: A Portrait*. Berkeley: U of California P.

Ramírez, Oscar, and Carlos Arce
1980 "The Contemporary Chicano Family: An Empirically Based Review." In *Explorations in Chicano Psychology*. Ed Augustine Baron, Jr. New York: Praeger.

Romo, Harriet
1986 "Chicano, Transitional and Undocumented Mexican Families: Perceptions of the Schooling of Their Children." In *Mexican Immigrants and Mexican Americans*. Eds Harley L. Browning and Rodolfo O. De La Garza. Austin, TX: CMAS Publications, pp 175-93.

Samora, Julian, and Richard Lamana
1967 *Mexican-Americans in a Midwest Metropolis: A Study of East Chicago*. UCLA Study Project Advance Report.

Sandefur, Gary D., and Marta Tienda
1988 "Introduction: Social Policy and the Minority Experience." In *Divided Opportunities: Minority Poverty and Social Policy*. Eds Gary D. Sandefur and Marta Tienda. New York: Plenum P.

Segura, Denise A., and Jennifer L. Pierce
1991 "Chicano Family Structure and Gender Personality: Chodorow, Familism, and Psychoanalytic Sociology Revisited." Unpublished paper.

Staples, R., and A. Mirande
1980 "Racial and Cultural Variations among American Families: A Decennial Review of the Literature on Minority Families." *Journal of Marriage and the Family*, 40:157-73.

Thomas, Darwin L., and Jean Edmondson Wilcox
1987 "The Rise of Family Theory." In *Handbook of Marriage and the Family*. Eds Marvin B. Sussman and Suzanne S. Steinmetz. New York: Plenum P.

Trevino, Fernando, Dorothy A Trevino, Christine A. Stroup, and Laura Ray
1988 "The Feminization of Poverty among Hispanic Households." Paper presented at the Seminar on Persistent Poverty among Hispanics, Trinity U, San Antonio, TX.

U. S. Bureau of the Census
1989 *Current Population Reports, Series P-20, no 438.* "The Hispanic Population of the United States: March 1988." Washington, DC: Government Printing Office.
1991 *Current Population Reports, Series P-20, no 499.* "The Hispanic Population of the United States: March 1990." Washington, DC: Government Printing Office.
1991 *Statistical Abstracts of the United States: 1991.* (111th ed). Washington, DC: Government Printing Office.

U. S. Department of Labor
1991 "Women of Hispanic Origin in the Labor Force." Women's Bureau. Washington, DC: Government Printing Office.

Valdivieso, Rafael, and Cary Davis
1988 *U. S. Hispanics: Challenging Issues for the 1990's.* Washington, DC: Population Reference Bureau.

Vega, William A.
1990 "Hispanic Families in the 1980s: A Decade of Research." *Journal of Marriage and the Family*, vol 52, (November):1015-1024.

Wagner, Roland, and Diana Shaffer
1980 "Social Networks and Survival Strategies: An Exploratory Study of Mexican-American, Black, and Anglo Female Family Heads in San Jose, California." In *Twice a Minority, Mexican American Women in the United States*. Ed Margarita Melville. St Louis, MO: Mosby, pp 173-90.

Wells, M. J.
1976 "Emigrants from the Migrant Stream: Environment and Incentive in Relocation." *Aztlán: International Journal of Chicano Studies Research*, 7:267-90.

White, Alfred
1971 "The Apperceptive Mass of Foreigners as Applied

to Americanization: The Mexican Group." M. A. Thesis: U of Southern California. Reprinted by R & E Research Associates.

Whitford, Linda
1980 "Mexican American Women as Innovative Behavior." In *Twice a Minority: Mexican American Women in the United States.* Ed Margarita Melville. St. Louis, MO: Mosby.

Ybarra, Lea
1982 "When Wives Work: The Impact on the Chicano Family." *Journal of Marriage and the Family*, vol 44, (February):169-78.

Zavella, Patricia
1984 "The Impact of Sun Belt Industrialization on Chicanas." *Frontiers*, 8.1:21-27.

Zavella, Patricia
1987 *Women's Work and Chicano Families.* Ithaca: Cornell UP.

Roots and Resistance: The Emergent Writings of Twenty Years of Chicana Feminist Struggle

Teresa Córdova

Chicana feminists have struggled to find their voices—have struggled to be heard. Our struggles continue but our silence is forever broken. We are telling our stories and we are recording our triumphs and, by virtue of our presence, we are challenging our surroundings.

This paper is an overview of the development of writings of Chicana feminists. As such, it cannot be exhaustive. It can be a statement to the reader that Chicana writing has developed out of personal and political struggle, a fact which shapes the very nature of that writing and the impact that Chicana writers have had in political, literary, and social science circles.

This paper focuses on the many self-identified Chicanas whose political roots originate from the Chicano movement of the 1960s and 1970s. As such, these roots are based in a political knowledge of the historical emergence of the Chicano people and their connection to their Indian ancestry. They are based on an understanding of the legacy of 500 years of resistance and on an understanding of contemporary dynamics of class and race relations in U. S. society, particularly the Southwest, known as Aztlán. The analysis presented by Chicanas is an important dimension added to assess the experiences of Chicanos and thus constitutes a perspective that is the intersection of class, race, and gender.

The Struggle to Speak

Chicanas were never passive nor entirely submissive to cultural constraints, yet these constraints did limit the emergence of Chicana voices; early efforts to speak began by identifying the cultural definitions that discouraged them. Chicanas were born into a culture of silence where, like children, we were to be seen, not heard. Or stated more dramatically, "Chicanas traditionally, have been tortilla-makers, baby-producers, to be touched but not heard" (Chávez 1972, 82). The Catholicism brought to us by missionaries influenced many of our world views and taught us the values of piety, humility and bearing our crosses in silence, for "blessed are the meek who would inherit the earth." Consuelo Nieto noted:

> For the most part, the Church has assumed a traditional stance toward women. It has clearly defined the woman's role as that of wife and mother, requiring obedience to one's husband . . .
>
> Marianismo (veneration of the Virgin Mary) has had tremendous impact upon the development of the Chicana. Within many Chicano homes, La Virgen—under various titles, but especially as La Virgen de Guadalupe—has been the ultimate role model for the Chicano woman.
>
> Mary draws her worth and nobility from her relationship to her son, Jesus Christ. She is extolled as mother, as nurturer. She is praised for her endurance of pain and sorrow, her willingness to serve, and her role as teacher of her son's word. She is Queen of the Church.
>
> Some Chicanas are similarly praised as they emulate the sanctified example set by Mary. The woman par excellence la mother and wife. She is to love and support her husband and to nurture and teach her children. Thus may she gain fulfillment as a woman. (1974, 37)

Thus, in our struggles to speak, the first major contradiction we encountered was between our desires to bring forth our voices and the traditions that our politics committed us to protect and preserve. Chicano activists in El Movimiento invoked these traditions and told a growing number of feministas that they were "anti-family, anti-cultural, anti-man and therefore anti-Chicano movement." (Nieto-Gómez 1974b, 35).

It was the contradictions that Chicanas encountered within the Chicano movement, therefore, which most shaped a feminist ideology decrying que nos dicen, "el problema es el gabacho, no es el macho." Within the Chicano movement Chicanas struggled for political equality and escape from the relegated tasks of dishwashers, secretaries, and rucas. Adelaida Del Castillo, for example, in response to a question on why there is an interest in Chicana feminism said, "A lot of Chicanas were sincerely feeling exploited if not alienated by certain organizations of the Chicano movement in the types of jobs that she was being given or relegated to" (1974, 8). Another Chicana activist's description of male/female relations was quoted from *Hijos de Cuahtemoc*

> When a freshman male comes to MECHA (Movimiento Estudiantil Chicano de Aztlán—a Chicano student organization in California), he is approached and welcomed. He is taught by observation that the Chicanas are only useful in areas of clerical and sexual activities. When something must be done there is always a Chicana there to do the work. "It is her place and duty to stand behind and back up her Macho." . . . Another aspect of the MACHO attitude is their lack of respect for Chicanas. They play their games, plotting girl against girl for their own benefit. . . . They use the movement and Chicanismo to take her to bed. And when she refuses, she is a vendida (sell-out) because she is not looking after the welfare of her men. (Vidal 1972)

It was a bold move for Chicanas to reject the role restrictions placed upon them and an even stronger step to suggest that the "triple oppression" (Hancock 1971, 168) of Chicanas should be an issue within the movement. Most of the Chicana writings during the late 1960s and early 1970s (primarily in Chicano movement newspapers and publications) were replete with responses to Chicanos and "loyalist" Chicanas who claimed that the feministas were being divisive to the movement and products of "Anglo bourgeois feminism." As Nieto-Gómez points out, "The Chicana feminist has had to struggle to develop and maintain her identity . . ." (1974b, 34).

However, some Chicanas viewed the search for identity as an "Anglo-bourgeois trip. The 'Loyalists' could only see the 'Feministas' as ambitious, selfish women who were only concerned with themselves at the cost of everyone else." Nieto-Gómez then quotes an anonymous "loyalist" who expressed her concern in a California State University Northridge student newspaper, *Popo Femenil*, in an article entitled, "Chicanas Take Wrong Direction."

> Since when does a Chicana need identity? If you are a real Chicana then no one regardless of the degrees needs to tell you about it. The only ones who need identity are the vendidas, the falsas, and the opportunists. The time has come for the Chicanas to examine the direction they wish to take. Yes, we need recognition. Our men must give this to us. But there is danger in the manner we are seeking it. . . . We are going to have to decide what we value more, the culture or the individual (as Anglos do)? I hope it's not too late. (1974b, 35)

It was precisely this sentiment that prevailed at the First National Chicano Student Conference in 1969 when women declared that "it was the consensus of the group that the Chicana woman does not want to be liberated."

A Chicana activist from New Mexico shared a similar experience:

> [In 1971] I was being called a white woman for organizing a Las Chicanas group on the University of New Mexico campus. I was not only ostracized by men but by women. Some felt I would be dividing the existing Chicano group on campus (the United Mexican-American Students, UMAS), some were simply afraid of displeasing the men, some felt that I was wrong and my ideas "white" and still others felt that their contribution to la Causa or El Movimiento was in giving the men moral support from the kitchen. (Chávez 1972, 82)

This "feminist baiting," as García (1989) calls it, was a form of harassment that

> forced many Chicanas to suppress their convictions. The term "women's libber," a stigmatizing label, was used as a social label assigned to those who spoke out for women's rights in the Chicano movement. These castigated Chicanas were identified as man haters, frustrated women, and "agringadas," Anglo-cized. If they spoke out against sexual inequality, they were often effectively isolated, controlled and discredited . . . Nieto-Gómez 1974b, 36)

García also notes that feminist lesbians were subjects of even more severe "feminist baiting": "In a political climate that already viewed feminist ideology with suspicion, lesbianism as a sexual lifestyle and political ideology came under even more attack. Clearly, a cultural nationalist ideology that perpetuated such stereotypical images of Chicanas as 'good wives and good mothers' found it difficult to accept a Chicana feminist lesbian movement" (García 1989, 226).

Despite these early attempts to silence the voices of a developing feminist consciousness, feministas were very clear that their voices did not mean a disruption to the unity of La Raza though it may have meant a disruption to a false unity based on the submission of women. Instead, feministas argued, men and women struggling together is a stronger foundation for a successful Chicano movement.

> We must come to the realization that we have to work together in order to save ourselves. If the male oppressed the female, perhaps it is because he has been oppressed. We can't turn against them, and they can't turn against us. We have to help each other. Remember, what the system wants is that the movement divide itself into small factions so that eventually it will fall apart into dust. We don't want this to happen. You are my compañero as a Mexicano and I am your compañera as a Mexicana. We're together. As Chicanos we have the responsibility to look after each other. (Del Castillo 1974, 10)

Chicana feminists articulated a support for political unity:

> While it is true that the unity of La Raza is the basic foundation of the Chicano movement, when Chicano men talk about maintaining La Familia and the "cultural heritage" of La Raza, they are in fact talking about maintaining the age-old concept of keeping the woman barefoot, pregnant, and in the kitchen. On the basis of the subordination of women there can be no real unity. . . . The only real unity between men and women is the unity forged in the course of struggle against their oppression. And it is by supporting, rather than opposing, the struggles of women, that Chicanos and Chicanas can genuinely unite. (Vidal 1971, 31-32)

This unity, feministas argued, called for a fuller participation of Chicanas. Chicana feministas understood that one of their first needs as activists was to become an integral part of the movement as leaders, as conference speakers and not as "decorations." Chicanas did not accept the claim that there were no qualified Chicanas for these positions. "If we are not 'qualified', my brother, what are you doing to help us? What experiences and training are you providing us? What support do you give us that we may become articulate and politically sophisticated, and that we may develop the skills of negotiation and decision making?" (Nieto 1974, 41).

In response to the claim that they should postpone their cause for a later time, feministas proclaimed that it was "illogical to ask a woman to ignore and postpone her struggle as a woman" (Nava 1973). Chicana feminists rejected the claims that as "Raza women who are triply oppressed," they did not have the right to "struggle around their specific, real, and immediate needs" (Vidal 1971, 9). In fact, the Chicana activists of the early 1970s had very well developed notions of what those needs were and were very clear that they were distinct from those of Anglo feminists. Based on her experiences and her politics, rooted in the ideologies of the Chicano movement, feministas understood their oppression and their relation to Chicano men in a historical political economic context. Sosa Riddel writes:

> Exploitation of contemporary Chicanas begins in a very real sense with the Spanish conquest, regardless of what conditions were among the native peoples prior to the Conquest. . . . In word and in deed, the Spaniards relegated the native woman, and later the mestiza, to the lowest position in the structured society which came to dominate Mexico. (1974, 157-58)

In more contemporary terms, another Chicana writes,

> The Chicana's socio-economic class as a non-Anglo Spanish-speaking, low-income Chicana woman determines her need and therefore her political position. The low-income Anglo woman does not have to deal with racism nor is she punished because she speaks another language. The middle-class Anglo woman only shares with the Chicana the fact that they are both women. But they are women of different ethnic, cultural, and class status. All these factors determine the different socio-economic needs and therefore determine the different political positions of these women. (Nieto-Gómez 1974b, 39)

Despite the analyses that Chicanas put forward, Nieto-Gómez also states that "it can be truthfully said that she [the Chicana] has been ignored" (1974b, 34). Most of the Chicano writings of the 1970s did not include the words of Chicanas or at best included one or two articles which in some cases had been circulated in several locations. Chicano journals contained few works by Chicanas and had virtually no Chicanas on their editorial boards. In a couple of cases (see below) journals printed special volumes on Chicanas. Chicanas developed their own vehicles to circulate their ideas. *Regeneración*, edited by a Chicana, was first published in 1970. In addition to its many articles by Chicanas, *Regeneración* also published two special volumes by mujeres in 1971 and again in 1973. Another journal, *Encuentro Femenil*, was published out of the L. A. area in Spring 1973 and was another critical source for Chicana writings in the early seventies. *Imágenes de la Chicana* published two volumes out of Stanford University. A special volume in 1973 of *El Grito*, published in Berkeley, was devoted to Chicanas. Chicanas also wrote extensively in newspapers such as *Hijas de Cuahtemoc* and magazines such as *La Luz*. Occasionally, other collections of writings on "women" included writings by Chicanas; for example, *Sisterhood Is Powerful* included the essay by Longauex y Vásquez.

The issues articulated by Chicanas in these and other writings of the early 1970s included welfare rights, child care, health, birth control, sterilization, legal rights, prison experience of Chicanas, sex roles, images of Chicanas, heroines of history, labor struggles (mostly historical), and organizing themselves as Chicanas. They were also beginning to publish works of poetry and fiction.

Encuentro Femenil published two works in 1973 and 1974 by Alicia Escalante, the leader of the Chicano Welfare Rights Organization on her personal experiences in the welfare system. In 1973, *Regeneración* also published an article entitled "Chicana Welfare Rights Challenges Talmadge Amendment" and "Chicana Service Action Center" in the same issue (vol. 2, no. 3). Clemencia Martínez wrote "Welfare Families Face Forced Labor" (1972).

Child care was a frequent subject; Chicanas understood the problem of availability of adequate child care for working mothers with young children. Chicanas called for 24-hour government-funded child care that was controlled by the community (Vidal 1971, 33). Chicanas voiced additional childcare concerns for bicultural, bilingual centers where their children do not face discrimination.

In the area of health, Chicanas were acutely aware of the discrimination they faced.

> Anglo women contend with the cruel prejudice doctors have towards women patients. Chicanas must also contend with doctors' racism, insensitivity to the Chicano culture and the lack of bilingual medical staff. In addition, economics limit her choice of medical facilities to state and county health clinics which usually have inadequate health services. Depending on the availability of a bilingual volunteer among the patients, most doctors treat monolingual Spanish-speaking patients with less than adequate diagnosis. (Nieto-Gómez 1974b, 40)

Other Chicana writings from Texas and Los Angeles exposed the fact that Chicanas were being used as guinea pigs against their knowledge for birth control testing and that sterilization was being used as a means of population control of Chicanas. As Nieto-Gómez noted, "Darwinistic doctors who feel that the poor are the burden of the strong play God with the bodies of women. As a result, Chicanas are victims of constant malpractice. They are involuntarily experimented with, and involuntarily sterilized" (1974b, 40). Thus, the Chicana called for health clinics in the community that were "community controlled."

Many Chicanas asserted their concern for their control of their bodies through access to birth control and abortion. Showing an early inclination for forming coalitions with other Third World women, Chicanas joined a group of fifty African Americans, Asian Americans and other Latinas to say that "there is a myth that Third World women do not want to control our bodies, that we do not want the right to contraception and abortion. . . . We know that more Third World women die every year from illegal back-street abortions than the rest of the female population" (Vidal 1971, 32).

The extent to which the law serves the needs of Chicanas was also called into question by Chicana feminists. Del Castillo, for example, tells the story of a Mexican woman who was in the process of divorcing her husband when he broke into her house and raped her. She took her case to court but found that because she couldn't speak English she faced a situation of ridicule in which the lawyers and the judge laughed at her.

> That's an insult to me as a Mexican woman and to that woman and to all Chicanos because here is a Mexican woman who is hoping that she can depend on the law, on the judge, to set this matter straight and he laughs at her in addition to which he admonished her and tells her off for not knowing English. Furthermore, he wanted her to pay him, the husband, damages when he has raped her in front of her children! So is there in fact any justice, or does racism impede justice for us? (Del Castillo 1974, 9)

The experience of Chicana prisoners was also an issue for Chicana feminists. An article entitled "Chicanas in Prison" appeared in *Regeneración* in 1975 (Madrid), and another appeared in *Encuentro Femenil* in 1974 entitled "La Pinta: The Myth of Rehabilitation."

Chicanas wrote about sexual stereotypes (González 1973; Suárez 1973) and the "Chicana: The Forgotten Woman" (Delgado 1971). Bernice Rincón wrote "La Chicana: Her Role in the Past and Her Search for a New

Role in the Future" (1971). The articulation of identity also included establishing connection to historical heroines such as Lucy González Parsons (Sánchez n.d.).

The working class perspective of many Chicana feminists led them to an analysis of Chicana employment issues and labor struggles. Yolanda Nava wrote, again in *Regeneración* and *Encuentro Femenil*, on "The Chicana and Employment: Needs Analysis and Recommendations for Legislation" (1973a) and "Employment Counseling and the Chicana" (1973b). Anna Nietó-Gomez also wrote "Chicanas in the Labor Force" (1974a) and "The Needs of the Spanish Speaking Mujer (Woman) in Woman-Manpower Training Programs" (1974b). Laura Arroyo wrote one of the few articles by a Chicana appearing in *Aztlán*, entitled "Industrial and Occupation Distribution of Chicana Workers" (1973). A 1971 volume of *Regeneración* contained a testimonial by María Moreno, an agricultural worker. She entitled her statement, "I'm Talking for Justice."

Writings on education include Nieto-Gómez's "The Chicana: Perspectives for Education," Nieto-Gómez and Sánchez's *New Directions in Education: Estudios Femeniles de la Chicana*, and Corinne Sánchez, "Higher Education y la Chicana" (1973). The first and third of these appeared in *Encuentro Femenil*.

In addition to works already cited on the development of Chicana feminist consciousness, other Chicanas wrote about issues of inequality and of themselves as Chicana feminists. Francisca Flores wrote on the Conference of Mexican Women in 1971 in Houston (1971), and Lionela Sáenz wrote "Machismo, No! Igualdad, Sí!" (1972). In December 1972, an article appeared in *Ms.* magazine entitled "Women of La Raza Unite!" Linda Aguilar wrote on "Unequal Opportunity and the Chicana" in the *Civil Rights Digest* (1973), and Elena García wrote "Chicana Consciousness: A New Perspective, a New Hope (1973). An essay appeared in *La Raza* in 1973 entitled "El Movimiento and the Chicana: What Else Could Break Down a Revolution but Women Who Do Not Understand True Equality." Nieto-Gómez also wrote "La Feminista" (1974). Guadalupe Valdés-Fallis wrote "The Liberated Chicana: A Struggle against Tradition" (1974).

These and other concerns served the basis of not only Chicana activism but also of the further development of Chicana writings. Instead of yielding to the demands for our silence, Chicanas declared the existence and legitimacy of a Chicana feminism which the Chicano movement had to make room for and which was distinct from white feminism.

In light of the many struggles to speak and be heard, it is a great triumph that Chicanas have continued to speak and have continued to develop a rich collection of poetry, literature, humanities and social science writings. The benefits are there for those who hear the voices of Chicana writers.

Chicana Writings: 1975-1981

The mid-1970s marked the beginning of more systematic social science and historical analyses of the Chicana experience. During this period Chicana poetry and literature were also more extensively circulated beyond the confines of intimate sharings.

Chicana feminists continued to write about feminism. Flores addressed the issues of "The New Chicana and Machismo" (1975) and Nieto-Gómez continued as an important voice in her article "Sexism in the Movimiento" (1976). Rita Sánchez addressed the development of the Chicana voice in "Chicana Writer Breaking Out of Silence" (1977). González wrote in the *Social Science Journal* on "The White Feminist Movement: The Chicana Perspective" (1977) and Burciaga wrote on "The 1977 National Women's Conference in Houston: Gains and Disappointments for Hispanas" (1977). In 1977, Martha Cotera published *Chicana Feminist,* which was a collection of essays she had written between 1970 and 1977.

Many of the same social issues appeared as themes in these more developed analyses including an article on sterilization in *The Chicano Law Review* (Hernández 1976), images of Chicanas in popular culture and literature (Salinas 1975; 1979), "Raza Mental Health" (Carillo-Berón 1977), and "Chicanas in Politics" (Chapa and Gutiérrez 1977).

Articles appeared on the topic of Chicana psychology and counseling. Many of these were based on research projects and placed in journals of the respective disciplines. These included Teresa Ramírez Boulette's "Determining Needs and Appropriate Counseling Approaches for Mexican-American Women: A Comparison of Therapeutic Listening and Behavioral Rehearsal" (1976), "Dilemmas of Chicana Counselors" (Medina and Reyes 1976), and "Psychology of the Chicana" (Nieto Senour 1977).

Maxine Baca Zinn published several articles during this period and Martha Cotera published *Diosa y Hembra* in 1977. The period is additionally notable for the publication of several edited volumes of Chicana writings. These included Martínez Cruz and Sánchez's *Essays on La Mujer*, (1977), Melville's *Twice a Minority* (1980), Mora and del Castillo's *Mexican Women in the United States: Struggles Past and Present* (1980). *De Colores* published a special volume entitled *La cosecha: Literatura y la mujer chicana* (see Rita Sánchez 1977) as did *Frontiers: A Journal of Women Studies, "Chicanas in the National Landscape"* (1980).

The combination of these and other writings established four major points: (1) The Chicana is not inherently passive—nor is she what the stereotypes say she is; (2) She has a history rooted in a legacy of struggle; (3) Her history and her contemporary experiences can only be understood in the context of a race and class analysis; and (4) The Chicana is in the best position to describe and define her own reality.

Thus, the writings of this period are a logical and political extension of the previous one. Chicana writings in the second half of the 1970s are distinguished by more elaborate analyses and research and the emergence of poetry, fiction, and autobiographical testimonios. The starting point was the rejection of traditional images and the debunking of social science myths about the Chicana. The result is the redefinition of the Chicana—by the Chicana.

Beginning with the beginning, Chicanas challenged the belief that the creation of the mestizo people originated with the violation of "a passive woman who surrendered herself and her people to the conquerors" (Mujeres en Marcha 1983). A first major challenge came from Adelaida del Castillo in her article "Malintzin" (1977):

> Because history is notorious for depicting the female as being one of the main causes for man's failures, it's extremely important that we understand the ethics with which historians, most of whom have been men in the past, distribute blame and justice. Apparently, what seems to be involved here is an unconscious acceptance of morals which blindly depict the male force as one which generally strives to do good in spite of the ever-present influence of the opposite sex. Woman is perceived as being one whose innately negative nature only serves to stagnate man, if not corrupt him entirely. So just as Eve was chosen long ago by misogynistic men to represent the embodiment of the "the root of all evil" for western man, Mexico's first and most exceptional heroine, Doña Marina "La Malinche" now embodies female negativity (traición) for our Mexican culture (139).

Del Castillo further asserts that this negative portrayal of Malintzin occurs because of the misinterpretation of her role in the conquest of Mexico and because of "an unconscious, if not intentional misogynistic attitude toward women in general, especially toward self-assertive women" (139). Del Castillo provides another interpretation of the historical role of Malintzin that is tied to her religious beliefs, to a more complex assessment of her relationship to Cortés, and to the cultures of the various indigenous groups. Rather than accepting "La Malinche" as the embodiment of evil or, in the words of Octavio Paz, "the cruel incarnation of the feminine condition," Del Castillo refutes the image of passivity and violation. In doing so she lays the foundation for Chicanas to reject the legacy which Paz insinuates: "A woman's nature (the physical condition of her body) is by its very essence always being 'violated'" (143) (more on "La Malinche" later).

Chicana writers took on mainstream social science to dispel the belief that Chicanas were inherently passive. In the mid-1970s, Maxine Baca Zinn wrote articles in which she stated that "the passive, submissive, Mexican woman is a creation of social scientists and journalists who have taken for granted the idea that women are dependent and unproductive creatures" (Baca Zinn 1975a, 19). In her article "Chicanas: Power and Control in the Domestic Sphere," Baca Zinn reexamines Chicanas within the family to show that "they have had great impact on Chicano survival in an Anglo-dominated society" (1975a, 19). It is the mother's role within the family that helps preserve its stability and its source as a "refuge and protection from an oppressed society."

> Those characteristics of Chicanas which social scientists have interpreted as passivity, dependence and submissiveness have been part of a process to preserve the stability of the family. . . . Deference to males, and the "giving in" whereby women temporarily relinquish their control of domestic sphere matters, when males exercise their generalized authority, has not been submissiveness, but a mechanism for safeguarding the internal solidarity of the family. (1975a, 29)

Baca Zinn acknowledged that patriarchal relations exist within the family but asserts that, "women control family activities," that "Chicano families are mother centered," and that women within the families form bonds with other women "which nurture a collective sense of their own worth" (1975a, 29).

In the same year Baca Zinn published an article entitled "Political Familism: Toward Sex Role Equality in Chicano Families." She again pointed out the limits of social science perspectives on the Chicano family and refuted the notion that families change as a function of modernization and assimilation. Instead, she again highlighted the importance of family response to the experience of structural domination. To make her point, she described how Chicano families combine their value of La Familia de la Raza and carnalismo to join as a family unit "in ongoing struggles for racial justice. "Family involvement in the Chicano Movement, with its philosophy of justice, challenged sex role inequality within the family unit: "Political familism itself does not transcend sex role subordination. But within the varied expressions and manifestations of El Movimiento are changes in sex role relationships and family structure, as well as the seeds of new roles for the women and men of La Raza" (1975b, 24).

The prevalence of myths in the social science literature motivated a Chicana anthropologist, Margarita Melville, to compile a collection of articles about Chicanas. The purpose of *Twice a Minority* was "to modify the stereotypes of Mexican-American women found in much of the social science literature which often views females as passive sufferers."

The myth of passivity is not the only one with which Chicanas have had to contend.

> They say we are nonachievement oriented, inept, docile, apathetic, totally without aspirations; we allow ourselves to be exploited and physically and sexually abused; we are masochistic, self-belittling, self-abnegating, subservient, self-sacrificing, suffering martyrs; we are passive, dependent, possessive, depressive, and neurotic; we are producers of large families, ever fertile, dedicated super-mothers with boundless love and nurturance for all. They say we are sometimes passionate, sexy, voluptuous, darkeyed, hot-tempered beauties; other times we are chaste and sexually pure; we are "mamacitas": fat women surrounded by five or six little brown-skinned children, always cooking. This is what they say we are. Is that who we really are? (Vásquez and González 1981, 50)

The writings of this period are characterized by the debunking of social science myths about the Chicana reality.

> First of all, the Chicana stereotype must be challenged. A review of existing research reveals a lack of data and a distorted and inaccurate image of the Chicana. The small bank of knowledge that does exist on the Chicana has been collected mainly by Anglos, who have lacked sufficient understanding and sensitivity to the total culture of Mexicans living in the United States. This research has dysfunctional consequences for the Chicano because of the perpetuation of false and stereotypical images of the role and function of women within the Chicano community (S. González 1977, 70).

González goes on to argue that these stereotypical images created by Anglos have a detrimental effect on the Chicana because educational, health, welfare, and law enforcement institutions form policies based on these myths that affect Chicanas. "This has effectively barred them from a full and creative role in society."

The entrance of Chicana writers into social science circles has meant a challenge to the results and methodologies used by social scientists to depict Chicana reality. Chicana writers, such as Vásquez and González, have challenged the social deficit model whereby Chicanas are compared to an Anglo-determined ideal. They state:

> Much of the early social science literature concerning Chicanos has promoted negative stereotypes about origins, history, identity, and, in particular family patterns and sex roles. Many of the negative stereotypic portrayals have been perpetuated by misapplication of a "social deficit" model to the study of Mexican-American families. That is, social scientists have assumed that the Anglo norms are ideal and that deviation from those norms is pathological. (52)

During this period, Chicana writers laid the groundwork for even the more extensive social science research to emerge during the 1980s.

Thus, not only is the Chicana not just a "passive sufferer" or silent in her subordination, but she has been active in her resistance and survival. This is further highlighted in the second major theme of the writings of this period—that the Chicana has a history rooted in struggle.

The entire volume entitled *Mexican Women in the United States: Struggles Past and Present* (Mora and del Castillo 1980) was organized to document and appraise "Mexican women's participation in the struggle against national oppression, class exploitation, and sexism. The essays present the complexity and depth of her participation and attest to her leadership, courage, tenacity, and creativity." The editors also make the point that "popular notions" portray Chicanas as passive and apathetic, yet this ignores their history as laborers and activists.

This history includes Chicana participation in the Partido Liberal Mexicano (PLM), International Ladies and Garment Workers Union (ILGWU), the contemporary student movement, and of course as laborers. One author (Hart) points out that during the colonial period of "New Spain," the Spanish tradition of protecting women from the outside world was reserved for the "gente decente." Women of the "castas" and Indians, however, were laborers in the mines while more "lucky" ones worked as domestic help or selling goods in the market place (Mora and del Castillo 1980, 151). The Mexican woman has been in the fields, the factories, and the fights to free herself and her people.

Most of the Chicana writings of this and the previous period clearly demonstrate that Chicanas understood themselves as a function of their race and class experience, the third major theme of the period 1975-81. For example, two notable studies during this period describe the labor force participation of Chicanas, noting that they are concentrated as clerical, operatives, and service workers and that in comparison to Chicanos and Anglo men and women, their incomes were considerably lower (Arroyo 1973, 1977; Sánchez 1977). As a result of her research, Arroyo notes that "Chicana workers were found to be employed in the lowest paid categories of the labor force. Chicanas like other oppressed workingclass women, remain and are kept at the bottom of the economic ladder" (Arroyo 1977, 165). The working class consciousness of the Chicana writer was rooted in her own class background and her continued connection to the barrio. Sánchez states emphatically:

> The needs and interests of Chicano women in the barrio. . . . are concerned with subsistence, health care, medical attention, rent payments, food bills, physical abuse from their husbands and unemployment. It is imperative then that those few Chicano women attaining professional status or higher education recognize the low economic status of the majority of Chicano women and identify with their struggle rather than with middle class feminist aspirations, for most of us Chicano women have strong working class roots. (Sánchez 1980, 14)

The clarity of Chicana class and race consciousness is also evident in writings that distinguish their feminism from that of white feminism. The *Chicana Feminist* by Martha Cotera, for example, is replete with statements that differentiate Chicanas from middle-class white women and their respective feminisms. Many such statements were in response to the attacks that if Chicanas were fighting on behalf of their issues, they must be products of white bourgeois women. These defensive assertions gradually lessened, though writings continued in which Chicanas noted the racism that they experienced from white women (discussed below).

The passion and depth of Chicana writings originate from the need to survive, first, by deconstructing others' definitions of us, and then by replacing them with their own. The fourth theme being discussed here is embodied in the notion that the Chicana is in the best position to describe and define her own reality. In addition to political statements and history and social science analyses, the Chicana voice spoke through her poetry, literature, literary analyses and personal narratives.

Writing by the Chicana, by its very act, is a rebellious move against a traditionally imposed silence.

> Embodied in the act of writing is her voice against others' definitions of who she is and what she should be. There is, in her open expression and in the very nature of this act of opening up, a refusal to submit to a quality of silence that has been imposed upon her for centuries. In the act of writing, the Chicana is saying "No," and by doing so she becomes the revolutionary, a source of change, and a real force for humanization. . . .
>
> The Chicana, by voicing her own brand of expression has rejected the latter in favor of telling anyone who wishes to read her work, hear her voice, exactly what she is not, and who she, in fact, is. (R. Sánchez 1977)

The result is a new Chicana. "La Nueva Chicana" is captured in a poem by Viola Correa:

> Hey,
> See that lad protesting against injustice,
> Es mi Mamá.
> That girl in the brown beret,
> The one teaching the children,
> She's my hermana.
> Over there fasting with the migrants,
> Es mi tía.
> These are the women who worry,
> Pray, Iron
> And cook chile y tortillas.
> The lady with the forgiving eyes
> And the gentie smile,
> Listen to her shout.
> She knows what hardship is all about
> All about.
> The establishment calls her
> A radical militant.
> The newspapers read she is
> A dangerous subversive
> They label her name to condemn her.
> By the F.B. I. she's called
> A big problem.
> In Aztlán we call her
> La Nueva Chicana. (Sánchez 1977, 33)

The development of Chicana poetry parallels the formation of Chicana identity where she moves from refusing the boundaries that have defined and restricted her to celebrating the liberation of her spirit. Through Chicana poetry we can witness a journey that abounds with political and personal awareness.

As was true with many of the essays and narratives, the poetry reflected many of the same assertions against machismo, racism, and class exploitation. What emerges in Chicana writings is the pain, strength, and struggle of her existence. Bernice Zamora, for example, wrote a poem in 1977 entitled "Notes from a Chicana 'Coed'" in which she stands up to the macho rejection of her feminism. The following is an excerpt:

> To cry that the gabacho
> is our oppressor is to shout
> in abstraction, carnal.
> He no more oppresses us
> than you do now as you tell me
> "It's the gringo who oppresses you, Babe."

Zamora also wrote poems reflecting unequal treatment of men and women. In a poem entitled "Pueblo, 1950" from *Restless Serpents,* Zamora remarks on the different moralities applied according to gender:

> I remember you, Fred Montoya.
> You were the first vato to ever kiss me.
> I was twelve years old.
> My mother said shame on you,
> my teacher said shame on you, and
> I said shame on me, and nobody
> said a word to you

Zamora's poems are based on struggle, but they also "efface those rules of conventional society that establish artificial divisions among social groups" (M. Sánchez 1979, 146).

In a poem "On living in Aztlán" she writes,

> We come and we go
> But within limits,
> Fixed by a law
> Which is not ours . . .

While Chicanas challenged the aspects of their tradition that have oppressed them, they were also connected to their past. They expressed this in their poetry and often in the Spanish language. As an example, María Herrera Sobek wrote "Abuelas Revolucionarias" and "Mantillas." Chicana poets wrote about love and land, history and family. They affirmed parts of their identity and searched for others. According to poetry and literary critic Tey Diana Rebolledo, what is best about Chicana poets is "their concern and relationship to life around them and their integral connection with their surroundings" (1984a, 99). Rebolledo writes, "These poets may write about alienation, but in their poetry they build bridges, create legends and find unity" (99).

Some of the most notable poetry of the period was contained in the following anthologies: *Restless Serpents* (1976) by Bernice Zamora; *Bloodroot* (1977) by Alma Villanueva; and *Emplumada* (1981) by Lorna de Cervantes. Many regional poets were visible in New Mexico, northern and southern California, Texas, and the Midwest. Among the many included Silvia González, Inés Hernández Tovar, Olivia Castellano, Judy Lucero, Erlinda González, Ximena, Evangelina Vigil, Pat Mora, Angela de Hoyos, Denise Chávez, Margarita Cota-Cárdenas, Lucha Corpi, and Sandra Cisneros. Many of these poets published chapbooks or simply circulated their poetry among themselves. Two of the most important outlets for Chicana poetry were special volumes of *De Colores* published by Pajarito Publications out of Albuquerque and *Revista Chicano Riqueña.*

These are two of the major publications during a somewhat prolific period of Chicano and Chicana writings. The use of writing as a way to define our histories and realities was an integral aspect of the Chicano movement. Short stories and narrative literature help mark this period of Chicana writings.

During this period, poetry and literature emerged, as did literacy analysis. The analysis acknowledged that trained literary analysts were subject to dominant ideological criteria and ways of assessing poetry and literature. The writers called for a perspective that took into account the culture and experience of Chicanas. In 1979, Marta E. Sánchez wrote:

> One of the fundamental dangers facing Chicano critics is that most of us have been educated to respect the dominant intellectual and cultural values of mainstream criticism. We hence tend at times to mechanically apply traditional criteria to Chicano literature, and consequently we not only perpetuate but also authenticate those values, which we should examine critically for their cultural, psychological, and social implications. (1979, 141)

Indeed, Chicana critics argued that meeting the so-called standards of the University "would be destructive to our literature" (Zamora 1977a,16). Despite the fact that Chicana critics recognized that not adhering to the so-called standards would affect their ability to publish in mainstream outlets, they still insisted on developing a form of critic appropriate to the Chicano and the Chicana. Again quoting from Marta E. Sánchez,

> Indeed, we might benefit by thinking of minority literatures here in the United States as areas of study where categories in literary scholarship and research are yet to be defined. We can think of ourselves as critics who at present are undertaking to formulate theoretical and applicable criteria leading toward such a definition.

> The opportunity remains therefore to approach Chicano literature as a field challenging us to think in fresh terms . . . as an effort to locate and construct formal as well as ideological categories that may prove productive in studying Chicano narrative and poetry. (1979, 141)

The Chicana critic, according to Bernice Zamora, is faced with challenges because of the depth of Chicana poetry and narrative:

> Truth, because it is so painful, can only be taken in small portions we are told. But unveiling the truth for the Chicana critic is not so difficult as enduring the pain of how to present that truth to an already suffering people. The responsibility of Chicana critics to present it unveiled becomes more acute because of the compassion, the love, and carnalismo that abounds among Chicanos. So it is the truth of our literature that Chicana critics are left to deal with, and the truth and the pain of Chicano literature will have to be dealt with by methods that defy category. (1977a, 19)

Chicana poetry, literature, and literary criticism continued to defy categories and definitions. The result was an explosion of writings during the 1980s, to which we will turn momentarily.

The Struggle to Be Heard

To declare themselves was one thing. To be heard was another. That struggle undoubtedly continues and is tied to a past in which we had to create elaborate mechanisms to channel our voices. As an example, despite the move of many Chicanas into academic and literary circles (though unquestionably fewer than their share of parity), Chicanas have had to make concerted efforts to establish ourselves in Chicano and women's studies. An examination of both sets of efforts illuminates features of our struggles to be heard.

The National Association for Chicano Studies, formed in 1972, is the most important organization that brings together Chicano scholars "in order to encourage a type of research which it felt could play a key part in the political actualization of the total Chicano community" (from the Preamble). Yet, as was typical of most Chicano organizations at the time, the role of women was limited, often to the dance partners after the conference. By the early 1980s, few women remained in the organization, having opted not to fill these roles. Therewere, however, faculty women who had been long-standing members of NACS, such as Ada Sosa Riddel. The early 1980s marks the entry of a critical core of Chicana graduate students who were ready to be active members of NACS—as scholars. Their entry, however, was not automatic but required conscious, organized efforts to create space for Chicanas. The most notable example was the panel at the 1982 National Conference organized by Mujeres en Marcha from the University of California, Berkeley.

After a great deal of lobbying throughout the tenth annual conference, Mujeres en Marcha led a discussion during the final session of the last day of the conference in a packed room. The discussion raised three themes:

> 1. For a number of years, Chicanas have heard claims that a concern with issues specifically affecting Chicanas is merely a distraction/diversion from the liberation of Chicano people as a whole. What are the issues that arise when women are asked to separate their exploitation as women from the other forms of oppression that we experience?
> 2. Chicanas are confronted daily by the limitation of being a woman in this patriarchal society; the attempt to assert these issues around "sexism" are often met with resistance and scorn. What are some of the major difficulties in relations amongst ourselves? How are the relationships between women and men affected? How are the relationships of women to women and men to men affected? How do we overcome the constraints of sexism?
> 3. It is not uncommon that our interests as feministas are challenged on the basis that we are simply falling prey to the interests of white middle-class women. We challenge the notion that there is no room for a Chicana movement within our own community. We, as women of color, have a unique set of concerns that are separate from white women and from men of color. (Mujeres en Marcha 1983)

Interestingly, some of the same issues discussed were prevalent during the seventies, in particular the notion that Chicanas were divisive and duped by "white women." What seemed to be of particular significance to this panel is that the Chicanas pulled together a group of women and men to talk directly about some tough issues. Many of the men were honest in saying that they did not like the way women raised issues and that confrontation was "too narrow." Women responded by saying: "We're talking about opening up a dialogue without stepping on anybody's toes first, but I never once in my life heard a male say, 'I'm sorry for stepping on your toes.'

The men stepped on the toes first. Men are saying if there is a confrontation it is hard to communicate, but there has already been a confrontation" (Mujeres en Marcha 1983, 21). The most lively part of the discussion was centered around the question of what happens to us when we assert our objections to being "relegated to a status of inferiority and submission" (1). Chicana resistance was defined as inappropriate, as Teresa Córdova pointed out:

> When we defend ourselves against the dominance, we are additionally faced with a rationale that rejects our protests. We are faced with a discourse of dominance. It is a rationale, an ideology, that portrays dedicated, assertive women as inappropriately pushy or hostile. That is, it is an ideology which accepts women only as agreeably passive. La mujer does not need to be pushy or hostile, to be seen so by those who feel most threatened by her. Rather, women are embodied with a strength that can and should be utilized in the struggle against the very forces that oppress her. (Mujeres en Marcha 1983, 19)

Some of the discussion centered around whether Chicanas should be shaking up the status quo and causing conflict or whether they should refrain and thus avoid causing the defensiveness and discomfort from men. Again quoting from Córdova:

> The hegemonic discourse requires them [Chicanas] to be agreeably passive and they are considered out of place if they overstep this boundary. Many women asserted that if they were to achieve their dignity as scholars in a male-dominated world, then it would be necessary to refrain from being agreeably passive and instead assert their presence as thinking individuals. Because this is so challenging to assumptions long held about how the Chicana should behave, such assertion results in conflict. (Mujeres en Marcha 1983, 19)

While many of the men in the National Association of Chicano Studies were resistant to these issues, those who were present were at least making an effort to engage in dialogue with the women. The following statement indicates that at least some men realized that there was something fundamentally wrong with the way that they thought about women, and that this fact challenges them to how they think about themselves and one another:

> It seems to me that a lot of Chicano men in academia will deal with the whole question of sexism from the perspective of wanting a list that they can check off and say, "Well, I'm not doing this and therefore I'm taking the correct political line." And part of that is tied into the problem of how we think in certain ways and with a certain logic. That's the way we deal with other men and that's the way we deal with other women. That pattern of thinking itself has to be examined. We can't reduce the question of sexism to something you can quantify, or some kind of model or some kind of simple policy statement. We have to begin to look at where we as men are coming from and what we are feeling and thinking inside of ourselves in regards not only to women but to men also. I see a great deal of resistance to that. I find that most men want to see sexism as a policy decision only and that it is not tied into one's spirit and soul. In terms of men, we have to go back to step one and we have to look at ourselves and try to understand ourselves, and see what is going on inside ourselves and in our relations to people. We have to look at our patterns of thinking and see if we are trying to impose those patterns on someone else. (Mujeres en Marcha 1983, 23)

The final statements of the panel acknowledge efforts to come to terms with some of these issues and that change doesn't happen overnight. Yet members of Mujeres en Marcha insist that these "good intentions" are not used to avoid confronting the issue of sexism. In the words of Córdova:

> It is not necessary that one intends to act in a way that has hegemonic consequences. More often than not, the intention is not there. However, intention or not, the consequences remain. The point is, the pernicious assumptions and stereotypical understandings about Chicana women are deeply rooted. These assumptions and understandings have been perpetuated and sustained through history. . . . It is easy to operate on these assumptions and act accordingly. It is these assumptions, however, which comprise the systematic body of knowledge that serves to oppress us. . . . The point that we are making is that many of these underlying assumption have served as the basis for a hierarchical structure that places men on top, women on the bottom. We challenge this on the basis that it is hierarchical and therefore requires that someone be on the bottom. (Mujeres en Marcha 1983, 30-31)

Ironically, while women in NACS were insisting on the distinction between their feminism and that of white women, women of color were faced with the racism and class discrimination at the annual conference of the National Women's Studies Association and within the association generally. In 1982 Chela Sandoval wrote a report on behalf of the Women of Color who attended the 1981 NWSA conference. The group called themselves the National Third World Women's Alliance and the report was entitled "Feminism and Racism: A Report on the 1981 National Women's Studies Association Conference" (see Sandoval 1990).

The theme of the conference was "Women Respond to Racism." Immediately, Sandoval asks, "which women?" and notes that one of the essential problems of the women in the association is the assumption of homogeneity. While NWSA and the women's movement in general had been fraught with contradictions and limitations for women of color, many had hoped that this conference would make possible a dialogue to deal with the many differences. But as Sandoval points out, the conference structure itself was hegemonic imposing a structure that did not allow for collective discussion. And while white women had several consciousness raising groups to choose from, Third World women had one group set aside for them. This one group became the organizing mechanism for the Third World women to form a conference within a conference. It was here that women of color further articulated their anger and frustration with attempting to work with white women in the association.

On the fourth day of the conference, the Third World women initiated a coalition meeting with an equal number of white women—nearly two hundred women altogether. The enthusiastic meeting resulted in the following resolution:

> This has been a racist conference in its structure, organization, and individual interaction despite its theme. Be it resolved that . . . next year's conference be organized around the same theme, with the leadership of Third World women, in cooperation with NWSA organizers, and that the location of the next conference be changed from another rural area, Humboldt, California, to a place more accessible to Third World women, such as Los Angeles. (Sandoval 1990, 69)

According to Sandoval, "The coalition's resolutions were met with a great deal of irritation" and that for many, "the issue of racism was worn to the bone."

> By the last assembly meeting most delegates were ready to move onto, as they called it, "more pressing issues." The continued "haranguing" by the Third Word delegates was seen as "idiosyncratic," "selfish," and as "unnecessarily divisive to the movement." The resolution was not passed. In spite of the one successful coalition, by the end of the conference the division between Third World and white women had become intensified and cemented with antagonism. It was an ironic ending to a movement conference on racism. (Sandoval 1990, 70)

These same problems continued to plague the National Women's Studies Association as exemplified by the mass walkout of women of color at the 1990 conference. This 1981 conference, however, was significant for what has become a women of color alliance among Chicana, Puerto Rican, Latina, Asian, Native American, and African American women. The publication of *This Bridge Called My Back* (edited by Gloria Anzaldúa and Cherríe Morraga) in the same year signaled this alliance. We will return to a discussion of *This Bridge Called My Back* and the women of color alliance.

The struggles of Chicanas to be heard was waged both within Chicano studies and women studies circles. The result of confronting sexism, racism, and also classism resulted in the above-mentioned women of color alliances. It also resulted in the formation of a Chicana studies organization, Mujeres Activas en Letras y Cambio Social, and in an emphasis on the intersection of class, race, and gender, as exemplified by the NACS publication *Chicana Voices: Intersections of Class, Race, and Gender.*

In June 1982 Ada Sosa Riddel convened several women from northern California, including members of Mujeres en Marcha, to meet in Davis to discuss the formation of a Chicana academic organization. The majority of the women in the group were academics but considered themselves very much connected to community and concerned with social change. Thus, they settled on the name Mujeres Activas en Letras y Cambios Social (MALCS). In the ensuing months the group formulated the following preamble with both an English and a Spanish version:

> We are the daughters of Chicano working class families involved in higher education. We were raised in labor camps and urban barrios, where sharing our resources was the basis of survival. Our values, our strength, derive from where we came. Our history is the story of working people—their struggles, commitments, strengths, and the problems they faced. We document, analyze, and interpret the Chi-

> cano/Mexicano experience in the United States. We are particularly concerned with the conditions women face at work, in and out of the home. We continue our mothers' struggle for social and economic justice.
>
> The scarcity of Chicanas in institutions of higher education requires that we join together to identify our common problems, to support each other and to define collective solutions. Our purpose is to fight the race, class and gender oppression we have experienced in the universities. Further we reject the separation of academic scholarship and community involvement. Our research strives to bridge the gap between intellectual work and active commitment to our communities. We draw upon a tradition of political struggle. We see ourselves developing strategies for social change—a change emanating from our communities. We declare our commitment to seek social, economic, and political change through our work and collective action. We welcome Chicanas who share these goals and invite them to join us. (Mujeres Activas en Letras y Cambio Social 1984)

Through the persistence and resourcefulness of Sosa Riddell the group sponsored a working paper series and what has now become an annual event, the MALCS Summer Institute, where women gather for workshops and information. A Chicana research institute has been established at the University of California, Davis, and soon MALCS will release the first volume of its journal.

Many Chicanas worked in coalition with women of color, formed their own organization, and continued to work with their male counterparts in the National Association for Chicano Studies. The year after the "Unsettled Issue" panel, Chicanas informally met at the annual conference held in Ypsilanti, Michigan, to form the Chicana Caucus. One of their demands was that the 1984 conference, to be held in Austin, Texas, have Voces de la Mujer as its theme. The local site committee agreed and the stage was set for the twelfth annual conference of NACS to be devoted to Chicana voices. The number of Chicanas who spoke at or attended the conference was substantially higher than ever and marked the beginning of an irreversible presence of women in NACS.

The conference, however, was not without very tense politics between the men and the women, the result of which was a redefinition of those relations. Women were also able to hold their own in the attempted take over of the editorial committee despite the implications that quality of the proceedings was jeopardized. The Chicana caucus placements on the editorial committee ensured the publication of the proceedings of this conference entitled *Chicana Voices: Intersections of Class, Race, and Gender.* The first section of the volume contains the statements that were given at the plenary session on Chicana feminism. Chris Sierra spoke on the qualities of the university that reinforce inequality; Norma Cantú debunked the Adelita image; Cynthia Orozco discussed the previous role of Chicanas in Chicano studies, how gender explains the Chicana experience, and how feminism can play a role for change; and Alma García stated that Chicana studies should be brought "into the frame" of Chicano studies. The final paper in the first section is the tribute paid by the association to two labor activists: Emma Tenayuca and Manuela Solís Sager (Córdova et al. 1986). Additional articles from this collection will be among those discussed in the following section.

History and Social Science of the 1980s

In describing what has been the treatment of Mexicanos/as in California history, Antonia Castañeda says in reference to the impact of ideology on history: "Accordingly, California historians applied Anglo, middle-class norms of woman's proper behavior to Mexican women's comportment and judged them according to their own perceptions of Mexican culture and women's positions within that culture" (1990a, 8).

In another article, Castañeda makes the point even more emphatically:

> In studying North American imperial expansion, Chicano and other scholars have concluded that pejorative, racist stereotypes of Mexicanos, in particular, were an integral part of an ideology that helped justify the Mexican-American War as well as subsequent repression in the conquered territory (213). While the contemporary and historical literature purports to present accurate descriptions of Mexican women's experience and condition, it actually constructs stereotypic images which serve ideological purposes. . . . While these prejudices are evident in most accounts of Mexicanas, and while all the descriptions purport to present transhistorical or timeless images, the descriptions do, in fact, vary considerably across time in terms of the particular aspects of these stereotypes which are emphasized. These variations correlate with the changing need of the capitalist and imperialist system, its shifting relations to Mexicano culture and economy in California and the evolving ideology of the nature of women. (Castañeda 1990b, 215)

These kinds of biases—the authors of which are often influential members of history departments—and the common exclusion of Mexicana/Chicana experiences in historical documents have been obstacles for Chicana historians. Yet their drive to set the historical records straight and to document historical roots has resulted in the emergence of a cadre of Chicana historians. With their political roots in the Chicano movement, these women are and will continue to produce scholarship that incorporates the significance of race, class, and gender. Antonia Casteñeda, Deena González, Emma Pérez, and Vicki Ruiz are among the most notable Chicana historians. Though not an historian, Adelaida Del Castillo was one of the first Chicanas to facilitate historical collections.

Del Castillo wrote one of the first essays challenging the myth of La Malinche and replacing it with historical documentation that takes into account Quetzalcoatl, the Aztec religion and empire, and Marina Tenepal's personal life. Del Castillo, along with Magdalena Mora, edited the important volume *Mexican Women in the United States: Struggles Past and Present.* The volume was especially notable for the accounts of Mexicanas/Chicanas in the U. S. workplace, in particular the garment industry. Not only were the conditions described but so were the various forms of resistance, including the FARAH strike in the early 1970s and La Costura in Los Angeles (1922-39).

The collection also contained profiles of women active in resistance both historically and more recently. The book had a historical materialist emphasis, and Magdalene Mora was herself active in organizing undocumented female workers as exemplified by her work with the Toltec Foods strike in Richmond, California, in 1975. Her death in 1981, at the age of 29, and before she completed here Ph.D. in history at UCLA, was a loss to organizing efforts in the undocumented community and to the community of Chicana historians.

Del Castillo later edited another volume, *Between Borders: Essays on Mexicana/Chicana History* (1990). This volume was an outgrowth of a conference that was held in 1982, "Mexicana/Chicana Women's History International Symposium." Antonia Castañeda published the article "The Political Economy of Nineteenth-Century Stereotypes of Californianas," in which she views the stereotyping of Mexicanas in California as serving an ideological function to justify domination by the U. S. over Mexicanos. Ideological constructions varied. For example, Mexicanas were defined both as women of easy virtue and inferiority while another stereotype was cast of the landowning Californianas to justify the union of Anglos to these women.

> Irrespective of the view, the end result was the same. Mexicana or Californiana, both representations rendered women in California ignorant, vacuous and powerless. In both cases, her Catholicism and culture made her priest-ridden, male dominated, superstitious and passive. Undemocratic Spanish and Mexican governance made her ignorant. If Mexicana, however, her immorality and racial impurity established her lack of value and exacerbated her ignorance. As part of the conquered Mexican nation, the War confirmed her powerlessness. If Californiana, on the other hand, her racial purity, morality and economic worth elevated her status, making her worthy of marrying an Anglo while dispossessing her of her racial, historical, cultural and class roots. With marriage and a husband's possession of her property, elite Californianas forfeited their economic power. Finally, the Californiana's presence was abstracted to an era long past, her person romanticized. In either case, Mexicana or Californiana, the conquest was complete. (Castañeda 1990b, 227)

Castañeda further notes that other than these stereotypical accounts of Mexican women in California during the 1940s there is virtually no mention of the Mexicana.

> In the literature, Mexican women's historical existence is defined out of all but a few short years of the nineteenth century. Her presence is confined to the 1840's and left to the assumptions, perceptions and interest of Anglo-American entrepreneurs and filibusters who wrote about California in a period of American continental imperialism that resulted in the Mexican-American War. (Castañeda 1990b, 228)

Castañeda wrote about Spanish-Mexican women in California in the period prior to the U. S.-Mexico War, and Deena González wrote about Spanish-Mexican women in New Mexico in the period immediately following the war. In "The Widowed Women of Santa Fe: Assessments on the Lives of an Unmarried Population, 1850-80," González examines the lives of unmarried women at a time when the territory was being settled by unmarried Anglo men. Through her resourceful historical scholarship, she portrays women, though unattached to a male partner, as very attached to their families, not particularly interested in the outsiders, and able to find ways to enhance their sense of control over their environment.

> The majority [of unmarried women] did not marry the immigrants; women displayed minimal

> interest in easing men's transition to life in a new society. Instead, they sought stability in their own worlds; they sought to impose order on a world increasingly changed by easterners and their ways. For more and more of these women, the act of writing a will offered a measure of control over their circumstances. Spanish-Mexican women had followed the custom for generations; worldly possessions, however, meager, required proper care. The custom took on added significance in the postwar period. Its assumption of stability contrasted sharply with an enveloping sense of disorder; it promised children a continuity, a certainty, that their parents lacked. (D. González 1988, 44)

Long historical roots and a strong extended family facilitated the resistance of the unmarried Spanish-Mexican woman, whose numbers soared in the post-war period. Yet as González points out, the post-war period was only a precursor to the disruption that northern New Mexico communities would face.

Emma Pérez researches the early twentieth century. She focuses on revolutionary Mexican ideology and the contradictions of that ideology with respect to Mexicanas. She wrote, for example, "'A La Mujer': A Critique of The Partido Liberal Mexicano's Gender Ideology on Women," in which she describes the central importance that women played in the PLM, a revolutionary group that opposed Porfirio Díaz, yet critiques the limits of the ideology. Women, for example, were still seen as needing to be the nurturers for men, and feminism was seen as a threat to women's emancipation. Pérez suggests that accounts focusing on the critique of capitalism and of race, ignoring the role of gender ideology, fail to assess the way that ideology, especially family ideology, limits the roles of women to wives, mothers, and nurturers.

The labor activism of Chicanas continues to be a popular theme. Vicki Ruiz writes on organizing efforts among cannery workers and shows the ways that women's networks are used as a mechanism for social change. The 1939-45 union organizing that began with a walkout in August 1939 is the topic of her article, "A Promise Fulfilled: Mexican Cannery Workers in Southern California" (1990). She also wrote a longer treatment of cannery workers, *Cannery Women Cannery Lives: Mexican Women, Unionization, and the California Food Processing Industry, 1930-1950.* Noting that "most Mexican women have been wage earners at some point in their lives" (1987b, xviii), Ruiz traces the experiences of cannery workers:

> Since the late 1800s, Mexican women living in California have flocked to food processing plants, attracted to the industry because of seasonal schedules and extended family networks. The chapters that follow delineate the experiences of a generation of Mexican women cannery operatives who, from 1939-1959, took control of their work lives as member of the United Cannery, Agricultural, Packing and Allied Workers of American. (1987b, xviii)

She concludes by placing this history of UCAPAWA as an example of a long history of labor activism—a history of the "struggle of proud, courageous men and women joining together whenever possible to counter economic and ethnic oppression" (1990, 123).

Several of the above-mentioned articles appear in Del Castillo's most recent edited volume (1990). The themes in *Between Borders: Essays on Mexicana/Chicana History* "are basic to feminist studies":

> The relationship between female prescriptive norms and actual behavior; the influence of tradition and innovation in women's lives; the disjuncture between the theory and practice of the left as concerns the liberation of women; urbanization and labor force participation as a catalyst for cultural change; the patriarchal oppression of women; women's choices and sources of strength; and women as agents of social change. These topics take on a new significance when placed within the context of the historical past of Mexican women.

The title and table of contents tell us at least two things about Chicana history. One, history reinforces what the Chicano/a movement espoused, namely, that historical and cultural connections between the borders are integral to the Chicana experience. Two, male and non-Chicana females are continuing to add to the list of historical accounts on the Chicana experience. While many of these are excellent accounts, the history of Chicanas is still plagued with an inadequate number of Chicana historians.

Social Science in the 1980s

The Chicana family was one of the early topics tackled by Chicana sociologists (Baca Zinn 1975, 1980, 1982a, 1982b, 1983; Ybarra 1982, 1983). In contrast to the many social science treatments of the Mexican family as pathological, these Chicana writers brought forward the positive aspects of the Chicana family as a source of support and refuge from a hostile environment. Their research also showed family relations that were more equitable when the women worked outside the home. Later other Chicanas were more critical of the family, noting that household division of labor was unequal among both working class and professional households (Pesquera and Durán 1984) and that gender inequality in the household was connected to gender inequality in the workplace (Zavella 1987).

In her book on cannery workers in the Santa Clara Valley, Pat Zavella describes the patterns of occupational segregation of Mexicanas in seasonal cannery work, the formation of job-related networks, and their emergence from job segregation. She integrates the segregation in the workplace with a family ideology of inequality. Together, their experience in work and family reinforce the subordination of the Chicana.

Margarita Melville edited a volume on Mexicanas and work entitled *Mexicanas at Work in the United States.* In her opening essay, Melville states the importance of these research reports in undermining "accepted myths and misconceptions" about Mexicanas. Each of these essays, some of which are discussed below, offer much needed and well-documented research on the the work experiences of Mexicanas in the United States. The research presented by Lea Ybarra, for example, challenges a cultural explanation for the work limitations of Chicanas and instead emphasizes the socio-economic variables.

Denise Segura has also studied participation of Chicanas in the workplace and concluded that there is systematic concentration of Chicanas in the "secondary labor market" and gender-specific jobs in the "primary labor market." Within job categories, Chicana workers made less then their Chicano male counterparts or white workers. The labor segmentation of Chicanas creates a "triple oppression" that is reinforced by gender role socialization, racial discrimination by employers, the education processes, and the institutional constraints of labor market structuring.

Another sociologist, Marta López-Garza, is looking at Mexican and Central American women in Los Angeles and assessing the major variables that affect labor force participation. She has also initiated a study of the activities of Mexican and Central American women in Los Angeles' informal sector. This is a continuation of work that she has done on reconceptualizing women's economic activities through her work at the informal labor sector in Mexico (1986).

In addition to work that assesses Chicana labor force participation, Chicana social scientists are studying the work experiences of Mexicanas on the U. S./Mexico border. Rosalía Solórzano Torres, for example, notes that most studies on the immigration experience leave out the experience of women and in fact make assumptions about the immigration experience that completely ignore their existence. In her own study of "Female Mexican Immigrants in San Diego County," she observes that nearly two-thirds of the women she studied worked in the maquila sector prior to their immigration to San Diego County (1987).

Solórzano Torres also writes about Mexican maids in El Paso and describes the "stressful ordeal" of the informal arrangements surrounding their employment (1988). Vicki Ruiz writes in more detail about the Mexican domestic workers in El Paso. She concludes, "Though frequently victimized, Mexicana domestics are not victims, but women who meet each day with integrity and endurance" (1987a, 74). Mary Romero also studied rural urban migration and the role of domestic work in that transition (1987). Julia Curry Rodríguez has looked at the labor migration process in an article entitled "Labor Migration and Familial Responsibilities: Experiences of Mexican Women," in which she observes the extensive networking among the women (1988).

Many of the Chicana feminists of the 1970s moved into health and mental health to organize and work in community-based agencies and clinics. This is an important arena where research of Chicanas has been directly connected to policy and direct services. Juana Mora (1990), for example, has done extensive research on alcohol use patterns of Chicanas at the same time that she sits on the California State Alcohol Advisory Board, the Los Angeles County Commission on Alcoholism, and the national Latino Council on Alcohol and Tobacco. Elena Flores, who recently completed a dissertation on "Sexual Attitudes and Behavior among Mexican Adolescent Females" (1992), has also developed comprehensive perinatal programs for low-income Latina women and adolescents at Tuburcio Vásquez Health Center in Union City, California. Her clinical work reinforces her research, which has implications for culturally specific intervention and prevention programs for Latina adolescents regarding pregnancy, AIDS, and STD. Gloria Romero, along with Lourdes Arguelles, is conducting research on AIDS, Latinas, and implications for public policy.

A reoccurring theme in Chicana writings is the ways in which Chicanas have been active agents in either their work or home environment or both. Mary Pardo has studied women in East Los Angeles and writes about their activism at the grass-roots level (1990). In her study of "Mothers of East Los Angeles" (MELA), she describes how Mexican-American women used "'traditional' networks and resources based on family and culture into political assets to defend the quality of urban life" (Pardo 1990, 1). Pardo points out that the ways in which women of MELA have transformed their gender-related organizing experiences into political influences is similar to the activism of women in Latin America.

Increasingly, conditions in Los Angeles resemble third world communities where inadequate housing, polluted and hazardous environments, low wages, the presence of unwanted institutions and development projects, and disappearing neighborhoods are eroding the quality of urban life. These conditions, points out Pardo, are setting the stage for new conflicts in which "quality of life issues" will be contested. Women such as the "Mothers of East Los Angeles" will be working at the grass-roots level to take on issues that have now moved to center stage in the midst of urban restructuring. She concludes:

> The work "Mothers of East Los Angeles" do to mobilize the community demonstrates that people's political involvement cannot be predicted by their cultural characteristics. These women have defined stereotypes of apathy and used ethnic, gender, and class identity as an impetus, a strength, a vehicle for political activism. They have expanded their—and our—understanding of the complexities of a political system, and they have reaffirmed the possibility of "doing something." (Pardo 1990, 6)

The Personal as Profound

The "possibility of doing something" motivates Chicana writers. As Gloria Anzaldúa wrote in the foreword to the Second Edition of *This Bridge Called My Back*: "We are beginning to realize that we are not wholly at the mercy of circumstance, nor are our lives completely out of our hands. that if we posture as victims we will be victims, that hopelessness, suicide, that self-attacks stop us on our tracks. We are slowly moving past the resistance within, leaving behind the defeated images."

Anzaldúa also sees that Chicanas are not alone, and thus she reaches out for the connections particularly with other women of color. She and Cherríe Moraga edited this very special volume of "writings by radical women of color" and, in doing so, speak forcibly for "an uncompromised definition of feminism by women of color in the U. S." (xxiii). They see six major areas of concern for this women of color alliance:

> 1. How visibility/invisibility as women of color forms our radicalism;
> 2. The ways in which Third World women derive a feminist political theory specifically from our racial/cultural background and experience;
> 3. The destructive and demoralizing effects of racism in the women's movement;
> 4. The cultural, class, and sexuality differences that divide women of color;
> 5. Third World women's writing as a tool for self-preservation and revolution; and
> 6. The ways and means of a Third World feminist future. (xxiv)

The power of *Bridge* is in its alliances among radical women of color. It is a book about the relationships between women, and it is especially a book of predominantly lesbian voices—voices that speak of lesbianism as an act of resistance: "For a woman to be a lesbian in a male- supremacist, capitalist, misogynistic, racist, homophobic, imperialist culture, such as that of North America, is an act of resistance. (A resistance that should be championed throughout the world by all the forces struggling for liberation from the same slave master.)" (128). Cherríe Moraga makes the connection between the oppression she feels as a lesbian and that of her mother:

> When I finally lifted the lid to my lesbianism, a profound connection with my mother reawakened in me. It wasn't until I acknowledged and confronted my own lesbianism in the flesh, that my heartfelt identification with and empathy for my mother's oppression—due to being poor, uneducated, and Chicana—was realized. My lesbianism is the avenue through which I have learned the most about silence and oppression, and it continues to be the most tactile reminder to me that we are not free human beings.

Bridge represents an important coming out for lesbian women of color—an escape from the silence. For Moraga, it was also a coming out as a Chicana. The process that she describes in finding herself through her identification with other Chicanas and Latinas is a kind of "coming home" where "for once, I didn't have to choose between being a lesbian and being a Chicana; between being a feminist and having a family" (xviii). Moraga followed through in this soul searching which she shared with us in *Loving in the War Years* published in 1983. In the same year, she joined with other Latinas, Alma Gómez and Mariana Romo-Carmona, to edit a volume entitled *Cuentos: Stories by Latinas.* We will return to a discussion of later works by Gloria Anzaldúa.

Women of color writers exposed their souls to us in *This Bridge Called My Back* through their narratives and poetry. The collection also contained an essay from a Chicana literary critic in which she makes the connection between the myths of our culture and the curse of their legacy.

Norma Alarcón makes the connection between the myths of Malinche and contemporary Chicana identity in the essay, "Chicana's Feminist Literature: A Re-vision through Malintzin/or Malintzin: Putting Flesh Back on the Object." Her "excruciating life in bondage" is of "no account" but the created myth has "turned her into a handy reference point not only for controlling, interpreting or visualizing women, but also to wage a domestic battle of stifling proportions." In this "family quarrel," the myth of La Malinche not only "pervades" male thought (". . . mother-whore, bearer of illegitimate children, responsible for the foreign Spanish invasion . . . ") but that of female thought as well:

> As it seeps into our own consciousness in the cradle through their eyes as well as our mothers', who are entrusted with the transmission of culture, we may come to believe that indeed our very sexuality condemns us to enslavement. An enslavement which is subsequently manifested in self-hatred. All we see is hatred of women. We must hate her too since love seems only possible through extreme virtue whose definition is at best slippery. (Alarcón 1983, 183)

In her analysis, Alarcón illuminates the presence of the myth in several Chicana poems including those of Alma Villanueva, Lorna Dee Cervantes, Rina Rocha, and Judy Lucero and asserts, "The pervasiveness of the myth is unfathomable, often permeating and suffusing our very being without conscious awareness" (184).

The myth views women as "sexually passive" and "hence at all times open to potential use by men whether it be seduction or rape" (184). Women as "pawnable," therefore, do not have choice in their actions. Refusing sexual exploitation is rejection of the myth's legacy. This refusal, Alarcón argues, was difficult in her cultural context for the slave Malintzin whose "allegiance" to Cortés was "obedience" to a master. For the contemporary Chicana, this obedience is defined as "devotion" and rejection of this devotion, i.e., servitude, makes her a traitor.

Thus, Alarcón illuminates for us why the early Chicana feminists were called "vendidas" and the non-feminist Chicanas the "loyalists." Yet Alarcón also notes the prevalence of this theme in Chicana poetry and literature and the need to "demythify," thus raising several "sexual political themes":

1. To choose among extant patriarchies is not a choice at all;
2. woman's abandonment and orphanhood and psychic/emotional starvation occur even in the midst of tangible family;
3. woman is a slave, emotionally as well as economically;
4. women are seen not just by one patriarchy but by all as rapeable and sexually exploitable;
5. blind devotion is not a feasible human choice (this is further clarified by the telling absence of poems by women to the Virgin of Guadalupe, while poems by men to her are plentiful);
6. when there is love/devotion it is at best deeply ambivalent as exemplified by Rina Rocha in "To the penetrator":

> I hate the love
> I feel for you. (187)

For Alarcón, therefore, the Chicana must participate in "creating our own defined identity and reality as women." Feminism is thus a rejection of historical and mythical distortions of our reality. And though we may be charged with betrayal for our feminism, "the worst kind of betrayal lies in making us believe that the Indian woman in US is the betrayor" (Anzaldúa 1987). Chicanas insist on their female consciousness and their visions of existence in this world.

> Even as we concern ourselves with Third World women's economic exploitation, we have to concern ourselves with psychosexual exploitation and pawnability at the hands of one's brother, father, employer, master, political systems and sometimes, sadly so, powerless mothers. As world politics continues the histrionics of dominance and control attempting to figure out just who indeed will be the better macho in the world map, macho politics' last priority is the quality of our lives as women or the lives of our children. (Alarcón 1983, 189)

The betrayal that the Chicana commits is the betrayal of a system that oppresses her while pretending to protect her. The Chicana, through her writings, has rejected that system. Chicana writings, above all else, are defiance against definitions imposed on her--definitions that oppress her. Chicana writings are stands against patriarchy and injustice. They are, at the same time, self-discovery and redefinitions of Chicanas. The many unique emergent identities are evident in the Chicana writings.

The amount of poetry, literature, narratives, and plays by Chicanas exploded during the 1980s—making it difficult to discuss or even list them all. However, in addition to the bibliography at the end of this overview, there are other published bibliographies of Chicana writings. Norma Alarcón (1989) provides a thorough listing of Chicana writings in "Chicana Writers and Critics in a Social Context: Towards a Contemporary Bibliography." Lillian Castillo-Speed has also compiled a listing of Chicana studies sources in "Chicana Studies: A Selected List of Materials since 1980" (1990).

This is the decade that marked the publication of Gina Valdes' *There Are No Madmen Here* (1981); Pat Mora's *Borders* (1986); Denise Chávez's *Last of the Menu Girls* (1987); Ana Castillo's *Women Are Not Roses* (1984), *The Mixquiahuala Letters* (1986), *My Father Was a Toltec* (1988), and *Sapogonia* (1989); Sandra Cisneros' *House on Mango Street* (1985), *My Wicked Wicked Ways* (1987), and *Woman Hollering Creek* (1991); Margarita Cota-Cárdenas' *Puppet* (1985); Alma Villanueva's *The Ultraviolet Sky* (1988); Helena María Viramontes' *The Moth and Other Stories* (1985); Evangelina Vigil's *Thirty an' Seen a Lot* (1982); Lucha Corpi's *Delia's Song* (1989); Angelina de Hoyos' *Woman, Woman* (1985); Mary Helen Ponce's *Taking Control* (1987); Erlinda Gonzales Berry's *Paletitas de guayaba*; Cherríe Moraga's *Giving Up the Ghost* (1986); Gloria Anzaldúa's *Borderlands* (1987), and Alicia Gaspar de Alba, María Herrera-Sobek, and Demetria Martínez's *Three Times a Woman* (1989). Poetry by Cordelia Candelaria, Olivia Castellano, Carmen Tafolla, Carmen Abrego, Naomi Quiñónez, Inez Hernández and many many others add to the list of prominent Chicana writings. Arte Público Press has been especially significant in publishing the works of Chicanas. Bilingual Press is also an important outlet for Chicana writings. Revista Mujeres and Third Woman are Chicana/Latina journals that publish, not only Chicana writings, but a wealth of other Latina writers.

Just as it is impossible in this paper to describe every Chicana writing, it is equally difficult to capture each of their unique identities. There are, however, some general statements that can be made. The Chicana identity is often interspersed with a Mexicana identity, and the emergence is a result of the interplay between the two. Many of the writings reflect this bicultural/bilingual aspect. The mixing of the two languages, in fact, is a stylistic feature of Chicana writings. Other writers are more or less one or the other. Writers such as Lucha Corpi reflect a closer connection to Mexico; she is heavily influenced by Mexican and Latin American literary figures, and she writes primarily in Spanish. Gloria Anzaldúa writes in *Borderlands* about growing up on the U. S./Mexico border and how that translates into a mestiza consciousness. This consciousness evolves from straddling borders that are political, cultural, psychological, spiritual, and sexual.

As reflected in earlier discussions about La Malinche, Chicanas write stories and especially poems about legendary symbols of their culture including La Malinche, La Llorana, and La Virgen de Guadalupe. They also write about historical figures such as Sor Juana de La Cruz, and they feel very connected to Mexican painter Frida Khalo. Clara Lomas has written about the "Mexican Precursors of Chicana Feminist Writing" (1989) including Sara Estela Ramírez, Jovita Idar, and many more.

Chicana literary works reflect a connection to family especially abuelitas and mothers. Some of the writings are about the struggles of those relationships and others are an expression of the connectedness with them. Indeed, the connectedness with other women and the love and appreciation for other women is very prevalent in Chicana writings. Lesbian writers are very open in expressing their intimate and physical love with their lovers. In fact, sexuality is an important theme, again as a struggling with issues affecting that sexuality and as the expression of it. Catholicism, traditionalism, and male abuse are some of the reasons that Chicanas redefine their own sexualities. Rape, as a metaphor, has also been utilized by Chicana writers to symbolize their relegated status and the many violations against them (Herrera-Sobek 1988). A special volume of *Third Woman* was devoted to the sexuality of Latinas (vol. 4 1989) and Carla Trujillo edited a volume published by Third Woman Press entitled *Chicana Lesbians: The Girls Our Mothers Warned Us About.* In addition to their love for each other, Chicanas also share the journey of developing their love for themselves.

What is most striking about Chicana writers is the incredible amount of pain they have known and the honesty with which they express it. In this regard, Chicana writings are similar to those of other women of color who write "on the degradations and horrors that Racism inflicts" (Anzaldúa 1990b, xvii). Gloria Anzaldúa, again showing leadership in bringing together women of color, edited a volume entitled *Making Face, Making Soul: Haciendo Caras.* In this collection of poems, narratives and essays, women of color expose with deep honesty "how we 'work through' internalized violence, how we attempt to decolonize ourselves and to find ways to survive personally, culturally and racially" (xvii).

These writers expose the truth of their pain to such a degree that it is no longer possible to ignore the significance of the impact of oppression on the individual. As Anzaldúa says in her introduction: "We who are oppressed by Racism internalize its deadly pollen along with the air we breathe. Make no mistake about it, the fruits of this weed are dysfunctional lifestyles which mutilate our physical bodies, stunt our blood from our bodies, our souls" (1990b, xix).

Expressing this pain through writing is more than an expression of victimization, it is also the beginning of healing and the path to making it better. "The anthology is meant to engage the reader's total person. . . . The intellect needs the guts and adrenaline that horrific suffering and anger, evoked by some of the pieces, catapult us into. Only when all the charged feelings are unearthed can we get down to 'the work,' la tarea, nuestro trabajo—changing culture and all its oppressive interlocking machinations" (1990b, xviii). The writings of Chicanas and women of color remind us that not only is the personal political, but when experiences are expressed so deeply, the personal is profound. It is these experiences that can then form the basis of new theories and new methodologies which more accurately reflect what happens in the so-called margins. The new theories challenge the dominant culture's interpretation of the experiences of women of color and set the stage for a total reconsideration of all dominant theory, including dominant feminist theory.

Cultural Studies and Chicana Feminist Theory

The very articulation of the Chicana reality through her own voice is immediately, by its very nature, a voice of resistance and the foundation for oppositional consciousness. To speak is to oppose. To give voice to emotions is to expose the sham of complicity. The act of deconstructing and reconstructing Chicana images is a subversive move against years of ideological mistreatment.

What Chicanas speak is a function of their experiences. To speak about those experiences is to find themselves in opposition with those that would define them otherwise. The result, as evident in the writings described, is an identity of opposition. Chicanas write in opposition to the symbolic representations of the Chicano movement that did not include them. Chicanas write in opposition to a hegemonic feminist discourse that places gender as a variable separate from that of race and class. Chicanas write in opposition to academics, whether mainstream or postmodern, who have never fully recognized them as subjects, as active agents.

Resistance against the dominant culture is implied in the use of the term *Chicano*. Self-representation was a key demand in the movement, and the statement "Yo Soy Chicano" was a proclamation of pride and independence. The choices for symbolic representation, however, ignored the multiple dynamic identities of Chicanos and was especially exclusive of self-representations by Chicanas (Chabram and Fregoso 1990). Despite the early efforts by Chicanas to be recognized, the representation of the Chicano movement placed the male subject at the center and thus repressed Chicana oppositional forms (Alarcón 1990; Quintana 1990). Chicana self-declarations and redefinitions are all the more significant as cultural expressions in opposition to the representations of the Chicano movement. Norma Alarcón, for example, notes that seizing the definitions of the native woman is an important step toward seizing the "I" of even the feminist "we." Influenced by French feminists, Alarcón notes: "It is worthwhile to remember that the historical founding moment of the construction of mestiza(o) subjectivity entails the rejection and denial of the dark Indian Mother as Indian which have compelled women to often collude in silence against themselves, and to actually deny the Indian position even as that position is visually stylized and represented in the making of the fatherland" (1990, 252).

The ideological constructions of the native dark woman, says Alarcón, are even more alarming when one notes that the majority of maquiladora workers are dark women. Chicana writers redefine these ideological portrayals, and in doing so not only reconstruct what "I" and "we" mean, but also what "you" and "they" mean. Alarcón suggests that "traversing the processes may well enable us to locate points of differences and identities in the present to forge the needed solidarities against repression and oppression" (1990, 255).

Dominant discourses generally fail to allow for difference. White feminist theory, which tends to exclude the experiences of women of color, functions as a dominant discourse. Chela Sandoval, following the lead of Gayatri Spivak, calls this "hegemonic feminism" and juxtaposes it with "U. S. Third World feminism." Third world feminists object to hegemonic feminism's focus solely on the variable of gender, excluding the fundamental categories of race, class, and culture. "Ain't I a woman" is a question women of color have asked since Sojourner Truth first posed it to suffragettes. Aida Hurtado notes that racial conflict in the suffragette movement occurred because of the privileged relationship of white women to white men, a factor that continues to influence race relations between the two groups of women (1989).

For Chicanas, the situation in relation to white feminists is similar to that of Chicanos, in that their oppositional forms are repressed within each of the movements. The result is yet another component of the oppositional consciousness of the Chicana, serving as the basis for alliances with other women of color. The oppositional consciousness of Third World feminism, argues Sandoval, offers a "design for oppositional political activity."

> U. S. third world feminism arose out of the matrix of the very discourses denying, permitting, and producing difference. Out of the imperatives born of necessity arose a mobility of identity that generated the activities of a new citizen-subject, and which reveals yet another model for the self-conscious production of political opposition . . . in mapping this new design, a model is revealed by which social actors can chart the point through which differing oppositional ideologies can meet, in spite of their varying trajectories. This knowledge becomes

> important when one begins to wonder, along with late twentieth-century cultural critics such as Fredric Jameson, how organized oppositional activity and consciousness can be made possible under the co-opting nature of the so-called 'post-modern' cultural condition. (1991, 2)

Chicana writers have always written in opposition to mainstream theories and now write in opposition to postmodern theorists who claim to know that there is subjectivity beyond the center. For example: "Contemporary ethnographers continue to ignore Chicanos as theoretical speaking subjects in their deconstructive work. This occurs despite the fact that deconstructive ethnographers are willing to admit that it is no longer possible to write as though 'others' did not exist" (Chabram 1990, 238). The very essence of Chicana writings is to establish Chicanas as subjects and to replace all previous representations with self-representations.

The identity of opposition is formed in interaction. The act of redefining the experiences of Chicanas through the voices of Chicanas is an expression of resistance against all other definitions. When Chicanas confront hegemonic representations, they question the symbolic bases of power relationships. The expressions from the margins is a fundamental challenge to the orderings of power. This requires a challenge to sociosexual power as well, and therefore a stand against the perpetrator/victim dynamic that prevents the realization of collective work for the common good (Pérez 1991).

As a lesbian feminist, Emma Pérez postulates that "sexuality and our symbolic reading of sexuality is the core of the problem," which prevents a successful movement for freedom and justice (160). Drawing upon male psychoanalytic theory (notably Freud, Lacan, and Foucault) to describe male behavior and French feminist critics of those theories (especially, Cixous, Duras, Irigaray), Pérez brings in the elements of race, class, and culture to deconstruct patriarchal ideology within colonization. Pérez reevaluates the Oedipal complex, the point when men realize their sociosexual power, and describes what she calls the "Oedipal-Conquest-Complex." Where as Octavio Paz attempted in the *Labyrinth of Solitude* to explain what he considers the inferiority complex of Mexicans, Pérez maintains instead that he "reveals more about his own castration complex."

> Paz exhibits his own internalized racial inferiority. He holds far less power than that of his symbolic white father, *el conquistador*. On the other hand, his hatred of women, *las chingadas*, and all that is female, symbolically begins with this Oedipal-conquest-triangle. Here, the sexual, political, social, and psychological violence against *la india*—the core of the Chicana is born. This core has been plundered from us through conquest and colonization. (Pérez 1991, 168)

Pérez makes connections between this "Oedipal-Conquest-Complex" and the collusion that takes place between the white colonizer father and the Chicano against the Chicana. "For example, Chicanos who absorb the white-colonizer-European father's ways hierarchically impose those laws on Chicanas. Those Chicanos become a caricature of the white-colonizer father. One has only to look at any institution where Chicanos have been integrated to see how much many of them emulate the white father and exclude women, especially women of color" (Pérez 1991, 169).

This "conquest triangle" is only one part of the puzzle to understand why Chicanas "uphold the law of the white-colonizer European father, knowing the extent of damage and pain for Chicanas and Chicanos" (169). Pérez finds the answer in the perpetrator/victim dynamic that for women begins with "the molestation memory," the point when "girls realize that they do not have sociosexual power in relation to men" (162). The result is an "addiction" to patriarchy in which one fears "violating the father's orders" and in which an "entire social structure" betrays her if she refuses to succumb to patriarchal mandates.

This relationship is symbolized in the Luis Valdez' theatre production *Corridos*, which, Pérez asserts, reveals his male centrist anxieties and "eroticizes women's victimization." The story is about "Delgadina," a young woman who has refused the advances of her father, is placed in a tower without food or water and eventually dies. Despite her pleas to her mother, sister, and brother, "Each one fears violating the father's order, his sexual laws, so they each ostracize Delgadina" (171).

> The song tells us about a young woman's death when she challenges the sexual law of the father. She cannot, however, break from the law, happy and free to join with women who believe her, or a community who will allow her to be. There is no such community. Instead, a male-centralist society with male-identified women cannot even hear her language, her pain. They just know they cannot defy the father. (Pérez 1991, 172)

The incestuous language and behavior was already operating by the time the father commands Delgadina to allow his "penetration." According to Pérez, that "penetration" was not necessary to create "a memory of molestation" that enters her psyche and leaves the pain of inappropriate behavior that goes unchallenged—by anyone. "Like Delgadina, women live in this cycle of addiction/dependency to the patriarchy that has ruled women since the precise historical moment that they become aware that women's bodies are sexually desired and/or overpowered by the penis" (172).

This "memory of molestation" may result in repudiation of the molester but often "victims continue to repudiate and embrace the perpetrator in a persistent pattern through relationships until that addictive/dependent cycle is broken" (173). The answer, argues Pérez, is to "resist the perpetrator" in order to abandon "phallocentric law and order." Letting go of capitalist patriarchal notions of sexual law and order is necessary in order to create a collective in the common good. "Social sexual relations between men and women condoned by the patriarchy are inherently unhealthy and destructive most of the time" (173).

Pérez is concerned with fundamental social change and believes that it is impossible without fundamental challenge to the social sexual ideology of patriarchy. Chicanas defy this patriarchy when they can find "a specific moment of consciousness when they can separate from the law of the father into their own *sitio y lengua.*" The writings of women of color, according to Emma Pérez, "emerge from un sitio y una lengua (a space and language) that rejects colonial ideology and the by-products of colonialism and capitalist patriarchy—sexism, racism homophobia, etc." (161). Chicana writings are writings of resistance, reaffirmation, self-representation—a break from the cycle of perpetrator/victim. Chicana writings are also the process of recovery from that cycle.

The Challenges of Oppositional Consciousness

As Sandoval writes: "Any social order which is hierarchically organized into relations of domination and subordination creates particular subject positions within which the subordinated can legitimately function. These subject positions, once self-consciously recognized by their inhabitants, can become transformed into more effective sites of resistance to the current ordering of power relations." (Sandoval 1991, 11)

The self-conscious recognition that Chela Sandoval refers to is similar to the "historical moment" that Pérez describes when a Chicana can separate from the law of the father, i.e., from domination through authority, and find her own "sitio y lengua." Chicana writings, in their very essence, are representations of resistance. As Chicanas join in alliance with women of color, they are looking to extend their resistance to forge effective opposition to all forms of domination. Pérez refers to a "collective good" and Alarcón to "solidarities against repression and oppression."

Self-identified Chicanas remain committed to a legacy from the Chicano movement:

> We live in an era in which Chicanos are increasingly the most impoverished group in the United States. In the Southwest, Chicanos will soon be the largest minority population, yet we also remain the most marginalized group in all the sectors of US society. Given this historical profile and given the upsurge of conservative ideology, there is an urgency and a necessity for retaining the utopian and political dimensions of our intellectual practice. This progressive humanism is the legacy which we have inherited from the Chicano movement and which we seek to reactivate. (Chabram and Fregoso 1990, 210)

This upsurge of conservative ideology, however, makes the resistance not only more difficult but more important. Idealist notions of a more humanitarian society are the dreams that fuel opposition to hierarchical subjugation. If we take seriously the opposition expressed by Chicanas against classist, racist, sexist, and homophobic conditions, then we will join them in the oppositional political activity for the collective good.

Bibliography

Abrego, Carmen
1985 *Women in My Lost Dreams.* Not published.

Acosta, Teresa Palomo
1984 *Passing Time.* Not published.

Aguilar-Henson, Marcela
1983 *Figura cristalina.* Ed Norma Cantú. San Antonio, TX: M & A Editions.

Aguilar, Linda
1973 "Unequal Opportunity and the Chicana." *Civil Rights Digest,* vol 5, no 4 (Spring):30-33.

Alarcón, Norma
1983 "Chicana's Feminist Literature: A Re-vision through Malintzin; or Malinztin: Putting Flesh Back on the Object." In *This Bridge Called My Back.* Eds Gloria Anzaldúa and Cherríe Moraga. New York: Kitchen Table/Women of Color P, pp 182-190.
1985 "What Kind of Lover Have You Made Me, Mother? Towards a Theory of Chicanas' Feminism and Cultural Identity through Poetry." In *Women of Color: Perspectives on Feminism and Identity.* Ed Audrey T. McCluskey. Bloomington: Women's Studies Program, Indiana U, pp 85-110.

1989a "Making 'Familia' from Scratch: Split Subjectives in the Work of Helena María Viramontes and Cherríe Moraga." In *Chicana Creativity and Criticism: Charting New Frontiers in American Literature.* Eds María Hererra-Sobek and Helena María Viramontes. Houston: Arte Público, pp 147-59.

1989b "Tradutora, traditora: A Paradigmatic Figure of Chicana Feminism." *Cultural Critique*, vol 13 (Fall).

1989c "Chicana Writers and Critics in a Social Context: Towards a Contemporary Bibliography." *Third Women,* vol 4:169-78.

1990 "Chicana feminism: In the Tracks of 'the' Native Woman." *Cultural Studies,* vol 4, no 3 (October): 248-56.

Alarcón, Norma, Ana Castillo, and Cherríe Moraga, eds.

1989 *The Sexuality of Latinas.* Spec vol of *Third Woman.* vol 4.

Anzaldúa, Gloria

1983 "Speaking in Tongues: A Letter to Third World Women Writers." In *This Bridge Called My Back,* pp 163-74.

1987 *Borderlands, La Frontera.* San Francisco: Spinsters/ Aunt Lute.

1988 "Speaking in My Own Tongue." In *Changing Our Power: An Introduction to Women Studies.* Eds Jo Whitehorse Cochran, Donna Langston, and Carolyn Woodward. Dubuque, Iowa: Kendall/Hunt Publishing, pp 361-68.

1990a "Bridge, Drawbridge, Sandbar, or Island: Lesbians of Color Hacienda Alianzas." In *Bridges of Power.* Eds Lisa Albrecht and Rose M. Brewer, in cooperation with the National Women's Studies Association. Philadelphia: New Society Publishers, pp 216-31.

1990b *Making Face, Making Soul: Haciendo Caras.* San Francisco: Aunt Lute Foundation Books.

Anzaldúa, Gloria and Cherríe Moraga, eds

1983 *This Bridge Called My Back.* New York: Kitchen Table/Women of Color P.

Apodaca, María Linda

1977 "The Chicana Women: An Historical Materialist Perspective." *Latin American Perspectives,* vol 4, no 1-2.

1986 "A Double Edge Sword: Hispanas and Liberal Feminism." *Crítica,* vol 1, no 3 (fall):96-114.

Arroyo, Laura E.

1973 "Industrial and Occupational Distribution of Chicana Workers." *Aztlán,* 4.2:342-59.

1977 "Industrial and Occupational Distribution of Chicana Workers." In *Essays on La Mujer.* Los Angeles: UCLA Chicano Studies Center Publications, pp150-87.

Baca Zinn, Maxine

1975a "Chicanas: Power and Control in the Domestic Sphere." *De Colores,* 2.3:19-31.

1975b "Political Familism: Toward Sex Role Equality in Chicano Families." *Aztlán,* vol 6, no 1 (spring):13-26.

1980 "Employment and Education of Mexican-American Women: The Interplay of Modernity and Ethnicity in Eight Families." *Harvard Educational Review,* vol 50, no 1 (February):47-62.

1982a "Mexican-American Women in the Social Sciences." *Signs: Journal of Women in Culture and Society,* vol 8, no 2 (winter):259-72.

1982b "Qualitative Methods in Family Research: A Look inside Chicano Families." *California Sociologist,* vol 5, no 2 (summer):58-79.

1982c "Urban Kinship and Midwest Chicano Families: Evidence in Support of Revision." *De Colores,* 6.1-2:85-98.

1983 "Ongoing Questions in the Study of Chicano Families." In *The State of Chicano Research on Family, Labor, and Migration.* Ed. Armando Valdez, Albert Camarillo, and Tomás Almaguer. Stanford, CA: Stanford Center for Chicano Research, pp 139-46.

1984 "Mexican Heritage Women: A Bibliographic Essay." *Sage Race Relations Abstracts,* vol 9, (August):1-12.

Broyles, Yolanda Julia

1986 "Women in El Teatro Campesino." In *Chicana Voices.* Ed Teresa Córdova, et al. Austin: Center for Mexican American Studies, U of Texas, Austin, pp 162-87.

Broyles-González, Yolanda

1990a "The Living Legacy of Chicana Performers: Preserving History through Oral Testimony." *Frontiers,* 11.1:46-52.

1990b "What price 'mainstream'? Luis Valdez' Corridos on stage and film." *Cultural Studies,* vol 4, no 3, (October):281-93.

Burciaga, Cecilia P.

1978 "The 1977 National Women's Conference in Houston: Gains and Disappointments for Hispanas." *La Luz,* 7.11:8-9.

Candelaria, Cordelia

1984 *Ojo de la Cueva.* Colorado Springs, CO: Maize P.

n.d. "Notes on a Chicana-identified 'Wild Zone' of American Culture." In *Trabajos Monográficos: Studies in Chicana/Latina Research.* Ed Adaljuza Sosa Riddell. Davis, CA: MALCS Institute, forthcoming.

Cantú, Norma

1986 "Women, Then and Now: An Analysis of the Adelita Image versus the Chicana as Political Writer and Philosopher." In *Chicana Voices.* Ed Teresa Córdova et al. Austin, TX: Center for Mexican American Studies, U of Texas, pp 8-10.

Carrillo, Teresa

1986 "The Woman's Movement and the Left in Mexico: The Presidential Candidacy of Doña Rosario Ibarra." In *Chicana Voices.* Ed. Teresa Córdova et al. Austin: Center for Mexican American Studies, U of Texas, pp 96-115.

Carrillo-Berón, Carmen

1977 "Raza Mental Health: Perspectivas Femeniles." In *Persectivas en Chicano Studies.* Ed Reynaldo Flores Macías. Los Angeles: National Association of Chicano Social Science.

Castañeda, Antonia I.

1990a "Gender, Race, and Culture: Spanish-Mexican Women in the Historiography of Frontier California." *Frontiers,* 11.1:8-20.

1990b "The Political Economy of Nineteenth-Century Stereotypes of Californianas." *Between Borders: Essays on Mexicana/Chicana History.* Ed Adelaida R. Del Castillo. Encino, CA: Floricanto P, pp 213-36.

Castellano, Olivia
1980 *Blue Mandolin, Yellow Field*. Berkeley: Grito del Sol (quarterly books: year five, book three).
1983 *Blue Horse of Madness*. Sacramento, CA: Crystal Clear.
1986 *Spaces That Time Missed*. Sacramento, CA: Crystal Clear.
Castillo, Ana
1977 *Otro Canto*. Chicago: Alternativa Publications.
1979 *The Invitation*. np
1984 *Women Are Not Roses*. Houston: Arte Público.
1986 *The Mixquiahuala Letters*. Binghamton, NY: Bilingual P/Editorial Bilingüe.
1988 *My Father Was a Toltec*. Novato, Calif: West End P.
1989 *Sapogonia*. Tempe, AZ: Bilingual P/Editorial Bilingüe.
Castillo-Speed, Lillian
1987 "Chicana/Latina Literature and Criticism: Reviews of Recent Books." *WLW Journal*, vol 11, no 3 (September):1-4.
1990 "Chicana Studies: A Selected List of Materials since 1980." *Frontiers*, 11.1:66-84.
Castillo-Speed, Lillian, Richard Chabrán, and Francisco García-Ayvens, eds
1989 *The Chicano Periodical Index*. Berkeley, CA: Chicano Studies Library Publications Unit.
Cervantes, Lorna Dee
1981 *Emplumada*. Pittsburgh: U of Pittsburgh P.
Chabram, Angie C.
1990 "Chicana/o Studies as Oppositional Ethnography." *Cultural Studies*, vol 4, no 3 (October):228-47.
Chabram, Angie C. and Rosa Linda Fregoso, eds
1990a "Chicana/o Cultural Representations" *Reframing Alternative Critical Discourses, Cultural Studies*, vol 4, no 3 (October):203-16.
1990b *Chicana/o Cultural Representations: Reframing Alternative Critical Discourse* (Spec issue). *Cultural Studies*, vol 4, no 3 (October).
Chapa, Evey, and Armando Gutiérrez
1977 "Chicanas in Politics: An Overview and a Case Study." In *Persectivas en Chicano Studies*. Ed Reynaldo Flores Macías. Los Angeles: National Association of Chicano Social Science.
Chávez, Denise
1986 *The Last of the Menu Girls*. Houston: Arte Público P.
1989 "Heat and Rain (Testimonio)." In *Breaking Boundaries: Latina Writing and Critical Readings*. Eds Asunción Horno-Delgado et al. Amherst: U of Massachusetts P, pp 27-32.
Chávez, Jennie V.
1972 "Women of the Mexican-American Movement." *Mademoiselle* (April):82.
Chavira, Alicia
1988 "'Tienes que ser valiente': Mexicana Migrants in a Midwestern Farm Labor Camp." In *Mexicanas at Work in the United States*. Ed Margarita B. Melville. Houston: Mexican American Studies Program, U of Houston, pp 64-74.
Cisneros, Sandra
1980 *Bad Boys*. San José, CA: Mango Publication.
1985 *The House on Mango Street*. Houston: Arte Público P.
1986 "Cactus Flowers: In Search of Tejana Feminist Poetry." *Third Woman*, 3.1-2:73-80.
1987a *My Wicked Wicked Ways*. Bloomington, IN: Third Woman P.
1987b "Notes to a Young(er) Writer." *The Americas Review*, vol 15, no 1 (Spring):74-76.
1991 *Woman Hollering Creek and Other Stories*. New York: Random House.
Córdova, Teresa
1984 "Chicano Literature: Criticism and Analysis." In *The Chicano Struggle: Analyses of Past and Present Efforts*. Eds John A. García, Teresa Córdova, and Juan R. García, National Association for Chicano Studies. Binghamton, NY: Bilingual P/Editorial Bilingüe, pp 148-51.
Córdova, Teresa, Norma Cantú, Gilberto Cardenas, Juan García, and Christine M. Sierra
1984 *Chicana Voices: Intersection of Class, Race, and Gender*. Austin: Center for Mexican American Centers, U of Texas.
Corpi, Lucha
1980 *Palabras de Mediodía/Noon Words*. Trans Catherine Rodríguez-Nieto. Berkeley: El Fuego de Aztlán Publications.
1989 *Delia's Song*. Houston: Arte Público P.
Cota-Cárdenas, Margarita
1977 *Noches despertando inconscientes*. Tucson: Scorpion P.
1984 "Discursos de la Malinche". In *Third Woman*, 2.1:46-50.
1985 *Puppet*. Austin: Relámpago Books P.
Cotera, Martha P.
1977 *The Chicana Feminist*. Austin: Information Systems Development. (1100 East 8th St., Austin, TX 78702)
Curry Rodríguez, Julia E.
1988 "Labor Migration and Familial Responsibilities: Experiences of Mexican Women." In *Mexicanas at Work in the United States*. Ed Margarita B. Melville. Houston: Mexican-American Studies Program, U of Houston, pp 47-63.
Del Castillo, Adelaida R.
1974 "La visión chicana." *La Gente de Aztlán* (UCLA) vol 4, no 4 (March):8-10.
1977 "Malintzin Tenépal: A Preliminary Look into a New Perspective." In *Essays on La Mujer*. Eds Rosa Martínez Cruz and Rosaura Sánchez. Los Angeles: UCLA Chicano Studies Center Publications, pp 129-49.
1988 "An Assessment of the Status of the Education of Hispanic American Women." In *The Broken Web*. Eds Teresa McKenna and Flora Ida Ortiz. Claremont, CA: Tomás Rivera Center; Berkeley, CA: Floricanto, pp 3-24.
1990 *Between Borders: Essays on Mexicana/Chicana History*. Encino, CA: Floricanto P.
Del Castillo, Adelaida R., and María Torres
1988 "The Interdependency of Educational Institutions and Cultural Norms: The Hispana Experience." In *The Broken Web*, ed Teresa McKenna and Flora Ida Ortiz. Claremont, CA: Tomás Rivera Center; Berkeley, CA: Floricanto P, pp 39-60.

Delgado, Sylvia
1971 "Chicana: The Forgotten Woman." *Regeneración,* 2.1:2-4.
Durón, Clementina
1984 "Mexican Women and Labor Conflict in Los Angeles: The ILGWU Dressmakers' Strike of 1933." *Aztlán,* 15.1:145-61.
Elsasser, Nan, Kyle Mackenzie, and Yvonne Tixier Vigil.
1980 *Las Mujeres: Conversations from a Hispanic Community.* Ed Sue Davidson. New York: Feminist P.
Escobedo, Theresa Herrera, ed
1982 "Thematic Issue: Chicana Issues." *Hispanic Journal of Behavioral Sciences,* vol 4, no 2 (June):145-286.
Facio, Elisa "Linda"
1985 "Gender and Aging: A Case of Mexicana/Chicana Elderly." *Trabajos Monográficos,* 1.1:5-21.
1988 "The Interaction of Age and Gender in Chicana Older Lives: A Case Study of Chicana Elderly in a Senior Citizen Center." Renato Rosaldo Lecture Series Monograph, vol 4, pp 21-38.
Flores, Elena
1992 "Sexual Attitudes and Behavior among Mexican Adolescent Females." Unpublished Diss. Berkeley: Wright Institute.
Flores, Francisca
1971 "Conference of Mexican Women in Houston." *Regeneración,* 1.10:1-4.
Flores, Rosalie
1975 "The New Chicana and Machismo" *Regeneración,* 2.4:56.
Frontiers: A Journal of Women Studies
1980 (Special Volume: Chicanas en el ambiente nacional/ Chicanas in the National Landscape) vol 5, no 2, (summer).
García, Alma M.
1989 "The Development of Chicana Feminist Discourse, 1970-1980." *Gender and Society,* vol 3, no 2 (June):217-38.
García, Elena H.
1973 "Chicana Consciousness: A New Perspective, A New Hope." In *La Mujer en pie de lucha.* Ed Dorinda Moreno. México: Espina del Norte Publications.
Gaspar De Alba, Alicia, María Herrera-Sobek, and Demetria Martínez
1989 *Three Times a Woman.* Tempe, AZ: Bilingual Review P.
Goldsmith, Raquel Rubio
1985 "Shipwrecked in the Desert: A Short History of the Adventures and Struggles for Survival of the Mexican Sisters of the House of the Providence in Douglas, Arizona, during Their First Twenty-Two Years of Existence (1927-1949)." Renato Rosaldo Lecture Series Monograph 1 (summer):39-67.
Gómez, Alma, Cherríe Moraga, and Mariana Romo-Carmona, eds.
1983 *Cuentos: Stories by Latinas.* New York: Kitchen Table/Women of Color P.
Gonzales-Berry, Erlinda.
1991 *Paletitas de guayaba.* Albuquerque: El Norte Publications.
González, Deena J.
1988 "The Widowed Women of Santa Fe: Assessments on the Lives of an Unmarried Population, 1850-80." In *On Their Own: Widows and Widowhood in the American Southwest, 1848-1939.* Ed Arlene Scadrkon. Urbana: U of Illinois P, pp 65-90.
1992 "Masquerades: Viewing the New Chicana Lesbian Anthologies." In *Outlook,* (winter), pp 80-83.
1992 "Encountering Columbus." In *Chicano Studies: Critical Connection Between Research and Community.* Ed Teresa Córdova. National Association for Chicano Studies (March):13-18.
1992 "On Chicano and Chicana Studies: The Heartache behind the Story." Speech presented at the National Chicano/a Student Conference, Albuquerque, NM (April 11).
González, Juanita Helena
1973 "Sex Role Stereotypes." *La Luz,* vol 1, no 9 (January).
González, Rosalinda M.
1983 "Chicana and Mexican Immigrant Families, 1920-1940: Women's Subordination and Family Exploitation." In *Decades of Discontent/The Women's Movement, 1920-1940.* Eds Louise Scharf and Joan M. Jensen. Westport, CT: Greenwood P, pp 59-84.
1984 "The Chicana in Southwest Labor History, 1900-1975 (A Preliminary Bibliographic Analysis)." *Critical Perspectives of Third World America,* vol 2, no 1 (fall):26-61.
González, Silvia
1977 "The White Feminist Movement: The Chicana Perspective." *Social Science Journal,* 14.2:67-76.
Hancock, Velia G.
1971 "La Chicana, Chicano Movement and Women's Liberation." *Chicano Studies Newsletter,* (February-March):1, 6.
Hererra-Sobek, María
1979 "Mothers, Lovers, and Losers: Images of Women in the Mexican Corrido." *Keystone Folklore Journal,* 23.1:53-77.
1980a "La imagen de la madre en la poesía chicana." In *Mujer y sociedad en América Latina.* Ed Lucía Guerra-Cunningham, pp 253-61. Chile: Editorial del Pacifico. Article reprinted in *La Opinión* (Suplemento Cultural), Los Angeles (April 27):10-11.
1980b "La Chicana: Nuevas perspectivas." *La Opinión Literary Supplement, vol* 10 (June 22):14-15.
1981 "La mujer traidora: Arquetipo estructurante en el corrido." *Cuadernos Americanos* (Marzo-Abril): 230-42.
1982a "The Acculturation Process of the Chicana in the Corrido." *De Colores,* 6.1-2:7-16.
1982b "The Treacherous Woman Archetype: A Structuring Agent in the Corrido." *Aztlán,* vol 13, no 1-2 (spring-fall):9-39.
1982c "La unidad del hombre y del cosmos: Reafirmacción del proceso vital en Estela Portillo Trombley." *La Palabra,* 4/5:127-41.
1983 "Crossing the Border: Three Case Studies of Mexican Immigrant Women in Orange County in the 1980s." In *Second Lives: The Contemporary Immi-*

grant/Refugee Experience in Orange County. Eds Valerie Smith and Michael Bigelow. Costa Mesa, CA: South Coast Repertory.

1985 *Beyond Stereotypes: The Critical Analysis of Chicana Literature*. Binghamton, NY: Bilingual P/Editorial Bilingüe.

1987a "'La Delgadina': Incest and Patriarchal Structure in a Spanish/Chicano Romance-Corrido." *Studies in Latin American Popular Culture Journal*, vol 5, pp 90-107.

1987b "Systems in Conflict: Myth, Family and Industrial Society." In *1987 Hispanic Playwrights Project*. Costa Mesa, CA: Southcoast Repertory, pp 17-19.

1988 "The Politics of Rape: Sexual Transgression in Chicana Fiction." In *Chicana Creativity and Criticism*. Eds María Hererra-Sobek and Helena María Viramontes. Houston: Arte Público P, pp 171-81.

Hererra-Sobek, María, and Helena María Viramontes, eds.

1988 *Chicana Creativity and Criticism: Charting New Frontiers in American Literature*. Houston: Arte Público.

Hernández, Antonia

1976 "Chicanas and the Issue of Involuntary Sterilization: Reforms Needed to Protect Informed Consent." *Chicano Law Review*, vol 3, no 3, (1976):3-37.

Hernández, Lisa, and Tina Benítez, eds

1988 *Palabras Chicanas: An Undergraduate Anthology*. Berkeley: Mujeres en Marcha, U of California, Berkeley.

Hernández Tovar, Inés

1977a *Con razón corazón*. San Antonio: Caracol.

n.d. "Chicana Writers." In *Women in Texas*. Eds Rose Marie Cutting and Bonnie Freeman. Austin: U of Texas P.

1980 "The Feminist Aesthetic in Chicano Literature. " In *Third Women: Minority Women Writers of the U. S.* Ed Dexter Fisher. Boston: Houghton Mifflin.

1987 *Con razón corazón*. 2nd edition, enlarged. San Antonio, TX: M & A Editions.

1988a "Open Letter to Chicanas: The Power and Politics of Origin." In *Changing Our Power: An Introduction to Women Studies*. Eds Jo Whitehorse Cochran, Danna Lanston, and Carolyn Woodward. Dubuque, Iowa: Kendall/Hunt Publishing.

1988 "With Due Respects to la Llorona." In *Changing Our Power: An Introduction to Women Studies*. Eds Jo Whitehorse cochran, Danna Lanston, and Carolyn Woodward. Dubuque, Iowa: Kendall/Hunt Publishing.

Hoyos, Angela de

1975 *Arise Chicano! and Other Poems*. San Antonio, TX: M & A Editions.

1976 *Selecciones. Traducción del Inglés por Mireya Robles*. Veracruz, México: Taller Editorial, S.A.

1977 *Chicano Poems for the Barrio*. San Antonio: M & A Editions.

1979 *Selected Poems/Selecciones*. San Antonio: Dezkalz.

1980 *Arise Chicano! and Other Poems*. Rev and enlarged bilingual edition. Trans. into Spanish by Mireya Robles. San Antonio, TX: M & A Editions.

1985 *Woman, Woman*. Houston: Arte Público P.

Hurtado, Aída

1989 "Relating to Privilege: Seduction and Rejection in the Subordination of White Women and Women of Color." *Signs* (summer):833-55.

Lizárraga, Sylvia S.

1982a "Chicana Women Writers and Their Audience." *Lector*, vol 1, no 1 (June):15-16, 18.

1982b "La mujer ingeniosa." *Fem*, vol 8, no 34 (June-July):41.

1985a "The Patriarchal Ideology in 'La noche que se apagaron las luces.'" *Revista Chicano-Riqueña*, vol 13, no 3-4 (fall-winter):90-95.

1985b "Images of Women in Chicano Literature by Men." *Feminist Issues*, vol 5, no 2 (fall):69-88.

1985c "La mujer doblemente explotada: 'On the Road to Texas: Pete Fonseca'" *Aztlán*, 16.1-2:197-215.

1988 "Hacia una teoría para la liberación de la mujer." In *Times of Challenge: Chicanos and Chicanas in American Society*. Ed Juan R. García, Julia Curry Rodríguez and Clara Lomas. National Association of Chicano Studies. Houston, TX: Mexican American Studies Program, U of Houston, pp 25-31.

Lomas, Clara

1986a "Libertad de no procrear: La voz de la mujer en 'A una madre de nuestros tiempos' de Margarita Cota-Cárdenas." In *Chicana Voices*. Eds Teresa Córdova et al. Austin, TX: Center for Mexican American Studies, U of Texas, pp 188-94.

1986b "Reproductive Freedom: La voz de la mujer en 'A una madre de nuestros tiempos' de Margarita Cota-Cárdenas." In *Chicana Voices*. Eds Teresa Córdova et. al. NACS, pp 195-201.

1989 "Mexican Precursors of Chicana Feminist Writing." In *Multiethnic Literature of the United States: Critical Introductions and Classroom Resources*. Ed Cordelia Candelaria. Boulder: U of Colorado, pp 21-33.

López-Garza, Marta C.

1986 "Toward A Reconceptualization of Women's Economic Activities: The Informal Sector in Urban Mexico." In *Chicana Voices*. Eds. Teresa Córdova et al. Austin, TX: Center for Mexican American Studies, U of Texas, pp 47-65.

Martínez, Clemencia

1972 "Welfare Families Face Forced Labor." *La Raza*, 1.7:41.

Martínez Cruz, Rosa, and Rosaura Sánchez, eds.

1977 *Essays on La Mujer: Part One and Part Two*. Los Angeles: UCLA Chicano Studies Center Publications.

McKenna, Teresa, and Flora Ida Ortiz

1988a "Select Bibliography on Hispanic Women and Education." In *The Broken Web*. Eds Teresa McKenna and Flora Ida Ortiz. Claremont, CA: Tomás Rivera Center; Berkeley, CA: Floricanto, pp 221-54.

1988b *The Broken Web: The Educational Experience of Hispanic American Women*. Claremont, CA: Tomás Rivera Center: Berkeley, CA: Floricanto.

Melville, Margarita B., ed

1980 *Twice a Minority: Mexican-American Women: A History of Mexican Americans*. St. Louis, MO: Mosby.

1988a "Mexican Women in the U. S. Wage Labor Force."

In *Mexicanas at Work in the United States.* Ed Margarita Melville. Houston, TX: Mexican American Studies Program, U of Houston, pp 1-11.

1988b *Mexicanas at Work in the United States.* Houston, TX: Mexican American Studies Program, U of Houston.

Mora, Juana

1990 "Mexican American Women." In *Women, Alcohol, and Other Drugs.* Ed Ruth Engs. Dubuque, Iowa: Kendall-Hunt Publishing.

Mora, Magdalena

1981 "The Tolteca Strike: Mexican Women and the Struggle for Union Representation." In *Mexican Immigrant Workers in the U. S.* Ed Antonio Ríos-Bustamante. Los Angeles: Chicano Studies Research Center Publications, U of California, pp 111-17.

Mora, Magdalena, and Adelaida R. Del Castillo, eds

1980 *Mexican Women in the United States: Struggles Past and Present.* Los Angeles: UCLA Chicano Studies Research Center Publication.

Mora, Pat

1984 *Chants.* Houston: Arte Público P.

1986 *Borders.* Houston: Arte Público P.

Moraga, Cherríe

1981 "Third World Women in the United States–by and about Us: A Selected Bibliography." In *This Bridge Called My Back.* Eds Cherríe Moraga and Gloria Anzaldúa. Watertown, MA: Persephone P, pp 251-56.

1983 *Loving in the War Years: Lo que nunca pasó por sus labios.* Boston: South End P.

1986 *Giving Up the Ghost.* Los Angels: West End P.

Moraga, Cherríe, and Ana Castillo, eds

1988 *Esta puente [sic], mi espalda: boces de mujeres tercermudistas en los Estados Unidos.* San Francisco, CA.: Ism Press. Spanish Trans and adaption of *This Bridge Called My Back.*

Morales, Sylvia

1985 "Chicano-Produced Celluloid Mujeres." *Chicano Cinemas: Research, Reviews, and Resources.* Ed Gary D. Keller. Binghamton, NY: Bilingual Review P, pp 89-93.

Moreno, María

1971 "I'm Talking for Justice." *Regeneración,* 1.10:12-13.

Mujeres Activas en Letras y Cambio Social

1984 *MALCS Noticiero.* vol 1, no 1, (January).

Mujeres en Marcha, University of California, Berkeley

1983 *Unsettled Issues: Chicanas in the 80s.* Berkeley, CA: Chicano Studies Library Publications Unit.

Nava, Yolanda M.

1973a "The Chicana and Employment: Needs Analysis and Recommendations for Legislation." *Regeneración,* 2.3:7-9.

1973b "Employment, Counseling and the Chicana." *Encuentro Femenil,* 1.1:34-61.

Nieto, Consuelo

1974 "The Chicana and the Women's Rights Movement: A Perspective." *Civil Rights Digest,* 6.3:36-42.

Nieto-Gómez, Anna

1973 "The Chicana: Perspectives for Education." *Encuentro Femenil,* 1.1:34-61.

1974a "Chicanas in the Labor Force." *Encuentro Femenil,* 1.2:28-33.

1974b "La Feminista." *Encuentro Femenil,* 1.2:34-37.

1976 "Sexism in the Movimiento." *La Gente,* 6.4:10.

Nieto-Gómez, Anna, and Corinne Sánchez, eds

1974 *New Directions in Education: Estudios femeniles de la chicana.* Los Angeles: U of California.

Olivares, Yvette

1986 "The Sweatshop: The Garment Industry's Reborn Child." *Revista Mujeres,* vol 3, no 2 (June):55-62.

Ordóñez, Elizabeth J.

1980 "Chicana Literature and Related Sources: A Selected and Annotated Bibliography." *Bilingual Review,* vol 7, no 2 (May-August):143-164.

1983 "Sexual Politics and the Theme of Sexuality in Chicana Poetry." In *Women in Hispanic Literature: Icons and Fallen Idols.* Ed Beth Miller. Berkeley: U of California P, pp 316-39.

1984 "The Concept of Cultural Identity in Chicana Poetry." *Third Woman,* 2.1:75-82.

Orozco, Cynthia

1984 "Chicana Labor History: A Critique of Male Consciousness in Historical Writing." La Red/The Net, no 77 (January):2-5.

Portillo-Trambley, Estela

1975 *Rain of Scorpions and Other Writings.* Berkeley, CA: Tonatiuh International.

1976 "The Day of the Swallows." In *Contemporary Chicano Theater.* Ed Roberto H. Garza. Notre Dame: U of Notre Dame P.

Rebolledo, Tey Diana

1980 "The Bittersweet Nostalgia of Childhood in the Poetry of Margarita Cota-Cárdenas." *Frontiers,* vol 5, no 2 (summer):31-35.

Rincón, Bernice

1971 "La Chicana: Her Role in the Past and Her Search for a New Role in the Future." *Regeneración,* 1.10:5-18 and 2.4:36-39.

Sáenz, Lionela

1972 "Machismo, No! Igualdad, Sí!" *La Luz.* vol 1, no 2.

Salinas, Judy

1975 "The Chicana Image." *Popular Culture Association.* (ED106032)

1979 "The Role of Women in Chicano Literature." In *The Identification and Analysis of Chicano Literature.* Ed Francisco Jiménez. New York: Bilingual P/Editorial Bilingüe.

Sánchez, Corrine

1973 "Higher Education y la Chicana?" *Encuentro Femenil,* 1.1:27-33.

Sánchez, Marta

1979 "Judy Lucero and Bernice Zamora: Two Dialectical Statements in Chicana Poetry," In *Modern Chicana Writers.* Ed Joseph Sommers and Tomás Ybarra-Frausto. Englewood Cliffs, NJ: Prentice-Hall, pp 141-49.

Sánchez, Olga

n.d. "Lucía González de Parsons: Labor Organizer." *Imágenes de la Chicana,* vol 1, pp 10-12.

Sánchez, Rita

1977 "Chicana Writer Breaking Out of the Silence." In *La*

cosecha: Literatura y la mujer chicana, De Colores, vol 3, no 3. Albuquerque, NM: Pajarito Publications.

Sanchez, Rosaura
1977 "The Chicana Labor Force." *Essays on la Mujer.* Los Angeles: Chicano Studies Center Publications, U of California, pp 3-15.

Sosa Riddell, Adaljiza
1974 "Chicanas and El Movimiento." *Aztlán,* 5.1-2:155-65.

Suárez, Cecilia, C.-R
1973 "Sexual Stereotypes—Psychological and Cultural Survival." *Regeneración,* 2.3:17-21.

Trujillo-Gaitán, Marcela
1980 "The Dilemma of the Modern Chicana Artist and Critic." *De Colores,* 3.3:38-48. Rep. in *Heresies,* vol 8, 1979, pp 5-10, and in *The Third Woman.* Ed Dexter Fisher, pp 324-32. Boston: Houghton Mifflin.

Valdés-Fallis, Guadalupe
1974 "The Liberated Chicana—A Struggle against Tradition." *Women: A Journal of Liberation,* 3.4:20-21.

Vidal, Mirta
1971 "New Voice of La Raza: Chicanas Speak Out." In *International Socialist Review,* October, pp 7-9, 31-33.
1972 "Chicanas Speak Out. Women: New Voice of La Raza." In *Feminism and Socialism.* Ed. Linda Jenness. New York: Pathfinder P, pp 48-57.

Vigil, Evangelina
1978 *Nade y Nade.* San Antonio, TX: M & A Editions.

Villanueva, Alma.
1977 *Bloodroot.* Austin, TX: Place of Herons P.
1978 *Mother May I?* np: Motheroot Publications.

Zamora, Bernice
1976 *Restless Serpents.* Menlo Park, California: Diseños Literarios.
1977a "The Chicana as a Literary Critic." *La cosecha: Literatura y la mujer chicana,* 3.9:16-19.
1977b "Notes from a Chicana 'Coed'." *Caracol,* vol 3, no 9.

Cuban Women in the United States

María Cristina García

The history of Cuban migration to the United States can be divided into two distinct periods: the nineteenth century migration, from 1868 to 1898, prompted in part by the wars of independence against Spain; and the post-1959 migration, prompted by the Castro revolution. While Cubans have emigrated to the United States at other times, primarily in responding to various political and economic crises in their country, the overwhelming majority have emigrated during these two periods. Most of the literature on the Cuban communities focuses on the post-1959 migration, due to its recent nature. A number of sociological, political, and economic studies have emerged over the past three decades, analyzing the factors that compelled the Cubans to emigrate, as well as the different variables that affected their adaptation to the United States: socioeconomic levels, political status, geographic distribution, education, fertility rates, and the group's race, sex, and age composition. A fewer number of studies exist on the Cuban communities of the late nineteenth century, and these focus primarily on the cigar-making communities of Tampa and Key West and their role in the Cuban independence efforts and the U. S. labor movement.

Most histories of the Cuban communities have paid little attention to the women's experience; in most texts, women are merely a footnote, not even mentioned in the indexes. Since most scholars have failed to see them as co-creators of their communities, little attention has been focused on their economic, political, or cultural contributions. However, in recent years, a few scholars have begun to fill this void in Cuban history, mostly with sociological studies of sex roles and women's changing employment patterns in the United States (Casal and Prieto 1981; Ferree 1979; Prieto 1977, 1984; Mariña 1978; Sullivan 1984; Lisandro Pérez 1985, September 1986). While these studies concentrate on the post-1959 migration, a few studies have also emerged on the women's experience in the nineteenth century (Estrade 1987; Hewitt 1985, 1987).

The following essay is a historical narrative that analyzes the role Cuban women played in their communities: first, during the late nineteenth century, in Key West and Tampa; and second, in Dade County, Florida, in the decades following the Castro revolution. Because the experience of the Cubans who arrived during the "Mariel boatlift" of 1980 was radically different from that of the earlier emigrés, special attention is also focused on the women's experience during this latest and most controversial migration.

The Migration of 1868-1898

Cuban migration to the United States began during the second half of the nineteenth century, prompted by the social, political, and economic turmoil on the island. By the end of the first year of the Ten Years War (1868-78), an estimated 100,000 Cubans, of every race and socioeconomic class, had emigrated to the United States, Europe, Central and South America, and the Caribbean (Pérez 1978, 129). Those who emigrated to the United States scattered around the country. Some, particularly the middle and upper classes, settled in the northeast in such cities as New York, Philadelphia, and Boston; the majority, however, settled in the southeastern United States, in Key West, Tampa, Jacksonville, and New Orleans.

Beginning in the 1860s, various cigar manufacturers relocated to Florida as a means of escaping the political turmoil on the island as well as circumventing the heavy U. S. tariffs on their products. Among the first to emigrate was Vicente Martínez Ybor, who established his El Príncipe de Gales cigar factory in Key West. He was followed by other cigar manufacturers, and within a decade Key West emerged as the major cigar manufacturing center in the United States (Pérez 1978, 130). Their factories attracted thousands of Cuban workers, who, faced with unemployment in Cuba in the midst of war, chose to emigrate to the United States, taking their wives and children with them. By 1870 over 1,000 Cubans had settled in Key West, and by 1873 they constituted the majority of the population (Poyo 1979, 290). Almost 80 percent of the Cubans in Key West, fourteen years and older, worked in the cigar factories, and 18 percent of the workers were black or mulatto (Poyo 1986, 47).

Many emigré women were forced to work outside the home to supplement their family's income. They worked as seamstresses, laundresses, servants, cooks, midwives, peddlers, grocers, and boardinghouse keepers. By the 1870s Cuban women in Florida had a higher labor participation rate than women on the island (Hewitt 1985). More women worked in the cigar industry than in any other trade, however, especially in Key West, where they constituted 9 percent of the cigar work force (Hewitt 1987). While men performed the highly skilled tasks of cutting, filling, rolling, classing, and selecting, women worked at semiskilled tasks, especially as *despalilladoras,* or tobacco-strippers. Over time, however, more and more women gained access to the skilled occupations traditionally held by men. By 1890 women comprised up to one-quarter of all hand-rollers in some factories in Tampa, working alongside the men, and there was at least one case of a woman lectora, occupying the most prestigious position in the cigar factory (Hewitt 1985).

Whether they settled in Florida or New York, most Cubans perceived themselves as temporary exiles and planned to return to their homeland, once it became feasible to do so. While they struggled to survive in the United States, they assisted in the liberation efforts. Throughout the Ten Years War, Cubans raised money for the rebel forces and recruited volunteers for filibustering expeditions, which sailed from Florida and the Bahamas carrying munitions. Rebel leaders, forced to flee from Spanish authorities, took refuge in the emigré communities. Women in Tampa opened their homes to dozens of rebels of the Ten Years War, including such heroes as Martín Herrera, Nestor Carbonell, Serafín Sánchez, Fernando Figueredo, Guillermo Sorondo, Ramón Rivero, Justo Carrillo, Carolina Rodríguez, and Rosalía Barrios (Hewitt 1987).

Women also established their own organizations to assist the independence movement, among them the *Hijas del Pueblo* in New Orleans and the *Junta Patriótica de Damas de Nueva York.* These organizations raised money to buy supplies for the rebel forces and rallied public support for the Cuban cause. In New York in 1869 Emilia Casanova, wife of author Cecilio Villaverde, founded the *Liga de las Hijas de Cuba,* which sent a petition with over 300 signatures from Cuban women on the island to French author Victor Hugo, asking him to publicly speak on behalf of the Cuban cause (Estrade 1987, 176).

The Pact of Zanjón, which ended the Ten Years War, temporarily postponed the Cubans' hopes for independence. The 1890s, however, ushered in a new period in revolutionary activity: a struggle that received much of its impetus from the emigré communities abroad. José Martí and other revolutionary leaders began visiting the emigré communities in 1891 to gather moral and financial support. It was in Key West in 1892 that Martí announced the formation of the *Partido Revolucionario Cubano* (PRC), which had the sole purpose of assisting the liberation efforts. Hundreds of PRC chapters, or *juntas,* were established in the United States, the Caribbean, and Central and South America to collect funds for the rebel army.

In the United States, the cigar workers were the backbone of the PRC, donating one day's pay on a regular basis to their local chapter. For the women cigar workers, this was even more of a sacrifice, since they earned much less than their male counterparts and received fewer benefits. Long active in trade unionism, the labor leaders strongly discouraged strikes once the war began in 1895, so as to not distract the community from the war effort and destroy the army's financial base.

Women played a key role in the Partido Revolucionario Cubano. Martí envisioned women—as well as blacks and trabajadores—as full participants in Cuba's future society, and the PRC was to serve as their introduction to egalitarianism. Of the 200 clubs that constituted part of the PRC, 25 percent were women's clubs (Estrade 1987, 178-79). By 1898 Key West had the most *clubes femeninos,* with eighteen chapters; Tampa had fifteen clubs; and New York had eleven. Three clubs emerged in New Orleans; two in both Ocala (Florida) and Philadelphia; and Jacksonville had one club. Outside the United States, the clubes femeninos emerged in Mexico, the Dominican Republic, Colombia, Costa Rica, Haiti, Honduras, El Salvador, Jamaica, and Venezuela. According to one historian, these were the first women's political clubs to emerge in Latin America during the last half of the nineteenth century (Estrade 1987, 175). Total membership in the clubes femeninos reached close to 1,500 by the end of 1898 (Estrade 1987, 179). Eight "mixed" clubs of both male and female members were also established, the majority of them in Tampa.

Most of the clubes femeninos were named after male revolutionary heroes, such as Carlos Manuel de Céspedes, Antonio Maceo, Tomás Estrada Palma, Calixto García, but especially José Martí. A smaller number were named for females heroes, such as Mariana Grajales, Mercedes Varona, Carolina Rodríguez, Flor Crombet, Lorenza Díaz Marcano, Evangelina Cossío Cisneros, and Adriana Loret de Mola. Oftentimes the names the women chose for their clubs reflected the role they perceived for themselves in the liberation effort: roles such as *Protectoras de la Patria* ("Protectors of the Nation"), *Auxiliadoras de la Revolución* ("Assisters of the Revolution"), *Hermanas de Martí* ("Sisters of José Martí"), *Obreras de la Independencia* ("Workers of Independence"), and *Protectoras del Ejército* ("Protectors of the Army").

Women elected to the directiva of the clubs tended to be the wives, sisters, mothers, or widows of the most important male leaders of the Partido Revolucionario Cubano or the rebel army. The clubes femeninos were comprised of both working-class and middle-class women, but the directiva usually came from the middle class; unlike their working-class sisters, middle-class women did not have to concern themselves with wage earning and were able to dedicate all their energies to the independence cause (Hewitt 1987). Some clubs, however, were comprised almost entirely of female cigar workers. Women also directed the work of the clubes infantiles, or youth groups, that emerged in many communities. Because of social conventions, however, the clubes femeninos usually elected a man to represent them at the meetings of the local PRC chapter. These meetings usually erupted into heated arguments, which were regarded as improper for female participants.

The clubes femeninos organized dances, picnics, raffles, auctions, banquets, rallies, and parades, through which they promoted the idea of independence and raised money to supply and feed the rebel army. For these events, women prepared food, sewed banners, wrote speeches, and organized entertainment. More than a few women distinguished themselves as orators. Each event usually raised anywhere from $100 to $1,000; one club, the *Hijas de Martí* in New York, collected over $8,000 during 1896 and 1897 (Estrade 1987, 184).

Apart from their active fund-raising and propaganda work, the women assisted the revolution in more subtle ways. As their men took off to fight in Cuba, the responsibility of supporting their families fell on their shoulders. Finding time to paint banners and prepare banquets became even more of a sacrifice, but many women successfully raised families, worked outside the home, and contributed to the cause. They often neglected their own personal comfort in order to contribute more money to the PRC. Throughout the war, as more and more Cubans sought refuge in their communities, the women also took in the homeless and collected clothes and set up soup kitchens. They took in widows, orphans, wounded soldiers, and other victims of the war. They housed medical supplies and even weapons and ammunition, and they opened their homes to the rebel leaders who made periodic visits to the exile communities to rally support.

Following the signing of the Treaty of Paris, the emigrés had to decide whether to return to Cuba or remain in the United States. Despite their victory, the war had devastated Cuba's economy, and thousands of people were left homeless or unemployed. Most working-class Cubans, in particular the cigar workers, opted to remain in the United States, where they had steady employment. Over the years they had established ties to their communities in spite of their nationalism; and while they were torn by their desires to return home, they realized that they could fare better economically if they remained in the United States. Many of those who repatriated following the war returned to Florida within a few years, due to the political and economic chaos on the island. They were joined by hundreds of new immigrants who chose to seek economic opportunities in the United States while Cuba rebuilt itself.

At the end of the war, most PRC clubs dissolved, their mission essentially fulfilled. The emigrés now channeled their energies into improving their domestic environment and especially their working conditions. The Cubans had a long tradition of militant trade unionism. Radicalized by Spanish anarchism and socialism, the trabajadores rejected the American labor movement for its lack of vision as well as for its overt racism. Instead of joining the Knights of Labor or the International Cigarmakers Union, they created their own organizations to address not only immediate concerns such as wages and benefits, but long-term issues such as the class struggle. The constant movement of immigrants between south Florida and Cuba during the last half of the nineteenth century ensured the continued radicalization of Cuban labor (Poyo 1986, 50-54).

As early as the 1870s and 1880s, Cuban cigar workers in Key West walked off the job on several occasions, protesting layoffs and wage reductions. In 1878 they succeeded in creating the first cigar worker's union in Florida, the *Unión de Tabaqueros*, which became an umbrella organization for various smaller unions of cigar makers, selectors, classers, and strippers. The Unión, however, enjoyed limited success. Concerned about the violence and labor unrest, Vicente Martínez Ybor relocated his factory to Tampa in 1886, where he obtained large tracts of land for "Ybor City," his new company town which he modeled after Pullman, Illinois. Other cigar factories followed, and Tampa replaced Key West as the center of the cigar manufacturing trade. As in Key West, the Cubans dominated the cigar-making industry. By the turn of the century, 111 million cigars were handrolled annually in Tampa's factories (Mormino 1982, 339).

While there were over a dozen labor strikes in Tampa between 1887 and 1893, Cuban labor leaders placed a moratorium on strikes during the war of 1895-98 so the community could concentrate its energies on the war. Once the war ended, however, the trabajadores resumed their unionization efforts and labor protests. The first major strike occurred in 1899: the so-called *huelga de la pesa*. By that year the first generation of patrones such as Martínez Ybor had died, and the cigar industry had become increasingly dominated by American interests. In an attempt to increase production and efficiency, the new cigar manufacturers introduced weight scales. A worker was now expected to produce a certain number of cigars from a specific amount of filler. The Cuban cigar makers protested, and the manufacturers enforced a lockout of their plants, displacing over 4,000 workers. Faced with no income, over 1,400 left Tampa for Havana. Local police, in collusion with management, arrested and detained 12 Cuban labor leaders. After a few months, however, management was forced to concede to the Cuban workers.

Confident after their victory, the workers formed *La Sociedad de Torcedores de Tabaco de Tampa*, more popularly known as *La Resistencia*. Although American labor unions such as the AFL continued to try to unionize the Cuban workers, the latter remained resistant. The 1899 protest, however, was the Cubans' last successful strike. Beginning in 1900, American conglomerates such as the Havana American Company began to take a harsher stand against labor activity (Mormino 1982, 353-54). In 1901 Tampa witnessed one of the longest labor strikes in its history, lasting almost seventeen months. During this period, local police and vigilantes used violence and intimidation to threaten the protesters. Immigrants were evicted by landlords, strikers were arrested for vagrancy, and union funds were frozen by banks. La Resistencia's president and treasurer were forcibly deported to Honduras (Mormino 1982, 355).

Female cigar makers struck alongside the men for higher wages, better benefits, and union recognition (Hewitt 1985). The women of the community assisted the protesters in countless ways. They set up soup kitchens, or cocinas económicas, to feed the striking cigar workers and their families, and they collected clothes, food, and medicine for them. When male strike leaders were abducted, deported, or forced to flee the community, the women called upon Florida governor, W. Sherman Jennings, and demanded that he put an end to the violence. When strikers were arrested by local police, the women marched upon police headquarters and demanded that Tampa's mayor intercede. When the strikers were evicted from their homes because of their inability to pay rent, women took families into their homes.

Despite their efforts, the strike ultimately failed. Over the next few decades, women would again be called to support the cigar workers, especially during the strikes of 1910, 1920, and 1931. These strikes involved not only the Cuban workers, but the Italian cigar workers who immigrated to Tampa during this period, and Cuban and Italian women worked alongside each other to rally support from the community.

After 1930, automation eliminated most of the skilled positions in the cigar industry, thus ending a way of life for an entire generation of trabajadores. The jobs that remained at the factories were the unskilled tasks that were traditionally performed by female workers; and women soon outnumbered men in the cigar industry. With automation, however, the factories no longer provided women with opportunities for occupational mobility, as they had for previous generations (Hewitt 1985). Henceforth, unless women trained to be teachers or nurses, they could not aspire to any jobs other than the unskilled and semiskilled positions in local industries.

The 1959-1973 Migration

The post-1959 migration from Cuba constitutes one of the largest migrations in recent U. S. history. Over half a million Cubans immigrated to the United States from 1959 to 1962 and during the federally sponsored "freedom flights" of 1965 to 1973. An additional 125,000 Cubans migrated during a six-month period in 1980, during the so-called "Mariel boatlift." Almost 100,000 more Cubans arrived in the United States in between these official periods of migration, immigrating via third countries or arriving clandestinely on small craft in the Florida Keys.

The revolution affected people of all classes, and with each year the migration became more representative of the Cuban population as a whole. The first people to leave Cuba were those who were most radically affected by the revolution: the political leaders, government officials, and military officers of the Batista regime, and the Cubans of the upper socioeconomic class who feared retribution because of their positions of privilege. They were followed by members of the middle class: professionals such as doctors, lawyers, engineers, and teachers; as well as merchants and craftsmen.

Following the Cuban Missile Crisis in October 1962, travel from Cuba to the United States ceased for a three-year period, resuming in late 1965 with the establishment of the federally sponsored "freedom flights." From 1965 to the termination of the flights in 1973, the migration became less concentrated among the middle-to-upper classes and became more representative of the working class. During the early 1960s, 31 percent of the Cubans who arrived in the United States held professional or managerial occupations; by 1970, only 12 percent were professionals or managers, and 57 percent were blue-collar, service, or agricultural workers (Pedraza-Bailey 1985, 18). The only group that remained under-represented in the 1959-73 migration were black Cubans. While the 1953 Cuban census revealed that close to 27 percent of the population was black or mulatto, by 1970 only 2.6 percent of the Cubans in the United States were black (*Censos de Población* 1953, 49; Aguirre 1976, 104). This underrepresentation was understandable due to the social welfare programs instituted by the Castro regime, which initially improved the quality of life of many black Cubans. In addition, many black Cubans feared emigrating because of the social and institutional racism in the United States. It was not until the Mariel Boatlift of 1980, in which blacks and mulattoes constituted up to 20 percent of the arrivals, that the Cuban emigré population became more representative in race.

The overwhelming majority of the Cubans settled in Dade County, Florida. Despite the federal government's intensive resettlement efforts, Cubans returned to live in south Florida where the climate was more temperate and reminded them of home. South Florida was also home to a small Cuban community: compatriots who had emigrated during previous political tenures. With Cuba less than a hundred miles away, they also had easier access to news from their homeland. By 1980 the national census revealed that more than 52 percent of the 803,226 Cubans in the United States lived in the Miami-Ft. Lauderdale area alone (Pérez summer 1986, 130). The only city with a larger Cuban population was Havana.

The U. S. government granted the Cubans refugee status and welcomed them with a comprehensive assistance program, which was unparalleled in all of American immigration history. The Cuban Refugee Program, initiated during the Kennedy administration, dispensed over $957 million in relief by 1973, through job training and education programs, loans, medical care, surplus food distribution, emergency relief checks, as well as a resettlement program. By providing these resources to needy refugees, the federal government hoped to facilitate their adaptation and assimilation into American society. The Cubans, however, did not perceive themselves as traditional immigrants but rather as "exilados" and "temporary visitors." They left Cuba for a variety of social, economic, and political reasons, and most hoped to return to their homeland once a more democratic government was in place.

A reunion of grandmother and granddaughter in Miami. (Courtesy of the *Texas Catholic Herald*.)

The emigration restrictions of the Cuban government prohibited men of military age (fourteen to twenty-six), certain technicians, as well as political prisoners from leaving the island. Consequently the Cuban population revealed an over-representation of both women and elderly (Pérez September 1986, 132-33). Women responded to their changed circumstances by entering the labor force in record numbers. Prior to the revolution only 13 percent of Cuban women, fourteen years and older, worked outside the home, concentrated mostly in the teaching professions and clerical work, or in working-class occupations such as domestic service and factory operation (*Censos de Población* 1953, 183). As early as 1970, however, Cuban women were the largest proportionate group of working women in the United States. Of white Cuban exile women sixteen years and older, 0.5 percent worked outside the home. Labor participation was even higher among black Cuban women, at 55.8 percent (Casal and Prieto 1981, 316-17). Women expanded their roles to include wage earning, not as a response to the feminist movement or the social currents of the 1960s but to ensure the economic survival of their families. This trend continued over the next decade: by 1980, 55.4 percent of Cuban women sixteen years and older worked outside the home, as compared to 49.9 percent of the total U. S. population (Pérez 1985, 8-9).

Women's participation in the labor force defied traditional middle-class concepts of respectability. In prerevolutionary Cuba, the wife and homemaker was the

A common scene from the Mariel boatlift. (Courtesy of the *Texas Catholic Herald.*)

feminine ideal, and most women sought personal realization in the home rather than the workplace. It was not uncommon for women to seek professional or specialized educations, but they gave up their careers once married to fulfill the feminine ideal and enhance their family's prestige. There were always exceptions; some women successfully combined both family life and careers, but they were always the small minority. Most married women chose to and were expected to remain at home, tending to familial responsibilities. For these women, employment was justified only in times of economic crisis, and then only on a temporary basis until the crisis was resolved. Manual labor was also prohibited to them, since it was considered improper and unworthy of their social status.

Most working-class women also remained at home, although in smaller numbers. The feminine ideal was a luxury few working-class families could afford. If women remained at home it was usually because no employment was available or because they were pushed out of their jobs by men. Even so, a single-income household, determined by choice rather than circumstance, was the ideal most working-class families aspired to since it was a symbol of upward mobility; and women often used their incomes to facilitate their family's entrance into the middle class.

In the United States, however, "exile" blurred class distinctions, and economic necessity forced most emigrés to adapt their attitudes concerning women's roles. Cubans suffered radical downward mobility during their first years in the United States, particularly the middle classes. Due to the Cuban government's restrictions on what they could take out of the country, most arrived with little or no money and few personal belongings. While they waited for Castro's overthrow, they had to concern themselves with the mundane aspects of day-to-day living: they had to find jobs and housing, buy groceries, and enroll their children in school. Cubans, both male and female, worked at whatever employment they found, regardless of their socioeconomic status, their training, or education. A two-income household was crucial to their economic security; and in those families where the men were prohibited from emigrating, women had to be the principal wage earner.

Cuban women often found their first jobs more readily than men because they were willing to work for even lower wages. These jobs, for the most part, were unskilled or semiskilled labor that did not require fluency in English or contact with the general public. Women found jobs as factory operatives, seamstresses, domestics, janitors, cooks, dishwashers, waitresses, sales attendants and cashiers, manicurists, and in other service occupations. In south Florida, women found jobs sorting shrimp in warehouses by the Miami River, a work so tedious and painful that they nicknamed it *la Siberia.* Still others found their first jobs as agricultural workers in *las tomateras,* or the fruit and vegetable fields outside the city. The garment industry and textile manufacturing were also important employers during the 1960s. Thousands of women trained in *las factorías* of northwest Miami, cutting material or sewing at the machines, and became the backbone of this industry. By 1980, 85 percent of garment workers were Cuban, mostly women (Arboleya 1980, 5).

With thousands of Cuban women seeking employment, the Cuban Refugee Center in Miami created vocational training programs specifically for them. In 1964 the program *Aprenda y Supérese*, or "Training for Independence," was established by the center to help single women and heads of households become self-supporting. In two-month sessions these women received intensive English instruction and training in any of a number of marketable skills: hand-sewing, sewing-machine work, clerical office work, nursing assistance, housekeeping and domestic service, and even silk-screen art work. In addition the women received a monthly stipend of $9 to cover bus transportation to and from the center, and their children were supervised in federally funded day-care centers, staffed by graduates of the program. After participants passed the course, the Cuban Refugee Center assisted the women in finding employment, usually resettling them to other parts of the country. *Aprenda y Supérese* trained more than 3,000 Cuban women and was so successful that it became a model for the amended Aid to Families with Dependent Children (AFDC) Program during the Johnson administration in 1968.

Women also encountered opportunities in the teaching profession, in which they contributed to the accommodation of thousands of refugee children into the Dade County School System. By 1961, 3,500 refugee children attended public schools, and 3,000 attended Catholic parochial schools (Walsh 1966, 287). In that year, Dade County established a Cuban Teacher Training Program to prepare aspiring teachers for positions in the rapidly growing school system. The Cuban teacher assistants, the majority of whom were women, spent up to eight hours per day in a classroom, assisting in curriculum planning, teaching, supervising, and acting as interpreters for the refugee children; by night they took English and education courses to prepare for their certification exams. Once certified, the new teachers headed their own classrooms in Dade County schools or were relocated to school systems around the country.

While educated women might seemingly have had an advantage over their less-educated sisters, their opportunities in the United States were initially limited. Many had the skills necessary to succeed in the labor market, but they had neither the experience nor the language fluency their employers required. English-fluency was critical in occupations such as teaching, library science, and office work that dealt with the general public. Although many women studied English as part of the school curriculum in Cuba, few were sufficiently fluent to hold such visible jobs. Professions such as law, medicine, engineering, and the sciences also required that they pass qualifying examinations before entering into practice. Preparation for these exams involved additional coursework, and with families to support, children to raise, and households to manage, few women could invest time or money in preparing for these exams. It was not uncommon, therefore, to find educated women working in factories and service occupations, regardless of their being overqualified. Like working-class women, they took whatever employment was available to ensure the economic security of their families.

As each year decreased their chances of returning to Cuba, women began to work towards improving the quality of their lives in the United States. Many returned to school to either revalidate their professional credentials or train for a more marketable career, accommodating language courses and college curriculums into their busy schedules.

To assist each other in these efforts, women helped found and maintain professional organizations that served as clearinghouses of information on job and educational opportunities. These organizations served emigrés—both women and men—in multiple ways: they served as forums for the scholarly discussion of ideas and lobbied for various political and professional interests before the state legislature; but most importantly they served as support networks of colleagues, experiencing similar sets of problems and challenges who assisted each other in reestablishing their careers in the United States. In most of these organizations, however, women comprised a minority, reflecting the realities of the profession itself; the associations of exile doctors and lawyers, for example, always had a predominantly male membership. In other organizations, such as the *Colegio Nacional de Bibliotecarios en el Exilio* for librarians, and the *Colegio Nacional de Farmacéuticos en el Exilio* for pharmacists, women comprised at least half of the membership, since these professions were traditionally open to women.

El exilio taught women to be resourceful and to work together within their families, neighborhoods, and community. As their spheres of responsibility expanded, they found new and innovative ways of balancing the work at home with the workplace. Out of their common need, they created networks of family, friends, and neighbors to exchange services: they took care of each other's children and took turns doing the grocery shopping; they served as interpreters for one another; and some even shared the expenses of major appliances, which they traded from house to house. Elderly women, in particular, played a crucial role in this community; in three-generation households, the elderly supplied an additional income from either their outside employment or from public assistance (Pérez spring 1986, 13-16). More importantly, they played a crucial role in child rearing and home maintenance, allowing their daughters, granddaughters, and neighbors to go out and find work. These networks of family and friends were crucial to the working woman, since although women expanded their roles to include wage earning, their spouses did not expand their roles to include housework.

Some entrepreneurial women turned these services into lucrative businesses, catering to the needs of women who entered the workplace: they created daycare centers, housekeeping and delivery services, laundries and dry cleaners, home ateliers and dress shops, beauty parlors, and even driving schools. Cubans discovered that any business that made life easier for the working woman had a good chance of succeeding. Some of the most successful businesses founded on this principle, for example, were the *cantinas:* subscription home-delivery food services, which brought hot meals of lechón asado, boliche, arroz con pollo and other Cuban specialties every evening to homes throughout the city. While cantinas existed in pre-revolutionary Cuba, they were never as popular as in Miami or in other Cuban enclaves. Women with little time or energy to prepare large family meals gave their patronage to the cantinas; these allowed them to spend time with their families while enjoying the traditional meals that they were accustomed to. Over time, as more and more women went out into the workplace and remained there, these and other Cuban-owned businesses thrived and became permanent fixtures in the community: reminders of the impact of emigration on women's roles.

While women's participation in the labor force had a notable impact on the economic success of both their families and the larger community, their participation in the political activities of the community was less obvious.

During the first decade, exile politics were concerned more with Cuba than with the United States. Hundreds of political organizations emerged in Miami, Union City, New York, Los Angeles, and Chicago to lead the counterrevolution, so many organizations that even the State Department was unable to catalogue all the groups and their activities (García 1990, 178-206). The only factor these groups shared in common was their opposition to the Castro government; each, however, promoted a different political agenda for Cuba. Exile political groups employed different strategies in the war against Castro: they published reports and documents that discredited the government; they organized rallies, marches, and demonstrations; they lobbied for stronger trade and diplomatic policies against Cuba; and a small number even trained and equipped men for covert paramilitary actions against the island.

Women, for the most part, were excluded from these organizations, since politics was considered male domain. The vast majority of women were also too preoccupied with domestic and economic responsibilities to be full-time advocates of la causa cubana. While men concerned themselves with revolution and with returning to Cuba, women concerned themselves with "exile" and with the here and now—raising their families, providing an additional income, and managing household resources to make ends meet. If men were able to dedicate time to these political commitments, it was usually because women carried more than their share of the domestic burdens.

Women were just as concerned about their homeland, but tradition cast them into a marginal and supportive role. They could always be counted on to do the thankless and tedious work of sewing or painting banners, preparing food for protesters at demonstrations, writing letters and making phone calls, and marching in demonstrations. As important consumers, they were periodically called upon to boycott products of countries that traded with Cuba, or as one exile newspaper put it, to serve as "economic guerrillas." Women may not have donned military garb and trained in the Everglades, or lobbied congressmen and foreign dignitaries, or shared in the political decision making, but they provided the community support structure that was vital to this campaign.

There were exceptions. A handful of political organizations emerged that were exclusively for women, among them the *Unión de Mujeres*, the *Cruzada Femenina Cubana*, the *Movimiento Femenino Anticomunista de Cuba*, and the *Organización de Damas Anticomunistas Cubanas*. These organizations, however, offered no real political alternatives. They functioned as auxiliaries and provided moral and financial support to different men's organizations by participating in their rallies and fundraisers, organizing public relations campaigns and membership drives, and even sponsoring memorial services for the men who died for *la causa*. While women's political organizations drew little attention and were overshadowed by the more vocal male organizations, they served an important purpose: they provided women with a forum of their own where they could seriously and freely discuss questions and ideas, as well as their hopes and fears about life in exile. Through these organizations women exercised their political voice and offered support to the campaign against Castro.

Younger women, particularly those studying at colleges and universities, tended to have greater opportunities for political expression than their mothers. Influenced by the civil rights movement, the feminist movement, and the student activism of the 1960s and early 1970s, they joined various student political groups and staged protests and demonstrations. Some of these younger women, influenced by the radicalized milieu of the sixties, came to adopt a more tolerant view of the revolution and began to work for the normalization of relations between both countries. Women also played key editorial roles in such political journals of the seventies as *Areíto, Nueva Generación, Joven Cuba, Krisis*, and ¡*Cuba Va*! which analyzed la problemática cubana and the plight of Cubans in the United States.

By the early 1970s, most political organizations dissolved as emigrés became frustrated with their inability to alter the social and political realities in Cuba. The growing apathy did not signify an increasing tolerance for the Castro regime, but rather a growing intolerance for the infighting and the political intrigues that characterized exile politics. Emigrés abandoned these organizations and concentrated instead on improving their lives in the United States. Petitions for citizenship increased significantly during the seventies. As the emigrés bought homes, paid taxes, and sent their children to school, they developed ties to their communities in spite of their original intentions; citizenship became a logical step in this accommodation. Of the hundreds of organizations that emerged during the 1960s, only a handful persisted into the 1980s, each with a substantially smaller membership.

One political issue, however, continued to evoke passionate response in the community: the plight of political prisoners in Cuba. While emigrés disagreed on many things and political organizations evolved and dissolved, the issue of human rights in Cuba transcended the various ideologies and factions. Numerous coalitions emerged, dedicated to calling world attention to the plight of political prisoners in Cuba. Perhaps the most notable of these groups is the nonprofit organization, Of Human Rights, founded in 1961 by Elena Mederos González (1900-1981) at Georgetown University in Washington, D.C., to monitor human rights abuses in Cuba. For over twenty years this organization evaluated the Cuban scene and published annual reports, which were sent to congressional leaders, journalists, and universities around the United States. Other groups included the "Committee to Denounce Cruelties to Cuban Political Prisoners," the *Centro de Derechos Humanos del Movimiento Demócrata Cristiano*, and *El Movimiento Mujeres Pro-Derechos Humanos*.

Women played a crucial role in this political campaign, since it was their fathers, husbands, sons—and sisters—who were imprisoned in Cuba. They wrote letters and sent petitions to Amnesty International, Americas Watch, the International Red Cross, and the P.E.N. clubs; they met with presidents, congressmen, and foreign dignitaries; and they held press conferences with writers and journalists. They organized fund-raising banquets to raise money for their publicity campaign; they arranged special memorial services to pray for the prisoners; and they helped erect monuments honoring the prisoners in parks and public areas, to keep them in the community's consciousness. It took years, however, to see the fruits of their work; it was not until the late 1970s and early 1980s that the Castro government finally began to release thousands of political prisoners.

The case of Martha Valladares, wife of political prisoner Armando Valladares, best illustrates the frustrating and lengthy process most family members endured. From the moment she arrived in the United States in 1969, Martha Valladares worked unceasingly on her husband's behalf; she wrote letters, gave interviews, met with government officials both in the United States and abroad, and even persuaded French president François Mitterand to personally intercede. She collected and published her husband's poetry, which was smuggled out of Cuba, and personally promoted his creative work in Europe and Latin America to call attention to his condition and that of other political prisoners. International pressure finally forced the Cuban government to reevaluate her husband's case. Armando Valladares, internationally acclaimed poet and author, was finally reunited with his wife in Paris in 1982 after twenty-two years in prison.

Not all who labored in this campaign had personal ties to the prisons in Cuba. One woman in Miami, Ester Martínez, with no relatives in prison herself, founded the House of the Cuban Ex-Political Prisoner to provide temporary food, clothing, and lodging to recently released prisoners who had no relatives in the United States (Zaldivar 1980, 14-15). Women, in particular, were drawn to this cause, because it represented family reunification. In lobbying for the release of political prisoners, they worked for the reunion of husbands and wives, parents and children. This cause also provided them with a socially acceptable forum for political expression: women could express their dissent against the Castro government in a dignified way, without succumbing to the messy brawls of other political organizations. While men's organizations struggled for power and fought over leadership and abstract ideologies, this cause concerned itself with the welfare of others and demanded selfless dedication and cooperation, traits culturally associated with their gender.

If judged by male standards, then, women had a limited participation in exile politics during the 1960s and 1970s. They were excluded from the more important political organizations; they created few viable organizations of their own, which received neither media attention nor funding; and few women ever emerged as prominent spokespersons for the political interests of the community. Women's participation, however, must be evaluated on its own terms, especially in light of the social obstacles they encountered. While women exercised a greater economic role in this community than in the homeland, they were still not regarded as the intellectual equals of men, and hence were not consulted in any political decision making. Politics was also not considered a respectable forum for women, since it involved competition, debate, and bargaining, and so men felt justified in excluding them from their activities. In spite of these obstacles, women found numerous ways of expressing their opinions and of working for their political ideals. However, because they worked in supportive and cooperative roles rather than leadership positions, their contributions remained anonymous. Their work was not any less significant than the men's, but they received few rewards and no glory.

Despite these social obstacles, during the 1980s a number of women distinguished themselves in local politics, serving in Miami's city government. One woman, Republican Ileana Ros-Lehtinen, was elected to fill the House seat long held by the late Democratic congressman Claude Pepper. Ironically, as women were excluded from exile politics, they carved a niche for themselves in ethnic politics, that is, the domestic policy making of their city. Working with other racial and ethnic groups, they addressed issues of importance to the community as a whole: issues such as crime, racism, education, taxes, utilities, and urban development. As representatives of the Cuban community at the local level, they also addressed issues of specific importance to their fellow emigrés.

Cuban women were perhaps most influential in cultural matters, specifically preserving *cubanidad*, or those customs, values, and traditions associated with being Cuban. Preserving *cubanidad* became a cultural mission in the emigré community: an attempt to preserve those values they regarded important for the distant day when repatriation became possible. Over time, however, as the exiles resigned themselves to a lengthy, if not permanent stay in the United States, preserving *cubanidad* became important to establish the cultural boundaries which would allow the Cubans to survive as a distinct community.

Women reinforced *cubanidad* at both the family and community levels. As parents they were traditionally responsible for instilling cultural values in their children and grandchildren, making sure that they learned to speak Spanish as well as appreciate their cultural heritage. With this goal in mind, they established after-school programs in churches, schools, and community centers to teach children the basics of Cuban history, geography, and culture for a few hours each day. On the community level women created cultural organizations that sponsored activities for the general public, such as lectures and seminars, literary contests, scholarship programs, variety shows, festivals, and parades to encourage study and pride in *la tradición nacional.*

One of the oldest and most respected of such organizations is the *Cruzada Educativa Cubana,* founded in 1962 by Dr. María Gómez Carbonell. The Cruzada sponsored an annual Cuban Culture Day in Miami each November 25, during which they presented the Juan J. Remos Award in recognition of the cultural and educational contributions of Cuban exiles. On July 11, they commemorated Cuban Teacher Day, during which they presented the José de la Luz y Caballero Award, named after the renowned nineteenth-century Cuban teacher and philosopher. During the sixties, the Cruzada also sponsored a Spanish-language radio program called "La Escuelita Cubana," written and narrated by Gómez Carbonell, which discussed important people and events in Cuban history.

Cultural organizations were never exclusively created for women, but because of the traditional association of "culture" with the female sphere, women outnumbered men in most of these groups. Ironically these organizations provided women with yet another forum for political expression, since preserving *cubanidad* was as much a political statement as a celebration of the cultural heritage. In sponsoring lectures and concerts, as well as in observing significant events of Cuban history, they promoted an appreciation and assertion of national values and ideals. Every cultural activity became a celebration of the past and a symbolic indictment of the present realities in Cuba. Men who took part in the organizations were usually attracted by the political overtones of the activities. Women, on the other hand, were attracted by the commitment to family and education. That the organizations provided a socially acceptable forum for the promotion of their political ideals was an added benefit.

In their mission to preserve *cubanidad*, women also published newspapers and magazines, wrote essays, articles, and editorials for the Cuban exile press, and a small few even had their own radio and television shows. Through these media, they educated the public on a variety of cultural and historical topics; they entertained them with stories and interviews; and they offered them practical advice about life in exile. Women, however, did not achieve as visible a representation in journalism, radio, and television as they did in cultural organizations, since men dominated the communications media. Of a sample of 665 periodicals published by Cuban exiles during the past thirty years and housed at the Cuban Exile Archives of the University of Miami, roughly 10 percent were published, edited, or directed by women (see Varona 1987). The percentage of female contributors varied, however, depending on the type of publication; political newspapers employed few or no women, while the so-called women's magazines usually had a predominantly female staff.

The impact of exile on women's roles, as well as on their interests and concerns, can be traced in these periodicals. About half of the newspapers and magazines published by women during 1959 to 1973, for example, focused on traditionally "female topics": homemaking, child rearing, fashions, and entertainment. Women's publications in Cuba prior to the revolution focused on the same topics (see Valdés 1982). By the late 1970s, however, women had expanded their participation in the community, and consequently their periodicals began to address nontraditional topics. Women demanded more than just homemaking tips or advice on how to raise good Cuban children; they also needed information on job and educational opportunities, the economy, international affairs, and community services. Significantly, over two-thirds of the periodicals directed by women in exile were published after 1973, when direct emigration from Cuba ceased. By this date most Cuban emigrés had established new homes and careers in the United States and had adapted their lives to the realities of exile. After 1973 women directed small local newspapers such as *La Prensa Comunitaria, Las Noticias de Hialeah,* and *Broward Latino,* which informed Spanish-speaking residents on community events and provided city and county news. They published business and professional newsletters; and a small number even published political tabloids.

As their spheres of influence expanded, women also demanded more of their organizations. The Cuban Women's Club, for example, founded in 1969 as a social club for middle-class women, diversified its activities to retain the participation of its wage-earning members (Niurka 1978, 8). Modeled after the elite *Liceo Cubano* in Havana, the Cuban Women's Club sponsored social and cultural activities such as luncheons, conferences, art exhibitions, and literary contests. Members also became actively involved in local

Cuban-American playwright Dolores Prida.

charities and fund-raising activities, just as women of their social class were expected to do in Cuba. By the mid-1970s however, members demanded that the club do more than just organize social and charitable events; they wanted the club to address issues pertinent to their careers and their new roles in society. By the late seventies, conferences addressed such issues as bilingual education, voting and political representation, salaries and the workplace. The CWC also expanded its membership to include women of the "new immigration" from Central and South America, who faced similar problems and challenges in the United States. The CWC ceased to be an exclusive Cuban social club; by 1980 it had over 300 members of various nationalities and professional and educational backgrounds.

Several business and professional organizations also emerged in south Florida during the 1970s and 1980s, reflecting women's permanent shift into the workplace. Groups such as the *Comité de Mujeres Latinas*, the *Latin Business and Professional Women's Club*, and the *Coalition of Hispanic American Women* were created by younger women, graduates of American colleges and universities who regarded themselves as Cuban Americans as well as Cuban exiles. Membership in these groups was not dependent on cubanidad; rather, since they shared the same interests and concerns as Anglo-American women and other Latinas, all women of the community were welcomed.

The Latin Business and Professional Women's Club was founded by Cuban women in 1969 as a local chap-

Cuban-American novelist, Margarita Engle.

ter of the National Federation of Business and Professional Women's Clubs, the oldest women's organization in the nation, which encourages women's political and professional development. As a chapter of a national women's organization, the LBPWC promotes a broader agenda. Most of their local dues go to underwrite the work of lobbyists in Washington, who promote such issues as child care legislation and women's rights to abortion. The LBPWC is a good example of how Cuban emigré women have begun to place their concerns within a broader spectrum and have begun to perceive themselves as part of the American mainstream.

The Coalition of Hispanic American Women was founded in 1979 by former members of the LBPWC, who wanted to create a women's organization that focused entirely on the local community in south Florida. Both CHAW and the LBPWC address the problems all women in the American work force face: unequal pay, inadequate child care, discrimination, and sexual harassment. Their workshops teach women how to have equal access to education, social services, and the judicial system. However, they also discuss issues relevant to the larger Latino community as well: bilingual education, immigration reform, affirmative action, and domestic violence. Both organizations sponsor a scholarship program to assist needy students attend college. CHAW also sponsors a "Spanish seminar" for women who have recently immigrated to south Florida and need assistance in finding employment and in learning English. Today young business and professional women raised in bilingual and bicultural settings such as Miami are more apt to join organizations such as CHAW and the LBPWC than those created by their mothers in the 1960s.

The exile experience, then, forced women to expand their participation in the community: in labor and the economy, in politics, and in the life of the community. To deal with the problems and challenges of life in a new country, they created social, familial, and professional networks that fostered a sense of community and strove to overcome the political divisions among emigrés. Women reconciled the past with the present and promoted an appreciation of the Cuban cultural heritage while contributing to their families' adaptation into the mainstream. They helped to create a strong and stable ethnic community with ties to two countries and two cultures.

While most women initially went out into the work force on a temporary basis, wage earning became a permanent part of their lives. They immigrated to the United States during a time when two-income households became a necessity for most American families and when the feminist movement made it socially acceptable for women to seek personal realization outside the home. As a consequence Cuban women continue to demonstrate high rates of participation in the work force; the largest proportion work in either clerical occupations or as factory workers (Pérez 1985, 16). Similar to other women in the general population, Cuban women earn less than Cuban men, but studies show that they earn more than any other female population in the United States (Pérez 1985, 14).

This shift in roles and responsibilities has had tremendous impact on the Cubans' economic "success" as a group; by 1980 their median family income was almost equal to that for the total U. S. population (Pérez summer 1986, 13). This was an important accomplishment for a community of predominantly first-generation immigrants. Women's high participation in the labor force played a crucial role in raising the median family income, and without their contributions these statistics would have been much different. Their participation also had negative social consequences, however, especially on the structure of the family; while their new roles brought them independence and power, it also strained marriages, since many men felt threatened by these nontraditional relationships. By 1980, census figures showed that Cuban women also had the highest divorce rates in the United States: 9.3 percent of Cuban women fifteen years and older identified themselves as divorced in the 1980 census, as compared to 7.3 percent of the total U. S. population (Pérez summer 1986, 8-9).

The "Mariel" Migration

The Cuban migration of 1980, more popularly known as the "Mariel Boatlift," provides one of the most fascinating case studies in recent immigration history, not only for the circumstances of the migration, but for the controversy it engendered. In April 1980, in a renewed effort to externalize dissent, Fidel Castro opened up the port of Mariel and invited Cuban emigrés in the United States to sail to Cuba to pick up their relatives. Thousands of emigrés took advantage of the opportunity and sailed to Cuba on yachts, sailboats, shrimpers, and even freighters, hoping to bring their relatives back with them to the United States. 124,776 Cubans were transported to the United States, from April to October 1980 (Bowen 1980, 78). More than half the people who arrived in the United States had no friends or relatives, however. For every relative the emigrés brought back with them, they were forced to carry at least a dozen others who were total strangers. The Cuban government used the boatlift as a means of exporting the discontented as well as all those who they believed posed a threat to their society.

The Cubans of Mariel differed from the Cubans who arrived during the earlier migrations in age, place of origin, race, and sex. The Mariel population was younger by about ten years (averaging thirty years of age), contained a higher percentage of blacks and mulattoes (roughly 20 percent), and reflected a wider geographic distribution (Boswell, Rivero, and Díaz 1988, 1-22). Unlike the 1965-73 migration, this migration was predominantly male: almost 70 percent (Boswell, Rivero, and Díaz 1988, 5). Despite these socioeconomic differences, the Cubans of Mariel had much in common with the working-class Cubans who emigrated during the final years of the "freedom flights," especially in their occupational history: they were predominantly craftworkers and factory operators, followed by professional and technical workers (Bach, Bach, and Triplett 1981-82, 29-48; Portes, Clark, and Manning 1985, 37-59).

The Mariel migration was most distinctive, however, in how it was perceived by the federal government and the larger society. Unlike the Cubans who immigrated from 1959 to 1973, the Cubans of Mariel were not regarded as legitimate refugees. Although the overwhelming majority cited political reasons for their emigration (Portes, Clark, and Manning 1985, 42), federal authorities determined that under the terms of the 1980 U. S. Refugee Act, the Cubans did not qualify for refugee status nor for the special assistance this status bestowed. Instead the government granted the Cubans a temporary "entrant" status, which allowed them to stay in the United States, to seek employment, and receive a limited amount of public assistance, but they were not entitled to the benefits received by their compatriots under the Cuban Refugee Program, nor were they entitled to the same rights as permanent residents or citizens. For the next four years, the Cubans' legal status remained undefined. It was not until December 1984 that the federal government finally determined that the Cubans of Mariel qualified for U. S. citizenship.

Public opinion, however, had long turned against the Cubans of Mariel. During the first months of the migration, the press uncovered Castro's plot to rid the island of its "undesirables"–persons with criminal records, patients from mental asylums, prostitutes, drug addicts, vagrants, alcoholics, and homosexuals–and the American public recoiled in horror. Some press reports estimated that as many as 26,000 of the Mariel immigrants had criminal records, and letters poured into the White House from all over the country demanding that the Mariel Cubans be expelled from the United States. Americans not only feared for their security but resented that the new immigrants would be over-represented on the relief rolls. The Cubans had arrived during one of the most serious economic recessions of the past thirty years, and they would most probably require extensive public assistance. Americans did not want to have to compete with the "dregs of Cuban society" for limited resources and employment opportunities.

While the presence of so many criminal offenders was indeed alarming, the press greatly exaggerated their numbers. According to most government estimates, from 2,000 to 5,000 (or less than 4 percent of the roughly 125,000 immigrants) had committed serious felonies in Cuba (Boswell, Rivero, and Díaz 1988, 3); and the U. S. Immigration and Naturalization Service detained over 1,000 of the more serious cases to await deportation. The overwhelming majority of Cubans with criminal records served time for lesser crimes, such as stealing food or trading on the black market, or for "crimes" which were not even recognized in the United States. Under Cuba's *ley de peligrosidad,* Cubans could be incarcerated for any form of "social deviancy" such as drug addiction or homosexuality.

Americans failed to understand the true social composition of the Mariel migration: that the vast majority of the new immigrants were decent, law-abiding citizens who simply wanted better economic opportunities and the ability to enjoy social and political freedoms. Instead Americans bitterly accused the Carter administration of allowing the United States to become the dumping ground for Cuba's criminals. They pointed to the rising crime rates in cities where the Cubans settled. In Miami in 1980 alone, crime rose 66 percent, and one-third of those arrested for murder were Cubans who arrived during the boatlift (Ojito and Román 1990, 8).

The Cubans of Mariel were caught in the middle of this controversy. Wanted neither by their homeland nor their host society, they were discriminated against in housing and employment and in social situations. Offers for sponsorship dropped radically after news of the criminal element was published. While the exile community of south Florida responded generously at first, raising millions of dollars for relief and resettlement efforts, many emigrés also turned against their compatriots, afraid that their golden reputations might be tarnished. Between these Cubans and the earlier emigrés lay twenty years of social and ideological differences, and the older emigrés worried that the new immigrants would never adapt to this democratic and capitalistic society. As news of the criminal element spread, emigrés also became reluctant to sponsor the Cubans and even to offer them jobs. They coined a special term—*marielito*—to distinguish themselves from the new arrivals, a term that quickly became a pejorative in the community.

Among the new immigrants, women and children fared better—at least in finding sponsors. In general American sponsors were more apt to open their homes to single women, or to families, rather than to the young single males who comprised the majority of the arrivals. Although an in-depth study of their accommodation has yet to be completed, it is probable that the women of Mariel encountered less difficulty in finding employment than their male counterparts. Over the past thirty years the garment industry and the service sector has readily absorbed a large percentage of the female immigrants who arrived in south Florida from the Caribbean and Latin America. Given the marielitos' notoriety, it is also probable that employers were more willing to hire women than men because they were regarded as "safer." Like their sisters who arrived in earlier periods, the women of Mariel found their first jobs as domestics, seamstresses, cooks, dishwashers, waitresses, and in other service occupations.

Having lived for twenty years in revolutionary Cuba, women were accustomed to playing many roles: they raised families and worked outside the home; they participated in their neighborhood "Committee for the Defense of the Revolution" (CDR); and during times of economic austerity, they provided volunteer labor in factories and rural areas. Those who settled in south Florida settled in a community where women also had a high participation in the labor force and where they were politically conscious and played an active role in the cultural life of their community. Thus, while the economic and political systems in which they functioned were different, their experiences were fairly compatible. Unlike their sisters, however, the women of Mariel did not have to assume new roles; rather, they had to adapt to the new context in which these roles were performed.

Women who had friends or relatives in the United States adapted more readily to their new environment, benefiting from the experience of the older emigrés. They could count on this familial network to help them find work, a place to live, and schools for their children. The network provided them with contacts when they had questions or problems, and they had friends to talk to when they felt angry, bewildered, or frustrated. Thus they were more easily absorbed into the enclave. Women with no friends or relatives in the United States, on the other hand, felt helpless and alienated. Apart from the trauma of having to adapt to a new society, they had to live with the contempt of their Cuban and American neighbors. They were more likely to remain unemployed and less likely to feel personal fulfillment in their new lives.

In 1990 the Cubans of Mariel celebrated their tenth anniversary in the United States. Despite the tremendous odds against them, they have made modest economic gains and revealed the same democratic and entrepreneurial spirit as the earlier emigrés. By 1986 over one-fourth of the immigrants were self-employed; and in a three-year period, from 1983 to 1986, their unemployment had been halved, from 27 percent to 13.6 percent. By 1990, 5.6 percent were unemployed, a figure comparable to the rest of the nation (Reveron 1990, 4). A survey in April 1990, sponsored by the *Miami Herald* and WTVJ-Channel 4, revealed that the Cubans of Mariel were much like their compatriots politically, as well. They strongly opposed ending the U. S. trade embargo against Cuba; and they strongly identified with the Republican party (Santiago 1990, 1). Only a small percentage of the Mariel Cubans actually voted, however, since less than 15 percent had become naturalized.

Over the past ten years the emigré community has developed a grudging respect for the Cubans of Mariel. The term marielito has slowly ceased to be a pejorative, and among some immigrants it is even used for self-identification, as a symbol of pride. The Mariel generation has exhibited great solidarity in the face of public hostility. Bound together by a common experience, they have revitalized the cultural landscape, strengthening the use of Spanish in the community and reintroducing customs and traditions the older emigrés had forgotten.

Bibliography

Aguirre, Benigno E.
1976 "Differential Migration of Cuban Social Races: A Review and Interpretation of the Problem." *Latin American Research Review*, 11:103-24.

Arboleya, Carlos
1980 "The Cuban Community, 1980." Records of the Cuban-Haitian Task Force, Jimmy Carter Library, Atlanta.

Bach, Robert L., Jennifer B. Bach, and Timothy Triplett
July 1981-January 1982 "The Flotilla 'Entrants': Latest and Most Controversial." *Cuban Studies/Estudios Cubanos*, 11/12:28-48.

Boswell, Thomas D., Manuel Rivero, and Guarioné M. Díaz, eds.
1988 *Bibliography for the Mariel-Cuba Diaspora.* Paper No. 7. Gainesville: Center for Latin American Studies, U of Florida.

Bowen, Robert, ed.
1980 *A Report of the Cuban-Haitian Task Force.* Washington, DC: Cuban-Haitian Task Force (November 1). Records of the Cuban-Haitian Task Force, Jimmy Carter Library, Atlanta.

Casal, Lourdes, and Yolanda Prieto
1981 "Black Cubans in the United States: Basic Demographic Information." In *Female Immigrants to the United States: Caribbean, Latin American, and African Experiences.* Eds Delores M. Mortimer and Roy S. Bryce-LaPorte. RIIES Occasional Papers No. 2, Research Institute on Immigration and Ethnic Studies, Smithsonian Institution, Washington, DC.

Censos de población, viviendas y electoral, informe general República de Cuba
1953

Cortázar, Mercedes
1990 "Contactos profesionales." *El Nuevo Herald*, pp C1, C8.

Estrade, Paul
1987 "Los clubes femeninos en el Partido Revolucionario Cubano (1892-1898)." *Anuario del Centro de Estudios Martianos*, 10:175-201.

Ferree, Myra Marx
1979 "Employment without Liberation: Cuban Women in the United States." *Social Science Quarterly*, 60:35-50.

García, María Cristina
1990 "Cuban Exiles and Cuban Americans: A History of an Immigrant Community in South Florida." PhD Diss Austin: U of Texas

Hewitt, Nancy A.
1985 "Workers' Culture and Women's Culture: Class and Gender in Ybor City." Paper presented at the Oral History Association Conference, Pensacola, October 31-November 2.
1987 "Cuban Women and Work: Tampa, Florida, 1895-1901." Paper presented at the meeting of the American Historical Association, Washington, DC, (December 29).

Mariña, Dorita Roca
1978 "A Theoretical Discussion of What Changes and What Stays the Same in Cuban Immigrant Families." *Cuban Americans: Acculturation, Adjustment and the Family.* Eds José Szapocznik and María Cristina Herrera. Washington, DC: The National Coalition of Hispanic Mental Health and Human Services Organization.

Mormino, Gary R.
1982 "Tampa and the New Urban South: The Weight Strike of 1899." *Florida Historical Quarterly*, 60:337-56.

Niurka, Norma
1978 "La mujer cubana en la encrucijada: Una entrevista con María Hernández." *El Miami Herald.* (March 11):8.

Ojito, Mirta, and Iván Román
1990 "Exito y progreso de los refugiados." *El Nuevo Herald*, p A1.

Pedraza-Bailey, Silvia
1985 "Cuba's Exiles: Portrait of a Refugee Migration," *International Migration Review*, 19:4-33.

Pérez, Lisandro
1985 "The Cuban Population of the United States: The Results of the 1980 U. S. Census of Population." *Cuban Studies*, 15:1-18.
1986a "Cubans in the United States." *The Annals of the American Academy of Political and Social Science*, 487:126-37.
1986b "Immigrant Economic Adjustment and Family Organization: The Cuban Success Story." *International Migration Review*, 20:4-21.

Pérez, Louis A.
1978 "Cubans in Tampa: From Exiles to Immigrants, 1892-1901." *Florida Historical Quarterly*, 57:129-40.

Portes, Alejandro, Juan M. Clark, and Robert D. Manning
1985 "After Mariel: A Survey of the Resettlement Experience of the 1980 Cuban Refugees in Miami." *Cuban Studies/Estudios Cubanos*, 15:37-59.

Poyo, Gerald E.
1979 "Key West and the Cuban Ten Years War." *Florida Historical Quarterly*, 57:289-307.
1986 "The Impact of Cuban and Spanish Workers on Labor Organizing in Florida, 1870-1900." *Journal of American Ethnic History*, vol 5.

Prieto, Yolanda
1977 "Women, Work, and Change: The Case of Cuban Women in the U. S." *Latin American Monograph Series*, Northwestern Pennsylvania Institute for Latin American Studies, Mercyhurst College.
1984 "Reinterpreting an Immigration Success Story: Cuban Women, Work, and Change in a New Jersey Community." PhD Diss New Brunswick, NJ: Rutgers U.

Prohías, Rafael J., and Lourdes Casal
1973 *The Cuban Minority in the U. S.: Preliminary Report on Need Identification and Program Evaluation.* Boca Raton, FL: Florida Atlantic U.

Reveron, Derek
1990 "Se disipó el temor de que refugiados fueran cargas." *El Nuevo Herald*, p B4.

Santiago, Ana E.
1990 "Volverían a Cuba los de Mariel?" *El Nuevo Herald*, pp A1, A14.

Sullivan, Teresa
1984 "The Occupational Prestige of Women Immigrants: A Comparison of Cubans and Mexicans." *International Migration Review*, 18.4:1045-1062.
1968 *Training for Independence: A New Approach to the Problems of Dependency.* U. S. Cuban Refugee Program, Social and Rehabilitation Service.

Valdés, Nelso P.
1982 "A Bibliography of Cuban Periodicals Related to Women." *Cuban Studies/Estudios Cubanos*, 22:73-80.

Varona, Esperanza B.
1987 *Cuban Exile Periodicals at the University of Miami Library: An Annotated Bibliography.* Madison, WI: SALALM.

Walsh, Bryan O.
1966 "Cubans in Miami." *America*, 114:286-89.

Zaldivar, Raquel Puig
1980 "Freedom to Suffer." *Nuestro*, pp 14-15.

Historical Vignettes of Puerto Rican Women Workers in New York City, 1895-1990

Altagracia Ortiz

Introduction

In 1951 Matilde Rodríguez Torres sold her four-poster, mahogany bed (her most treasured possession), the rest of her simple furnishings, her pigs and poultry, and her small, wooden house in the town of Cayey, Puerto Rico, and with her five children came to New York City to join her husband. Although she expected to be just a housewife when she emigrated to this city, she found herself working both at home and in different garment factories throughout her life in New York. "Doña Matí," as her friends and customers called her, was an expert seamstress, so during the 1950s and 1960s she did not have difficulties finding employment when she needed it. In the meantime, as a working mother she knew all too well the burdens of the "double-shift." Even though she had trained all of her children and a niece to help with the housework, she ultimately felt responsible for the running of the household. After working eight, sometimes nine hours, she would come home and surpervise the evening meal or prepare the next day's supper, wash clothes in her bathtub and hang them to dry on a clothesline outside her kitchen window. During the weekends with her daughters' help, she shopped, cleaned house, and ironed. In the 1970s when garment factories began to close, she sold Avon products, jewelry, and even *bolita* (illegal numbers) to help support her family. As she grew older in spite of advanced osteoporosis, painful arthritis, colon cancer, and a bad heart condition, she continued to emotionally take care of her adult children, babysit her grandchildren, and keep house for her husband. For almost 40 years, Matilde Rodríguez Torres was a paid and unpaid Puerto Rican worker in New York City. In 1990 she returned one last time to her hometown on the island, and died there two years later, amid the white and purple orchids she had recently begun to grow.

The story of Matilde Rodríguez Torres, my mother, is but one of the many stories of women who migrated from Puerto Rico to the United States in the last 100 years in search of a better economic life. There are countless others, not only of Puerto Rican women (*puertorriqueñas*) from the island, whose personal and working lives have been transformed by the migration experience, but of U. S.-born puertorriqueñas who have worked for wages at different jobs and for no pay at maintaining links with their families, communities, and cultural heritage. And, then there are the stories of women who are prevented from earning sufficient incomes because of unemployment, underemployment, or social conditions (i.e., lack of adequate English-language skills, education, childcare), and are forced to depend on public assistance or *chiripeo* (informal economic activities) to help their families survive. The lives of these women are separated by different eras, class distinctions, racial backgrounds, sexual orientations, opposing social, religious, and political ideologies, and sometimes by contrasting cultural environments—since some of these "new ricans," or Puerto Rican Americans also come from ethnically mixed families. Nevertheless, these lives are joined together by a unique migration history that gives meaning to their individual stories and binds their experiences in a very special way. Only a few of these stories have been recorded so far, mainly in the form of oral histories and biographical sketches. Coupled with emerging empirical social science research, however, these personal narratives allow for a reconstruction of the work history of puertorriqueñas that already illuminate certain patterns as their story unfolds in this country. Some of these patterns bind them to other women's experiences—particularly to other immigrant women, who like them, have struggled throughout the century in households and factories. Other trends speak solely of the reality of puertorriqueñas, since their labor history has been so inexorably tied to the colonial manifestations on their island, a territorial possession of the United States.

This relationship between Puerto Rican women's work and North American colonialism began immediately after the occupation of the island by Yankee troops in 1898, when Puerto Rico's economy experienced a period of expansion and slight diversification caused by infusions of U. S. capital. As a result of these economic changes greater numbers of women entered the paid labor force. In addition to their traditional jobs as domestics and farmhands, women now were employed as hat makers, needleworkers, and tobacco strippers (Colón-Warren et al. 1986; González Garciá 1990; Tirado 1989-1990). But, these increased employment opportunities did not tremendously improve work conditions for women on the island in the years that followed; women continued to work long hours, sometimes in very unhealthy conditions (as was the case in the tobacco industry), for extremely low wages in a sex-segregated labor market (Rivera 1986). The economic crisis of the 1930s in Puerto Rico, in the meantime, not only reduced the number of jobs available to women but also worsened work conditions for them, as evidenced by Caroline Manning's 1934 report on *The Employment of Women in Puerto Rico*, which exposed the oppression of workers in various trades (Manning 1934; Baerga 1989). After World War II the Puerto Rican government, still under U. S. tutelage, attempted to rejuvenate the island's economy by wooing more North American-owned, labor-intensive industries, a policy change resulting in the introduction of establishments that largely employed women. This increase in jobs, however, did not result in comparatively higher wages, greater employment opportunities, or better working conditions for women (Acevedo 1990; Acosta-Belén 1986; A. Ortiz, forthcoming), although, as on scholar has observed, gender discrimination in the workplace has declined somewhat since 1950 (Ríos 1990).

One response on the part of puertorriqueñas to the limitations imposed on them by the island's colonial economy has been to immigrate to the mainland of the U. S. in the hope of obtaining better employment opportunities. At the very beginning of the century, the number of women traveling to the U. S. was small, but as the economy of this country began to expand and demand more low-wage, semi-skilled labor in the 1920s, Puerto Rican women were drawn to industrial meccas, such as New York City, to fulfill the labor market needs of North American capitalists. Often they worked at home or in garment shops doing needlework for wages that were only a few pennies more than in those of homeworkers in Puerto Rico. But, during the Great Depression, as had been the case on the island, the wages of these workers were critical in keeping Puerto Rican communities alive in the city.

The economic boom that followed World War II brought about a large migration wave of puertorriqueñas that now included many more unskilled workers and housewives. The latter, like my mother, came expecting to take care of their children and depend on husbands for support but soon found that the financial needs of their families in this city required that they join the formal, paid labor force. Together with women who expressly came to find better employment opportunities here, they entered a sexually and racially segregated labor market, offered them only dirty, back-breaking, low-wage factory jobs. Most of these were in the garment industry, where Puerto Rican women quickly became the sustaining work force. By the early 1960s, however, this industry began to experience contractions and relocations, and over the next two decades puertorriqueñas were caught in web of factory job losses, increasing sub-contracting, declining wages and benefits, and competition from immigrant workers from other parts of Latin America, the Caribbean, and Asia who were forced to accept even lower wages and more horrendous work conditions. This essay provides some insights in the work experiences of Puerto Rican women in New York City, focusing specifically on the the contributions some of these workers made to the development of their communities and to the garment industry of this city. Parts of the essay also examine some of the problems working puertorriqueñas have encountered in New York City.

First Workers in America, 1890-1930

There is very little information on Puerto Rican migrant women who came to North America at the beginning of the twentieth century, but the biographical sketches of the more notable women who sailed to these shores during the period from 1895 to about 1935, and the statistical data presently available, provide an enlightening—even if limited—framework for the early history of Puerto Rican women workers in the United States (A. Ortiz 1989). The first women to arrive, for example, stayed in this country for periods of time, returned to Puerto Rico, and sometimes sojourned again in the United States. This pattern of circular migration was to become a major characteristic of Puerto Rican migrations to the mainland throughout the twentieth century (Hernández-Alvarez 1967). Many of these women were well educated, had extensive work experiences on the island, and even if they came for only brief periods of time, made an energetic commitment to the formation of a Puerto Rican community in New York City.

One of these migrant women was Lola Rodríguez de Tío, a woman who first migrated to New York City just before the turn of the century, when a Puerto Rican community hardly existed at all. Rodríguez de Tío, a leading poet in Puerto Rico, had been forced into exile because of her anticolonialist stance against Spain and her support of the movement for independence for the island (Mendoza de Tió 1975). In Puerto Rico she and her husband, Bonifacio Tío Segarra, a publisher and fellow poet, had entertained in their home many political revolutionaries, liberal reformers, and intellectuals; and it was presumably at one of their famous social gatherings that Rodríguez de Tío first recited her militant poem, "La Borinqueña" (Ribes Tovar 1976). Probably written in 1868 for Ramón Emeterio Betances, the leader of the unsuccessful Lares' Revolt of the same year, "La Borinqueña" was an unequivocal call to arms. In it Rodríguez de Tío demanded:

> ¡Despierta, borinqueño
> (Wake up, borinqueño),
> que han dado la señal
> (they have given the signal)!
> ¡Despierta de ese sueño
> (Wake up from your sleep)
> que es hora de luchar
> (it is time to fight)!
> ¡A ese llamar patriótico
> (When you hear the patriot's call),
> no arde tu corazón
> (doesn't your heart stir)?
> (Mendoza de Tió 1974)

Rodríguez de Tío's dedication to the cause of Puerto Rican and Cuban independence made her a very welcomed political worker among revolutionary exiles in New York City. Caribbean patriots, such as José Martí, Sotero Figueroa, Pachín Marín and Modesto A. Tirado, soon befriended her, and she ardently worked with them for the national liberation of Spain's last colonies in North America. In 1896 Rodríguez de Tío was made honorary president of one of the revolutionary political clubs in the city, *Club Político Ruis Rivera* and the following year she became secretary for another revolutionary group, *Club Caridad* (Cuevas 1969; Ribes Tovar 1972). And sometime before she left for Cuba in 1898, Rodríguez de Tío also helped found the *Liga Antillana* (Antillian League), an association of Cuban and Puerto Rican women tobacco workers. In 1903 she returned to New York one last time for an eye operation, yet still managed to find time to do cultural work by reciting some of her newest poems and playing some danzas puertorriqueñas, melodic piano waltzes of the times, by two of Puerto Rico's most famous composers, Manuel Tavares and Juan Morel Campos, to her friends in this city (Vega 1980).

Although Lola Rodríguez de Tío's two visits to New York were extremely short, her political and intellectual activities—especially readings from her poems—helped nourish the early social life of the city's nascent Puerto Rican community However, it was Rodríguez de Tío's struggle on behalf of independence for the Spanish Antilles and her spirited march "La Borinqueña" that have immortalized her among new generations of *independentistas* in the United States. "La Borinqueña," for example, is the rousing anthem that is played at many radical independentista and socialist meetings and conventions, instead of the officially more peaceful national anthem of Puerto Rico. There is also the story that when María Haydeé Torres, the celebrated political prisoner of the *Frente armado para la liberación nacional* (Armed Front for the National Liberation of Puerto Rico) (FALN), was being sentenced at one of her trials for the alleged bombing of a Mobil Oil building in 1977, she turned her back to the judge and sang Rodríguez de Tío's "La Borinqueña" (New Movement n.d.; *New York Times* 20 May 1980). The legacy of Rodríguez de Tío's political ideology and work, thus, continues to permeate the life of the Puerto Rican community in the United States.

Another Puerto Rican migrant woman who lived in the United States for only a couple of years, yet while here dedicated herself to the growth of the Hispanic community, was Luisa Capetillo. Like Rodríguez de Tío, Capetillo left a legacy of radicalism; but Capetillo's political ideology revolved more around the rights of labor and feminist issues than on the immediate liberation of Puerto Rico from colonial rule. Capetillo's commitment to improving the lives of Hispanic workers and of women in the United States, however, was no less important. Capetillo was born in Arecibo, a town on the northern coast of Puerto Rico, either in 1880 or 1882 to a French mother and a Spanish father. As a child she learned to read French fluently and had access to French and European socialist and naturalist writings, which helped shape her ideas about the value of men and women as workers and created in her a tremendous dedication to working class struggles in Puerto Rico (Azize 1985). Indeed, long before she arrived in the United States in 1912, Capetillo had established a reputation as a labor organizer and essayist throughout the island (Valle 1990). Around 1910 she began writing for the official organ of the *Federación Libre de los Trabajadores* (Free Federation of Workers), *Unión Obrera* (Workers' Union), and, conscious of the special needs of women workers, started a tabloid, which she simply called *La mujer* (The Woman), this same year (Azize 1985). In New York she collaborated in the publication of *Cultura obrera* (Workers' Culture) and other labor newspapers, and in 1913, while in Tampa, Florida, she worked for *La unión de Tampa* (The Tampa Union), where she continued to defend the rights of workers and women (Valle 1975). In Tampa she also wrote numerous treatises that later became part of one of her most famous works, *Influencias de las ideas modernas* (The Influence of Modern Ideas), and she published a second edition of a book that had originally been published in 1911, *Mi opinión sobre las libertades, derechos y deberes de la mujer: como compañera, madre y ser independentista* (*La mujer en el hogar, en la familia, en el gobierno)* (My Opinion on the Liberties and Responsibilities of Women: As Companion, Mother, and Individual [The Woman in the Home, the Family, and in Government]).

This publication, long regarded as one of the earliest tracts of feminist ideology in Puerto Rico, recognized that marriage "*tal como es*" (as it was then) was oppressive to women: brides had to be virgins, though grooms did not; wives had to be faithful, but husbands did not; and wives were always held responsible for the upkeep of the home and for sustaining the marriage. Capetillo opposed this oppression so intensely that, although she had four children by a man whom she must have loved "freely" (because she advocated this), she never married him. She also was one of the first supporters of divorce as a way out for a woman who found herself married to a husband who was not patient, sweet, loving, loyal, and helpful around the house. In this book, however, Capetillo gives plenty of advice to women on how to make their marriages more "harmonious"—certainly very contradictory advice considering her own negative ideas about this institution and her own style of life (Capetillo 1911). She chose to be independent financially, working hard all her life not only at writing and labor organizing, but by reading to cigar workers in tobacco factories, and during her final stay in New York in 1919 by providing room and board for migrant lodgers (Vega 1980).

Felisa Rincón Marrero de Gautier, who years later was elected mayor of San Juan, an office she held uninterruptedly from 1946 to 1968, was another early migrant worker in New York City. "Doña Felisa," as she came to be called by her political constituents, was born in Ceiba, Puerto Rico, in 1897. Her father, a lawyer, and her mother, a school teacher, both died when Rincón de Gautier was eleven and so she took on the responsibility of raising seven brothers and sisters. Having learned the skill of sewing from her mother at an early age, Rincón de Gautier became an expert seamstress who eventually developed a steady clientele of affluent customers (Ribes Tovar 1972). In the early 1930s she sailed to New York in order to learn more about the garment business. There she found employment as a cutter in a fashion shop on Fifth Avenue but soon returned to San Juan where she opened up her own dress shop (Gruber 1972). Rincón de Gautier visited New York several times after this, at first in connection with her dressmaking business and later as an influential political leader, but she did not reside in the United States again. Nonetheless, various North American organizations recognized her political and social work both on the island and on behalf of Puerto Ricans here: in 1954 the Union of American Women of New York awarded her the title Woman of the Americas; in 1958 and again in 1960 she was granted honorary degrees by Marymount College in Milwaukee and Temple University in Philadelphia, respectively; in 1961 New York City's Hebrew Philanthropic Federation bestowed on Rincón de Gautier the Madeleine Borg Award (Ribes Tovar 1972).

Pioneering Workers, 1920-1940

The contributions that many of these temporary migrant workers made to the origins and early development of the Puerto Rican community in New York City are invaluable, but those of women who came and established a permanent settlement of puertorriqueños in this city are truly historical prisms through which the socio-political and economic activities of the Puerto Rican people in this country can be traced. The life stories of four of these women—Victoria Hernández, probably the city's first music agent and entrepreneur; Carmela Marrero Zapata, the first Catholic nun from Puerto Rico to serve the expanding Latino settlement in Brooklyn; Pura Belpré, the first puertorriqueña employed by the New York Public Library to work in its East Harlem Branches; and Josefina Silva de Cintrón, a cultural and political leader among the Spanish-speaking people of the city—reflect the yearnings of a community desirous of social and cultural growth. The lives of these pioneering women workers vary greatly, but they were all united in their dedication to creating a Puerto Rican community that could be proud of its Latin American heritage and values. Clearly they were not "conventional women," as one biographer points out; they were all highly educated when compared to other women migrants of the times and they appear to have done more public work than other women of the period (Sánchez Korrol 1988). Nevertheless, they were women who decided—like many migrating *boricuas* (Puerto Ricans) during these years— to settle in this country and help build a new Puerto Rican nation in exile.

The first of these women to arrive in New York City was Victoria Hernández. Although the daughter of a poor Afro-Puerto Rican tobacco worker, she was raised by a grandmother who initiated her into the world of music from the time she was born. At an early age she learned to play the violin and cello, and when the family could afford a piano, she played this instrument, too. In 1919 she came to New York City with her two brothers, Rafael and Jesús. Both of her brothers went on to become successful performing artists, but Hernández chose to stay in the background and guide their careers. This decision was inspired by her belief that a professional musician had natural talents and romantic inclinations that she felt she lacked as a woman. Hernández, therefore, taught music to help support her brothers. But in 1927 she bought a small music store from a Jewish owner in East Harlem. By 1929 she advertised her business, *Casa Hernández,* as the only Puerto Rican-owned music store in the city.

Although she dreamt of using her business as an avenue to pressing and marketing records herself, Hernández had to settle for a dealership contract with Victoria Records Company, when the 1929 crash wiped out her store's profits. As agent for Victoria Records, however, she figured prominently in the Hispanic community of East Harlem, always searching for new talent, booking musicians for recording sessions, and laying out money to recording artists until they received their contract payments. In exchange, Hernández charged a fee, a cut from their record sales. Her shrewd business dealings on behalf of Latino musicians earned her the title of *Madrina* (godmother); but when she withheld payments from musicians, they called her *La Judía* (Glass 1991). This epithet probably had less to do with stereotypes about Jews than with the prevalence of ethnic conflicts between Jews and Hispanics in East Harlem during the 1920s and 1930s. During these years as Latino entrepreneurs began to buy businesses in the area, Jewish gangs threatened and harassed them (Glasser 1991). In 1926 this conflict escalated when the ice cream cart of a Hispanic *piragüero* was attacked by some Jews and a riot broke out.

In spite of the ethnic tensions and competition that existed in the music business in East Harlem at this time, Casa Hernández flourished and permitted Rafael to dedicate himself exclusively to the writing and performing of Latin music. Besides financially supporting him, Victoria Hernández also assisted in recording some of his songs, managing his quartet, not surprisingly called *Grupo Victoria* (Victoria's Group), and organized many of his other activities. In Casa Hernández Victoria provided a a small quiet room with a piano for Rafael, where he composed many patriotic songs. It was in this room that he played for the first time his now famous *Lamento Borincano,* which has come to nostalgically symbolize the plight of the uprooted Puerto Rican migrant in North America. The work of Victoria Hernández as music agent, entrepreneur, and constant supporter of Latino musicians, especially her brother, was profoundly important to the cultural and economic life of the Puerto Rican community during this period. It is true that her interest in the music business probably was not altogether altruistic; yet, as one scholar has noted, "commercial incentives went along with family and ethnic pride in helping struggling artists" (Glasser 1991). And it was certainly Victoria Hernández's pride in her brother's musical talents that led her to support him throughout the years so that Rafael had the time, security, and peace to produce some of most beautiful songs in the Latino repertories of the times. What is regretable is that Victoria Hernández's traditional gender ideas about professional musicians prevented her from creating and performing similar works.

While we may question the work of business entrepreneurs as laudatory "community-building work" in the Hispanic communities of New York City, certainly the altruism and dedication of the work of Carmela Zapata Marrero, or Sister Carmelita as she came to be called, is beyond reproach. Born in Cabo Rojo, Puerto Rico, in 1907 into a relatively prosperous land-owning family, she arrived in the United States in 1923 to train as a missionary in the Trinitarian Order of the Catholic church. After two years at the Convent of the Holy Trinity in Georgia, Sister Carmelita was assigned to the order's Court Street Center in Brooklyn, which then only served the Polish, Irish, Lithuanian, Chinese and Filipino worshippers in the area. Puerto Ricans had yet to arrive; and when they did, Sister Carmelita recalled that: "During those years it was when they use to put them . . . out—dispossess them—and it was very hard. And I thought it was my duty to save every Puerto Rican that I found—from anything. I felt that terrible. . . . I remember seeing them on the sidewalk, with all their children, and their beds, and all their things. . . . Then we had no welfare" (quoted in Sánchez Korrol 1988). But Sister Carmelita wasted no time taking care of her flock. She contacted official politicians at city hall and power brokers in the Spanish-speaking *barrios,* including *boliteros (*numbers' runners), for financial aid. She found jobs for the unemployed and food and shelter for the destitute. She acted as translator or mediator for those who needed to communicate with the larger non-Hispanic society. In time, through her work at Casita María, a settlement house she helped found in East Harlem, and through her close contacts with individual children, Sister Carmelita was able to inspire a new generation of Puerto Ricans to go on to lead very productive lives in North America (Ribes Tovar 1972). Sister Carmelita became an excellent role model herself, completing in her middle years her bachelor's and master's degrees at the University of Puerto Rico soon after the Catholic church transferred her there in the 1940s. After a few years of service on the island, Sister Carmelita, at her own request, was relocated once again to New York City, where she continued to shepherd the progress of the Puerto Rican community in this city. She retired in the early 1970s due to ill health; by then, Sister Carmelita had created a series of religious and social networks that had not only helped in the birthing of this community but also came to serve as a linkage between the first Puerto Rican migration wave that occurred after World War I and the subsequent migrations of the post-World War II decades.

Another woman who spearheaded the growth of the Puerto Rican community in New York City, and whose work also connected two different historical periods was Pura Belpré, an imaginative and active librarian who worked in the city during the 1930s and early 1940s and again in the 1960s. Belpré was born in Cidra, Puerto Rico, in 1899 to a Puerto Rican mother and Martinican father, who because of his contracting business was forced to move his family throughout the island. Belpré's family finally settled in San Juan, and there she attended the University of Puerto Rico for a year before migrating to North America. Her decision to stay in Manhattan was rather fortuitous, for Belpré had come just to celebrate her sister's wedding ceremony. But the New York Public Library offered her a position in the Countee Cullen Branch in Harlem, and so she decided to stay for a while. This was the year 1921; in the next few years Belpré completed her training as a professional librarian first at the New York Library school (1924-25) and then at the Seward Library Branch in Manhattan (1925-29). Soon after this, Belpré was appointed to the 115 Street Upper Manhattan Branch and not long after to the East Harlem Aguilar Branch, where she eventually became a children's librarian (L. López 1976). It was at this branch that Belpré first developed a series of storytelling sessions for the Hispanic children of the neighborhood in order to encourage them to read. Belpré began by reciting to the children stories and tales that she had heard as a child in Puerto Rico; later she designed colorful puppets to animate her folktales. Belpré's storytelling became so popular that she often gave recitations at Casita María and throughout the Harlem district schools just to entertain the children. Out of this experience came her first published children's book, *Pérez y Martina: A Puerto Rican Folktale* (1932), one of the island's most endearing tales about the love between a little mouse and a lovely cockroach.

But Belpré was not just a children's librarian; she also was liaison to the Hispanic community and to North American organizations seeking to ease the social integration of the new settlers into the life of the city. The Catholic and Evangelical churches, for example, requested her help in setting up preparatory classes for high school students who had the potential of attending college; and some of the founders of Casita María, many of whom were Irish humanitarians who knew little Spanish, asked for her assistance in learning the language and culture. She not only created various cultural programs for this settlement house but for other social centers, such as the Union Settlement, Madison House, and the Educational Alliance of the city of New York (Sánchez Korrol 1986). Belpré also worked very closely with the Latino community itself. Bernardo Vega, an educated tobacco worker from Puerto Rico, who recorded important events relating to puertorriqueños in the city during these years, remembers that Pura Belpré managed to find a *cuevita* (little room) in her library for the members of *Puerto Rico Literario,* a literary and political club founded in 1929 that met regularly to study and discuss Spanish literature and independentista politics (Vega 1980). The club, consisting of Vega and Belpré and a handful of other Latinos—mainly poets, journalists, and other writers and professionals—was a symbol of a Spanish-speaking community that was emerging in an East Harlem still predominantly populated by other ethnic groups.

Belpré left the New York City Public Library system in 1945 soon after she married Dr. Clarence Cameron White, an African-American tenor, violinist, and conductor. Her husband's active performing career appears not to have permitted Belpré the opportunity of combining a private and public life, but on occasion she gave lectures and talks on Hispanic cultural themes. In 1946 Belpré also wrote her second children's book, *The Tiger and the Rabbit and Other Tales,* America's first published collection of Puerto Rican folktales. Upon her husband's death in 1963, Belpré returned once again to the work she loved best—to children's library services. This time Belpré collaborated with another Puerto Rican librarian, Lillian López, the coordinator of the South Bronx Project, to organize a bilingual educational program within the Mott Haven Library Branch, which included her famous storytelling sessions, puppetry, and other cultural services for Latino children (De Montreville 1978; López and Belpré 1974). During these years Belpré also continued to write her charming folktales—*Juan Bobo and the Queen's Necklace* (1962); *Santiago* (1969); *Ote: A Puerto Rican Folk Tale* (1969); *Dance of the Animals: A Puerto Rican Folk Tale* (1972); *Once in Puerto Rico* (1973); *The Little Horse of Seven Colors* (1976)—all of which brought children of New York City a sense of the uniqueness of the Hispanic world and its values.

For her dedication to the Puerto Rican culture and educational advancement of her community, Belpré was granted the Mayor's Award for Arts and Culture in 1977. In 1983 the *Agrupación Femenina Hispano-americana* (Hispanic-American Women's Association) also commemorated her contributions to the city of New York at the *Museo del Barrio,* Harlem's Hispanic Museum (Centro de Estudios Puertorriqueños, Vertical File, Belpré). Belpré died in 1972, leaving behind a legacy of joy in her children's stories and of a genuine commitment to the cultural life of the Puerto Rican nation in this country.

While Sister Carmelita and Pura Belpré dedicated their energies to poor and working-class Puerto Ricans in New York City, Josefina Silva de Cintrón's efforts were principally aimed at the Hispanic professional and middle-class sector. Her most important contribution to the pioneering Puerto Rican community was the establishment of a journal, *Artes y Letras (*Arts and Letters), which she published monthly between 1933 and 1945. The primary function of this publication was to disseminate information about Hispanic culture and society in the United States; thus it provided its readers with the literary works of Spanish authors and celebrations of the successes of Latino literati in Spain and Latin America. The journal also was a social register for the elite segment of the Hispanic population in the city, recording their family triumphs and activities, such as graduations, weddings, travels, and obituaries. Of special interest are the articles and other information earmarked for the women of this class during these years. There were essays on "feminine values," on children and the family, and on women's community services and conferences. These and other articles in *Artes y Letras* reveal without question a preoccupation with middle-class values and way of life. However, under Silva de Cintrón's editorship, the journal also raised issues of concern to the entire Hispanic community; in 1936, for example, it questioned the discriminatory testing of school children in Harlem. And it always gave space to the activities of neighborhood-wide religious and social organizations. But, in general the journal addressed itself to an audience that was highly educated and well placed throughout the city of New York (Sánchez Korrol 1986). As founder and editor of *Artes y Letras,* Josefina Silva de Cintrón chronicled the life of this sector of the Hispanic community, illustrating the economic and social diversity of Latinos in this city during the late 1930s and early 1940s.

The individual life stories or personal histories of these migrant women provide important documentation for reconstructing the work history of the Puerto Rican community in the United States. These biographical vignettes indicate that this history is much older than it has been presumed—its roots stretching back into the late nineteenth century. More significantly, as was the case of women among other immigration groups (Seller 1975; Loo and Ong 1982; Ewen 1985; Sanchez 1987; Acosta-Belén 1988; Cohen 1992), the work of puertorriqueñas played a crucial role in the origins and development of the Puerto Rican community in New York City during its early years. Many of these women, for example, struggled to recreate in a variety of ways the sense of community or *pueblo* (town) they had left behind—a sense of community that had fortified them as workers on the island. Thus, Rodríguez de Tío, by kindling connections with other Latino poets and literary figures in New York, forged an ambience for Spanish arts and letters among Hispanics in this city, and by establishing a dialogue with other freedom fighters, sustained the idea of an independent Puerto Rican nation. Hernández, Belpré and Silva de Cintrón likewise sought to preserve cultural ideals and institutions they believed enriched the lives of Puerto Ricans everywhere. In the meantime, Sister Carmelita revitalized the spiritual and social bonding that had always defined life in poor *barriadas* or neighborhoods in Puerto Rico, because she truly believed that this spirit of *caridad* or neighborly caring would help her people survive the hardships of ghetto life in New York City. And the more radical Capetillo brought her socialist battles against capitalism to Puerto Rican workers in the United States, maintaining that a new economic system would someday liberate working men and women on the island and the mainland.

The work of these women—and those of Hernández, Sister Carmelita and Belpré—stand out in this respect; they also created a rich cultural oasis that historically connected not only Puerto Ricans of different eras, but Puerto Ricans with other ethnic groups in this city as well. Indeed, the presence of these women in the Puerto Rican settlements during these early years provided such an enduring and stabilizing force that the Puerto Rican community was able to survive the critical years of the Great Depression and lay a solid foundation for its first large expansion immediately after World War II (Rodríguez et al. 1980). Much more research needs to be done on the individual experiences of migrant women in the Hispanic communities of New York City during these early years in order for us to detail fully the work history of puertorriqueñas in this country. There is, however, a growing body of information on women needleworkers who emigrated from Puerto Rico between 1920 and 1940 that allows us to more completely detail the history of this vital part of the Puerto Rican community in New York.

This information indicates that needleworkers worked both at home and in the factories. The homeworkers earned their living by picking up bundles of unfinished garments—dresses, blouses, skirts, undergarments, handkerchiefs—at an agent's warehouse or local factory, and sometimes with the aid of young daughters, sisters or other adult females, completing these garments at home. Some of these women dedicated themselves exclusively to homework because they believed that a woman's most important role was to take care of her family personally—a concept that was not unusual for the women of the times. Puerto Rican mothers, therefore, found the making of garments at home somewhat advantageous. Homework had other advantages for puertorriqueñas: it did not require fluency in the English language, travel to far-away places, or expensive machinery or tools (Sánchez Korrol 1983). But, these presumed "advantages" made it that much easier for these workers to be exploited in New York City, for this industry was notorious for its extremely low wages and long hours (A. Ortiz 1990).

The first Puerto Rican needleworkers became visible in the city's factories in the mid-1920s. Although very little is known about them, a 1925 census of the city showed that 600—that is, 17.2 percent of the 3,496 women listed as living in the Puerto Rican community of East Harlem during these years—worked in the production sector of the city's economy as skilled seamstresses (Sánchez Korrol 1980). Accounts of the 1930s and 1940s have not yielded statistical information regarding the exact numbers of Puerto Rican women involved in the garment industry of the city during these years. But, the records of the Department of Labor of the government of Puerto Rico, which in 1930 established an employment office in Harlem, indicate that from 1930 to 1936 1,612 Puerto Rican women were placed in factory jobs—about 40 percent of all women serviced by this agency. They were classified as needleworkers or hand sewers, machine operators, and miscellaneous factory workers (Chenault 1938).

During these years women garment workers of New York City were confronted by a variety of problems. Finding a job was always difficult, but a few already had jobs when they arrived here. Some were recruited in Puerto Rico by employers of nonunion shops, who promised these women jobs on their arrival to the city in order to undermine the unionization attempts of the ILGWU in the area. Others found employment through friends and relatives. Most had to walk the unfamiliar streets of the city or search through the few Spanish newspapers for the want ads that advertised "Se necesitan operadoras" (Sewing Machine Operators Needed). The fact that many did not speak or understand the English language well or did not know how to travel through the city compounded their work problems. To help each other, puertorriqueñas in the needlework industry developed an informal system of networking, consisting of friends and relatives who helped them find employment, travel to distant places, and communicate with English-speaking coworkers and employers (Sánchez Korrol 1980).

This personal network system, however, did not assist Puerto Rican women factory workers in resolving the problems that prevailed throughout the garment industry during these early years. Most garment workers still earned very low wages and suffered deplorable working conditions. The factories of the times were firetraps because of their poor ventilation and heating systems; they were also cold in the winter and hot in the summer. The hours were long; sometimes they worked fourteen hours a day during the busy season (Wertheimer and Nelson 1975). Puerto Rican women also struggled against the problems that eventually resulted in the demise of the garment industry of New York City: the increased use of job contractors, relocation of businesses out of the city, and the deskilling of the better paid shops. Some Puerto Rican workers joined the ILGWU during the 1920s expecting to ameliorate these conditions through union activity. The ILGWU admitted them but did not begin to actively organize them until the 1930s when over 2,000 Puerto Ricans were recruited. Most joined Dressmakers' Local 22, but others were found in Children's Dressmakers' Local 91, Beltmakers' Local 40, Embroiderers' Local 66, Knitgoods Workers' Local 155, and Neckwear Workers' Local 142. The ILGWU organized the Puerto Rican women in these shops, because it found that Puerto Rican nonunion workers hired themselves out for lower wages than those the union had contracted for its members. Although Puerto Rican women also worked as "floor girls" and in finishing, they were not organized until later years, perhaps because they did not pose a threat to the existing white labor force.

Joining the ILGWU did not help Puerto Rican women garment workers resolve their work problems either. They continued to be employed in low-paying shops as semiskilled operators, finishers, pinkers, examiners, and cleaners. There is no evidence that the ILGWU attempted to negotiate better contracts between them and their employers. Moreover, the union totally ignored the issue of wage discrimination, and so these women continued to be paid wages that were lower than those of non-Hispanic white women. The union also paid little attention to complaints that bosses fined or threatened Puerto Rican women with loss of their jobs if they were critical of conditions in the factories or to charges of sexual harassment. One Puerto Rican woman, nonetheless, succeeded in getting the ILGWU to take up her case and was awarded a meager sum for her boss's transgressions (Laurentz 1980).

The ILGWU also did not effectively deal with the intrinsic problems of the needlework trades—deskilling, subcontracting, and relocation—which increasingly had begun to affect garment workers during this period. By the 1930s deskilling already was prevalent in certain jobs, such as those in the highly skilled and well-paid tailoring shops. The innovation of section work had permitted employers to use semiskilled workers by dividing complex manufacturing operations into simpler sewing tasks. Manufacturers of top of the line garments, particularly those in the coat and suit businesses, no longer needed to hire expert tailors who commanded higher wages than section workers. Originally when these manufacturing changes began to transform this industry, Jewish and Italian immigrant women were hired as section workers, but with the upward mobility of these ethnic groups, migrant puertorriqueñas and African-American women migrating from the South began replacing them in the factories and earned the lower wages that section workers were paid at this time. While deskilling allowed these new unskilled and semiskilled workers to enter the garment labor market, it also prevented them from becoming professional tailors and seamstresses and thus from earning higher wages in this industry. But, even if deskilling had not begun to affect the better paid shops, the dominance of the tailoring and cutting trades by men, coupled with the discrimination that existed against people of color in general, would have excluded Puerto Rican women from employment in the higher paid sectors of the garment industry.

Job contracting and relocation, too, made their appearance by the 1930s. By hiring independent subcontractors, who often used nonunion labor to produce garments at lower wage rates, clothing manufacturers were able to greatly cut labor costs. Garment businesses likewise relocated to places outside of New York City—first to nearby Connecticut, New Jersey, Pennsylvania, and later to the southern United States and Puerto Rico, to avoid the slightly higher wages that the ILGWU had negotiated for its members. There is almost no empirical documentation on the impact these problems had on the Puerto Rican work force during these years, but one researcher concludes that the relocation of dress manufacturers outside of New York "tended to undermine the security of . . . Puerto Ricans who found thousands of positions in the New York City dress trade" (Laurentz 1980). Many of these women worked in the making of inexpensive cotton dresses, an industry which usually paid an average of 72.5 cents an hour in the city at that time. Since labor costs outside of New York were lower—on the average of 38.7 cents an hour—dress manufacturers moved. Close to 350 businesses relocated their factories to places outside the metropolitan area (Vernon 1960).

Unfortunately, the ILGWU's policies and strategies during these years did not enable Puerto Rican women garment workers to counteract the continual denigration and decimation of jobs in this industry. The position of the union was a disappointment to its members, which at this time included a group of radical Hispanic dressmakers who attempted to organize a Spanish-speaking local in order to challenge the union leadership in Dressmakers' Local 22 of the early 1930s. These workers criticized the administration of Charles Zimmerman, head of the local, for not helping them and forcing workers to vote for Zimmerman's "clique." They demanded that the leaders of the ILGWU recognize their right to organize and allow them to select their leaders. The propaganda they distributed to their fellow workers called for the election of sympathetic candidates who would best represent their interests. A 1933 appeal sought their support with the exhortation:

> Spanish dressmakers let us fight with all our strength for the election of the left group candidates. They represent our platform for the enforcement of the decision on the minimum prices in all shops, for the immediate attention of our complaints, for reduced dues to the unemployed dressmakers, against taxes, for the demands of the finishers, pinkers, and examiners and the unity of all workers of the trade. (Zimmerman Collection 1933)

The ILGWU refused to recognize these workers as a separate unit of the union, even though Italian workers had been allowed to create their own locals: Local 89, the Italian Dressmakers' Union; and Local 48, the Italian Cloakmakers' Union. After these locals were established the ILGWU leadership decided not to fragment union membership any further. The radicalism of these Hispanic laborers probably was another factor in the ILGWU's refusal to grant Spanish-speaking workers a separate local. The ILGWU leadership under President David Dubinsky was anxious to create a unified, malleable membership that would quietly continue to accept the union's definition of "industrial peace." This tenet had become part of the union's ideology following the sanguine strikes of 1909 and 1910, when union leaders agreed not to strike in exchange for recognition by employers as the collective bargaining agency of garment workers in the United States (Foner 1965; Meyerson 1969). Radical workers were critical of this policy, particularly at a time when the crisis of the 1930s had placed extra burdens on them. Dubinsky and other union leaders, on the other hand, sought to control the rank and file more than ever. Although Spanish-speaking workers were not granted their own local, Dubinsky appointed Saby Nehama, a Sephardic Jewish agent in Dressmakers' Local 22, to organize Hispanic workers into a special department. In addition, at the 1934 ILGWU annual convention Nehama and Zimmerman arranged to get two Puerto Rican women recognized as bona fide delegates (Laurentz 1980). Thus, the leadership of the ILGWU checkmated the Hispanic radicals of Local 22 and may have prevented them from becoming a viable source of leadership during a period when these workers were feeling the full effects of the Great Depression.

Workers of the Great Migration, 1945-1960

After World War II Puerto Rican women workers migrated to New York City in greater numbers. Through their labor as householders, community workers, or wage workers, they sustained their families and the Hispanic *barriadas* of the city. Although the bulk of these migrants were married women, there were single workers who came alone in search of employment. Among these was a gifted young woman who had been employed in Puerto Rico as a rural school teacher. Unable to continue her profession in New York, she worked in a variety of jobs throughout the city. But, one day in the summer of 1953 she was found unconscious in an East Harlem street. She had no identification and was taken to Harlem Hospital, where she died later that day. Because no one claimed her body, she was photographed, given a number, and then quietly buried in an unmarked grave in Potter's Field, the municipal cemetery of the city. After searching for her for days, her sister, Consuelo, recognized her picture at the morgue, claimed her remains, and with the help of friends and relatives, sent them to Puerto Rico for burial in the town of Carolina. There, with all the dignity and recognition she so well deserved, Julia de Burgos—poet, teacher, journalist, political activist, and factory worker—was finally laid to rest (Ribes Tovar 1972). Burgos died as she once predicted in "Poema para mi muerte" (Poem for my death) (1941) "alone and abandoned, on the thickest rock of a deserted island," at the age of thirty-nine after struggling for years to survive as a worker in New York City (Matilla and Silén 1972).

In Puerto Rico, however, Burgos had produced some of her finest work as a poet and as a teacher. Although born into a very poor rural family in 1914, by the age of nineteen she had acquired a teaching degree at the University of Puerto Rico in 1933. This certificate allowed Burgos to get a teaching job in a small town in the interior of the island; she also began to publish some of her poems in the local newspapers. By 1940, the year of her first departure for New York, Burgos had published three of her collections of poems: *Poemas exactos a mí misma* (Poems Exactly True to Myself) (1937); *Poema en veinte surcos* (Poem in Twenty Furrows) (1938); and *Canción de la verdad sencilla* (Song of Simple Truth) (1939). In these poetry collections Burgos exhibits her dramatic skills as a poet: she beautifully conveys images of the world of nature (rivers, seas, land, flora, fauna, stars, moon, and sky); she flowingly combines the intellectual with the emotional; and she wisely describes human passions and obsessions (love, death) (González 1961). Through her poems we rejoice in her loves, rise with her patriotism, bend with her sadness, and empathize with her concerns, especially with her hatred for racism, war, dictatorships, and the oppression of women (Quiroga 1980). In "A Julia de Burgos" (To Julia de Burgos), probably her best known poem in the United States, Burgos creatively expresses her feminist ideology by establishing a dialogue between the woman who is as free as Rocinante (the quixotic steed) and the woman who lives by social conventions.

Interestingly, Burgos calls the unliberated woman in the poem, Julia, a woman who is a "cold doll of social prevarication," a "honey of polite hypocrisies." Burgos calls her "selfish" and a "prim ladylike lady." She belongs to her husband, curls her hair, and paints her face; she is a "housewife, resigned, submissive/ ruled by the prejudices of men . . . " But, this was not the real Julia de Burgos. The real Julia de Burgos was "the essence" in the poem—"the living spark of human truth." She was a woman who believed that she had "life, strength . . . "; that she belonged to "no one, or to everyone, because to everyone, everyone. . . " she gave herself in "pure feeling and thought" (Flores and Flores 1986). Indeed, the real Julia de Burgos was a woman who defied the social conventions of her time. She diligently embraced her work as a student and a teacher, and on the island rose above the poverty of her childhood years. Burgos' love for Puerto Rico also led her to support the pro-independence revolutionary ideology of Pedro Albizu Campos' *Nacionalista* (Nationalist) Party during the 1930s and 1940s. And when her first marriage failed, she remarried. With her second husband she went to Cuba, where she continued her studies at the University of Havana and wrote poems that earned the admiration of scholars and intellectuals, such as Juan Bosch and Pablo Neruda. In 1940, she stayed in New York for a brief period of time, only to return alone in 1946.

Life was hard for Julia de Burgos in New York. In spite of her academic training, teaching credentials, and literary fame, she was unable to find employment in any of the city schools. Burgos did some writing and translating for Hispanic journals and newspapers and produced a few new poems, but mostly she supported herself by working as a clerk in stores and offices and as a seamstress in factories (Ribes Tovar 1976). When Burgos found time, she worked with other *independentista* (pro-independence) followers at gatherings of the wing of the Nationalist Party of Puerto Rico in New York for the island's liberation from United States' colonialism, and she collaborated with literary friends at the *Círculo de Escritores y Poetas Ibero-americanos* (Circle of Iberian-American Writers and Poets) (Vega 1980). Unfortunately, the insecurities of temporary jobs and low pay, the long periods of unemployment, the hostility of the environment that discriminated against the color of her dark skin—all contributed to the increasing bouts of alcoholism and depression that led to her death on that summer's day (Fernández Olmos 1982). In at least one analysis of her life in New York, Burgos is portrayed as a victim of the migration experience (Estévez 1989). Yet, Burgos' greatness lies in the fact that in spite of her overwhelming problems, she continued to work till the very end and to write beautiful and meaningful poetry that spoke of the realities of puertorriqueñas both on the island and mainland.

The life of Julia de Burgos is one of the few recorded stories of Puerto Rican women in New York City after World War II. Although there are some mini-biographies of artists Esther Comas, Rita Moreno and Myrta Silva; of community organizers Evelina Antonetty, founder of United Bronx Parents; of Luisa Quintero, journalist; of Patricia Rodríguez, founder of the Organization of Puerto Rican Notaries; of entrepreneurs Celia Vice (bookstore and real estate owner), Mercedes Llado (clothing factory owner) and Rosa Merced (advertising agency owner) (Ribes 1968); of ministers and teachers (Sánchez Korrol 1988, forthcoming), there is only one full-length biography of a migrant worker (Ribes Tovar 1974). Likewise we lack major analytical studies of those women whom the economy classifies as "workers," women in the formal paid labor force. The scanty literature that exists focuses on workers in the garment industry, since large numbers of migrating puertorriqueñas were absorbed by the expansion of this industry in New York City during the late 1940s and the decade of the 1950s. During these years puertorriqueñas were incorporated into almost all of the needle trades and subsequently into the ILGWU. An accurate and complete assessment of the total numbers of these workers in either the garment industry or the union locals in New York City also is not available. We do know, however, that many of these women were greatly affected by the conditions the entire garment business was experiencing at the time, and some were aware that the industry, in spite of its short-lived period of expansion was exhibiting a continual spiral of decline. This decline began with the natural adjustment in the consumer market that followed World War II, reducing retail consumption of garment wear, a condition further aggravated by increased competition from foreign imports in clothing (especially in neckwear, skirts, blouses, scarves and sweaters) and by the introduction of longer lasting materials (i.e., acetates, nylons and polyesters) (Laurentz 1980).

These market and technological changes had a tremendous impact on the garment industry of New York City during this period. Clothing manufacturers, for example, widened their use of the deskilling and subcontracting practices they had introduced in earlier decades, since these were still profitable ways of cutting down labor costs. The trend toward relocation to areas where labor and other costs were cheaper also continued unabated during these years. Garment businesses, noticeably those in the lower price bracket of men's and women's apparel industries, began to move in greater numbers to New Jersey, Massachusetts, Pennsylvania, Ohio, Texas, California, and increasingly to other countries to avoid New York City's high production costs (Vernon 1960). The reaction of clothing manufacturers to the changing economic conditions of the times ultimately affected Puerto Rican women workers, who experienced exploitation and discrimination more than ever.

Many of these women joined the ILGWU during these years and worked within its locals with the same high expectations as garment workers of previous generations. Some, like Rosie Flores, a young seamstress who worked in a factory in East Harlem, joined the union because they felt the ILGWU made a difference in their lives. In 1959 Rosie Flores happily enumerated her benefits as a union member:

> We get sick pay and holidays. . . . We even get paid when we have a baby—$150 for the time off and doctors' bills! And such a difference in the work, too. Not just getting paid more, but more relaxed (work). In the shops that don't have union it's always a fight to get your work. . . . In our shop we divide it up, so whatever work there is for the day, we have some. And then we get a minimum of $42.50 a week no matter what, but most of the time it's lots more, usually $70 or $80. (quoted in Wakefield 1959)

Rosie Flores's past experiences in nonunion shops made her only too glad to belong to the union. Carlotta Rodríguez, a Puerto Rican labor organizer in East

Harlem, also believed in membership in the ILGWU. During the 1950s she helped Joseph Piscitello, who was the official union organizer for the Harlem area, to mobilize workers in the remaining sweatshops to become members of the union. Many other workers supported the ILGWU and the organizational work that it was doing in Spanish Harlem and in other parts of the city (Helfgott 1959; P. Rodríguez 1993).

However, by the end of the 1950s some Puerto Rican workers began to express dissatisfaction with the ILGWU's conservative leadership and its policies. In 1957 a group of them rejected the ILGWU as their bargaining agent and along with African-American workers demonstrated in front of union headquarters. These protestors were convinced that the union had not negotiated a fair contract for them, and so they petitioned the National Labor Relations Board to decertify the ILGWU as their labor representative. The following year there was another demonstration against the union, involving some 200 employees of Plastic Wear, Incorporated, members of Local 132 of the Bronx, who criticized the ILGWU's leaders for conducting meetings in English, when 80 percent of its membership spoke only Spanish. They also picketed the union headquarters. In 1958 there was a second protest—this one at the Q-T Knitwear Company factory in Brooklyn. In this case Puerto Rican workers accused the ILGWU of establishing an alliance with employers that was detrimental to their interests —in other words, of negotiating a "sweetheart" deal. Carrying signs that read "We're Tired of Industrial Peace. We Want Industrial Justice," they marched around the factory expressing their disappointment with ILGWU policies (Hill 1974).

The ILGWU, in the meantime, quickly dismissed the demands of these workers and initiated a publicity campaign to place the union in a favorable light. The first of these efforts was a report prepared in 1959 by Roy B. Helfgott (then research director of the New York Joint Board of the ILGWU) for the New York State Commission against Discrimination, announcing that the ILGWU had successfully integrated almost all Puerto Rican female skirt makers into Local 23. Helfgott praised the organizational work of the union, noting that Local 23 had begun to organize Puerto Rican women in the late 1940s, after these workers became the predominant labor force in this industry. The report also noted that the union already had a Spanish-speaking business agent in this local to handle the problems of Sephardic Jews, who up until then had constituted the bulk of its membership. The increase in the number of Hispanic workers, however, led Local 23 to appoint three other Spanish-speaking business agents—all Sephardic Jews—to facilitate communication with Puerto Rican and other Latin American women. In 1949 the ILGWU created in this local the position of educational director, who was to be fluent in Spanish and whose main function was to set up a special educational program, including English instruction classes for members who wanted to acquire English language skills. The union leadership believed this would help Puerto Ricans get jobs in the better price shops, where little Spanish was spoken, and hence facilitate the integration of Puerto Rican workers into full participation in union membership activities (Helfgott 1959).

Among the activities the local offered its members, Helfgott reported were lectures, visits to historic sites, an annual spring dance, and the annual weekend outing to the Pocono Mountains for the shop's chairpersons, a few of whom were puertorriqueñas. Through these social activities the union hoped to create feelings of solidarity and cohesiveness. The union, Helfgott also noted, initiated a program of "political education" in Local 23 in order to develop union consciousness and leadership among Puerto Rican women workers. They were urged to participate in elections and signature drives to support bills that protected the interests of labor. A significant part of this program envisioned the development of a core of Hispanic leaders who would become active in union affairs. To keep its entire local membership informed of union activities and benefits, Helfgott added, the ILGWU distributed its Spanish version of *Justice*, the union's bimonthly publication. Local 23 also ran a counseling program to help Puerto Rican women with individual problems, but Helfgott did not clarify if these workers used this service. Finally, Helfgott's report emphasized that in spite of some remaining problems, such as those of membership retention, payment of dues, and full participation in union activities, the vast majority of Puerto Rican skirt makers were members of the local and some of these women were active in leadership positions in the local's executive board and its various committees (Helfgott 1958).

Notwithstanding Helfgott's glowing report on Puerto Rican women in Local 23, other research indicates that the ILGWU instituted discriminatory policies and practices that resulted in the subordination of puertorriqueñas and other Hispanic women in the occupational ladder of the industry and in the leadership structure of the union (see Hill 1974). This discrimination was especially obvious in the lack of representation of Puerto Ricans in the top leadership positions of the union (Fitzpatrick 1971). Jewish men and to a lesser extent Italian males had held these positions in the past with the support of a largely Jewish and Italian coalition of male and female garment workers, but as the numbers of these early ethnic workers began to decline, the leaders of the ILGWU established an exclusionary electoral process that prevented other groups from occupying important decision-making posts. The eligibility rules for candidates for president, secretary-treasurer, or member of the general executive board were the strictest among all of the labor unions in the nation (Meyerson 1969). This severely limited the number of challengers, especially among the newcomers to the union. Since special political groups or caucuses could not be convened in the union until three months before the annual convention, it was difficult for contending candidates to meet with the rank and file to present their platforms. Those in office, however, could meet with the members as often as they wished. Exclusivism in appointment methods also prevented Puerto Rican women from becoming local managers or agents in the lower ranks of the ILGWU. Vacancies, transfers, or new appointments were deliberately given to Jewish members of the union and sometimes to Italians in order to balance out the power structure of the old members. Even in areas such as East Harlem where Puerto Rican garment workers were clearly in the majority, the union did not alter its policy and maintained a non-Puerto Rican male representative. Thus Puerto Rican women were excluded from full participation in union activities, while the Jewish and Italian male leadership continued to stay in power.

The ILGWU also revealed its discriminatory attitudes towards Puerto Rican workers during the 1950s by continuing to blatantly disregard the language needs of the Spanish-speaking members of the union. Although in 1954 it allowed another Spanish club within Dressmakers' Local 22 to be organized in order to meet the needs of its members, and it regularly translated its newspaper into Spanish, the ILGWU rejected the request for a Spanish language local once again, still claiming this would be detrimental to the garment labor movement. Yet the ILGWU permitted the two Italian locals to continue to operate until the mid-1970s in spite of the New York State Anti-Discriminatory Act of 1945 and the Equal Employment Section of the Civil Rights Act of 1964, both of which had declared all nationality locals illegal (Hill 1974). The Italian locals controlled some of the better paid jobs in the industry and constituted a source of power for the remaining Italian workers. The ILGWU likewise did not appoint a Spanish-speaking agent to the Harlem area, where a good number of the workers did not speak English. Piscitello, who had been the union organizer in that district since 1933 when the Italians constituted the bulk of the work force in that area, knew no Spanish. He, himself, admitted that:

> That is a problem . . . because they can't understand English, a lot of them, and we can't make them understand about the things they should have and why they should have a union. . . . But you see, Puerto Ricans, they don't have the education that we have. . . . They're just not educated, you see, except for some elite like Miss [Carlotta] Rodríguez here. But mostly they're backward. (quoted in Wakefield 1959)

Puerto Rican workers resented this kind of attitude on the part of the union representatives, and their 1957 and 1958 protests against the union clearly demonstrated this. They demanded a union that appointed local leaders who would be more sensitive to their needs. The union answered by continuing to appoint or keep agents like Piscitello, by denying Puerto Rican women the right to organize their own local, and by refusing to translate contracts and minutes for the Spanish-speaking membership, which consisted mainly of adult Puerto Rican women, many of whom had family responsibilities and thus were unable to attend school after work to learn English.

The ILGWU also did not enable capable Puerto Rican garment workers to advance to higher skilled and better paid positions in the top of the line shops located in New York City. The policy of the union for the most part was to ignore the undemocratic processes that had been instituted in the shops and in the locals to select workers for higher training. Originally a worker was trained in a skilled trade by a friend or was recommended by the local union officials. Will Herberg, who in the early 1950s conducted a study on ethnic relations in the dress industry, claimed that the union had tried to get Jewish and Italian skilled workers to "bring up" Puerto Rican women into the better paid shops. These attempts failed, and Herberg believed that "ethnic clannishness"—the reluctance of the "old timers" to accept Puerto Ricans as their equals, was mainly responsible for this exclusion. Herberg added, nonetheless, that there was no "oppression" of Puerto Rican women in the garment industry and that their advancement was not "altogether barred." It was his opinion—but he did not substantiate it—that Puerto Rican workers were not interested in advancing themselves in the skilled trades anyway (Herberg 1953). The consequences of these discriminatory attitudes were summarized in 1959 by Helfgott, who also studied the women's and children's apparel industries during the 1950s. Helfgott observed that in the dressmakers' crafts Puerto Rican women were found in the less skilled, lower priced jobs and that in this industry they were not advancing to higher positions as rapidly as other groups had done. He concluded his study by stating that in the better paid shops "with few exceptions . . . they did not become highly skilled tailor-system workers on dresses or 'cloaks.' As a result, a shortage of skilled sewing machine operators is developing" (Helfgott 1959).

Even when the problem of trained, skilled workers became acute during the 1960s, the union did not adopt a favorable position regarding the advancement of Puerto Rican women in the garment trades. At the 1962 congressional hearings before a House Sub-committee on Education and Labor investigating discrimination in the ILGWU, President Dubinsky and other union officials insisted that it was not the union's responsibility to train workers (Congressional Record 1962). Later, when the federal government recommended subsidization of training programs in the garment industry in order to create employment opportunities for Hispanics and other people of color in the city, the ILGWU objected on the grounds that this could cause instability, since this was an industry that depended greatly on inexperienced labor. Union leaders believed that workers who needed specific skills could be trained by individual employers or they could learn the trade at the Fashion Institute of Technology High School, where the union held "grading" (skill improvement) classes. As a result of the ILGWU's opposition, federally funded programs that could have helped Puerto Rican women acquire the skills needed for advancement in the garment industry, were not implemented. Thus puertorriqueñas continued to perform unskilled and semiskilled work that paid at a much cheaper rate than skilled craft work; and most were unable to enter into the better paid trades for lack of advanced skills (Hill 1974).

This brief analysis of Puerto Rican garment workers in this country, although limited by its particular time and place and by the paucity of available documentation, has tried to shed some light on the experiences of one of the most important sectors of the Puerto Rican community in New York City. The complete story of puertorriqueñas in the needle trades in New York City, as well as in other places throughout this country, has yet to be told; but we can already isolate several important dimensions regarding their work in this region of the country. First and foremost, we should reiterate the fact that migrant women from Puerto Rico began entering garment factories and other needlework establishments long before the "Great Migration" wave of the 1950s. This is worth emphasizing since most popular accounts of the Puerto Rican migrations to the United States usually only record the arrival and contributions of women workers who came in the post World War II period (see Mills 1950; Senior 1965; Fitzpatrick 1965). The placement of pioneering Puerto Rican garment workers in different Spanish-speaking communities of the city of New York during the first few decades of the twentieth century is important because it can help us to appreciate in greater depth the role women workers played in establishing and nurturing a migrant labor community in America. Through the consistency of their hard work and their dedication to their families, migrant needle and garment workers from Puerto Rico supported economically and spiritually a new community abroad. Accounts of the lives of individual Puerto Rican needle workers who migrated to New York from 1920 to 1950 and settled in Manhattan's Lower East Side, Brooklyn's Navy Yard section and the emerging Spanish Harlem at this time attest to this spirit of community building and "puertorriqueñidad." (Centro de Estudios Puertorriqueños 1984).

Studies on the work experiences of puertorriqueñas in the garment industry of New York City also may allow us to illustrate more completely the salient links—as well as the incongruities—in women's labor history in America in the twentieth century. Indeed, in many ways the experiences of Puerto Rican women workers in the garment industry were similar to those of earlier workers, for, like the first European immigrant women who preceded them, Puerto Rican women had to endure the insecurities and hardships of seasonal exploitative work in an industry that was highly competitive and subject to volatile market changes. Many of the gender problems that puertorriqueñas encountered in the ILGWU similarly had defined the relations between white men and women in the factories, locals, and the leadership structures of the union in the past (Kessler-Harris 1977). However, the entrance of Puerto Rican women, who represented an ethnically and at times racially different component, in what traditionally had been a predominantly white labor force, singularly exposed them to discriminatory attitudes and policies on the part of white workers, bosses, and the union. This resulted in personal humiliations and limitations that denigrated them as workers and as puertorriqueñas. In this sense the experiences of these migrant women were quite different from those of Jewish and Italian women who had had a cultural commonality with other workers, many of the garment bosses, and the ILGWU leaders (Waldinger 1986).

The labor participation of Puerto Rican women in the garment industry differs from that of previous women workers in one other significant respect: they were the first workers to feel the impact of the increasing relocation and internationalization of this industry—economic transformations that began to affect garment businesses as early as the 1960s. Not surprisingly the next few decades witnessed a dramatic decline in their numbers in this industry, a work pattern that has been accompanied by high unemployment rates and declining labor participation rates in general (Ríos 1984; Maymí 1977; Cooney and Colón-Warren 1980). How did puertorriqueñas cope with these new economic changes and fluctuations in the garment industry? We can only partially answer this question here: some of them used the public services available to all workers during these moments of economic distress; others continued to work (often "off-the-books" and far below minimum wage) in some of the remaining factories and sweatshops (Smith 1980). Only a few were able to retrain for other jobs, because most lacked education and English language skills (Bose 1986). Unexplored as of yet are the lives of workers who earned their livelihood doing *chiripeo* (informal economic activities) by making and selling custom-made garments, *capias* (mementos given to guests at showers, weddings or birthdays), flowers, foods, cosmetics, plastic-wares or selling bolita as did my mother.

Declining Labor Force Participation, 1960-1980

As this essay has indicated in its examination of the experience of Puerto Rican garment workers, most of the women who have migrated from Puerto Rico to the United States have come to the Middle Atlantic region to work in industries generally classified as secondary, unstable, low-wage, and that have been part of the declining sectors in this country's economy. Hence, many puertorriqueñas have not been able to find decent, steady, reasonably priced work here. Workers from the island, have arrived and departed from the American labor market in this geographic area in concert with the expansion or contraction of these industries during periods of economic prosperity and regression (or depression) characteristic of this century. Many of these workers came, worked for periods of time when there were plenty of jobs, but returned to Puerto Rico when they found themselves hopelessly unemployed (Hernández-Alvarez 1968). And many of those who stayed became part of yet another work pattern characterizing Puerto Rican women's labor history in America in recent decades, namely the declining rate of the labor participation of puertorriqueñas in the U. S. labor market. This decline first became noticeable in the 1960 U. S. population census, which showed a rate of 36.3 percent as compared to 38.9 percent in 1950 (the highest percentage ever). By 1970 the labor force participation rate of puertorriqueñas was down almost ten points (29 percent), the lowest of any female group except for Native-American women, who had a slightly lower participation rate of 25.5 percent (Cooney 1979; Cooney and Colón-Warren 1980). Although the 1980 census showed an increased labor force participation of 40.1 percent, this figure was still much lower than that of white American women, whose participation rate was by now almost 50 percent (49.4 percent) (Ríos 1984). This declining labor force participation trend of puertorriqueñas in the United States has intrigued scholars concerned with the economic well-being of women and their families in the Puerto Rican community. In their research these investigators have attempted to answer three crucial questions: first, is the declining labor force participation rate of Puerto Rican women uniform across the nation or does this phenomenon vary by region; second, what are the factors that explain this unusual trend in women's labor history in America; and third, what are the relationships between Puerto Rican women's declining labor force participation and the economic situation of their families and their community?

In a series of studies conducted during the late 1970s and early 1980s Rosemay Santana Cooney of Fordham University and a number of co-researchers provided some startling replies to these questions. Their investigations focused on the labor force participation of working age (14+ years) puertorriqueñas (at least 100 in each sample), residing in fifty-six cities in states where there were large concentrations of Puerto Ricans (i.e., New York, New Jersey, Pennsylvania, Illinois, California) between 1960 and 1970 (Cooney 1979; Cooney and Colón-Warren 1979; Cooney and Colón-Warren 1980; Cooney and Min 1981; Cooney and Ortiz 1983; Ortiz and Cooney 1984). In these studies Santana Cooney and her associates compared the individual characteristics of Puerto Rican women (regency, assimilation, age, education, marital status, fertility, size of family) with regional labor market conditions (i.e., operative work demand, industry mix, unemployment rate, median female earnings) prevalent in these cities. They concluded that "the overall effect of socio-economic [or individual] characteristics of Puerto Rican females . . . was small and insignificant . . . In contrast, unfavorable labor market conditions and large declines in central-city industries in which Puerto Ricans are concentrated are part of the answer." (Cooney and Colón-Warren 1980). In the Middle Atlantic region, for example, the decline of labor-intensive nondurable industries has had an extremely negative effect on the labor force participation of puertorriqueñas, not only during 1960s, but during the 1970s and 1980s as well (Wagenheim 1975; Cooney and Colón-Warren 1979; Colón-Warren forthcoming). Specifically, in 1950 the garment industry of New York City employed a total of 72 percent of all Puerto Rican working women as operatives; by 1980 they accounted for only 25.5 percent of all Puerto Rican women in the labor force (Ríos 1984). Meanwhile the labor force participation of puertorriqueñas in other areas across the country increased wherever market conditions were favorable (V. Ortiz and Cooney 1984). The decline in the labor force participation rate of puertorriqueñas, therefore, is not a national trend but must be measured in light of labor demands of the economy or economies of a particular region.

Relating the rate of labor participation of these women to their family status, Cooney and her researchers found that in cities with larger numbers of families headed by women, there was a correspondingly lower level of labor participation on the part of Puerto Rican women. This certainly was the case in the New York metropolitan area between 1960 and 1970:

> In 1960, the participation of Puerto Rican female heads was noticeably higher than nonheads (52.8 as compared to 34.9). But, by 1970, these differences had disappeared, with Puerto Rican female heads having a participation rate of 28.4 and Puerto Rican female nonheads 29.5. Even after adjusting for other factors such as fertility, education, and age, the participation rates were very similar. What these analyses show is that the decline in Puerto Rican female participation was slight for Puerto Rican females who were not household heads, while the decline among female heads was dramatic—24.4 percentage points. (Cooney and Colón-Warren 1980)

More significantly these statistics demonstrate the decline of Puerto Rican women's labor force participation rate at least in this region of the country was very closely related to the lack of participation of puertorriqueñas who headed families. And why were Puerto Rican women head of families not able to participate in the New York metropolitan area labor market as effectively as they had done in the past? The answer, Cooney reminds us in her essays, is imbedded in the unfavorable market conditions that beset this region of the country during these years.

Conclusion

Contemporary studies, based on the more recent census and ethnographic accounts of Puerto Rican women in the Middle Atlantic states, have not dramatically altered this grim socioeconomic picture of life for women heads of family (or household) in this section of the country (Bose 1986; Barry Figueroa 1991; Colón-Warren forthcoming). On the contrary, they not only present a negative prognosis of the labor force participation of these women but of other Puerto Rican women workers presently in the labor market. For those women who were able to gain an education or retrained and gained entrance into the clerical and service sectors are now becoming increasingly unemployed due to contractions in the economy and budget cuts (Bose 1986; Ríos 1989; Colón-Warren forthcoming; Bose forthcoming). This labor market scenario coupled with the continued rate of growth—as of yet unexplained—of woman-headed families in the Puerto Rican community has created great concern for the viability of this community in the next century. Without adequate employment opportunities, education, or public assistance programs, many of the families headed by women are more and more living at or below poverty levels. Many argue that the continued economic deterioration of Puerto Rican women-headed families has contributed to increased poverty in the Puerto Rican community (Colón-Warren forthcoming). The most strategic solution to this problem, advocated by some, is to educate and continue to retrain Puerto Rican women so they can successfully compete in the United States labor market (García 1989). Thus, the history of puertorriqueñas, in or out of the labor market, continues to be inextricably connected to the heartbeat of their community—a community that they helped forge back in the first decades of the twentieth century, that they nourished with hard work and love in later years, and that now seems to depend on them once again for its survival.

Bibliography

Acevedo, Luz del Alba
1990 "Industrialization and Employment: Changes in the Patterns of Women's Work in Puerto Rico." *World Development*, 18.2:231-55.

Acosta-Belén, Edna
1988 "From Settlers to Newcomers: The Hispanic Legacy in the United States." In *The Hispanic Experience in the United States*. New York: Praeger, pp 81-106.
1986 *The Puerto Rican Woman: Perspectives on Culture, History, and Society*. New York: Praeger.

Azize, Yamila
1985 *La mujer en la lucha*. Rio Piedras, PR: Editorial Cultural.

Azize Vargas, Yamila
1989 "A Commentary on the Works of Three Puerto Rican Women Poets in New York." In *Breaking Boundaries: Latina Writings and Critical Readings*. Eds Asunción Horno-Delgado, Eliana Ortega, Nina M. Scott, and Nancy Saporta Sternbach. Amherst: U of Massachusetts P, pp 146-65.

Baerga, María del Carmen
1989 "Women's Labor and the Domestic Unit: Industrial Homework in Puerto Rico during the 1930s." *Centro de Estudios Puertorriqueños Bulletin*, vol 2, no 7, (winter):33-39.

Barry Figueroa, Janis
1991 "A Comparison of Labor Supply Behavior among Single and Married Puerto Rican Mothers." In *Hispanics in the Labor Force: Issues and Policies.* Eds. Edwin Meléndez, Clara Rodríguez, and Janis Barry Figueroa. New York: Plenum.

Benmayor, Rina, Ana Juarbe, Blanca Vázquez Erazo and Celia Alvarez
1988 "Stories To Live By: Continuity and Change in Three Generations of Puerto Rican Women." *Oral History Review*, vol 16, no 2, (fall), pp 1-46.

Bose, Christine E.
n.d. "Entangled Gender: Poverty, Geography, and Latinas in the U. S.," forthcoming.
1986 "Puerto Rican Women in the United States: An Overview." In *The Puerto Rican Woman: Perspectives on Culture, History, and Society.* Ed Edna Acosta-Belén. New York: Praeger, pp147-69.

Boujouen, Norma
n.d. "Menea esas manos: Factory Work, Domestic Life, and Job Loss among Puerto Rican Women in a Connecticut Town." In *Gender, Labor, and Migration: Puerto Rican Women Workers in the Twentieth Century.* Eds. Altagracia Ortiz and Palmira Ríos. Philadelphia: Temple UP, forthcoming.

Capetillo, Luisa
1911 *Mi opinión sobre las libertades, derechos y deberes de la mujer: Como compañera, madre, y ser independiente (la mujer en el hogar, en la familia, en el gobierno).* San Juan, PR: Times Publishing Co.

Centro de Estudios Puertorriqueños
1984 "Nosotras trabajamos en la costura; Puerto Rican Women in the Garment Industry" (radio documentary). New York: Oral History Task Force Project.
n.d. *Vertical File: Belpré.*

Chenault, Lawrence Royce
1970 *The Puerto Rican Migrant in New York City.* 1938 Repr New York: Russell & Russell.

Cohen, Miriam
1977 "Italian-American Women in New York City, 1900-1950: Work and School." In *Class, Sex, and the Woman Worker.* Eds Milton Cantor and Bruce Laurie. Westport, CT: Greenwood P, pp 120-43.
1992 *Workshop to Office: Two Generations of Italian Women Workers in New York City, 1900-1950.* Ithaca: Cornell UP.

Colón-Warren, Alice
n.d. "Puerto Rican Women in the Middle Atlantic Region: Employment, Loss of Jobs, and the Feminization of Poverty, 1970-1980." In *Puerto Rican Women Workers in the Twentieth Century: New Perspectives on Gender, Labor, and Migration, 1900-1990.* Ed Altagracia Ortiz. Philadelphia: Temple UP, forthcoming.

Colón-Warren, Alice, Margarita Mergal and Nilsa Torres
1986 *Participación de la mujer en la historia de Puerto Rico (las primeras décadas del siglo veinte).* New Brunswick, NJ: Rutgers U and U of Puerto Rico.

Cooney, Rosemary Santana
1979 "Intercity Variations in Puerto Rican Female Participation." *Journal of Human Resources*, 14.2: 222-35.

Cooney, Rosemary, and Alice Colón-Warren
1980 "Work and Family: The Recent Struggle of Puerto Rican Females." In *The Puerto Rican Struggle: Essays on Survival in the U. S.* Eds Clara E. Rodríguez, Virginia Sánchez Korrol, and José Oscar Alers. New York: Puerto Rican Migration Consortium, pp 58-73.

Cooney, Rosemary Santana, and Alice E. Colón-Warren
1979 "Declining Female Participation among Puerto Rican New Yorkers: A Comparison with Native White Non-Spanish New Yorkers." *Ethnicity*, vol 6, no 3, (September):281-97.

Cooney, Rosemary Santana, and Kyonghee Min
1981 "Demographic Characteristics Affecting Living Arrangements among Young Currently Unmarried Puerto Rican, Non-Spanish Black, and Non-Spanish White Mothers." *Ethnicity*, vol 2, (June):107-20.

Cooney, Rosemary Santana, and Vilma Ortiz
1983 "Nativity, National Origin, and Hispanic Female Participation in the Labor Force." *Social Science Quarterly*, vol 64, no 3, (September):510-23.

Cuevas, Carmen Leila
1969 *Lola de América.* Hato Rey, PR: Ramallo Bros.

De Montreville, Doris, and Elizabeth D. Crawford, eds
1978 *Fourth Book of Junior Authors and Ilustrators.* New York: H. W. Wilson.

Ewen, Elizabeth
1985 *Immigrant Women in the Land of Dollars: Life and Culture on the Lower East Side, 1890-1925.* New York: Monthly Review P.

Fernández Olmos, Margarite
1982 "From the Metropolis: Puerto Rican Women Poets and the Immigration Experience." *Third Woman*, 1.2:40-51.

Fitzpatrick, Joseph P.
1971 *Puerto Rican Americans: The Meaning of Migration to the Mainland.* 1965 Repr. Englewood Cliffs, NJ: Prentice Hall.

Flores, Angel, and Kate Flores, eds
1986 *The Defiant Muse: Hispanic Feminist Poems from the Middle Ages to the Present.* New York: Feminist P.

Foner, Philip S.
1965 *History of the Labor Movement in the United States.* 4 vols. New York: International Publishers.

Garciá, Karen Marie
1989 "Migrant Puerto Rican Women in the U. S. under Economic Stress: A Theoretical Framework for a National Study." PhD Diss. U of Massachusetts.

Glasser, Ruth
1991 "Qué vivío tiene la gente aquí en Nueva York: Music and Community in Puerto Rican New York, 1915-1940," PhD Diss Yale U.

González, José Emilio
1961 "La poesía de Julia de Burgos." *Julia de Burgos, criatura del agua: Obra poética.* Eds Consuelo Burgos and Juan Bautista Pagán. San Juan, PR: Instituto de Cultura Puertorriqueña, pp 11-59.

González García, Lydia Milagros
1990 *Una puntada en el tiempo: La industria de la aguja*

en Puerto Rico (1900-1929)*. Río Piedras: CEREP/CIPAFO.

Gruber, Ruth
1972 *Felisa Rincón de Gautier: The Mayor of San Juan.* New York: Dell.

Helfgott, Roy B.
1958 "Puerto Rican Integration in a Garment Union Local." *Proceedings of the Tenth Annual Meeting of the Industrial Relations Research Association,* vol 10, pp 269-275.
1959a "Puerto Rican Integration in the Skirt Industry in New York City." In *Discrimination and Low Incomes: Social and Economic Discrimination against Minority Groups in Relation to Low Incomes in New York State.* New York: Studies of New York State Commission Against Discrimination, New School for Social Research.
1959b "Women's and Children's Apparel." In *Made in New York: Case Studies in Metropolitan Manufacturing.* Ed Max Hall. Cambridge, MA: Harvard UP, pp 21-134.

Herberg, Will
1953 "The Old-Timers and the Newcomers: Ethnic Group Relations in a Needle Trades' Union." *Journal of Social Issues,* vol. 9, (summer):12-19.

Hernández-Alvarez, José
1968 "Migration, Return, and Development in Puerto Rico," *Economic Development and Cultural Change,* vol 16, no 4, (July):574-87.
1967 *Return Migration to Puerto Rico.* Berkeley: U of California, Institute of International Studies.

Hill, Herbert
"Guardians of the Sweatshops: The Trade Unions, Racism, and the Garment Industry." In *Puerto Rico and Puerto Ricans: Studies in History and Society.* Eds. Adalberto López and James Petras. New York: John Wiley & Sons, pp 384-416.

International Ladies' Garments Workers' Union Archives. Zimmermann Collection, Box 33.

Kessler-Harris, Alice
"Organizing the Unorganizable: Three Jewish Women and Their Union." In *Class, Sex, and the Woman Worker.* Eds. Milton Cantor and Bruce Laurie. Westport, CT: Greenwood P, pp 144-65.
1982 *Out to Work: History of Wage Earning Women in the United States.* Oxford: Oxford UP.

Laurentz, Robert
1980 "Racial Ethnic Conflict in the New York City Garment Industry, 1933-1980." PhD Diss New York State U at Binghamton.

Lochner, Frances Carol, ed
1978 *Contemporary Authors,* vols 73-76. Detroit, MI: Gale Research, p 51.

Loo, Chalsa and Paul Ong
1987 "Slaying Demons with a Sewing Needle: Feminist Issues for Chinatown's Women." In *From Different Shores: Perspectives on Race and Ethnicity in America.* Ed Ronald Takaki. New York: Oxford UP, pp 186-91.

López, Adalberto, and James Petras, eds
1974 *Puerto Rico and Puerto Ricans: Studies in History and Society.* New York: Wiley.

López, Lillian
1976 *Interview with Pura Belpré.* New York: Columbia U Oral History Project, (February 14), (April 4).

López, Lillian, with Pura Belpré
1974 "Reminiscences of Two Turned-on Librarians." In *Puerto Rican Perspectives.* Ed Edward Mapp. Methuchen, NJ: Scarecrow P, pp 83-96.

Manning, Caroline
1934 "The Employment of Women in Puerto Rico." U. S. Department of Labor, Women's Bureau. *Bulletin of the Women's Bureau No 118.* Washington, DC: Government Printing Office.

Matilla, Alfredo, and Ivan Silén, eds
1972 *The Puerto Rican Poets: Los poetas puertorriqueños.* New York: Bantam.

Maymí, Carmen R.
1977 "Puerto Rican Women Working Together." In *Puerto Rican Women in the United States: Organizing for Change.* Washington, DC: National Conference of Puerto Rican Women, pp 10-12.

Mendoza, Tió Carlos F., ed
1974 *Contribución al estudio de la obra poética de Lola Rodríguez de Tío (1843-1924).* San Juan, PR: n.p.
1975 *Investigaciones literarias: Lola Rodríguez de Tío.* 5 vols. San Juan, PR: n.p.

Meyerson, Michael
1969 "ILGWU: Fighting for Lower Wages," *Ramparts,* vol 8, no 4, (October):51-55.

Mills, Charles Wright, Clarence Senior and Rose Kohn Goldsen
1950 *Puerto Rican Journey: New York's Newest Migrants.* New York: Harper & Row.

Muñiz, Vicky
n.d. "The Defense of the Neighborhood as a Response to Urban Revitalization and Gentrification: Puerto Rican Women Struggle for Homes and Identities." Ph.D. Diss. U of Syracuse, forthcoming.

New Movement in Solidarity with Puerto Rican and Mexican Revolutionaries, eds
1980 *Have You Seen La Mujer Revolucionaria Puertorriqueña? The Poetry and Lives of Revolutionary Puerto Rican Women.* N.p.

New York Times
1980 May 20.

Ortiz, Altagracia
1989 "Historical Perspectives on Feminism and the Puerto Rican Woman." *Journal on Women's History,* vol 1, no 2, (fall):166-78.
1988 "The Labor Struggles of Puerto Rican Women in the Garment Industry of New York City, 1920-1960." *Cimarrón,* vol. 1, no 3, (spring):39-59.
1989 "The Lives of *Pioneras*: Bibliographic and Research Sources on Puerto Rican Women in the United States." *Boletín del Centro de Estudios Puertorriqueños,* vol 2, no 2, (winter):41-47.
1984 "Puerto Rican Women in the Needle Trade." *The Hispanic Monitor,* vol 1, no 7, (August):5-6.
n.d. *Puerto Rican Women Workers in the Twentieth Century: New Perspectives on Gender, Labor and Migration, 1900-1990.* Philadelphia: Temple UP, forthcoming.

1990 "Puerto Rican Workers in the Garment Industry of New York City, 1920-1960." In *Labor Divided: Race and Ethnicity in United States Labor Struggles, 1835-1960*. Eds Robert Asher and Charles Stephenson. Albany: State U of New York, pp 105-25.

Ortiz, Vilma, and Rosemary Santana Cooney
1984 "Sex-Role Attitudes and Labor Participation among Young Hispanic Females and Non-Hispanic White Females." *Social Science Quarterly*, vol 65, no 2, (June):392-400.

Quiroga, Carmen Lucila
1980 "Julia de Burgos: El desarrollo de la conciencia femenina en la expresión poética," PhD Diss New York U.

Ribes Tovar, Federico.
1968 *El libro puertorriqueño de Nueva York; Handbook of the Puerto Rican Community*. New York: El Libro Puertorriqueño.
1974 *Lolita Lebrón, la prisionera*. New York: Plus Ultra.
1976 *One Hundred Oustanding Puerto Ricans*. New York: Plus Ultra.
1972 *The Puerto Rican Woman: Her Life and Evolution throughout History*. New York: Plus Ultra.

Ríos-González, Palmira N.
1990 "Work and Industrialization in Puerto Rico: Gender Division of Labor and the Demand for Female Labor in the Manufacturing Sector, 1950-1980." PhD Diss Yale U.
1989 "Puerto Rican Women and the New York City Labor Market." In *Towards a Puerto Rican/Latino Agenda for N.Y.C.* New York City: Institute for Puerto Rican Policy, vol 9, pp 51-56.
1984 "Puerto Rican Women in the United States Labor Market." Paper presented to "Nosotras Trabajamos en la Costura," Puerto Rican Women in Garment Industry Conference. Sponsored by the Centro de Estudios Puertorriqueños, New York City.
1985 "Puerto Rican Women in the United States Labor Force." *Line of March*, (fall):43-56.

Rivera, Marcia
1986 "The Development of Capitalism in Puerto Rico and the Incorporation of Women into the Labor Force." In *The Puerto Rican Woman: Perspectives on Culture, History, and Society*. Ed Edna Acosta-Belén. New York: Praeger, pp 30- 45.

Rodríguez, Clara E.
1979 "Economic Factors Affecting Puerto Ricans in New York." In *Labor and Migration under Capitalism: The Puerto Rican Experience*. Ed History Task Force, Centro de Estudios Puertorriqueños. New York: Monthly Review P, pp 197-221.

Rodríguez, Clara, Virginia Sánchez Korrol and José Oscar Alers, eds
1980 *The Puerto Rican Struggle: Essays in Survival.* New York: Puerto Rican Migration Research Consortium.

Rodríguez, Pereta
1993 "Growing Up in the International Ladies' Garments Workers' Union." *Visión: El Periódico del Barrio*, 5.4:6-7.

Sánchez, George
1990 "Go After the Women: Americanization and the Mexican Woman, 1915-1929." In *Unequal Sisters: A Multi-Cultural Reader in U. S. Women's History*. Eds Ellen C. DuBois and Vicki L. Ruiz. New York: Routledge, pp 250-61.

Sánchez Korrol, Virginia
1986 "The Forgotten Migrant: Educated Puerto Rican Women in New York City, 1920-1940." In *The Puerto Rican Woman: Perspectives on Culture, History, and Society*. Ed Edna Acosta-Belén. New York: Praeger, pp 170-79.
1983 *From Colonia to Community: The History of Puerto Ricans in New York City, 1917-1948*. Westport, CT: Greenwood P.
1988 "In Search of Unconventional Women: Histories of Puerto Rican Women in Religious Vocations before Mid-Century." *Oral History Review*, vol 16, no 2, (fall):47-63.
1979 "On the Other Side of the Ocean: The Work Experiences of Early Puerto Rican Migrant Women." *Caribbean Review*, vol 8, (January):22-28.
1980 "Survival of Puerto Rican Women in New York before World War II." In *The Puerto Rican Struggle: Essays on Survival in the U. S.* Eds Clara E. Rodríguez, Virginia Sánchez Korrol, and José Oscar Alers. New York: Puerto Rican Migration Consortium, pp 47-57.
1967 "Towards Bilingual Education: Puerto Rican Women Educators in New York City Schools, 1947-1967." In *Puerto Rican Women Workers in the Twentieth Century: New Perspectives on Gender, Labor and Migration, 1900-1990*. Ed Altagracia Ortiz. Philadelphia: Temple UP, forthcoming.

Seller, Maxine S.
1975 "Beyond the Stereotype: A New Look at the Immigrant Woman." *Journal of Ethnic Studies, vol* 3, no 1, (spring):59-68.

Senior, Clarence Ollson
1965 *The Puerto Ricans: Strangers—Then Neighbors.* Chicago: Quadrangle.

Smith, Carole Joan
1980 "Immigrant Women, Work, and Use of Government Benefits: A Case Study of Hispanic Women Workers in New York's Garment Industry." PhD Diss Adelphi School of Social Welfare.

Tirado Aviles, Amilcar
1989 "Notas sobre el desarrollo de la industria del tabaco en Puerto Rico y su impacto en la mujer puertorriqueña, 1898-1920." *Centro de Estudios Puertorriqueños Bulletin*, 2.7:19-29.

U. S. Congress House Committee on Education and Labor
1963 88th Cong., 1st session. "Testimony of Herbert Hill before Sub-committee on Education and Labor of August 17, 1962." *Congressional Record*, vol 109, part 2, pp 1569-572.

Valle, Norma
1975 *Luisa Capetillo*. San Juan, PR: n.p.
1980 *Luisa Capetillo: Historia de una mujer proscrita.* Rio Piedras, PR: Ediciones Huracán.

Vega, Bernardo
1980 *Memorias de Bernardo Vega: Contribución a la historia de la comunidad puertorriqueña en Nueva York.* Ed. César Andreu Iglesias. Río Piedras, PR: Ediciones Huracán.

Vernon, Raymond
1960 *Metropolis, 1985: An Interpretation of the Findings of the New York Metropolitan Region Study.* Cambridge, MA: Harvard UP.

Wagenheim, Kal
1975 *A Survery of Puerto Ricans on the U. S. Mainland in the 70s.* New York: Praeger.

Wakefield, Dan
1959 *Island in the City: The World of Spanish Harlem.* Boston: Houghton Mifflin.

Waldinger, Roger
1985 "Immigration and Industrial Change in the New York City Apparel Industry." In *Hispanics in the U. S. Economy.* Eds. George J. Borjas and Marta Tienda. New York: Academic, pp 323-49.
1986 *Through the Eye of the Needle: Immigrants and Enterprise in New York's Garment Trades.* New York: New York UP.

Wertheimer, Barbara, and Anne H. Nelson
1975 *Trade Union Women: A Study of Their Participation in New York City Locals.* New York: Praeger.

A Socio-Historic Study of Hispanic Newspapers in the United States

Nicolás Kanellos

The Nineteenth Century

Throughout the last two centuries Hispanic communities from coast to coast have supported newspapers of varying sizes and missions, running the gamut from the eight-page weekly written in Spanish or bilingually to the highly entrepreneurial large-city daily written exclusively in Spanish. Since the founding in New Orleans in 1808 of *El Misisipí*, probably the first Spanish-language newspaper in the United States, the Hispanic press has had to serve functions hardly ever envisioned in Mexico City, Madrid, or Havana. Besides supplying basic news of the homeland and of the Hispanic world in general, advertising local businesses, and informing the community on relevant current affairs and politics of the United States (often through unauthorized translations of the English-language press and/or news agencies), Hispanic periodicals have offered alternative information services, presenting their own communities' views of news and events. At times this information has taken a contestatory and challenging posture vis-à-vis the English-language news organizations and U. S. government and cultural institutions. Furthermore, the newspapers led the effort to preserve Hispanic language and cultural identity in the face of the powerful assimilationist forces prevalent in American society. Most of the Hispanic press, whether small weekly or large city daily, assumed a leadership role in cultural resistance and on issues regarding the homeland and the United States. Indeed, they battled to protect the very real economic and political interests of the local Hispanic community, whether regarded as a community, an internal colony, or a racial barrio.

The Hispanic press played its leadership role during the last two centuries, often in concert with the Church and social organizations and often without regard to its own commercial and financial survival. The press sponsored patriotic and cultural celebrations. It organized the community for social and political action for such purposes as founding Spanish-language schools and community clinics. It led the fight against segregation and discrimination and collected funds for flood victims, refugees, and other needy and displaced persons. The press featured editorials and letters to the editor in support of community needs.

Historically, the Hispanic press always functioned as a purveyor of education, high culture, and entertainment. During the nineteenth century and the first half of the twentieth, it became the principal publisher of literature including poetry, literary prose, and even serialized novels in its pages. The newspapers relied on two basic ways to preserve the culture of the local community and elevate its level of education. One called for the publication of works by local writers. The other entailed reprinting works by writers in the homeland and from throughout the Hispanic world. As an extension of this mission, many newspapers founded publishing houses and some even opened bookstores to further disseminate Hispanic intellectural and artistic thought.

The significance and implications of the growth and spread of the Hispanic press to the Hispanic community were outstanding: it pointed to the considerable economic resources dedicated to this effort; it indicated large-scale involvement and cooperation of hundreds of intellectuals, creative writers, political figures, and businessmen; and it succeeded in producing and distributing the writings of important political and literary figures of the day. Notable among the writers were Mexican novelist Mariano Azuela, Dominican writer and journalist Pedro Henríquez Ureña, Puerto Rican independence patriot and writer Pachín Marín, Cuban patriot and writer José Martí, Mexican philosopher and educator José Vasconselos, and scores of others who in the past were active and known in U. S. Hispanic communities but unknown in the homelands. The works of these intellectual and artistic giants and of many others whose writings are still generally unknown contributed significantly to Hispanic identity, history, and culture in the United States. They also provide the basis for U. S. Hispanism in the twenty-first century. The Hispanic press has assisted enormously in rediscovering and bringing to light their work.

The Southwest

In the area that later became known as the Southwest even before the Mexican-American War, Hispanic newspapers were already carrying on and promoting political activities, as Luis Leal pointed out in his article "The Spanish Language Press: Function and Use" (Leal 1989). The interests of the press and the local community were intertwined. Newspapers became responsible for assuring that these interests were clearly presented and delineated. For instance, Santa Fe's *El Crepúsculo de la Libertad* (The Dawn of Liberty) headed up a campaign in 1834 for the election of representatives to their Mexican Congress, and it also served as a forum for Antonio Martínez's defense of the civil rights and land ownership rights of the Taos Indians. And after the Mexican-American War, as Leal noted (1989), the Spanish-language press defended the rights of the Mexican inhabitants in what had become the new territories of the United States.

On the foundation laid by such newspapers as El *Crepúsculo de la Libertad, La Gaceta de Texas* (1813; The Texas Gazette) and *El Mexicano* (1813; The Mexican), numerous Spanish-language newspapers were founded, and they began to offer an alternative to the flow of information from Anglo-American sources during the transition from Mexican to U. S. government following the Mexican-American War (1846-48). This was only logical, for it was their specific business mission to serve the interests of the Mexican (-American) and Hispanic communities. The important commercial centers of Los Angeles and San Francisco supported dozens of periodicals at this time, including *La Estrella de Los Angeles* (The Los Angeles Star) and *El Clamor Público* (The Public Clamor) during the 1850s and Los Angeles's *La Crónica* (The Chronicle) from the 1870s to the 1890s; San Francisco's *La Voz de México* (The Voice of Mexico) from the 1860s to the 1890s, *La República* (The Republic) from the 1870s to the 1890s and *La Voz del Nuevo Mundo* (The Voice of the New World) in the 1870s and 1880s. Of course, the port cities were not the only populations that supported Spanish-language newspapers. Hispanic journalism also flourished in inland towns and villages, especially in New Mexico, where virtually every sizable town had its own weekly, including Bernalillo, Las Cruces, Mora, Santa Fe, Socorro, and Las Vegas.

While the newspapers published various types of creative literature at this time, it is noteworthy that one of the expressions of this period was a serialized novel that illustrated the clash of Mexican and Anglo-American economic and cultural interests. "Las Aventuras de Joaquín Murieta" (The Adventures of Joaquín Murieta), based on the life of the legendary social bandit, was one such serialized novel published in Santa Barbara's *La Gaceta* (The Gazette) in 1881. Murieta's pursuit of vengeance on the Anglo-American newcomers surely coincided with popular resentment among the Californios then losing their lands and rights.

José Martí.

New York

Although in the Southwest the Spanish-language newspapers intensely felt the need to defend the Mexican community, such was not he case for the newspapers serving the communities of Hispanic immigrants to New York during the same time period. There the Spaniards, Cubans, Mexicans, and other Hispanic immigrants founded periodicals that provided more for the typical interests of immigrants: news from the homeland, coverage of local Hispanic affairs and business, and also the preservation and enrichment of the Spanish lan-

Office of Los Angeles' *La Crónica* (center).

guage and Hispanic culture in the alien environment. Of continuing concern in these papers were the wars of independence from Spain and the transition from colonial status to self-determination in Spanish America. The earliest newspapers on record were *El Mensajero Semanal* (The Weekly Messenger; 1828-31), El *Mercurio de Nueva York* (The New York Mercury; 1828-33), *La Crónica* (The Chronicle; 1850), and *La Voz de América* (The Voice of America) in the 1860s.

It was not until the end of the nineteenth century that the periodicals began to multiply in New York, undoubtedly responding to increased Hispanic immigration and the political and cultural fervor that developed in the Cuban, Dominican, and Puerto Rican communities, which were raising funds for and promoting the revolutionary ideologies of independence from Spain for their homelands. In this regard, the most noteworthy institution was the Cuban newspaper *La Patria* (The Homeland; 1892-98), in whose pages can be found essays by the leading Cuban and Puerto Rican patriots. The newspapers like *La Patria* served not only as forums for revolutionary ideas but were actually tools of organization and propaganda around which many of the expatriate conspirators rallied. Many of the Spanish-language literary books published in New York at this time were also related to the Cuban independence struggle. The title of Luis García Pérez's *El grito de Yara* (The Shout at Yara; 1879), in fact, commemorated the Cuban declaration of independence from Spain. Desiderio Fajardo Ortiz's *La Fuga de Evangelina* (The Escape of Evangelina; 1898), told the story of the young Cuban heroine Evangelina Cossío's attempts to free her father from imprisonment by the Spaniards and of her own escape to freedom in New York and involvement in the organizing effort.

Active in organizing support among the Hispanic communities and in publishing in *La Patria* and the other periodicals at this time were the revolutionary leaders Francisco González "Pachín" Marín, a Puerto Rican, and the Cuban hero José Martí, who was also carrying out similar functions in the Cuban communities of Tampa-Ybor City and Key West. "Pachín" Marín, a typesetter by trade, was instrumental in producing many political and literary publications. A poet and essayist, Marín has left us an important essay, "Nueva York por dentro: Una faz de su vida bohemia" (New York on the Inside: One Side of Its Bohemian Life), in which he sketches life in New York from the perspective of a disillusioned immigrant. The essay represents perhaps the earliest document in Spanish to elaborate this theme, which will increasingly grow in importance throughout the twentieth century. This may very well mark the beginning of Hispanic immigrant literature, at least on the East Coast.

An early Puerto Rican contribution to Hispanic journalism was *La Gaceta Ilustrada* (The Illustrated Gazette), published by Francisco Amy in the 1890s. And writing in the newspapers of New York at this time were the important Puerto Rican literary and patriotic figures Eugenio María de Hostos, Ramón Emeterio Betances, Lola Rodríguez de Tío, and Sotero Figueroa.

The most widely circulated weekly was *Las Novedades* (The News; 1893-18), whose theater, music, and literary critic was famed Dominican writer Pedro Henríquez Ureña. Other periodicals publishing at this time were *El Porvenir* (The Future) and *Revista Popular* (The People's Magazine), according to an article published in *La Patria*. Just how many other periodicals existed at the end of the nineteenth century is not known, but probably there were not many more, judging from the size of the population. Nevertheless, the number that existed played a prominent role in the cultures and lives of Hispanics in the Northeast.

The Twentieth Century

The turn of the century brought record immigration from Mexico to the Southwest and Midwest because of the Mexican Revolution of 1910. The appropriation by the United States of the former Spanish colonies in the Caribbean after the Spanish-American War resulted in an increase of immigration from Cuba and Puerto Rico. The Spanish Civil War also sent a host of new Spanish expatriates to New York, Tampa, and even Chicago. In the Southwest from 1910 until World War II, immigrant workers and upper-class and educated professionals from Mexico interacted with the Mexican-origin U. S.

Lola Rodríguez de Tío.

residents who had been somewhat cut off from the evolution of Mexican culture inside Mexico. It was a period, too, when elites from throughout the Spanish-speaking world were drawn to the great U. S. urban centers of New York and Los Angeles, thus lending a broader international and cosmopolitan perspective to the urban Hispanic communities. It was the period when Spanish-language periodical literature flourished throughtout the Southwest, Midwest, New York, and Tampa. New York, Los Angeles, and San Antonio even supported competing dailies vying to serve a heterogeneous public, made up of diverse social classes, diverse Hispanic nationalities, and immigrants of varying status: economic refugees, political refugees, and citizens, as was the case for Mexican Americans and, after 1907, for Puerto Ricans. Of course, then as now, the vast majority of Hispanics were laborers of one sort or another.

The Southwest

In the Southwest, the educated political refugees played a key role in publishing and other social and intellectual activities that defined and solidified the urban Mexican immigrant/Mexican-American communities. From their upper-class, expatriate perspective, these intellectuals and entrepreneurs created and promoted—and here the newspaper was essential—an ideology of a Mexican community in exile, or a "México de afuera" (Mexico on the outside). They intended that the culture, religion, politics, and ethos of Mexico were to be, if not duplicated, at least continued in the foreign land until the revolution ceased and the internal politics in Mexico changed sufficiently to allow them to return to their *patria*, or fatherland.

From within the context of this conservative world view, the Spanish language had to be protected from the threat of erosion from speaking English, and Hispanic culture had to fend off assimilation to the Anglo-Saxon culture and what they considered to be its looser morality, especially the more liberated role of women in the society. All of this was usually couched in nationalistic terms of defending Mexican identity and its illustrious heritage, not only against the influence of a culture that at first seemed superior in its technological and economic success, but against the real aggression of racism and political and economic exploitation. This position was well stated by Clemente Idar in an editorial in his Laredo newspaper, *La Crónica* (The Chronicle), on November 26, 1910:

> Nosotros no predicamos el antagonismo de razas, sólo nos interesamos por la conservación y la ilustración de la nuestra para que ésta deje de ser mal vista mientras no ensanche sus facultades físicas e intelectuales. En los Estados Unidos de Norte América, el problema de razas es cuestión de color, y nosotros que pertenecemos a una raza latinizada multicolor, al inmigrar a este país con toda nuestra ignorancia, nos colocamos en una atmósfera decidida y tradicionalmente hostil. . . . Los americanos, con rarísimas excepciones, a todos aquellos de nosotros que somos ciudadanos de su mismo país, no nos creen capaces de ser buenos, cumplidos y leales ciudadanos, y el resultado es, que con esa suposición, casi se deja al mexicano mendigo de nacionalidad. Pues ya que así son los hechos, estrechémonos todos los mexicanos por los santos lazos de sangre, y como latinos, seamos tan unidos como los anglo-sajones; luchando con denodado ardor por la exaltación de nuestra estirpe mexicana por las vías de la cultura, de la intelectualidad y de la moralidad.
>
> *[We do not preach the antagonism of the races ("race" in Spanish also means "culture"), as we*

are only interested in the preservation and education of our own so that it will no longer be looked down upon for not improving its physical and intellectual abilities. In the United States of North America, the problem of race is a question of color, and we who belong to a multicolor Latinized race, upon immigrating to this country with all of our ignorance, find ourselves in a decidedly and traditionally hostile environment. . . . With rare exceptions, the Americans do not believe that those of us who are citizens of their country are capable of being good, responsible and loyal citizens, and the result is that, because of that belief, Mexicans are practically without a nationality. Well, those being the facts, let all of us Mexicans pull together with the holy ties of blood, and as Latins let us be as united as the Anglo-Saxons, fighting with valiant ardor for the glory of our Mexican heritage in the areas of culture, intellectual pursuits and morality.]

There was no clearer expression of a cultural nationalism and no clearer battle lines drawn for Anglo-Mexican conflict than in the areas of race, culture, thought, and morality. A decade later the same themes were still being expressed in an editorial published in the February 27, 1921, edition of *El Heraldo*, de México. This time however, part of the blame for the prejudice was placed upon the Mexican Revolution and what the elites thought was the negative impression created by uneducated working-class immigrants. The writer's elite and educated identity is apparent, and the counter-revolutionary theme is linked to culture and race conflict here in the United States:

> ¿Por qué? Porque en esta tierra, bien lo sabéis y algunos quizás lo resentís, por infundados prejuicios de raza, —que no es del caso comentar— no el público culto, que ése a todos hace justicia; pero sí el que sólo nos conoce por falsas informaciones periodísticas y a través de calumniosas y ofensivas cintas cinematográficas cree que todos los mexicanos somos de la hez que ha removido la funesta revolución.
>
> *[Why? Because in this land, you know it well and some of you resent it, because of unfounded racial prejudice—which does not merit comment on this occasion—not in the educated public, which is just to everyone, but certainly in that public that only knows us from false periodical information and through defamatory and offensive movies and that believes that all Mexicans are the lowlifes that have been removed by the unfortunate revolution.]*

Among the most powerful of the political, business, and intellectual figures in expressing the ideology the "México de afuera" was Ignacio E. Lozano, founder and operator of the two most powerful and well distributed daily newspapers, *La Prensa* (The Press) and *La Opinión* (The Opinion). This future magnate settled in San Antonio in 1908 and in 1913 founded *La Prensa*. In 1926 he founed *La Opinión* in Los Angeles. He brought to Hispanic journalism in the United States a professionalism and business acumen that resulted in the longevity for his two newspapers. In fact, *La Opinión* has survived and remains viable to the present. Lozano hired well-trained journalists, notably appointing Teodoro Torres as editor. Considered the "Father of Mexican Journalism," Torres wrote and taught in his field and founded schools of journalism after returning to Mexico from exile. *La Prensa's* publishing house also issued two of Torres's novels, one of which was a biting satire of the revolution: *Como perros y gatos* (Like Cats and Dogs).

In the pages of his newspapers Lozano also published the essays and editorials of one of the most eloquent and active promoters of the ideology of exile, Nemesio García Naranjo, who had been President Victoriano Huerta's minister of education. The ideas of men like Torres and García Naranjo reached thousands in San Antonio, the Southwest and Midwest, as well as interior Mexico, through a vast distribution system that

Issue of *La Opinión*.

included newsstand sales, home delivery, and mail. *La Prensa* also set up a network of correspondents throughout the United States who reported on current events and cultural activities of the Mexican community in exile and other Hispanics in such far away places as Detroit, Chicago, and even New York.

Businessmen, intellectuals, and exiled politicians such as Lozano, Torres, and Nemesio García exercised leadership of the diverse Mexican/Mexican-American communities in the urban centers precisely because they dominated newspapers, magazines, and books and because they were the prime movers in mutualist societies and other community organizations. Their charitable work, including the founding of Mexican schools, clinics, hospitals, and insurance, as well as their cultural leadership, provided cohesion and respect for their heritage–even if it were an elite version of Mexican/Hispanic culture and history. The businessmen reaped the benefits of an isolated and specialized market for their products. They shaped and cultivated their market as efficiently for cultural products and the print media as they did for material goods, Mexican foods, and specialized services for immigrants. While the businessmen and entrepreneurs became wealthier, the intellectuals earned prestige, renown, and decision-making power. Thus, for real business and cultural purposes, the ideology of exile in many ways further isolated the community, which had to battle assimilation to ensure the survival of Mexicans as a cultural group in an alien environment.

The Mexican community thus obtained needed goods, information, and services that were often denied by the larger society through official and open segregation. The writers, artists, and intellecutals also provided entertainment in the native language for the Mexican community, which was not offered by Anglo-American society. As for the creation of Spanish-language theater by many of the journalists, it should be remembered that many theaters and movie houses were also segregated and off limits to Mexicans at this time.

The role of the journalist as a leader in the Mexican community was emphasized by Daniel Venegas in an editorial in the April 17, 1927, edition of his newspaper, *El Malcriado* (The Brat), upon the occasion of the founding of a Mexican newspaper association in Calfiornia:

> Los periodistas deben ponerse, con su agrupación, al frente de las demás socie-dades mexicanas, como guiadores hacia un porvenir de afectiva solidaridad y verdadero patriotismo para todos los exiliados. Es decir, para realizar la dignificación no solamente de los trabajadores mexicanos –también los periodistas son trabajadores– residentes en una tierra extraña, sino por manera muy especial la de la Patria.
>
> *[The journalists should place themselves, with their association, at the head of the other Mexican societies as guides to a future of warm solidarity and patriotism for all of the exiles. That is to say, this is to achieve the dignity of not only Mexican workers–journalists are also workers–residing in a strange land, but also of the Homeland in a very special way.]*

Venegas argued that the one significant role played by the newspapers was fomenting the ideology of exile. In his view, the newspapers helped to dignify the character of Mexicans and Mexico. He also suggested the role of the newspapermen as community leaders. These newspapermen, like Venegas himself, were to carry out their intellectual and cultural task not only through their journalism, but also in writing novels, poetry, and plays for production and publication.

In the editorial offices of *La Prensa* in San Antonio and Los Angeles's *La Opinión* and *El Heraldo de México* (The Mexican Herald), some of the most talented writers from Mexico, Spain, and Latin America earned their living as reporters, columnists and critics, including such writers as Miguel Arce, Esteban Escalante, Gabriel Navarro, and Daniel Venegas. These and many others used the newspapers as a stable source of employment and as a base from which they launched their literary publications in book form or wrote plays

Gabriel Navarro.

and revues for the flourishing dramatic stages. Various newspaper companies themselves established publishing houses and marketed the books of these authors and others. The Casa Editorial Lozano, an outgrowth of San Antonio's *La Prensa*, not only advertised the books in the family's two newspapers to be sold via direct mail, but also operated a bookstore in San Antonio. *El Heraldo de México* also owned and operated a bookstore in Los Angeles. In addition to the publishing houses owned by the large dailies, in the same cities and in smaller population centers there were many other smaller companies operating, such as Laredo Publishing Company, Los Angeles's Spanish American Printing, and San Diego's Imprenta Bolaños Cacho Hermanos.

The largest and most productive publishing houses were located in San Antonio. Leading the list was the Casa Editorial Lozano, owned by Ignacio E. Lozano. Issuing and distributing hundreds of titles per year, it was the largest publishing establishment ever owned by a Hispanic in the United States. Another was the Viola Novelty Company, owned by P. Viola and associated with his two satirical newspapers, *El Vacilón* (The Joker) and *El Fandango* (The Fandango), active from 1916 through at least 1927. The Whitt Company, run by the descendants of an English officer who had remained in Mexico after his tour of duty under Maximilian's reign, still exists today but only as a printer. And another was the Librería Española, which today survives only as a bookstore. These houses produced everything from religious books to political propaganda, from how-to books (such as Ignacio E. Lozano's *El secretario perfecto)* to novels and books of poetry. Many of the novels produced by these houses were part of the genre known as "novels of the Mexican Revolution." Their stories were set within the context of the revolution and often commented on historical events and personalities, especially from a conservative or reactionary perspective, so that they may also be considered as exile literature.

Typical of the novels attacking the revolution and certain of its political leaders were Miguel Bolaños Cacho's *Sembradores de viento* (Sowers of the Wind; 1928), Brígido Caro's *Plutarco Elías Calles: Dictador bolchevique de México* (Plutarco Elías Calles: Bolshevik Dictator of Mexico; 1924) and Lázaro Gutiérrez de Lara's *Los bribones rebeldes* (The Rebel Rogues; 1932). Other authors of this very popular genre included Miguel Arce, Conrado Espinosa, Alfredo González, Esteban Maqueos Castellanos, Manuel Mateos, Ramón Puente, and Teodoro Torres, but the most famous was Mariano Azuela, whose masterpiece, *Los de abajo* (The Underdogs), helped establish the standards of modern Mexican literature. It was first published in 1915 in a serialized version in El Paso's newspaper *El Paso del Norte* (The Northern Pass) and was issued later by the same newspaper in book form.

Although most of the novels published during these years concerned political and counter-revolutionary topics, there were others that focused on the experiences of working-class Mexicans and Mexican Americans in the United States. In fact, some of these titles can be considered forerunners of the Chicano novel of the 1960s in their identification with the working-class Mexicans of the Southwest, their use of popular dialects, and their political stance toward the government and society of the United States. The prime example of this new sensibility was written by Los Angeles newspaperman Daniel Venegas. His novel, *Las aventuras de don Chipote o Cuando los pericos mamen* (The Adventures of Don Chipote; or, When Parakeets May Suckle Their Young; 1928) is a humorous picaresque account of a fictional immigrant Mexican, a country bumpkin who travels through the Southwest, working here and there at menial tasks and hard labor and encountering one misadventure after the other. He becomes the victim of rogues, con men, the authorities, and his foremen during his search for the mythic streets lined with gold that the United States is supposed to offer immigrants. *Don*

Daniel Venegas.

Chipote is a novel of immigration, a picaresque novel, and a novel of protest all wrapped up into one, and it is furthermore a historical document recording the language and customs of Mexican workers in the 1920s. In the autobiographical passages of the book, Daniel Venegas shows himself to be proud of having been a laborer, as he recounts his own experiences in crossing the border, working on the railroad, and chafing at the customs and attitudes of his Mexican-American brothers.

Venegas also published (he wrote each entire issue himself) the satirical weekly newspaper *El Malcriado* (The Brat) in Los Angeles during the 1920s. It was a chatty periodical that employed worker's dialect and openly identified with Chicanos, the term used both in the newspaper and in his novel. Venegas also wrote plays and headed up a vaudeville company that performed to working-class audiences in Los Angeles, which revealed once again his class stand as departing significantly from his elite brethren among the writers and newspaper publishers.

The novels were an important expression of the ideology of exile and of nationalism, but there was another genre more traditionally identified with and central to Hispanic newspapers that became essential in forming and maintaining community attitudes. It was the *crónica,* or chronicle, a short weekly column that humorously and satirically commented on current topics and social habits. It owed its origins to Addison and Steel in England and to José Mariano de Larra in Spain, but it was cultivated extensively throughout Mexico and Spanish America. In the Southwest, it served purposes never imagined in Mexico or Spain. From Los Angeles to San Antonio and up to Chicago, Mexican moralists assumed pseudonyms and satirized the customs and behavior of the Mexican colony coming under the influence of the dominant Anglo-Saxon culture. The columns were filled with jokes, anecdotes, and popular speech, making them a real mirror of the social environment from which they sprang. It was the cronista's job to fan the flames of nationalism and to enforce the ideology of "México de afuera" and to battle the Anglo-Saxon immorality and Protestantism. Another job was to protect against the erosion of the Spanish language with almost religious fervor. Using such pseudonyms as El Malcriado (The Brat [Daniel Venegas]), Kaskabel (Rattle Snake [Benjamín Padilla]), Az.T.K. (The Aztec), and Chicote (The Whip), the cronistas were literally whipping and stinging the community into conformity as they commented on how the common folk mixed Spanish and English or poked fun at them for being overly impressed with Yankee ingenuity and technology.

Women, in particular, were a target for these chroniclers, apparently because the men were worried that their wives, daughters, and girlfriends would imitate Anglo women and assume some of the leadership and responsibility heretofore reserved for men in Hispanic culture. This was symbolized by the more masculine haircuts of flappers, their smoking in public, and their higher hemlines during the liberal Roaring Twenties. But more subtly, women were in short supply in the Mexican immigrant communities, and their assimilation to Anglo culture would lead the way to their intermarriage with Anglos. The circumstance posed a very real threat to the genetic and cultural survival of the Mexican community. The most hostile of the satirists of women was without a doubt Julio G. Arce (1870-1926), who used the pen name Jorge Ulica in his syndicated "Crónicas Diabólicas" (Diabolical Chronicles). He satirized women adopting such American customs as giving surprise parties and celebrating Thanksgiving. He attacked them for being domineering their husbands and for entering the workplace as secretaries and picking up "masculine prerogatives," which could only be learned from American women "wearing the pants" in the family. He even went to the absurd extreme in one of his crónicas of writing a court scene in which a wife is exonerated for killing her husband by defenestration because she is embarrassed by his backward Mexican ways.

Julio G. Arce was an expatriate Mexican who had been a newspaper editor and publisher in Culiacán and later in Guadalajara. He escaped from Mexico in fear of losing his life because of his political stances, which were often expressed in his *Diario de Occidente* (The Daily Westerner). After arriving in San Francisco in 1915, he swore he would never return to Mexico, so

Leonor Villegas de Magnón.

bitter was he at the revolution. That same year he began work for San Francisco's *La Crónica* (The Chronicle) and later became its editor and buyer, changing its name to *Hispano América* (Spanish America) in 1919. Arce's "Crónicas Diabólicas" column, first published in *La Crónica*, became so popular they were syndicated throughout the Southwest. Their popularity was rivaled only by the columns of expatriate Guadalajara journalist Benjamín Padilla, whose crónicas were also syndicated.

Despite the campaign against women's liberation waged by Arce and others, there is a sound record of journalistic and even feminist intellectual activity in the newspapers of the Southwest. Among the first manifestations of this are the editorials and other publications of teachers such as Sara Estela Ramírez (1881-1910) and Leonor Villegas de Magnón (1876-1955) in Laredo's *La Crónica*, and in Ramírez's own periodicals, *Aurora* and *La Corregidora*. There was also El Paso's short-lived newspaper *La Voz de la Mujer* (1907) and newspapers founded by revolutionaries, the Bermúdez sisters, in San Antonio. An important woman cronista, poet, and novelist was San Antonio's María Luisa Garza, who used the pen name of Loreley in her columns in *La Prensa*. But one of the most interesting women in the tradition was Lucía Eldine Gonzales (1853-1942), a native of Johnson County, Texas, who was married to social journalist Albert Parsons. Under the name Lucy Parsons, she authored numerous poems, articles, and editorials in support of labor, socialist, and anarchist organizations

Purchasing *La Prensa* on the streets of New York in the early 1960s. (Courtesy of the Justo A. Marté Collection, Center for Puerto Rican Studies Library, Hunter College, CUNY.)

and causes. She became one of the most prominent reformers and labor organizers in the late nineteenth and early twentieth centuries and one of the original founders of the Industrial Workers of the World (IWW). In 1873 she moved with her husband to Chicago, which became the base for most of her writings and activities.

Much of this journalistic and literary activity in the Southwest came to an abrupt end with the Great Depression and the Repatriation of the 1930s. Both circumstances caused the forced and voluntary repatriation of Mexican immigrants. A large segment of Southwest Mexican society disappeared over a period of some ten years. With the economic distress brought on by the Depression and the loss of markets in the depopulated Mexican communities, numerous periodicals and publishing ventures failed. It was not until the 1960s that small weeklies would begin to flourish again in Mexican-American communities.

New York

In New York, the period from the turn of the century up until the Depression was one of increased Hispanic immigration from the Spanish-speaking world and one of interaction of the various Hispanic nationality groups once in the metropolis. While Spaniards and Cubans made up the majority of the Hispanic community, this period saw increased migration of Puerto Ricans to the city, facilitated by the Jones Act of 1917, which declared Puerto Ricans to be citizens of the United States. From the 1930s to the 1950s Puerto Rican migration to the city assumed the proportions of a diaspora, as economic conditions worsened on the island and the United States suffered a shortage of manpower during World War II in the heart of its manufacturing industry. Also in the 1930s, a new wave of Spanish immigration was registered as refugees from the Spanish Civil War were drawn to New York's Hispanic community. At the turn of the century Spanish and Cuban journalists dominated the print media environment in the city. The first decade of the century saw the founding of *La Prensa* (The Press), a daily whose heritage continues today in *El Diario–La Prensa* (The Daily–The Press) born of the fusion of *La Prensa* with *El Diario de Nueva York* (The New York Daily) in 1963. Also being published during the decade were *Sangre Latina* (Latin Blood) at Columbia University, *Revista Pan-Americana* (Pan American Review), and *La Paz y el Trabajo–Revista Mensual de Comercio, Literatura, Ciencias, Artes* (Peace and Work–Monthly Review of Commerce, Literature, Sciences, and Arts). Even as far north as Buffalo there were journalistic enterprises, such as *La Hacienda* (The State), founded in 1906.

Among the various specialized weeklies that appeared in the city over the next two decades, one merits special attention: *Gráfico* (The Graphic). What was notable about the newspaper, aside from including numerous photos and illustrations, was that in its early years it was an openly declared "amateur" enterprise written and directed by writers and artists, many of whom were involved in the Hispanic professional stage in Manhattan and Brooklyn. The founders of *Gráfico* felt that as amateurs they could better defend community interests, especially those of Spanish Harlem. Professional Spanish-language newspapers, which depended greatly on advertising, could not deal with controversial social and political issues. *Gráfico* was founded in 1927 under the editorship of Alberto O'Farrill, an important playwright and comic actor of the *teatro bufo cubano* (Cuban blackface musical farces). As such, *Gráfico* was replete with theater and entertainment news, as well as poems, short stories, essays, and crónicas by the leading Hispanic writers in the city. In reality, *Gráfico* was more of a magazine that, in addition to covering general and community news, commented on the artistic and cultural life of the community. Among the most important literary pieces to be found in the newspaper were those of Alberto O'Farrill himself. However, after a few years when O'Farrill no longer edited the newspaper, *Gráfico* became more of a conventional newspaper, more interested in hard news than in theater and literature.

Gráfico also published some of the most notable cronistas living in New York under such pseudonyms as Maquiavelo (Machiavelli) and O'Fa (O'Farrill himself). As in the Southwest, these cronistas labored to solidify the Hispanic community; a more difficult task in New York because of the various Hispanic national origins—and races—of the Hispanics there. The cronistas in New York were also protecting the purity of Hispanic culture against the dangers of assimilation, and they voiced the social and political concerns of the community by correcting and satirizing current behavior. Whereas in the Southwest the immigrant writers and entrepreneurs promoted a "México de afuera," in New York they often attempted to create a "Trópico en Manhattan" (a Tropics or Caribbean culture in Manhattan).

Despite its initial dedication to the world of arts and entertainment in its first years, *Gráfico* documented an intense Hispanic nationalism and the need to defend the civil rights and culture of the Hispanic community. The two cultures causing the most conflict to the Hispanic community were the Anglo-New York environment (they called Anglo-New Yorkers "americanos") and the New York Jewish environment in Harlem (Hispanic immigrants had followed upon the trail of European Jewish immigrants in Harlem). *Gráfico* printed the following editorial in English (this was the only portion of the paper in which English appeared) and Spanish on July 31, 1927:

> We want to make this weekly publication an efficient instrument dedicated to the defense of the Spanish-speaking population of Harlem and a vehicle for mutual understanding and compensation between the two main racial groups living in this section.
>
> We do not expect financial compensation. The cooperation given to GRAFICO will not be used for individual aggrandizement. Ours is amateur and disinterested journalism.
>
> We feel the immediate necessity of taking up important issues pertaining to our common defense instead of leaving them to be defended by any individual that may betray us as it happened oftentimes. We stanchely [sic] believe that, whoever wants something well done, must do it himself.
>
> With our numerical strength, with our prestige as civilized human beings, with our unity in aspirations and our efforts for the common good, we shall reach as good moral, social and economic standards as any other racial group living in this community.

And on the same editorial page appeared the following plea to the Jewish merchants of Harlem (as previously noted, Hispanics used the term "raza," or races to refer more to culture than to physiology or color):

> "Hath not a Jew Eyes? Hath not a Jew hands?" The Jewish merchants and business men of the Harlem section should not antagonize and create friction with our racial group. The fact that we are mostly working men and women victims of industrial slavery does not justify any attack, abuse or humiliation from anybody.
>
> The bulk of the Spanish-American population in this city lives in Harlem. It is a matter of a few years more and Harlem will be known as the Spanish centre in New York.
>
> As a natural outcome of the concentration of our racial group, the commercial, professional and social activities of the Spanish element are becoming wider and wider.
>
> All other racial groups that came before to the country took advantage of the blooming and prosperous times, having today a better financial standing than we have. But we feel confident that in a few years our people will overcome all the stumbling blocks that may

come their way, and be as well to do as any other citizen in the country. For we do not lack the intelligence and ability to do so.

It must be clearly understood that we aim not to create race prejudice. We want no hindrances in the social and commercial intercourse of the two races. We are ready to condemn any unjustified or uncalled for action on the part of our conationals, but will come forward to defend our rights, our lives and homes whenever they will be at stake. "For sufferance is (not) the badge of our tribe. . . ."

In addition to protecting the Hispanic portion of the Harlem community in competition with another immigrant group, the editorial also voices an ideology that departs significantly from the "México de afuera" and the ideology of exile so often voiced in the Spanish-language newspapers of the Southwest. The Hispanic community in New York saw itself at this point as the most recent of immigrant groups bent on pursuing, if not assimilation and the American Dream, most certainly a permanent place in the melting pot of economic opportunity. The Hispanics were here to stay; they were not just awaiting the end of the revolution and times more propitious for their return to the homeland, as were the expatriate Mexicans in the Southwest. The fight for their civil rights and their plea or warning in the English-language editorial are more understandable in this light. Rarely was such an editorial published in English at this point in history in the Southwest.

There are also notable differences in the Spanish- and English-language versions of these two editorials. Notably absent from the English-language version is the attack on "todos los periódicos hispanos que han venido aquí con el estribillo de defender los intereses de la Colonia" (all of the Hispanic newspapers that have come here with the refrain of defending the interests of the colony), probably because of the desire not to air dirty laundry outside the community. More importantly, in Spanish the first editorial ends with the words "ya que estamos condenados a prolongar nuestra residencia aquí" (being that we are condemned to prolong our residence here). It seems that the writer or writers elaborated in English the immigrant's theme of searching for a better life in the United States, but in Spanish made somewhat of an about-face, touching upon the ideology of exile or at least indicating an unwilling sojourn in the United States. When one takes both English and Spanish versions into account, the stance is ambivalent, neither as militantly separatist as the ideology expressed in the Southwest, nor quite that of the Europeans immigrating to stay, to become American citizens, to trade the old culture and language for the new in order to succeed in the American melting pot.

An issue of New York's *Gráfico*.

The attitudes towards the English language seems to have differed as well. In O'Fa's crónica "Pegas Suaves" of February 27, 1927, and elsewhere, he uses Anglicisms in his Spanish to reflect daily usage in the community; except for the word *express*, referring to the express subway train, he does not set the English terms apart in quotation marks or italics, nor does he satirize their use. Some examples follow:

1) Son las tres de la mañana; a esta hora como de costumbre abandono el suave y delicado alambre de mi caucho. . . . (It's three in the morning; and as is my custom I abandon the soft and delicate wire of my couch. . . .)
2) Me meto las manos en los bolsillos, saco los cinco pennies que tengo de ciñuelo y entre la vacilación de que si convierto en metálico el nickel o no. . . . (I put my hands into my pockets and pull out my last five pennies and not deciding whether to

exchange the pennies for a nickel. . . .)
3) Altravieso el hall chiflando mi valsesito. . . .
(I cross the hall whistling a little waltz. . . .)

While Daniel Venegas in *El Malcriado* and in *Las aventuras de don Chipote* mimicked the speech of working-class Chicanos, he went to pains to italicize Anglicisms. He was among the most liberal of the Southwestern cronistas. Julio G. Arce, on the other hand, attacked such unpure Spanish with biting satire, for it represented the beginnings of assimilation and loss of identity, as well as low-class behavior. O'Fa, assuming the persona of a common penniless worker, was not sensitive to these linguistic rules. Neither were many of the other cronistas in New York, where competition and conflict between Anglos and Hispanics did not have a long and bloody history. This soil was never part of the Mexican homeland, as was true in the Southwest. The cultural nationalism expressed in New York was not as acrid and widespread as it was in the Southwest at this juncture in history. Then too, the stigma against speaking Spanish and being an immigrant was not as strong in New York as it was among Anglos in the Southwest. As far as the Spanish language was concerned, when evoked as a topic in the newspapers in New York as well as in the Southwest, it was always a motive for pride and nationalism, as can be appreciated from the following excerpts from a poem by Alfonso Muñoz, "Canto a la Raza—El idioma español" (A Canto For Hispanic Culture—The Spanish Language) published in New York's *El Heraldo* (The Herald) on November 14, 1917:

Alberto O'Farrill.

Si en cada ser humano, la palabra,
fiel trasunto
de su espíritu, el idioma lo es del alma
nacional;
. . . .
Porque pinta vigoroso con sus frases
y oraciones
de antiguas generaciones
su poder extraordinario:
La intrepidez del guerrero
y esforzado caballero
temerario! . . .
Lo aguerrido de sus huestes,
el honor de los blasones;
el flameo de banderas, gallardetes
y pendones
y todo legendario
de la Raza
lleno de vida y luz:
El fulgor centelleante del casco y de
la coraza;
los chasquidos del acero y los golpes de
la maza . . .
¡Y el suspiro de la dama, de rodillas en
la cruz!
. . . .
Y por esa valentía,
y por esa gallardía
y por esa suficiencia,
fue la lucha denodada por la
santa Independencia,
que es de Libertad y Patria una
divina amalgama . . .
y es la llama
y es el fuego
que inflamó a los corazones del uno y
otro confín
y es Maldonado y es Riego,
y es Bolívar como es Juárez
y Maceo y San Martín!
. . . .
Y como una maravilla,
se escucha un rumor de besos
que haciendo un pueblo de dos,

los estrecha y los enlaza.
Es el Habla de Castilla!
Es el alma de la Raza
y es lo eterno! . . . . Como es Dios!

If in every human being, the word is a
faithful copy
of his spirit, such is language to the
national soul;
. . . .
because it paints with its phrases
and sentences
ancient generations
with extraordinary power:
The intrepidness of the warrior
and determined knight
who is fearless! . . . .
His war-seasoned troupes,
the honor of his coat of arms;
the fluttering flags, banners and pendants
and all the legendary
of the People.
full of life and light:
the shining of the helmet and the breastplate;
the clanging of steel and the blows of
the mace. . . .
And the sigh of the lady kneeling before
the cross!
. . . .
And by that valiance,
and by that bravery
and by that sufficiency,
was known the struggle for
holy Independence,
which is a divine amalgam of Freedom
and Fatherland. . . .
and it is the flame
and it is the fire
that burned in the hearts from border
to border
and it is Maldonado, and it is Riego,
and it is Bolívar as it is Juárez
and Maceo and San Martín!
. . . .
And as in a marvel,
the sound of a kiss is heard
which makes one people out of two,
it embraces them and entwines them.
It is the Language of Castille!
It is the soul of the People
and it is eternal! . . . As is God!

But the "eternal" Spanish language of the poem was just one of a hundred or so languages spoken on the streets of the city. New York was a veritable Tower of Babel that had drawn peoples from the far corners of the earth and where many languages could be heard every day in public. There was not in New York, as in the Southwest, this sense of two major groups, the Anglos and the Mexicans, confronting each other, locked in a mortal embrace over time and existing at the expense of each other. There was not that prevailing ideology of supposed Anglo superiority for having defeated and colonized a backward people of mixed racial heritage. Nor was there that sense of guilt that lies below the surface among Anglos in the Southwest for having dispossessed a people of their lands and heritage.

However, Hispanics in New York were aware of racial and cultural prejudice, and they did not hesitate to fight back, with the newspaper editorials taking the lead in the defense of the community, as can be seen from the following editorial published in *Gráfico* on August 7, 1927:

> La gran mayoría de nuestros detractores olvidan que los ciudadanos residentes en la vecindad de Harlem gozan de las prerrogativas y privilegios que lleva consigo la ciudadanía americana. Somos casi en nuestra totalidad naturales de Puerto Rico y otros, ciudadanos por naturalización. Cualquiera que esté identificado con la historia de este país, sabe que cuando hablamos de elementos extranjeros hablamos de nosotros mismos, pues no son otra cosa los habitantes de esta joven nación. Son los Estados Unidos una nación joven y creemos que la obra del acrisolamiento de las razas que la integran indica claramente que sus componentes pertenecen a todas las razas y a todas las naciones. De modo que nos hacemos tontos y ridículos al querer tildar a cualquier persona que con nosotros convive de extranjero.
>
> Muchos de los individuos que tratan de atropellar a nuestros conciudadanos en esta localidad, no fueron mejores que ellos antes de aprender aquí las costumbres y maneras del país. Se necesita ser ciego para no ver en cualquier individuo de los que ya se llaman ciudadanos completos, los ribetes de su antigua patria y de sus antiguas costumbres. Indica un grado muy pobre de inteligencia que se haga caballo de batalla el grito estúpido de unos cuantos intolerantes para combatir a ciudadanos dignos, especialmente cuando éstos respetan los derechos y prerrogativas de sus semejantes.

Nosotros, por supuesto, no participamos de este odio intransigente y no vamos a hacer bandera de combate de las animosidades y de los prejuicios que pudiera levantarse alimentando odios que a nada pueden conducir. Sin embargo, nos parece juicioso y muy prudente llamar la atención a todos los que están al presente sembrando vientos que muy pronto pueden redundar en tempestades.

Los últimos choques ocurridos entre habitantes del barrio y entre algunas autoridades que, también han bajado a lo común e ignorante en su juicio acerca de nuestra Colonia, nos hacen salir a la palestra dispuestos a arrostrar las consecuencias que vayan envueltas por nuestra justa y razonable defensa.

The great majority of our detractors forget that the citizens residing in the Harlem vicinity enjoy the prerogatives and privileges that American citizenship brings. We are almost all originally from Puerto Rico and the rest of us are naturalized citizens. Whoever identifies himself with the history of this country knows that when we speak of foreigners, we are talking about ourselves, because that is what the inhabitants of this young nation are. The United States is a young nation and we believe that the melting pot of peoples that it constitutes clearly indicates that its components belong to all of the cultures and all of the nations of the world. Thus we are making fools of ourselves when we try to categorize anyone here as a foreigner.

Many of the individuals who attempt to knock down our co-citizens in this locale were no better than them before learning the customs and ways of this country. One has to be blind not to see in any of those individuals who call themselves complete citizens the fringes of their old country and their old customs. It is indicative of a low level of intelligence to beat that old war horse with the stupid cry of a few intolerant people trying to oppose our dignified citizens, especially when ours respect the rights and prerogatives of others.

We, of course, do not participate in this intransigent hate and we are not going to wave the battle flag of animosities and prejudices that would further feed hate and serve no other purpose. Nevertheless, it seems to us judicious and prudent to call attention to all those who are currently blowing air that could soon turn into a storm.

The recent clashes between inhabitants of the barrio and some authorities who have also lowered themselves to the common and ignorant judgment about our colony have obligated us to take up the forum ready to brave the consequences implied in our just and reasonable defense.

The above editorial also points to another major difference, of course, between the Puerto Rican and Mexican communities and their identities vis-à-vis the United States. The editorial writer was claiming his community's rights of citizenship, and from that basis he was also appealing to the melting pot theory. The ideology of exile among Mexicans in the Southwest left no room for citizenship nor was it interested in promoting a Mexican addition to the American stew. Instead it promoted a return to Mexico, the American experience posited as only temporary. But citizenship and melting pot pluralism did not translate to assimilationism for the Puerto Ricans. Already possessed of citizenship, the pressure was off to assimilate, at least officially. They were thus quite different from European immigrants and the European's pursuit of an American identity. Given the paucity of documents and study, it is still too early to reach any conclusions about how American citizenship affected the overall identity of a Hispanic community which derived from so many different Hispanic nationalities. We do know that there have been many Hispanics who have tried to pass as Puerto Ricans for the protection that citizenship offers. Whether the Spanish Harlem of 1927 was almost totally made up of U. S. citizens of Hispanic origin as the editorial claims may be debatable.

The Depression did not cause the massive repatriation of Hispanics from New York as it did from the Southwest. Instead hard economic times brought even more Puerto Ricans to the city, a trend that intensified during World War II, when the northeastern manufacturing and service industries experienced manpower shortages. During the 1930s and 1940s immigration increased, as refugees of the Spanish Civil War streamed into Hispanic population centers, such as New York, Tampa, and Puerto Rico. In New York, newspapers were founded to serve the new migrants and immigrants. They also reflected a renewed interest in working-class culture, labor organizing, and even socialism. In the pages of *Vida Obrera* (Worker Life; 1930), *Alma Boricua* (Puerto Rican Soul; 1934), *España Libre* (Free Spain; 1943) and *Cultura Proletaria* (Proletarian Culture; 1943) was to found an important body of literature that reflected the life interests, not of an elite and educated class, but of common working people and their battles against worker exploitation and their struggles toward accommodation into an alien society. In these newspapers appeared autobiographical sketches, anecdotes, and stories, quite often in a homey, straightforward language that was not any less replete with pathos and artistic sensibility.

The first truly significant writings in English by a Puerto Rican began to appear in newspapers in the late 1930s. The columns of Jesús Colón are considered landmarks in the development of Puerto Rican literature in the continental United States, because they foreshadowed the working-class and racial identity that characterized much of New York Puerto Rican (Nuyorican) writing that appeared in the 1960s and that prevails today. Colón was born in 1901 into a working-class family in Cayey, Puerto Rico. At the age of sixteen Colón stowed away on a ship that landed in Brooklyn. In New York he worked at a series of jobs that exposed him to the exploitation and abuse of lower-class and unskilled laborers. Becoming involved in literary and journalistic endeavors while working as a laborer, Colón tried to establish a newspaper and wrote translations of English-language poetry. Of Afro-Puerto Rican heritage, Colón encountered discrimination because of his skin color. In response to this racism he became active in community and political activities. He also became a columnist for the *Worker*, the publication of the national office of the Communist party. In addition, Colón founded and operated a small publishing house, Hispanic Publishers (Editorial Hispánica), which published history and literary books as well as political pamphlets in Spanish. A selection of Jesús Colón's newspaper columns and essays appeared in 1961 under the title *A Puerto Rican in New York and Other Sketches.* In this volume Colón documented (1) the creation and development of a political consciousness, (2) his own literary development and worth, (3) advocacy for the working-class poor, and (4) the injustices of capitalist society, in which racial and class discrimination are all too frequent and individual worth hardly seems to exist. The whole collection is richly expressive of a social humanistic point of view. With the exception of the socialist and working-class Spanish-language newspapers mentioned above, many of Colón's writings, because of their political content, would not have been welcomed in other community-based Spanish-language newspapers, which were typically operated by an immigrant of the entrepreneurial class. But Colón's stance and writings are totally consistent with the points of view expressed in *Vida Obrera, Cultura Proletaria,* and the early years of *Gráfico.*

Jesús Colón. (Courtesy of the Jesús Colón Collection, Center for Puerto Rican Studies Library, Hunter College, CUNY.)

Tampa

The history of Spanish-language newspapers in Tampa diverges somewhat from that of the periodicals in Hispanic communities in other parts of the United States. At the end of the nineteenth century, the Tampa area experienced the transplanting from Cuba of a large segment of the cigar-manufacturing industry. The owners of various cigar companies engineered this large-scale venture for the following reasons: (1) in order to avoid the hostilities of the Cuban wars for independence from Spain; (2) to relocate closer to their principal market, the United States, and also avoid excise taxes; and (3) to attempt to avoid the problems of dealing with labor unions that were organizing this industry in Cuba. In 1886 they began building their factories in the mosquito-infested swamps just east of Tampa in what came to be Ybor City, a town named after the principal cigar manufacturer, Rafael Ybor. The owners were not able to escape the labor unrest that characterized the industry in Cuba and only partially did they escape the repercussions of the of the wars of independence, which were followed upon by the Spanish-American War.

The Tampa-Ybor City Hispanic community became divided more or less along the lines of ethnicity, nationality, and class. There the owners and managers of the cigar industry were made up mostly of Spaniards, conservative and sympathetic toward the European colonial power. Their actions in Tampa were dictated quite often by noblesse oblige, which resulted in their providing many cultural amenities and work benefits for their workers. The cigar workers themselves were mostly Cuban and Asturian and other working-class Spaniards. The ethnic and racial divisions were reflected in the establishment of various mutualist societies: the Centro Español (Spanish Center), the Centro Asturiano (Asturian Center), the Círculo Cubano (Cuban Circle), and the Sociedad Martí-Maceo (Martí-Maceo Society), the latter being a center for Afro Cubans, who were not welcome in the other clubs and who now experienced increased discrimination from two divergent sources: Anglos and Hispanics.

All of the above class, race, and ethnic divisions were reflected in periodical literature. First and foremost, there were the periodicals that served the interests of the owners of the cigar factories, such as *La Revista* (The Magazine), which was directed by Rafael M. Ybor, the son of the owner of the largest and most important factory. On the other side of the equation were the periodicals that served the interests of the workers and unions: *Federación* (Federation), *Federal* (Federal), *El Internacional* (The International), and *Boletín Obrero* (Worker Bulletin). Some of the ethnic societies also issued periodicals, such as *El Cubano* (The Cuban), the biweekly review of the Círculo Cubano. The Afro Cubans were given very little coverage in any of the Tampa newspapers. There were other periodicals that promoted ethnic unity in the Hispanic community. Out of these efforts came such publications as *Tampa Ilustrado* (Tampa Illustrated) and *La Gaceta* (The Gazette), whose unifying effort was "Latin" rather than Hispanic and even including Tampa's Italian community. To this day *La Gaceta* is published trilingually: English, Spanish, and Italian

Summary

Before World War II there existed two large categories of Spanish-language newspapers in Hispanic communities in the United States: (1) the dailies and (2) the weeklies and biweeklies. The dailies were large business enterprises in the major urban centers: San Antonio's *La Prensa*, Los Angeles's *La Opinión* and *El Heraldo de México*, and New York's *La Prensa* and *El Diario de Nueva York*. They distributed their papers in other towns, cities, and states, and they also maintained a corps of correspondents in the major Hispanic communities in the country. It should also be noted that before the Second World War, as now, these enterprises counted on a clientele made up largely of immigrants and recent arrivals, as opposed to Americans of Hispanic descent. In other words, the dailies depended on a population whose principal mode of obtaining information was the Spanish language. In addition to depending on large, urban populations, these dailies existed necessarily in cities that were ports of entry where the Hispanics settled in "colonies," barrios, or ghettos making up a more or less homogeneous market. Such a market was something that these newspapers' ideologies of exile and ethnic solidarity incidentally or subtly promoted. A few of these enterprises also expanded into publishing and distributing books, some of which were written by their own journalists, editors, and owners, and this easily extended their intellectual leadership and influence. Of course, such genres as the "novel of the Mexican Revolution"—a clear forerunner, it may be added, of the Cuban exile novel of the last thirty years—and the political tracts that were published in book form also promoted quite heavily the ideology of exile maintained by the elites.

From the mid-nineteenth century there existed literally hundreds of small weekly newspapers in the Southwest, and from the latter part of the nineteenth century on, numerous others in New York and Tampa. The small weekly was the most representative type of Hispanic periodical, because its modest staff and equipment made publication possible even in the smallest of communities. They provided the most important local, regional, national, and home-country news, in addition to providing literature, entertainment, and political and cultural commentary. To this day they are the most popular and frequently published Hispanic periodicals, maintaining a flexibility that mirrors the evolution of the community. They are the most likely to serve the interests of a particular segment of a heterogeneous Hispanic community in a large city. In Houston today, for instance, various ethnic communities subscribe to their own papers: the Mexican Americans to *El Sol* (The Sun) and *El Mexica* (The Aztec), the Cubans to *Información* (Information), and the general Hispanic population to *La Voz* (The Voice); in Chicago, the Mexicans have *La Raza* (The Race) and the Puerto Ricans have *El Puertorriqueño* (The Puerto Rican). After World War II some of these weeklies began publishing in bilingual format while others were born that are published just in English. Today, local and national monthly magazines in English are an outgrowth of this tradition, although such national ones as *Hispanic, Vista,* and *Nuestro* (Ours) specifically promote a national Hispanic identity (and market). But before the Second World War, the weeklies were the staunchest axis of cultural and linguistic resistance to assimilation. By the end of the nineteenth century in New Mexico, on the other hand, newspapers publishing bilingually even had a Hispanic and Anglo clientele subscribing to the same bilingual periodicals, which reflected the larger Hispanic population figures and greater political and economic power of Hispanics.

As seen above, there were various types of weeklies. Some, like *El Cubano* of Tampa's Círculo Cubano and Milwaukee's *El Mutualista* (The Mutualist), were organs of the mutualist societies. Others were related to lay religious groups, such as Indiana Harbor's *El Amigo del Hogar* (The Friend of the Home) of the Círculo de Obreros Católicos San José (The Saint Joseph Catholic Workers Circle) and *El Bautista* (The Baptist). Among the most interesting and lively were the satirical reviews, such as San Antonio's *El Fandango* and *El Vacilón* and Los Angeles's *El Malcriado*. Other tabloid or magazine type weeklies, such as New York's *Gráfico* and *Ecos de Nueva York* (New York Echoes) and Tampa's *Tampa Ilustrado*, emphasized cultural commentary and were likely to feature the crónicas by such writers as O'Fa (Alberto O'Farrill), Maquiavelo, Latiguillo, and Samurai. And throughout the country there were numerous periodicals related to unions and labor struggle: *Huelga General* (General Strike) in Los Angeles (1911-14), *La Unión Industrial* (Industrial Union) in Phoenix (1912-15), *El Obrero* (The Worker) in San Antonio, *El Obrero Mexicano* (The Mexican Worker) in El Paso, and those already mentioned in New York and Tampa. A number of political weeklies of great historical significance were also published in the United States: the Flores-Magón brothers' *Regeneración* (Regeneration), spreading the ideology of revolution for Mexico from Los Angeles, San Antonio, and Kansas City; Sara Estela Ramírez's *Aurora* and *La Corregidora* in Laredo, which presented the ideology of the Mexican Revolution; New York's *La Patria* and *Cuba y América*, supporting the wars of independence from Spain of its Caribbean island colonies; Brownsville's *El Porvenir* (The Future; 1898), and New York's Spanish *España Libre* (Free Spain; 1943), against Spanish fascism. Estela Ramírez's papers, Andrea and Teresa Villarreal's newspaper in San Antonio, and *La Voz de la Mujer* in El Paso at the beginning of the century were important precursors of Chicana feminism. These were certainly forerunners of the militant newspapers that sprung up during the 1960s and 1970s to support the Chicano movement and Hispanic identity and civil rights. In Lansing, Michigan, a weekly even resuscitated the title of "Regeneración." The famed newspaper of César Chávez's United Farm Workers was *El Malcriado*. Other periodicals inherited the grassroots, folksy, and satirical perspective of *El Vacilón* and *El Malcriado*, such as Los Angeles's magazine *Con Safos* (Safety Zone) and San Antonio's Caracol and *El Magazín*. In fact, the late 1960s and early 1970s was a period of renewed flourishing of the Hispanic periodical in the United States, and it merits a detailed study beyond the limits of the present article.

Summarizing further, Spanish-language newspapers had been published in the United States since the beginning of the nineteenth century, but it was not until the 1920s and 1930s that they actually flourished, especially in California, Texas, Tampa, and New York. During these years of flourishing there seems to have existed a national Hispanic consciousness at the same time that there also existed a sense of resistance to acculturation and assimilation. In the elite society of publishing, there was an integration of writers, publishers, and cultural workers from throughout the Spanish-speaking world. In the Southwest and the Midwest, the personnel, context, and culture of Mexico predominated, while in New York and Tampa the culture and references of Spain and Cuba prevailed. During the 1920s and 1940s the Puerto Rican influence in New York was felt more and more, but it should be remembered that New York always maintained a cosmopolitan and international Hispanism, regardless of the population size of one group compared to another.

It is evident that much of the Hispanic periodical production was influenced by the great political movements in the various Hispanic countries of origin and, furthermore, various Hispanic newspapers in the United States were founded to promote or were products of these political movements: wars of independence, revolutions, civil wars. While in the Southwest the Great Depression and the repatriation of Mexicans were catastrophic for the newspapers, in New York and Tampa the Depression and the Second World War interrupted and retarded their development but did not bring about their destruction.

As regards Mexican, Puerto Rican, Cuban, or Hispanic nationalism and the historical resistance to Anglo-Saxon culture, in editorials one can easily find the same sentiments among any Hispanic group living in the United States today, as the excerpt from the following editorial indicates.

> El que tus padres o tus abuelos hayan nacido en México, debe ser un gran motivo de justo orgullo para ti, pues México con su historia antigua, que es heroica, con su antiquísima cultura aborigen y el mantenimiento de la paz por más de cincuenta años, es el país de mayor prestigio en América Latina.
>
> Honra a tu país de origen, conservando sus costumbres, estudiando su historia y sintiéndote orgullosamente mexicano sobre todas las cosas.
>
> Nadie puede ser lo que no ha nacido para ser. Si conoces la historia de la Patria de tus ancestros, no tienes por qué sentirte inferior a nadie y por lo tanto no hay para qué quieras ser de la raza que no eres.
>
> *That your parents or grandparents were born in Mexico should be a motive of deserved pride for you, being that Mexico, with its ancient history, which is heroic, with its ancient aboriginal culture and its maintaining more than fifty years of peace, is the most prestigious country in Latin America.*

Honor your country of origin by maintaining its customs, studying its history and feeling proudly Mexican above everything else.

No one can be what they were not born to be. If you are familiar with the history of the homeland of your ancestors, there is no reason to feel inferior to anyone and, therefore, there is no reason for wanting to be of a race that is not yours. (*Tribuna de América* [The Tribune of the Americas; Chicago], 5 March 1989)

For Further Reading

Arce, Julio G.
1982 *Crónicas diabólicas de "Jorge Ulica."* Ed Juan Rodríguez. San Diego: Maize.

García, Richard A.
1977 "Class, Consciousness, and Ideology: The Mexican Community of San Antonio, Texas, 1930-1940." *Aztlán,* vol 8 (fall):23-69.

"Jesús Colón"
1989 In *A Bio-Bibliographic Dictionary of Hispanic Literature of the United States.* Ed Nicolás Kanellos. Westport, CT: Greenwood P.

Kanellos, Nicolás
1989 "Daniel Venegas." In *The Dictionary of Literary Biography,* vol 82: *Chicano Writers.* Detroit, MI: Gale, pp 271-74.

Leal, Luis
1987 "The Spanish Language Press: Function and Use." *Americas Review,* vol 17, no 3-4, pp 157-62.

Medeiros, Francine
1980 "*La Opinión*: A Mexican Exile Newspaper; A Content Analysis of Its First Years, 1926-1929." *Aztlán,* vol 11, no 1 (spring):65-87.

❖

Religious Faith and Institutions in the Forging of Latino Identities

Anthony M. Stevens-Arroyo and Ana María Díaz-Stevens

Background

Nearly 100 years before the Pilgrims landed at Plymouth Rock in Massachusetts, the Christian faith was first brought by Spanish explorers and missionaries to lands now under the U. S. flag. Any consideration of religion among Latinos in the United States today must begin from the premise that not only are our language and cultural traditions different from those of the English-speaking Americans, so also is our religious sentiment and expression.

In order to better understand religion and its manifestations among Latinos, this article distinguishes between belief which is the individual assent to religion, and church which is the institution—Catholic or Protestant—that is organized to promote this belief and defend its interests in society and in politics. In the ideal order, belief and church ought to combine perfectly, but throughout history, there has been dissonance between them. In the case of Latinos, their beliefs have been filtered through church institutions generally controlled by priests and ministers with different social class origins or even from another culture. Latinos have encountered dissonance between their native belief and the institutional churches that controlled faith expression. Hence, understanding religion—the combination of faith and institutional practice—requires examination of both aspects of Latino experiences.

Likewise, it will be useful to understand that the institutions have wide agendas in addition to purely ecclesiastical matters. Religion attends to spiritual needs in its rites, prayers, and catechetical instructions, but it also cares for material needs by providing food, clothing, housing, and modes of social and political organization. Inasmuch as religion's ministry to material needs is motivated by spiritual convictions of faith, it is not easy to separate one order from the other. Conflict between church and state has often resulted from contradictory interpretations of appropriate roles for attending to material needs. In some cases, instead of serving the status quo, religion can become critical of state attention to material needs.

Although they have assumed much importance in today's United States, the original Spanish settlements in California, Texas, and Florida were peripheral to the overall colonizing enterprise of Spain. This notion of "peripheral" is intended to include the technical meaning used in world-systems analysis. In economic terms, each of these regions was in a dependent position within the economic exchanges of the Spanish colonial world with Europe until the dawn of the nineteenth century. Dependency in economic matters resulted in an inferior social and political standing as well. Unable to keep its own wealth or even in some cases to generate any profit, the periphery of the Caribbean and the lands north of Mexico were relatively powerless in the Spanish colonial world.

Racial distinctions in Spanish America helped legitimate economic differences. Although there were always exceptions to the rule, in general social power was accessible on the basis of approximation to whiteness and Spanish identity. European-born whites, called *gachupines* in Mexico and *mojados* in nineteenth century Puerto Rico, were assigned maximum political and social influence. The American-born *criollos,* often descendants of the original *conquistadores* and richer than the newly arrived from Spain, gradually lost social prestige in the colonial world. It was not uncommon for the Europeans and the criollos to intermarry, parlaying advantages of birth and wealth to form a ruling class in the colonies.

The native Indians, even when able to retain a biological purity, were forced by evangelization practices to submit to general Spanish social norms. But European diseases devastated these populations, particularly in the Caribbean. Black slaves from Africa were imported to perform the hard labor in the mines and

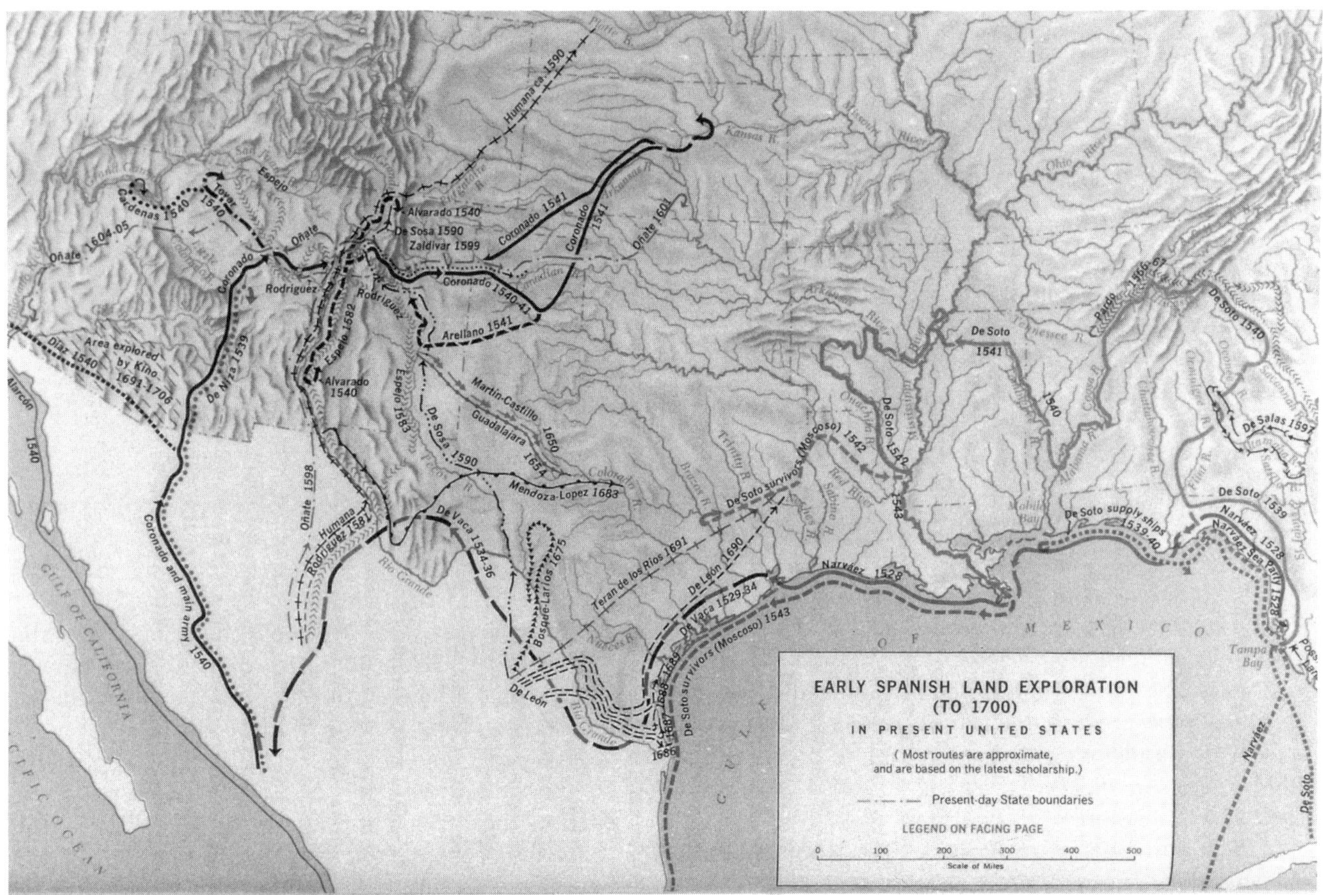

Early Spanish land exploration. (Courtesy of the U. S. Department of the Interior and National Park Service.)

on the plantations of the Caribbean and parts of Mexico. From these mixtures were produced three basic types: the *mestizo,* or Indian and European progeny; the *mulato,* or African and European offspring; and the *zambo,* from Indian and African stock.

Those in power in the periphery often aspired to belong to the upper classes of the urban centers. Such class-motivated behavior in pursuit of economic interests not only divided center from periphery, but also split the periphery itself into upper and lower classes. In imitation of the metropolitan centers, the chief power relationship in the periphery was based on race. Yet in the peripheries of Puerto Rico, Florida, California, and the continental Southwest, these social and racial differences were not as highly demarcated as in the colonial centers. From a practical point of view, the dependent economies in the peripheries required every capable person to contribute. There was more of an opportunity for mestizos to exercise in the periphery a social role usually reserved in the centers for whites alone. In a sense, life in the periphery was more of a meritocracy than in other areas of Spanish America. Thus Latinos have a different tradition from much of Latin America. And although neglected by some who study colonial Spanish America from the perspective of the centers of power, the Latino periphery deserves specialized attention.

Inasmuch as the Catholic church was closely tied to the Spanish colonial apparatus, this institution suffered the fate of parallel institutions in the same areas. There were always fewer schools, hospitals, convents, monasteries, and churches in the periphery, just as there were fewer banks, roads, shops, and stores. This did not mean that the religious beliefs of the inhabitants at the frontiers were less fervent than in the great cities of Spanish America. But the church institutions had fewer resources and less influence in preserving and developing this faith. Accordingly the numbers and ability of clergy, the quality of services, and the condition of church buildings suffered at the periphery.

Racial differences were also reflected in religion, since separate books were kept to record baptisms, marriages, and deaths among white and non-white Catholics well into the nineteenth century in virtually all the colonies. People of Indian or African ancestry were generally barred from sitting with the European and criollo population during services. Mestizos and some mulatos could sometimes enter into the upper-

Drawing of free black militia that were stationed in the Spanish colonies in Florida (1795).

class world as lesser ranked clergy or as servants within convents and monasteries to the priests and nuns of upper-class birth. But bishops—the highest rank of clergy—were chosen exclusively from the white upper classes.

Yet these racial distinctions in religion, as in other matters, were weaker in the periphery than at the centers of Spanish America. Social mobility free from some of the more rigid constraints of race and class characterized the practice of religion at the frontier, where any Christian was eagerly welcomed from among the scant Hispanized population. The practice of religion in the periphery was more racially tolerant than in the class-conscious cities, and Indians, blacks, and mixed-race peoples enjoyed a higher level of acceptance from Catholicism at the periphery. Moreover, in attention to material needs, the church at the periphery was frequently in conflict with government policies, arguing for more action on behalf of the poor, who were also the racially mixed population. Hence, among the people who were to become Latinos, the roots of religion were often deeper than their loyalties to Spain.

The Foundation of the Churches

Puerto Rico

The oldest of the territories settled by the Spaniards and now under the U. S. flag is Puerto Rico. First visited by Columbus on his second journey in 1493, the island was not colonized until August 12, 1509, when the hidalgo Juan Ponce de León arrived on the shores of Burenke or Borinquen (the native Taíno name), with some twenty colonists from Hispaniola. In his bull, *Romanus Pontifex* (1511), Pope Julius II erected the first dioceses in America, and the bishop named for San Juan, Alonso Manso, was the first prelate to arrive in the New World, setting foot in his see on December 25, 1513. Manso also ordained the Seville-born Bartolomé de las Casas, who went on to become the famous defender of the Indians. The faithful bishop of Puerto Rico lived to ordain the first American-born priest, Luis Ponce de León, son of the governor, on August 31, 1527. His episcopacy also witnessed the first Catholic school in Puerto Rico in 1523, when the Dominican friars opened Santo Tomás de Aquino. Less gloriously, Bishop Manso of Puerto Rico was the first Inquisitor General in America (1519), a post he eventually recognized as impractical in Puerto Rico, and it was abolished at his death in 1539. His successor, Rodrigo de Bastidas (1541-67), scion of a wealthy family of Hispaniola, was the first native-born American to be elevated to the rank of bishop.

Thus Puerto Rico has the distinction as home to many of the first Catholic institutions in lands presently under the U. S. flag. But more important to Puerto Rico's historical importance was its role in providing a transition from the medieval forms of conversion to the approaches implemented later on the American continents. Medieval conversion depended on feudal concepts of authority. By converting the native ruler, it was thought, all his subjects would automatically adhere to the faith. Divine intervention by miraculous appearances of the Blessed Virgin Mary and/or the saints was expected to legitimate such acceptance. Thus, religious authority in the society rather than the faith of the individual figured centrally in the medieval conversion process.

The role of the church in providing conversion *en masse* was closely tied to the state recognition of power, and only Christians could be lords. The legal device utilized in Puerto Rico and the Caribbean was the *encomienda*, which had grown from a medieval institution. By the contract of the encomienda, the people in a newly settled territory enlisted a protector—even if he did not belong to the nobility. In exchange for such protection, the inhabitant freely accepted the protector as if he were a feudal lord.

The oldest church in Puerto Rico, the convent of Porta Coeli in San Germán.

As early as 1511, the Dominican superior in Hispaniola, Antón de Montesinos, denounced the encomienda—supposedly a voluntary arrangement of defense—as being enslavement and contrary to the Gospel. This cause of Montesinos, who later became superior of the Dominican school in San Juan (1521), was taken up by Bartolomé de las Casas.

Despite its basic injustice, the encomienda was more benign than the *repartimiento,* which was a purely punitive institution consigning enemies conquered in battle to forced labor. It was to the advantage of conquistadores to provoke the Indians to violence, because that legitimated the repartimiento, and rumors of cannibalism among certain peoples automatically became justification for enslavement. Both by encomienda and repartimiento, the Spaniards subdued the Taínos of the Caribbean and sought justification from the Catholic religion. But the Gospel instinct of defending the poor from injustice was reborn in the Caribbean and has been a part of Latin American Catholicism since.

The first significant reform of this system was the plan of the Jeronymite Fathers who were commissioned by Cardinal Cisneros, regent for the new king, Carlos V, in 1517. The Jeryonimites instituted villages for the natives, close to but separate from the Spaniards. This was the model for the *reducción,* a kind of Indian reservation.

Under supervision of the clergy, the Indians were expected to work partially for the Spaniards but to gradually acquire the faith through instruction in their own language from missionary priests who lived among them. This task of missionary work was assigned to members of a religious order on the basis of their special preparation for such a special role. While the Franciscans were the early favorites in work with the Indians, the Dominicans, Jesuits, Benedictines, and Augustinians all had commissions at different times and in different places.

Puerto Rico's first governor, Juan Ponce de León, was a man of singular tolerance for the times, and he sought to enhance the role of the church in Puerto Rico in the hopes of avoiding native uprisings. But although Ponce de León sought a peaceful coexistence with the native Taínos of Puerto Rico, greed and disease unwound his careful efforts. Intrigue at the Spanish court took the governorship away from him briefly in 1509-10, and permanently after 1512. He eventually died in Havana, Cuba, on May 20, 1521, from wounds received in Florida while trying to start all over again in the colonial enterprise.

By the time Ponce's colleague Bishop Manso died in 1539, Mexico and Perú had been opened up by the Spanish conquistadores. The abundance of gold and easy wealth on the continent relegated Puerto Rico and the rest of the Caribbean to a peripheral role in the colonial system. Few settlers could be attracted to the island, preferring instead to continue on their journey to Perú. Such was the experience of Gaspar Flores and his wife, who lived briefly in Puerto Rico before going to Perú, where their daughter and later saint, Rose of Lima, was born.

From 1539, when the erection of the fortress of San Felipe del Morro was begun, until the dawn of the nineteenth century, Puerto Rico was a military outpost on the Spanish main. San Juan became a walled city when construction was completed in 1630, and the island was a bulwark against pirates and marauders from a hostile Britain or France. Puerto Rico had virtually no other participation in the colonial system, having become only peripheral to the Spanish Empire. In fact, after 1586 the island depended for its economic activity upon the *situado,* a subsidy derived from the bullion shipped from Mexico and Perú.

In a rural society populated largely by former soldiers, former sailors, and still active pirates and privateers, religion had an uphill task among the Spanish settlers. While the fortress city of San Juan had its parish churches, the outlying regions suffered from lack of clergy. Parish churches were not found in rural settlements, only *hermitas,* or shrines. Derived from medieval practice, these were small chapels cared for by laypersons. Sacraments and the celebration of mass were occasional affairs, prompted by infrequent visits by an overworked clergy. The shrines, however, allowed for expression of devotion, communal recitation of prayers, and celebration of special occasions. All of these were directed by laypersons who could recite prayers for the neighbors.

It was in these rural surroundings that the native and mixed-blood peoples most often came to know Catholicism. Disease and exploitation had launched a precipitous decline in the physical presence of the native Taínos. In 1515 there were 14,636 Taínos—about half the estimated number from when the Spaniards first landed in 1509. The Taínos survived biologically by intermarriage with the settlers, adopting Spanish ways, including the acceptance of Catholicism. The census of 1778 recorded only 2,302 pure Indians left on the island.

But even if today some 17 percent of Puerto Rico's population is identifiably of Taíno origins in a biological sense, the Taínos have been culturally extinct since the sixteenth century. Because of this, Puerto Rican folk Catholicism is strikingly different from the Mexican experiences. Precisely because of the destruction of Taíno culture in the transition from medieval practices of evangelization and colonization, Spain adopted new modes of preserving the natives and their societies. The New Laws of Burgos (1542) were key in this process and provided for the survival of an Indian religious substratum among Latinos of Mexican origin.

Blacks were imported from Africa as slaves to replace the moribund Taínos as a cheap labor force. Between 1607 and 1633, 2,240 slaves were brought to Puerto Rico. And while eventually there were considerable numbers of freed blacks as well, the subordinate position of Africans in the society made the Catholic religion an instrument of domination. In 1765, on the eve of the large-scale sugar cultivation which was to considerably expand the island's population, there were 5,037 black slaves, or 10 percent of the island's inhabitants out of a total 39,846 persons. The number of free blacks and mulattos may be estimated at about another 10 percent of the island's people, scattered in fifteen towns, most of which had less than 1,000 inhabitants.

Africans and their descendants, even if freepersons, were considered inferior—legally, economically, and culturally—to white Spaniards. This racism was also present in the policies of the institutional church towards the believers under its care. But the African instincts for religion assumed new and complex forms alongside the imitation of Spanish Catholicism. Consequently, within the Puerto Rican folk religion are many African customs and traditions, adding a dimension to the Caribbean experience not widely found among Mexican-origin people.

Florida

The present area of Florida was initially part of the Spanish colonies. Ponce de León was the first European whose entry into the present-day United States can be historically documented. Ponce's expedition landed in Florida on Easter Sunday, March 17, 1513. Contrary to a legend of dubious origin, Ponce was not looking for a miraculous fountain to restore his youth, but for a mythical place called Bimini by the Taínos of Puerto Rico. He encountered instead the Seminole Indians, whose techniques of warfare inclined them to resist Spanish intrusions.

Florida was also the site for the first use of the *requerimiento,* which had been ordered by Ferdinand and Isabella in 1513. A legal text announcing the peaceful intentions of the Spanish and inviting Indians to accept Christianity, the requerimiento was intended to insure the rights of the Indians. But in practice the requerimiento was a farce. Because it was proclaimed in Spanish to natives who did not understand this language, the requerimiento communicated nothing to the people it was supposed to defend. Instead it legitimized ruthless conquest by the conquistadores who were quick to interpret Indian non-response as rejection of Christianity.

The fierceness of the Florida Indians produced the first Catholic martyr in the United States, when Luis Cancel,

Pedro Menédez de Artés, explorer of La Florida.

the Dominican former prior of Santo Tomás in San Juan, was killed while attempting to preach the gospel on Florida's shores in 1549. His martyrdom was tribute to the intrepid spirit of Catholic missionaries, who often sought to divorce themselves from association with the greed and cruelty of the conquistadores. But the Indians frequently were unable to make such distinctions, viewing all Christians alike.

For the Spaniards, Florida extended virtually the entire Atlantic coast of North America, well beyond the borders of the present-day state. An ill-fated expedition with 600 men, including Fray Antón de Montesinos, attempted settlement in the Chesapeake Bay in 1526. But the site had to be abandoned the following year. In this region, the British founded the Jamestown Colony eighty-one years later.

After initial failures, the Spanish under Pedro de Menéndez finally established the settlement at St. Augustine in the northern part of the present state of Florida in 1565. The church that survives there is today the oldest sacred Christian building in the United States in continuous use.

The Creek Nations in northern Florida received the faith more readily than their Seminole cousins in the south. The first episcopal visit to any of today's United States occurred in 1606 when Juan Cabezas de Altamirano, Bishop of Havana, came to St. Augustine and its 1,200-some converts. In 1674 Havana's Bishop Gabriel Díaz Vera Calderón confirmed 13,152 Catholics and celebrated a synod. In a serious effort to foster the faith, the synod outlawed the Indian game of lacrosse, which was partly a pre-Christian religious festival.

The settlement of Pensacola on the Gulf Coast met with slow success. Founded April 25, 1693, by Andrés de Pes and Fray Carlos Sigüenza y Góngora, it was scarcely developed beyond an outpost meant to prevent the British or French from using Florida as a base from which to attack Spanish caravels carrying gold and silver back to Europe.

Harassed and pillaged by the British from the Carolinas (1702, 1704), the Spaniards lost much of the land north and west of Pensacola to the French in 1719, when they laid claim to Louisiana on both sides of the Mississippi. The first bishop resident in Florida was Francisco de San-buenaventura Martínez, auxiliary of Havana, who arrived in 1735. But after invasion and devastation of Havana by the English from Georgia (1740), Florida was eventually ceded to England by Spain in 1763 in exchange for the British-held Havana, captured during hostilities. And although Florida was restored to Spanish rule briefly after the foundation of the United States, it never achieved anything but peripheral importance to the Spanish colonial system. Pensacola was invaded and occupied by General Andrew Jackson in 1818. In 1821, President Monroe demanded the Spanish surrender Florida forever. Most of the remaining Spanish subjects departed and the area was populated by U. S. citizens, who brought black slavery and Protestantism with them.

New Mexico

Spanish entry into what is now the U. S. Southwest began with explorations from Florida by Narváez (1526), Nuñez Cabeza de Vaca (1528), Vásquez de Coronado (1539) and De Soto (1539-1542), who were able to distinguish Amichal (Texas) from the Mississippi Valley (French Louisiana). But these explorations, like the expedition into California by Rodríguez Cabrillo (1542) were largely motivated by search for fabled wealth and did not produce any settlements.

What is now New Mexico was systematically colonized by Juan de Oñate from northern Mexico in 1582. In 1598, a church was established giving permanence to the settlement and in 1610 Santa Fe became the capital of the colony. The Spaniards sought to establish cattle-ranching in this dry and sparse land, not unlike parts of the Iberian meseta. The encomienda, which had now been reduced by royal edicts to little more than a tributary system, nonetheless forced local natives to participate in the fragile economic system in order to obtain Spanish currency for what essentially were taxes to Spanish land-grant holders.

Entrusted to the care of Franciscan missionaries, New Mexico was elevated ecclesiastically to a missionary province under the diocese of Durango, México, in 1622. Because of its peripheral importance to the Spanish Empire, as long as Nuevo México was part of México, Santa Fe remained under the Diocese of Durango.

New Mexico spurred evolution of missionary institutions that transcended the transitional modes employed in Puerto Rico. By the seventeenth century, four modes of church establishment were common in New Mexico and in most of the Spanish colonies in North America. First, there was the parish church in the city, a repetition of European practice and frequently accessible only to Spaniards and white criollos. Second, was the mission, a monastery for religious order priests. This mission was walled to protect it from marauders and maintain the religious cloister. Inside was a church, however, that was open to the people of the surrounding area. The mission also included industries like leather tanning, tool-making forges, and various forms of food processing. Styled on the Jeronymite Reforms of 1517, it was a reducción, or reservation, which allowed the Indians to gradually assimilate both Christian faith and Spanish technology. Third, was the village church built among the Indians of the reducción, without the walls of protection. Fourth, was the hermita, or local shrine visited on occasion by priests on horseback.

San Francisco de la Espada Mission, San Antonio, Texas.

The success or failure of each of these particular models was usually subject to the reaction of the different Indian groups encountered. For instance, the Navajo of New Mexico adapted to the Spanish presence. They adopted sheep raising as a mode of economic participation, and although they were not without frictions with colonial rule, they prospered as Hispanicized Indians. The Apaches, on the other hand, proved to be fiercely resistant, fighting not only the Spaniards but also the United States military.

The desire of the missionaries to divorce themselves from the military often meant that the church missions were vulnerable to attack, either from the British or French or from revolt by the Indians. In 1680 the Pueblo Indians revolted at Taos, killing many friars and temporarily driving the Spaniards out of New Mexico. Diego de Vargas negotiated peace and in 1692 reestablished Santa Fe.

New Mexico was the first permanent penetration of Spanish settlement into what is now the southwestern United States. From New Mexico, as radiating from the spokes of a wheel, were to come most of the remaining colonial churches. This position of New Mexico as distributor of people to West Texas, Colorado, and California, while receiving new migration from Mexico, continued until the first half of the twentieth century. The distinction between the criollos of New Mexico and the newly arrived immigrants from Mexico in the twentieth century led to the adoption of the term "Hispanos" among descendants of colonists who had come directly from Spain and not from post-independence Mexico. However, this term, which has historical meaning, has also been used to emphasize racial and social distinctions.

Texas

The ferocity of the Indians in what is now Texas discouraged colonization. Predictably the natives were described as cannibals, thus making them liable to enslavement. The name for the region, "Texas," is said to derive from the native word for "ally," i.e., against the Apaches, which eventually displaced the Spanish official name for the region, "New Philippines." Encouraged by the report of de La Salle (1682), the French had moved westward from Louisiana at the mouth of the Mississippi River into Texas towards the end of the seventeenth century. Determined to drive them out, the Spaniards embarked on a serious colonizing effort, founding a series of missions along a river system named after San

Antonio in 1691 by Fray Damián de Massanet. This led to the establishment of the mission San Antonio de Valero (the Alamo) on May 1, 1718, by Martín de Alarcón and the Franciscans Félix Isidro de Espinoza and Antonio Olivares. With additions of a fort and the villa of Bexar in 1720 and additional missions founded by the Blessed Fray Antonio Márgil de Jesús, this has become the modern city of San Antonio, Texas.

The colony in San Antonio desperately sought civilian settlers to make the presidium that had been established for purely military purposes into an economically prosperous colony. In 1729-31, colonists from the Canary Islands were recruited to build a civilian population. This ambitious plan, like others launched in other places, had only limited success. It was not until Mexican independence in 1821, a hundred years later, that Texas pacified the Indians, especially the Comanches, to a level that permitted solid economic activity. Cattle raising provided a spur to Texan vitality in the band of settled lands that stretched from Corpus Christi on the Gulf Coast and westward through San Antonio to El Paso on the New Mexico border. It was from this coastal base that the Spanish field marshall Bernardo de Gálvez led two campaigns against the British (1779, 1780) at the time of the U. S. War of Independence. The present city of Galveston, Texas, is named in his honor.

Yet the achievement of peace with the Indians and expulsion of the British did not bring peace to Texas. U. S. filibusters and farmers violated territorial borders with alarming frequency. In search of booty or lands for cotton farming, these pressures were not unlike those that had forced the ceding of Florida by Spain in 1821. Eventually this formed the backdrop for the Texan War of Independence (1835-36).

Arizona and California

In 1681, the Tyrol-born Jesuit Eusebio Kino, received permission to establish missions in the Sonora Valley in northern Mexico on the borders of present-day Arizona. Pushing north towards the Gila River into what was called Pimería Alta, Kino founded San Xavier del Bac near Tucson in 1700, where evidence of contact with the Pacific coast was discovered. Following trails established by Indian commerce, Kino arrived in California in 1702. Kino himself was a gifted scholar, astronomer, and mathematician whose exploits made him a representative of the Enlightenment under Catholic vision. By arrangement with the Spanish Crown in 1697, Kino financed the missionary effort with a subsidy called the Pious Fund, a sort of ecclesiastical version of Puerto Rico's military *situado*. Thus, Arizona and California settlements were relatively insulated from the greed and militarism of the conquistadores.

The suppression of the Company of Jesus in 1767 meant that the Jesuits had to surrender their missions. The Pious Fund was appropriated by the Crown. The Franciscan Junípero Serra inherited the task of founding missions among the Indians of California. He arrived in San Diego in 1769, where he began to mold the reducción into the famous string of California missions.

Aided by a Spanish government anxious to prevent Russian advances down the Pacific coast from Alaska, Serra founded twenty-one missions in all, stretching from San Francisco in the north to San Diego in the south. These missions functioned as self-contained economic units, producing food, raw materials for export, and manufacturing the basic items of clothing, shoes, and domestic tools internally. Each had its school, where learning was largely by rote, although reading and writing were taught at rudimentary levels. This education, however, was religious in purpose and content and was organized around agricultural cycles, permitting long recesses during productive seasons.

Although the Catholic church has seen fit to elevate Junípero Serra to the ranks of the beatified in 1990, there is a continuing debate about the use of Catholicism to obliterate native religious belief and much of Indian culture. The Franciscans were inclined to use corporal punishment against Indians who refused to work, who missed mass, or became inebriated. The paternalism towards the natives that had begun in the Caribbean was continually repeated. While the missionaries showed interest in native languages, often preaching and catechizing in the Indian tongue, the purpose was to install Spanish as the official language. Native Indian lan-

San José de Tumacacori Mission, Arizona.

San Luis Rey de Francia Mission, Oceanside, California. (Photo by Henry F. Witney, 1936, W.P.A.)

guages were considered inadequate for the expression of the Catholic faith. By insisting that doctrinal orthodoxy was possible only in Spanish, the imperialistic agenda of domination was fostered by religion.

Whatever the morality of this missionary practice, it resulted in acceptance of the faith in such a way that the Spanish language and the new religion became identical with the new culture produced by the encounter of Indians with Spanish technology and civilization. Ironically the poorer elements of society often remained more loyal to the faith preached by the missionaries than the upper classes, who were characteristically more interested in this world than in the next. Among Latinos today, particularly those of a rural background, the Catholic religion and the Spanish language are so intertwined in a cultural complex that preserving the one is equivalent to preserving the other.

California of the nineteenth century had a rich agricultural potential, and only the limitations of a weak Mexican state in the aftermath of the War of Independence (1810-21) prevented the full development of this region from periphery into an economic center of Mexico. Enlisting the expertise of a Hungarian count, the government of California initiated a wine industry that presently ranks among the world's finest producers. But these and other successes also provoked conflicts between the Hispanicized Indians of the missions and the Mexican criollos or Californios. Thus a class distinction, largely expressed in racial terms, was introduced into the colony, dividing it internally on the eve of U. S. conquest, much as the similar concept of Hispanos divided New Mexico.

Formation of Religious Traditions

Traditional religion for today's Latinos developed far from the accelerated pace of urban life in the rural areas, where the people devised their own ways of relating to the spiritual world. Close to the cycles of nature and committed to an often difficult struggle for subsistence, the people at the frontiers of the colonies fashioned religious expression around the two things without which this existence would have been impossible—land and family. And since family went far beyond the father-mother-siblings nucleus to include grandparents, uncles, aunts, cousins, etc., the religious expression that emerged was ultimately communal in nature. Even today, after continual North American control and the virtual disappearance of a village way of life, a look at traditional religious practices entails consideration of the family (extension, continuation, demise) and the cultivation of the land.

These traditions are so rooted in a communal identity and ethnic origins that at times they operate more as culture than as faith commitment. That is to say, people practice them out a sense of loyalty to tradition rather than a consciously religious choice. Yet it would be an oversimplification to deny religious meaning to such traditions. More than "folklore" (i.e., quaint customs that are vestiges of the past), these traditions form the core of what is now called "popular religiosity," because it projects the unarticulated premises of faith and religious commitment. Traditional religion is, therefore, a form of faith unique to those marginated by social forces, but it is faith nonetheless.

Traditional Latino Catholicism is related to the rites of passages, imparting a particular dimension to reception of the sacraments of baptism, confirmation, matrimony, the anointing of the sick, and Christian burial. But while in yesteryear as today, parents usually sought the baptism of their children in the church, the initiation of an individual as a Christian began immediately upon birth and was imparted by the midwife. This precautionary measure was instituted to safeguard against the danger of dying without the sacrament at a time of high infant mortality rates. Isolation and lack of ecclesiastical care transformed a precautionary measure into a common practice, so midwives often baptize infants before they turn to the priest for a "formal" baptism. This baptism is called *Bautismo de agua* and the practice is referred to as *echar el agua.*

In the countryside the midwife, called *comadrona* or *partera,* was godmother to all the children of the town on account of this "unofficial" baptism. A child often had two sets of godparents, one *de agua* and one *de iglesia o pila.* To these are added the sponsors at the time of confirmation, a sacrament that in Puerto Rico is commonly referred to as *obispar,* because it was one of the few occasions in a rural Catholic's life that he or she encountered a bishop (*obispo*).

Because of the security provided to children who had been initiated into the Christian life through bautismo de agua, oftentimes the parents postponed the other baptism until the *compadres* were ready economically speaking to make the required offering and pay for the celebration, which conferred social prestige. Baptism was important because it presented an excellent opportunity to the parents to extend familial ties to a friend or strengthen the bonds of the family with a brother, a sister, or some other relative by making that person a *compadre* or *comadre.* By inviting an individual to be a co-parent to a child, the parents were also indicating that they wanted to enter into a relationship of trust and obligation. Sometimes parents would seek someone of influence in the community in order to insure the child a certain amount of economic security in the absence of the parents. The common saying *el que no tiene padrino no se bautiza* is rooted in this practice.

This new and unique obligation is called *compadrazgo.* The obligation falls upon the adults so that in effect they become blood relations, as close as brothers and sisters. Adoption of a child under compadrazgo confers equal treatment with natural children, and the baptismal relationship implicitly carries this potential for raising a godchild as one's own. Birthdays and holidays such as Christmas necessitate gift giving between those spiritually related by baptism.

The celebration of the sacrament now known as reconciliation and that of First Holy Communion were oftentimes less spectacular. The child was often taught by an adult member of the family or a local catechist the main points of the Catholic faith. When he or she was thought to be ready, the individual was presented to the priest for examination and first confession. It was usual for a child to go through three confessions before approaching the altar for the reception of the Eucharist. Confession meant for the child that as an individual he or she had entered the "age of reason" and therefore was held accountable before God and the community for his or her actions. Children were told that they were no longer innocent and that every transgression henceforth was punishable. Fear of offending the Supreme Being, parents, and elders was very real, as was that of provoking their anger. On the other hand, there was always the assurance that through a good confession things could be set right once again.

Confirmation in the Mexican-ruled Southwest or Spanish-ruled Puerto Rico was imparted to the very young, somewhere between baptism and first reconciliation. Again, as with baptism, there was always fear that a child would die without the sacraments, and since the bishop's visits were very rare, it became customary to confirm all those who had been baptized, young and old alike.

The function of Christian maturity, fulfilled by confirmation in other more settled places, was supplied at least for female children, through *el quinceaños* or *el debut.* This custom of formally presenting or introducing young female daughters to society is customary among the middle and upper classes and has become a very elaborate affair, in many cases reaching excesses. It is customary for the debutante to dress in a formal white gown not unlike a wedding dress, to be escorted by a male friend and to be accompanied by "a court" of her best friends. In an attempt to bring some religious significance to this celebration, some families have opted for attendance at Mass and the reception of the sacraments preceding the secular celebration.

Due to consanguineous ties, many postponed marriage in the Church until the first child was born. It was

A Chicago teenager and her mother, Adalid Esther and Adalid Chapa, prepare for the fiesta de quinceaños. (Photo by Lloyd DeGrane, Chicago Católico. Courtesy of the Catholic News Service.)

usually easier to secure the necessary dispensation once there was proof that the union had been consummated, and what better proof than the birth of a child. The couple also realized that they had to seek to *arreglar el matrimonio* if they wanted the child to be baptized. Church marriage usually meant that the bride's parents had to provide her with proper attire (a white dress); a *desposorio,* a small celebration for the intimate family the day before the wedding; and the *bodas,* or big celebration on the day of the wedding. The groom had to provide an offering for the priest for the celebration of the ceremony and dispensations (if they were required) and *las arras,* usually twenty silver pieces for the bride, symbolizing his ability and willingness to support and provide for the future household. It was customary for the father of the bride to fatten several hogs and a calf for a daughter's marriage and to provide the feast with music and drink as well. Everybody in town was invited, as everybody in town was somehow related to the bride and/or groom. Baptisms and marriages were occasions to visit with one another, to catch up on the latest news or gossip, and to renew old bonds.

The first pregnancy of a young married woman was always a joyous occasion. The mother-to-be was rewarded by being pampered by family members and most especially by the husband. Perhaps this was the one occasion that she was so treated, since life in the countryside offered very little luxury to anyone. But during pregnancy, women could indulge themselves a bit more by appealing to other's sympathies and guilt through the yearnings, or *antojos.* Invoking antojos can be interpreted as very subtle manipulation by the woman not only to seek sanction for giving in to cravings, desires, and whims, but to procure other peoples' assistance in doing so. Most often the antojos were related to food, and oftentimes a husband was awakened in the middle of the night to be told his wife wanted some difficult-to-acquire "delicacy." Everyone would give in to a pregnant woman's antojos, because it was believed that to do otherwise would create undue anxiety and harm not only to the woman but to the unborn child. People went as far as believing that an unfulfilled antojo could even result in a miscarriage or the deformation of the fetus.

The *comadrona* was called upon not only at the birth of the child but also during the pregnancy. Most often lacking formal education, these *comadronas* were expert at observing. From the expectant mother's behavior and appearance, the best among them learned to diagnose how well she was carrying the baby, if it was going to be a difficult pregnancy and birth, measures to prevent or minimize risks, and even the gender of the child.

Oftentimes the comadrona was also the town healer or *curandera.* As a healer she employed not only her expertise as a herbalist and massager but added on a wide repertoire of prayers in a rite called *santiguos y despojos.* For *alumbramientos,* or births, the midwife would usually ask for very little assistance from others. Usually the husband, children, and other members of the household would be asked to wait in another room. An older child, grandmother, or aunt was asked to prepare a broth, which usually was made from an old hen that had been kept especially for that occasion. This broth was both ritualistic and pragmatic, providing nourishment for the women. After all, they were both to engage in very painful labor oftentimes for hours or even days. Some comadronas would enjoy a hearty cup of sugary black coffee or a few swallows of *ron cañita,* clandestine rum, to ward off against the early morning chill.

If both the curanderas' medicine as well as that of the town physician failed, then it was time for the *rezador* to appear. This person (male or female) would be sought to pray over the ill person, asking divine intercession for his or her cure, and if this was not possible, then *la gracia de un buen morir* (resignation and a good death). There were special prayers for *los moribundos.* Sometimes a person would make it known that he or she would not die until a specific matter was settled between himself/herself and another person. If not present, the person was sought and brought before the dying person, where differences would be reconciled. There were times when what the dying person wanted was simply a favor from a special someone—perhaps to do on his behalf something he had committed himself to but could not fulfill now that he was dying or to care for loved ones after he was dead.

When it became apparent that death was inevitable, the family and friends would be asked to gather around the person's bed to help him or her take leave of his or her temporal existence. The prayers were initiated by the rezador and followed by everyone present, at times even the dying person if still conscious. Someone would go for the priest to administer the sacrament then known as extreme unction and today referred to as the anointing of the sick.

At death, a special attire called la *mortaja* was prepared. The corpse would remain in the home overnight and during that time people would be permitted to come and pay their respects. This was called *velar al muerto* or *velorio,* and there would be some eating and drinking. But this was also a time for prayers for the repose of the soul of the person who died and all the departed souls. Every year this day would be commemorated by an anniversary velorio, where a rezador and the friends and family would be invited back. For special velorios the *rezador* would be asked for a *velorio cantado,* where the *decenario de difuntos* or ten decades of the holy rosary with special prayers for the dead were sung. A simple wooden box was sought, and the closest of kin would carry the remains of the dear one to the town church and cemetery, where the priest would officiate the last ceremonies, and a close relative or friend would be asked to give the final farewell in a sort of homily known as *despedir el duelo*. The *dolientes* would return home to comfort one another over a family meal, and for an additional eight days they would come together again to pray for the respose of the soul, thus completing *la novena*, or nine days of prayers.

Death was not seen as the end, but as a new beginning. The closest members of the family, however, would be expected to mourn the person's departure by wearing dark clothes and abstaining from dancing and other such festivities for a period of time in accordance with the traditions of that family and community. This was done out of respect and love for the departed one and for the benefit of his or her soul. Sometimes widows, orphans, mothers, or other relatives would vow to wear black or not to cut their hair for the rest of their lives. These are called *promesas*, from the Spanish meaning "promise."

But promesas need not be connected to death, and oftentimes they are not. A promesa may be made in order to ask for any special blessing or in thanksgiving for one received. It may include wearing special attire such as black clothing, the habit of a saint, not cutting one's hair, or doing special works of mercy or penance. The promesa may be temporary or for life. There are times when one person makes a promesa that another person is asked to fulfill. In this instance, the second person is not bound by it and can either disregard it or substitute it for something else. Once a promesa is made, however, people feel a need to comply, no matter who made the original commitment. Connected to promesas is yet another custom—the wearing, usually around the neck, of medals of saints or a much shortened version of the cloth scapulars of religious orders.

In addition to these rites of passage, Latino Catholicism celebrated annual feasts that were tied to agricultural and pastoral cycles. Given the diversity of economic patterns in Puerto Rico, with sugar and coffee, and in Texas, New Mexico, and California with cattle raising, sheep herding, and farming, it would be impossible to describe in detail each of these cycles with its regional variations. A few major feasts may be indicated, however.

The cycle for planting and pasturage usually began in early February and was initiated by the Feasts of the Purification of Mary (*Nuestra Señora de Candelaria*) and of St. Blaise. These two feasts coincided with the clearing of the land for planting and the spring mating of the herds. As in Spain and much of Europe, fire and light are associated with Candlemas and blessing with candles for St. Blaise, but coincided with the old Roman feast of Lupercalia, which celebrated the fertility of flocks of sheep. These layers of meaning, both Christian and pre-Christian, were carried over to the New World. In New Mexico, for instance, where sheep raising was a major industry, the February feasts occasion the celebration of the *Pastorela,* in which the central role of shepherds in the Christmas events is reenacted, usually with small children.

Easter brought springtime feasts, with special attention to vicarious identification with the sufferings of Christ. Good Friday, with its emphasis on fasting and pain, sometimes supplanted Easter Sunday in the focus of Christian celebration. The Penitentes of New Mexico scourged themselves publicly on Good Friday in reparation for sins. The May feast of the Finding of the Holy Cross (May 3) coincides with the month dedicated to the Blessed Virgin Mary and both allow for the introduction of femininity into festivals of the spring. These include various processions, often with young women assuming important roles, in which a statue of Mary is crowned with flowers or a prominent cross is similarly decorated.

Summertime feasts included St. John the Baptist (June 24) and Our Lady of Mt. Carmel (July 16); of relevance to maritime settlements, they include various forms of bathing and blessing of waters. The Feast of St. James the Apostle (July 25) has rich roots in Iberian practice, where this feast reenacted symbolically the centuries-long wars between Christians and Moors. In the New World the feast of St. James is likewise celebrated by donning costumes reminiscent of a Spanish past and contrasting that with local pre-Christian dress.

The harvest season was marked by celebrations of prominent feasts such as St. Michael the Archangel (September 29), St. Francis of Assisi (October 4), Our Lady of the Rosary (October 7), and St. Rafael the Archangel (October 24). These liturgical feasts would often be matched with particular harvest or other autumn agricultural practices. The feasts of All Saints (November 1) and All Souls (November 2) carry resonances of pre-Christian rites of communicating with the dead, particularly in Mexican-influenced areas.

In addition, each town has its patron saint, so that the village would often add a week of festivities not unlike medieval feasts that symbolically united the different classes in a common Christian belief and practice. Civic, religious, and even ribald elements of parades, processions and carousing were brought together, celebrating the community as much as the saint's life and works.

The most important cycle was that of Christmas, which began in Mexican culture areas with the Feast of Our Lady of Guadalupe (December 12) and ends the second Sunday of January called "Bethlehem's Octave."

Celebration of the Three Kings Day sponsored by the Puerto Rican Workers Mutual Aid Society. (Courtesy of the Jesús Colón Papers, Center for Puerto Rican Studies, Hunter College, CUNY.)

The Christmas cycle features distinctive music and special foods, making it the richest segment of Latino popular religiosity. The sixteenth-century Spanish missionary use of miracle plays, or *actos sacramentales,* has significantly affected many of these celebrations.

In places of Mexican influence, the *posadas* are observed both for religious ritual and musical expression. The entire village is involved in a dramatic reenactment of the journey of Joseph and Mary to Bethlehem, where Jesus was born. In the days before Christmas, those dressed as the holy couple go from one house to another, accompanied by the villagers bearing lighted candles and sometimes the statues of Joseph and Mary. After being ritually refused entry, they finally enter the last selected house, where pastries and hot chocolate are consumed amid communal singing. On Christmas Eve the final stop is the parish church, where the midnight mass, or *misa de gallo*, is celebrated. The liturgical celebration of the liturgy is submerged between the more elaborate celebration of the posadas and the subsequent public party, which includes the breaking of the *piñata* in a public place so that children receive their first Christmas gifts from the community, rather than from "Santa Claus."

The nine consecutive days before Christmas are celebrated with masses at dawn, called *misas de aguinaldo.* In Puerto Rico the *aguinaldo* has become a musical form of particular creativity, allowing native instruments and improvised versification in a popular style. Both in Puerto Rico and in Mexican-influenced areas, Christmas Day itself is marked by a meal for the extended family rather than with gifts for children.

The Feast of the Holy Innocents (December 28) carries with it customs inherited from the Canary Islands and the general framework of the Feast of Fools connected historically to the Roman Saturnalia. Children are given adult roles to play and promises are made in jest, much like April Fool's Day in North American experience. Persons foolish enough to lend items on the Feast of the Holy Innocents may never have them returned.

The Feast of the Epiphany, or Three Kings Day, is the traditional time of gift giving to children. Fresh cut grass is placed in a box underneath the bed. At night the kings pay their visit, the horses eat the grass, and in the morning, the children awake to find gifts left in the boxes by the grateful kings.

In Puerto Rico the entire Christmas cycle coincides with the time between the last harvest of sugar and the new planting. With little agricultural work available as well as the increased wealth due to payment for labor during harvest, household festivities are common. This is the social basis for the *parranda,* in which musicians and singers visit homes in the area, eating and drinking in each as reward for offering merriment.

This description of the formation of religious traditions for Latinos would not be complete without noting that such celebrations were rooted in a rural reality. These feasts were generally scorned by upper classes in these regions. On occasion, bishops censured or even condemned the revelry as not sufficiently ecclesiastical. On the other hand, given the remoteness of the people from populated centers and in light of the scarcity of clergy to attend to the sacramental needs of the people, these religious celebrations represented the social dimensions of faith for most people. The practice of the shrine, or hermita was often carried over to home altars and devotional tables where flowers, offerings, lighted candles, and statues in effect made a part of the home a private chapel. When people were too poor to buy expensive statues from Spain, they made their own out of local materials, thus giving rise to the art of the *santos,* or home-made religious figures.

The rosary was the principal form of prayer in the countryside, principally because it required knowledge of only a few formal prayers easily memorized. Often each of the mysteries of the rosary was preceded with an introduction or gloss that contained elements of poetry and local belief.

The mid-nineteenth-century movements of anticlericalism in Mexico and Spain distanced the upper classes still further from these traditional expressions of Catholicism. With such antagonism towards the Church, especially among those agitating for governmental reforms, these expressions of the common people were sometimes targeted for attack and eradication. In Puerto Rico, agitation for separation from Spain and the island's independence formed the basis for a nationalist sentiment that endured until the U. S. invasion of 1898. With the Catholic church's identification with Spanish rule,

A family celebrating Catholic mass. (Courtesy of the *Texas Catholic Herald.*)

A posada sponsored by the Sembradores de la Amistad in Houston, Texas, 1988. (Photo by Curtis Dowell, courtesy of the *Texas Catholic Herald*.)

Puerto Rican nationalism was generally held to be incompatible with Catholicism.

In various ways, however, the deep roots of traditional religious practice among the common people permitted a turnabout of this nationalist versus Catholicism dichotomy. Both in post-annexation New Mexico, where Father Antonio José Martínez (1793-1867) articulated a form of Catholic practice identified with the common people, and in Puerto Rico, where leaders like José de Diego (1866-1918) and Pedro Albizu Campos (1891-1965) advocated independence from the U. S. and Catholicism instead of Protestantism, popular religiosity acquired a powerful political significance.

Americanization, Protestantization and Americanizing Catholicism

To understand the religious dilemma of Latinos today, it is necessary to focus upon the processes of Americanization and Protestantization. Avoiding highly technical language, one can simply state that both terms describe a process of a change in values and in patterns of social behavior. "Americanization" refers to the political and legal aspects of this change and include the adoption of the English language. "Protestantization," on the other hand, is the remaking of religious organization and expression into the general mold of the Reformation. In terms of the religious institution, this means an egalitarian—if not also democratic—choice of church leaders; emphasis upon individual revelation through the reading of the Scriptures rather than a dependency upon tradition for discernment of the divine; exclusion from worship of devotions to Mary and the saints, as well as a paucity of religious symbols, medals, candles, etc. So much of popular culture in the United States reflects values deriving from the Protestant matrix that it is hard to avoid the conclusion, frequently expressed, that the culture of the United States is a Protestant culture.

There is nothing particularly threatening in such an assessment, anymore than to say that Spain or Italy have a Catholic culture. However, frequently Protestantization, and therefore Americanization, are categorized as more "modern" than Catholic values and culture. This presumption can be found even among many Latinos, as for instance the nineteenth-century Puerto Rican sociologist

Eugenio María de Hostos, who theorized that the Catholic religion represented mankind in its infancy, Protestantism was its adolescence, and agnosticism its adulthood. On the premise that the United States and its religion were more modern than Catholicism or Hispanic culture, Protestants believed that bringing Latinos to change their religious culture was beneficial for them and for the country. In this way, the Protestant religion legitimized military invasion in the nineteenth century, just as the Catholic religion had in the sixteenth and seventeenth.

The native religion (Catholicism) and native language (Spanish) were made targets for elimination or at least for subordination. In this, the English-speaking conquerors were scarcely different from the Spanish Catholics who, centuries before, had done the same with the Indians they met. The modes of subjugation, however, were more controlled and complex.

Catholicism is not a "pagan" religion, of course, and the Spanish language has centuries of accumulated literature that none of the Indian peoples enjoyed. But it is important to explain that under American rule, Catholicism was considered inferior to Protestantism, and the Spanish language was treated by state policies as the language of the ignorant. There is no way to explain or understand the shape of religion among Latinos today without accepting the complicity of the U. S. Government in this discrimination.

This subordination was not confined to religious and linguistic prejudice. In fact, the focus of discrimination was upon political and economic power. By installing a U. S. style of capitalism and controlling its operations so as to benefit English-speaking entrepreneurs, Latinos were impoverished in Texas, New Mexico, California, and Puerto Rico.

The economic activity in Texas and the conquered Mexican lands before the U. S. Civil War (1861-65) was generally limited to cattle ranching and subsistence farming. English-speaking people controlled local courts and agencies, and with the aid of government contracts and monopolies they undermined local control of the economy. In loans, for instance, they substituted the Anglo-American practice of total liability for interest payment to the renter, whereas the Spanish-based *partido* system had made both the giver and recipient of loans proportionately liable for losses and gains. A drought, diseased cattle, or inability to meet preestablished market quotas, made it possible for the newly arrived English-speaking Americans to take over ranches and farms that had belonged to the Spanish-speaking for centuries.

Moreover, since the sharing of communal rights to water and pastureland, guaranteed in land grants from Spain, did not conform to English common law as used by the United States, the basic ownership rights of ancestral lands was frequently questioned. In the sixty-odd years between the takeover of the Southwest by the U. S. government, the ownership of 35,491,020 acres was contested in courts. In these cases, only 2,051,526 were retained by Spanish-speaking owners. This means that Latinos lost 83 percent of the disputed lands. And even when they won, English-speaking lawyers often demanded to be paid in land, and the cash-poor Latinos were forced to oblige.

Despite its more developed agrarian capitalist economy, Puerto Rico in 1898 faced economic attack from U. S. businessmen and bankers, similar to what had been launched against Texas and New Mexico a half century before. But the centralization of capital that had brought relative prosperity after 1870 to a ruling elite of Spanish merchants and landowners made it easier for U. S. corporations and banks to supplant Spain. For instance, 85 percent of all farmland was controlled by a handful of U. S. sugar corporations within seventeen years of the 1898 invasion. Thus, the Puerto Rican patriots who had denounced Spain for such practices in the last quarter of the nineteenth century found themselves victims to a much more powerful and impersonal capitalism under the United States.

On the premise that everything funded by Spanish government funds was public property, U. S. rule brought claims that parish schools, rectories, cemeteries, hospitals, convents, and even church buildings were town properties. Virtually stripped of its resources and with all Spanish clergy forced to leave the island to petition for reentry with a visa, institutional Catholicism in Puerto Rico was literally bankrupted. The Church had to go to the Supreme Court of the United States in 1908 to salvage its material resources.

Not satisfied with crippling institutional Catholicism, the state actively sought to promote the Protestant religion by linking it to the public school system by hiring missionaries as teachers. The first several secretaries of education on the island, a post appointed by the island U. S. governor, not an elected post until 1948, were always Protestant, even when they were native Puerto Ricans. English was proclaimed the official language of the island in 1911 and continued as the language of instruction in public schools until 1948. Holidays with a Catholic cultural tie such as the Epiphany or Three Kings Day were eliminated from school calendars. Recruitment for teachers was limited to Protestant affiliated colleges in the United States, ignoring native Puerto Ricans until the Depression made it too costly to rely on non-Puerto Ricans. These measures in Puerto Rico were not substantially different from those previously employed to the same purposes in the Mexican-conquered territories of the Southwest and Pacific Coast.

Just as the U. S. government saw it a religious duty to foster Protestantism in the newly conquered island,

Protestant leaders saw it a patriotic duty to serve as missionaries. The Comity Agreements signed in New York in 1898 and 1900 efficiently divided Puerto Rico into districts so that Protestants would not compete against each other in seeking converts. The Presbyterian, American Baptist, Congregational, and Methodist Episcopal churches were among the first to assume the Puerto Rican missions, and the same denominations were especially active among Mexicans as well.

It is important to state, however, that such mutual favoritism between state and Protestantism should not dim the luster of the faith expressed by these missionaries, any more than the defects of the conquistadores should detract from Spain's contributions to America. They may have been linked to unseemly government policies, but in the light of faith they served religion generously.

Protestant missionary work in all of the conquered lands assumed three basic patterns. First, there was the work of the missionary board from its headquarters in the United States that provided personnel and financial support for the work of preaching, teaching, and eventually church building. These funds came mostly from the English speaking members of the church, rather than from the new Spanish-speaking converts in the region.

Second, there was the conversion of natives—even resigned Catholic priests—to the Protestant faith, who often proved themselves to be more effective in ministry than the English-speaking missionaries. Thus, money came from the church mission board controlled by the English-speaking, while the preaching and ministration of the new churches came from Spanish-speaking converts. Such arrangements were not contradictory, but they did produce conflicts. Given the gradual impoverishment produced by the U. S. takeovers, the viability of self-financing grew less rather than greater for most Protestant churches until mid-century. Thus, the effective work of the converts was always subordinated institutionally to the control by non-Latino missionaries. Put in other terms, power was always given by the institution to native English-speakers to a degree much greater than to the Spanish-speaking counterparts, even though the churches depended on the converts for their early effectiveness.

By the 1950s, this conflict was somewhat alleviated by a division between pastoral care and social concerns. The institutional agencies were requested to supply the funds for attending to the materials needs of Latinos—things like schools, settlement houses, financial and legal assistance agencies, etc. On the other hand, the strictly pastoral care concerns of preaching and worship were relegated to the native Spanish speakers. Traces of this compromise is evident in the apparent contradiction that native Spanish-speaking ministers tended to be more conservative than the English-speaking in the 1960s and 1970s. But the so-called conservative native Spanish speakers may have avoided social justice issues in order to guard a hard-won autonomy in pastoral matters.

Third, the rapid rise of Pentecostalism in the twentieth century has engulfed the initial beginnings of Protestantism among Latinos. The earliest recorded conversion of a Latino to Pentecostalism was when Salomón Feliciano Quiñones, a Puerto Rican migrant worker in Hawaii, who had accepted the Methodist faith while in Puerto Rico, converted to Pentecostalism in 1905. After working in California for his new faith, he returned to his native Puerto Rico in 1916 where his family helped to found Pentecostalism on the island. But even if Feliciano Quiñones was not the first convert, he was the first Spanish-speaking leader of Pentecostalism. By 1930 there were half as many Puerto Ricans who were Pentecostal as there were Puerto Ricans who were Protestant. In a sense, all Pentecostalism among Spanish speakers can be traced to this Puerto Rican beginning. The Puerto Rican Pentecostal churches have sent missionaries to New York, Texas, California, and New Mexico, and perhaps, more importantly, to other Latin American countries. Today, both among Latinos in the United States and in several Latin American countries, Pentecostalism is the fastest growing religion.

The Catholic church was a part of the "Americanization" impulse as much as the Protestant institutions. Leaders of the U. S. clergy, notably John Hughes, archbishop of New York, were full supporters of the War with Mexico in 1846. After the war, the Holy See named as bishop of Monterey and much of the rest of California, Joseph Sadoc Alemany, a native Catalán who had been driven from Spain by the secularization of church properties and was serving as Dominican superior in the United States. In 1850, the year of Alemany's appointment, California became a state, largely because the discovery of gold in 1848 had sent tens of thousands of English-speaking settlers to Northern California, which had passed under U. S. rule at the end of the War with Mexico. Alemany was elevated to archbishop of San Francisco in 1854 and his successor in Monterey was the Vincentian and fellow Catalán Taddeus Amat. The new bishop transferred his residence to Los Angeles, renaming the diocese. And in 1878, upon Amat's death, Francisco Mora became the last native Spanish-speaking bishop under the U. S. flag until 1960, when Luis Aponte Martínez (now cardinal of San Juan) was ordained an auxiliary bishop in Puerto Rico. The first Mexican-American bishop was Patricio Flores (1970), now archbishop of San Antonio, Texas. There are two Spanish-born auxiliary bishops in the United States today, Francisco Garmendia (1977) of New York and David Arias (1983) of Newark.

Bishop Patrick Flores of San Antonio receiving a donation for the promotion of Mexican American vocations, 1978. (Courtesy of the *Texas Catholic Herald.*)

The three Catalán bishops of California were chosen largely on their language affinity with the Latinos in their charge, but the expectation held over them by the body of U. S. bishops was for Americanization. Americanizing Catholicism was not invented for Latinos alone. It had been developed in serious and sometimes bitter conflicts among the English-speaking bishops of the United States in their dealings with European immigrant groups. Eventually the episcopate came to the conclusion that much—but not all—of European-based Catholic traditions had to be modified to conform with the Protestant matrix that was also the modern and Americanizing pattern of life and social organization. Liberal bishops wanted this assimilation to be accomplished as fast as possible, while conservatives intended to preserve cohesion as a Catholic group, for fear that assimilation as individuals would result in conversion to Protestantism. Curiously few of the bishops ever suggested that the democratizing trends urged in parish matters concerning non-English speakers should be applied to the selection of future bishops, or to the quasi-monarchical use of episcopal powers.

By the turn of the century in Los Angeles, not only had the original Spanish-speaking population lost political power and economic prosperity but the diocese was also effectively segregated into churches for the poor, Spanish-speaking, and the middle-class English-speaking Catholics. Amat's confiscation of Mexican Franciscan foundations and threats of excommunication aided this alienation of the Spanish-speaking congregation from institutional Catholicism. Such policies were strangely opposite from the East Coast dioceses, where the non-English-speaking newcomers were expected to adapt to the already established Catholicism in the United States. In California under Bishop Amat, the Catholic church lent its principal care to the English-speaking migrants and demanded the already established Spanish-speaking populace to adapt to the newcomers. Amat and his successors used financial resources for the English-speaking Catholics, principally in duplicating the kind of diocesan and parish structures common to the major East Coast sees of New York, Boston, and Philadelphia. California witnessed the building of Catholic schools, hospitals, convents, and seminaries—all for the English-speaking. The Spanish-speaking were expected to raise their own funds, although the church began a long court process against Mexico to restore the Pious Fund for ecclesiastical finances. When finally resolved in the twentieth century on the eve of the Mexican Revolution, the awarding of the Pious Fund could do little to save the vitality of the California missions.

Catholic discrimination towards Latinos was characterized by abrupt and inflammatory conduct from the bishops sent by the U. S. episcopate into the conquered territories of Texas, New Mexico, and later to Puerto Rico. The most outrageous of these prelates was Jean-Baptiste Lamy (1850-85) who became the first Archbishop of Santa Fe, New Mexico. French-born and trained in a Gallic Catholicism foreign to native religious expression, Lamy consciously set about extirpating continuity between Catholicism under Mexican rule and the new U. S. regime. He spied upon, publicly humiliated, and in

Father Antonio José Martínez.

1857 defrocked the native clerical leader, Father José Martínez of Taos, New Mexico. Martínez was already well respected for his writings and leadership (he was elected to the New Mexico legislature), and his high standing with the native Spanish-speaking clergy made him a rival to the archbishop's demand for total loyalty. Lamy's refashioning of New Mexican Catholicism to conform to the values of North American society were described approvingly by the novelist Willa Cather in *Death Comes to the Archbishop*, and the image of Martínez, like that of all Latinos, suffered from her bias. All of Lamy's successors until 1919 were of French ancestry and prohibited special apostolic funding for the Spanish-speaking population of New Mexico.

When the United States annexed Puerto Rico in 1898, the U. S. episcopate looked upon the island as if it were another New Mexico. One of Lamy's successors in Santa Fe, Placide Chapelle, recently named archbishop of New Orleans in 1897, assumed the role of apostolic delegate for Cuba and Puerto Rico, both ruled by U. S. military governors. James Blenck (1898-07), the Bavarian-born American citizen and protegé of Chapelle in New Orleans was appointed bishop of Puerto Rico at the insistence of the U. S. episcopate. Despite his crusade for Church properties, during his episcopate Blenck closed the local seminary and undermined native Puerto Rican political leaders who looked to Catholicism as a cultural and social defense against Americanization. Blenck banned the Christmas midnight mass (misa de gallo) in the San Juan Cathedral in 1898, considering it too rowdy and offensive to U. S. culture.

Bishop Ambrose Jones (1907-21) actively promoted the massive displacement of local clergy in favor of "missionaries" from New York and Philadelphia to found parish schools that still teach only English. Americanizing lay organizations like the Knights of Columbus were established among the wealthy, and English-speaking pastors were named in preference to the few native Puerto Rican priests who remained. The Catholic church thus openly promoted statehood for Puerto Rico. In 1917, testimony was received by Congress over the imposition of American citizenship on Puerto Ricans, only Blenck—somewhat repentant and now Archbishop of New Orleans—offered any opposition.

In Puerto Rico and in the Southwest, the native Latino clergy was depreciated, sabotaged, and rendered impotent by the policies of an Americanizing Catholicism. The severity and the mode of such disparagement varied in time and place, but the result everywhere was the same. The scarcity of native Latino priests cannot be attributed to a failure of Spanish Catholicism or some "defect" of Latino culture. This scarcity was courted by the institutionalized Catholic Church that wanted its clergy clearly identified with the Americanizing mission itself.

Deprived of native clerical leadership and impoverished by the grinding economic forces of occupation, lay reaction and defense of Catholic values became a defense of Latino culture as well. In New Mexico, the Penitentes became economic and political forces of resistance to U. S. domination. The Penitente Brotherhoods were modeled upon the pious lay organizations of Spain, meant to perform charitable works in a

Juan Bautista Lamy.

quasi-anonymous atmosphere and motivated by devotion to the suffering Christ. In New Mexico, Archbishop Lamy suppressed them, citing the Holy Week flagellations as superstitious excesses. This condemnation of a once-a-year rite, however, could not blind the people to the value of membership in the Penitentes. Often the Brotherhood served as a council of town elders, a local board of justice, and even as a credit union. In Puerto Rico, a lay preaching society called *Hermanos Cheos* was founded to counteract the activities of native Spanish-speaking missionaries by supplying a Catholic equivalent. Ironically their defense of Catholicism and Latino culture was sometimes resented by the Americanizing clergy as an encroachment upon clerical powers.

The biggest issue confronting Latinos, whether Catholic or Protestant, was native clergy. The social distance between a Catholic priest and his flock was considerable. To be a priest one had to be highly educated, speak English, and live celibate and outside of family. The Protestant minister was not required to live outside of family, but other demands, especially in formal education, were virtually the same. Only in Pentecostalism could one receive the spirit, remain within the family, and, with little formal education or knowledge of English, move into religious leadership.

The dilemma of Protestant and Pentecostal Latinos, however, was that in opting for a religious organization that suited certain social needs of the people, they had to turn their back upon centuries of Catholic liturgy and traditions that were interwoven with native Latino culture. Moreover, rather than encourage an accommodation with a Catholic culture, Protestant and Pentecostal churches in the United States adopted a hostility towards Catholicism matched only by the hostility Catholicism held toward Protestantism in Catholic countries. This dilemma became more acute in the 1970s and was echoed by a similar anxiety by Latino Catholic clergy in a rejection of North American Catholicism in favor of Latin American Catholicism.

The Catholic traditions derived from the Spanish experience tended to thrive most in small village and remote rural areas, where a North American clergy could not interfere with the established Catholicism of centuries. While the parish church and its sacramental distribution were always a part of such traditional Catholicism, the power of belief in the setting of home altar, local processions, and village customs coexisted with the institutional changes. Social distance, which made Latinos less important to the official churches, had the simultaneous effect of making the official churches less important to Latinos. These patterns were interrupted by mass migrations to urban centers of the United States that occurred after the two world wars.

Migration

The United States, it is said, is a "nation of immigrants." There have always been moments in history when large numbers of people have changed residence. Such mass migrations are usually spurred by natural disasters, political calamities like wars, or oppression for religious motives. Feeling the need to move, the immigrants search for a more attractive place to live. Such is the definition of the push-pull theory; one is pushed away from a region and pulled toward another. When the movement is between countries, the persons are emigrants from a country and immigrants to another; when the movement is between two regions of the same nation, the persons are migrants.

The Mexican Revolution of 1910 began to push Mexican nationals away from the devastation of their homeland and north across the borders of Texas and New Mexico into the United States. The fear that the mostly Latino population of New Mexico and Arizona would place their sympathies with the promise of a new Mexico stimulated the rapid incorporation of these territories as states in 1912.

But this predictable flow of immigrants north was greatly complicated in the aftermath of the First World War. The rapid industrialization of the Far West and the opening up of New Mexico's mineral wealth by the extension of the railroads created a new economy for the region. The boom of the roaring twenties, the beginning of the film industry in Hollywood, and the rapid development of Southern California brought more English-speaking migrants into what had been largely Latino-populated areas. When the Great Depression of 1929 devastated agriculture, the California-bound migration of "Oakies" intensified, as dramatized in Steinbeck's novels, especially *Grapes of Wrath.*

The arrival of English-speaking migrants in the 1930s further impoverished the local Latinos and the Mexicans who had come northward during the Mexican Revolution (1910-17). In order to find jobs, they began traveling along the railroads north and eastwards from Texas and New Mexico into states like Michigan, Ohio and Kansas, and into cities like Topeka and Chicago. Finding seasonal labor during the summers in northern fields, many of these Latinos then returned south and homeward to Texas and New Mexico for the winter.

The circulatory movement of laborers substantially altered the classic explanation of "push-pull" migration. Now the movement was virtually perpetual, and the economic relationships were interdependent. The Latinos found jobs in summer fields because they were willing to work for so very little under trying circumstances and in temporary jobs—conditions Euro-Americans would generally not tolerate. Yet Latino willingness to gather the crops was dependent on their near total impoverishment in native lands. Growers had no willingness or motivation to see these temporary migrant workers receive an education, join unions, or advance upward in the social scale because the economic viability of their farms depended upon cheap labor. Texas and New Mexico had little motivation to provide social services to Latinos, who spent their most productive months working in other states.

Migration no longer guaranteed economic upward mobility, as it had for European immigrants. Instead, migration was the ticket to permanent poverty. There were, of course, Latinos who worked in factories, and some migrant workers succeeded in putting down roots as permanent residents in northern cities. Often enough, such desirable jobs opened up because the war had caused a shortage of Euro-American workers for industry. Such urban dwellers formed the core of what became the Mexican-American barrios of the Midwest and California cities, and the Puerto Ricans in New York, Chicago, and parts of Ohio. City-bound Latinos were a source of cheap labor that was no longer available directly from Europe or from among the children of European immigrants.

Symptomatic of the poverty in which Latinos found themselves, especially in cities, was the development of antisocial modes of behavior. Unable to move upward in society towards "middle-class respectability" as white Americans had and unsuccessful in recovering the rural roots of Latino past prosperity because they lived in an urban slum, many young Latinos assumed new hybrid identities. Such was the pachuco of Southern California of the 1940s. Famous for his zoot suit, with its exaggerated lapels, tapered pants, and outlandish colors, the pachuco was described by a young Octavio Paz as a protester against Americanization and a Mexican past of oppression. The future Nobel Prize winner saw in the pachuco another of Mexican cultural masks, bravely disguising his conflict with a challenging and defiant outer pose.

In the adaptation to life in the United States, the differences between those recently arrived from Mexico and those who had been residents of conquered Mexico for generations began to fade. Except for the New Mexico Hispanos, whose disassociation from Mexicans was fraught with unfortunate racial overtones, second-generation Mexicans intermingled and were scarcely distinguishable from the descendants of the original colonists. In fact, only the question of citizenship (which was not readily apparent) and the ability to speak English (which was a subjective perception) socially distinguished Mexicans (i.e., born in Mexico) from Mexican Americans (born in the United States of Mexican ancestry).

The pachuco became a target for white groups fearing that his latent hostility would upset the existing dominance of an otherwise "docile" but growing Mexican-American population. The famous Sleepy Lagoon trial of 1942 was a bitterly racist attack on Mexican-American culture that was only partially remedied by a reversal of the original decision in 1944. In between the verdict and its overturning came the San Diego riots of 1943, which pitted the pachucos against U. S. Marines and the police in violent confrontations. The struggle was retold in more sympathetic tones in Luis Valdez's 1970s Broadway musical *Zoot Suit*, in which he made the pachucos forerunners of the militants of the Chicano movement.

The experiences of Mexicans in this circulatory migration were taken to a more dramatic level by Puerto Ricans. From the U. S. takeover in 1898 and gradually increasing until the Depression, migrants from Puerto Rico sought work in rural areas of the United States such as Lansing, Michigan; Hartford, Connecticut; and Vineland, New Jersey. The U. S. tobacco industry also recruited Puerto Ricans for work in urban centers. Indeed, New York City received 80 percent of all Puerto Rican migrants until the 1950s. Like the migrations from Texas and New Mexico into the Midwest and Southern California cities, the Puerto Ricans who came to New York before World War II, formed the core of the barrios in New York's Spanish Harlem, South Bronx, and Red Hook section in Brooklyn.

The radical transformation of this early Puerto Rican Pioneer Migration (1900-45) began when the island of Puerto Rico under Governor Luis Muñoz Marín adopted a large-scale economic industrialization plan called Operation Bootstrap. This program invited U. S. industries to locate factories throughout Puerto Rico to take advantage of the cheap labor there and—most importantly—the exemption from federal income taxes that was allowed because Puerto Rico was not a state of the Union. Muñoz Marín believed that the trickle-down effect of industrialization and its accompanying urbanization of the island would provide modernization to Puerto Rico more rapidly than statehood or complete independence.

The investments, massive as they were, could not supply jobs to all Puerto Ricans, however. Consequently, Puerto Ricans, convinced by their governor that industrial jobs were a ticket out of poverty, came to New York to work in that city's factories. Their numbers were unprecedented. From a yearly average of fewer than 4,200 Puerto Ricans in the previous decade, the average arrivals were more than 34,165 a year for the next eighteen years. If one calculates the children born in the United States to these migrants, it resulted in the transfer of nearly 40 percent of the island's entire population to the United States in less than two decades. This is the Great Puerto Rican Migration (1946-64). The rapid movement was aided by the use of airplane travel,

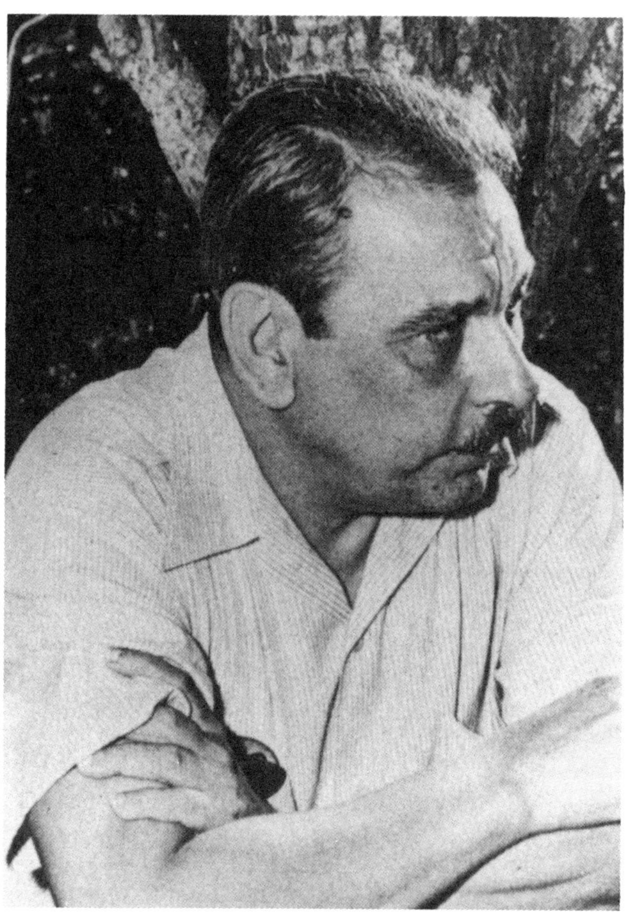

Luis Muñoz Marín. (Courtesy of the National Archives.)

which allowed Puerto Ricans to come north at low cost and in a matter of hours. Moreover, the popularization of electronic communications—radio, phonographs, telephones, and soon television—meant that the homeland was always present. The Great Puerto Rican Migration was a prototype of contemporary migration all over the world, in which the newcomers arrive by plane and scarcely leave behind their old country while working in the new country.

Most importantly, the Great Puerto Rican Migration was an early phase of what is now called the "global economy." The Puerto Ricans came to New York because they could not find work in Puerto Rico soon enough, yet New York needed cheap labor, because the investment in efficient new factories and modern equipment was being sent to Puerto Rico. Hence the migration of Puerto Ricans to the United States as cheap labor was accompanied by the migration of investment capital in search of cheap labor outside the United States. These structural patterns of the economy insured that the profits generated by Puerto Ricans in both places would never accrue to them. During the 1970s, New York would lose its tax base by the exodus of corporations to industrial havens in Puerto Rico and other parts of the world, and contrary to Muñoz Marín's original expectation, the island would never be able to tax these earnings, because the corporations threatened to go elsewhere.

Like the experience of the pachucos on the West Coast, the young Puerto Ricans growing up in alien New York City faced problems of cultural and social identity. Most of New York's housing is in rented apartments rather than single homes. The massive influx of Puerto Ricans to the city meant that the apartments in the original barrios were insufficient to accommodate the newcomers. Consequently Puerto Ricans moved into formerly Irish, Italian, and Jewish neighborhoods. Young and with children, used to residing with extended rather than nuclear families, and with different tastes in music and food, the arrival of the Puerto Ricans meant that the social complexion and type of services available in the neighborhood had to change. An added pressure was the racial perception of Puerto Ricans as more black than white. Once Puerto Ricans began to move into a community, seeking to escape poverty and slum conditions, the exodus of whites began. Landlords often took advantage of the Puerto Ricans' desperate need for housing to neglect maintenance and repairs, and the policies of residential building were focused away from more housing for the poor and towards government-subsidized middle-class dwellings. The turmoil and interracial conflicts within these changing New York neighborhoods is reflected in the Broadway musical and Oscar-winning movie *West Side Story*, based loosely on a Romeo and Juliet theme.

The early 1960s also brought a mass immigration of Cubans to the United States in response to the Cuban Revolution of 1959. Like the neighboring Puerto Ricans, Cubans had come in small but significant numbers to the United States to work in tobacco and other urban industries. The most famous of these migrations was the experiment at Ybor City, near Tampa, in which virtually an entire Cuban plant and its island village was relocated to Florida in the 1870s. These working-class Cubans brought with them a variety of African-influenced religion mixed with accretions from Spiritualism, called *Santería*. But this early Cuban migration was overwhelmed by what came after the Cuban revolution.

Three distinct groups emerge from the study of Cuban immigration after 1959. First were the very well-off and politically connected *batistianos* who had sided with a right-wing dictator and lost. Included in this group were some persons who participated in or even benefited from the wide-scale corruption of the Batista regime. They flocked to Miami, Florida, scarcely ninety miles away and refuge during the twentieth century for displaced presidents and their retinue, who often returned triumphantly to Cuba in a matter of months. Miami's weather was similar to that of the island, and the tourist industry there was connected to the nightclubs, casinos, and other enterprises that had flourished in Havana.

Second were largely middle-class professionals and business persons connected with American corporations operating in Cuba, often holding degrees from U. S. universities. These two groups, who had prospered before 1959, were the first targeted by the new government to be stripped of the privileges that accrued to them by pro-U. S. connections. The two groups also sent about 30,000 immigrants to Puerto Rico as well as larger numbers who went to Florida and other states. Many of the professionals moved to urban centers where Puerto Ricans and Mexicans were the majority. Because of their professional abilities, the Cubans quickly obtained positions in government and private agencies oriented towards Spanish speakers.

Third were the Cuban city and town dwellers, including fervent Catholics and Protestants, who came from working-class backgrounds and who had supported Fidel Castro's *26 de julio* Movement as a way to end corruption, install social justice, and restore constitutional rights. The Cold War implications of the Cuban revolution, spurred by the brinkmanship policies of John Foster Dulles, forced this third group into a difficult choice. Either they backed Castro and became allied with the Soviet Union or they rejected Castro and became partners with the ruling class that they despised. Most of these working-class Cubans stayed on the island and supported the revolution to varying degrees. But some departed, so that by 1970 there were about 800,000 Cubans in the United States and Puerto Rico. This constituted scarcely 9 percent of the total Cuban population—pale in comparison with the 40 percent of Puerto Ricans—but it was a substantial number that has made Cubans the third largest of the Latino groups today. Without the connections or the professional training of the first two groups, the working-class Cubans often settled outside Miami, as for instance in small factory towns in New Jersey.

This third group of Cuban exiles was urged on by religious conceptions that made communism incompatible with God and freedom. This group had split between those who chose the revolution and stayed in Cuba and those who rejected it for life in the United States. Predictably, those who came to the United States emphasized religious practice in their adjustments to life on the continent. The religious factor had been a decisive issue in the decision to leave Cuba, and it became a part of their identity as a "Cuban exile."

Thus, even if the first two groups reflected the weakness of religious practice in Cuba, the third group, which was the majority, was increasingly bound to faith and the institutional churches. (The most recent migrants of 1980, the *marielitos*, have a very different trajectory, having come from a country where Catholic practice has been decisively affected by the revolution). As will be discussed below in terms of other Latino groups, religion became for the Cubans in the United States a mode of preserving language, cultural identity, and the social values of the homeland. To these were added the heavy political baggage of an anti-Castro crusade. Lacking a political middle ground between the right wing and Marxism, the Cuban expression of institutionalized religion carries an ideological tilt to the right.

The Latino Parish before the Second Vatican Council

The institutional churches, Catholic and Protestant, were confronted by the need to provide a response in urban centers to the migrations of Mexican Americans, Mexicans, Puerto Ricans, and Cubans. The challenge was greatest to the Catholic church, which could claim the traditional loyalty of most of the migrants. But the influx presented great opportunity to the Protestant and Pentecostal churches as well.

The Catholic institution of the diocese is assembled from parishes. Although most parishes are divided territorially so that people residing in a certain district are expected to attend services and financially support the parish closest to them, Catholicism in the United States had an alternate mode of tending to immigrant groups. This was the national parish, which targeted as its congregation only those people of a particular nationality or language. Typically this national parish was ministered to by clergy who were native speakers of the language, most often priests from a religious order based in the homeland of the immigrants. Such an arrangement was of great advantage to the diocese, since the money for support was taken from the national group and the personnel for staffing the parish was not taken from the diocesan clergy. Moreover, the national parish was perceived as a temporary arrangement. Once the people learned English and became Americanized, they were supposed to abandon the national parish and enter into the existing territorial parishes.

National parishes abounded in the big city dioceses of the East Coast and the Midwest. In 1902 the New York archdiocese (which does not include Brooklyn or Queens) had 13 German churches, 2 French, 1 Bohemian, 4 Polish, 1 Maronite, 2 Slovak, 1 Hungarian, 11 Italian, and 1 Spanish. Philadelphia, Boston, Detroit, and Chicago were similar. In retrospect, sociologists argue that the national parishes allowed the immigrants continuity of a cultural and religious expression, without sacrificing a cohesive group identity. Eventually, assimilation for the immigrant was easier because the national parish allowed for an Americanizing Catholicism rather than an Americanization that was also a Protestantization.

Such division was not without its contradictions. The territorial parishes were afforded more diocesan resources, and the secular clergy provided most of the bishops in the United States. National parishes were left largely to the orders that staffed them, with no direct participation in diocesan governance. In practice the territorial parishes were dominated by the Irish, who arrived in this country already as English speakers and closer to assimilation as "Americans" than most other groups. Thus the Irish, who were by far the most numerous of the bishops, also determined the political influence of institutional Catholicism and controlled most of the resources of the church.

Conflict arising from several instances of discrimination led on occasion to schism and to the Cahensly affair of 1890-91, which disputed the financial control of missionary funds raised for non-English speakers and suggested episcopal nomination according to language group for the United States. In virtually all these conflicts, the (Irish) bishops won, but not always without cost to their relations with non-English speakers.

In the larger sees of the East Coast and Midwest, the end of the Open Door Immigration (1921-23) alleviated the conflictive nature of national parishes. By the 1950s, in fact, many had lost their congregations to assimilation, age, and residential mobility. Cardinal Spellman, who became ordinary of New York in 1939, decided against increasing the number of national parishes for the Spanish-speaking, which had grown to five in number. Instead he opted to turn existing territorial parishes into churches that ministered both to the English-speaking and Spanish-speaking congregations. This was accomplished by inviting Spanish-speaking clergy to join the parish staff and allowing use of existing facilities to the largely Puerto Rican faithful. When there were not enough Spanish-speaking clergy from religious orders to supply the rapidly growing need, Spellman sent the archdiocesan native English-speaking priests to learn Spanish.

This arrangement was an improvement over the national parish approach. Existing facilities and personnel were made bilingual, obviating the expenditure necessary to duplicate buildings and services. In a sense, the incoming Puerto Ricans simply replaced the outgoing English speakers and kept the parish vital and functioning. Unfortunately, however, the prejudice against Puerto Ricans on account of the (perceived) negative impact on changing neighborhoods was translated into an inferior portion of parish attention and resources. The masses and services provided in Spanish were frequently offered only in the basement church, usually inferior to the upstairs church, reserved for English speakers. Like segregated blacks in the United States, Latinos were separate, and not equal.

In Texas, New Mexico, and much of California and the western states, the national parish functioned differently. Unlike New York City, the newcomers to the area were not Spanish-speaking; they were the English speakers. The parishes for the Spanish-speaking community existing at the time of conquest were allowed to continue, usually under the ministry of Mexican clergy, but often without shared resources of the finances provided by English-speaking Catholics. Segregation of English and Spanish speakers was based on residential geography rather than on a juridic notion of national parish. And because of the gradual impoverishment of the original Spanish-speaking population, the economic segregation was highly effective.

In urban centers such as Chicago or Los Angeles on the other hand, the national parish for Mexican-origin Catholics followed the New York pattern. Often named after Our Lady of Guadalupe, patroness of Mexico, and usually staffed by Spanish-speaking missionary orders, these Mexican national parishes had an important advantage over the churches that serviced Puerto Ricans in the East. The clergy of the Mexican parishes were usually Mexican themselves, i.e., native clergy—Mexican, although not Mexican American. Puerto Ricans, on the other hand, were afforded clergy from Spain or U. S. priests who had learned to speak Spanish. Thus the Mexican national parishes and some of the territorial ones that remained under the charge of Mexican-based religious orders had not only a bilingual, but also a bicultural clergy; Puerto Ricans in New York, on the other hand, had a clergy that spoke their language but was not part of their culture.

Cubans who came to the United States after 1959 had significant numbers of native Cuban priests and ministers. In fact, 135 Catholic clergy against the revolutionary government were swiftly deported from Cuba in 1961, including Bishop Eduardo Boza Masvidal and 45 native Cuban priests. At the same time, *every single Methodist minister in Cuba had left voluntarily by the same year!* Cuban Catholics in south Florida did not rely on the national parish. Instead an impressive shrine to Our Lady of Charity of the Cove, patroness of Cuba, founded by Agustín Román, a dedicated Cuban priest from among the 1961 deportees, has supplied some of the functions of the national parish.

South Florida, to which most Cubans migrated, suffered from a chronic lack of priests, and the Cuban clergy was rapidly integrated (the Catholic term is "incardinated") into the existing institutional church. In 1979 Father Román was ordained auxiliary bishop of Miami.

By the time of the urban migrations in the 1950s and afterwards, Protestant churches already had established a modus vivendi between native English-speaking leaders and the native Spanish speakers. Mainline denominations like the Presbyterians, Methodists, and American Baptists provided social services in the cities to needy Spanish-speaking migrants. In time this produced converts who eventually formed a congregation and were provided a Latino minister from the already established churches of Texas, New Mexico, or some part of Latin America. Although this arrangement did not resolve the tensions between the dual structures of a controlling English-speaking institution and a Spanish-speaking parish, it did extend the concern for outreach to Spanish speakers beyond its previous geographical limits. In 1966 Dr. Jorge Lara Braud helped found the Hispanic American Institute in Austin, Texas, to train ministers for the Presbyterian church. Eventually Dr. Lara Braud was named director of the Faith and Order Commission of the National Council of Churches, and much of his progressive thinking passed into the organizational plans of major Protestant denominations, placing increased resources both at the disposition and under the control of the Spanish-speaking adherents themselves.

The Catholic church, through the National Council of Catholic Bishops, established a social concerns ministry to the migrant agricultural workers of the Midwest and Texas in 1948. Funded by what was called at that time the National Catholic Welfare Conference (known after 1968 as the United States Catholic Conference, or USCC), this office addressed the material and social needs of mostly Mexican and Mexican-American farmworkers in a social concerns apostolate. But it also provided for the pastoral care of mass and sacraments by coordinating the ministry on an interdiocesan basis. Most importantly, Archbishop Robert Lucey of San Antonio invited the clergy of northern dioceses, who ministered to the workers during the agricultural season, to accompany the Spanish speakers to their communities of origin in Texas during the winter.

This innovation introduced a modern social work dimension to ministry. The visits to Texas were intended to substitute a personal contact with the migrant workers for the impersonal ministry based entirely upon temporary factors of residence. The ministry to the Spanish-speaking population was enriched with sociological assessment of the material needs of the people as well as for patterns of migration. Lastly the need for cultural awareness on the part of church personnel was emphasized.

In the New York archdiocese, an Office for Spanish-American Catholic Action was founded in 1953 essentially to do for the Puerto Ricans what the Bishops' Committee on the Spanish-speaking had established for Mexican-origin peoples in the Midwest and Texas. Working closely with the Puerto Rican church and agencies of the island government, the New York office coordinated the social concerns apostolate with the resources of parishes which were primarily interested in pastoral care to Puerto Ricans. This office also established in 1957 the Institute for Intercultural Communications on the campus of the Catholic University of Ponce. Directed by Msgr. Ivan Illich, the institute at Ponce was the first Catholic center for cultural and apostolic training in the Spanish-speaking ministry of the United States.

Lay persons were also provided with apostolic training and given participation in pastoral care with the large-scale introduction of the Cursillo Movement after 1960. The *Cursillos de Cristiandad*, or "Little Courses in Christianity," were derived from a movement in Spain that utilized a retreat-type environment and instruction by lay persons to make a cultural Catholicism into a vital practice of the faith. While adhering to a strict subordination of the laity to the clergy in the hierarchic structures of Catholicism, the Cursillo nonetheless permitted lay persons certain functions that were traditionally assigned to clergy. Sociologically speaking, the factors of personal testimony and the emotional impact of group dynamics gave the Cursillo a Catholic version of a Protestant conversion experience.

Pentecostal religion grew and prospered in the urban environment. Unburdened of a rigidly hierarchical structure and capable of bestowing the ministry without extensive formal training, Pentecostalism reaped an immediate number of native leaders from among the Spanish speakers. While much of the cultural style—music, abandonment of Catholic traditions, rejection of devotions, medals, candles, processions, etc.—can be interpreted as antagonistic to Latino culture, there was great insistence upon the Spanish language and personal involvement. Moreover, the tight-knit, almost extended family structure of Pentecostal churches provided a generally congenial context for religious expression, even if aspects of this expression departed from some long-held norms.

Militancy

Militancy in the churches sounds like a contradiction: if the institution is dedicated to advocating love and belief in God, why should there be internal conflict? Yet, throughout history, religion has been a rallying cry that has nonetheless resulted in conflict, violence, and even bloodshed. The militancy described here is a conflict between believers over the use of church resources and related issues of representation within the councils of authority that make the decisions pertaining to these resources. As will be seen, Latino militancy initially sought greater representation for Latinos within the institutional churches, on the premise that Latino church leaders would make decisions that favored Latino believers. Gradually it became apparent that representation alone was not sufficient to change policies that subordinated Latinos within the churches.

In Puerto Rico the first success in what had been a century and a half struggle for a native Puerto Rican bishop was successfully completed after the 1960 elections on the island. The North American ordinaries, concerned at a rising tide of materialism in the wake of industrialization and urbanization, had denounced government-sponsored birth-control clinics. Declaring birth-control by artificial means a mortal sin, the bishops founded their own political party for the 1960 elections, Christian Action (PAC), and declared that any Catholic voting for Luis Muñoz Marín and his Popular Democratic party would be excommunicated.

The bishops were largely unsuccessful in making the PAC a viable party and the majority of the island Catholics voted for the popular governor, who won a resounding electoral victory. But the struggle was eventually couched in nationalistic terms, pitting a Puerto Rican leader against non-Puerto Rican bishops. Moreover this struggle had the unfortunate timing of coinciding with the campaign of John Fitzgerald Kennedy to be the first Catholic president of the United States. The bishops' threats against the freedom of Puerto Rican voters was exactly the opposite message that Kennedy attempted to convey about his own respect for the separation of church and state. With the active intervention of Cardinal Cushing of Boston, the Holy See removed the two North American bishops, sending one, McManus, into virtual retirement, and the other, John Davis, to Santa Fe, New Mexico, as archbishop there in 1964. Three new sees were created in Puerto Rico in 1964, and all bishops since have been native Puerto Ricans. This indigenization of the island's hierarchy had been sought for decades by the Arizmendi society, named after the only native Puerto Rican bishop under Spain (1809-14), and it became a presage for similar actions elsewhere.

The concept of indigenization in Catholicism came to full flower after the Second Vatican Council (1963-65). Liturgical reforms compelled celebration of the mass in the language of the people and urged incorporation of local musical and cultural expressions. These immediate alterations in what had been a virtually unchanging Catholicism since the sixteenth-century Council of Trent set in motion larger questions about the meaning of the church; the nature of relations between bishops, clergy, and laity; and the role of politics and social concerns within the traditional ministry of pastoral care.

In the United States, such profound questioning by Catholics about the faith and its institutions was complicated by the social and political upheavals of the late 1960s. The civil rights movement climaxed in the War on Poverty legislation of 1964, the Voting Rights Act of 1965, and the radical change in the immigration laws, which removed the quotas biased in favor of Europeans. As a result the federal government actively intervened in social affairs to advance interests of the poor, now called "minorities." Eventually the amount of representation and resource distribution for minorities became measures of institutional fairness. Moreover the rise of anti-Vietnam War feelings, the assassinations of Martin Luther King, Jr., and Robert Kennedy, and the counterculture movements of the time introduced self-doubt and skepticism into the social complexion.

Latinos, particularly young college-age Mexican Americans and Puerto Ricans in the United States, reacted to the opportunities and the radicalism by redefining themselves. If "Amerika" was corrupt and imperialist, the thinking ran, why should it define half of Mexican-American identity? But clearly the youth raised in the United States were not "Mexican" either, since they knew less of the Spanish language and Mexican history than the arriving Mexicans from across the border. Accordingly a new term was coined for the militant persons of Mexican descent who had been born (or at least raised) in the United States: they were "Chicanos." The homeland of the Chicanos was not Mexico but the historical home of the Aztecs before they migrated south about the year 1100 to present-day Mexico. This homeland, which coincided with parts of New Mexico and Texas, was "Aztlán." A new cultural identity and a new interpretation of Aztlán and its rightful heirs was developed by university professors who created a new field of studies about these Chicanos.

Puerto Ricans in the United States had little difficulty in recognizing Puerto Rico as their homeland, and in the radical spirit of the time, they identified with the cause of the island's total independence from the United States. Such independence was to be accomplished by adopting anti-imperialist socialism as an ideology. Puerto Rico already had many university professors who had developed alternative interpretations of Puerto Rican history, emphasizing the heroism of the Puerto Ricans and the imperialist nature of U. S. rule. These professors became part of the City University of New York and other colleges in urban centers where Puerto Rican studies were introduced.

The institutional churches could not escape the application of secular norms of social justice to ecclesiastical organizations. Moreover, the reforms of the Second Vatican Council had already produced far-reaching changes upon the previously secretive hierarchic policy-making apparatus of Catholicism, with ripple effects on other churches as well.

The 1967-68 strike of the United Farm Workers at Delano in California, led by the Mexican-American César Chávez, was the first Latino militancy to capture the national imagination. Supported by the still-popular Kennedy family and other prominent liberals, a boycott of table grapes gathered support for the workers and led to an eventual labor triumph.

Chávez was Catholic and utilized the motivational force of the Cursillo in mobilizing and maintaining the morale of the strikers. The strike also forced the Catholic church, which ministered to the needs of the farm workers, to take sides. Predictably the priests ministering to the social concerns of the workers sided with the strike; whereas the clergy who placed primacy upon pastoral care alone denounced Chávez and the cause. Ironically the conservative bishop of Monterey-Fresno, in whose jurisdiction Delano's events unfolded, was Aloysius Willinger, former bishop of Ponce, Puerto Rico.

In Los Angeles Mexican-American Catholics were angered that Cardinal McIntyre, the conservative archbishop, joined Willinger in a vitriolic denunciation of Chávez, including McCarthyite accusations of communism. Organized under the name *Católicos por La Raza,* this group began to gather embarrassing statistics about the property holdings of the archdiocese, its meager distribution of resources to Chicanos, and the growing numbers of Spanish speakers without pastoral care within Los Angeles. At the cathedral's televised midnight mass of Christmas 1969, Católicos por La Raza, were violently prevented from entering the church by armed sheriffs hiding in the wings of the vestibule at the invitation of the cardinal. McIntyre then proceeded to apologize to the congregation for the disturbance that had resulted in several serious and bloody injuries to the Chicanos, that this was necessary "to keep the rabble out."

The mass at St. Basil's Cathedral became a rallying cry for increased Chicano militancy. In the aftermath of the well-publicized words and actions of the cardinal, Bishop Antulio Parrilla of Puerto Rico, who was in California protesting the Vietnam War, celebrated mass for the Católicos in direct repudiation of McIntyre. In the aftermath of the confrontation there was public criticism of Cardinal McIntyre from Latinos, so, like the North American bishops of Puerto Rico after the 1960 debacle, he was "retired," although his policies towards Chicanos were never cited as the reason.

Nor was this the only victory for the church militants. When the UFW contract was not renegotiated and a second strike was declared in 1973, all the Catholic bishops in the United States supported Chávez through a statement issued by the NCCB. Similar support from the local church in El Paso for the Farah strike in 1972 presented a new kind of Catholicism that would stand with Chicanos and their social needs.

Conscious that Catholicism was capable of change and would respond more generously to Chicanos if church leaders were confronted with the people's needs, native Chicano priests became convinced of a need for unity in an organization that would address these needs across diocesan and ecclesiastical boundaries. In 1969, PADRES (*Padres Associados por Derechos Educativos y Sociales*) was founded in San Antonio, Texas. A year later, religious women founded a parallel group named *Hermanas,* to press for the same goals among women religious.

These groups played a most important role in the initial militancy of Latinos within the Catholic church. They assembled talented leaders, most of them young and aggressive. By periodic meetings, newsletters, and seminars, PADRES and *Hermanas* educated themselves about the needs of Latinos. They issued frequent whitepapers and documents analyzing the plight of the people and offering plans to the church to remedy these problems. In many places the Latino church leaders gained legitimacy in the eyes of civic leaders and the secular press. Latino priests and women religious, it was thought, speak better for Latino Catholics than non-Latino clergy. Moreover, PADRES and Hermanas represented a pool of capable leaders who often were the most qualified to implement the programs they had suggested. From the ranks of PADRES came some of the most committed Latino bishops: Patricio Flores of San Antonio, Juan Arzube of Los Angeles, Gilberto Chávez of San Diego, Roberto Sánchez of Santa Fe, and Ricardo Ramírez of Las Cruces.

PADRES had some contradictions, however, which lessened its importance by the end of the decade. First, only Chicanos were allowed membership. This excluded non-Latinos and even Spaniards, Puerto Ricans, and Cubans. Eventually, all Latinos and Spaniards were allowed to join, but the original division left scars that never healed, and Spaniards in the Northeast founded a rival organization, ASH (*Asociación de Sacerdotes Hispanos*). Second, the protesting and confrontational nature of PADRES meant that when its most talented members became members of the episcopate of directors of programs in local chanceries, they felt compelled to separate themselves from direct participation in PADRES on the grounds they could not protest to themselves. Third, success in practical recommendations that were implemented left PADRES without an agenda. Gradually the association was left with only the most radical proposals. Perceived as ungrateful for the lesser concessions that had been made, PADRES was labeled negatively, and its membership began to shrink as middle-of-the-road PADRES resisted the new agenda. Finally,

A conference of Roman Catholic Bishops discussing the needs of the Spanish speakers. Menlo Park, California, 1977. (Courtesy of the *Texas Catholic Herald*.)

like Hermanas, PADRES lost many members who resigned from the priesthood and religious life, often marrying and abandoning the ministry completely.

Despite these difficulties, it would be hard to overstate the importance of PADRES and Hermanas. They provided leadership for a specifically Latino agenda. They produced proposals to the Campaign for Human Development of the USCC, which, like the War on Poverty, sought to empower local groups of minority people seeking to improve the social conditions of the people.

But the most significant contribution to Latino militancy within the church by PADRES and Hermanas may have been the early matching of a paradigm taken from U. S. minority politics to the Latin American Theology of Liberation. The implementation of the Second Vatican Council's reforms in Latin America was charted in the historic meetings of the Latin American episcopate (CELAM) in Medellín, Columbia, 1967-69. Besides unifying liturgical expression and texts, the meeting also developed new definitions of how pastoral care and social concerns were to be merged in accordance with conciliar decrees. The innovative result of this new formulation of apostolate was called the theology of liberation.

Some have dwelt upon the use of Marxist dialectical class analysis to condemn liberation theology. But whatever its excesses, it has provided a new conception of the role of theology as justification to apostolic action, or praxis, as it is called. Not only did liberation theology incorporate social analysis as a critical ingredient for faith consideration, it also opened up the process of reflection to ordinary people whose experiences of hunger, pain, repression, etc., were considered valid for theological formulation. Lay persons were organized in small basic groups, or *comunidades de base,* to conduct this reflection and then to mobilize themselves for active participation in the betterment of social conditions. Nor were socialism and insurgent *guerrilla* movements excluded in Latin America from inclusion as valid forms of Christian response to injustice.

While PADRES and Hermanas never directly urged such political solutions for the United States, they did express solidarity with Catholics in Latin America who had taken up such causes. Invitations were extended to Latin American theologians to visit the United States and instruct Latinos in liberation theology. In this way there was an early and enduring connection between the militancy of Latinos within the Church and the most important theological movement since Vatican II. The theology of liberation gave a scope and profundity to Latino militancy that made it much more than a strident call for representational power and episcopal appointment for its members.

The first fruit of this matching of militancy with the theology of liberation produced the National Hispanic Pastoral Encounters, the first of which was held in Washington, D.C., in June 1972. The visit to an international conference in New York by one of the theologians from Medellín, Edgar Beltrán, a Colombian priest, sparked interest in a pastoral planning session for the leadership of the Archdiocese of New York. Sponsored by Fr. Robert L. Stern, director of the New York Office for the Spanish-speaking Apostolate, this pastoral meeting in New York took place in October 1971. It confirmed the direction Stern had taken towards indigenization of the ministry in New York and the opening up of the theological process to the laity, mostly Puerto Rican, in his charge.

The success of the New York experience argued for its repetition elsewhere, and Beltrán suggested a national meeting to produce maximum results in the swiftest possible time. PADRES and Hermanas were brought into the process early on, as well as catechists, directors of new programs such as the permanent diaconate, and traditional leaders from movements like the Cursillo. A newly formed national committee awarded representation to each diocese in a process that allowed matching numbers of clerical and lay delegates, selected both by the laity and the local bishop. Three major speakers were chosen: Bishop Raúl Zambrano of Facatitiva, Colombia, representing CELAM, where the theological process of pastoral encounter had been implemented; Bishop Patricio Flores, auxiliary of San Antonio, who was the highest ranking Latino clergyman on the U. S. mainland; and Virgilio Elizondo, a seminary professor of San Antonio, who had been an observer at Medellín on liturgical and catechetical matters. The Puerto Rican bishops, who had formed their own island episcopal conference affiliated with CELAM at the end of the council, were not invited.

The 1972 National Encounter made a series of forcefully expressed and carefully drawn recommendations. Although the NCCB took a year to issue its response, it adopted several of the recommendations. Principal among these were (1) the establishment of the Mexican-American Cultural Center (MACC) in San Antonio as a experimental model for pastoral training of clergy, religious, and laity; (2) recognition that different liturgical norms were required for the Spanish-speaking population in the United States; the eventual elevation of the social concerns agency, the Division of the Spanish-Speaking, to the level of a multifaceted secretariat within the U. S. Catholic Conference, with a mission to respond to pastoral as well as social concerns issues; and (3) acceptance of comunidades de base as a valid form of ministry.

Although the bishops expressly rejected the Encounter's call for a quota of native Latino members of the hierarchy, in practice, many sees where there were significant numbers of Spanish speakers named native Latino auxiliaries, some of whom later became ordinaries. The petition for married clergy was brusquely rejected, while the suggestion that Spanish-speaking national parishes should be elevated to equal rank with territorial parishes was left to local initiative. The Encounter also mandated the celebration of regional encounters and left the way open for subsequent national encounters, which have been held in 1977 and 1985, in Washington, D.C.

Protestant churches were not neglectful of the new theology and social militancy among Latinos. In fact, considering the smaller percentages of Latinos in the total membership of most Protestant churches, Protestant response may be considered to have been more

Hispanic bishops and Pablo Sedello, Secretary of the Hispanic Secretarial, pose at Encentro II. (Courtesy of the *Texas Catholic Herald.*)

generous than Catholic. The Presbyterian church supported the interdenominational organization Theology in the Americas, which promoted the theology of liberation throughout the United States. The United Methodist Church intensified its publications in the Spanish language and widened its pastoral training programs. Other denominations increased Latino representation, especially in the familiar areas of social concerns outreach and funding.

In general the mainline Protestant churches have responded well to the new sense of ecumenism that the theology of liberation engendered. Especially in Puerto Rico, progressive Protestant leaders frequently collaborate on social, political, and ecclesiastical matters with progressive Catholics. In fact, such cooperation among progressives of different denominations is more frequent than collaboration with conservative members of their own denominations. But the strong political overtones of liberation theology as it impacted upon the ministry to Latinos also produced a conservative backlash. Complicated by the perennial status question as to whether Puerto Rico will be a state, an independent republic, or remain a commonwealth, church leadership on the island is sharply divided along ideological lines in virtually every denomination.

Pentecostal and evangelical Christians in Puerto Rico and the United States have generally rejected liberation theology. In fact, in some places they actively seek to destroy it. This has insured that their antipolitical message carries with it an active rejection of a social concerns role for ministry among the people. In some instances Pentecostal ministers have moved to Evangelical or the Methodist and Baptist churches, where they preach in largely a Pentecostal style but pursue a social concerns apostolate more congenial with the new denominations than with Pentecostalism.

The Catholic church has also incorporated a Pentecostal movement within its orthodoxy, which has attracted many Latinos to reconversion as Catholics who worship as Pentecostals. The charismatic, nonhierarchial model of church instilled by this Catholic movement clashes with the vision of church promoted by the Cursillo. In some places a rapprochement between the two groups has been achieved; in others a significant hostility endures. This Catholic movement, moreover, competes with proselytism by Pentecostal churches among Latino Catholics.

Solidarity

The impact of the First National Hispano Pastoral Encounter of 1972 upon Catholicism was mixed. In some dioceses it opened the door for recognition to a Latino presence that had been hitherto ignored; elsewhere it added impetus to an already healthy presence; but there were also places where the final result of the encounter was a weakening of Latino militancy.

The recommendations of the encounter were of two types: first, those targeting the institutional church, particularly on the question of Latino representation at power levels and the elevation in importance of diocesan offices for the Spanish-speaking apostolate; second, those providing materials, leadership, training, and recognition to parish level movements, especially among the laity.

The institutional church works on a system of hierarchical influence, so that when an archbishop adopts a particular form of administration, the suffragan dioceses are likely to imitate in form—if not always in substance—the same reorganization. Because the encounter had gone directly to the national leadership of the U. S. bishops, this battle for the elevation of Offices for the Spanish-speaking community to chancery-level status was a nearly spectacular victory everywhere. Likewise the regionalization of pastoral training centers and the inter-diocesan pooling of resources afforded a measure of autonomy to such centers, inasmuch as they escaped control from any single diocese. Lastly, the directorship of both the offices and the centers almost always consisted of Latinos.

Archdioceses like San Antonio and Miami, where the overwhelming majority of the Spanish-speaking population were of a single national origin, effortlessly matched their particular culture to all pastoral efforts on behalf of Spanish speakers. Community-based movements, largely supported by the churches but run by Latinos themselves, have been a healthy result. In San Antonio, Communities Organized for Public Service (COPS) has succeeded in altering the city charter so as to eliminate at-large elections, which had been used to prevent Latinos from gaining representation in city offices. When district officials were required to live in the areas they represented in neighborhood voting, Latino spokespersons emerged, and Henry Cisneros was elected mayor of San Antonio twice. In Los Angeles, United Neighborhood Organizations (UNO) was a similar church-supported empowerment coalition. In 1990 a court decision in California eliminated at-large voting for a powerful city governance board, but it remains to be seen if Latino officials will gain the kind of prominence in California as resulted from a similar electoral change in Texas.

In other places, particularly in Newark and New York, there is less of a predominance of one group over the other, and promotion of Latino culture by the church was joined to encouragement of many national and ethnic groups. If the Latino culture projected by the church excludes other groups, it produces conflicts. Some

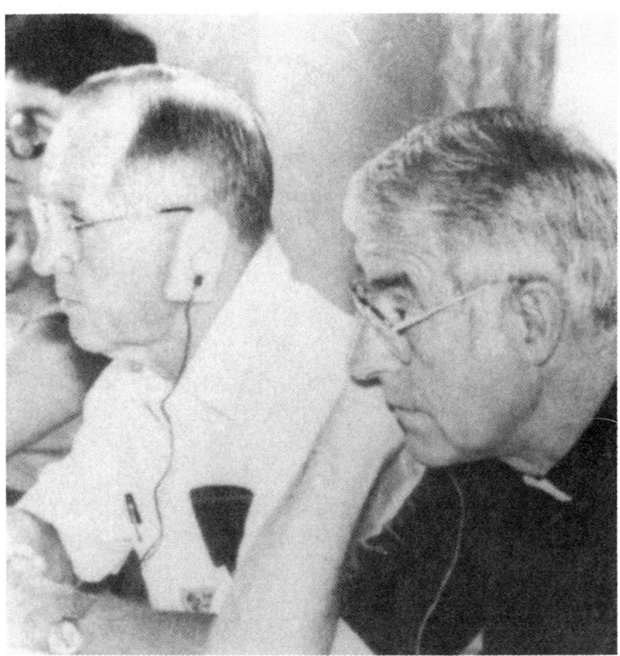

Bishops listen to interpreters at Encuentro III in Washington, D.C. (Courtesy of the *Texas Catholic Herald.*)

object to equating "Latino" or "Hispano" with one particular nationality, or minority with "the Spanish-speaking." But the adoption of a nationality-neutral term like "Hispano" then diluted the defense of culture implicit in the apostolate.

The biggest losers in this dilemma of post-encounter reorganization were the Puerto Ricans of New York and New Jersey. Although Puerto Ricans constitute some 65 percent of the total Latino population in these regions, alongside Dominicans and Colombians (New York) and Cubans (New Jersey), the dioceses adopted a nationality-neutral term of "Hispano" for the apostolate. Resources were shared with each group, leading to a proliferation of societies, fiestas, and official masses. For instance, in New York the sponsorhip of the San Juan Fiesta in honor of Puerto Rico's patron was reduced in importance as archdiocesan feasts for the patrons of Cuba, Dominican Republic, Colombia, Argentina, Perú, etc., were added to the official calendar.

The appointment of leaders to church posts and commissions also tended to be proportionate, so that conflicts developed among the Spanish-speaking groups over leadership that was then identified as "Puerto Rican," "Cuban," etc., usually to the detriment of effectiveness. None of the native Spanish-speaking bishops appointed in three dioceses of the area (Francisco Garmendia, New York; David Arias, Newark; René Valero, Brooklyn) were taken from the largest groups; two were Spaniards, the third was Venezuelan in background. This does not mean that any of these bishops were antagonistic to the people, but they were at a considerable disadvantage in mobilizing the people and fostering the militancy that produced the successes of the encounter and the empowerment of Latinos in predominately single-nationality regions such as San Antonio and Miami.

Lastly, in some dioceses cooptation of leadership and tokenism was used to debilitate the impetus of the encounter. These are terms that have technical meanings. Briefly put, cooptation of leadership reorients the accountablilty of persons with influence among the people so that the leader places a priority upon convincing the people of the correctness of institutional policies rather than presenting the people's needs before the institution. This cooptation takes places in various ways, both on account of institutional factors and personal needs. The institution may refuse funding, present impossible bureaucratic hurdles, or so dilute leadership functions among competing interests so as to forestall effectiveness. It may also appeal to personal ambition of the leader in order to minimize the challenge offered to the institution or rely upon psychological "burnout" to reduce the effectiveness of the leader.

Tokenism consists of a deliberate policy to elevate persons to positions of visibility but without real power to effect policy. In some instances the native Spanish-speaking bishop was selected from persons not at all active or even hostile to Latino militancy. This effectively decapitated the movements and created conflicts between the token Latino leader and the grassroots leaders. Often enough the grassroots people lost interest in a losing battle in which the letter but not the spirit of their requests for Latino representation had been met. Hence, in some places the estrangement from the church has been relatively high among the original leadership.

The conservative regimes of Ronald Reagan in Washington and of Pope John Paul II in Rome greatly constrained Latino militancy. In the first case, the social and political opportunities afforded Latinos as a minority group were underfunded or abolished. Perniciously, the social atmosphere that sought social justice by remediation of centuries of past injustices was replaced by belligerent opposition to affirmative action and active opposition to federal intervention in the economic system. In the case of the Catholic church, John Paul II initiated an effort at recentralization of power in the Vatican, an attack on theological pluralism, and the condemnation of liberation theology. Even with a Democrat, Bill Clinton, in the White House, it is not clear how Latinos will be affected by more progressive politics. Nor can one predict a change in Catholicism if a new pope were to be elected. But the change in Catholic policies along with political conservatism has diminished the effectiveness of the Latino militancy that was so successful during the 1970s.

Conservative forces have also had their effects upon the Protestant churches. The dispersal of major denominations from the centralized headquarters at 475 Riverside Drive in New York to parts of the Midwest was directed against liberal church leadership. The Moral Majority intrusion into politics during the 1980s has also politicized Pentecostals and Evangelicals towards the right wing, in a phenomenon that is likely to outlast its initiators. Nonetheless, the politicization of virtually all religions is an increasingly problematic circumstance. The greatest blow against vital work by mainline Protestant churches among Latinos has been the drying-up of funds previously dispensed for wide-ranging social action, often through local groups identified with radical Christianity.

Conclusions

This analysis has attempted to distinguish between religion as institution and religion as faith. Among Latinos the institutional churches have been challenged seriously with a wide range of issues. The response has been mixed, so that general statements about the Catholic church, Protestant denominations, or Pentecostalism must be qualified by references to particular parishes, dioceses, bishops, ministers, and governing boards. While institutional religion has not been completely negative towards Latinos, neither has it been completely positive.

On the positive side is the support in most institutional churches for reforms of the immigration laws as they affect Latinos. With few exceptions the churches have lobbied for the most favorable legislation to unite families, and simultaneously the churches have denounced extreme and harsh enforcement of deportation and other aspects of immigration law enforcement. The mobilization of public will and church resources for the Cuban refugees from Mariel in 1980 was a noteworthy example.

Some churches have actively supported the sanctuary movement, which sought to utilize the medieval tradition of church grounds as exempt from civil law. The U. S. government, however, infiltrated the sanctuary movement, spied on clergy defending undocumented immigrants, and prosecuted in civil court clergy and religious who defended sanctuary as a practice of religion.

Institutional support from the churches for Latino political issues like bilingual education, increased social spending for housing, drug prevention, aid to dependent families, etc., has been less consistent. AIDS has now become a killer of a heterosexual portion of the Latino community, and although there are many church ministries to victims of AIDS, this ministry has not yet acquired an apostolic focus upon Latinos. Yet, with some exceptions, Latinos have entered into a new ecumenism, so that Protestant and Catholic Latinos frequently unite on public issues. Moreover, religion is one of the few fronts where representatives from each of the Latino groups meet with some semblance of national unity as a united ethnic group. While political groups are still divided as Chicanos, Puerto Ricans, and Cubans, the churches have achieved a viable modus vivendi among all these groups as "Latinos" or "Hispanos."

Religion as faith, however, has been alive and well. Instead of disappearing or waning as some secularists predicted, religion has grown significantly stronger among the underprivileged Latinos in the United States. In some neighborhoods, where drug addiction, crime, and broken homes and families abound, the churches remain as the only stabilizing institution that faithfully addresses Latinos. More open and less distant than government or schools, the churches of virtually every denomination constitute a bulwark of morality and continuity.

In some places the dedication to the support of movements, to the empowerment of neighborhoods, and to the education of Latino leadership make the church into a powerful agent of change. In all these situations religion preserves the Spanish language and much of native Latino culture. More study is needed to properly assess the dimensions of religion among Latinos, but there is clear evidence that the seeds of faith planted nearly 500 years ago by Spanish missionaries still flourish.

Bibliography

The Cushwa Center for the Study of American Religion at Notre Dame University is presently directing a study of the history of Catholicism among Latinos that will publish three volumes with the University of Illinois Press begining in 1994. Similar research is planned for some of the leading Protestant denominations (e.g., Justo González, ed. *Each in Our Own Tongue: History of Hispanic Methodism,* forthcoming). Together with the interfaith social science publishing project of the Program for the Analysis of Religion among Latinos (PARAL) based in New York's Bildner Center, there will soon be a series of major publications on Latino religion. Until these appear, however, the bibliographical sources must be compiled by examining different areas and various disciplines for materials focused upon Latinos and religion.

The most comprehensive history to date is Moises Sandoval, ed. *Fronteras: A History of the Latin American*

Church in the USA since 1513 (San Antonio: MACC, 1983), which is also volume X in the series, General History of the Church in Latin America, known best by its Spanish acronym CEHILA. There are denominational studies of different types written from institutional perspectives, such as Thomas Harwood's *History of New Mexico Spanish and English Missions in the Methodist Episcopal Church from 1850 to 1910 in Decades* (2 vols.; Albuquerque: El Abogado Press, 1910) and Carlos E. Castañeda's *Our Catholic Heritage in Texas* (7 vols.; Austin: Van Brockmann-Jones, 1936-50). These are valuable sources but do not carry either contemporary methodologies and more often than not treat the Spanish speaking in one region only and not all Latinos. Perhaps the best contemporary book on the emerging Latino reality is by Joan Moore and Harry Pachón, *Hispanics in the United States* (Englewood Cliffs: Prentice-Hall, 1985), which has a concise section on the churches (110-117).

General historical works that treat subjects related to religion and which offer insights into the processes discussed in the first parts of this article include the following:

Mestizaje

Lefage, Jacques
1976 *Queztalcoatal and Guadalupe: The Formation of Mexican Consciousness, 1531-1813.* Chicago: U of Chicago P.

Mörner, Magnus
1967 *Racial Mixture in the History of Latin America.* Boston: Little, Brown.

Ricard, Roberto
1966 *La conquista espiritual de México.* México: Editorial Jus, 1947. English trans. pub. as The Spiritual Conquest of Mexico. Berkeley: U of California P.

Evangelization

Borges Morán, Pedro
1987 *Misión y civilización en América.* Madrid: Editorial Alhambra.

Rivera Pagán, Luis
1990 *Evangelización y violencia: La conquista de América.* San Juan: Editorial Cemí. (Available in English translation from Westminister Press.)

Stevens-Arroyo, Anthony M.
"The Inter-Atlantic Paradigm: The Failure of Spanish Medieval Colonization of the Canary and Caribbean Islands." *Comparative Studies in Society and History*, 35:3 (July 1993) 515-43.

For the application of Wallenstein's notions of center-periphery to historical studies of the Southwest, see the excellent essay (33-54) by David J. Weber in *Myth and History of the Hispanic Southwest* (Albuquerque: University of New Mexico Press, 1987, especially footnote 71, where he points to the ground-breaking work by Thomas Hall). For the relationship of religion to social structures see Otto Maduro, *Religion and Social Conflicts* (Maryknoll: Orbis Books, 1982). Roland Robertson's explorations of globalization theory develop this relationship between religion and social structures, as does a chapter in his classic, *The Sociological Interpretation of Religion* (New York: Schocken, 1972, 78-112). The world-systems theory and religion is addressed by Robert Wuthnow in his 1980 article, "World Order and Religious Movements" in Albert Bergensen, ed. *Studies of the Modern World System* (New York: Academic Press, 57-75).

For the establishment of Catholicism in Puerto Rico see the work of Father Vicente Murga Sanz, especially his book on Juan Ponce de León (1971). The brothers Salvador and Augustín Perea published useful books (1936, 1971) with rich data on the colonial church. See also Antonio Cuesta Mendoza, *Historia eclesiástica del Puerto Rico colonial, 1508-1700* (Santo Domingo: Colección Arte y Cine, 1948) and Cristina Campo Lacasa, *Historia de la Iglesia en Puerto Rico* (San Juan: Instituto de Cultura Puertorriqueña, 1977). The sections on religion by the eighteenth century Spanish priest Iñigo Abad y Lasierra in his *Historia geográfica, civil y natural* (1789, repr. 1970) are highly descriptive of Catholicism in Puerto Rico. The contemporary works of the Jesuit historian Fernando Picó, especially his *Libertad y servidumbre* (Río Piedras: Ediciones Huracán, 1981), update this traditional data with modern insights into the role of religion among Puerto Ricans in mountain towns. Edward Berbusse (*The United States in Puerto Rico, 1898-1900*, Chapel Hill: University of North Carolina Press, 1966) and Charles Beirne (*The Problem of Americanization in the Catholic Schools of Puerto Rico*, Río Piedras: Editorial Universitaria, 1975) provide analysis of how U. S. domination affected institutions such as the church and its parochial schools. The best overall work on a changing island society in the 1950s is Julian Steward's editorship of *The People of Puerto Rico* (Urbana: University of Illinois Press, 1956).

The study of Catholicism until the 1960s by Elisa Julián de Nieves (*The Catholic Church in Colonial Puerto Rico, 1898-1964*, Río Piedras: Ediciones Edil, 1982) is not only complete, but it is an island-published book with a rare advantage for a mainland scholar, because it is written in English. Coupled with the many monographs of Puerto Rican sociologist of religion Samuel Silva Gotay, there is a growing body of literature on religion in Puerto Rico written with a contemporary methodology. The prize-winning mansucript, *Oxcart Catholicism on Fifth Avenue* by Ana María Díaz-Stevens, published by the University of Notre Dame Press in 1993, offers a synthesis of the sociological functions for Catholic religion on the island and for its migrants to New York City.

Donald T. Moore's *Puerto Rico para Cristo* (Cuernavaca: CIDOC, Sondeos n. 43, 1969) is also written in English and offers a wealth of information on the establishment of Protestantism and Pentecostalism on the island of Puerto Rico, with important perspectives on the Comity Agreement. Emilio Pantojas García provides a more critical evaluation in monograph. Luis Rivera Pagán has analyzed the thought of Protestant theologians of Puerto Rico in *Senderos teológicos* (Río Piedras: Editorial la Reforma, 1989).

The works of Herbert Eugene Bolton, especially his classic *The Spanish Borderlands: A Chronicle of Old Florida and the Southwest* (New Haven: Yale University Press, 1921), can be considered to have imparted a new direction to studies of the Spanish-speaking peoples on the U. S. mainland, although not always placing Hispanic culture or institutions in the most favorable light. Essentially Bolton and his many disciples made the geographical notion of frontier into a process, wherein personalities and social life were forced into new adaptations. See David J. Weber's, *The Spanish Frontier in North America* (New Haven: Yale University Press, 1992) for an example of this approach today. Gilberto Hinojosa, Carmen Tafolla, and Ricardo Santos are among the Latino historians who have paid special attention to the role of religion in this process. Francis J. Weber's *Readings in California Catholic History* (Los Angeles: Westernlore Press, 1967) provides a perspective on the Pacific coast.

Historians of Mexican-American communities include Richard Griswold del Castillo, Albert Camarillo, and Ricardo Romo, although none provide extended analyses of religious factors. Worthy of particular mention because of its emphasis upon women and the role of religion is Sarah Deutsch's, *No Separate Refuge* (New York: Oxford University Press, 1987). Likewise, Félix Padilla's studies of Chicago provide insightful commentary on the sociological functions of religious organizations in that city.

For insight into the Penitentes of New Mexico, see:

Chávez, Fray Angélico OFM
    1974 *My Penitente Land.* Albuquerque: U of New Mexico P.
Espinosa, J. Manuel
    1993 "The Origin of the Penitentes of New Mexico: Separating Fact from Fiction." *The Catholic Historical Review*, vol 29, no 3 (July):454-77.
Steele, Thomas J., and Rowena A. Rivera
    1985 *Penitente Self-Government.* Santa Fe: Ancient City.
Weigle, Marta
    1976 *Brothers of Light, Brothers of Blood; The Penitentes of the Southwest.* Albuquerque: U of New Mexico P.

For the formation of religious traditions, the best and most recent work is C. Gilbert Romero's, *Hispanic Devotional Piety* (Maryknoll: Orbis Books, 1991). However, the title is misleading, because this work focuses exclusively on Mexican-origin traditions. The Spaniard Pablo Garrido and various works by the Episcopal priest Pedro Escabí detail the rich creative thrust of religous traditions on the island of Puerto Rico. Jaime Vidal has a short but powerful explanation of Hispanic Caribbean customs in Part IV of *Nueva Presencia* (Newark: Archdiocesan Office of Pastoral Planning, 1988). Ana María Díaz-Stevens has written on this general subject and details sociologically the functions of many customs. The ever useful volume by Joseph P. Fitzpatrick of Fordham, *Puerto Rican Americans: The Meaning of Migration to the Mainland* (2d ed. Englewood Cliffs: Prentice-Hall, 1982), offers valuable commentary on the practice of religion both in Puerto Rico and in New York.

The Spanish origins for all these traditions are best traced in the work of Luis Maldonado, who has participated in efforts at the Mexican American Cultural Center in San Antonio, Texas, in a series of monographs that frames contemporary customs within their historical and liturgical origins.

Curanderismo and Spiritism in the Caribbean are explained in a socio-historical analysis by Joan Koss, "El por qué de los cultos religiosos: El caso del Espiritismo en Puerto Rico" (Revista de Ciencias Sociales [San Juan] Vol. 16 [March 1972]: 61-72. See also Allan Harwood's, *Rx: Spiritist as Needed* (New York: Wiley & Sons, 1977) for how this religious sentiment is utilized by social workers in New York. The newly published *Speaking with the Dead: Development of Afro-Latino Religion among Puerto Ricans in the United States* by Andrés I. Pérez y Mena (New York: AMS Press, 1991) is particularly valuable to understanding the creation of new religious forms as different Latino groups increase contacts in northern cities. *El monte* by the Cuban-born Lydia Cabrera remains a classic, if nonacademic, desciption of African religious practices found among Cubans. The dissertations by Orlando Espín focuses this rich Cuban experience within a theological context.

Studies of Mexican migration gained visibility with Manuel Gamio's *Mexican Immigration to the United States* (Chicago: University of Chicago Press, 1930) and Carey McWilliams's, *North from Mexico: The Spanish-Speaking People of the United States* (New York: J. P. Lippincott, 1948; repr., New York: Greenwood Press, 1968). For similar early work on the Puerto Rican migration, see C. Wright Mills et al., *The Puerto Rican Journey* (New York: Harper, 1950); Elena Padilla, *Up from Puerto Rico* (New York: Columbia University Press, 1959); and Dan Wakefield, *Island in the Sun (Boston: Houghton Mifflin, 1959*). The religious dimensions of the Cuban migration after 1960 are dramatically drawn by Leslie Dewart in his controversial *Christianity and Revolution* (New York: Herder & Herder, 1963). A more sober assessment of the Cuban immigration to the United States can be found in David Longbrake and Woodrow Nichols, *Sunshine and Shadows in Metropolitan Miami* (Cambridge, MA: Ballinger, 1976) and José Llanes, *Cuban Americans* (Cambridge, MA: Abt, 1982).

A comprehensive study that places Mexican migration in a wider context is Leo Grebler et al., *The Mexican-American People* (New York: Free Press, 1970). This collection features important early studies on Hispanic religious movements by Patrick McNamara, who subsquently became a trailblazer in the study of religion among Mexican Americans. A similar role for Puerto Ricans in New York was exercised by Jesuit sociologist Joseph P. Fitzpatrick.

These early studies have gradually been eclipsed by a host of more specialized works by authors who examine the phenomenon of Latino migration from myriad perspectives. See publications by Alejando Portes, Lisandro Pérez, Joan Moore, Julián Somora, Manuel Maldonado Denis, Clara Rodríguez, Frank Bonilla, and Ricardo Campos. However, the analysis of religion is usually incidental for these authors, who are more skilled in other areas.

The militancy of Chicanos is examined in works by Rodolfo Acuña, Juan Gómez-Quiñones, Matt S. Meier, and Feliciano Rivera. Puerto Rican militancy in the United States is described by Alberto López in *The Puerto Rican Papers* (Indianapolis: Bobbs-Merrill, 1973). A special focus upon the function of religion in this militancy is found in Armando Rendón's *Chicano Manifesto* (New York: Macmillan, 1971) and even more extensively by David F. Gómez in *Somos Chicanos: Strangers in Our Own Land* (Boston: Beacon Press, 1973). However, the best overall treatment of religious militancy remains the anthology *Prophets Denied Honor* (Maryknoll: Orbis Books, 1980) by Antonio M. Stevens-Arroyo.

More recent studies of Church militants in dissertations by Ana María Díaz-Stevens, Gilberto Cadena, Lawrence Mosquera, Alberto Pullido, and Michael Candelaria—most of whom are involved in current research projects with PARAL—offer evaluative perspectives on this period of Latino militancy. (See also David Abalos' work *Latinos in the United States: The Sacred and the Political*, University of Notre Dame Press, 1986.)

For contemporary theological expressions of Hispanic ministry see:

Deck, Alan Figueroa
1989 *The Second Wave.* Mahwah: Paulist P.
González, Justo
1990 *Mañana: Christian Theology from a Hispanic Perspective.* Nashville: Abingdon.
1988 *The Theological Education of Hispanics.* New York: The Fund for Theological Education.
Issasi Díaz, Ada María, and Yolando Tarango
1988 *Hispanic Women: Prophetic Voice in the Church.* San Francisco: Harper & Row.

❋

On Hispanic Identity

Félix M. Padilla

Introduction: The Sociology of Hispanic People

For the last twenty years the concept of Hispanic or Latino (also referred to here as Latinismo or Hispanismo) has been drawn to the attention of increasing numbers of people in the United States. As Puerto Ricans, Mexican Americans, Cubans, and other Latin American immigrants and descendants identify themselves and others in the idiom of Latino or Hispanic similarity and/or differences, several issues stand out. First, it is clear that the term Hispanic or Latino (hereafter referred to as simply Hispanic) means quite different things to different people. Second, regardless of its specific meanings and connotations, the word Hispanic and its variations carry heavy emotional freight, causing wide acceptance or rejection by those so labeled.

In spite of the manifestation and salience of what I shall term a Hispanic ethnic-conscious identity and behavior, there is little clarity on the meaning of this form of group identification. It has become common for social scientists to refer to Puerto Ricans, Mexican Americans, Cubans, and other Spanish-speaking groups, either as individual ethnics or as a wider population, as "Hispanics" without explaining the process by which they become "Hispanic." A classic example can be found in Burma's study (1954). Although Burma's book suggests to represent an analysis of Hispanismo or some form of a collective identification developed by Spanish-speaking groups in this country, his book is actually an accumulation of facts about several distinct groups of "Spanish Americans," and about Filipinos as well. A similar approach used in the examination of a "Hispanic group identification" is evident in two studies specifically about Chicago's Spanish-speaking populations: *The Political Organization of Chicago's Latin Communities* by Walton and Salces (1977) and *Aquí Estamos* by Lucas (1978). In both cases the idea of Hispanismo as a singular, all-embracing form of identity for this population is never examined. In Walton and Scales the only mention of this concept is found in a footnote at the outset of their discussion: "Here we shall use the term 'Latin' to describe Chicago's Spanish-speaking population in the aggregate since, according to our data, it [the Latino term] is most preferred" (1977, 1). On the other hand, Lucas says flatly:

> "Popularly, the term Latino has been used quite often to describe this population [the Spanish-speaking], and related cultural manifestations. It will be used in this report." (1978, 2)

In effect, studies on Puerto Ricans, Mexican Americans, Cubans, and other Spanish-speaking groups have taken for granted the specific changes of ethnic identification among this multiethnic population that at times result in the manifestation of a distinct, all-embracing, wider Hispanic ethnic identity and consciousness. To date social scientists have failed to make a conceptual distinction between behavior that is Hispanic related and behavior that is the expression of individual and separate Spanish-speaking ethnics. In other words, there is little conceptual precision on the meaning of the concept of Hispanic when used as an expression of a particular form of multi-group identity and behavior.

By using the concept of Hispanic synonymously with the individual experience of the separate Spanish-speaking ethnics (i.e., using Hispanic to mean Mexican American or to mean Puerto Rican), or as an inclusive category (i.e., using Hispanic to mean the collective experience of different groups) without explaining the process through which they are Hispanicized, social science has failed to examine the empirical characteristics and boundaries of Hispanic group consciousness and solidarity and important issues that an investigation of this type of multiethnic identification may raise. Further, this focus has detracted from examining the different social forces, conditions, organizations, and individuals in the larger society as well as those that take place in local Spanish-speaking *barrios* (neighborhoods), which may encourage or influence the emergence of Hispanic ethnic identity and solidarity. Finally, the traditional approach to examining the concept of Hispanic has neglected to investigate and analyze the shared cultural, political, and economic histories of Mexican Americans, Puerto Ricans, Cubans, and other Spanish-speaking groups, and has thus obscured such innovations as Hispanismo that may develop in these historical contexts.

In short, I argue that it is too simple to assume that behaviors of Mexican Americans, Puerto Ricans, Cubans, and Central and South Americans as individual groups or as comprising a collective group response are not necessarily expressions of Hispanic ethnic consciousness. In the first place, the degree of correspondence, if any, should be tested empirically and not assumed as a priori. In the second place, the difference between behavior that is an expression of Hispanic ethnic consciousness and behavior that represents the expression of a distinct Mexican-American experience, or a distinct Puerto Rican experience, or a distinct Cuban experience, or of any other individual Spanish-speaking group, ought to be reconciled by an appropriate theory of ethnic consciousness and identification.

Toward this end, this chapter provides a way of examining the concept of Hispanic as a form of ethnic-conscious identity and behavior, using the experience of Chicago's heterogeneous Spanish-speaking population for analysis. I provide a case study of a particular instance when Mexican-American and Puerto Rican community-based organization leaders and their constituents crossed over the boundaries of their respective ethnic identities and communities and formed a wider Latino Unit. (The selection of Mexican-American and Puerto Rican community organizations for the study was done exclusively for methodological reasons. Primarily, there were no more than three or four Cuban community organizations and/or Central and South American organizations servicing this other component of the Spanish-speaking population of the city of Chicago. Thus, to have included them in the study would have given it conceptually irrelevant style or sample.)

The case study illustrates the various factors, inside and out of the Puerto Rican and Mexican-American communities, that led to the ethnic change manifest in the emergence of a new Hispanic ethnic identity in an American urban setting. This chapter is part of a larger study in which I combined historical data (i.e., organization archives, accounts found in the literature, newspaper articles, and other relevant information) with interviews of community organization leaders to reconstruct the sequence of developments in American and Spanish-speaking institutions and organizations, which help to explain the process by which the concept of Hispanic has become another form of ethnic group identification and consciousness in the city of Chicago (Padilla 1985).

The emphasis on Chicago's Spanish-speaking population is best explained by the recognition that this city is one of the few that historically has had large numbers of Puerto Ricans, Mexican Americans, and Cubans sharing the same urban space and its accompanying institutions and structures. Until recently, to speak of Hispanics in New York was equivalent to speaking about Puerto Ricans. In the Southwest, using the term Hispanic often referred primarily to Mexican Americans. And in the Southeast, in particular Miami, the term Hispanic has been used in reference to Cubans. Chicago, on the other hand, represents the hub for these various groups. When used in Chicago, the term Hispanic designates many people and actions.

This chapter is divided into two major parts. The first section provides an empirical definition for the concept of Hispanic, showing that Hispanic ethnic identification represents a special form of group identity and behavior produced out of the intergroup relations or multigroup interaction of at least two Spanish-speaking groups. This section also shows that the manifestation of a Hispanic ethnic-conscious identity is operative within specific situational contexts rather than at all times. This situational dimension of Hispanic identification implies that particular contexts determine whether the individual national/cultural identity of Puerto Ricans, Mexican Americans, Cubans, and Central and South Americans or the all-embracing Hispanic identification is most appropriate or salient for social action at that point in time.

The second section presents the case of one organizational attempt made in the city of Chicago during the early 1970s to unite people with different ethnic identities (Mexican American and Puerto Rican) under one Latino ethnic unit. First, this case examines the process by which Mexican Americans and Puerto Ricans created a wider Latino ethnic frame in order to acquire employment opportunities for Spanish-speaking workers in two American corporations, Illinois Bell and Jewel Tea. Although both Illinois Bell and Jewel Tea had received federal funds to train and hire "minorities," neither Mexican Americans nor Puerto Ricans had been considered in their overall plans. It became clear to both groups that the best way to gain access to job opportunities in the two corporations was by working as one group. It was believed that this approach would prevent Illinois Bell and Jewel Tea from playing one group against the other by hiring members of one group and then claiming to have hired "Hispanics."

This case also examines the significant role played by the federal Affirmative Action policy in contributing to these two Spanish-speaking ethnics mobilizing as one Hispanic unit. The Affirmative Action policy provided the legal sanction for Mexican Americans and Puerto Ricans to claim and challenge, as one Hispanic group, the unfair hiring practices of Illinois Bell and Jewel Tea. Believing that they were victims of a system that discriminated against them because it viewed them as "Hispanics," the Puerto Ricans and Mexican Americans mobilized as a Hispanic group to overcome the assigned stigmas.

Situational Latino Ethnic Consciousness

At the outset of the kind of examination presented in this chapter, one is immediately confronted with the task of answering the following question: When is Hispanic ethnic identification the actual expression of a wider, all-embracing unit rather than the distinct and separate identities of Puerto Ricans or Mexican Americans? As a starting point, I will suggest following the interpretation of "black consciousness" by Jim Pitts, a professor at Northwestern and a colleague and friend, that Hispanic ethnic identity be viewed as a social product: "purposive action and interpretation of actions operating in social relationships" (1974, 672). From this point of view, Hispanic ethnic identification and consciousness may not be viewed as the action taken by a group of Mexican Americans or Puerto Ricans operating independently of one another. In other words, any action or behavior that does not include the intergroup social relations or affiliation of two or more Spanish-speaking groups is not considered an expression of Hispanic ethnic consciousness and identity. Hispanic ethnic-conscious behavior, rather, represents a multigroup generated behavior that transcends the boundaries of the individual national and cultural identities of the different Spanish-speaking populations and emerges as a distinct group identification and affiliation.

On the whole, Hispanic ethnic behavior represents another form of group consciousness among Spanish-speaking populations in the United States. It represents the tendency toward sentimental and ideological identification with the language group, as in *"Nosotros somos hispanos porque hablamos el mismo idioma"* (We are Hispanic because we speak the same language). It also signifies the expression, in certain circumstances, of devotion and loyalty to the wider concern of Spanish speakers, while in most other instances, individual Puerto Rican and Mexican-American ethnic ties and sentiments continue to call for the expression of separate group affiliations and loyalties. Viewed somewhat differently, the Hispanic-conscious person sees himself as a Hispanic sometimes, and as a Puerto Rican, Mexican American, Cuban, and the like at other times.

Members of the Spanish-speaking community-based organizations in Chicago that I interviewed for this study gave frequent and eloquent expressions to this type of sentiment. The following is a typical example of situational-collective solidarity by one of the study's respondents: "Here [in Chicago] we have a combination of different Hispanic populations and groups; however, in each community the majority takes care of its own first. . . . I try to use Hispanic as much as I can. When I talk to people in my community, I use Mexican or Mexican American, but I use Hispanic when the situation calls for issues that have citywide implications, issues that hit us all the same way."

While using the case of the building of a new school in one of the city's Mexican-American communities as an example of his views, another respondent also reflected the situational dimensions of the Latino conscious person. "In Pilsen [a Mexican-American community] you have a Hispanic movement when they are talking or confronting the city. But in issues such as the Benito Juárez High School, you did not find a Puerto Rican being the spokesperson for the group that was putting pressure on the city to build the new school."

Another conceptual formulation of Hispanismo as a situational type of group consciousness and identity was expressed by a community organizer from one of the initial areas of Mexican-American settlement in the city. A strong supporter of Saul Alinsky's grassroots organizing principles, which aim to empower residents of local neighborhoods, this respondent sees the Hispanic ethnic form of group identity operative in those instances when the concerns and interests of both Mexican Americans and Puerto Ricans are at stake. "When we move out of South Chicago and people from South Chicago are to have a relationship with the West Town Concerned Citizens Coalition [a community-based organization located in the Puerto Rican community], it will have to be around issues that affect them equally. We cannot get South Chicago to get mad at West Town if West Town doesn't support their immigration situation [the issue of documented workers]. That is a Mexican issue or problem that cannot be resolved through a Hispanic effort. We wish that other groups would support these efforts, but we understand. But we can get the people from South Chicago to come and talk to Westtown about jobs, about things that are hitting everybody."

In an interview with a newspaper reporter, one of the first Spanish-speaking members of Chicago's Board of Education gave further credence to the emergence of a distinct, situational Hispanic identity in this major midwestern city. While speaking on behalf of bilingual education in the Chicago schools, this board member indicated supporting a "bicultural program which would provide the Hispanic child with a solid Hispanic identity, varying by nationality of neighborhood" (*Chicago Reporter* 1975, 6).

These various ideological expressions suggest that there are at least two interdependent levels of ethnic organization that are in operation among Spanish-speaking groups: one level is localized in particular communities of the city (e.g., the individual Puerto Rican identity or Mexican-American identity) and the other manifests itself at the level of the city-at-large around issues that pertain to two or more groups (i.e., Hispanic). Both limited and spatially inclusive conceptual elements of ethnic identities are necessary ingredients for a complete understanding of the play of forces in the municipal polity that influences the expression of Hispanic ethnic identity and behavior among Spanish-speaking groups. A discussion of these forces follows in the second section.

These various examples also point to the shift from a traditional cultural and national population-group frame of reference between Puerto Ricans and Mexican Americans to a behavior strategy frame, which views Hispanic ethnic consciousness and identity generating out of intergroup social participation. The perception of Hispanic ethnic identity becomes an understanding that has meaning for the inter-social action of the people concerned, but this meaning is clearly contained in the social situation in which the interaction is taking place. (Hispanic ethnic consciousness and identity don't just occur simply because one is born Puerto Rican or has Mexican-American parents. It must be developed over time within the context of intergroup association.) It seems from these examples that the decision of Spanish-speaking groups about when to construct an inclusive collective group identity and come to share a consciousness-of-kind as "Hispanics" is based on the groups' assessment of their goals and their options to attain those goals.

Hispanic Ethnic Mobilization: The Spanish Coalition for Jobs

"Ethnic mobilization is," according to sociologist Susan Olzak, "the process by which groups organize around some feature of ethnic identity (for example, skin color, language, customs) in pursuit of collective ends" (1983, 355). From this point of view, Hispanic ethnic mobilization and Hispanic ethnic identity represent two empirically distinct processes: Hispanic ethnic identity symbolizes basic identification with a language population, while Latino ethnic mobilization represents the actual organization of two or more Spanish-speaking groups. Thus, while the Spanish language may serve as a characteristic symbolizing the major cultural similarity of Mexican Americans and Puerto Ricans, it is not sufficient to bring about a "Hispanic" response among various Spanish-speaking groups to their collective needs and wants. This language commonality can be excited into Hispanic ethnic mobilization by certain external stimuli, e.g., governmental and public policies that were designed to redress ethnic discrimination and inequality. The third section of this chapter examines certain process in the 1970s that created the conditions necessary for Hispanic ethnic mobilization in the Midwest metropolis. The discussion emphasizes the interplay between features of political development and expansion and sociopolitical characteristics shared by Puerto Ricans and Mexican Americans.

Before entering into this discussion, it is appropriate to make a few statements on the Puerto Rican and Mexican-American communities of Chicago. Mexican Americans are considered Chicago's first group of Spanish-speaking people, having arrived in the city during the period of World War I. The majority of newly arrived Mexicans established settlements in three areas of the city: South Chicago, Back of the Yards, and the Near West Side. According to historian Año Nuevo de Kerr, "The three neighborhoods [have] persisted with one significant change. South Chicago and Back of the Yards remained intact, while under the pressure of urban renewal [during the 1960s] half of the Near West Side community had moved a few blocks south" (1975, 22). This other area is called the Pilsen community. Figure 1 shows the geographic distribution of these communities in the city.

During this period of initial immigration, the Mexican community grew very quickly. In 1916 already 1,000 newcomers lived in Chicago, and by 1930 this number had increased beyond the 20,000 mark (Taylor 1932). The major areas of Mexican settlement were located near particular industries where the newcomers found employment: (1) South Chicago (steel), (2) Back of the Yards (packing houses), and (3) Near West Side (railroad). The great majority of Mexicans who comprised the first wave of immigrants to Chicago were overwhelmingly young, male, unskilled, and not prepared for the urban conditions of the new society. Many of the immigrants came to Chicago on their own; most, however, were recruited directly by employers and transported to Chicago via railroad cars. Despite being hired primarily as strikebreakers

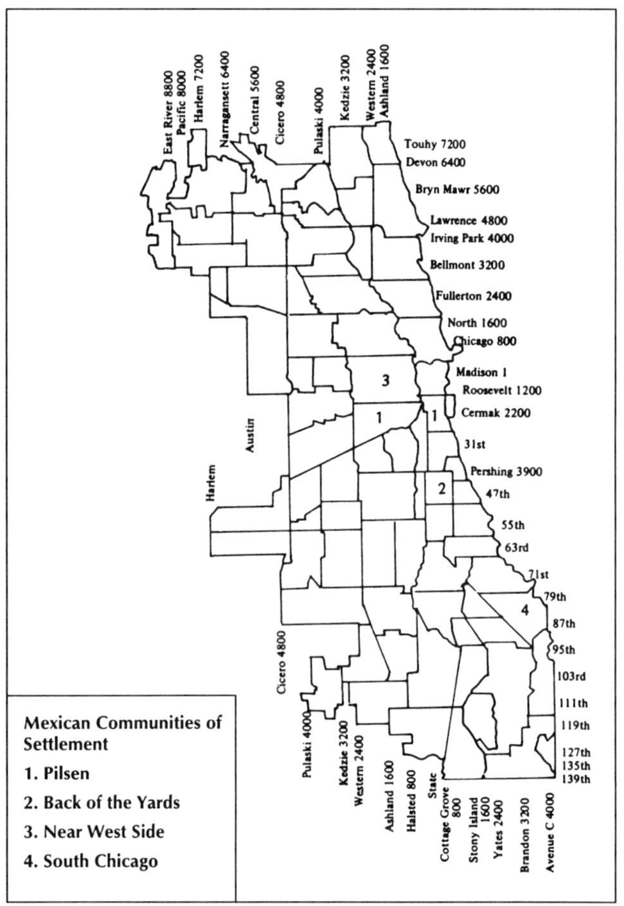

Figure 1. Map #1.

and hardly ever in permanent and steady employment, many of the Mexican newcomers did manage to become part of the labor force of those industries noted above, though not on an equal basis with other workers and always as the last hired and first fired. It was primarily the labor shortages created by World War I and the industrial expansion of the urban economy during this period that created the conditions that allowed for the marginal integration of Mexican labor in these structures. Although they were usually employed in the most unskilled jobs and paid the lowest wages among the workers, the integration of Mexican newcomers in the steel mills, packing houses, and railroad industries has been viewed as comparable to the experience of earlier European immigrants. Año Nuevo de Kerr (1976) noted, for instance, that it appeared Mexicans were following the traditional road toward assimilation into American life.

Hopes and thoughts of assimilation were quickly shattered, however, by the major and most obvious and devastating incident in Mexican labor exploitation in Chicago, as well as in other parts of the country where Mexicans had established communities of settlement. The incident was the result of The Great Depression of the early 1930s, and it involved the collaboration of American immigration officials and welfare agencies from the state of Illinois and the city of Chicago in rounding up and returning Mexican workers and their families, regardless of their legal citizenship status, to their homeland. This process, known as repatriation, was undertaken, according to these officials, as a relief measure. As the 1930s came to a close the Mexicans who survived repatriation were few in number. According to Taylor (1932), the number of Mexicans was reduced from nearly 30,000 in the late 1920s to just 7,000 in 1940. Año Nuevo de Kerr estimated the number of Mexican residents in Chicago in 1950 at 24,000, the majority of them were newly arrived immigrants (1975, 32).

Like many ethnic groups, Mexicans responded to their conditions in Chicago by developing voluntary social organizations and associations. The dispersed geographic location of Mexican settlements in the city caused these social organizations to develop primarily along neighborhood lines. Viewed in a different way, the early newcomers did not develop structures to deal with their collective, citywide situations. In the 1950s several groups were finally established to coalesce and politicize the different neighborhoods under one collective "Mexican ethnicity." The focus of these structures was Chicago's "Mexican-American" population, and their major goal was the assimilation of this generation into the larger American society. In other words, the new generation of Mexican newcomers to Chicago from Mexico and the Southwest was not part of the agenda of the new "Mexican-American Organization" of the period. In fact, it was not until the mid-1960s that organizational efforts were started in the Pilsen community to claim the allegiance of all the city's Mexican and Mexican-American residents.

Puerto Rican immigration to Chicago started in the late 1940s, increased substantially during the 1950s, and reached its highest proportion in the 1960s. According to the 1960 census, the first official enumeration of Puerto Ricans in Chicago, there were 32,371 Puerto Ricans living in the city. Ten years later, this number more than doubled to a total of 78,963 residents: the Puerto Rican population increase between 1950 and 1970 was, indeed, substantial.

During this twenty-year period, several sizable Puerto Rican neighborhoods, usually of a few square blocks each, sprang up in various parts of the city. Beginning with the initial group of Puerto Rican immigrants in the 1940s, Puerto Rican newcomers to Chicago usually settled in or near the center of the city north of the Mexican areas of settlement (Padilla 1947). In a series of articles for the *Chicago Sun-Times*, reporters Watson and Wheeler (1971) indicated that there were several major initial communities of Puerto Rican settlement in northside areas during the 1950s (1971). For example, they identified Lakeview, Near North Side, Lincoln Park, and Uptown as the prominent communities of Puerto Rican settlement. The two writers also added that Puerto Rican migrants had settled in the Woodlawn community in the city's south side. Figure 2 shows the geographic location of the leading communities of Puerto Rican settlement in Chicago in the 1950s.

By 1960, the major Puerto Rican neighborhood in the city began to take shape. A large Puerto Rican enclave, located in the West Town and Humboldt Park communities on the city's near northwest side, popularly known as the "Division Street Area," was formed. Although a few of the neighborhoods that emerged as distinguishable areas of Puerto Rican settlements in the 1950s remained the core of the Chicago Puerto Rican community in the following decade, the Division Street Area served new arrivals as the leading area of first settlement throughout the 1960s and 1970s. In fact, to this day the Division Street Area continues to be

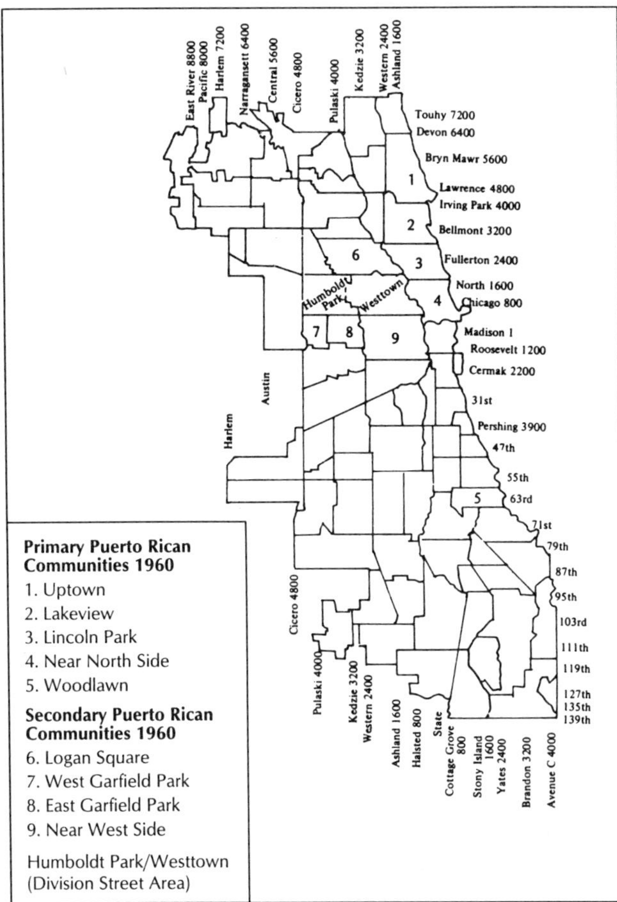

Figure 2. Map #2.

defined by residents as well as outsiders as the city's Puerto Rican neighborhood.

The massive immigration of Puerto Ricans to Chicago and other metropolitan areas began during a period of modern industrial and technological growth and expansion. During this post-World War II "modern era," nationwide social and economic changes and technological developments were reducing the importance of manufacturing as a provider of new jobs in the major, older cities of the Midwest as well as in the Northeast. For Puerto Ricans this meant that they were immigrating to the United States about the same historical period when the traditional, unskilled, and semiskilled jobs, which had represented the initial step or phase of integration into American institutional life for large numbers of European immigrants, were undergoing steady decline as major economic activities in many cities and were being replaced with white-collar and professional jobs. Major American cities were changing their manufacturing, industrial economies to a service economy. Such an economy services people, requiring workers to possess a certain level of education to understand how to "service." For those who lacked educational training, their service took place in jobs like restaurants, hotels, and the like.

These economic and technological shifts and expansions have meant concentration of Puerto Rican workers in nonindustrial, poorly paid, menial, and dead-end jobs. Elena Padilla's study of the first group of Puerto Rican immigrants to Chicago in the late 1940s, for example, shows that many of the newcomers were employed in the restaurant business as bus boys, sweepers, kitchen help, waiters, and the like (1947). Padilla also discovered that other Puerto Rican workers were employed in the business sector as messengers and delivery men, while another worked in stock rooms and packaging areas of many stores. Finally, another large number, according to Padilla, came to work in jobs in the janitorial labor force of the city.

Twenty years after their arrival, Puerto Rican workers had made few gains in the jobs they held. They were still concentrated essentially in the same job categories as in the previous decade. According to one of the reports of the U. S. Immigration and Naturalization Service, by 1960 the majority of Puerto Rican workers were employed in three leading unskilled categories: "operatives and kindred" (45.7 percent), "laborers" (13.7 percent), and "service workers" (11.7 percent) (U. S. Immigration and Naturalization Services 1968).

The employment of Puerto Ricans in noncompetitive economic sectors caused very little friction with the white workers. In effect, racial antagonism between the two groups became related to social, political, and community-related concerns.

From the outset, housing discrimination and police injustice became leading forces shaping group relationships between Puerto Ricans and whites in the city. As for the former, Puerto Ricans were trapped in the most deteriorated and run-down residential sections in their communities of settlement not only because of poverty but also because of a stringent pattern of housing discrimination. In terms of police relations, from the start police officers treated Puerto Ricans in Chicago with a great deal of resentment and enmity; Puerto Ricans became victims of police racism and brutality in Chicago.

This particular form of initial contact between Puerto Rican newcomers and the white society during the 1950s and 1960s accelerated the growth of Puerto Rican consciousness in the city. The Puerto Ricans' ethnic identity underwent considerable evolution and growth, converting whatever residual homeland regional/town differences may have existed between the arrivals into a sense of peoplehood. Manifestations of Puerto Rican peoplehood and consciousness were operative in a variety of ethnic-conscious attitudes and organizations: Puerto Ricans were forced to develop and staff a parallel set of personal and social services, neighborhood businesses, and communication networks to meet the tastes and needs of a growing Puerto Rican population.

The most significant organizational response among Puerto Ricans during this period was their development of community organizations. Several community organizations developed that sought principally to provide guidance and leadership for neighborhood residents.

In sum, during the immigration period, individual Puerto Rican and Mexican-American ethnic boundaries were clearly evident in the actions and behavior of each national and cultural group. They lived in separate areas of the city. Both groups established their own social organizations in the face of the treatment they received from the larger society. Just as important, Puerto Rican and Mexican-American social organizations were developed to ensure continuity with the cultural way of life each group had left in their homeland. One can suspect that while at times Puerto Ricans and Mexican Americans were in contact and were tolerant of one another, their daily life was still demarcated by individual ethnic boundaries. National and cultural ethnicity was a basis for personal trust for individual Mexican-American and Puerto Rican residents, and the personal bonds promoted by ethnic conscious-of-kind were vital to social interaction and mobilization in the individual communities, for otherwise the residents had little reason for crossing their respective lines. This began to change in the 1970s as the hardening dimensions of urban-based inequality (continued shrinking of the industrial job base in the city) gave rise to more apparent similarities among Puerto Ricans and Mexican Americans. The influence of Affirmative Action programs, for example, contributed immensely to the organization or mobilization of these two groups as "Hispanics."

Affirmative Action

The leading factor for exciting Hispanic ethnic mobilization among Puerto Ricans and Mexican Americans in Chicago was the federally legislated Affirmative Action policy. This policy represented the instrument or mechanism used by leaders from the two communities to make claims against institutions and structures found to be discriminating against Spanish-speaking workers at the city-wide level. Viewed another way, Affirmative Action provided the critical base for the Mexican-American and Puerto Rican leadership to advance the interests of their populations collectively rather than as individual or separate Puerto Rican or Mexican-American ethnics. Affirmative Action enabled two non-united groups to transcend the boundaries of their individual ethnic groups and assert demands as a Hispanic population or group.

That Affirmative Action was of great importance for the formation, development, and the growth of a Hispanic identity and agenda is clearly reflected in a memo sent by the chair of one community organization from a Puerto Rican neighborhood to social service agencies and officials in Spanish-speaking communities of the city during spring 1971. The memo called attention to the "full rights citizens from Latin America have, including the protection of the government against the dehumanization of conditions of Latinos" (Spanish Coalition for Jobs 1971, 1). The same memo stated that the two leading priorities of the "Latino community" were specifically directed at the implementation of the Affirmative Action policy by all employers:

> 1. All federal agencies, state and private, which administer federal funds, be compelled to adhere to the 1964 and 1968 Civil Rights Statutes and other federal laws to hire Latinos at all levels with direct federal criteria enforcement.
> 2. In the enforcement of full rights of American citizenship according to the U. S. Constitution and Federal Statutes—that all Affirmative Action plans filed by private companies be made public record. That a doctrine of community participation in the processing and implementation of the Affirmative Action plan of particular interest to us Latinos—be a federal requirement for compliance. (1971, 1)

The importance of Affirmative Action to the development and growth of a Hispanic identity and mobilization was also expressed in an interview by the present executive director of the Spanish Coalition for Jobs (a discussion on this organization is presented later). The Spanish Coalition for Jobs was started because of Affirmative Action. This was in the early 1970s when a group of Hispanic Manpower Service agencies throughout the city of Chicago became concerned mainly with the utility companies and major chain stores "where we did not see Hispanic or our brown faces working there." The courts were not implementing the Affirmative Action policy as it applied to Latinos. However, the act was there to be used and to force employers to carry it out. So Affirmative Action gave birth to the Spanish Coalition for Jobs.

In the same interview she added: "We needed no longer to theorize and speculate on the matter of job discrimination. We knew that equal employment opportunity could be significantly advanced via the provisions of Affirmative Action."

Fundamentally, the Affirmative Action policy provided Puerto Rican and Mexican-American leaders the legal sanctions with which to seek meaningful responses and resolutions to the various grievances of Spanish-speaking people in general. Opening doors long closed to both Mexican-American and Puerto Rican workers was a necessary first step. Making sure that those who were formerly locked out had a real opportunity to compete—that is, not only enter but to also move upward—was the thrust of the Mexican-American and the Puerto Rican leadership that came to form the Spanish Coalition for Jobs. Affirmative Action was the key to creating an organization or initiative with a Hispanic boundary whose aims were to achieve goals for both Mexican Americansand Puerto Ricans.

The Spanish Coalition for Jobs

In June 1971 a total of twenty-three Puerto Rican and Mexican-American local organizations, including nine employment referral agencies from the Pilsen, South Chicago, Lakeview, and Westtown/Humbolt Park communities, formed a coalition to enforce the implementation of Affirmative Action as it applied to all Spanish-speaking workers in the city. The Spanish Coalition for Jobs (La Coalición Latinoamericana de Empleos), as this coalition was named, had its roots in issues of employment—namely, job discrimination. Several of the coalition's member employment agencies had discovered over time that a large number of their Spanish-speaking referrals to certain American firms were not being hired or accepted as trainees as stipulated by the Affirmative Action policy. This concern was expressed in one of the Spanish Coalition reports: "Employers were giving two or three token jobs to the referral agencies to satisfy them, but very few of these companies ever considered hiring significant number of Latinos. . . . As consumers we were welcomed, but as candidates for jobs we were ignored" (Spanish Coalition for Jobs, unpublished). In a proposal submitted by the Spanish Coalition for Jobs to the Rockefeller Foundation the same feelings are expressed: "The racist attitude of employers triggered us into utilizing our consumer power as a tool or bargaining device . . . to compete in the job market" (1972). The Spanish Coalition for Jobs was established within this context of employers' negation of servicing "Hispanic" workers. It can be said that the Spanish Coalition for Jobs became the enforcer of resources to which Hispanic workers in Chicago were entitled.

Illinois Bell

Although the Spanish Coalition for Jobs could depend on a legal statute to make claims on behalf of Mexican-American and Puerto Rican workers collectively as well as on its network of existing community organizations and agencies, the organization also needed an event, issue, or threat to mobilize its mass base as one "Hispanic unit." The organization's support system, in itself, in other words, was simply not sufficient to excite political action or mobilization as one Hispanic group. The Coalition's mass-based membership had to be convinced that functioning as "Hispanics" was more advantageous or productive in some instances than working as individual Mexican-American or Puerto Rican ethnics.

The event was provided during a community meeting on August 5, 1971, at the Association House, an organization located in the Puerto Rican community of Westtown. The meeting was called by Illinois Bell officials to discuss the different services that the telephone company was offering its "Spanish-speaking customers." During the meeting, one Illinois Bell official acknowledged that in fact his corporation had not readily employed Spanish-speaking workers in the past. Several representatives from the Spanish Coalition for Jobs, among many in attendance, used this moment to politicize the meeting participants, estimated at about 300. Members from the Coalition made the case that Illinois Bell had a terrible history of job discrimination against Spanish-speaking workers.

Although very few material or tangible benefits were gained from the meeting, the Spanish Coalition for Jobs won a symbolic victory. The representatives from the telephone company agreed to an initial negotiation meeting to discuss the job issue with the members of the Spanish Coalition for Jobs.

The first formal meeting between the two opposing groups was held September 15, 1971; once again the meeting was held at the Association House. According to the *Chicago Sun Times,* after a list of demands was presented by the coalition, 115 jobs for Spanish-speaking workers were offered while the other demands were not recognized. The coalition refused to accept the company's offer and the following day conducted a mass demonstration as a "Latino group" at the Illinois Bell office downtown (1971, 13).

This exchange of negotiations followed by protest tactics is indicative of the year-long adversarial relationship developed between the Spanish Coalition for Jobs and the Illinois Bell Telephone Company. Fundamentally there would be negotiations, and when those broke down, picketing would begin at the homes of Illinois Bell officials and executives by members of the Spanish Coalition. The offices of the telephone company also became sites for demonstration and picketing.

Finally, on June 14, 1972, the Illinois Bell Telephone Company signed an agreement with the Spanish Coalition for Jobs. Under the terms of agreement, according to one local newspaper, it was expected that Illinois Bell would hire at least 1,323 Latinos by the end of 1976, including two top-level executives (*Booster Newspaper* 1972, 2). The promise of 1,323 additional Spanish-speaking workers was virtually a fulfillment of the Spanish Coalition's main demand. The *Booster Newspaper* further reported that the Spanish Coalition was pleased "with a provision in the eight-point agreement calling for regular reviews by the coalition of the company's progress toward achieving its hiring goals" (1972, 3).

Jewel Tea Company

In order to sustain the Spanish Coalition for Jobs as representative of the city's "Hispanic" working class, it became necessary for the organization to work on several issues that affected Mexican Americans and Puerto Ricans. Fundamentally, the approach of "interrelationship of issues" is basic to the Saul Alinsky philosophy of community organizing on which the Spanish Coalition for jobs was founded. Alinsky's discussion of building "People's Organizations" stressed the interrelationships of problems and maintenance value of many issues: "The conventional community council—which means practically all community councils—soon discovers the problems of life are not wrapped up in individual cellophane packages, and because the community council cannot and does not want to get down to the roots of the problems, it retreats into a sphere of trivial, superficial amelioration. The people judge the agency by its programs and soon define the agency as insignificant" (1969, 60).

The program of a real people's organization calmly accepts the overwhelming fact that all problems are related and that they are all progeny of certain fundamental causes, that ultimate success in conquering these evils can be achieved only by victory over all evils. In keeping with this approach, the Jewel Tea Company became the Spanish Coalition's second target of confrontation, as it also was found to discriminate against Spanish-speaking workers.

By the time Jewel emerged, the Spanish Coalition for Jobs seemed to have been halfway down the road from protest to negotiation. It had not yet achieved the regularized access to public and private officials necessary for a bargaining relationship; however, it was assumed that the protest tactics employed against Illinois Bell demonstrated the legitimacy of the organization's grievances, so that it was no longer necessary to dramatize an issue in order to gain hearing from targets. As one of the Spanish Coalition for Jobs' organizers commented: "The coalition received the recognition that made it a respectable organization. People in government and private business were taking a serious look at us."

In March 1972 members of the Spanish Coalition for Jobs met for the first time with representatives from Jewel Tea Company. The major demands presented to Jewel officials were: "(1) A job training program for Latinos, (2) an increase of Latino workers, (3) the hiring of Latinos to administrative positions, (4) a greater increase in participation by community residents in the supervision of how Latinos were being processed for employment" (quoted in *El Informador Newspaper* 1973, 3). These negotiations broke down after several hours of bargaining when Jewel officials rejected the Spanish Coalition for Jobs' demands. In a news release, the coalition called Jewel's response to their demands a "rejection of Latino community and a callous lack of corporate responsibility to the community."

It was not until an entire year of bargaining negotiations with the food chain's official had elapsed that the Spanish Coalition resorted to protests as a way to secure perquisites for its constituents. The coalition's first mass demonstration, in the form of a boycott against Jewel, began Saturday April 13, 1973, at 9:00 a.m. A local community newspaper reported that the "members from the Spanish Coalition for Jobs met at the front of Jewel's 14 stores for several hours distributing leaflets and urging shoppers not to buy at Jewel" (*El Informador Newspaper* 1973, 3). The same newspaper report noted that the positive reaction of the shoppers could be measured by the large number who boycotted the supermarkets. It was also indicated that the real test and effect of the boycott occurred the following day when the Jewel store, located on Damen and

North Avenues in the Puerto Rican neighborhood of Westtown, closed down at 3:00 p.m. because people refused to shop at that particular store. After several months of picketing and the shoppers' boycott of Jewel stores in the Spanish-speaking neighborhoods of the city, Jewel signed an agreement with the Spanish Coalition for Jobs late in the summer of 1973.

In sum, the Illinois Bell and Jewel controversies provided both material and symbolic benefits to the Spanish Coalition network organizations and their members. The job-opening and job-training agreements secured from the two companies by the Spanish Coalition for Jobs are clearly material, for the ability to secure employment or a better-paying job improves the economic position of individual beneficiaries. The individual economic gains may contribute indirectly to community stability, in the form of increased financial support for local businesses, to cite one example.

On a more symbolic level, these successes demonstrated that adoption of a "Hispanic ethnic identity" can alter institutional racist practices and thus can contribute to the development of feelings of political effectiveness as one Hispanic group. In general, the symbolic benefit of these events demonstrated the efficacy of situational Hispanic ethnicity by influencing those institutions whose policies affected the wider interests of Puerto Ricans and Mexican Americans in the city of Chicago. Puerto Ricans and Mexican Americans in Chicago have learned how to be fluid in the ways they define themselves and their interests. They have come to recognize the power of their specific ethnic identification as individual Puerto Ricans or Mexican Americans, but they also have come to experience the benefits of identifying themselves as belonging to one Hispanic group during some situations.

Conclusion

In sum, the information presented in this chapter indicates that the concept of Hispanic has evolved in the lives of some Spanish-speaking groups as an "ethnic principle of organization": it is generated out of a myth of common origin (based on language similarity) and broader social conditions not in themselves "ethnic" at all and brings together people who believe that their conditions can be served as one group. Hispanic ethnic identification is fabricated out of shared cultural and structural similarities and functions according to the needs and wants of Spanish-speaking groups. The information also reveals that the organization of a larger Hispanic ethnic unit is, indeed, a clear case of a mobilized ethnic contender. Hispanic ethnic mobilization represents an attempt on the part of Spanish-speaking groups to mount a competitive front in pursuit of emerging resources and rewards as well as those that might appear to be shrinking. There are certain situations in which Mexican Americans, Puerto Ricans, Cubans, and other Spanish-speaking groups may find a competitive edge in Hispanic ethnic mobilization rather than as individual ethnics. Finally, this chapter presents more than a picture of a group of aggrieved Spanish-speaking individuals banding together as a wider Hispanic unit to fight for their dues. It is also an examination of how the availability of a government policy facilitated the expression of grievances by two Spanish-speaking ethnics in the form of a wider Hispanic unit.

Overall, this chapter showed that Hispanic ethnic identification is a mix of both internally generated dynamics and of pressure from the external environment. Shared structural similarities and generalized beliefs about the causes (e.g., cultural or language discrimination) and possible means of reducing circumstances (e.g., organization of a larger Hispanic unit) are important preconditions for the emergence of Hispanic ethnic solidarity and mobilization. An increase in the extent of or inequality in commonalities among two or more Spanish-speaking groups and the development of an ideology must occur prior to Hispanic ethnic mobilization. The meaning of this explanation is that before Hispanic ethnic action is possible within a collectivity of various Spanish-speaking groups, a generalized belief (or ideological justification) is necessary concerning at least the causes of discontent and, under certain conditions, the modes of redress. In the same way the explanation is based on the premise that Hispanic ethnic mobilization cannot be perceived as occurring without a certain external stimulus. In the case of Mexican Americans and Puerto Ricans in Chicago, the federal Affirmative Action policy represented that necessary stimulus. This policy provided previously non-united, culturally distinct, resource-poor groups with clear objects for effectiveness, focusing their wider hostility and pressure on a common target. The Affirmative Action policy supported, and, in a way encouraged, the organization of Puerto Ricans and Mexican Americans into one Hispanic boundary or "community of interests." The presence of this legal forum, from which Puerto Ricans and Mexican Americans could make "Hispanic claims and demands," contributed to the creation of this broader and stronger power base.

One final concern needs to be addressed here: why Hispanic and not a working-class movement involving blacks, since they, too, represent another aggrieved "minority" population? It is often assumed that since Spanish-speaking groups share certain commonalities with blacks, particularly those stemming from the commonly shared urban economy, a class or "minority" boundary would be more beneficial for the advancement of these wider interests. The advantage of a Hispanic boundary is that it is based on certain cultural markers and symbols that the actors are able to recognize, and they imply some evaluation of the behavior of the persons so categorized in terms of what people expect of them. The set of meanings generally attached to Hispanic ethnic solidarity is more clear-cut than other cues; thus, overall there is less ambiguity about the relationships among individual Spanish-speaking ethnics. In other words, Hispanic ethnicity is construed as the set of meanings that actors attribute to certain symbols, signs, or cues by means of which they are able to identify Spanish-speaking persons as members of this "cultural innovation." Once the symbols have been recognized and interpreted and the Hispanic ethnic identity thereby established, then the actor has available a set of expectations of the person's behavior toward him or her. The Hispanic ethnic boundary, therefore, has significance in that it exists as a wide representation that is not only common among a designed set of people but is also shared by them, so that the shared perceptions can become the basis of an understanding between them in their social relationships.

The "minority" cleavage, on the other hand, lacks all of these features. Interaction and solidarity between Spanish-speaking groups and blacks, therefore, is more likely to be quite ambiguous and problematic. In the same way that the Hispanic boundary calls for the assessment of the appropriateness of its functions as a wider unit for two or more Spanish-speaking groups, the idea of a minority cleavage also requires the adoption of specific meanings and practices for those groups concerned. For a minority cleavage to occur, in other words, there must be, at the very least, a minimal level of adherence to a set of rules governing interaction and relationships between the members of the different groups composing the unit. These rules will constitute a deeply ingrained understanding, transcending the cultural or ethnic differences that divide the groups while at the same time binding them at the level of a basic social contract.

Instead of seeking those cues or markers that can provide precision and definition to "minority-related behavior and expectations," both Spanish-speaking and black leaders in Chicago have tended to direct most of their energies to explaining why a bond between the two groups is simply not probable. While black leaders view Hispanics as racists, the Spanish-speaking leadership cries misunderstanding of their ethnicity as well as foul or betrayal on the part of blacks for not fairly distributing minority-related opportunities and rewards to all minorities. This dispute was the major focus of an article, "Competition, Cultural Differences Split Black and Latino Groups in Chicago," published in 1979 by the *Chicago Reporter*, a magazine that focuses on racial issues in the city. Blacks generally claim, according to the report, that relations between themselves and Hispanics are particularly "strained by cultural differences and a peculiar brand of race consciousness among Hispanics, many of whom shy away from close associations with Blacks" (1979, 1). Spanish-speaking leaders respond to these charges by maintaining that blacks simply do not understand their ethnic needs and interest such as bilingual education. There are times when "Hispanic" interests run counter to the interest of blacks—e.g., support for bilingual education is often perceived as a move against school desegregation (a policy strongly supported by blacks), since the former schooling program requires the concentration of Spanish-speaking students in the same school. In addition, Spanish-speaking leaders make the claim that certain government agencies and programs controlled by blacks receive federal funds to aid all minorities but spend them almost exclusively on blacks. One Spanish-speaking leader is quoted as saying in the report: "The Urban League gets all this government money to fight city problems, but the only time they remember Latinos is when they want to sell tickets to one of their banquets. The rest of the time we don't exist" (1979, 6).

It is quite obvious that these discrepant perspectives reflect differences in ethnic background and orientation; they also reflect opposing group interests related to the rights and obligations in minority-related behavior and action. While members of both ethnic groups agree on the relative social significance of the minority boundary, they are in disagreement as to the normative basis and interfactional prerogative of this wider cleavage. Again, whatever is involved in the assessment of the minority boundary for social action, it must be carried out in the context of certain specific and meaningful markers and symbols. Behaviors, attitudes, actions, and gains must all be predefined before groups can engage in minority-related activities.

Bibliography

Alinsky, Saul

1969 *Reveille for Radicals*. New York: Vintage.

Año Nuevo de Kerr, Louise

1975 "Chicano Settlement in Chicago: A Brief History." *Journal of Ethnic Studies* 2.4:22-32.

1976 *The Chicano Experience in Chicago, 1920-1970.* Unpublished PhD Diss, Chicago: U of Illinois, Chicago Circle Campus.

Booster Newspaper

1972 "Bell Telephone Co. Increases Its Number of Latin Employees." Chicago, IL (June 17).

Burma, John H.
1954 *Spanish-Speaking Groups in the United States.* Durham, NC: Duke UP.
Chicago Reporter
1979 "Reporter Survey Identifies 18 Latino Leaders Considered Most Influential in Their Community." Vol 4, no 7, pp 6-9.
Chicago Sun Times
1971 "Latinos Beset Bell Aides with Job Demands." (September 15.)
El Informador Newspaper
1973 "Boicott a la Jewel por tiempo indefinido." Chicago, IL (May 13).
Enloe, Cynthia H.
1980 *Police, Military and Ethnicity: Foundations of State Power.* New Brunswick, NJ: Transactions.
Lucas, Isidro
1978 *Aquí Estamos: An Overview of Latino Communities in Greater Chicago.* Report to Chicago United.
Olzak, Susan
1983 "Contemporary Ethnic Mobilization." In *Annual Review of Sociologists.* Eds. Ralph H. Turner and James F. Short. Vol 9, pp 355-74.
Padilla, Elena
1947 "Puerto Rican Immigrants in New York and Chicago: A Study in Comparative Assimilation." Unpublished dissertation. Chicago: U of Chicago.
Padilla, Félix M.
1985 *Latino Ethnic Consciousness: The Case of Mexican Americans and Puerto Ricans in Chicago.* Notre Dame, IN: U of Notre Dame P.
Pitts, James
1974 "The Study of Race Consciousness: Comments on New Directions." *American Journal of Sociology,* vol 80, pp 665-87.
Spanish Coalition for Jobs
1972 *Proposal to the Rockefeller Foundation.*
1971 "Acute Depression in the Latin American Community." Memo, (spring).
n.d. "History of the Spanish Coalition for Jobs." Up.
Taylor, Paul S.
1932 *Mexican Labor in the United States: Chicago and Calumet Region.* Berkeley: U of California P.
U. S. Immigration and Naturalization Service
1968 *Annual Report of the U. S. Immigration and Naturalization Service.* Washington, DC: Government Printing Office.
Walton, John, and Luis M. Salces
1977 *The Political Organization of Chicago's Latino Communities.* Evanston, IL: Northwestern U Center for Urban Affairs.
Watson, J., and C. N. Wheeler
1971 "The Latins." *Chicago Sun Times,* Chicago, IL (September):12-20.

Mass Communication and Hispanics

Federico A. Subervi-Vélez

with Charles Ramírez Berg, Patricia Constantakis-Valdés, Chon Noriega, Diane I. Ríos and Kenton T. Wilkinson

As can be observed in other parts of this volume, methodical writings by sociologists, anthropologists, and historians about Hispanics in the United States can be traced back to the early part of this century. There are even some historical narrations about Mexicans in the Southwest during the 1800s. The field of mass communication, which itself is only about half a century old, cannot yet claim credit for many writings about Hispanics. Nevertheless, as this chapter demonstrates, there is a distinctive body of literature that can be classified liberally under the rubric of "mass communication and Hispanics." Stemming from a variety of disciplinary perspectives, writings about Hispanic representations and participation in film, television, radio, newspapers, and magazines in the United States have been steadily growing, especially since the mid-1970s.

Anyone who has made serious inquiries about almost any topic within this distinctive subfield of communication would probably testify to the fact that learning about even a fraction of that literature can be quite challenging. Not because the writings themselves are particularly difficult or inadequate.

Instead, the major obstacle lies in the ability to first identify and then gain access to the scattering of pertinent material. Since there are few places where courses are taught and research is conducted on Hispanics and the mass media, there are also not many places to turn to for learning about and gaining access to resources on or about mass communication as applicable to this ethnic group. Comprehensive and up-to-date library collections on this subject may be, at best, in an embryonic stage.

One of the purposes of this chapter is therefore to introduce the reader to the fundamental literature on the subject of mass communication and Hispanics. A concomitant goal is to provide a succinct overview account of this part of Hispanic life in the United States.

Before proceeding, two parameters of the chapter require explanation. First, this work focuses primarily on mass communication as it pertains to newspapers, magazines, film, radio, television, and advertising. Excluded are discussions on books, the music recording industry, and theater. Each could qualify, in some respects, under the heading of mass communication. But these topics deserve extensive and separate treatment and can not be accommodated within the space constraints of this chapter.

Also, writings about the representations and participation of Hispanics in theater have been centered within that discipline (Kanellos 1990) and ought not to be under the umbrella of mass communication. The same can be said about Hispanics in literature. On the other hand, methodical writings about Hispanics in the book publishing and the recording industries are so scarce that we can only hope that adequate documentation will be developed for presentation in some other publications.

Second, this chapter deals with mass communication and Hispanics primarily in the United States. Thus, we review issues related to portrayals of Hispanics and the media oriented to them in this country. However, some discussions are indispensable regarding portrayals of Latin Americans and about financial, programming, and other pertinent linkages between U. S.-Hispanic media and foreign corporations, particularly in Mexico and Puerto Rico. Yet, detailed analyses of the media of those countries are excluded.

The chapter is divided into two major parts. The first concentrates on the treatment of Hispanics in U. S. mainstream mass media: print media particularly newspapers, the film industry, television, and advertising. The focal point is to explain representations of Hispanics in the media that are primarily oriented toward the dominant society, Anglos, or "whites." In other words, we examine how Latinos have been portrayed, depicted, and stereotyped over the years in the channels of mass entertainment and information. A complimentary purpose of this section is to explain the treatment of Latinos in the workplace of these media. To the extent that literature was available, brief discussions are made about Hispanics' employment or lack of participation in the print news and television industries.

The second part of the chapter focuses on various Hispanic-oriented print and electronic media whose main audience are Spanish- and/or English-speaking Hispanics in the United States. Our aim is to review historical developments of some of these media and their principal content characteristics and audience. For selected media institutions highlighted here, we also point out some data about the corporate foundations and the ethnicity of the owners or principal executives.

Treatment of Hispanics in Mainstream Media

The treatment of one ethnic group by another is quite often influenced by economic and/or political factors within and between the nations, states, or regions from which the groups come. Domination of one group by another can both cause and affect extended animosities between groups. When such relations shift from positive to negative (or vice versa) between the dominant (usually political and economic) sectors of the regional/ national groups, the relations between the respective ethnic populations also change.

This general axiom is certainly applicable to the relations between the United States and Hispanic countries and, by extension, to the relations between Anglos and Latinos outside and within the U. S. The mainstream mass media—which so often reflect the prevalent perspectives of the dominant sectors of society—have historically replicated those views in their treatment of Hispanics. Therefore, an avenue for partially understanding contemporary Latino life in the United States is the assessment of messages that the media are constantly disseminating about them.

There are two related reasons why media become the focus of analysis. First, at all levels of society they are the most pervasive sources of news and information. For many people they are also the most relied upon source for entertainment. Second, the messages presented by the media may have significant effects on the audience, especially regarding events, topics, and issues about which the audience has no direct access or experience. Thus, for millions of people in this country, a significant part of the information they receive and the notions they develop about Hispanics may often be products of mass-mediated messages. While a comprehensive treatment of the topic of "media effects" is beyond the scope of this work, it is imperative to stress that there are conditions under which media may have maximal influence on the audience—conditions that are germane to the critical discussion that follows about the mainstream media's treatment of Hispanics.

One of those conditions occurs when the viewers do not have other sources of information or experiences that provide a standard against which to assess the media messages. To the extent that non-Hispanics live segregated lives with limited opportunities to interact effectively with a variety of Hispanics in constructive or productive ways, the mediated images of Hispanics will be among the most important sources for non-Latinos to learn and interpret who and how Hispanics are. Another factor that contributes to make the symbolic media more influential is when the values or views presented by the media are recurrent (Berry and Mitchell-Kernan 1982). As summarized in this chapter and discussed in detail in the cited works, the values and views presented about Latinos are both predominantly negative and recurrent across media and time.

Lastly, it should be stressed that the treatment of Latinos in mainstream media has its impact on Hispanics, who suffer the potential impact of the recurring negative imagery. For example, they face the psychological pain that emerges due to the negative portrayals and lack of recognition of their own people and values. They also have to endure the social scorn that emerges when the treatment they receive from other people, and sometimes from those of their own ethnic background, is consciously or unconsciously based on stereotyped notions disseminated by the media.

With this in mind, we now discuss how newspapers, films, television and advertising have treated Hispanics and how they have presented some notions of the Latino experience in the United States.

Newspapers

Mainstream newspapers were probably the first major means of mass communication through which fragmented and distorted news, information, and images of Hispanics were conjured, created and/or promulgated. While much has changed from the early depictions, the treatment and employment of Hispanics in these newspapers is still far from adequate in this American media institution.

Portrayals

Evans' (1967) study of the roots of three popular stereotypes (the "Indian savage," the "Mexican bandit," and the "Chinese heathen") reveals that "the Anglo image of the Mexican as a bandit is largely an outgrowth of the Manifest Destiny policy of the early 1800s" (69). His review of nineteenth-century English-language American newspapers in California and Texas discusses how circumstantial events related to economic and political relations between the people who inhabited the expansive Mexican territories of the southwest and the Anglo-European settlers and gold prospectors led the latter group to create stereotypes of the former in order to justify the conquest of that region. The political, religious and economic beliefs of Anglo-European superiority were constantly revealed as they depicted the native American and Mexican inhabitants as people destined to be conquered and unworthy of keeping their lands and resources. After the conquests of the southwestern territories, the mainstream press of the twentieth century continued a pattern of false depictions of Hispanic people. In other instances the mainstream press simply ignored the mainstream experiences of Hispanics. The most blatant act of negative stereotyping occurred during the 1940s by exploiting social and economic tensions between Hispanics and Anglos in Los Angeles. The press gave undue prominence to Mexican-Americans in crime news. Alarmist headlines and stories blaming these Hispanics for many of the city's social ills were a hostile correlate of the 1943 "Zoot-suit riots" and their aftermath (see McWilliams 1949).

In subsequent decades, changing journalistic standards of increased professionalism, balance, and objectivity helped diminish such blatant anti-Mexican racism. Yet negative, limited, and/or inadequate portrayals of Hispanics in newspapers of the latter half of this century have been systematically documented. One of the first studies in this area was Fishman and Casiano's analysis of Puerto Ricans in *The New York Times* and *The New York Post* (1969). They also studied the Spanish-language dailies *El Diario* and *El Tiempo* (Fishman and Casiano 1969). The authors found that the English dailies showed little interest in Puerto Ricans, who were referred to with negative attributes and covered primarily in terms of their community needs or problems (for which solutions were infrequently offered). The same was not true in the Spanish dailies where more positive and solutions-oriented stories were observed.

Negative and biased coverage of Mexican-Americans was also evident in a handful of unpublished masters theses regarding pre-trial criminal news reporting (Valdéz 1970) and general reporting (Lee 1973; Sánchez 1973). Also, Chavira (1975, 1977), comparing immigration and deportation news in the *Los Angeles Times* and the Spanish-language daily *La Opinión* during the 1930s, 1950s, and 1970s found that the plight of Mexicans was covered much more sympathetically and humanistically in the latter paper (see also A. Arias 1985).

Yet some improvements have been made, at least according to the two most recent studies of the mainstream press. In the most systematic and quantitatively oriented study of the coverage of Hispanic-Americans in the English-language dailies of Santa Fe (New Mexico), Tucson (Arizona), and Salinas, San Bernardino, Stockton, and Visalia (California), Greenberg et al. conclude (based on their two-week sample) that "sports news and photo coverage get high marks for their inclusion of local Hispanics," and that "local news coverage exclusive of sports gets a passing grade—good, not excellent, but better than it is currently receiving credit for." They add, however, that "editorial coverage and bulletin listings of Hispanic people and activities are below average and in need of considerable attention" (1983, 223).

The most promising assessment was provided by VanSlyke Turk, Richstad, Bryson Jr., and Johnson. In their study of *The Albuquerque Journal* and the *San Antonio Express*, they found some examples of parity in the inclusion of Hispanics as they conclude that "Hispanics and Hispanic issues are . . . present in the newspaper newshole in proportion to their presence in the population" (1989, 113). They also found that in comparison to stories about Anglos, Hispanic stories were adequately treated in terms of length and placement. However, as was the case in previously cited studies, Hispanics were much too prominently reported as "problem people," e.g., in judicial and crime news, news of riots, and accident and disaster news (see also Gutiérrez 1978b, 1980; Lewels 1974; and Wilson and Gutiérrez 1985).

In spite of these studies, the prognosis of Hispanic treatment in mainstream newspapers has consistently remained culturally insensitive and nonsupportive. Based on his observations and personal experiences, Charles A. Ericksen, founder and editor of *Hispanic Link, Inc.*, summarized that "the relationship between 20 million Americans crowded under the umbrella 'Hispanic' and the nation's establishment print media sprawls across the spectrum from non-existent to quaint, to precarious, to outright antagonistic" (1981, 3). Ericksen then identifies six dimensions of mainstream press irresponsibility: "the press will not allow Hispanics to be authorities on general issues"; "the press will not even allow Hispanics to be authorities on issues where Hispanics have the obvious expertise"; "the press still views the Hispanic community in stereotype"; "the press fails to provide Hispanics with information of critical interest and importance to their welfare and progress"; "the press does not hire enough Hispanics or other reporters and editors with Hispanic cultural awareness and expertise"; and "the press tends to smother those Hispanics they do hire." For each dimension, Ericksen provides various examples to support his case. For instance, regarding the press viewing the Hispanic community as stereotype, he states:

> Traditionally, non-Hispanic reporters have attached negative adjectives to the word "barrio." For example, Houston's barrios were described in a series one of its papers ran some months ago as places where "shoppers haggle and Latin rhythms blare." A Chicago reporter described New York's Spanish Harlem as "grim, rat-infested." A *Christian Science Monitor* writer chose the words: "the often-steamy barrios (sic) East Los Angeles." (Ericksen 1981, 7)

A decade following Ericksen's critique of the mainstream press, David Shaw's nine- article series in the *The Los Angeles Times* assessing the status of reporting about and hiring of minorities found many of the same situations and problems discussed by Ericksen. The headline of the first story summarized the issue: "Negative News and Little Else. By focusing on crime, poverty and aberrant behavior newspapers fail to give a complete portrait of ethnic minorities" (Shaw 1990a, A1). An example of continued stereotyping presented by Shaw (1990d) is the use of the word "aliens" (which can make Latinos seem "inhuman—strange outcasts from another world") instead of "illegal immigrants" or "undocumented workers." "Heller's (1992) analysis of how Hispanics were covered in the *Chicago Tribune, Los Angeles Times, New York times, San Antonio Light,* and *Washington Post* during late August of that year found that even though on occasions there were some positive stories about Latinos, the predominant pattern was negative" (Heller 1992,18-26).

In trying to understand some of the reasons that lead to the continued fragmentation and distortion of news about Hispanics and other minorities, Ericksen, Shaw, Lewels, Gutiérrez, and others who have written on this subject would probably agree that the lack of Hispanics in newsrooms and management is one the major factors to be considered. Thus, we turn to some data on the employment of Hispanics in selected mainstream media across America.

Employment

Wilson and Gutiérrez point out that when the first counts of minority participants in the mainstream press were conducted in the early 1970s, these constituted less than 2 percent of the total (1985). About a decade later, in 1984, the total had only made it to 5.8 percent among the approximately 1,750 daily newspapers in the nation. As low as these figures are, one must realize that they are for all minorities, which means that the situation for Hispanics is far more dismal. This problem continues even today, according to the most recent study of the National Association of Hispanic Journalists (NAHJ) (see Arocha and Moreno 1993). Based on the NAHJ's fifth annual survey (for which 100 newspapers with circulations over 100,000 were queried and 57 responded), Hispanics accounted for a mere 4 percent of the general labor force of those newspapers. Of this group of Hispanic journalists, only 4 percent were managers. The numbers did not represent dramatic changes from the NAHJ's previous surveys nor from other studies on the subject. In 1991, the American Society of Newspaper Editors (ASNE) had surveyed 1,545 newspapers (of which 65 percent responded) and found that approximately 1,349 Hispanics were employed in those newspapers and constituted a scant 2.4 percent of the workforce of about 55,714.

In addition to the problem of low numbers, Hispanics who have succeeded in gaining employment in journalism encounter various burdens often related to their ethnicity. As suggested by Ericksen, Hispanic reporters face unwarranted challenges of their latitude and credibility as professional journalists (1981, 5-11). He points out that while too often Hispanics are considered lacking the acumen to write about issues other than ethnic problems or strife, they are also perceived as too partial for "objective" in-depth reporting about educational, economic, and other type of policy issues of importance to their community. Moreover, many Hispanic journalists are burdened with requests to be the translators for situations beyond their reporting duties. For example, to assist in answering Spanish-language business calls or correspondence not related to their department. Yet these tasks and Hispanics' bilingual abilities usually go without compensatory pay (for more on this topic see Committee on Minorities 1982; Gutiérrez 1981; Wilson and Gutiérrez 1985; Shaw 1990f).

Given these current employment figures and practices, we can understand one of the factors related to the inadequate treatment of Hispanics in newspapers. However, due to the slow process of newsroom integration and the limited sensibilities of many Anglo reporters and editors, it will be some time before Hispanics make sufficient inroads to professional positions that will allow them to improve the portrayals of their communities.

In spite of the difficulties described above, many newspapers have been increasing the hiring of Latino and other ethnic minority journalists and improving the working environment for them, especially with respect to training, promotions, and distribution of assignments. These efforts have also included second-language courses (e.g., Spanish) and racial and ethnic awareness workshops for all employees of the newspaper. In the late 1980s some newspapers, such as *The Los Angeles Times* and *The Fresno Bee*, began publishing weekly supplements in Spanish. This practice, which is quite recent in these papers, has been going on with mixed success since the 1840s in various locations, especially in border towns (see Wilson and Gutiérrez 1985). A more extensive discussion of the Hispanic-oriented print media is provided below.

To conclude this section, it is imperative to point out that the concerted efforts of organizations such as the National Association of Hispanic Journalists, the National Hispanic Media Coalition, the Hispanic Academy of Media Arts and Sciences, and the National Association of Hispanic Publications have been major factors in the push for positive changes and will undoubtedly contribute to the improvement of both the portrayal and employment of Hispanics in the media.

Films

While newspapers were probably the first mass medium to widely disseminate images of Hispanics, their circulation and influence were more limited than the reach and impact of films. Since the inception of this medium, stereotypes of minority and ethnic groups have been a standard feature of motion pictures.

Portrayals

Hispanics have been regularly stereotyped in films dating back to the early days of silent cinema. Early westerns, such as the so-called "greaser" films like *Bronco Billy and the Greaser* (1914), instituted in films the Mexican or half-breed bandit, one of several Mexican stereotypes that Pettit (1980) says derives from western dime novels. By the early 1920s, the six major Hispanic stereotypes were well established in Hollywood movies. Following Pettit (1980) Woll (1980) and Wilson and Gutiérrez (1985), they have been delineated by Berg (1990) as follows:

> **El Bandido**—the ubiquitous Mexican bandit present in a host of Hollywood westerns, he is dirty, unkempt, and unshaven, wearing a sombrero and bandoleros. He is treacherous, shifty, and dishonest; his reactions are emotional, irrational and usually violent; his activities are criminal and antisocial.
>
> **The Half-Breed Harlot**—*the bandido's* female counterpart, another stock figure in the movies, especially westerns. She wears a low-cut blouse with shoulders exposed, a rose behind her ear, and a multicolored ruffled skirt. She is lusty, hot-tempered, and sexually promiscuous.
>
> **The Male Buffoon**—the second-banana comic relief: Pancho in "The Cisco Kid," Sgt. García in Walt Disney's "Zorro," Ricky Ricardo in "I Love Lucy." The character is funny due to the difficulty he has in assimilating. Since he is simple-minded and backward, he is incapable of observing the social conventions of American society—and that's the joke. Ricky Ricardo's explosions into Spanish are only one instance of a Hispanic character becoming laughable because of an inability to master standard English.
>
> **The Female Clown**—Here the strategy is to neutralize the Half-Breed Harlot's sexual threat by making her an object of comic derision. Examples include the dizzy "Mexican Spitfire" portrayed by Lupe Vélez in a number of films of the 1930s and the exaggerated antics of Carmen Miranda in Hollywood musicals of the 1940s.
>
> **The Latin Lover**—initiated by Rudolph Valentino in *The Four Horsemen of the Apocalypse* (1920), this figure is dashing and magnetic. He brought to screen lovemaking an exotic combination of the suave and the sensual, of tenderness mixed with sexual danger. He has been a remarkably consistent movie type and has been played by Latin stars such as Cesar Romero, Gilbert Roland, Ricardo Montalban, and Fernando Lamas.
>
> **The Dark Lady**—mysterious, virginal, inscrutable, and aristocratic, she is marginal because she is so different from Anglo women, with whom she is often contrasted. The Dark Lady is circumspect and aloof, where the Anglo woman is direct and forthright, reserved, where her Anglo sister is boisterous; opaque, where the Anglo is transparent. The best example is Dolores Del Rio in a number of films in the 1930s and early 1940s. By making both the Latin Lover and the Dark Lady the possessors of a sexual mystery lacking in the Anglo, Hollywood stereotyped by idealization.

While the overall thrust of Hollywood's portrayal of Hispanics has been quite uniform, political and economic forces have accounted for several well-differentiated stages in the history of that depiction. In the beginning, Hollywood stereotyped with impunity. Even before the appearance of the "greaser" films, Hollywood was portraying Mexicans as vengeful, cruel, and violent (Lamb 1975). For a time, with the beginning of World War I there was a shift away from negative Mexican stereotypes. But afterwards the same stereotypical patterns continued, and derogatory depictions of Mexicans and Mexico led the government of Mexico to threaten to boycott such films (Delpar 1984). Hollywood's response was to change the setting of many films from Mexico to some fictional Latin American country. For example, the setting of Harold Lloyd's comedy *Why Worry?* (1923), about an American hypochondriac who finds himself in the midst of revolutionary turmoil in what is obviously Mexico, is set in "Paradiso." Hollywood continued to adjust its productions to take Mexican objections into account, but the results were often just as stereotypical. The producers of *Viva Villa!* (1934) got the approval of the Mexican government for the film's shooting script, although the movie itself is full of mean-spirited, hateful, and moronic Mexicans (Woll 1977; Delpar 1984).

The Second World War quickly reversed such imagery, however, as Hollywood hastened to solidify relations with Mexico and Latin America against the Axis powers. An era of "Good Neighborism" (1939-45) followed, in which Latin America and Latin Americans were portrayed positively, if rather two-dimensionally. Typical of the change was *Juarez* (1939), a Hollywood-ized biography of the Mexican revolutionary leader, and the Disney studio's animated travelogues *Saludos Amigos* (1943) and *The Three Caballeros* (1945). It was this era that saw the rise of Latin stars such as María Montez, Ricardo Montalbán, Fernando Lamas and Carmen Miranda (Hadley-García 1990).

Carmen Miranda.

In many ways the period immediately following World War II was the most interesting in terms of how Hollywood dealt with Hispanics and Hispanic themes. Two major postwar genres predominantly featured Hispanic characters and issues: *film noir,* a group of dark, bleak films with betrayal as a central theme, and the social melodrama, movies that directly addressed social problems. Of the *films noirs,* those treating Hispanics included Billy Wilder's *Ace in the Hole* (also known as *The Big Carnival* 1951), Orson Welles's *Touch of Evil* (1958), and Ralph Nelson's *Requiem for a Heavyweight* (1962), films that critique the massive corruption within the Anglo world.

There were a number of social melodramas that dealt with Hispanic issues. Notable among them was *Salt of the Earth* (1954), a joint venture by blacklisted Hollywood filmmakers (screenwriter Michael Wilson, director Herbert Biberman, producer Paul Jerico), depicting in gritty terms a miner's strike in New Mexico. *The Lawless* (1954) was another Chicano-centered film made by a blacklisted filmmaker, Joseph Losey. Two boxing films should be noted here, the formulaic *Right Cross* (1950, directed by John Sturges), with Ricardo Montalbán as a Chicano fighter with an anti-Anglo chip on his shoulder, and the much more intriguing *The Ring* (1952, directed by Kurt Neumann), starring Lalo Ríos as a young man trying to box his way out of East L.A. Irving Pichel's *A Medal for Benny* (1945) and William Wellman's *My Man and I* (1952) both condemned the hypocrisy within the Anglo mainstream. Surprisingly, *Giant* (1957), a blockbuster directed by George Stevens, was one of the most progressive of all these films, indicting not only racism, but patriarchy, the imperialistic bent of America's westward expansion, the class system, and the social construction of manhood.

From the 1960s to the present, Hollywood's stereotyping of Hispanics could be placed into two broad categories: repeated and countered. In the main, Hollywood continued its policy of stereotyping Hispanics. The *bandido* stereotype, for example, could be found in a number of film genres. Updated variations included the young Puerto Rican toughs in *West Side Story* (1961) and the well-meaning courtroom drama *The Young Savages* (1961) (for one of the few analyses of Puerto Ricans in Hollywood film see (Pérez 1990), as well as the East L.A. Chicano gang members in *Colors* (1988). Perhaps the most widely seen example occurred in the opening of Steven

West Side Story.

Spieberg's *Raiders of the Lost Ark* (1981). In the film's first fifteen minutes, Indiana Jones, somewhere in South America in 1936, is menaced by all manner of Latino culprits. He is abandoned (an Indian carrier leaves the Jones expedition screaming hysterically), betrayed (one of his remaining native guides tries to shoot him in the back, the other leaves him for dead in the underground passageway), and threatened (a tribe of Latin American Indians chases and tries to kill him). Another example of a widely seen recent Hollywood film featuring the bandido type in a number of Latin American bad guys is *Romancing the Stone* (1984), with a particularly corrupt villain played by Mexican actor Manuel Ojeda. The other five Hispanic stereotypes had similar Hollywood incarnations during the same period.

But during this time there was a promising development, namely the countering of such pervasive imagery. This stage was precipitated by the emergence of a number of talented Hispanics who began working behind the camera. Because of them, the opportunity for opposing long-standing Hollywood stereotypes became a reality. The narrative strategy of these filmmakers was to revise standard Hollywood genres. Familiar story formulas were given an ethnic twist, which subverted standard Hollywood practice and promoted a more pluralistic view of the world. A good example of this sort of counter-imagery could be noted in Leon Ichaso's *Crossover Dreams* (1985), a Hispanic rendition of the well-known show-biz success story. An ambitious New York salsa musician (Rubén Blades) turns his back on his friends, his *barrio*, and his roots to achieve mainstream success, but fails to make it in the big time. In the film's final scene, the character swallows his pride, returns to his old neighborhood, and asks his old partner to start another salsa band. The film thus critiques dominant notions of the American Dream as well as celebrates and reaffirms traditional Hispano values.

A more problematic version of the same story was Luis Valdez's *La Bamba* (1987), whose compliant rock 'n' roll hero Richie Valens (Lou Diamond Phillips) conforms to mainstream requisites for success (he even changes his name) to facilitate his rise to stardom. Much more powerful was Valdez's first feature, *Zoot Suit* (1981), a filmed version of his hit stage play of the same name. It was an assault on Hollywood in its form (a provocative combination of broad comedy, courtroom melodrama, social criticism, Brechtian distancing devices, and song and dance) and on the justice system

Luis Valdez, playwright-film director.

in its content (a depiction of Los Angeles's notorious Sleepy Lagoon trial).

Director-turned-producer Moctezuma Esparza revised the western genre in *The Ballad of Gregorio Cortez* (1982, directed by Robert M. Young), based on Américo Paredes's account of the real-life exploits of the man who eluded the Texas Rangers around the turn of the century. The film tells the story from multiple perspectives and manages an even-handed account while at the same time reveals the prejudice prevalent in Texas at that time. It remains the most eloquent reversal of the *bandido* stereotype yet put on film. Esparza also produced Robert Redford's *The Milagro Beanfield War* (1988), an earnest though less-than-successful attempt to portray an entire New Mexico community—both Anglo and Chicano—during a municipal crisis.

Another notable film of this "counter-image" phase was Gregory Nava's *El Norte* (1984), a retelling of the familiar coming-to-America story from the point of view of a Central American brother and sister fleeing political oppression in their homeland. By impressively combining graphic realism with lyrical magic realism, the film deftly depicts both the danger and the hopefulness of their flight. Cheech Marin's *Born in East L.A.* (1987), about the deportation to Mexico of a Mexican-American, is a comic inversion of the same story. In its own raucous way, it manages to cast a knowing eye at the contradictions inherent in America's definition of citizenship (Noriega 1991). Finally, there is the Chicano version of *Goodbye, Mr.Chips*, Ramón Menendez's *Stand and Deliver* (1988). The film was based on the true-life story of Jaime Escalante, a courageous and visionary East L.A. high school math teacher (played by Edward James Olmos, who was nominated for a Best Actor Academy Award for the role). Using humor, threats, and shrewd psychology, Escalante inspires his students to master calculus and in so doing gives them a positive sense of self-worth and a key to self-actualization.

As remarkable as these counter-imagery strides have been, however, it remains to be seen whether this trend will continue. After the advancements of the 1980s, production on Hispanic themes in movies initiated by Hispanics has slowed down considerably since the peak period of 1987-88. There is no comparison with African-American filmmaking, for example, which has witnessed an unprecedented explosion during the same

Moctezuma Esparza.

time period. In 1991, for example, there were nineteen African-American-directed feature films released by Hollywood. In contrast, between 1988 and mid-1991 only one Latino-directed film was made, Isaac Artenstein's independently produced *Break of Dawn*, and it never found a mainstream distributor.

Television

Not surprisingly the treatment of Hispanics on mainstream television has not been sharply different from that in the film industry. Although there have been occasional breaks with stereotypical imagery, in some respects the portrayal has been more debilitating of Hispanic culture and life. In addition, the situation is worse in the scarce numbers of Hispanics employed in front of or behind the cameras. This summation is quite evident from even cursory watching of American television. It has also been documented in various writings originating from government, academic, and professional circles, which are overviewed in this section beginning with the main literature regarding portrayals and employment. The section ends with a synopsis of the efforts being made by Hispanic organizations seeking to improve media treatment of Hispanics.

Portrayals

Since television's widespread inception in the late 1950s, the masters of television images have been less than fair in the portrayals of Hispanics. Reyes's brief review of the Hispanic image on network television from 1951 through 1983 lends qualitative support to this judgment (1983). For example, the first "prominent" Hispanic male buffoon (as classified by Berg 1988, 1990) was seen for many years on the "I Love Lucy" show (CBS 1951-1961) where Lucille Ball's husband, Ricky Ricardo, played "the good-looking, excitable, short tempered Cuban band leader who spoke with an accent and occasionally rattled off expletives in Spanish" (L. Reyes 1983, 11). Interestingly, in "Desi and Lucy: Before the Laughter," a two-hour special broadcast on February 20, 1991, on CBS, he is stereotyped as an irresponsible Latin lover. Other Hispanic male buffoons have been Pancho, the sidekick to the Cisco Kid in the syndicated series (1951-1956) "Cisco Kid"; José Jiménez, the Puerto Rican bumbling doorman and elevator operator in "The Danny Thomas Show" (NBC 1953-71); and Sgt. García in the "Zorro" series (ABC 1957-59). The last of the successful (in terms of ratings and continuity) Hispanic male buffoons on network television was probably Freddie Prinze, who in "Chico and the Man" (NBC 1974-78) played Chico, a Hispanic "streetwise kid working in a garage with a bigoted old man" (L. Reyes 1983; for other commentaries and critiques of this series see Berger 1976; Davidson 1974; Gutiérrez 1974; Woll and Miller 1987).

Edward James Olmos.

After the termination of this program shortly after Prinze's suicide in early 1977, Hispanics as major comic characters in successful network programs have been very few and far between. CBS came up with an innovative strategy to market its "Latino odd couple" sit-com "Trial and Error" (1988). It was simulcast in Spanish on Spanish-language radio stations. The show centered around two unlikely roommates: Tony (Paul Rodríguez), a T-shirt salesman on Los Angeles's Olvera Street, and John (Eddie Vélez), a newly graduated Puerto Rican lawyer working in an established law firm. The comedy was strained and the series never gained acceptance; it only attracted 8 percent of the available audience (Valle 1988). Much more noteworthy was the short-lived "I Married Dora" which had a brief run on ABC during the fall 1987 season. An admirable attempt to center a situation comedy around a Salvadoran woman, it reversed cultural fields by making Dora (Elizabeth Peña) smart and self-assured and her uptight, "open-minded" Anglo husband the butt of many jokes because he held stereo-

Ricardo Montalbán.

typical ideas about Hispanics. The series dealt meaningfully with Latino immigration to the United States and the misconceptions the two cultures often have about one another. However, it was canceled before establishing a consistent tone and finding an audience.

The Hispanic *bandidos,* i.e., bandits, criminals, and lawbreakers, were also adapted promptly and prominently by television. The Hispanic "stock bandido, spitfire or peon" (Reyes 1983) was common in innumerable western cowboy series. Also, the numerous urban counterparts have been constantly present, starting with "Dragnet" (NBC 1951-59 and 1967-70) and "Naked City" (ABC 1958-59 and 1960-63), as part of the detective and police dramas. Most recently they were quite salient in the underworld activities (especially regarding drug traffic and dealings) in "Hill Street Blues" (NBC 1981-1986) and "Miami Vice" (ABC 1984-89).

Mainstream television has allowed a few law-enforcer or lawmaker Hispanic stereotypes. From "The Cisco Kid" and "Zorro" in the 1950s to more recent shows such as "CHiPs," "Miami Vice," and "L.A. Law," some relatively positive Hispanic male figures have been shown. One notable early example was Walt Disney's "The Nine Lives of Elfago Baca" (1958). Based on the exploits of the New Mexican-American lawman, the mini-series was an all-too-rare instance of television depicting a Chicano hero. More often Hispanics have been cast in secondary or insignificant roles. For example, Beale points out how on "Hill Street Blues" the Hispanic officer who is second-in-command is "often given little to do and is generally dull or a buffoon" (1986, 136).

Most attempts at centering a law enforcement series around a Hispanic character have been disappointing. "Juarez" (1988) was conceived as a gritty portrayal of the life of a Mexican-American border detective (it was shot on location in El Paso). ABC lost confidence in the project, however, and suspended production after only two episodes (of the six initially ordered) were completed. That episode was subsequently broadcast with little fanfare and soon forgotten. NBC's "Drug Wars: The Kiki Camarena Story" (1990) was replete with updated *bandido* stereotypes and so offensive to Mexico that it issued formal complaints about the miniseries (which went on to win an Emmy). Paul Rodríguez's private investigator in "Grand Slam" resulted in little more than yet another instance of the comic buffoon.

In contrast, Edward James Olmos's Lt. Martin Castillo in "Miami Vice" is one of the most positive Hispanic characters in television history. Because Olmos was initially reluctant to take the part (he turned down the role several times before finally accepting), the show's producers gave him complete control over the creation and realization of Castillo. He fashioned a dignified, honorable character of quiet strength and considerable power, thereby helping to offset the show's facile stereotyping of villainous Latin American drug smugglers. Finally there was the formidable presence of Victor Sifuentes (Jimmy Smits) on "LA Law," who provided the law firm (and the series) with a healthy dose of social consciousness.

Other stereotypes of Hispanics on television could be reviewed, as could the occasions when some Hispanic actors (e.g., Ricardo Montalbán) and actresses (e.g., Rita Moreno) have been called upon to play, when hired, a variety of roles beyond the usual stereotypes. It is crucial, however, to also point out what has been most neglected: regular positive roles for Hispanic women and, equally important, the Hispanic family. This is one of the areas in which Hispanics on television have been worse off than on film. In this respect, they have also fared much worse than African-Americans.

According to Reyes, during the early 1950s, Elena Verdugo starred in the comedy series "Meet Millie," but not as an Hispanic woman. Instead, she played "an all-American girl." Reyes points out, "The image of the Hispanic woman has been usually relegated to the overweight *mamacita,* the spitfire or señorita, and the suffering mother or gang member's girlfriend" (1983, 12). He adds that images of "strong, self-reliant, attractive, all knowing" Hispanic females were notable in Linda Cristal's role as Victoria Cannon in "The High Chaparral" (NBC 1967-71) and Elena Verdugo as nurse Consuelo in "Marcus Welby, M.D." (ABC 1969-76). More recently this shortage of strong Latina characters remains the predominant pattern. Two notable exceptions are the previously discussed character of Dora in "I Married Dora" (ABC 1987) and Pilar in "Falcon Crest" (CBS 1987-89)—the latter played a character who managed to be more than a simple two-dimensional love interest and was a forceful businesswoman.

Hispanic families have also been absent from the center stages of mainstream network television. In "The High Chaparral," a Mexican cattle-ranching family was "very prominently portrayed alongside the gringo family" (Reyes 1983, 12). After that series, consequential inclusions of Hispanic families have eluded long runs on the small screen. "Viva Valdez," a poorly conceived and received situation comedy about a Chicano family living in East Los Angeles was aired on ABC only between May 31 to September 6, 1976.

It was not until spring 1983 when ABC aired "Condo" that a middle-class urban Hispanic family was first introduced to TV viewers in the United States. That situation comedy series featured "a textbook WASP and an upwardly mobile Hispanic who find themselves as condominium neighbors on opposite sides of almost every question, yet who are faced with impending family ties" (Subervi-Vélez 1990, 311). This modern-day Romeo and Juliet—in the very first episode the oldest Anglo son and a Hispanic daughter fall in love, elope, and begin a series of adventures that embroil the families in joy and sorrow—was also short-lived, as its quality declined and ratings faltered against the competition of CBS's "Magnum, P.I." and NBC's "Fame." Yet during "Condos'" twelve episodes, another TV first was set as the featured Mexican American family was shown interacting as equals with an Anglo family, which sometimes acceptingly participated with them as Hispanics (Subervi-Vélez 1990).

On March 6 of the following year, ABC tried Norman Lear's "a.k.a. Pablo," another situation comedy that was centered on Hispanic comedian Paul Rodríguez but also featured his working-class family. However, Pablo's pungent jokes, often about Mexicans and Hispanics in general, irked enough Hispanics and others whose strong protest to the network contributed to the show's cancellation after only six episodes (Bunnell 1984; Friedman 1985; Knudsen 1984; and Prida 1984). The wealthiest urban Hispanic family ever featured was in another sitcom, "Sánchez of Bel-Air" on the USA Cable Network. In this program, the nouveau riche Sánchez family faced numerous social class and cultural challenges after they move from the barrio to live in one of the most upscale areas of Los Angeles. The program ran only thirteen episodes between 1986 and 1987. As of this writing, mainstream network television has no Hispanic "Huxtables," "Windslows," or even "Jeffersons."

Until very recently, the absence of notable Hispanic female figures and families was also evident in the soap opera genre, which neglected blacks, Latinos, and most other ethnic minorities. In the early 1990s, "Santa Barbara" was the only soap opera with recurring roles for Hispanics, five of which were regularly included. Payne indicates that according to Jerry Dobson, one of the show's writers, a commitment was made to have a Hispanic family "because there are large numbers of Latinos in Santa Barbara" (1985, 27). Payne adds that "while originally the only Hispanic character with a major storyline was Santana (who was played by a non-Hispanic actress), Cruz (A. Martínez), the lead Hispanic male character was promised a major storyline, replete with romance" (1985, 27). The producers of the show kept their promise as Cruz was given a major story line and viewers were introduced to his family circle. Unfortunately, this soap opera went off the air on January 5, 1993.

One other program with a prominent Hispanic female was "Dangerous Women," where actress María Rangel was one of six main characters. She played the role of an ex-convict Hispanic woman who, after being unjustly jailed for murdering her abusive husband, works as a prison warden seeking to reform the abuses of the penitentiary system. The show was a one-hour syndicated nighttime soap opera/drama that aired in various major markets such as Los Angeles, New York, Chicago, Phoenix, Minneapolis, San Francisco, and Houston. Prior to this show, the only other prominent role for a Hispanic female was found in the daytime soap opera "Rituals," 1984-85, also short lived.

Studies originating from government, academic, and professional circles corroborate the previous findings and reveal additional shortcomings about the treatment of Hispanics on mainstream television. In 1977 and 1979, the U. S. Commission on Civil Rights published two reports on the portrayals and employment of women and minorities in television. While many results were reported with aggregated data on all minorities, specific findings about "people of Spanish origin" [sic] were noted in the 1977 report. For example, from the content analysis of one sample week of programming during fall 1973 and 1974, only three Hispanics, all males, were found in "major" roles; twelve Hispanic males and one female were found playing minor roles. The highest occupation shown was a lawyer in a minor role.

The first academically based systematic analysis of this subject was conducted by Greenberg and Baptista-Fernández (1980), who examined sample weeks of commercial fictional programming during three television seasons (1975-76, 1976-77, and 1977-78). Among the 3,549 characters with speaking roles observed in the 255 episodes coded, they were able to find only "53 different individuals who could reliably be identified as Hispanic-Americans. . . . [These] constitute slightly less that 1.5 percent of the population of speaking TV characters" (1980, 6). Summarizing their findings, Greenberg and Baptista-Fernández state that Hispanic characters on television were "with dark hair, most often with heavy accents"; and "women are absent and insignificant" (1980, 11). Also, that the characters were "gregarious and pleasant, with strong family ties"; "half work hard, half are lazy, and very few show much concern for their futures"; and "most have had very little education, and their jobs reflect that fact" (1980, 11).

Mainstream television's neglect of Hispanics was similarly documented in a report commissioned by the League of United Latin American Citizens (LULAC) and prepared by Public Advocates, Inc. (1983). In the Public Advocates' audit of all sixty-three prime time shows during the first week of the fall 1983 television season (September 26-October 2), Hispanics played 0.5 percent (3 characters out of 496) of the significant speaking roles and only 1 percent (10 characters out of 866) of the those who spoke one or more lines. With the exception of Geraldo Rivera, there was "a total absence of positive Hispanic characters" (1983, 3). Comparing the networks, CBS was consistently the worse (one Hispanic character out of 212); ABC and NBC "showed significant decreases in the percentage of Hispanics portrayed" (1983, 3). Also, on ABC, "Two-thirds of all speaking parts for Hispanics were criminals"; on CBS there were "no Hispanics in any significant speaking roles"; and on NBC "only one of its 189 (one-half of 1%) significant roles included an Hispanic" (1983, 4).

The very low percentage of Hispanic participation in television was also found in a study by Lichter, Lichter, Rothman, and Amundson (1987). Upon analyzing 620 episodes of prime-time series randomly selected from the Library of Congress's holdings from 1955 to 1986, they observed that "since 1975, nearly one in ten characters have been black (from a low of under 1 percent in the 1950s), while Hispanics have hovered around the 2 percent mark for three decades" (1987, 16). Furthermore, in almost every comparison Lichter et al. made of the social background (e.g., education, employment) and plot functions (e.g., starring role, positive/negative portrayal, having committed a crime) of the white, black, and Latino characters, this latter group was consistently worse off.

The previous findings were again reaffirmed in the most recent studies of this topic. In the National Commission on Working Women's (1989) examination of thirty network entertainment programs in which minority characters were featured, only nine Hispanics (five women, four men) were found; in the same shows there were sixty-five Blacks, three Asians, and one native American. The NCWW qualitative commentaries of some of the scenes that included Hispanics found occasional redeeming contributions by some the leading characters (1989, 33-36). A more optimistic view on redeeming participation of minorities and the fading away of their stereotypes on television was provided recently by Tyrer (1991). But Gerbner's study of 19,642 speaking parts appearing in 1,371 network and cable television programs between 1982 and 1992 found that "Latino/Hispanic characters are rarely seen. Only in game shows do they rise significantly above 1 percent representation" (Gerbner 1993, 4)

Public television has fared just slightly better than the commercial networks. In his brief overview of Latinos on television, Beale (1986) summarizes some past offerings of the Public Broadcasting System (PBS). For example, he indicates that "'Sesame Street,' '3-2-1 Contact,' and 'The Electric Company,' children's shows produced by Children's Television Workshop for PBS, regularly feature Hispanic role models, adults as well as children" (1986, 137-38). Beale also points to the airing of Latino-themed dramas and films such as Jesús Salvador Treviño's "Seguín," Robert M. Young's "Alambrista," Moctezuma Esparza and Robert M. Young's "The Ballad of Gregorio Cortéz," and Gregory Nava's "El Norte," adding that "PBS deals with a broader range of Hispanic issues than the commercial networks, which are obsessed with immigration and revolution in their documentary treatment of Latino themes" (1986, 138).

This trend has continued. More recently PBS has broadcast Luis Valdez's "Corridos!" (1987), dramatizations of traditional Mexican narrative ballads, Jesús Salvador Treviño's "Birthright: Growing Up Hispanic" (1989), interviews with leading Hispanic writers, Isaac Artenstein's "Break of Dawn" (1990), a docu-drama based on the life of singer and Los Angeles radio personality Pedro J. González, and Hector Galán's hard-hitting documentaries "New Harvest, Old Shame" (1990) and "Los Mineros" (1991). Also of notice was the series "Americas" (1992), the National Geographic Special "The Mexicans: Through Their Eyes" (1992), and occasional episodes on Hispanics in series such as "P.O.V." (point of view), "The Territory" and "American Experience." However, exemplary series such as "Villa Alegre," "Carrascolendas," and "Qué Pasa, U. S. A." have been canceled due to lack of funds or low ratings. The lack of funding is certainly at the core of the problem as "only about 2% of funds for television production allocated by the Corporation for Public Broadcasting in the past fourteen years have gone to produce programs specifically geared to the Hispanic communities of the United States" (Treviño 1983). Even in early 1993, no nationally broadcast shows for or about Hispanics are regularly scheduled on PBS. Also, shows related to or about Hispanic children were scarce in both mainstream television as well as Spanish-language TV (see Subervi-Vélez and Necochea 1990; Subervi-Vélez and Colsant 1993).

The final area of interest regarding the images of Hispanics in mainstream television is news coverage. Ironically, researchers of media news content have themselves shown little concern for this population. Among the scores of articles published about the characteristics and biases of television news, not even one has given systematic attention to portrayals of Hispanics in newscasts. For studies that have focused on the major network news, part of the problem may be the few stories broadcast about Hispanics. For example, the U. S. Commission on Civil Rights report mentions in passing that in the 230 stories examined from fifteen network news programs aired between March 1974 and February 1975, "4 men of Spanish origin" were identified as newsmakers (1979, 51); but no further explanation is given about who or why they were in the news. The commission's 1979 update, for which fifteen newscasts from 1977 were coded, makes very brief mention about two stories related to Hispanics. The handful of studies published systematically analyzing Hispanics in the news have all focused on print media.

Based on these findings it is very easy to agree with Greenberg and Baptista-Fernández's view: "In essence, it seems that television has yet to do much with, or for, the Hispanic-American either as a television character or as a viewer. It might be improper to characterize them as invisible, but the portrayal is blurred or certainly hard to follow" (1983, 11).

Employment

Behind the cameras and in the offices, the treatment of Hispanics is likewise inadequate. From the first reports of the U. S. Commission on Civil Rights (1977, 1979) to more recent configurations of minority employment in the broadcasting industry (e.g., Stone 1988; and Bielby and Bielby 1987, 1989), Hispanic participation has been and continues to be extremely small, much below Hispanic population proportions, and it is inferior to that of African-Americans. For example, in the Civil Rights Commission's 1977 report, the average number of "Spanish origin" persons employed by forty stations surveyed in 1971 was 1.4 percent for males and .56 percent for females; in 1975 the respective figures were 2.2 percent and 1.14 percent. In the Commission's 1979 update based on the 1977 data, these latter averages remained unchanged. These averages based on aggregate data for various positions and localities hide the more negative situation that existed with respect to Hispanics in decision making versus nondecision making positions.

Stone's findings, based on a 1987 study of 375 television stations across the country, showed, not surprisingly, similar figures with respect to the percentages of Hispanics in television news staffs (1988). In fact, the average for Hispanic females in these capacities was lower, 0.9 percent, while for males it remained at 2.2 percent. However, in his discussion of the placement of minorities on the "talent track," Stone observes:

> On the talent track, minority women are as likely as non-minority men and women to be reporting or anchoring. But minority men are much less likely than minority women to have jobs that put them on the air as reporters or anchors. So although black, Hispanic and other minority women are winning on the talent track but tending to lose on the managerial track, minority men [including Hispanics] are double losers. They are underrepresented in both pipelines to advancement in broadcast news. (1988, 18)

The aforementioned NAHJ study (see Arocha and Moreno 1993) confirmed this as it found that in 1992 Hispanics were only 6 percent of the television news staffs and merely 3.3 percent of the radio news workforce. However, there were notable differences among independent television stations where 22.2 percent of the general workforce was Hispanic as compared to 4.2 of network affiliates. For radio, in contrast, Hispanics were better represented in the major markets where they accounted for almost 12 percent of the staffs compared to small percentages in the other markets.

Finally, Bielby and Bielby's 1987 and 1989 reports suggest that when it comes to writing the scripts for television, Hispanics have been given minimal opportunities. Their studies, which aggregate data for all minorities, show participation at rates of at best 3 percent for minority writers for prime-time series.

In spite of the bleak picture summarized in this synopsis of Hispanic portrayals and employment in mainstream television, there is evidence that some changes have taken place throughout the years. One of the forces contributing to the gradual changes has been the complaints and protests of concerned individuals and organizations. In her study of how various advocacy groups have impacted prime-time television, Montgomery discusses the efforts and struggles of Latino groups (1989, see especially 55-65). For example, she states that Justicia was a national Mexican-American organization "active in media reform campaigns during the early sixties and seventies"; other organizations such as the National Latino Media Coalition, La Raza, the League of United Latino American Citizens (LULAC), and the Mexican-American Anti-Defamation Committee "focused on grassroot efforts for reforming local television, although they [also] made some moves to change entertainment television" (1989, 55).

In summary, as with the case of the mainstream film industry of the United States, Hispanics have been neglected and poorly depicted in a television industry oriented to the dominant society. The future of the treatment of Latinos in this medium may be contingent on some inroads that individual actors and actresses make. It may also depend on the continued process of organized activities being carried out by advocacy and Latino community groups.

Advertising

Wilson and Gutiérrez state that "advertisers have reflected the place of racial minorities in the social fabric of the nation by either ignoring them or, when they have been included in advertisements for the mass audience, by processing and presenting them so as to make them palatable salespersons for the products being advertised" (1985, 113). While no systematic studies have yet been conducted on Hispanic advertising images across time, there is some evidence to support these authors' proposition. For years Hispanics have been practically invisible in mainstream advertising and by extension in the employment opportunities in this industry (there are no accurate figures of Hispanic employment in this field). When Hispanics have been included in ways palatable to the Anglo majority society, their images have often been quite offensive to fellow Hispanics. Martínez's (1969) work, which discusses various examples of the derisive commercials at the time, pointed out the

> Granny Goose chips featuring fat gun-toting Mexicans; and advertisement for Arid underarm deodorant showing a dusty Mexican bandito spraying his underarms after a hard ride as the announcer intoned, "If it works for him it will work for you"; a magazine advertisement featuring a stereotypical Mexican sleeping under his sombrero as he leans against a Philco television set; . . . a Liggett & Meyers commercial for L&M cigarettes that featured Paco, a lazy Latino who never "feenishes" anything, not even the revolution he is supposed to be fighting. (as cited in Wilson and Gutiérrez 1985, 115-16)

In 1967 the most controversial advertisement with a "Hispanic character" was the Frito Bandito—the Mexican bandit cartoon figure utilized repeatedly by the Frito-Lay Corporation in their television and print promotions of corn chips. In discussions about advertising racism and mistreatment of Hispanics, this example is often cited because of the complaints it generated among Hispanics, especially among Chicano activist and civic groups. Thanks in part to the public protests against Frito-Lay (see Rasberry 1971a, b) and activists' threatened boycotts of television stations airing the commercials, the Frito Bandito figure was discontinued in 1971. The public objections by Hispanics during the 1970s (Montgomery 1989), including the position paper by Latino media activists Reyes and Rendón (1971), led to some positive changes in the media during the 1970s just at the dawn of the so-called "Hispanic decade." Then, as advertising and marketing companies began to recognize the profitability of this growing sector of society, Hispanic-oriented strategies began to emerge in these industries.

Hispanic Oriented Media

Unlike any other ethnic group in the history of the United States, Latinos have had a broad range of mass media directed at them. Beginning with the border newspapers of the 1800s up to present-day inroads in telecommunications, Hispanics have worked hard at establishing and maintaining print and electronic channels through which they can be informed and entertained in ways more relevant to their particular populations and cultures. While most of the Hispanic-oriented media have been in the Spanish language, many have been bilingual, and in more recent times, fully English-language products have been specifically directed at Latinos. Likewise, Hispanics have been owners and producers of a number of mass media institutions oriented to them. However, a significant part of such media have been majority- or partially-owned and operated by Anglo individuals or corporations. In whatever the language or ownership, one of the common aspects of all these media is that in their portrayals via images or words, and in their general employment practices, Latinos have been treated much more adequately. In these media, Hispanic life in the United States has been and continues to be presented and reflected more thoroughly, appropriately and positively.

Newspapers

The Early Years

The Spanish-language press within the national boundaries of the United States had its beginnings in 1808 in New Orleans, Louisiana, with *El Misisipí*, a four-page commercial and trade oriented "publication printed primarily in Spanish, but with English translations of many of the articles and almost all of the advertising" (Wilson and Gutiérrez 1985, 175). According to these authors, the paper, which was started by the Anglo firm William

H. Johnson & Company, appeared to be a business venture, its content was heavily influenced by events outside the United States and it was directed toward Spanish immigrants—characteristics similar to those of other Hispanic-oriented publications that followed.

Prior to the inauguration of *El Misisipí*, dozens of Spanish-language newspapers and periodicals, founded by the Spanish conquerors and settlers and the Mexican pioneers of the times, were published in the southwestern territories that belonged to Mexico until the 1860s. In fact, the very first printing press in the Americas was brought to Mexico from Spain in 1535. Thus, for over four centuries, "Hispanic" publications have circulated in this part of the world; some have lasted various decades, while others just an edition or two. Among the U. S. Hispanic-oriented newspapers, the majority have been published in Spanish, but many have been bilingual, and a few have been in English but specifically directed at the regional or national Hispanic populations. These and other details of the past and present history of the Spanish-language press in the United States have been documented by various authors such as Chacón (1977), Cortés (1987), Del Olmo (1971), Fitzpatrick (1987), Gonzáles (1977), Griswold del Castillo (1977), Gutiérrez (1977, 1978a), Gutiérrez and Ballesteros (1979), Hester (1979), MacCurdy (1951), Medeiros (1980), Rendón (1974), Ríos and Castillo (1970), Ríos (1972), Shearer (1954), Straton (1969), and Wagner (1937).

Ignacio E. Lozano, Sr.

The Early 1990s

In 1991, five Spanish-language newspapers were published daily—two in New York, two in Miami, and one in Los Angeles. Basic information about the history, ownership, editorial policy, and circulation of these is presented in the following pages.

La Opinión (Los Angeles) began publishing on September 16, 1926, by Ignacio E. Lozano, Sr., a Mexican national who wanted to provide news of the native homeland as well as of the new country for the growing Mexican population in southern California. Lozano went to Los Angeles after working during four years in two Texas newspapers and being owner and editor of his own paper—*La Prensa* of San Antonio—from 1913 to 1926 (see special edition of *Americas Review* 1989). The move to California was the result of Lozano's view that there were greater Mexican readership needs and opportunities on the West Coast.

From its beginning, *La Opinión* was owned and operated by Lozano and his family, which in 1926 formed Lozano Enterprises, Inc. This company also published *El Eco del Valle*, a weekly tabloid distributed in the San Fernando Valley since 1985. On September 28, 1990, 50 percent interest in Lozano Enterprises was purchased by the Times Mirror Company. This major media conglomerate has interests in broadcasting and cable television, book and magazine publishing, and publishes *The Los Angeles Times*, *Newsday* (New York), and five other newspapers nationwide. With this association, *La Opinión* acquired financial resources that enabled it to continue improving its product. In spite of this new financial affiliation, the Lozano family maintained a majority on the board of directors and continued its full editorial policy and operational control.

As of March 31, 1991, *La Opinión's* circulation was assessed by the Audit Bureau of Circulations at 109,558 Monday through Saturday, and 81,773 on Sundays. The vast majority of *La Opinión* newspapers were sold in street stands and a variety of neighborhood stores. Only about 1,300 copies were delivered to home subscribers, and approximately 1,000 were sent by mail. According to a 1990 profile of the newspaper's readers, the majority were Mexican and Mexican American (66 percent), but increasingly Central American (15 percent) and South American (5 percent), as reflective of the immigration influx of the last two decades. In an effort to better serve the Hispanic community as well as

Peter Davidson.

increase its visibility and potential future subscribers, in January 1991 the marketing director of *La Opinión*, initiated this paper's participation in the Newspapers in Education Program. With this program *La Opinión* was being used for instructional purposes in over forty-eight classes in twenty-five schools.

La Opinión is a broadsheet paper of approximately 48 pages daily; the Sunday edition consists of about 88 pages, including a 32-page, tabloid-style TV guide. Apart from the daily news, opinions, sports, entertainment, and advertising sections, *La Opinión* had special supplements on various weekdays. For example, Thursdays: "Comida," a food supplement; Fridays: "Deportes locales," with expanded news about local sports such as the soccer clubs, "Panorama," a tabloid entertainment section, and "De viernes a viernes," a calendar section with special events of the week. On Sundays, there were various special sections such as "Encuentro," dealing with arts and literature, "Comentarios," with editorials and op-ed columns and opinions, "Viajes," regarding travel and leisure, "Acceso," a lifestyle section, "TV guía," a television listing guide, and "Tiempo extra," a sports pull-out section.

In mid-1991, approximately 500 people worked in *La Opinión*, 40 of them (including 8 translators) in the editorial department. In addition to its 15 reporters, it subscribed to four major news wire services, United Press International (United States), EFE (Spain), Notimex (Mexico), and Agence France Press (France). While reporters regularly cover the greater Los Angeles area, no foreign correspondents were permanently located in Latin America or elsewhere.

El Diario-La Prensa (New York) started in the summer of 1963 from the merger of two newspapers; *La Prensa* and *El Diario de Nueva York*. The former had been operating since 1913 under the ownership of José Campubrí, a Spaniard who kept the paper until 1957, when it was purchased by Fortune Pope. Pope, whose brother was the owner of *The National Enquirer,* was also the owner of the New York Italian paper *Il Progreso* and of WHOM-AM, which later became WJIT-AM, one of the most popular Spanish-language radio stations in New York. In 1963 Pope sold *La Prensa* to O. Roy Chalk, who had been owner of *El Diario de Nueva York* since he purchased it in 1961 from Porfirio Domenicci, a Dominican who had started *El Diario* in 1948.

With both papers under his control, Chalk, an American Jewish businessman president of Diversified Media, merged *El Diario-La Prensa,* which he directed from 1963 until 1981, when he sold it to the Gannett Company, a major media conglomerate which at the time owned a chain of ninety English-language papers. In 1989, El Diario Associates, Inc., was formed by Peter Davidson, a former Morgan Stanley specialist in newspaper industry mergers and acquisitions. This new company then bought *El Diario-La Prensa* from Gannett in August of that year for an estimated $20 million (Glasheen 1989). Carlos D. Ramírez, a Puerto Rican from New York who had been publisher of this newspaper since 1984, stayed on board to participate as a partner of El Diario Associates, Inc.

In mid-1991, approximately 139 persons worked at this newspaper, about 44 of these in the editorial department (writing and editing the news, sports, editorials, and opinions). The newspaper's reporters regularly covered city hall, Manhattan, the Bronx, Brooklyn, and Queens, but *El Diario* also relied on the Associated Press (AP) news wire services for some of the state and local news. The other major wire news sources it received were EFE (Spain), Notimex (Mexico), Agence France Press (France), and Deutsche Press Agenteur (Germany). Also, two foreign correspondents covered events in Puerto Rico and the Dominican Republic.

Within its daily average of 56 tabloid-size pages *El Diario-La Prensa* published—in addition to the daily news, opinions, sports, entertainment, and advertising sections—a pull-out supplement each day of the week.

Mondays: "Deportes" (details of weekend sporting events); Tuesdays: "Artes y Ciencias" (arts and sciences); Wednesdays: "Buen Vivir" (food and supermarket specials); Thursdays: "Comunidad" (community developments and events); Friday: "Espectáculos" (entertainment); and for the Saturday-Sunday edition: "Siete Días" (summary of the week, and reviews and opinions on diverse topics such as literature, poetry, movies, and politics). During the calendar year, a bridal supplement and another ten to twelve special supplements were published related to events such as the Puerto Rican Parade, the Dominican Republic Parade, Thanksgiving Day, Christmas, New Year's Day, etc.

Based on the Audit Bureau of Circulations assessment of March 31, 1991, the circulation of *El Diario-La Prensa* was 54,481 from Monday through Friday, and 36,786 for the combined Saturday-Sunday (weekend) edition. Given the difficulty of home delivery in the city of New York and the transient characteristic of many residents, the newspaper depends almost entirely on "point sales," i.e., street sales. Since their beginnings, *La Prensa* and *El Diario de Nueva York* had been primarily directed at the Puerto Rican, Spaniard, and Dominican communities in New York. Presently *El Diario-La Prensa* caters to a more diverse Hispanic population which, although still principally Puerto Rican, is increasingly more Dominican and Central and South American. Veciana-Suárez, writing about the editorial policy of *El Diario-La Prensa*, states that "the primary focus of the editorial, without a doubt, is on Hispanic issues, whether local, national, or international" (1987, 28). She also indicates that the newspaper has a five-member editorial board that spans a broad range of the political spectrum and gives the paper "a definite independent editorial policy" according to Veciana-Suárez's citation of publisher Ramírez (1987, 28).

Noticias del Mundo (New York) began publishing on April 22, 1980, by News World Communications, Inc., an organization founded in 1976 by the anti-communist crusader Rev. Sun Myung Moon and his Unification Church International. News World Communications also publishes *The Washington Times*, the *New York City Tribune*, and various other publications including *Ultimas Noticias*, a daily newspaper in Uruguay. Although now *Noticias del Mundo* functions more independently from its staunch conservative founder, author Veciana-Suárez cites editor in chief José Cardinali as stating: " We are against dictatorships. . . . We cannot abide Marxism" (1987, 21). She adds that the editorial stands are "decidedly conservative in international affairs and pro-Hispanic on domestic issues (1987, 21).

Noticias del Mundo is a broadsheet-size newspaper with an average of 20 pages published from Monday through Friday. Difficulty in home delivery also makes this newspaper depend primarily on "point sales." Their promotional flier *More Than Just News* (c. 1987) states it is indicated that *Noticias* "publishes four editions which serve the primary market areas of New York City, New Jersey, Los Angeles, and San Francisco" and that "each edition reaches into secondary areas such as Philadelphia and Connecticut on the East Coast and San Jose, Las Vegas, Palm Springs/Indio and San Bernardino on the West Coast" for total distribution in twenty-two cities. Yet its circulation as of mid-1991 was reported at 32,000 in the New York metro area, and for their new routes in New Jersey and Boston (started in fall 1990), the figures were 7,300 and 2,450, respectively. None of these circulation figures and territorial claims could be verified as the circulation is not audited by the industry's standard for these matters—the Audit Bureau of Circulations.

In addition to the typical news, opinions, sports, entertainment, and advertising pages, *Noticias del Mundo* had regular weekly sections on legal orientation (Mondays), community focusing on Puerto Rico and Cuba (Tuesdays), woman's page (Wednesdays), religious page and community focusing on Peru and the Dominican Republic (Thursdays), and entertainment and restaurants (Fridays). On Tuesdays 2,000 copies of *Noticias* were distributed to five high schools, which participated in the Newspaper in Education Program. According to a *Noticias del Mundo* fact sheet, when the paper participated in that program in 1986, it became the first Spanish-language newspaper in the United States to do so.

In mid-1991, approximately 150 persons worked at this newspaper, about 55 of these in editorial department. Major Hispanic population centers in New York and surrounding cities are regularly covered by the newspaper's staff. Its principal sources of wire news services included the United Press International, Associated Press, Reuters, and EFE. The newspaper had regular freelance contributors and commentators throughout Latin America and Spain, who acted as their foreign "correspondents." *El Nuevo Herald* (Miami) was started in November 21, 1987, as a new and improved version of *El Miami Herald*, which had been continuously published since March 29, 1976, as an insert to *The Miami Herald*. Both the Spanish-language and the English-language newspapers are owned by the Miami Herald Publishing Company, a subsidiary of the Knight-Ridder newspaper chain, which has holdings in twenty-nine newspapers across the United States.

In 1987 the Miami Herald Publishing Company recognized the geometric growth of the Hispanic populations in South Florida and, with the support and approval of the Knight-Ridder Corporation, began assessing what Hispanic readers wanted in their Spanish-language daily. The outcome of the study was *El Nuevo Herald*, which moved to a separate building from that of its English-language counterpart to begin publishing from a location closer to the Hispanic community. Other improvements included a 150 percent increase of the daily news space (which now runs approximately 34 pages daily and 50 on Sundays), more and better coverage of Cuban and Latin American events and communities, and the use of color in the more modern formats, graphics, and layout. Also expanded was the news staff, which increased from 23 to more than 65 in mid-1991. An additional 2,500 persons worked for the two Herald newspapers, which share the advertising, marketing, and circulation departments.

As could be expected, given the demographics of Miami and southern Florida, since its beginnings, the principal readers of *El Nuevo Herald* are immigrant Cuban and Latin American populations residing in that area. This paper, in contrast to its New York counterparts, reaches the majority of its readers via home delivery. The June 1990 circulation, as verified by the ABC, was 102,856 Monday through Saturdays, and 118,756 on Sundays. This broadsheet newspaper also published special weekly sections in addition to the standard sections, including a travel section (Sundays); "Vida Social," about social life (Tuesdays); "Gusto," a food section (Thursdays); "A la carte," restaurant listings (Fridays); "Diseñado para vivir," a real estate section; and an automotive section (Saturdays). During the year, an additional fifty special topic sections may be published.

Aside from the news gathering by its own staff, *El Nuevo Herald* benefits from the work of its English-language partner, including use of translated stories from the international correspondents. For major stories, *El Nuevo Herald* may send its own reporters to Latin America. Also, *The Miami Herald* may use stories gathered by *El Nuevo Herald's* foreign or local reporters. The major news wire services for *El Nuevo Herald* were the Spanish-language version of the Associated Press, Agence France Press, Reuters, and EFE. Syndicated information services from various major newspaper are also subscribed to.

Since the 1987 reorganization, *El Nuevo Herald* did not publish editorials. Instead it had its own policy regarding the op-ed page, where various prominent Cuban and Latin American columnists write about politics and other topics. The majority are about Hispanic issues or Cuban interpretations of national or international events. Veciana-Suárez wrote about the *Herald's* op-ed policy prior to the change: "When dealing with politics, [the columns] tend to be anti-communist and conservative, a reflection of the overwhelming feeling of Miami's Cuban community" (Veciana-Suárez 1987, 41). This general policy holds today. Prior to the 1987 reorganization, *El Nuevo Herald* only published translations of editorials that appeared on the same day in the *Miami Herald*. At the time, the editor of *El Nuevo Herald* was a member of the English-language paper's editorial board and participated in the discussions about the subjects and points of view. Political candidates were also endorsed in unison by *The Herald's* board.

Diario Las Américas (Miami) was founded on July 4, 1953, by Horacio Aguirre, a Nicaraguan lawyer who had been an editorial writer for a Panamanian newspaper—*El Panamá-América*, directed by Dr. Harmodio Arias, a former president of that country. Part of the financial support needed for starting *Diario Las Américas* was made possible by a Venezuelan builder/investor and two Pensacola, Florida, road builders, who also believed in the founder's mission. The paper is published by The Americas Publishing Company, which is owned by the Aguirre family. *Diario Las Américas* remains the only Spanish-language daily owned and operated by Hispanics without full or partial partnership with Anglo corporations.

This broadsheet newspaper published 28 pages Tuesday through Friday and approximately 45 on Sundays (it was not published on Mondays). In mid-1991, the respective circulation for these days were 66,770 and 70,737, as indicated in a sworn statement filed with the Standard Rate and Data Service. While a few papers are sold at newsstands, practically all of the circulation is based on home delivery, including 13,367 mail subscriptions in major U. S. cities and various locations outside the Florida area. Since its beginnings, the principal readers of *Diario Las Américas* have been the Latin American residents of the Miami and southern Florida. After the massive migration of Cubans from their island in the 1960s, these became the major clients of the paper. A reader profile conducted in 1990 for the paper by Strategy Research Corporation shows that 79.2 percent of *Diario's* readers were born in Cuba; 8.5 percent of the readers were born in Nicaragua (*Diario Las Américas* 1990, 3).

The Cuban and Latin American interests of that readership were evidently reflected in the strong international—particularly Latin American—news coverage of the paper. Those interests were even more notable in the editorial policy of *Diario*. Veciana-Suárez quotes publisher and editor Horacio Aguirre as saying: "Since the fall of Cuba, we consider that one of the biggest problems we face is the Russian-Soviet border 90 miles from here. . . . And we now have Central America in a precarious situation" (1987, 34). She goes on to point out that "Aguirre's political leanings are reflected clearly and eloquently in *Diario's* editorials," which he writes and describes as "moderately conservative with a strong defense of individual rights" (1987, 34). These perspectives are typically expressed in the many opinion columns from various Spanish-speaking writers and the translated columns of well-known Anglos.

To provide the international news of interest to its readers, *Diario Las Américas* relied more on the news wire services of UPI, AP, AFP, EFE, Agencia Latinoamericana (ALA), Editors Press, and a few other syndicated services. In addition to its news, opinions, sports, and advertising pages, it had various special weekly sections such as "Vida Sana," about health (Wednesdays); "De la cocina al comedor," regarding food and cooking (Thursdays); "Sábado Residencial," a home section (Saturdays); "Viajes y turismo," the travel and tourism pages (Sundays); and the restaurant feature "Buen Provecho" and automotive section "Automovilismo" (Fridays). *Diario Las Américas* had a staff of 20 reporters and editorial department employees, and an additional 100 people worked at the other parts of the production of this paper.

The preceding pages have only provided some of the basic information about the history, ownership, editorial policy, and circulation of the *major* Spanish-language daily newspapers presently being published in the United States for its Hispanic populations. At least these five enterprises seem to be reaching and serving their respective Hispanic communities while maintaining some stable circulation and advertising. Additional discussions about the business of this print media, their market, readership, and advertising possibilities are found in articles such as those by Glasheen (1989), Gresh (1988), Rangel (1981), and Pisano and Splan (1984).

To assess with more depth the performance of these newspapers in the diverse Hispanic world, the reader is advised to make further inquiries about some of the controversies regarding the political and economic forces that influence the structure and content these newspapers, and the functions they play in society. Such discussions about these newspapers are found in the works by Brown (1980), Golden (1991), McCardell (1976), Sterling (1984), Veciana-Suárez (1987, 1990) and Vidal (1980). Also, see Subervi-Vélez (1988) for the only empirical study that has been conducted on the political content of these newspapers. This latter work, which analyzes the aforementioned Spanish-language daily newspapers' coverage of the 1984 presidential elections, found that these dailies appear to be more partisan than their Anglo counterparts. It was also observed that while most of the Hispanic population outside of Miami may be liberal or inclined to vote for the Democratic party, only *La Opinión* and *El Diario-La Prensa* gave relatively more support in news stories and editorials to the Democrats than to the Republicans.

In addition to these five major dailies, in mid-1991 there were five more daily publications serving the U. S. Hispanic communities. The oldest was the Spanish-language page of *The Laredo Morning Times.* This seven-day-a-week *news page* has been published continuously since 1926. Also produced in the United States is *El Heraldo de Brownsville* (Texas), published seven days a week by *The Brownsville Herald.*This is a 6-page broadsheet edition inaugurated November 11, 1934, by Oscar del Castillo, who was founder and editor since its beginning until his death January 19, 1991. Marcelino González was the director of this paper serving the Texas Rio Grande Valley region. As of March 31, 1991, this newspaper had an ABC-audited, paid circulation of 3,701 weekdays and 4,436 Sundays.

The three other daily publications were *El Fronterizo, El Mexicano*, and *El Continental*—the morning, afternoon, and evening editions, respectively, published by the Compañia Periodística del Sol de Ciudad Juárez. *El Fronterizo*, published since 1943, was the largest of the three, with six daily sections each of approximately 8 pages. As of mid-1991 its circulation was approximately 36,000 Monday through Sundays. *El Mexicano*, published since 1950, is more condensed and contains about 10 pages; its circulation figures were 29,000 Monday through Saturdays. *El Continental*, founded in 1933, had only 8 pages and a Monday through Saturday circulation of 8,000. While all three newspapers had as major clients the Mexicans and U. S. Hispanics in El Paso and surrounding communities, they were published in Ciudad Juárez by the Organización Editorial Mexicana, representing seventy-eight newspapers in that country.

One final newspaper that during the late 1980s and early 1990s had occasionally published on a daily schedule is *El Mañana* (Chicago). It was founded in May 1971 by Gorki Tellez, who at the time was a community activist and owner of a small truck catering business. Financial difficulties have restricted the continuity and success of this newspaper's daily publication effort.

Aside from the aforementioned dailies, it is estimated that across the nation over 250 newspaper-type publications directed especially to the diverse Hispanic populations in the United States are produced from as frequently as twice a week to once or twice a month. Many of these publications have been and still are the product of extraordinary efforts of individuals in their local communities. The irregular and transitory nature of their products, which often have very limited circulation, has made it very difficult to develop any comprehensive and updated directory of all such newspapers.

Nevertheless, an edition of the *Hispanic Media & Markets* guide, produced by the Standard Rate and Data Service (1991), listed 101 of the most enduring of these publications. Our analysis of the information in the "Community Newspaper" section of this directory yielded the following data: Spanish was the main language of publications with 74 titles; 24 were bilingual and 3 were printed in English with a Spanish-language page. Of the first group, 58 were published at least once a week, and of these weeklies 19 were produced in California. It was also observed that 45 of the Spanish-language weeklies were distributed for free, and only 6 reported selling most of their papers; this data was not indicated for 7 of the titles. Thirty-two of these Spanish-language weeklies indicated circulations of over 20,000 copies; 12 circulated between 10,000 and 20,000 copies; the remainder printed 5,000 or less. Two of the bilingual periodicals were published by major English-language newspapers, both in California. *Nuestro Tiempo*, with a paid circulation of about 100,000 and free delivery of over 354,000, is published fifteen times per year by the *Los Angeles Times*. *Vida en el Valle*, which circulated 30,000 free copies in the San Joaquín Valley, is produced by *The Fresno Bee*. The trend of Spanish-language papers being published by major English-language dailies was expanded when *The Chicago Tribune* began publishing the weekly *Exitos* in Miami in 1991 and also Chicago as of September 16, 1993. Another trend is that independently owned and operated Spanish-language weeklies are being distributed by major English-language dailies: such is the arrangement between *La Raza* and *The Chicago Sun Times*.

Finally, it should be mentioned that dozens of Spanish-language newspapers from Spain, Mexico, Puerto Rico, Venezuela, Columbia, Chile, and numerous other Latin American countries also reach the newsstands in U. S. cities with large Hispanic populations. While few, if any, of these are published with the Latin American immigrant or U. S. Hispanic as primary clients, they are important sources of information widely sought and read, especially by the most recent of the immigrants.

Réplica.

Magazines and Other Periodicals

Long before the turn of the century, a variety of publications that can be classified as "U. S.-Hispanic-oriented magazines" have been produced in this country. The rich history of these publications can be observed in the holdings of major libraries such as the Benson Latin American Collection at the University of Texas at Austin and the Chicano Studies Collections of the University of California at Berkeley, Los Angeles, and Santa Barbara. Alejandra Salinas (1990) compiled a partial listing of 137 titles of past and present Hispanic magazines, journals, and newsletters. While a comprehensive anthology of all such publications is still lacking, even a cursory review of the titles would show that culturally oriented magazines have abounded, as have many with political, social, education, business and entertainment topics. Cortés (1991, 11-12) briefly mentions the following among those that have ceased to publish but were prominent during the last thirty years: Los Angeles's iconoclastic *La Raza* (1967-75), Denver's establishmentarian *La Luz* (1971-81), the National Council of La Raza's policy-oriented *Agenda* (1970-81), and New York's (later Washington's) feature-oriented *Nuestro* (1977-84). Another recent but short lived national magazine was *Más* (1989-93). Although copies of these now can only be found in some libraries, dozens of others magazines, especially consumer-oriented publications, are attempting to fill the demands of the Hispanic readers.

The 1991 edition of the *Hispanic Media and Markets* guide of the Standard Rate & Data Service provides descriptions of advertising-related information of sixty-five titles under its section on "consumer magazines." While this catalog contains indispensable data for marketing and advertising interests, it is neither comprehensive nor the most accurate listing of U. S. Hispanic-oriented magazines. For example, the list includes many specialty magazines (such as in-flight publications for Latin American airlines), magazines published in Puerto Rico primarily for Puerto Ricans, and various other titles for which U. S. Hispanics are not the primary targets. On the other hand, it excludes titles of smaller magazines and various academic journals with limited state or regional circulation. Nevertheless, based on the data in the SRDS publication and other information about this field, highlights can be provided about eight Hispanic-

Más.

oriented magazines with national circulation that are produced and published in the United States. Three are published in Spanish, three in English, and two are bilingual. It should be observed that the distribution figures indicated in this section are divided into paid, free, and "controlled" circulation. The difference between the second and the third terms is that under controlled circulation the magazine knows who it gratuitously sends the publication to, thus it has some knowledge and control of the demographics of its audience. This is usually not the case under "free" circulation of magazines that are placed in public places for readers to pick up at will. Some publications also have their circulation verified; for magazines this is usually done by the Business Publications Audit (BPA).

Of the Spanish-language magazines, the oldest is *Temas,* which has been published on a monthly basis continuously since November 1950 in New York City by Temas Corporation, whose main partners are Spaniards and U. S. Hispanics. It circulated over 110,000 copies per month, of which 106,000 were paid purchases. *Temas* averaged 62 pages measuring 8.5 by 11 inches and featured articles on culture, current events, beauty, fashion, home decorations, and interviews with personalities of various artistic and academic backgrounds of interest to the Spanish speaking populations in the United States. This general-interest family oriented magazine was founded by its publisher and editor José de la Vega, a Spaniard, who claims that *Temas* is the only national magazine published in Castillian Spanish without trendy "idioms." Given this editorial style, many of its articles are reprinted in high school and university reading packages across the country.

The second Spanish-language magazine is *Réplica,* founded in 1963 by Alex Lesnik, a Cuban immigrant who still owns the publication. From its base in Miami, this monthly magazine had as of March 1991, a circulation (BPA verified) of 110,745 nationwide, of which approximately 96 percent was controlled—targeted to reach bilingual, bicultural, affluent, opinion makers and other influential Hispanics in the United States. In its 50 pages measuring 8.5 by 11 inches, there are a variety of articles on topics such as travel, fashion, sports, entertainment, and news events related to Latin America and the Caribbean Basin.

Among the most recent of the Spanish-language magazines is *La Familia de Hoy.* This larger-size magazine measuring 10 by 13 inches and averaging 86 pages was founded with an issue dated March/April 1990. It was published six times a year in Knoxville, Tennessee, by Whittle Communications, which is half-owned by Times-Warner Corporation, a major U. S. media conglomerate. The circulation, approximately 165,000 and BPA verified, also relied on complimentary controlled subscriptions provided mainly to beauty salons, doctors, dentists, and similar qualified offices in the top thirty-three markets with high Hispanic populations and clientele. Its home circulation was about 3,000.

The three English-language magazines that merit particular notation are *Hispanic, Hispanic Business,* and *Hispanic Link. Hispanic* published its premier issue in April 1988. According to one of its promotional pages, the major focus of this "magazine for and about Hispanics" is on contemporary Hispanics and their achievements and contributions to American society. Thus, the stories cover a broad range of topics such as entertainment, education, business, sports, the arts, government, politics, literature, and national and international personalities and events that may be of importance and interest to Hispanics in the United States. *Hispanic* is owned by Hispanic Publishing Corporation based in Washington, DC. This is a family company of chairman and founder Fred Estrada, a native of Cuba. His son, Alfredo, was the current publisher. The first publisher was Jerry Apodaca, a Mexican American and former governor of New Mexico. A total of 150,000 copies of *Hispanic,* which measures 8.5 by 11 inches and averages 66 pages, were

Charlie Erikson.

printed for each of the eleven monthly issues produced per year (the December-January magazine was a combined number). The BPA audits indicate that approximately 40,000 copies were for paid subscriptions, and the majority of the remainder are for controlled distribution directed to, among others, the U. S. Hispanic Chamber of Commerce and the Hispanic National Bar Association. Also, 1,500 copies were distributed across 300 schools which participate in a special academic-oriented program known as America's Hispanic Education Achievement Drive (AHEAD).

Hispanic Business, according to its own promotional material, is "the oldest established business magazine oriented toward the U. S. Hispanic market." It is published in Santa Barbara, California, by Hispanic Business, Inc., under the directorship of Jesús Chavarría, editor and publisher, a Mexican American who started this magazine in 1979 as a newsletter which turned to regular monthly publication in 1982. This magazine, averaging 56 pages and published in a format measuring 8.5 by 11 inches, has a circulation recently certified at 150,000. Over 90 percent of this distribution is controlled. Special monthly topics include, among others, the December issue which focuses on statistics and trends in the Hispanic media markets; the June issue on the Hispanic Business 500, the annual directory of the largest Hispanic-owned corporations in the United States; and the July edition, which looks at Hispanics in the mainstream television, film, music, and related entertainment businesses. The magazine also tracks the Hispanic market, the progress of Hispanic professionals, managers and executives and legislative issues of concern to Hispanics.

The third English-language Hispanic-oriented publication is *Hispanic Link.* Although it is a newsweekly and not a "magazine" per se, it is a very important and influential publication that provides a succinct summary of the major issues and events related to education, immigration, business, legislative, political, policy, and economic concerns of the Hispanic populations in the United States. Weekly summary columns include "Arts and Entertainment" and a "Media Report." It averages 8 pages measuring 8.5 by 11 inches and is published weekly (fifty weeks per year) in Washington, D.C., by Hispanic Link News Service, Inc. *Hispanic Link* was founded by Charles A. Eriksen, his son Hector, and his Mexican wife Sebastiana Mendoza in February, 1980, as a column service for newspapers. In September 1983 it inaugurated a national newsweekly. Although it only claims approximately 1,200 subscribers, its circulation and readership is much higher as it reaches many libraries, Hispanic organization leaders, people in corporations with major responsibilities toward Hispanics, journalists, Hispanic advocacy groups, and influential government officials working with or interested in legislation and policy issues related to Hispanic populations. *Hispanic Link* solicits columns from various journalists and experts on subjects concerning Hispanics and distributes three columns per week via *The Los Angeles Times* syndicated news service to more than eighty-five newspapers in the U. S. and over ten newspapers in Latin America. By the beginning of 1994 *Hispanic Link* will be a non-profit corporation to pursue more journalism education objectives, including the continuation and expansion of its year-long paid internship program allowing aspiring Latino journalists to specialize on education, health, and political concerns related to Hispanics.

The two most notable bilingual magazines are *Vista* and *Saludos Hispanos. Vista,* with its headquarters in Coral Gables, Florida, started in September 1985 as a monthly supplement insert to selected newspapers in locations with large Hispanic populations. *Vista* which is published by Horizon—a U. S. communications company—was published in English on a weekly basis from late 1989 through June 1991. Financial problems resulting from the general national economic situation, particularly insufficient advertising support, made it return to its monthly schedule at this latter date. Since then, in addition to its English-language articles, it incorporated "mosaico"—a Spanish-language supplement with three stories in this language. Another change since June 1991 is that it has increased to 32 pages on average (when it was weekly it averaged 12 pages). *Vista* with its format measuring 9-1/8 by 11 inches, is aimed at informing, educating, and entertaining Hispanic-American readers with stories that focus on Hispanic role models, positive portrayals of our people, and cultural identity. In February 1991, Arturo Villar, the first publisher, and Harry Caicedo, editor, (both of Cuban heritage) were dismissed from *Vista* after a series of disagreements with the Board of Directors. At the time, Vista's two largest shareholders were Hycliff Partners, a New York investment group that owned 28 percent, and Time-Warner Inc., which held 25 percent (*Wall Street Journal* 1993). It was purchased by Fred Estrada who, as indicated above, is also the owner of Hispanic magazine. In November 1992, Gustavo Godoy, who has many years of experience in the broadcast news business (see below under Television) became the publisher. As of fall 1991, *Vista* was being inserted in thirty-one different newspapers in eight states—Arizona, California, Colorado, Florida, Illinois, New Mexico, New York, and Texas, and had a total circulation, which is ABC certified, of approximately 1,075,000 copies. Due to the high incidence of bilingualism within Vista's readership, and the bilingual characteristics of a significant part of the Hispanic market at large, Vista offers a dual language (English-Spanish) format and in May 1993 began distribution of four regional editions which include local editorials in Spanish.

Saludos Hispanos, "the official publication of the United Council of Spanish Speaking People," is owned by Rosemarie García-Solomon, a Mexican-American. When it began publishing in September 1985 it was a quarterly magazine, but in January 1991 it turned to six publications per year with a national circulation of approximately 300,000. Since this date it has also been changing its distribution from being a free insert in selected newspapers to direct paid subscription to individuals and sales at magazine stands. Nevertheless, a significant part of its circulation still goes to about 3,000 schools, universities, organizations, and various institutions in California, Florida, Illinois, New York, and Texas, which use the magazine for educational purposes. One reason for *Saludos Hispanos's* educational value is that within its average 92 pages, which measure 9 by 12 inches, it publishes side by side Spanish and English versions of most of its stories. Furthermore, it stresses positive role models for and about Hispanics. In addition to articles on the feature topic, the regular departments include, among others, "role models," "music," "careers," "earth watch," "university profile," "fashion," "law and order," "museums," and "food." Another educational distinction of this publication company is its *Saludos Hispanos Video Magazin*—a three-part video program that has been used by over 4,000 schools and organizations for recruitment and retention of Hispanic youth in the educational system. According to its promotional page, the video, available in English and a Spanish-language dubbed version, is designed to motivate Hispanic youth to stay in school, improve relationships, and to stress the importance of cultural pride and self-esteem as keys to success.

In addition to the publications highlighted above, there are dozens of Spanish-language consumer magazines with specialized topics related to parenthood, fashion, hobbies, social, cultural, and political interests. All are readily available in the United States via subscriptions and/or magazine racks in Hispanic communities in major cities. Examples of these are *Buenhogar, Cosmopolitan, Geomundo, Hombre del Mundo, Harper's Bazaar en Español, Mecánica Popular, Selecciones del Reader's Digest, Tu Internacional,* and *Vanidades Continental,* just to name a few of the most popular. As can be observed by the titles, some are Spanish-language editions of English-language publications. Regardless of where these are produced, be it Spain, the United States, or Latin America, they have as primary clients any and all Spanish-speaking populations. Other specialized magazines in Spanish and/or English are produced with the U. S. Hispanic as the primary client. For example, *Automundo, Buena Salud, Career Focus* (also targeted to African-Americans), *Embarazo, Hispanic American Family, Hispanic Youth-USA, Mi Bebé, Ser Padre, Teleguía, TV y Novelas USA, Una Nueva Vida*, the northeastern U. S. edition of *Imágen,* and the Hispanic youth oriented automobile publication *Lowrider*.

Furthermore, there are the journals with specialized topics related to academia, professions, and organizations. Among the current academic journals we can mention *Aztlán, The Americas Review, Bulletin of the Centro de Estudios Puertorriqueños, Hispanic Journal of Behavioral Sciences, Journal of Hispanic Policy*, and *Latino Studies Journal.*

And finally, there are state and regional publications aimed at the respective Hispanic and/or Spanish-speaking populations. Examples of these are *Avance Hispano* (San Francisco), *Cambio!* (Phoenix), *Eko* (Houston), *La Voz* (Seattle), *Miami Mensual* and *Bienvenidos a Miami, Tele Guía*, and *Lea* (directed at Colombians residing in the United States). In these cities and dozens of others with large Hispanic concentrations, one can even find Spanish and/or Hispanic Yellow Pages telephone directories. As can be discerned from this section, the number of magazines and other periodicals available to Hispanics in the United States is very extensive and diverse. No other ethnic minority population in this country has such an array of printed materials. The same is true regarding electronic media as presented in the following section.

Electronic Media

"Hispanic broadcasting comes of age," proclaimed *Broadcasting* magazine in a 1989 special report reviewing the growth, financial status, and related developments of Spanish-language radio and television. Why such assessment? One reason is because the number of stations, companies, and organizations related to Spanish-language radio and television in this country has grown, as have the options of content offered by these. Radio, for example, not only offers *rancheras* and *salsa,* but also top 40, *mariachi, norteña,* Tex-Mex, Mexican hits, adult contemporary, contemporary Latin hits, international hits, Spanish adult contemporary, romantic, ballads, traditional hits and oldies, folkloric, regional, boleros, progressive Tejano, merengue, and even bilingual contemporary hits. Television is no longer song and dance shows with some novelas and old movies. It is also drama, talk-shows, comedy, news, investigative journalism, sports, contemporary movies, entertainment magazines, dance videos, and many specials from all over the world. All of these options have been brought by the search for new markets by both Hispanic and Anglo entrepreneurs and the combined growth of the Hispanic population and its purchasing power. In fact, in some markets the Hispanic audience for selected Spanish-language radio and television stations has been larger than that of many well-known English-language stations (e.g., Los Angeles KLVE-FM and KWKW-AM more than KNX-AM and KROQ-FM) (Puig 1991). The "coming of age" that was evident in 1989 is even more evident in this section assessing the past and present of Hispanic-oriented electronic media in the United States.

Radio

Spanish-language radio programs transmitted from within the boundaries of the United States began as early as the mid-1920s—almost immediately after the inauguration of commercial broadcasting in this country. Since then, radio directed especially to the U. S.-Hispanic market has grown "from an occasional voice heard on isolated stations in the Southwest and on big city multilingual stations to a multimillion-dollar segment of the broadcast industry" (Gutiérrez and Schement 1979, 3). Today there are hundreds of Spanish-language radio stations, a couple of Hispanic commercial and public radio owners' associations, various specialized news services, and at least five major advertising representatives for this expanding market.

Pedro Ganzález.

The Early Years

While Hispanic-oriented radio is now quite diversified and can be found in almost every community with an established Hispanic population, its development was limited and difficult. In their accounts of the history of this ethnic medium, Schement and Flores (1977) and Gutiérrez and Schement (1979) indicate that Spanish-language radio started in the mid-1920s, when English-language radio stations began selling time slots to Latino brokers. These brokers, some of whom had previous radio experience in Mexico, "paid the stations a flat rate for the airtime, sold advertisements to local business and programmed the broadcasts themselves. The difference between what they took in from advertising and paid to the station for the airtime was their profit" (Gutiérrez and Schement 1979, 5). During the early days of radio, the stations that sold those slots and the time frames that were made available to brokers, depended on the local market competition among stations and the profitability of the various airtimes. Invariably, space for foreign-language programming was provided primarily during the least profitable time (i.e., early mornings or weekends) and by stations seeking alternative avenues for revenue.

One of the best-known pioneers of Spanish-language radio in California was Pedro J. González, about whom two films have been made, the documentary *Ballad of an Unsung Hero* (1984, Paul Espinosa, writer and producer) and the full-length feature *Break of Dawn* (1988, Isaac Artenstein, director). According to the interviews and documents gathered by Producer Espinosa, between 1924 and 1934 González was responsible for shows such as "Los Madrugadores." This program was broadcast from 4:00 to 6:00 a.m. primarily on Los Angeles station KMPC, which thanks to its 100,000-watt power, could be heard at that time all over the Southwest—even as far as Texas—thus reaching thousands of Mexican workers as they started their day. The dynamics of González's show and his progressive political stands made him a threat to the establishment, resulting in trumped-up rape charges against him in 1934. He was convicted and condemned to six years in San Quentin prison, released in 1940, and immediately deported to Mexico. In Tijuana he reestablished and continued his radio career until the 1970s, when he returned and retired in the United States. Many others across the Southwest followed Pedro's footsteps in the new medium.

In San Antonio, Paco Astol was an early voice heard on Spanish-language radio as emcee for the program "La Hora Commercial Mexicana" on English-language station KMAC. Astol was a well-known theater personality on stage at the Nacional and other theaters. As gathered during interviews by Kanellos (1990), in 1952 Astol also began doing soap operas in Spanish on Cortez's KCOR, acted in a radio dramatic series "Los Abuelitos," and emceed a quiz show "El Marko." In 1956 Astol moved on to Spanish-language television where he served in various writing, directing, and acting roles. He has also worked for San Antonio radio KUKA doing "El Mercado del Aire" (Kanellos 1990, 93).

Even through the early brokerage system, Spanish-language radio thrived. By the late 1930s numerous stations carried Spanish-language programs either full time or part time. In response to the market demands, in 1939 the International Broadcasting Company (IBC) was established in El Paso, Texas, to produce and sell Spanish-language programming to various stations and brokers across the country. As a result of the efforts of services like the IBC and the work by dozens of independent brokers, by 1941 it was estimated that 264 hours of Spanish were being broadcast each week by U. S. broadcasters (Arheim and Bayne 1941).

Gutiérrez and Schement (1979), citing sources who have written of the early days of radio, indicate that ethnic-language programming, especially in Spanish, proved economically successful, as the emotional impact of an advertising message wrapped in the music and drama of the listener's native language was more appealing than the same message in English. Therefore, from the beginning, the goal behind foreign-language programming was the same as with English-language broadcasting: to make profits via advertising. In Texas Raúl Cortez was one of the earliest Chicano brokers who eventually was successful enough to establish and operate his own full-time Spanish-language station—KCOR-AM, a 1,000 kilowatt "daytime only" station in San Antonio—which went on the air in 1946. Nine years later, Cortez ventured into the Spanish-language television industry (see below). Gutiérrez and Schement indicate that after World War II, Anglo station owners and Hispanic brokers saw the increasing opportunities in Hispanic market via Spanish-language radio. This allowed some brokers to follow Cortez's lead and became owners of full-time stations. Most, however, were made employees of the stations they had been buying time from. Such were the initial stages of Spanish-language radio programming and stations.

From the 1950s to the 1970s, Spanish-language radio was in transition. During those decades, this radio format continued to grow but began moving away from the brokerage system in favor of the more independent, full-time stations in AM and subsequently in FM—many transmitting up to twenty-four hours per day. In terms of the content, the early "broker" years were characterized by poetry, live dramas, news, and live music programming. Most of the live music was "Mexican," and the majority of the news was from foreign countries, predominantly from Mexico. As musical recordings became more common, this less expensive form of programming replaced the live music, allowing brokers and the stations to keep more of their profits to themselves. During the transition years, "personality radio" was at its best; brokers and announcers who had control over their programs and commercials became popular themselves. By the late 1960s the format became more tightly packaged and was less in the hands of individual radio stars. Music was selected by the station management to give a consistent sound throughout the programs. These broadcasts had less talk than before and were very much like other music-oriented English-language programs. In the 1970s the stations' growth also brought increased attention to format programming on the air and to sophisticated marketing techniques on the business side. One interesting note about Spanish-language broadcast stations is that almost all the announcers came from Latin America, in spite of the growth of the Hispanic audiences (Grebler, Moore, and Guzmán 1970). No research has been done to explain this employment practice; perhaps it was because station managers perceived that the Spanish of U. S. Hispanics was of poorer quality.

The phenomenal expansion of Spanish-language radio in the United States, especially during the late 1980s, is illustrated by the following figures. In 1974 there were 55 stations that broadcast in Spanish at least half of their air time, and there were an additional 425 that broadcast in this format less than half of their air time (Gutiérrez and Schement 1979). By 1980, the respective numbers were 64 and 436 (Schement and Singleton 1981). In 1986 there were a reported 73 stations that broadcast over half their time in Spanish (no comparable figures were provided for part-time Spanish-language stations).

The Early 1990s

According to the Standard Rate & Data Service's (1991) *Hispanic Media and Markets* guide, as of June 1991 there were 35 AM and 112 FM full-time Spanish-language radio stations and an additional 77 AM and 16 FM stations that dedicate a significant part (but not the majority) of their broadcast time to Spanish programming. This SRDS data, however, is less comprehensive than the 1991 *Broadcasting Yearbook*, which lists 185 AM and 68 FM stations transmitting full time in Spanish. Under this publication's "special programming" section, an additional 197 AM and 203 FM stations are listed as airing Spanish programs at least a few hours per week. Regardless of which source one chooses to view, the statistics provide indisputable evidence that Spanish-language radio is a powerful and growing ethnic medium in the United States. (For brief accounts of the history, ownership, audience, and programming of the most popular Spanish-language radio stations in New York, Los Angeles, Chicago, South Florida, and Texas during the early 1980s, see Veciana-Suárez 1987.)

While these numbers attest to a remarkable growth of the Hispanic-oriented radio industry, Hispanic *ownership* of these radio stations has not followed similar patterns. According to Schement and Singleton (1981), in 1980, of the 64 primary Spanish-language radio stations identified in their study, only 25 percent were owned by Latinos. In the top markets (e.g., New York, Los Angeles, Chicago, Miami, San Antonio) Latinos owned only about 10 percent of these types of stations. Primary Spanish-language radio (PSLR) are stations that transmit in this language 50 percent or more of their broadcast day. After discussing figures on ownership of assets and employment statistics at the various levels of a station's hierarchy, Schement and Singleton conclude that "PSLR stations can be described as owned and operated predominantly by Anglos" (1981, 81) (see also Gutiérrez and Schement 1981, 1984).

More recent statistics gathered by the National Association of Broadcasters and the Minority Telecommunications Development Program (MTDP) of the National Telecommunications and Information Administration on minority-owned and -controlled broadcast stations shed some additional light on the issue of Hispanic control over radio stations.

Apparently these two agencies used different criteria for identifying or classifying Hispanic-owned and -controlled radio. Otherwise, it seems that the number of Hispanic-owned radio stations more than doubled between 1986 and 1990. However, MTDP data suggest that there has been a decline between 1990 and 1991. It will be important to observe future statistics from this same source to assess which way the market is going. One other fact to keep in mind when considering these statistics is that they are not indicators of the programming language of the Hispanic-owned stations; it is unclear whether Spanish or English is used full or part time. It is only coincidental that all of the Hispanic-owned stations listed in the radio directory in the 1990-91 MTDP report are primarily Spanish-language stations. This fact allows for an approximate calculation of the current percentage of Hispanic-owned PSLR. In 1991, the 58 AM and the 21 FM stations listed in Table 1, constitute 32 percent and 31 percent respectively, of the Spanish-language AM and FM stations listed in the *Broadcasting Yearbook* that same year. Altogether this represents a slight increase from the 25 percent assessed by Schement and Singleton (1981) ten years ago.

Another important issue about the ownership of Hispanic-oriented radio is the trend toward concentration of various stations, particularly the most profitable ones, under major corporate groups. The oldest and largest of these (in number of stations owned) is *Tichenor Media System, Inc.*, a family-owned private company based in Dallas, Texas, which presently owns eleven full-time Spanish-language radio stations in the following locations: New York (WADO-AM), Miami (WQBA-AM and FM), Chicago (WIND-AM and WOJO-FM), San Antonio (KCOR-AM), Houston (KLAT-AM), Brownsville-Harlingen-McAllen (KGBT-AM and KIWW-FM), and El Paso (KBNA-AM and FM). Tichenor also has partial ownership of another Spanish-language station in Corpus Christi (KUNO-AM). This company was started in 1940 by McHenry Tichenor, a successful Anglo newspaperman who in 1941 bought his second radio station in South Texas, which at the time broadcast half a day in English and half a day in Spanish. This was the family's first venture in the Hispanic market. According to a Tichenor Media System summary sheet, the expansion into the Spanish radio field began in 1984 when, "under the directions of the second and third generations of the Tichenor family, the Company restructured its Corporate goal and formed Tichenor Spanish Radio." At the time,

TABLE 1

Hispanic-Owned and Controlled Radio Stations

	1982	1983	1984	1985	1986	1990	1991
AM	33	31	31	29	35	64	58
FM	13	9	8	8	9	24	21

Sources: 1982-86 data: National Association of Broadcasters, Department of Minority and Special Services, 1986; 1990–1991 data: Minority Telecommunications Development Program of the National Telecommunications and Information Administration, U. S. Department of Commerce, October 1991.

the non-Spanish language broadcast properties, including television, were divested to allow for the new ventures into the Hispanic market. In 1990, *Spanish Radio Network* was formed in partnership with SRN Texas, Inc. (a wholly-owned subsidiary of Tichenor Media System) and Radio WADO, Inc., in order to purchase the Miami and the New York stations. As of this writing, the Tichenor company with McHenry Taylor Tichenor, Jr., as president, continues to seek new stations in major Hispanic markets, particularly in Los Angeles. This corporate goal can be understood in light of the fact that in 1991, five of the company's stations were among the nation's top ten in billings for this market and accounted for as much as $21.4 million in revenues (Lopes 1991; see also *Broadcasting* 1991a). Assessments of major Spanish-language radio in previous years also show the prominence of the Tichenor stations and other groups listed below (see Mendosa 1990a; Russell 1988 and 1989).

A second group of Spanish-language radio stations—(the largest in terms of audience reached) is *Spanish Broadcasting System* (SBS). It was started in 1983 by Raúl Alarcón, Jr. This company, the only radio group company whose proprietors are Hispanics, presently owns six stations in the top three Latino markets: Los Angeles (KLAX-FM and KXED-AM and FM), New York (WSKQ-AM and FM), and Miami (WCMQ-AM and FM), plus a station in Key Largo, Florida (WZMQ-FM) which retransmits the Miami station's signals. The first of these KLAX (which until August 1, 1992 was KSKQ) had the distinction of being the top station—outranking even the most popular English-language stations in the fall 1992 and Winter through Summer 1993 Arbitron ratings among equal time periods and demographics. According to Lopes (1991), the combined AM/FM stations were also among the top ten in billings in 1991, accounting for $23.1 million in revenues for SBS. Mendosa states that Alarcón has been successful in acquiring so many stations because this entrepreneur is extremely "persistent in taking advantage of several options that the FCC makes available to minority broadcasters" (1990b, 58). By way of a brief explanation of the FCC policy, consider that on May 25, 1978, the FCC issued a statement of policy on minority ownership of broadcasting facilities, the purpose of which was to correct the "dearth of minority ownership" (FCC original) in the industry and enhance diversity of programming. The following are three provisions that SBS has been able to capitalize on: (1) an "enhanced credit" policy for minorities applying for permits to construct new stations; (2) mainstream broadcasters threatened with revocation of their licenses can sell to minority-controlled business at 75 percent of fair market value rather than risk losing almost everything; and (3) broadcasters selling to a minority can defer and sometimes totally avoid the taxes on any profits from the sale (Mendosa 1990b). In addition to its own stations, SBS is the national sales representative for six stations in Texas, six in California, and three in Illinois. The company also develops revenues from its SBS Promotions (e.g., of concerts, sporting events, supermarket tie-ins, and on-air contests) and from Alarcin Holdings in real estate. In 1990 SBS's combined capital reached $32.3 million, making it, according to *Hispanic Business* (1990), the 52nd largest Hispanic company in the United States.

Lotus Communications Corporation owns a third group of Spanish-language radio stations. The flagstaff operation

McHenry Tichnor.

is KWKW-AM, a station that has been serving the Hispanic community in Los Angeles and vicinities since 1942. It was purchased by Lotus in 1962 for approximately $1 million. The price was and is a reflection of the large audience it attracts, especially among the Mexican and Mexican American populations of that region. A recent audience estimate placed the number of listeners at over 1 million (at least during one day-part, i.e., time segment), making it among the largest in the United States and a few Latin American cities. Other Spanish-language stations owned by Lotus are KOXR-AM in Oxnard (bought in 1968), WTAQ-AM in Chicago (since 1985), and KGST-AM in Fresno (since 1986). All 4 of these stations are identified as "La Mexicana" in their respective markets because the music, programming, and the disc jockeys follow a Mexican format in idioms, accents, and modisms. Another distinctive programming feature of these stations is that they broadcast Los Angeles Dodger baseball games and retransmit these to 148 stations in Mexico. Lotus owns 10 other radio outlets in the United States, all of which are English-language stations. In addition, under Lotus Hispanic Reps, this company is sales representative to approximately 100 Spanish-language radio stations in the United States. The president of Lotus Communications is Howard Kalmenson; the vice president is Jim Kalmenson. Both are Anglos, as are the other owners of the company. In 1991, billings for KWKW on its own made it the single most profitable Spanish-language station in the country. According to Kalmenson, the success of this station has helped fund the growth of the entire company, which continues its operations with no capital debt.

Amancio V. Suárez.

A fourth Spanish-language radio group is *Radio América*, founded in 1986 when brothers Daniel and James Villanueva, of Mexican heritage, bought station KBRG-FM in the San Francisco Bay Area. In 1988 they acquired station KLOK-AM in the San Jose/San Francisco area. Lopes (1991) estimates that these two stations had net billings of $3.4 million in 1991. According to a fact sheet provided by the corporate management, KLOK was bought "using a separate shell company–Bahia Radio." The fact sheet ads that at the end of 1991 the Villanuevas, under a separate company called Orange County Broadcasting, purchased station KPLS-AM in Los Angeles. A distinctive characteristic of this station, with 20 percent ownership by Fernando Niebla, also of Mexican decent, is that it was the first "all talk" Spanish-language station in the Los Angeles and Southern California area (there were four "talk" stations in the Miami market). Daniel Villanueva also had minority (20 percent) interests with Washington, D.C.'s Los Cerezos Broadcasting Company, which owns WMDO-AM and WMDO-TV Channel 48-a Univisión affiliate.

Yet another Spanish-language radio group is the *Viva América* company, which was started in 1989 with 49 percent ownership by Heftel Broadcasting and 51 percent ownership by Mambisa Broadcasting Corporation. Heftel owns stations in Los Angeles (KLVE-FM and KTNQ-AM). Mambisa is divided among Amancio V. Suárez, his son Amancio J. Suárez, and cousin Charles Fernández, all of whom are of Cuban descent. In Miami, the Viva America Media Group owned two stations (WAQI-AM and WXDJ-FM). In addition, under the corporate heading of the Southern Media Holding Group presided by Amancio V. Suárez, it was also linked to *Mi Casa*–a monthly Spanish-language newspaper. In spite of its recent entry into the market, the Viva América stations earned $10.1 million in billings in 1991, almost duplicating the figure of the previous year; the two Heftel stations were the top in the Spanish-language radio market, totaling $16.3 million for the same year (Lopes 1991).

A final group of stations that is especially distinct from the aforementioned ones is the nonprofit *Radio Bilingüe* network in California. Efforts to establish this network date to 1976 when Hugo Morales, a Harvard Law School graduate of Mexican-Mixtec Indian heritage, Lupe

Ortiz y Roberto Páramo, with the collaboration of a group of Mexican peasants, artists, and activists sought to use radio to improve life and sustain the cultural identity of farm workers of the San Joaquin Valley (see Corwin 1989; and Downing 1990). With the significant backing of a grant from a Catholic charity, KSJV-FM was launched in Fresno, California, on July 4, 1980. It transmits a variety of music programs plus a diversity of information related to health, education, immigration, civic action, and the arts. Supported primarily by donations from community members, businesses, and some foundations, the Radio Bilingüe network now reaches across central California as KSJV programming is rebroadcast over KMPO-FM in Modesto, KTQX-FM in Bakersfield, KUBO-FM in Imperial Valley, and KHDC-FM in Salinas. KSJV programming is also beamed 24 hours a day via two satellite systems–a KU-Band system and a C-Band system. The C-Band systems allows any of the 400 interconnected to public radio stations in the U. S. and Puerto Rico to have access to the Fresno based KSJV programming which is available to commercial and noncommercial stations. Affiliate KUBO-FM, started in El Centro in April 1989 producing some of its own independent programming. Radio Bilingüe sponsors the "Viva El Mariachi" music festival, which serves as an important fundraiser for the network. One of the distinctive features of this network is the operational and programming support it receives from innumerable volunteers, who produce diverse music and public service programs in English, Spanish, and bilingual format. Radio Bilingüe is presently the largest noncommercial producer of Spanish-language and bilingual programs. Another feature of Radio Bilingüe is its news service, "Noticiero Latino" which is described below.

Due to the increased pressures in the commercial and public radio markets, two organizations serving the interests of this sector were established in 1991. The first was American Hispanic-Owned Radio Association (AHORA), which started with fifty-five Hispanic station owners concerned with the competition for the Hispanic market and with the rapid pace at which Spanish-language radio stations are being bought by non-Hispanics. According to *Broadcasting Magazine*, AHORA, under the direction of Mary Helen Barro (majority owner of KAFY-AM in Bakersfield, California), seeks to "increase the number of business opportunities for Hispanic broadcasters and to attract more Hispanic talent to broadcasting"; its agenda also includes encouraging the government to include Spanish-language radio stations in government media buys (1991b, 40).

With June 1991 as its organization date, another professional radio group is the Hispanics in Public Radio (HPR). A press release provided by Florence Hernández-Ramos, general manager of KUVO-FM in Denver, Colorado, indicates that this "nonprofit professional organization designed to provide a forum for the expression of the needs and interests of Hispanic Americans involved with public radio" proposes to "represent the interests of Hispanic-controlled public radio stations with the goal of improving the financial resources of the stations." The inaugural press release also indicates that HPR's main activities will be "information sharing, joint fundraising, training, and program development."

The Radio News and Other Program Providers

Although some stations produce everything they broadcast, including news and commercials, many stations depend on various companies dedicated to packaging programs for the Spanish-language radio market. Two types of providers merit special attention: those that provide news services and the ones that provide "full-service."

Among the major news service providers, the oldest is *Spanish Information Systems* (SIS), inaugurated in 1976. From its headquarters in Dallas, Texas, it distributes via satellite to 43 stations nationwide five-minute Spanish-language news programs seven days a week. SIS also transmits a 15-minute radio magazine Monday through Firday at noon. This magazine includes segments on current affairs, sports, cooking, health, show business and beauty. Additional sportscasts are also distributed to its affiliates. SIS has operating offices in Dallas, New york and Los Angeles. It is a subdivision of the Texas State Networks, the oldest and largest state radio network in the country with 55 years in the English-language news network industry.

A second radio news provider is *Radio Noticias,* which began in 1983 as a division in Spanish of United Press International (UPI), once one of the major wire series in the world. From its base in Washington, DC, Radio Noticias distributes to forty-two affiliated stations a five-minute news program on an hourly basis seven days a week. It also provides one-minute headline news and a fifteen-minute talk program called "Mesa Redonda" which is distributed Fridays for broadcasting during weekends.

A third news provider is *Noticiero Latino,* produced by Radio Bilingüe in Fresno, California. This news service, which began in 1985, is unique in that it is the only Spanish news service produced by a nonprofit network in the United States whose proprietaries and coordinators are Latino residents of this country. It is also unique because it is exclusively dedicated to informing and helping to interpret events in the United States, Latin America, and the Caribbean that are related to Hispanics in the United States; for example, immigration, civil rights, health, education, culture, and successes of Hispanics. Using information gathered by its local reporters and network of correspondents in the United States, Mexico and Puerto Rico, Noticiero Latino offers a daily eight- to ten-minute news program which is transmitted Monday through Friday by telephone line as well as via the C-Band and KU-Band satellites. Noticiero Latino's news services are used by more than forty stations in the United States, one in Puerto Rico, and another thirty in Mexico. The Mexico links are facilitated through the Instituto Mexicano de la Radio's Programa Cultural de las Fronteras and through Radio Educación.

Among the "full-service" providers of Spanish-language programming, the oldest and largest is *Cadena Radio Centro* (CRC)—a network founded in 1985 in Dallas, Texas. CRC is a subsidiary of *Grupo Radio Centro,* a Mexican company listed in the *New York Stock Exchange* and controlled by the Aguirre family, which also owns 9 radio stations and has more than 100 affiliates. In the United States the president of Cadena Radio Centro is Barrett Alley and the vice-chairman is Carlos Aguirre—a controlling family heir. This U. S. radio network offers its news services every hour to 80 affiliated Spanish-language stations linked via satellite. CRC programming service operates seven days a week with two information lines. One transmits its five-minute news reports; three of these daily transmissions originate directly from Mexico City, and another three focus on Latin American news. The other line transmits a variety of programs including "En Concierto" (prominent Hispanic artists introducing their music), "Cristina Opina" (opinions by Cristina Saralegui on a wide range of subjects), "Hablando de deportes" (a live sports call-in talk show), and news of special events. All or some of these programs are purchased by affiliated stations, depending on the local or regional interests. CRC was taped to broadcast the world's biggest sporting event—the 1994 World [soccer] Cup.

With its starting date in March 1991, the most recent Spanish-language radio program provider is Hispano U. S. A. which claims to be the first Hispanic-owned and -operated Spanish network service. According to a company informational brochure, *Hispano U. S. A.* sells twenty-four daily hours of "Spanish radio programming for the 90's, designed for cost-efficient station operations which benefits resident as well as absentee ownership." The programming, which is transmitted via satellite, features "top 40 Hispanic dance tunes," national and international news including sports, and weekend special reports. Nine months after its start-up, Hispano U. S. A. had contracted with eighteen stations covering the southern United States from California to Florida.

Another major provider of Spanish-language radio programs is CBS Hispanic Radio Network (CBSHRN). This special events network was founded in 1990 by Columbia Broadcasting System. According to a company fact sheet, CBSHRN was created "to sell, affiliate and produce Spanish-language broadcasts of the Crown Jewels [i.e., the play-off games and World Series] of Major League Baseball to the United States and Latin America." It also transmits National Football League postseason and Super Bowl games, world soccer championship games, and more recently entertainment specials such as "Navidad Mágica en Disneyland." The programs are provided via syndication free of charge to affiliates in exchange for carrying the network's commercials; local commercials are allowed between selected breaks. For 1992 the network planed to offer more entertainment programs. CBS Hispanic Radio Network started its Spanish-language programming in Latin America in the mid 1970s with baseball specials. When it began in the United States it was affiliated with Caballero Hispanic media representatives to provide such programs to the stations represented by Caballero, but in 1990 it established its own syndication network.

The most recent radio program provider is Latino USA, an English-language "radio journal of news and culture." The weekly service offers Hispanic perspectives to many of the most important news events of the week, as well as interviews, commentaries, and features stories on a diversity of topics related to Hispanics. Its inaugural program was launched on July 2, 1993, from the University of Texas at Austin where it was developed with major grants from the Ford Foundation and the Corporation for Public Broadcasting. It is distributed free of charge to over 155 public radio stations nationwide. The program is facilitated by satellite on the Extended Program Service (EPS), and to both commercial and noncommercial radio stations via cassette through the Longhorn Radio Network. The executive producer is Dr. Gilberto Cardenas, director of the Center for Mexican American Studies at the University of Texas; María Martin is senior producer; María Hinojosa is the host, and Vidal Guzmán is the marketing and production manager.

In sum, as of 1991, Spanish-language radio stations, whether owned by Hispanics or Anglos, could be heard in practically every region of the United States. In some major metropolitan cities with large concentrations of Hispanics (e.g., New York, Los Angeles, Miami, Chicago, San Antonio and Houston), Hispanics have a variety of such stations to choose from, each with a distinct format and music to please almost any of the major Latin American and U. S. Hispanic musical traditions. Through the news and other programming services, Hispanics in the U. S., be they Spanish speakers, English speakers, or bilingual, also have many opportunities to keep ties to their countries of origin, enjoy the diversity of entertainment shows, and be part of the news and cultural developments events in this country as well as around the Latin world.

Television

Just as was the case for radio, Spanish-language television transmissions started almost as soon as they began in the English-language medium. Since the 1940s, entrepreneurs have found a significant market and profits transmitting to the Hispanic populations in the United States. Spanish-language television has grown enormously from the early days of a few brokered hours on some English-language stations in San Antonio and New York. In 1991, over $332 million in advertising was spent on the three broadcasting networks and various cable companies that make up Spanish-language television. These businesses differ considerably—some operate independently, while others have corporate ties to both U. S. and Mexican media. Yet since its inception, the structure of this medium has been strongly related to Mexicans and Mexican media.

The Genesis Years: 1950s to Early 1960s

The first Spanish-language television station in the United States was San Antonio's KCOR-TV Channel 41, which began broadcasting in 1955. But a few years before this and other similar stations started, a number of Spanish-language radio entrepreneurs recognized the potential of the Spanish-speaking television audiences and pioneered the way by producing special TV programs. Following the pattern used in the early stages of Spanish-language radio, time was brokered for these programs in the nascent English-language stations in selected cities. One of the earliest of such Spanish-language television programs was "Buscando Estrellas," which began in 1951 produced and hosted by José Pérez (Pepe) del Río, a Mexican national of Spanish heritage. With Pioneer Flour Mills of San Antonio, Texas, as the primary commercial sponsor, this weekly entertainment and variety talent-search show lasted approximately three years. It was broadcast live on Sunday afternoons initially from the studios of KERN Channel 5—an English-language station in San Antonio. "Buscando Estrellas" brought to Texas a variety of talent from Mexico and provided opportunities for local amateurs to present their artistic aspirations to the public at the recording studios and to the television viewing audiences. Another characteristic of this precursor of U. S.-Hispanic television was that its production and broadcasting location rotated every thirteen weeks to three other Texas cities: Corpus Christi, Harlingen, and Laredo. In each city, Joe Harry sold the concept of the show and brokered time for it from English-language stations, which found it profitable to sell those slots. Between 1956 and 1961, Pepe del Río hosted another popular Spanish-language program in San Antonio: "Cine en Español," which featured old movies brought from Mexico, Spain, and Argentina. Broadcast from the studios of KERN, those movies were quite popular among the Spanish-speaking audiences of the time. In New York, the precursors of Spanish-language television were the well-known radio personalities Don Pessante and Don Mendez. Some anecdotal evidence indicates that during the late 1940s they may have hosted the very first U.S.-Hispanic-oriented television entertainment programs by brokering time on one of the English-language channels (9, 11, or 13).

More anecdotal evidence was obtained about another Hispanic-oriented program in New York during the early 1950s: "El Show Hispano" which aired on the once-commercial WATV Channel 13 between 11:00 a.m. and 12:00 a.m. on weekends (this station later became WNJU Channel 47; see below). This program began in early 1952 and lasted for approximately two years; it was brokered by an Anglo who also saw the potential audience and profit among the growing Hispanic populations in New York. One of the distinctive features of this show, which was co-hosted by Don Mendez and Aníbal González-Irizarry, was that in addition to its musical and comic segments, it also had a fifteen-minute news section. González-Irizarry was responsible for this part of the program, making him probably the first Hispanic television newscaster in the early stages of this medium in the United States. In addition to working on the weekend television scene, González-Irizarry was a well-known disc jockey and newscaster on two of the early Spanish-language radio stations in New York (WWRL and WBNX). When he returned to Puerto Rico in 1955, Aníbal González-Irizarry eventually became the most prominent and respected anchorman on Puerto Rican television for over twenty years on WKAQ Channel 2.

During the 1960s, part-time Spanish-language programs in English-language stations also emerged in various other cities with large concentrations of Hispanics, such as Los Angeles, Houston, Miami, Phoenix, Tucson, and Chicago (Valenzuela 1985a, 129). Most often such programs—sponsored primarily by a local company—would be the outcome of personal efforts of Hispanic entrepreneurs, many of whom had experiences with radio. Some stations provided time for these in order to seek alternative sources of profits and/or to comply with FCC requirements of public service programs to serve community needs and interests.

The Formative Years

Between the 1960s and the end of the 1980s, the Spanish-language television industry in the United States was dominated by three networks: Spanish International Network—subsequently Univisión—, Telemundo, and

Galavisión. Local and regional enterprises became national and international operations which themselves were part of other mega-industrial interests. It should be pointed out that Telemundo's entry into the Spanish-language television market introduced real competition to this industry for the first time. For example, in 1988, a domestic production began as the two networks fought for the coveted advertising dollars. The potential gold mine offered by the exponential growth of the U. S. Hispanic populations was a driving force in the formation of and competition among those television ventures. This potential did not go unnoticed by primarily English-language broadcasting and cable companies which developed special series and cable operations to profit from Hispanics all across the United States as well as the Latin American markets south of the Rio Grande. From its beginnings up to this medium's fifth decade in United States, it continues to have a substantial foreign connection in the corporate structures, on-camera and off-camera personnel, and in programming (*Foreign Connection* 1989; Mydans 1989).

Spanish International Network: 1960s to 1986

The experiences of the Hispanic television entrepreneurs and their part-time Spanish-language television programs eventually led the way to establish separate stations especially directed at the Hispanic viewers. As mentioned above, the first primarily Spanish-language television station in the United States was San Antonio's KCOR, which transmitted on Channel 41 using the newly created ultra high frequency (UHF) band. The principal pioneer behind this effort was Raúl Cortez, the same owner of KCOR-AM, which was itself the first Hispanic-owned and -operated Spanish-language radio station in the United States. KCOR-TV began in 1955 broadcasting between 5:00 p.m. and midnight. Emilio Nicolás, one of the first general managers of the station, recalls that approximately 50 percent of the programs were live variety and entertainment shows that featured a host of the best available talent from Mexico. Many of these shows took place from the studios of Cortez's radio station which aired these programs simultaneously. Movies and other prerecorded programs imported primarily from Mexico accounted for the rest of the early offerings of Channel 41.

Although the station was very popular among the Mexican and other Spanish-speaking residents of San Antonio and vicinity, Nicolás recalls that advertisers did not acknowledge this market and failed to use it extensively for commercial promotions. During those early years of the medium, Hispanic viewers were not accounted for in the standard ratings services. One reason for this, according to Nicolás, was that in the 1940s and 1950s Mexicans were cautious in either acknowledging their heritage or exposure to Spanish-language media for fear of blatant discriminatory practices. Thus, after spending heavily in the live talent imported from Mexico and receiving limited financial support from the advertising agencies, Cortez was forced to sell the television station to Anglo interests. He kept the KCOR call letters for his radio station but the television station's were changed to KUAL. The station continued some Spanish-language programs, and in 1961 these call letters changed again to KWEX, when Channel 41 was sold to Don Emilio Azcárraga Vidaurreta and his financial partners, who then went on to establish the first Spanish-language television network.

Until his death in 1972, Don Emilio Azcárraga Vidaurreta was the most prominent media magnate in Mexico. With his family he owned and operated a significant part of the country's commercial radio system and the emerging Telesistema Mexicano, S.A. (Sociedad Anónima), broadcasting empire (see Mejía Barquera et al. 1985; Mejía Barquera 1989; Miller and Darling 1991; and Trejo Delarbe 1988). In the United States Don Emilio, his son Emilio Azcárraga Milmo, and Reynold (René) Anselmo became central figures for not only the purchase of San Antonio's Channel 41 but also the establishment of the largest and most influential businesses related to Spanish-language television broadcasting. The complex history of these corporations have been documented by various authors (see Beale 1988; Cox 1969; de Uriarte 1980; González 1978; Gutiérrez 1979; Gutiérrez and Schement 1981, 1984; Seijo-Maldonado 1989; Valenzuela 1985a, b; and Wilkinson 1990a, b, 1991).

From the works of these authors it can be summarized that the most significant development of Spanish-language television in the United States began when Spanish International Communications Corporation (SICC) was initiated and organized by René Anselmo and bankrolled by Azcárraga Vidaurreta along with minority investors having U. S. citizenship. Since SICC (which at one point was called Spanish International Broadcasting Corporation—SIBC) was to hold the licenses of the stations, the corporation was structured so that Azcárraga Vidaurreta, a Mexican citizen, would own only 20 percent of the company. Most of the other partners were U. S. citizens so as to conform with Federal Communication Act Section 310, which "prohibits the issuing of broadcast licenses to aliens, to the representatives of aliens, or to corporations in which aliens control more than one-fifth of the stock" (Gutiérrez 1979, 141). Anselmo, a Boston-born Italian-American and associate of Azcárraga's Mexican media, was the main U. S. person in the ensuing enterprises. Among other principal U. S. citizens of SICC at the time were Frank Fouce, owner of Los Angeles Spanish-language

Jorge Ramos and María Elena Salinas of "Noticiero Univisión," the Monday through Friday evening news broadcast.

movie houses, including the famous Million Dollar Theater; and Edward Noble, an advertising executive in Mexico City. After obtaining KWEX, the SICC with the assistance of a few other partners bought Los Angeles station KMEX Channel 34 in 1962. Gutiérrez points out that "although there is a limitation in the amount of stock a foreign national can hold in a broadcast license, there apparently is no such restriction on U. S. television networks" (1979, 144). Thus, in 1961 Don Emilio and Anselmo established the sister company Spanish International Network (SIN) to purchase and provide programming, virtually all of which originated from Azcárraga's production studios at Telesistema (later known as Televisa) in Mexico. The other function of SIN was to provide advertising sales for the SICC stations.

Over the next ten years the licensee corporation went through a series of expansions, mergers, and reorganizations as it added three other stations: WXTV Channel 41 in New York (1968); WLTV Channel 23, Miami (1971); and KFTV Channel 21, Fresno/Hanford (1972). The network was also extended with stations owned by some principals of SICC/SIN: under the company Bahía de San Francisco it was KDTV Channel 14, San Francisco (1974) and under Legend of Cibola (later known as Seven Hills Corporation) it was KTVW Channel 33, Phoenix (1976). In addition, SIN had the affiliation of five stations owned and operated by corporations not related to SIN/SICC; these were located in Albuquerque, Chicago, Corpus Christi, Houston and Sacramento. Furthermore, SIN had four stations owned and operated by this company's parent corporation Televisa, S.A. From their locations on the Mexican border at Juárez, Mexicali, Nuevo Laredo, and Tijuana, these stations served U. S. cities at El Paso, El Centro, Laredo, and San Diego, respectively.

Until the mid-1970s, most of these stations shared the programming that came primarily from Mexico's Productora de Teleprogramas (ProTele, S.A.), a company created and controlled by Televisa as its export subsidiary. SIN imported and licensed taped shows, movies, and other programs that would be transported to the Los Angeles station, sent to San Antonio, and then passed along in a "bicycle type network" to the other owned and affiliated stations. In September 1976 SIN became the first major broadcasting company, preceding CBS, ABC, and NBC, to distribute programming directly to its affiliates via domestic satellite. The SIN signal reached the San Antonio station from Mexico City by terrestrial microwave, and from there it was distributed by the Westar satellite (Gutiérrez and Schement 1981; see also Valenzuela 1985a, b). That same year another related company, Univisión, had been started by Televisa to provide the live, direct Spanish-language programming to Spanish-speaking audiences worldwide, but particularly to the United States. A major incentive for this new company was to sell advertising in Mexico for SIN programs that would be aired in both countries. Between 1978 and 1979, live interconnections were established via satellite among eleven of SIN's stations. In 1979, as cable connections became more readily available, another precedent was established as SIN began paying cable franchise operators to carry its satellite signals. Then in early 1980, SIN's outlets expanded further as the network was granted permission to establish low-power television (LPTV) stations (those whose signals only reach a radius of approximately twelve to fifteen miles), beginning with Denver affiliate K49TE Channel 49, which at the time served just as a retransmitter with no local programs. Another LPTV was licensed to Los Cerezos Television Company, Washington, D.C. Additional LPTVs were licensed in Austin, Bakersfield, Hartford, Philadelphia, and Tucson. Altogether, by 1983 the Spanish-language television stations represented by SIN/SICC were reaching over 3.3 million Hispanic households across the United States. Advertising for the stations was sold in the United States, Mexico, and other Latin American countries.

Although KMEX had turned a profit in 1964, most of the SICC stations did not operate in the black until a decade or more after they began operations. Nevertheless, the Azcárragas and their fellow investors recognized the growth potential of the Spanish-speaking television audience and market in the United States and were willing to subsidize the station group. When SICC did eventually generate profits, many of them found their way back to Mexico through the SIN pipeline. A falling out between Frank Fouce, one of SICC's principal investors, and René Anselmo, one of the creators and president of both SICC and SIN, led to a long and bitter stockholder derivative lawsuit (CV 76 3451, 1976), which took over ten years to settle (Crister 1987). A second legal action against SICC was initiated at the FCC in 1980, when a group of radio broadcasters (the now defunct Spanish Radio Broadcasters Association) charged that the company was under illegal foreign control. In January 1986 a judge appointed by the FCC ruled not to renew the licenses of the thirteen SICC stations and ordered their transfer to U. S.-based entities. This decision was followed by numerous legal appeals and challenges (these have been summarized by Seijo-Maldonado 1989; and Wilkinson 1991).

In terms of programming content, Gutiérrez and Schement (1981) state that "by 1979 SIN was feeding over 64 hours of programming to eight affiliates by Westar II satellite, 50 hours of which came from Televisa. The remainder was originated in the United States or imported from Venezuela, Spain, Argentina, or Brazil. The network feed consisted primarily of *novelas* (soap operas), variety shows, and the news [the program *24 Horas*]] from Mexico City" (1980, 196). From the 1960s to the 1970s, Hispanic programs made within the United States usually consisted of public affairs programming and local newscasts, some of which were acclaimed for their excellent coverage of issues of concern to the local Hispanic communities. In addition, some of the special programs at the time included, as summarized by Gutiérrez, "salutes to Latin American countries produced on location by Radio Televisión Española, New Jersey's Puerto Rican Day parade, a Fourth of July Special from Miami and New York, and live coverage of the OTI [Organización de la Televisión Iberoamericana] Latin song festival"; there were also sporting events such as boxing matches, soccer, and world cup competitions (1979, 153-54). In fact, SIN began carrying selected games of the World Cup Soccer Championship in 1970. At first these were shown on closed circuit television and in rented theaters; regular broadcasts began in 1978.

Among the network's various programs, "Noticiero SIN," the national news program, merits a special historical review because of its development and impact in the United States and Latin America. One of the pacesetters in this area was Gustavo Godoy, a native of Cuba who in Miami worked with CBS's affiliate television station as a producer and with ABC's affiliate in the news department. From there he went on to WLTV Channel 23, and then with the SIN network news. In sharing some of his recollections of the early years of the "Noticiero SIN," he indicated that from the start, the network established that there would be a standard of local newscasts from 6:00 to 6:30 p.m., followed by the national program from 6:30 to 7:00 p.m., in order to provide viewers with one solid hour of news focusing on events and people related to the Hispanic and Latin American communities. During its beginning the national news program was produced at the television studios of the School of Communication at Howard University in Washington, D.C. On June 14, 1982, the national news department was transferred to Miami, where it continued productions until January 1987, when it was moved to Laguna Niguel in Southern California when Hallmark Corporation bought the network (see below).

While regional newscasts were done from San Antonio and some of the larger stations, for the international news gathering activities, news bureaus were established, beginning in 1982, in Washington, New York, El Salvador, Argentina, Mexico, Puerto Rico, Israel, and London. The satellite uplink operations, which had been in San Antonio since 1976, were also moved to Laguna Niguel in January 1987, where they remained for four years.

There were a number of special programs produced by the SIN news department including "Temas y Debates," a talk show that started in 1982 in Washington, D.C., and continues to this day. "Temas y Debates" airs interviews with government and public personalities who are important newsmakers and interpreters for the week. Another notable accomplishment of the SIN news was its coverage of U. S. and Latin American political developments. The first U. S. national election night coverage in Spanish was in 1968; similar reports followed in subsequent years. Starting with the 1981 elections in Miami, in which two Hispanic candidates were finalists for mayor of that city, "Noticias 23" and "Noticiero SIN" began giving ample time to present and analyze in Spanish the campaigns, issues, and personalities of the time at a network level. Entrance and exit polling was also conducted by the stations and the network to share their projections and predictions of the electoral outcomes, especially among the Hispanic populations. At each station and the network level, there was also a very strong campaign for voter registration. In 1984 SIN launched "Destino '84" which further promoted voter registration, and through a series of special programs and reports, it gave ample coverage to the presidential elections in the United States. Cameras and reporters followed the candidates and events of the primaries, the conventions, and the final campaign up to election night. That year, the NBC network sent a camera and reporter to SIN news to follow-up the trends in Hispanic voting at the national level. (For an analysis of Univisión's and Telemundo's coverage of the 1988 presidential elections in the U. S. see Constantakis-Valdés 1993). Godoy and his staff proceeded with similar coverages in Latin America, including the polling activities beginning with the 1984 congressional and presidential elections in El Salvador, where their surveys were quite accurate in predicting the voting results. In subsequent years ample coverage was given to elections and more exit polls were conducted in Guatemala, Peru, Honduras, Columbia, Costa Rica and many other locations. In 1985, the first summit meeting between U. S. president Reagan and the Soviet Union's president Gorbachev was covered live from Geneva, Switzerland. According to Godoy, thanks to SIN's live satellite transmissions from Latin America, these crucial electoral processes were placed in an international spotlight, creating public attention that may have contributed to an increased sense of honesty and balance in such events. The amplitude and time of "Noticiero SIN"'s live coverage of these Latin American developments have not been matched by any English-language network in the United States. The same can be said about the telethons to benefit victims of the earthquakes and other natural disasters in Chile, Colombia, Puerto Rico, and Mexico.

One of the most significant internal turmoils in the history of "Noticiero SIN" began to take place in 1986 when the Mexican parent company, seeking to exert stronger control of the U. S. news activities, considered absorbing the "Noticiero" under Televisa's new international news enterprise ECO (Empresas de Comunicaciones Orbitales). This action was prompted when Azcárraga established ECO to optimize the gathering and production of television news for his Univisión and for additional subscribers in the United States and Latin America (Lozano 1988). In August 1986, Godoy, who was then executive vice president for news at SIN, was informed that there would be limited funds for the coverage and conducting of polls related to the elections in the Mexican state of Chihuahua. This was interpreted as an attempt to suppress uncloaking of electoral corruption and mismanagement by the main Mexican political party—the Partido de la Revolución Institucional (PRI).

In November 1986, Televisa's Jacobo Zabludovsky, who for sixteen years had been anchorman for that company's "24 Horas" news program, was appointed to take charge of the SIN news operations in the United States. Shortly after Godoy and approximately thirty-five others at SIN resigned, to protest Televisa's and indirectly the Mexican Government's interventions (Nordheimer 1986). Without ever having established an operational office in the United States, Zabludovsky was eventually "prevented from working as president of ECO due to charges by Latino journalists and politicians about the Televisa news division's constant praise of the Mexican government" (Lozano 1988, 5). By then, Godoy had formed his own news production company Hispanic American Broadcasting Corporation, which from 1987 to 1988 provided news for competing network Telemundo (see below under Telemundo). Lozano indicates that "in the end, former UPI chief Luis G. Nogales replaced Zabludovsky as president of ECO, and started a radical restructuring of Noticiero Univisión" along with editor Sylvana Foa, who stressed that the intention was to follow "the American TV networks' style at the start of Noticiero Univisión" (1988, 5).

From SIN to Univisión under Hallmark: 1986 to 1992

When the FCC appointed judge ruled not to renew the thirteen SICC licences and ordered the transfer to U. S.-based entities, an intense and controversial bidding war ensued in the same court that had heard the stockholder suit. it culminated in July, 1986 when Hallmark Cards, Inc., and its 25 percent partner, First Capital Corporation of Chicago, won with a $301.5 million bid for the SICC licenses and properties. The losing bidder was TVL Corporation directed by a group of Hispanic investors, who submitted a higher bid ($320 million) but whose financing was less secure. TVL's principal investors were Raúl R. Tapia, a partner in the Washington, D.C., law firm of Tapia & Buffington and former deputy special assistant of Hispanic affairs during President Jimmy Carter's administration; Alfred R. Villalobos, vice-chairman and president of a management company; David C. Lizárraga, chairman, president, and chief executive officer of TELACU; and Diego C. Ascencio, former ambassador to Brazil and assistant secretary of state for consular affairs (Broadcasting 1986; Wilkinson 1991). Other Hispanic notables who at some time expressed an interest in acquiring SICC were Miami politician Raúl Masvidal, investor Enrique (Hank) Hernández, and Los Angeles surgeon and Republican party leader Tirso del Junco (Rivera Brooks 1986). Among the unsuccessful Anglo bidders, there were producers Norman Lear, A. Jerrold Perenchio, and the former U. S. ambassador to Mexico, John Gavin. Legal challenges of the sale process brought by losing bidders were not resolved until April 1991.

As various appeals were being deliberated in federal court and at the FCC, SIN and SICC were renamed Univisión on January 1, 1987. That same month the national news program Noticiero Univisión (formerly Noticiero SIN) returned to Miami, along with other Univisión operations. In February, the cable service Galavisión, which was not included in the deal, split from Univisión and remained under the control of Televisa and Univisa. In July of that year, Hallmark and First Capital paid $286 million for the five original SICC stations and in August obtained actual control of the channels. Later San Francisco station KDTV was purchased for an additional $23.6 million, and the Phoenix station was bought for $23 million. In February 1988, the SIN network was also acquired by Hallmark for an additional $274.5 million. With the transition, both the station group and the network continued operations under the name Univisión Holdings, Inc., of which Hallmark became sole owner by February 15, 1988.

Under the parent company Hallmark Cards, Inc., the Univisión owned and operated Spanish-language television group consisted of 10 full-power stations and 4 low-power stations and it counted on the affiliation of 10 full-power and 11 low-power stations plus 566 cable carriers that operated in forty of the fifty states plus the District of Columbia. Because of the dynamics of the Hispanic media market and industries, the composition of this network continues to change. Tables 2A and 2B list the Univisión network group composition as of fall 1993 after the most recent transitions (see below). The satellite used for program transmissions is the SATCOM 1R. Two stations in Guadalajara and Sonora, Mexico, purchased some Univisión programs but were not owned by the network.

Between 1988 and May 1992 the president of the Univisión television station group was Joaquín Blaya, a native of Chile, where he worked as a journalist, radio newscaster, disc jockey, and production manager. Prior to this position he was an account representative at WXTV in New York, and eventually president and general manager of station WLTV in Miami. During that time, Blaya was also acting president of Univisión Holdings, which included Univisión Publications, Univisión News, and the Univisión Network and its various components. Three other key directors at that time were Raúl Torano, senior vice president for sales and marketing executive of the network, the stations, and *Más*; Rosita Perú, senior vice president for programming; and Ray Rodríguez who was responsible for international co-productions and talent management functions. Perú is a Buenos Aires-educated native of Lima, Perú; the family roots of the other two are from Cuba. Another important appointment by Hallmark was that of Guillermo Martínez as news director and vice president of Univisíon news. Martínez, a native of Cuba, had been a journalist and editorial writer for The Miami Herald, and for a few months news director at WLTV.

In its continued expansion in this country, on March 9, 1991, Univisión inaugurated its state-of-the-art-technology network television center in Miami's West Dade County. The 139,000 square-foot facility housed many of the network's departments, including news, special events, merchandising, programming, talent relations, sports, programming development, and its regional sales office. The operations, news, and promotions departments, formerly based in Laguna Niguel in Southern California, moved to the Miami facilities during summer of that same year amid protests from Mexican Americans who feared a greater Cuban influence on Univisión's news, programming, and personnel (Bergsman 1989b).

For the expansion of its national and international news coverage, Univisión's news department, under the direction of Guillermo Martínez, hired sixteen additional correspondents to work in the United States and Latin America (Shiver 1990). To improve the network's knowledge of Hispanic public opinion, Univisión enlisted the services of Sergio Bendixen and his survey research company, Bendixen Associates. Bendixen started doing research for SIN in 1985 and worked for Univisión until 1992 conducting surveys related to political opinions and orientations of the general public and particularly Hispanics.

In terms of the other programs, a 1991 fact sheet about Univisión stated that these were "obtained from various Latin American sources, but an increasing amount were produced by Univisión, as well as by independent producers, in the United States" and that

TABLE 2A

The Univisión Spanish-Language Television Group, Owned & Operated Stations, Fall 1993

Station		City, State
Full-Power		
KLUZ	41	Albuquerque, NM
KUVN	23	Dallas/Ft. Worth, TX
KFTV	21	Fresno, CA
KCEC	50	Lakewood, CO
KMEX	34	Los Angeles, CA
WLTV	23	Miami, FL
KTVW	33	Phoenix, AZ
KWEX	41	San Antonio, TX
KDTV	14	San Francisco, CA
WXTV	41	Secaucus, NJ (New York)
WUNI	27	Shrewsbury, MA (Boston)
Low-Power		
K30AK	30	Austin, TX

( ) Indicates adjacent major city served.

approximately 44 percent of the programs were U. S. based. Univisión is on the air twenty-four hours a day, seven days a week.

When Blaya was with Univisíon, he stated in an interview with Hispanic Business, that the company's "main thrust of the program development in the United States [was] to address . . . 'the born-again Hispanic' "—the young Hispanics who were not watching Spanish-language television; adding that Univisión was "not a Latin American television network in the United States. 1dots [It was] an American television network that speaks Spanish" (Mendosa 1991, 18). At the time, the following were some of the programs, in addition to "Noticiero Univisión" and "Temas y Debates," that exemplify this mold. For debates and presentations related to public issues, there was "Cristina," a talk-show hosted by Cuban-born Cristina Saralegui—Univisión's version of Oprah Winfrey—in which issues and subjects formerly taboo in the Hispanic community are discussed. Other programs were: "Portada," a news magazine hosted by Puerto Rican Ana Azcuy that was "a Spanish-language version of an investigative report program similar to general market's '20/20,' and, "Noticias y Más," a live daily show with stories that did not make the main evening news program but were carried in this more "sensationalist" show for general public interest.

For comedy, games, and variety, Hallmark's Univisión at the height of its U. S. productions, had "Corte Tropical," a zany situation comedy portraying a Latin-style pursuit of the elusive American dream, produced by Cuban Mimi Belt-Mendoza. "Sábado Gigante," a variety-game show which was top-rated in the United States and many Latin American countries, featuring games, contests, talent searches, celebrity guest appearances, and musical entertainment. It was hosted by Chilean Mario Kreutzberger, familiarly known as Don Francisco. There was a daily afternoon show, "Hola América," in which viewers called in to play and compete for prizes, also featuring news briefs and interviews with celebrities, some of whom sang or performed in brief comedy sketches. It is hosted by Jose Rondstadt (a cousin of famous Mexican-American singer Linda Rondstadt); Maria Olga Fernández, a native of Chile; and Cuban-born Maty Monfort-Novia.

For the younger Hispanic-American viewers, Univisión produced "Cita con el Amor" (a Spanish-language version of "The Dating Game") which was hosted by Venezuelan Henry Zakka. There was also the prime-time talk-entertainment shows "Desde Hollywood" and "El Show de Paul Rodríguez." The former was hosted by Luca Bentivoglio, a Venezuelan born of Italian parents, featuring interviews with celebrities, show business news, and gossip. The latter, a late-night show, carried the name of its host, a Los Angeles Mexican-born comedian who did occasional comedy sketches and conducted interviews with guests from the world of entertainment.

TABLE 2B

The Univisión Spanish-Language Television Group, Affiliated UHF Stations, Fall 1993

Station		City, State
Full-Power		
WCIU	26	Chicago, IL
KORO	28	Corpus Christi, TX
KCEC	50	Denver, CO
KINT	26	El Paso, TX
KXLN	45	Houston, TX
KNVO	48	McAllen, TX
KREN	27	Reno, NV
KCSO	19	Sacramento, CA
KSMS	67	Salinas, CA
WMDO	48	Washington, DC
W46AR	46	Milwaukee, WI
KVER	4	Palm Desert, CA
KBNT	19	San Diego, CA
K07TA	7	Santa Barbara, CA
Low-Power		
K52AY	52	St. Louis, MO

This list does not include re-transmitter locations.

Joaquín F. Blaya, president of Telemundo (formerly Univisión).

Another late-night show is "Charytín International," which carried the name of popular Puerto Rican singer and host. In this weekly show Charytín also brought artists for interviews, singing, or participating in comedy sketches.

Aside from these regularly scheduled programs, by late 1991 Univisión also produced a number of musical and variety specials. The most popular of these were the national (U. S.) and international OTI song festivals, which have been telecast since 1972, and "Premio Lo Nuestro a la Música Latina," the annual Spanish-language version of the "Grammy" awards. This latter special which was produced in conjunction with *Billboard Magazine*, started in May 1989. Other specials accentuated Mother's and Father's Day, beauty pageants, Hispanic achievements, and heritage days in the United States, and national independence days in the Americas. For 1992, this included programs related to the quincentennial commemoration of Columbus' exploration of the Americas. Under the theme "Encuentro con lo Nuestro," Univisión scheduled 200 historical vignettes that explored key elements of the commemoration, 41 capsules on past and present Hispanic achievements, and another half-dozen special shows.

When the results of the Nielsen Ratings research (jointly funded by Univisión and Telemundo—see Bergsman, 1989c) came in by late 1992 the results were not as expected, especially in terms of viewership of the local productions. This brought various cancelations which coincided with another change in ownership of Univisión. Some of the details of those changes, which developed at the closing of this chapter, are presented below under *Transitions: 1993 and the Future.* Table 3 presents a typical schedule by program types and hours of Univisión's 24-hours-a-day, 7-day-per-week programming in fall 1993. When one compares these figures to similar data from two years ago (see Subervi 1993), the most significant change is found in the increased hours of talk, variety, comedy shows.

Telemundo: 1986-1992

While SIN and SICC were developing their powerful and far-reaching dominion, the growth and market potential of the Hispanic audience was being recognized by other interested parties such as Saul Steinberg, chairman of the board and chief executive officer (CEO) of Reliance Capital Group, L.P.; and Henry Silverman, the eventual president, CEO, and director of the Telemundo. Together with their investment partners, they founded the Telemundo Group, Inc., which is currently the second largest Spanish-language television network in the United States. Some discussions of this network

TABLE 3

Program Types and Hours of Each During a Typical Week. Univisión Network, Fall 1993

Type of program	Hours of broadcast during a typical Weekday	Saturday	Sunday
Novelas	10.0*	-	-
Talk/variety/comedy	8.5**	16.0†	7.0§
Music videos	-	1.0	1.0
Movies	2.0***	2.0	6.0§§
News, news magazine	2.5****	1.0‡‡	1.5§§§
Cartoons/children's shows	.5	2.0	2.0
Sports	-	.5	4.0§§§§
Religious/paid/etc.	.5	1.5	2.5

Legend

* 2.5 hours are repeated, fewer hours on Fridays, replaced with movies
** 2 hours are repeated
*** 6 hours on Fridays
**** .5 hour repeated
† 6.5 hours are repeated
†† .5 hour repeated
§ 2 hours are repeated
§§ 4 hours are repeated
§§§ .5 hour repeated
§§§§ .5 hour repeated

and its financial underpinnings have been published by several authors from which we draw for this section (see Beale 1986; Bergsman 1986; Berry 1987; Kilgore 1988; Valenzuela 1985a; and Wilkinson 1991). The most detailed financial accounts stem from the Telemundo Group's own corporate prospectus (Drexel Burnham Lambert 1987).

The organization of the Telemundo Group, Inc., began in May 1986, when Reliance Capital Group, L.P., acquired John Blair & Company, a diversified communication business. Blair had fallen potential prey to corporate raiders after an attempt at expansion left it overburdened with debt. Telemundo, as the successor to Blair, thus obtained stations WSCV Channel 51 in Miami and WKAQ Channel 2 in San Juan, Puerto Rico, which had been purchased by Blair in 1985 and 1983, respectively. Prior to its acquisition by Blair, WSCV was an English-language subscription television station. The station in Puerto Rico had been a major component of the Fundación Angel Ramos media enterprises and had its own island-wide retransmitter and affiliation network under the name adopted for the U. S. group–Cadena Telemundo (for an analysis of the mass media in Puerto Rico, see Subervi-Vélez et al. 1990). The WKAQ facilities consist of 250,000 square feet of operations space, including three master control rooms and nine fully equipped modern studios. On December 24, 1986, Reliance completed its acquisition of 100 percent of the outstanding common stock of Blair. Altogether, Reliance paid $325 million ($215 million of it for Blair's debt retirement) and immediately began selling off properties not connected to Spanish-language broadcasting. (According to the *Wall Street Journal*, due to its own debts, Reliance considered raising capital by selling the Puerto Rico station for $160 million in November 1988, but the sale was not consummated at that time.) The change of name to Telemundo Group, Inc., was officially established on April 10, 1987. This company went public with offerings of common stock and bonds during the summers of 1987 and 1988.

Prior to forming the Telemundo Group, Reliance had entered the Hispanic media market in April 1985 with its ownership interests in Estrella Communications, Inc. This latter company had been formed in January of that year for the purpose of buying Channel 52 in Los Angeles. Under the call letters KBSC and the corporate name SFN Communications, Inc., this station was owned by Columbia Pictures and A. Jerrold Perenchio who had launched it in the late 1970s to compete with KMEX for the Los Angeles Hispanic audience. At the time KBSC split its broadcast schedule, offering approximately ninety-five hours a week in Spanish. The remaining hours were sold to other programmers. According to Valenzuela, "in 1980 KBSC offered a pay-television service (ON-TV) in English at night and switched to full-time Spanish-language programs during the day" (1985a, 131). He adds that much of that station's Spanish-language programming was supplied by government station Channel 13 of Mexico. When KBSC was put on the market in 1985, Reliance Capital, a large shareholder of Estrella Communications, Inc., purchased a greater proportion of the stock for $38 million and began operating the station with new call letters KVEA. In December 1986 Reliance had spent $13.5 million to buy out the remaining minority holders of Estrella Communications, Inc., including some shares held by Hallmark Cards.

The third major component of the Telemundo Group was WNJU Channel 47 licensed in Linden, New Jersey, and serving the metropolitan New York area. This station was founded by Ed Cooperstein who had been the general manager of its predecessor–the English-language WATV Channel 13, which had started in the early 1960s in New York. That station soon underwent a series of ownership and programming changes. While in 1965 WNJU was primarily an Anglo station transmitting in the evenings, it also broadcast some Spanish-language variety shows. According to some historical internal files of the station, by the end of that year and in early 1966, "slightly half of WNJU-TV's programming catered to the Hispanic market." In 1971 the station was bought by Columbia Pictures via its subsidiary Screen Gems, which also owned WAPA Channel 4 in Puerto Rico. With the new structure, WNJU had access not only to Columbia's repertoire of films regularly marketed to Latin America, but also to a great variety of Spanish-language programs from Puerto Rico's WAPA. From these and other sources, WNJU broadcast was 60 percent Spanish-language programs such as *novelas*, live musical variety shows, sports, news, and community public affairs. Despite the new options for programs, Channel 47 faced numerous financial difficulties during its early years, leading to the firing of founder and general manager Ed Cooperstein in 1972, who was eventually replaced by Carlos Barba (Valenzuela 1985a). The challenge was even greater after SIN's WXTV Channel 41 was inaugurated in 1968 and began competing for the New York-New Jersey Hispanic audiences, which at the time had limited access to the UHF receivers. In 1980 Columbia relinquished its holdings to the station as it was purchased jointly by A. Jerrold Perenchio, Norman Lear, and other investors under Spanish-American Communications Corporation (SACC). These new owners planned to feature primarily sports and entertainment on prime time, but due to commitment problems they continued to run the Spanish-language programming–WNJU's strongest time block totaling seventy-four hours per week. It was because of the strength of the Spanish-language programs and Hispanic audience that WNJU was bought for approximately $75 million in December 1986 from Perenchio, Lear and SACC by Steinberg and his Reliance Capital Group.

The growth of Steinberg's television network continued in August 1987, when Telemundo bought out (for $15.5 million) National Group Television, Inc., the license holder of station KSTS Channel 48 serving the San Jose and San Francisco area. For the Houston/Galveston market, Telemundo invested $6.43 million to obtain the outstanding stock of Bluebonnet, which operated KTMD Channel 48 in that area in 1988. Another significant Hispanic market penetration came that year when Telemundo won over the affiliation of Chicago's WSNS Channel 26, which had been associated with Univisión. Until then, Telemundo's link to Chicago had been WCIU Channel 26. A year later entry was made into San Antonio with the affiliation of KVDA Channel 60. In August 1990 Telemundo paid nearly $3 million to purchase 85 percent of the stock of Nueva Vista, which operated KVDA. With these stations, its affiliations, and cable linkages, the Telemundo network was firmly established and potentially available to over 80 percent of Hispanic households in the United States.

During the early years the Telemundo stations shared some novelas and entertainment programs made available from WKAQ Channel 2 in Puerto Rico. It also imported other novelas from Brazil, Mexico, Venezuela, Argentina, and Spain. In 1987, of the thirty hours of weekly network programming, twenty hours consisted of novelas. A variety of movies and entertainment shows were also imported from these countries. From mid-1987 through 1989 "Super Sábados" was among the programs broadcast via satellite from the studios in Puerto Rico. This five-hour variety and game show had a large audience following on the island since 1984. Telemundo also broadcast international sports competition, particularly soccer matches. One of the distinct characteristics of this network's programming was the prompt venture to make local productions a large percentage of the offerings. A notable first was the start-up in July 1988 of "MTV Internacional"—a one-hour Spanish-language version of the MTV network's programming. Aimed at the bilingual Hispanic-American youth market, this new show was hosted in Spanish by Daisy Fuentes, a native of Cuba. It featured rock music videos by groups performing in both Spanish and English, music news, artist interviews, and concert footage. (This show, syndicated by Viacom Latino Americano, a division of Viacom International, Inc., was also seen in many Latin American countries.) Another first for Telemundo was the novela "Angélica, Mi Vida," produced in Puerto Rico. This soap opera, launched in August 1988, was specially directed to and based on the local audiences as "the plot appealed to regional Hispanic differences by webbing Mexican, Puerto Rican and Cuban immigrant families into [the traditional] novela elements: passion, power struggles, love and desire" (Seijo-Maldonado 1989, 26). One additional program, which is no longer on air, also deserves mention: "Feria de la Alegria," a contest and game show with audience participation. It was the first live Spanish-language television show of its kind broadcast on weekdays in the continental United States.

From 1987 to mid-1988, the "Noticiero Telemundo," the national news segment for this group's stations, was produced in Hialeah, Florida, by the Hispanic American Broadcasting Corporation (HBC). This company was founded by Gustavo Godoy (formerly at SIN news; see above) with the financial assistance of Amancio V. Suárez (of the Viva América radio group). Godoy's newscasts for Telemundo began on January 12, 1987, and marked the first national transmission for the emergent Telemundo. However, HBC's telecasts were short-lived when, in January 1988, Telemundo acquired this production company and facilities as part of their network building strategy. Between May 1988 and May 1993, Telemundo had a a co-production venture with Ted Turner's Cable News Network. "Noticiero Telemundo-CNN" combined news videos with Spanish-speaking journalists, camera crews, and news anchors, who used as their headquarters the CNN facilities in Atlanta, Georgia. From 1988 through 1990, Godoy became general manager of KTVW, a Univisión station in Phoenix, from which he returned to Telemundo, where he was president and director of news operations.

By January 1992 the Telemundo Group owned and operated Spanish-language television network in the United States six full-power stations and four low-power stations. It also owned the channel in San Juan, Puerto Rico, which was the network's only VHF station. Furthermore, Telemundo counted on the affiliation of six full-power and sixteen low-power stations), plus seven cable carriers that operated in fourteen of the fifty states plus the District of Columbia. Three other stations affiliated to Telemundo transmitted from Tijuana, Juárez, and Matamoros to serve the U. S. Hispanic communities in San Diego, El Paso, and McAllen/Brownsville, respectively. Tables 4A and 4B list the Telemundo network group composition as of fall 1993 reflecting the most recent transitions (see below). In 1992, the Telemundo network had the potential of reaching approximately 84 percent of the U. S. Hispanic households. At the time, the satellite used for program transmissions and station connections was the Spacenet II.

In addition to his duties as chairman of the board of Reliance Holdings Group, L.P., Steinberg assumed the role of President, CEO, and director of Telemundo when Silverman left the company in February 1990. In 1991, upon the resignation of the network's vice president Car-

TABLE 4A

The Telemundo Spanish-Language Television Group, Owned & Operated Stations, Fall 1993

Station		City, State
Full-Power		
KTMD	48	Houston, TX
KVEA	52	Los Angeles, CA
WSCV	51	Miami, FL
WNJU	47	New York, NY
KVDA	60	San Antonio, TX
KSTS	48	San Francisco, CA
WKAQ	2	San Juan, Puerto Rico
Low-Power		
K11SF	11	Austin, TX
K49CJ	49	Colorado Springs, CO
K60EE	60	Midland/Odessa, TX
K61F1	61	Modesto, CA
K60EE	60	Odessa, TX
K15CU	15	Salinas, CA
K47DQ	47	Sacramento, CA
K52BS	52	Santa Fe, NM
K52CK	52	Stockton, CA

TABLE 4B

The Telemundo Spanish-Language Television Group, Affiliated UHF Stations, Fall 1993

Station		City, State
Full-Power		
WSNS	44	Chicago, IL
KFWD	52	Dallas/Ft. Worth, TX
KUDB	59	Denver, CO
KSWT	13	El Centro/Yuma, CA
XHIJ	44	El Paso, TX
KMSG	59	Fresno, CA
KLDO	27	Laredo, TX
KBLR	39	Las Vegas, NV
XHRIO	2	McAllen/Brownsville, TX
WTGI	61	Philadelphia, PA
XHAS	33	San Diego, CA
KHRR	40	Tucson, AZ
Low-Power		
K59DB	59	Albuquerque, NM
KO8LQ	8	Alice, TX
W12CD	12	Altamonte Springs, FL
W67CI	67	Atlanta, GA
W19AH	19	Boston, MA
K49AY	49	Cheyenne, WY
K66EB	66	Corpus Christi, TX
KVAW	16	Eagle Pass, TX
W13BF	13	Hartford, CT
K13WE	13	Kingsville, TX
K46CS	46	Lubbock, TX
K49CD	49	Midland, TX
W07BZ	7	Orlando, FL
K64DR	64	Phoenix, AZ
K44DA	44	Plainview, TX
K48EJ	48	Salt Lake City, UT
K27EI	27	Santa Maria, CA
W65BX	65	Springfield, MA
KO8LU	8	Sunnyside, WA
W35AQ	35	Syracuse, NY
W57BA	57	Tampa, FL
K51BG	51	Victoria, TX
W42AJ	42	Washington, DC
K17CJ	17	Yakima, WA

los Barba (who became the president of Venevisión International and in 1992 the president and chief operating officer of the Univisión Television Group, Inc.), Telemundo created a three-member office of the president. The directors were W. Gary McBride, network president responsible for all network activities including programming, promotion, market research, marketing, and network sales; Donald M. Travis, station group president responsible for overseeing Telemundo's seven owned and operated stations and local and national spot sales; and Peter J. Housmann II, president of business and corporate affairs who was responsible for finance, legal, human resources, affiliate relations, and engineering. At that time, no person of Hispanic heritage was either member of the board of directors or in the highest echelons of this network. The main facilities, measuring 50,000 square feet and containing five production studios, was located in Hialeah, Florida, in the former building of the Hispanic American Broadcasting Corporation.

The "Noticiero Telemundo-CNN" arrangement, as discussed previously, continued (until May 1993). However, Telemundo also had its own news bureaus in Mexico, New York, Washington, and in Miami for coverage of the Caribbean and Central America. To supplement its knowledge of Hispanic community, Telemundo periodically commissions studies inquiring about numerous issues such as quality of life, economic concerns, discrimination, bilingual education, the political status of Puerto Rico, the free trade agreement with Mexico and Canada, and relations with Cuba.

In late 1991, Telemundo broadcasted approximately 126 hours a week between 7:00 a.m. to 1:00 a.m. The majority of domestically produced offerings were news programs and talk, variety, and comedy-type shows. A fact sheet from that year stated that "more than 50 percent of all programming aired on the network is produced in the United States at the company's production center in Hialeah, Florida, as well as at owned stations in Los Angeles and Puerto Rico." It adds that "these programs are directly targeted to the needs and lifestyles of Hispanic Americans." When the network was launched, it claimed that U. S.-based programming, especially for U. S. Hispanics, would be a key to Telemundo's long-term strategy, which sought to differentiate itself from Univisión and win the viewership of the more acculturated Hispanics (Kilgore 1988). In addition to the national and local news programs and the "MTV Internacional," Telemundo has more various programs intended to meet its strategy. The most prominent—"María Laria" (formerly "Cara a Cara")—has been a talk-show hosted by Cuban-born María Laria. This program, Telemundo's own version of the "Oprah Winfrey show," has covered controversial topics such as abortion, drugs, sex, religion, politics, crime, and AIDS. Another domestic program has been "Occurió Así," a daily newsmagazine show hosted by Enrique Gratas, a native of Argentina. This investigative news reporting program has utilized the network's news bureaus in New York, Los Angeles, and Latin America to probe "the news behind the news that shape our world." In mid-1991, Telemundo was also broadcasting "El Magnate," another locally produced *novela* in the form of a dramatic series with the backdrop of modern Miami. Except for "María Laria" and the national news, the others originated in Florida.

At the height of its formative years, Telemundo also embarked on the production of specials. One of their more popular offerings was "Esta Noche con Usted," (presently, "Esta Noche Con Cecilia Bolocco"), a four-times-a-year series of "in-depth, one-on-one interviews with noted Latino personalities in film, music, television, the performing arts, science and business." This one-hour program was being hosted by the former Miss Universe, Chilean Cecilia Bolocco, who had also been co-anchor to the "Noticiero Telemundo-CNN." "Columbus Day," another special for 1992, focused on the theme of the quincentennial anniversary of the navigator's voyage to the Americas. That voyage and related activities taking place in Spain during 1992 was featured in the weekly cultural magazine "Línea América" produced by EFE, the national news agency of Spain. In addition, Telemundo produces and/or distributes a number of specials such as "Carnaval Internacional de Miami," featuring musical and artistic highlights of the carnival; and the "Miss Hispanidad" beauty pageant, which draws from contestants to the Miss Universe pageant. Other musical and variety specials were regularly imported from Venezuela, Mexico, Argentina, and Spain. Future plans for Telemundo include increased local productions, some of which may themselves be exported to Latin America. Table 5 presents a typical schedule by program types and hours of Telemundo's programming in fall 1993. By then it had increased to approximately 133 hours per week as it broadcast 19 hours per day (7-2:00 a.m. Monday-Friday and 8-3:00 a.m. weekends). The most notable change from programming from mid-1991 (see Subervi 1993), is a decrease in the time allocated for movies during weekdays and Saturdays. However, more time is given to talk, variety, comedy shows on weekdays and Saturdays, while on Sundays these types of programs receive less time.

In November 1991 the Telemundo Group also became involved in a different type of venture—the collaborative promotion of the first Spanish-English bilingual credit card. The bank issuing the Visa and Master Cards was the People's Bank of Connecticut. The Telemundo stations informed the public that the network was part of a financial service targeted primarily to Hispanic-Americans. The service was distinct in that it provided bilingual applications, customer information and assistance, as well as the lower than average interest rates.

Galavisión: 1979-1992

Until the Azcárragas and Televisa reacquired Univisión in 1993 (see below) the third major player in Spanish-language television in the United States was Galavisión. This television company was launched in 1979 under the parent company of Univisa, Inc., a subsidiary of Mexico's Televisa. At that time, Galavisión was a premium cable service offering recently produced Spanish-language movies along with coverage of select sporting events and special entertainment shows. In early 1988 it had only 160,000 subscribers. But in September of that year, after the entry of Telemundo network and the consolidation of Hallmark's Univisión network, Univisa started to convert Galavisión's cable operations to an advertising-based basic cable service. This change expanded Galavisión's audience substantially as potentially 2 million cable subscribers can then receive Galavisión's programs.

The new format offered twenty-four-hours-a-day programming via a network feed provided by the Galaxy I and Spacenet 2 satellites. In addition Galavisión expanded to over-the-air offerings when it affiliated stations KWHY Channel 22 in Los Angeles, KTFH Channel 49 in Houston, KSTV Channel 57 in Santa Barbara, and low-power retransmitters in seven other cities. KWHY and KTFH were converted from English-language sta-

TABLE 5

Program Types and Hours of Each During a Typical Week Telemundo Network, Fall 1993

Types of program	Hours of broadcast during a typical Weekday	Saturday†	Sunday
Novelas	6.0	-	-
Talk/variety/comedy	2.0	2.0	3.0
Music videos	1.0*	1.0*	-
Movies	6.5**	7.0	8.5
News, news magazine	3.0	-	-
Cartoons/children shows	1.5	4.0	1.5
Sports	-	3.0	2.0
Misc. (educational/religioius/paid)	1.5***	3.0††	3.0§

Legend
* Fridays and Saturdays only, Saturday is repeat of Friday's program
** 4 hours only on Fridays
*** Fridays only
† on air 20 hours on Saturdays
†† one hour is for local programming
§ 1.5 hours dedicated to local programming

tions; KSTV was licensed for the first time for Galavisión. Some stations broadcasted Galavisión part time (typically from 3:00 p.m. to 2:00 a.m.) while others had twenty-four-hour coverage. (The method of delivery for Galavisión reverted to cable only when Televisa regained control of Univisión. See below under Transitions: 1992-93).

Galavisión, operated under the separate entity of what was then SIN, Inc., and was not included in the sales of SICC and SIN to Hallmark. During those years, Univisa operated from Los Angeles where it was parent to other companies, including Video Visa, a videocassette distributor; and in Mexicali, Mexico: Plasticus, a videocassette manufacturing operation that produced more cassettes than Sony, Kodak, or 3M and also operated the world's largest video dubbing facility, Central de Video, S.A. de C.V. (see Bergsman 1989a).

Until early 1992, the structure of Galavisión continued as described above in terms of the principal directors, the Univisa, Inc., subsidiary companies, the stations owned and operated as well as the affiliate linkages. The principal executives at the time were president Jaime Dávila, a native of Mexico; vice president of broadcasting operations Stuart Livingston, native of the United States; and Vera González, a native of Guatemala, who was national director of cable operations. As of late 1991, the Galavisión network affiliates in the United States consisted of 3 full-power UHF stations and 7 low-power stations. In addition, programming was provided via cable affiliations with 228 systems across the United States. Through its Mexican network, Galavisión's programs were also seen most everywhere in that country as well as in Latin America, Western Europe, and Northern Africa.

In terms of programming, Galavisión executives stated that the network intended to tailor its offerings primarily to Hispanics of Mexican and Central American origin. They felt that Univisión and Telemundo attempted to reach too diverse an audience by broadcasting coast to coast; Galavisión was therefore concentrating its efforts west of the Mississippi River where its target audience typically resided (Besas 1990). Thus, Galavisión provided "unfiltered" Mexican television to the United States twenty-four hours-a-day, seven days a week. In 1992, The major block of daily programs, thirteen hours, consisted of news from the ECO system (Empresas de Comunicaciones Orbitales). Via satellite, ECO links a news production center in Mexico City to the rest of Latin America, Europe, and the United States. Movies were transmitted two hours per weekday and eighteen hours on weekends. *Novelas* were broadcast about four hours each weekday, but none of those novelas or the other shows are made in the United States with Hispanic Americans. Table 6 presents a typical schedule by program types and hours of Galavisión's 24-hour-a-day, 7-day-per-week programming in fall 1993. The most notable change from programming from mid-1991 (see Subervi 1993), is that on weekends there are fewer movies but more music video programs.

Galavisión's parent company Televisa saw the U. S. Hispanic market as one of the top growth areas for the next decade and thus continued to make inroads into this market. As summarized below, the most dramatic thrust was the repurchasing of Univisión.

The Formation of Other Hispanic-Oriented TV Companies and Program Ventures

While the aforementioned networks were dominating the majority of the U. S. Hispanic audience in terms of general programming, several companies were seeking their own niche in this market. One of the first to do so was *International TeleMúsica, Inc.*, which produced a show featuring international music videos, entertainment news, promotions, and life-style segments. Hosted by Alex Sellar, a Spaniard, and Pilar Isla, a native of Mexico, the show was produced in Hollywood using various California landscapes for settings. The target audience was the Hispanic and Latin American youth. In 1990 Jesús Garza Rapport, executive vice president of TeleMúsica, started this company with full financial backing from Radio Programas de México (RPM). A Mexican company, RPM owned thirty and operated fifty radio stations in that country and also owned one television station in Guadalajara, Mexico. RPM owners Clemente Serna and family were among the principal contenders for acquiring the Red 7, a group of Mexican government stations to be sold to the private sector. After experimenting during 1990 in RPM's Channel 6 in Guadalajara, TeleMúsica's first two-hour show in the United States was telecast

TABLE 6

Program Types and Hours of Each During a Typical Week
Galavisión Network, Fall 1993

Types of program	Hours of broadcast during a typical Weekday	Saturday	Sunday
Novelas	6.0*	-	-
Variety/comedy	4.0**	4.0	5.0
Movies	-	4.0	2.0
ECO news/magazine	12.0***	7.0	6.0
Music videos	-	6.0	2.5
Cartoons/children's shows	-	-	5.5
Sports	2.0****	2.0	3.0
Documentary	-	1.0	-

Legend
* 3 hours are repeated
** 5 hours on Wednesdays, 8 hours on Fridays
*** 13 hours on Wednesdays, 10 hours on Thursdays and Fridays
**** 0 hours on Wednesdays and Fridays, 4 hours on Thursdays

in September 1991 from Miami on the Univisión network. That same month, distribution began for five separate one-hour shows to air Monday through Friday aimed at the Mexican market via the Red 7 network. In October the weekday shows reached the five South American affiliates—Ecuador, El Salvador, Nicaragua, Guatemala, and Costa Rica—via the Pan American international network satellite launched by René Anselmo. Puerto Rican John Figueroa, vice-president of affiliate relations, indicated that the shows reached their targeted youth audience even beyond the locations where TeleMúsica was licensed, as evidenced by the fan club correspondence from all over Latin America.

Another company seeking to form its niche in the U. S. Hispanic market in 1991 was Viva television Network, Inc. in an information brochure of the company, it claimed to be "the first U. S. latino owned national cable television network." At the time, Viva's aim was to provide sixteen-hour daily Spanish-language (and some English-language) programs such as documentaries, public affairs, music, sports, comedy, news, children's shows, art films, and movies catered to the eighteen to forty-nine year old Hispanic audience. The chief executive officer and one of the founders was Mark Carreño, a native of Cuba who has served as executive director of the Latino Consortium, a nationally syndicated network based at KCET-TV, the Los Angeles Public Broadcasting Station. Other founders and executive staff included chief operating officer Guillermo Rodríguez, a native of Puerto Rico who had worked with KMEX-TV and Lorimar Telepictures; and vice-president of international operations Esteban de Icaza, of Mexican heritage, who had been president of Azteca films, the foreign distribution company of the Mexican Government. De Icaza's connections with that company and Imevisión, Mexico's educational television company, helped Viva obtain exclusive rights for telecasting selections from these companies' movie and video libraries, as well as Immevisión's newscasts. For program delivery, Viva was going to sublease a transponder from the General Electric cable satellite and enter in agreements with multisystem cable operators in major Hispanic markets.

Home Box Office's *Selecciones en Español* was another significant venture to capture a niche in the U. S.-Hispanic television audience. In January 1989 this service was inaugurated to provide HBO and Cinemax cable subscribers the option of Spanish-language audio for the telecast motion pictures and even some sporting events such as boxing matches. This service is the brainchild of Lara Concepción, a native of Mexico, who after eight years of trying was able to persuade HBO's executives that there was a viable Hispanic market for such service (Arias 1990). The turning point for Concepción's efforts came shortly after the box office success of the Hispanic-themed movie "La Bamba." Following a market study that further convinced HBO that it could expand its business with the Spanish-speaking audience, HBO scheduled about ten Spanish-dubbed movies per month in 1989. At first, Selecciones en Español was provided to 20 HBO and Cinemax cable operators in five cities: El Paso, Miami, New York, San Antonio, and San Diego. Shortly thereafter, the service was requested by an additional 35 cable firms and later by another 15 (Valle 1989). By the end of 1989, HBO expanded its dubbed activities and was offering an average of twenty movies per month in Spanish. In 1991, Selecciones en Español was carried by 182 cable systems within the United States. HBO and Cinemax cable operators had three methods for delivering this service: a channel dedicated to Selecciones, a second audio program (SAP) channel available to stereo television sets or to video cassette recorders with multiple channel television sound (MTS), and an FM tuner in which the affiliates can transmit the second audio feed via an FM modulator, i.e., cable subscribers listen to the Spanish soundtrack on their FM radio.

Based on the formidable success with the U. S. Spanish-speaking audience, HBO launched in October 1991 HBO-Olé Pay-TV service in Latin America and the Caribbean Basin. This allowed cable subscribers in over twenty Latin American countries prompt access in Spanish to HBO's movies and other shows supplied by Warner Brothers; 20th Century-Fox; and Columbia TriStar International Television, which provides feature films from Columbia Pictures and TriStar Pictures. (The sports cable network ESPN also began providing Spanish-language telecasts for the Latin American market in January 1991 but had not provided this service for the U. S. Hispanic audiences.)

Long before HBO started applying the SAP and related technologies to establish their particular niches in the Hispanic market, other Anglo television businesses had successfully used Spanish-language audio to provide selected programs to their audiences. In Los Angeles, one of the most successful ventures with SAP was Fox's affiliate KTLA Channel 5. This station, owned by the Tribune Broadcasting Company, was the pioneer in taking advantage of the Federal Communication Commission's 1984 rule authorizing broadcasters and cable providers to split up the single soundtrack into four audio channels. Henceforth, the first track was for the English audio, the second for stereo, the third for any alternate language, and the fourth for data transmission. In October of same year of the FCC ruling, KTLA broadcast the movie (*2,001: A Space Odyssey* and began offering the "The Love Boat," "McMillan Wife," "Columbo," and "McCloud" in Spanish via the third audio channel. Dubbed editions of these programs were readily available because some Hollywood producers had a long-standing policy of dubbing many of their programs for their Latin American markets (Valle 1991). Then in February 1985, KTLA hired Analía Sarno-Riggle to be the Spanish interpreter of the "News at Ten," which airs Monday through Friday from 10:00 to 11:00 p.m. While in 1984 the pilot program with three other interpreters had not succeeded, the public response to Sarno-Riggle was formidable, as she developed an accurate technique to provide the Spanish-speaking viewers an adequate representation of what they were getting on the screen. She also established her own "audio personality,"not just a mimic of the people she was interpreting.

Given her success, especially as evidenced by ratings among Hispanic viewers, by July 1985 KTLA made Sarno-Riggle a regular staff employee and committed to continue the service. A native of Argentina, Sarno-Riggle considered her own simulcast interpretations an alternative to Univisión's and Telemundo's news. She believed it offered access to a larger and more diverse amount of local news, which may be preferred by some assimilated Hispanics or by those who simply wish to be informed on the same issues their neighbors are tuned into. Subsequently, KTLA assigned her to the Hollywood Christmas parade and various other specials. The station also expanded its offerings of Spanish-language audio for more of its prime-time programs such as "Airwolf," "Magnum, P.I.," and "Knight Rider." These programs were also among those dubbed for foreign distribution by their producers. In early 1992, KTLA scheduled approximately twenty hours per week of Spanish-language audio.

The Hispanic audience ratings of KTLA did not go unnoticed by other stations and networks in Los Angeles and elsewhere. The SAP was promptly adopted by various other Anglo broadcasters in large Hispanic markets, including the Tribune Broadcasting Company's Chicago and New York stations WGN Channel 9 and WPIX Channel 11. Even some nonprofit stations began this language option. For example, KCET Channel 28 hired Sarno-Riggle for ten months to do the Spanish-language audio for "By the Year 2000," a weekly half-hour public affairs program for Southern California. Also, under Sarno-Riggle's guidance, on January 14, 1991, New York station WNET Channel 13 began the second audio for "The MacNeil/Lehrer News-Hour." Bolivian native Oscar Ordenes was the Spanish-language voice for this show, which in the United States was being carried by thirty-three Public Broadcasting System stations either via SAP or as a separate show repeated later in the evening. In addition, thirty-two cities in twenty-six Latin American countries received videos of this version of the "MacNeil/Lehrer News Hour" by way of the United States Information Agency's Worldnet information program.

Finally, English-language musical programs specifically oriented toward U. S. Hispanics are also made their debut when in June 1991 MTV launched "Second Generation," a half-hour mix of videos, comedy, and entertainment news aimed primarily at second generation Hispanics in the United States. Hosted by New York Puerto Rican Andy Panda and Colombian Tony Moran, this program was broadcasted by thirty-one primarily English-language stations from the East to the West Coast.

Transitions: 1992-1993 and the Future

A combination of factors affected considerable change in the U. S. Spanish-language television industry in 1992 and 1993. Most consequential was a change in ownership at the Univisión network. In early April 1992 Hallmark Cards Corp. announced that it had entered an agreement to sell the network to an investor group comprised of A. Jerrold Perenchio (a previous owner of the Spanish-language station WNJU in New Jersey, and an unsuccessful bidder for Univisión when Hallmark purchased it in 1986); and two of the richest and most influential media magnates in Latin America, Emilio Azcárraga Milmo (the controlling owner of the Mexican media conglomerate Televisa) and Gustavo and Ricardo Cisneros (of the powerful Venezuelan broadcast corporation Venevision). Hallmark claimed it was streamlining its media holdings after acquiring a cable television system in 1991 (Cencom Cable Associates) but the company's dissatisfaction with the return on its Univisión investment was well-known. The ownership arrangement that was announced in April 1992 and approved by the FCC in September 1992 had Perenchio owning 76% of the television station group and 50% of the network with Azcárraga and Cisneros each holding 12% of the station group (to conform with U. S. foreign ownership laws) and 25% of the network. A concomitant outcome of this change of ownership was that Televisa's (and Univisa's) Galavisión network which was primarily delivered via cable with a few UHF retransmitters (see above) terminated its contracts with the few stations that were broadcasting its signals over the air. Thus, it became an exclusively cable delivery system just as it was when it started operations in 1979. This change helped reduce the competition that would have resulted between two of Televisa's own media subsidiaries—Univisión and Galavisión.

Between the sale's announcement and approval of the sale of Univisión to Televisa, protests were made from within and without the industry. The internal dissent originated an employee-buyout offer. Network president Joaquin Blaya had not been forewarned of the sale, and within two months left his post to become president of Telemundo. He was followed by José Cancela, then manager of WLTV in Miami; José del Cueto, Univision's domestic sales chief; and Filiberto Fernández, vice president for business development (Lopes 1992). Blaya cited the new owner's plan to scale back U. S. production of Spanish-language shows as the reason for his departure. Objections originating from outside the industry also focused on program production. The National Hispanic Media Coalition, the National Puerto Rican Forum and the G.I. Forum are Hispanic political organizations, which along with Telemundo, filed petitions with the FCC to deny transfer of the Univisión stations to the Perenchio-Azcárraga-cisneros group. The petitioners' argued that allowing the Latin Americans in would stifle competition between the networks, reduce the level of U. S. production as more imported programs flowed in and reduced the number of U. S. Hispanics employed in the industry. In its decision, the FCC emphasized Perenchio's experience as a media owner, found the sale to conform with U. S. law, denied the petitions and approved the license transfer (7 FCC Rcd. 6672; 1992).

At the time of this writing, the Univisión programs were seen in 18 Latin American countries and reached 91 percent of all U. S. Hispanic households through 36 broadcast affiliates and more than 600 cable affiliates. The Univisión Television Network was headed by Jaime Dávila, chairman and chief executive officer; Ray Rodríguez, president and chief operating officer; Raúl Toraño, president of network sales; Stuart Livingston, vice president and director of affiliate relations; and Guillermo Martínez who continues as vice president of news and sports. For the Univisión Network Limited Partnership, the operating company for the network, the managing directors were Ricardo Cisneros, Fernando Diez Barroso, A. Jerrold Perenchio, and Stephen Rader. The Univisión Television Group, Inc., a separate entity that holds the licenses for the stations, was headed by A. Jerrold Perenchio, chairman and chief executive officer; Carlos Barba, president and chief operating officer; and George Bank, executive vice president and chief financial officer.

Early in 1993, as the petitioners had predicted, the new owners of Univisión did terminate several shows and reduce the network staff. Since staff reductions and other changes are typical occurrences during ownership transitions, it is dangerous to speculate on the role played by foreign ownership. The Nielsen Hispanic Television Index's first release of national ratings in mid January assisted the Univisión management's production cutback decisions. U. S.-produced shows eliminated due to poor ratings were the aforementioned programs "Charytin Internacional" and "Portada," and "Al Mediodia," a mid-day talk show which had linked studios, hosts and callers-in from several Univisión studios nationwide. Staff reductions associated with these cancellations terminated 70 employees, and two or the three shows were replaced with Televisa programs (Puig 1993a, 1993b).

The Nielsen Hispanic Television Index was first proposed in 1989 in order to generate more accurate measurements of television viewing by U. S. Hispanics. Funded principally by Univisión and Telemundo which hope to garner higher advertising rates, the index is also partially supported by advertising agencies and advertisers such as (Anheuser-Busch and The Clorox Company). The index, which measures viewing of English as well as Spanish-language program viewing, employs "people meters" placed in 800 Hispanic households which were chosen for how representative they were in terms of language spoken in the home and geographic location ("Nielsen releases" 1993). The November 1992 national ratings placed only 4 Telemundo programs in the Spanish-language top 20 with the highest showing in 7th place. It must be emphasized, however, that success in a few key markets–such as KVEA's strong showing in the May 1993 Los Angeles sweeps–can sustain Telemundo as a strong competitor.

Neither network was on solid financial footing in late 1993. The Univisión purchase was executed with shaky financing in spite of the investors' strong portfolios ("The secrets" 1993). In 1992 the company continued a three-year string of losses by posting a $39 million loss on revenues of $200 million. A planned $140 million issue of subordinated notes was announced in April 1993; potential investors were warned of Univisión's highly leveraged position (Cole 1993). Nevertheless, the expectations of improved market share and profits for the network is evident as it continues to invest in technology as with the October 1993 purchase of nearly $2 million in digital equipment for the Univisión produced programs, post-production, and broadcast operations. One month earlier, a programming investment had been made when the network and the television group agreed to extend their arrangement with Cable News Network (CNN) for broadcast news services.

On the business side, Telemundo was forced by a group of its investors into involuntary bankruptcy in June 1993. The network had been negotiating with bond-holders since it had failed to make a payment on its $283 million debt in February 1992 (Ozemhoya 1993). Several junk bonds issues were made in the late 1980s to raise operating capital and to finance station acquisitions; the network was still operating in the red when the bonds came due. In terms of its principal executives, Saul Steinberg continued as chairman of the board. Juaquín Blaya was made president and CEO. Peter Housman remained as president of business and corporate affairs, while José Cancela was appointed president of the station group.

The financial difficulties notwithstanding, the optimism for recovery and growth at Telemundo is evident in various ways. By fall 1993, the network reached 85.4 percent of Hispanic television households in 53 markets on the U. S. mainland. It also reached practically all of Puerto Rico by way of its owned and operated station

WKAQ Channel 2 on the island (programming in this station, however, is significantly different from that shown in the U. S.). Some of the network produced programs are now syndicated to international markets. Furthermore, in June 1993, Telemundo leased two C-band transponders on Hughes Communications' Galaxy IV satellite for the transmission of the network's programs. The same month, Telemundo signed an agreement with Major League Baseball to produce a weekly baseball magazine show for the network. One month earlier, in May, in an effort to generate greater cash flow for Telemundo, president and CEO Juaquín Blaya set in motion a 24-hour international news effort in collaboration with the British Broadcasting Corporation (BBC) and Reuters. Telemundo's five year news production agreement with CNN ended in May 1993. The new partnership will rely on Reuters' international news gathering resources, BBC World Service Television's distribution network and Telemund's on-and-off screen talent. The new service will compete with Noticiero Univisión which continues to be distributed internationally by the new ownership, with the aforementioned ECO service, and "Canal de Noticias NBC," a 24-hour, Spanish-language news service by NBC which was launched in March 1993.

News is not the only area in which English-language media corporations are attempting to penetrate Spanish-language markets. A second wave of entertainment programming from the libraries and studios of major Hollywood producers and cable programmers is washing over Latin American markets. ESPN International, HBO Olé and TNT Latin America have been joined by "Marte TV," a co-production effort by Warner Bros. and Marte TV of Venezuela; "Cine Canal," a movie channel organized as a joint venture between a pay television system operators in Latin America and paramount, MGM, Universal and 20th Century Fox; "MTV Latin America," a new 24-hour music video service which also targets U. S. audiences; a Spanish-language version of the USA Network; and "Tele-Uno" a joint venture between Spelling Entertainment and several South American cable TV operators. Two new services created by U. S. Hispanic and Latin American interests are La Cadena Deportiva, a rival sports channel to ESPN and GEMS, a series originating from RCTV in Venezuela which concentrates its efforts on female audiences.

An economic upturn and return to political democracy in may Latin American countries has combined with rapid growth of pay television systems in many of the region's major cities to attract media companies which have been eager to globalize since the 1980s. The financial returns on the new services were minimal or non-existent as of late 1993, but like the U. S. Spanish-language networks, the investors are hoping to profit in the longer term as markets mature.

Regardless of the free trade agreement between the United States, Mexico, and Canada the media industries in these countries and the communication flows between them and the rest of the the hemisphere are likely to expand through the next century. The U. S. Hispanic-oriented media owned by Latinos, Anglos, or combination of business interests including those from Latin America will also grow assuming three conditions are met: first, that mainstream media continue to exclude or be discriminatory in their portrayals and employment of Hispanics; second, that there is a steady or increasing number of Hispanics seeking information and entertainment content that satisfied their distinct needs—including the maintenance of their language and their identity as people with valued heritages from Puerto Rico, Mexico, Cuba, etc.; and third, that entrepreneurs and businesses—continue recognizing the monetary and cultural profits to be made from Hispanic diversity. Given the patterns of this chapter, the demographic changes mentioned elsewhere in this volume, and the profitability of at least some of the media mentioned above, it seems likely that Latinos in the United States will continue to have numerous channels of communication directed especially to them.

Summary

The first part of this chapter made evident that since the 1840s Latinos and their life in and outside of the united States has been portrayed in predominantly limited, stereotyped and unfavorable ways in print, film, television and advertising. While significant positive changes occurred throughout the years,the overall balance is still on the negative side, not so much due to blatant injurious stereotypes but to the absence of the variety of Hispanics and their values as they exist across all sectors of society. Clearly, there are also serious and continuous underrepresentations in the employment of Latinos and other minorities in America's media industries. From the every day selection, production and dissemination of news to the conceptualization, creation and production of entertainment, the proportion of Hispanics i the workforce is significantly smaller in the media than it is in society at large.

The second part of this chapter showed that Hispanic-oriented media in the U. S. have an extensive history developing closely at par and even sometimes ahead of mainstream media. This was shown to be true for print media from the 1800s to the still emergent cable and satellite transmissions and ventures. As we move to the twenty-first century, Spanish-language and English-language media directed at Hispanics in the United States, and more recently directed towards Latinos in Mexico, Central America, the Caribbean, and South America, will continue to grow as such media are deemed profitable by national (U. S.) and international companies exploring and exploiting the global communications markets.

What remains to be seen and assessed is whether or not Hispanics within the United States will be at the forefront of developing the new content and media affecting their lives. Indeed, who will be deciding the quality and diversity of Hispanic images or content related to Hispanics in mainstream and Latino-oriented media? And, who will be among the prominent financial beneficiaries of the profits made from the media particularly directed at Hispanics? Answers to these and other inquiries are left to the next generation of students and scholars who follow the trails of the authors cited in these pages.

In guiding the work that still needs to be done, we conclude by stressing two educational and employment solutions that merit prompt attention. First, communication as well as general educational curriculum in the United States should incorporate systematic analysis and discussions of how the mass media treat Hispanic—including Latin Americans, and other ethnic minorities (see Subervi-Vélez 1993). Future generations of students—especially those who will eventually participate in the image industries—must be ever more aware of the causes and consequences of stereotyping and other forms of discriminatory inclusions and exclusions of selected segments of society. While this is especially needed with respect to mainstream media, attention should also be given to English-language as well as Spanish-language media directed to Hispanics. At times they too portray with stereotypes an exlcusions Hispanics and "others," especially those of darker skin colors and/or lower social classes. Second, employment practices in the mainstream media should eradicate past discrimination procedures and make room for people of all ethnic backgrounds—particularly those who are cognizant of and sensitive to the diversity of the growing multiethnic and multicultural populations. Again, the same applies for Hispanic-oriented media regardless of the language in which it is produced or its ownership-Hispanic or other wise. The richness and positive diversity of the Hispanic heritages should be a prime goal of all media in the United States.

Bibliography

Americas Review, The

1989 *La Prensa*: nine articles about the past and present history of the San Antonio newspaper in a special issue of *Americas Review*, 17.3-4:121-84.

Anonymous

1990 "Interview with Tomas Ybarra Frausto: The Chicano Alternative Film Movement." *Centro*, 2.8.

Arias, Armando A., Jr.

1985 "Mass Mediated Images of Undocumented Mexicans." Paper presented at the annual conference of the Western Society of Criminology, Reno, Nevada.

Arias, Carlos

1990 "Lara Concepción: 'Cerebro' de Programación en Español de HBO." *Noticias del Mundo*, (February):B9.

Arias, M. Beatriz

1982 "Educational television: Impact on the Socialization of the Hispanic Child." *Television and the Socialization of the Minority Child.* Eds G. L. Berry and C. Mitchell-Kernan. New York: Academic P, pp 203-211.

Arnheim, Rudolf and Martha C. Bayne

1941 "Foreign Language Broadcasting over Local American Stations." *Radio Research 1941*. Eds P. Lazersfelf and F. Stanton. New York: Duell, Sloan & Pearce.

Beale, Steve

1986 "Trumoil and Growth." *Hispanic Business*, (December):52.

1988 "A Hallmark in the Takeover of Spanish TV." *Hispanic Business*, (May):21.

Berg, Charles Ramirez

1988 "Images and Counterimages of the Hispanic in Hollywood." *Tontantzin: Chicano Arts in San Antonio*, 6.1:12-13.

1989 "Immigrants, Aliens, and Extraterrestrials: Science Fiction's Alien 'Other' as, (Among *Other* Things) new Hispanic Imagery." *CineACTION!*, 18:3-17.

1990 "Sterotyping in Films in General and of the Hispanic in Particular." *Howard Journal of Communications*, 2.3:286-300.

Berger, Arthur Asa

1976 *The TV Guided American.* New York: Walker & Co.

Bergsman, Steve

1986 "New Blood, Fresh Money." *Hispanic Business*, (December):36.

1988 "New & Improved " *Hispanic Business*, (December):42-50.

1989a "Univisa's World View." *Hispanic Business*, (April):22-23.

1989b "Controversy Hits L.A.'s Spanish Television." *Hispanic Business*, (September):42-48.

1989c "Item: Networks Invest in Nielsen Ratings." *Hispanic Business*, (December):38-41.

Berry, Gordon L., and Claudia Mitchell-Kernan

1982 "Television as a Socializing Force within a Society of Mass Communication." *Television and the Socialization of the Minority Child*, New York: Academic P, pp 1-11.

Berry, John F.

1987 "The New Order at Blair." *Channels: The Business of Communications*, (April):53-56.

Besas, Peter

1990 "Univisa Setting Up Hispano Network in U. S." *Variety*, vol 41, (March):560.

Bielby, William and Denise Bielby

1987 *The 1987 Hollywood Writers' Report: Unequal Access, Unequal Pay.* Commissioned by the Writers Guild of America, West, Los Angeles, CA.

1989 *The 1989 Hollywood Writers' Report: Unequal*

Access, Unequal Pay. Commissioned by the Writers Guild of America, West, Los Angeles, CA.

Blosser, Bettsy J.

1988 "Ethnic Differences in Children's Media Use." *Journal of Broadcasting and Electronic Media,* 32.4:453-470.

Border, Jeff

1989 "Investors in Spanish Daily Hope to Add Gloss." *Crian's Chicago Business,* (October 2):54

Broadcasting

1989 "The Coming of Age of Hispanic Broadcasting: Special Report." (April 3).

1991a "Mac Tichnenor: Banking on Hispanic Radio." (May 13):87.

1991b "Hispanic Owners Band Together." (May 20):40.

Brown, Cynthia

1980 "Stong-Arming the Hispanic Press." *Columbia Journalism Review,* (July/August):51-54.

Bunnell, Robert

1984 "A.K.A. Pablo: ABC's New Latino Comedy Series." *Nuestro,* (April):15-16.

Chacon, Ramon

1977 "The Chicano Immigrant press in Los Angeles: The Case of El Heraldo de Mexico, 1916-1920." *Journalism History,* 4.2:48-9.

Chavira, Ricardo

1975 "Reporting in Two Los Angeles Dailies of Mexican Deportation and Emigration from the United States." Unpublished Masters Thesis, California State U, Northridge.

1977 "A Case Study: Reporting of Mexican Emigration and Deportation." *Journalism History,* 4.2:59-61.

Committee on Minorities

1982 "Minorities and Newspapers. A Report by the Committee on Minorities for the American Society of Newspaper Editors," (May).

Cortes, Carlos

1987 "The Mexican-American Press." *The Ethnic Press in the United States: A Historical Analysis and Handbook.* Ed S. M. Miller. New York: Greenwood P, pp 247-60.

1991 "Power, Passivity and Pluralism: Mass Media in the Development of Latino Culture and Identity." Paper presented at the Hispanic History and Culture Conference, U of Wisconsin, Milwaukee, (April).

Corwin, Miles

1989 "A Voice for Farm Workers." *Los Angeles Times,* (August 20):3, 33.

Cox, Dorrit Sue

1969 "Spanish-Language Television in the United States: Its Audience and its Potential." Unpublished Master's Thesis, U of Illinois.

Crister, Greg

1987 "The Feud that Topp led a TV Empire." *Channels: The Business of Communications,* (January):28.

CV 76 3451

1976 *Fouce Amusement Enterprises, Inc., Metropolitan Theaters Corporation vs. Spanish International Communications Corporation.* United States Federal District Court, Central District of California, Los Angeles. Case Number CV 76 35411 IH, (November 4).

Davidson, Bill

1974 "The Reformation of Chico and the Man." *TV Guide,* vol 22, (November 23):25-9.

Del Olmo, Frank

1971 "Voices for the Chicano Movement." *Quill,* (October):8-11.

Delpar, Helen

1984 "Goodbye to the Greaser: Mexico, the MPP DA, and Derogatory Films, 1922-26." *Journal of Popular Film and Television,* 12.1:34-40.

de Uriarte, Mercedes

1980 "Battle for the Ear of the Latino." *Los Angeles Time Calendar,* (December 14):5.

Diario Las Americas

1990 "Reader Profile, 1990." Miami, FL: *Diario Las Americas.*

Downing, John D.H.

1990 "Ethnic Minority Radio in the United States." *Howard Journal of Communications,* vol 2, (spring):135-48.

Drexel, Burnham Lambert

1987 *Prospectus: 2,000,000 Shares: Telemundo Group, Inc., Common Stock,* (August 19).

Ericksen, Charles A.

1981 "Hispanic Americans and the Press." *Journal of Intergroup Relations,* 9.1:3-16.

Evans, James

1967 "The Indian Savage, the Mexican Bandit, and the Chinese Heathen." Unpublished Doctoral Thesis, U of Texas at Austin.

Fishman, J. and H. Casiano

1969 "Puerto Ricans in Our Press." *Modern Language Journal,* 53.3:157-62.

Fitzpatrick, Joseph

1987 *The Puerto Rican Press. The Ethnic Press in the* United States: A Historical Analysis and Handbook. Ed S. M. Miller. New York: Greenwood P, pp 303-14.

Foreign Connection

1989 "The Foreign Connection: From Mexico to Miami." *Broadcasting,* (April 3):44-6.

Friedman, Norman

1985 "A.K.A. Pablo: Mexican American Images for Television." *Exploration in Ethnic Studies, vol* 8, pp 1-10.

Gandy, Oscar H., Jr., and P. W. Matabane

1989 "Television and Social Perceptions among African Americans and Hispanics." *Handbook of International and Intercultural Communications.* Eds M. K. Asante and W. B. Gudykunst. Newbury Park, CA: Sage, pp 318-48.

Gersh, Debra

1988 "An Underserved Market." *Editor & Publisher,* (September 17):16-17, 42.

Glasheen, Janet

1989 "Betting on Print." *Hispanic Business.* (December):42-44.

Golden, Tim

1991 "Hispanic Paper Defies the Ad Slump." *New York Times,* (April 22):C1, 6.

Gonzales, Juan

1977 "Forgotten Pages: Spanish-Language Newspapers in the Southwest." *Journalism History,* 4.2:50-1.

Gonzalez, Arturo R.
1978 "A Case Study of KMEX." Unplished Master's Thesis. California State U at Northridge.
Graves, Sherryl B.
1982 "The Impact of Television on the Cognitive and Affective Development of Minority Children." *Television and the Socialization of the Minority Child.* Ed G. L. Berry and C. Mitchell-Kernan. New York: Academic P, pp 35-67.
Grebler, Leo, Joan Moore and Ralph Guzman
1970 *The Mexican-American People.* New York: Free Press.
Greenburg, Bradley s.
1980 "Gratifications from Television Viewing and Their Correlates for British Children." *The Uses of Mass Communications: Current Perspectives on Gratifications Research.* Beverly Hills, CA: Sage, pp 71-92.
Greenburg, Bradley S., Michael Burgoon and Judee Burgoon
1983 *Mexican Americans and the Mass Media.* Norwook, NJ: Ablex.
Griswold del Castillo, Richard
1977 "The Mexican Revolution and the Spanish-Language Press in the Borderlands." *Journalism History,* 4.2:42-7.
Guernica, Antonio and Irene Kasperuk
1982 *Reaching the Hispanic Market Effectively.* New York: McGraw-Hill.
Gutiérrez, Félix F.
1974 "Chico and the Racist. Review of Southern California" *Journalism History,* (fall/winter):1-3.
1976 Spanish-Language Radio and Chicano Internal Colonialism." Unpublished Doctoral Thesis, Stanford U.
1977 "Spanish-Language Media in America: Background Resources, History." *Journalism History,* 4.2:34-41.
1978a "Reporting for La Raza: The History of Latino Journalism in America." *Agenda,* vol 8, (July-August):29-35.
1978b "Through Anglo Eyes: Chicanos as portrayed in the News Media." Paper presented to the Association for Education in Journalism.
1979 "Mexico's Television Network in the Untied States: The Case of Spanish International Network." Proceedings of the Sixth Annual Telecommunications Policy Research Conference. Ed H. S. Dordick. Lexington, MA: Lexington, pp 135-59.
1980 "Latinos and the Media in the United States: An Overview." Paper presented to the International Communication Association, Acapulco, Mexico.
1981 "Breaking through the Media Employment Wall." *Agenda,* 11.3:13-16
1989 *Latinos and the Media. Readings in Mass Communication.* Ed. M. Emery and T. C. Smythe. Dubuque, IA: W. C. Brown, 7th ed.
1990 "Advertising and the Growth of the Minority Market." *Journal of Communication Inquiry,* 14.1:6-16
Gutiérrez, Félix F. and Ernesto Ballesteros
1979 "The 1541 Earthquake: Dawn of Latin American Journalism." *Journalism History,* 6.3:79-83.
Gutiérrez, Félix F. and Jorge R. Schement
1977 "Chicanos and the Media: A Bibliography of Selected Materials." *Journalism History,* 4.2:52-55.
1981 "Problems of Ownership and Control of Spanish-Language Media in the United States: National and International Policy Concerns." *Communication and Social Structure: Critical Studies in Mass Media Research.* New York: Praeger, pp 181-203.
1984 "Spanish International Network: The Flow of Television from Mexico to the United States." *Communication Research,* 11.2:241-258.
Gutiérrez, Félix F. and Clint C. Wilson Jr.
1979 "The Demographic Dilemma." *Columbia Journalism Review,* (January/February):53-55.
Hadley-Garcia, George
1990 *Hispanic Hollywood: the Latinos in Motion Pictures.* New York: Citadel.
Hester, Al
1979 "Newspapers and Newspaper Prototypes in Spanish America, 1541-1750." *Journalism History,* 6.3:73-8.
Hispanic Link
1989 "Latinos Tally 25% of U. S. Growth." *Hispanic Link Weekly Report,* 7.41:1, 6
In Re Spanish International Communications Corporation.
1986 *Federal Communication Commission release no 86D-1,* (January 3).
Kanellos, Nicolas
1990 *A History of Hispanic Theater in the United States: Origins to 1940.* Austin, TX: U of Texas P.
Keller, Gary D.
1985 *Chicano Cinema: Research, Reviews and Resources.* Binghamton, NY: Bilingual Review P.
1985 "The Image of the Chicano in Mexican, United States, and Chicano Cinema: An Overview." *Chicano Cinema.* Binghamton, NY: Bilingual Review P, pp 13-58.
Kilgore, Julia Kay
1988 "Take Two." *Hispanic Business,* (December):52-58.
Kim, Young Y.
1988 *Communication and Cross-Cultural Adaptation.* Philadelphia, PA: Multilingual Matters.
Knudsen, Erik
1984 "Pablo Is Much Like Me." *Nuestro,* (April):17-18.
Korzenny, Felipe and Kimberly Neuendorf
1980 "Television Viewing and Self-Concept of the Elderly." *Journal of Communication,* 30.1:71-80.
Lamb, Blaine P.
1975 "The Convenient Villain: The Early Cinema Views the Mexican American." *Journal of the West,* 14.4:75-81.
Lee, Sylvia Anne
1973 "Image of Mexican Americans in San Antonio Newspapers: A Content Analysis." Unpublished Masters Thesis, U of Texas at Austin.
Lewels, Francisco J.
1974 *The Uses of the Media by the Chicano Movement: A Study in Minority Access.* New York: Praeger.
Lichter, S. Robert, Linda S. Lichter and Stanly Rothman
1987 "Prime-Time Prejudice: TV's Images of Blacks and Hispanics." *Public Opinion,* (July/August):13-16.
Lopes, Humberto
1991 "Viva Leads Miami in Spanish Radio." *Hispanic Business,* (December):42-3.

Lozano, Jose Carlos
1988 "Issues and Sources in Spanish-Language TV: The Case of Noticiero Univisión." Unpublished monograph, Department of Journalism, U of Texas at Austin.
MacCurdy, Raymond
1951 *A History and Bibliography of Spanish Language Newspapers and Magazines in Louisiana, 1808-1949.* Albuquerque: U of New Mexico P.
Martinez, Thomas
1969 "How Advertisers Promote Racism." *Civil Rights Digest*, (fall):5-11.
McCardell, Wallin S.
1976 "Socialization Factors in El Diario-La Prensa, the Spanish-language Newspaper with the Largest Daily Circulation in the United States." Unpublished Doctoral Thesis, U of Iowa.
McWilliams, Carey
1949 *Blood on the Pavements. North from Mexico*. Ed. C. McWilliams. New York: J. B. Lippincott.
Medeiros, Francine
1980 "La Opinion: A Mexican Exile Newspaper: A Content Analysis of Its First Years, 1926-1929." *Agenda*, 11:87.
Mejia Barquera, Fernando
1989 *La industria de la radio y la television y la politica del estado Mexicano*. Vol 1, pp 1920-960. Mexico, D.F.: Fundacion Manuel Buendia.
Mejia Barquera, Fernando, et al.
1985 *Televisa: El Quinto Poder*. Mexico, D.F.: Claves Latinoamericanas.
Mendosa, Rick
1990a "Radio Revenues Rock and Roll." *Hispanic Business*, (December):26-27.
1990b Media Consumers but Not Owners." *Hispanic Business, (*December):52-65.
1991 "Blaya Beams It Up: Exclusive Interview. Hispanic Business, (October):16-22.
Miller, Marjorie and Juanita Darling
1991 "El Tigre." *Los Angeles Times Magazine*, (November 10):24-29, 51.
Miller, Randall M.
1980 *The Kaleidoscopic Lens: How Hollywood Views Ethnic Groups.* Englewood, NJ: Jerome S. Ozer.
Minority Telecommuncations Development Program of the National Telecommunications and Information Administration, U. S. Department of Commerce
1991 "Compilations by State of Minority Owned Commercial Broadcast Stations. Minority Telecommuncations Development Program of the National Telecommuncations and Information Administration, U. S. Department of Commerce, Louis Camphor III, Telecommuncations Researcher." Unpublished report, (October).
Montgomery, Kathryn C.
1989 *Target: Prime Time: Advocacy Groups and The Struggle over Entertainment Television.* New York: Oxford UP.
Mydans, Seth
1989 "Charges of Bias in Spanish-Language Television." *New York Times*. (August 24).
National Association of Broadcasters
1986 "Minority-Owned and Controlled Broadcast Station Totals in the Continental United States, (excluded Hawaii, Puerto Rico, and U. S. Territories). Part II of Minority Broadcasting Facts." Department of Minority and Special Services, National Association of Broadcasters. Unpublished report.
National Commission on Working Women
1989 "Unequal Picture: Black, Hispanic, Asian, and Native American Characters on Television." Published monograph. Washington, DC: National Commission on Working Women of Wider Opportunities for Women.
Newman, M. A., M. B. Liss and F. Sherman
1983 "Ethnic Awareness in Children: Not a Unitary Concept." *Journal of Genetic Psychology*, 143:102-112.
Nordheimer, John
1986 "Resignations Upset Hispanic TV News Program." *New York Times, (*Late City Edition). (November 4):C17.
Noriega, Chon
1991 "Cafe orale: Narrative structure in Born in East L.A." *Tonantzin*, 8.1:17-18.
Payne, Andrea
1985 "Minorities on Soaps: Are They Treated Fairly?" *Soap Opera Digest*, vol 10, no 3, (January 29):20-27.
Perez, Richie
1990 "From Assimilation to Annihilation: Puerto Rican Images in U. S. Films." *Centro*, 2.8:8-27.
Pettit, Arthur G.
1980 *Images of the Mexican American in Fiction and Film.* College Station: Texas A & M UP.
Piers, E.V.
1969 *Manual for the Piers-harris Children's Self-Concept Scale*. Nashville, TN: Counselor Recordings and Tests.
Pisano, Vivian M. and Claire Splan
1984 "The Hispanic Media: Alive and Well and Printing in the U. S. A." *Lector*. (May/June):5-7.
Powell, Gloria J.
1982 *The Impact of Television on the Self-concept Development of Minority Group Children. Television and the Socialization of the Minority Child.* G.L. Berry and C. Mitchell-Kernan. New York: Academic P, pp 105-131.
Prida, Dolores
1984 A.K.A. Pablo-Watching and Waiting. *Nuestro*, (April):45.
Public Advocates, Inc.
1983 "The Network Brownout: A National Hispanic Network Audit." Unpublished paper prepared upon request by the League of United Latin American Citizens, Washington, DC.
Puig, Claudia
1991 "Off the Charts." *Los Angeles Times*, Calendar Section, (April 7):89-90.
Rangel, Jesus
1981 "Hispanic Print Media—Alive and Growing." *Agenda*, 11.3:10-12.
Rasberry, William
1971a "How about Frito Amigo?" *Washington Post*, (June 2):A19.

1971b "Who's the Real Bandito?" *Washington Post*, (June 7):A23.

Reich, K.
1986 "Doubling of U. S. Latinos by 2020 Forecast." *Los Angeles Times*, (September 26):I1, 26.

Rendon, Armando B.
1974 "The Chicano Press: A Status Report on the Needs and Trends in Chicano Journalism." Published mimeograph. Washington, DC.

Reyes, Domingo Nick and Armando B. Rendon
1971 "Chicanos and the Mass Media." National Mexican Anti-Defamation Committee, 1971.

Reyes, Luis
1983 "The Hispanic Image on Network Television: Past and Present." *Caminos*, (March):10-16.

Rios, Herminio
1972 "Toward a True Chicano Bibliography, Part II." *El Grito: A Journal of Contemporary Mexican-American Thought, vol* 5, (summer):40-7.

Rios, Herminio and Guadalupe Castillo
1970 "Toward a True Chicano Bibliography: Mexican-American Newspapers, 1848-1942." *El Grito: A Journal of Contemporary Mexican-American Thought*, vol 3, (summer):17-24.

Rivera Brooks, Nancy
1986 "SICC Rejects Latino Group's Bid for Spanish-Language Stations." *Los Angeles Times*, (Part IV):1.

Rubin, A.
1977 "Television Usage, Attitudes and Viewing Behaviors of Children and Adolescents." *Journal of Broadcasting*, vol 21, pp 355-369.

Russell, Joel
1988 "Something in the Air." *Hispanic Business*, (December):60-66.
1989 "Media Deal of the Year." *Hispanic Business*, (December):24-30.

Salinas, Alejandra
1990 Unpublished computer listing of Hispanic publications. Benson Mexican American Studies Library, U of Texas at Austin.

Sanchez, Leo Anthony
1973 "Treatment of Mexican Americans by Selected U. S. Newspapers, January-June." Unpublished Masters Thesis, Pennsylvania State U.

Santillan, Richard and Federico A. Subervi-Velez
n.d. *Mexican Americans and Republican Presidential Campaigns in California. Ethnic and Racial Politics in California.* Ed M. Preston and B. Jackson. Berkeley, CA: Institute of Governmental Studies. Forthcoming.

Schement, Jorge Reina
1976 "Primary Spanish-Language Radio as a Function of Internal Colonialism: Patterns of Ownership and Control. Unpublished Doctoral Thesis." Stanford, CA: Stanford U.

Schement, Jorge Reina and Loy A. Singleton
1977 "The Origins of Spanish-Language Radio: The Case of San Antonio, Texas." *Journalism History*, 4.2:56-58, 61.
1981 "The Onus of Minority Ownership: FCC Policy and Spanish-Language Radio." *Journal of Communication*, vol 31, no 2, (spring).

Seijo-Maldonado, haydee
1989 "History of Spanish-Language Television in the United States." Unpublished communication monography, U of Illinois at Urbana.

Shaw, David
1990a "Negative News and Little Else." *Los Angeles Times*, (December 11).
1990b "Asian-Americans Chafe against Stereotype of Model Citizen." *Los Angeles Times*, (December 11).
1990c "Newspapers Struggling to Raise Minority coverage." *Los Angeles Times*, (December 12).
1990d "Despite Advances, Stereotypes Still Used by Media." *Los Angeles Times*, (December 12).
1990e "Seattle Times uses Direct Approach in Minority Coverage." *Los Angeles Times*, (December 12).
1990f "What's the News? White Editors Make the Call." *Los Angeles Times*, (December 13).
1990g "Stereotypes Hinder Minorities' Attempts to Reach managerial Ranks." *Los Angeles Times*, (December 13).
1990h "Amid L.A.'s Ethnic Mix, the Times Plays Catch-Up." *Los Angeles Times*, (December 14).
1990i "The 'Jackie Robinson Syndrome': A Double Standard." *Los Angeles Times*, (December 14).

Shearer, James F.
1954 "Periodicos espanoles en los Estados Unidos." *Revista Hispanica Moderna*. Vol 20, pp 45-57.

Shiver, Jube, Jr.
1990 "Keeping Univisión Alive." *Los Angeles Times*, (February 19):D1, 4.

Standard Rate and Data Service
1991 "Hispanic Media and Markets." Vol 4, no 1, (March 28).

Sterling, Mary Ann
1984 "Spanish-Language Print Media in the United States: A Case Study of La Opinion." Unpublished Master's Thesis, U of Southern California.

Stone, Vernon A.
1988 "Pipelines and Dead Ends: Jobs Held by Minorities and Women in Broadcast News." *Mass Comm Review*, 15.2-3:10-19.

Straton, Porter A.
1969 *The Territorial Press of New Mexico, 1834-1912.* Albuquerque: U of New Mexico P.

Stroman, Carolyn A.
1986 "Television Viewing and Self-Concept among Black Children." *Journal of Broadcasting and Electronic Media*, 30.1:87-93.

Subervi-Velez, Federico A.
1986 "The Mass Media and Ethnic Assimilation and Pluralism: A Review and Research Proposal with Special Focus on Hispanics." *Communication Research*, 13.1:71-96.
1988 "Spanish-Language Daily Newspapers and the 1984 Elections." *Journalism Quarterly*, 65.3:678-85.
1990 *Interactions between latinos and Anglos on Prime-Time Television: A Case Study of Condo. Income and Status Differences between White and Minority Americans: A Persistent Inequality*. Ed S. Chan. Lewiston, NY: Edwin Mellen P.
1993a "Mass Communication and Ethnic Minority Groups:

An overview course." *Pluralizing Journalism Educatino: A Multicultural Handbook*. Ed C. Martindale. New York: Greenwood P, pp 159-72.

1993b *The Democratic and Republican Parties' Latino-oriented mass Communication Strategies during the 1988 Elections. Latinos and the 1988 Elections.* R.O. de la Garza. Boulder, CO: Westview P.

Subervi-Vélez, Federico A., and collaborators

1993 "Media." *The Hispanic American Almanac.* Ed. Nicolás Kanellos. Detroit: Gale Research, pp 621-74.

Subervi-Velez, Federico A., Richard Herrara and Michael Begay

1987 "Toward an Understanding of the Role of the Mass Media in Latino Political Life." *Social Science Quarterly,* 68.1:185-96.

Subervi-Velez, Federico A., Nitza Lopez-Hernandez and Aline Frambes-Buxeda

1990 *Mass Media in Puerto Rico. Mass Media and the Caribbean.* S. H. Surlin and W. S. Soderlund, New York: Gordon & Breach, pp 149-76.

Subervi-Velez, Federico A. and Juan Necochea

1990 "Television Viewing and Self-Concept among Latino Children: A Pilot Study." *Howard Journal of Communications,* 2.3:315-29.

Subervi-Velez, Federico A., and Susan Colsant

1993 "The teleivsion worlds of Latino children." *Children and Television: Images in a Changing Socio-Cultural World.* Ed G. L. Berry and J. K. Asamen. Newbury Park, CA: Sage, pp 215-28.

BegaTan, Alex S. and G. Tan

1979 "Television Use and Self-Esteem of Blacks." *Journal of Communication,* 29.1:129-35.

Television/Radio Age

1984 "Spanish Spending Power Growing Dramatically, but Consumers Retain Special Characteristics." *Television/Radio Age,* (December):A3-A14.

Trejo Delarbe, Raul, ed

1988 *Las redes de Televisa.* Mexico, DF: Claves Latinoamericanos.

Trevino, Jesus Salvador

1983 "Latinos and Public Broadcasting: The 2% Factor." *Caminos,* (March):25-27.

Tyer, Thomas

1991 "Stereotypes Fading from Small Screen." *Electronic Media.* (July 8):29, 34.

U. S. Commission on Civil Rights

1977 "Window Dressing on the Set: Women and Minorities in Television." Washington, DC: Government Printing Office.

1979 "Window Dressing on the Set: An Update." Washington, DC: Government Printing Office.

Valdez, Ruben V.

1970 "A Case Study in Pretrial Criminal News Reporting: The Rio Arriba County Courthouse Raid of June 5, 1967, Involving Reies Lopez Tijerina." Unpublished Masters Thesis, West Virginia U.

Valenzuela, Nicholas A.

1985a"Organizational Evolution of a Spanish-Language Television Network: An Environmental Approach." Unpublished Doctoral Thesis, Stanford U.

1985b "The Evolution of Spanish-Language Television in the United States as Related to Panama at: Transborder Telecommunications Policy Issues." Paper presented at the 13th Annual Telecommunications Policy Research Conference, Airlie, VA, (April).

Valle, Victor

1988 "The Latino Wave." *Los Angeles Times,* Entertainment Section, (April 2):1, 11

1989 "HBO-Cinemax Experiment in Bilingual TV." *Los Angeles Times, (*May 1):D1,6

VanSlyke Turk, Judy, Jim Richstad, Robert Bryson Jr. and Sammye Johnson

1989 "Hispanic Americans in the News in Two Southwestern Cities." *Journalism Quarterly,* 66.1:107-13.

Veciana-Suarez, Ana

1990 *Hispanic Media: Impact and Influence.* Washington, DC: Media Institute.

Veciana-Suarez, Ana

1987 *Hispanic Media, USA.* Washington, DC: Media Institute.

Wagner, Henry R.

1937 "New Mexico Spanish Press." *New Mexico Historical Review,* 12:1-140.

Wall Street Journal

1988 "Sale of WKAZ-TV Station in Puerto Rico Is Arranged." *Wall Street Journal Western Edition,* (November 14):B6.

1991 "Vista Magazine Names Tosteson to Top Posts, after Firing Publisher." (February 19).

Weiland, A,. and R. Coughlin

1979 "Self-Identification and Preferences: A Comparison of White and Mexican-American First and Third Graders." *Journal of Cross-Cultural Psychology,* 10:356-65.

Wilkinson, Kenton T.

1990a "The Forgotten Factor in the Sale of Spanish International Communications Corporation to Hallmark Cards: The Influence of Mexico's Economy and Politics." Paper presented at the 7th annual Intercultural and International Communication Conference, Miami, FL, (February).

1990b "Recent Developments in the Evolution of Spanish-Language Television in the United States." Unpublished political science monograph, U of California at Berkeley.

1991 "The Sale of Spanish International Communications corporation: Milestone in the Development of Spanish-Language Television in the United States." Unpublished Master's Thesis, U of California at Berkeley.

Williams, Linda

1985 *Type and Stereotype: Chicano Images in Film.* Chicano Cinema. Ed G. Keller. Binghamton, NY: Bilingual Review P, pp 59-63.

Wilson, Clint, Jr., and Felix F. Gutierrez

1985 *Minorities and the Media: Diversity and the End of Mass Communication.* Beverly Hills, CA: Sage.

Woll, Allen

1980 *The Latin Image in American Film.* Los Angeles: Latin American Center Publications, U of California.

Woll, Allen L. and Randall M. Miller
1987 *Ethnic and Racial Images in American Film and Television: Historical Essays and Bibliography.* New York: Garland.

Zohoori, A.R.
1988 "A Cross-Cultural Analysis of Children's Television Use." *Journal of Broadcasting and Electronic Media,* 32.1:105-13.

Index